Early Massachusetts Marriages

PRIOR TO 1800

Edited by Frederic W. Bailey

Three Books in One

With the Addition of

PLYMOUTH COUNTY MARRIAGES

1692 — 1746

CLEARFIELD

Reprinted for
Clearfield Company by
Genealogical Publishing Co.
Baltimore, Maryland
2008

Originally published
Book One: New Haven, Connecticut, 1897
Book Two: New Haven, Connecticut, 1900
Book Three: Worchester, Massachusetts, 1914

Reprinted, three volumes in one, with the
addition of *Plymouth County Marriages, 1692–1746,*
excerpted from *The Genealogical Advertiser,*
Volumes I–II, 1898–1899

Genealogical Publishing Co.
Baltimore, Maryland
1968, 1979, 1991, 1996

Library of Congress Catalogue Card Number 68-28249
ISBN-13: 978-0-8063-0008-5
ISBN-10: 0-8063-0008-6

Made in the United States of America

EARLY MASSACHUSETTS MARRIAGES

PRIOR TO 1800.

AS FOUND ON THE OFFICIAL RECORDS OF

WORCESTER COUNTY.

FIRST BOOK.

EDITED BY

FREDERIC W. BAILEY,

ED. "EARLY CONN. MARRIAGES," DESIGNER BAILEY'S PHOTO-ANCESTRAL RECORD, "THE RECORD
OF MY ANCESTRY." MEMBER AMERICAN HIST. ASSO., CONN. HIST. SO., NEW HAVEN
COLONY HIST. SO., N. Y. GEN. & BIOG. SO., SONS OF THE AMERICAN REV-
OLUTION (MASS.), MANAGER BUREAU OF AMERICAN ANCESTRY.

PUBLISHED BY THE

BUREAU OF AMERICAN ANCESTRY
FOR
Family Researches
FREDERIC W. BAILEY, MGR.
P. O. BOX 587. NEW HAVEN, CONN.

Abner Wood Middleborough 83

CONTENTS.

EARLY MASSACHUSETTS MARRIAGES.

PREFACE.

The earliest settlements in Massachusetts were along the coast line; and the territory which became the Counties of Essex, Middlesex, Plymouth and Barnstable, all in Eastern Massachusetts, and extending indefinitely westward and inland, plenty large enough for years to meet the needs of a slowly expanding colony. Except the few isolated companies that dared to penetrate the forests, press over the hills and beyond the nearest streams, and there trust themselves to the mercies of impulsive and hostile Indian tribes, a large majority of the inhabitants were content to reach out gradually by mastering their immediate foes and subduing by degrees the neighboring wilds, all the while keeping within easy reach of the sure aid which at any time might even there become necessary.

The territory now embraced in Worcester County was occupied here and there long before its organization in 1731. In the steady march of civilization those sturdy ancestors to whom, through warfare or distant journeyings this region had become familiar, had marked out a number of its most fertile spots for settlement that were later so oft left by will to worthy sons and daughters, who there found for themselves permanent and happy homes. Such localities may now be known by the ancient townships, dating back even as early as 1653, when Lancaster was organized and named.

But the interesting and impressive feature of our early and colonial life in Massachusetts, here so briefly told, is that prior to any thought of an organized township, the Christian church, fulfilling to the letter the Gospel spirit, "where two or three are gathered together," had already planted and erected its church, around and in which might center the best aims and ambitions of the humblest community. It gathered the isolated and scattered households for miles around together in an assembly, holy in its purpose and far reaching in its aim. At home in the wilderness it brought to each lonely fireside comfort, consolation, good cheer. Its all pervading life and light conquered as nothing else could the red savage in his forest den, persuading even him to submit to its precious ordinances. The faithful pastor kept peculiar oversight of all these people from a supreme sense of duty which was not strictly and conscientiously fulfilled if somehow every name was not recorded by him among his baptisms, on his list of membership, or the eligible among those by him joined in the sacred bonds of matrimony.

Now to these old records of the early Church, carefully gathered by the clergy, mutilated as they sometimes are by years of usage, genealogists have been greatly indebted. And it seems very strange that town

authorities have not seen fit more generally to secure copies of these
perishable books and papers, not alone for their better protection, but
that the town records might by their aid be made even more complete.
Especially evident is this, so well is it known how oft the church records
will contain marriages of town people never recorded elsewhere, or the
baptism of children whose names at birth never reached the town clerk.
It can hardly be said, however, that the Colony or State of Massachusetts itself has ever been indifferent to the importance of this subject,
if we may judge from the number of enactments which its Assembly
from time to time has passed.   Indeed, fortunate is the man who, seek-
ing for his ancestry, is drawn in the search to the old Bay State, since,
of all the ancient States, its records as a whole, thanks to an interested
people, are the most complete and satisfactory.

For instance we find (and we use as our authority, and to which we
are indebted for numerous dates, etc., "Report on the Custody and Condition of the Public Records," by Carroll D. Wright), that as early as September 9, 1639, "It was ordered that records be kept of the days of
every marriage, birth and death of every person within this jurisdiction." Mass. Rec., Vol. I, p. 276. June 14, 1642, another step was
taken to secure complete and perfect record, when "clerks of the writs
in the several towns were hereafter to record all births and deaths and
deliver a return of the same yearly to the recorder of the court belonging to the jurisdiction in which they lived. Persons authorized to marry
were to return the names of persons married by them, and the date
when married, to the recorder of the court nearest their habitation. Such
recorders were to faithfully and carefully enroll such births, marriages
and deaths as shall thus be committed to their trust." Mass. Rec., Vol.
II, p. 15. November 3, 1692. At this time defects in the previous enact-
ment were wisely met when " Every justice and minister was ordered
to register all marriages solemnized before any of them and make a
return quarterly to the clerk of the Sessions of the Peace, to be by him
registered." Prov. Laws, Vol. I, p. 61.

In 1693 town clerks were ordered to register births and marriages.
In 1695 justices and ministers were ordered to return within three
months the names of all persons married by them, to the clerk of the
town, he being ordered to register the same.   While on December 1,
1716, " Every town clerk was ordered to give in a list of marriages to
the clerk of the Sessions of the Peace annually in April, and every
clerk of the court was to record the same." Prov. Laws, Vol. II, p. 60.

These several enactments supplementing each other clearly show
how well Massachusetts has sought to do its full duty in the preservation of valuable family data, and explains not only how it is that each
town possesses so much of this kind, but also why it is that in the
various counties of the state the County Clerk or Clerk of Courts, as
called, should have in his possession marriage records as herein found.

Worcester County, organized with this law already in force, began
to receive from the various towns within its limits such records as both

justices of the peace and ministers possessed. It did not secure the earlier records, which, of course, had gone to the clerk of the county from which Worcester was taken—Middlesex—nor did the law probably secure complete obedience in every case, as it might had some penalty been attached, but it did result in the preservation in compact form of valuable data of ancestors now so earnestly sought for, and which town clerks themselves might not be able from their records to supply.

The period between 1731 and 1785 is covered by two large books filed away in the office of the Clerk of the Courts. The marriages are entered apparently in the order of their reception from the different towns, and not according to any systematic arrangement. The name of the minister or justice of the peace in many cases is recorded, though we have noted herein only such Rev. as occasionally appears. The puzzling handwriting, together with the fact that no index exists, and no order or arrangement in the books, has made the search therein most difficult, and the searcher has, after a fair trial, given up in despair of any reasonable results therefrom.

The following records have been most carefully copied and compared. In a few cases the names could not be determined, and such are marked with an (?). The first and oldest book is contained in this issue. A copy of the second book is on file for reference in hopes of publication at some future day.

FREDERIC W. BAILEY.

New Haven, Conn., September 7, 1897.

EARLY MASSACHUSETTS MARRIAGES.

Incorporated 1731. Taken from Middlesex County.

The County records begin with the following marriages. Where and by whom performed is not stated. It is presumed that most of them occurred in Worcester.

Noah Mason & Kezia Mascroft,	Dec. 9, 1736
Thomas Converse & Abigail Fay,	Nov. 3, 1737
Stephen Cary & Mercy Frame,	June 22, 1739
Ebenezer Fay & Thankful Hide,	Sept. 19, 1739
Richard Dresser & Dorothy Marcy,	Nov. 12, 1741
Jeremiah Streeter & Eunice Rice,	April 28, 1742
Samuel Roger & Captivity Peter,	June 29, 1742
Stephen Davis & Esther Haw,	Nov. 9, 1742
Jabez Nichols & Hannah Mirick,	Jan. 4, 1742-3
John Stacy, Jr., & Abigail Allen,	Nov. 1, 1743
Jacob Huntley & Lydia Allen,	April 22, 1744
John Harding & Washts (?) Rice,	Feb. 26, 1744-5
Solomon Pagon & Hannah Chekeys (Indians),	July 10, 1745
Benjamid Hide & Dorcas Dyer,	Nov. 21, 1745
Caleb Harding & Hannah Weld,	Dec. 26, 1745
Edward Simpson & Anna Bond,	May 15, 1746
Joseph Perry & Lois Gilburt,	Jan. 6, 1746
Thomas Moores & Ruth Nichols,	April 24, 1747
Tilly Rue & Mary Buckminster,	Nov. 2, 1748
Oliver Heyward, Esq., & Anna Hinds,	June 8, 1749
Benjamin Wood & Mehitabell Hamilton,	Sept. 13, 1749
John Bell & Susannah Hinds,	Nov. 17, 1749
Oliver Woolcot & Abigail Mills,	Jan. 11, 1749
Thomas Tucker & Hannah Hill,	July 20, 1749
Samuel Leech & Mary Simson,	June 20, 1749
Benjamin Scott & Lydia Johnson,	Sept. 7, 1749
Icchabod Robbins & Zerviah Rice,	Dec. 27, 1749
Elijah Bartlett & Bathsheba Gilburt,	Jan. 11, 1749
Arthur Tucker & Mary Sabins,	May 17, 1750
Jeremiah Woodbury & Jerusha Tucker,	March 22, 1750
Samuel Bascom & Sarah Barns,	Sept. 18, 1750

Benjamin Jennings & Elizabeth Gilburt,	Nov. 8, 1750
William Witt & Abigail Killam,	Nov. 29, 1750
Nathaniel Bartlet & Dorothy Harwood,	July 5, 1750
Joseph Marsh & Abigail Symons,	May 17, 1750
Benjamin Lee & Esther Baker,	June 28, 1750
Beriah Haws & Patience Warner,	Nov. 15, 1750
Thomas Holdin & Ruth Baker,	March 21, 1750
Josiah Bacon & Abigail Holden,	March 21, 1750
Nathan Newton & Experience Stow,	June 5, 1750
Elnathan Newton & Jemima Joslin,	June 19, 1750
Isaac Newton, Jr., & Sarah Collins,	Aug. 17, 1750
Benjamin Morse & Mary James,	Oct. 26, 1750
William Lewis & Mercy Pike,	Dec. 10, 1750
Jonas Woods & Elisabeth Newton,	Dec. 12, 1750
Nathaniel Stacy & Mary Withirbee,	Jan 10, 1750
Timothy Barret & Dinah Witt,	Jan. 24, 1750–51
Nathan Brigham & Martha Gleason,	Feb. 6, 1750–51
Elijah Bellows & Martha Joslin,	Feb. 20, 1750–51
Samuel Adams of Grafton & Elizabeth Gould of Sutton,	Nov. 1, 1750
James Whipple of Grafton & Lydia Powers of Littleton,	Nov. 29, 1750
William Hatfield & Elizabeth Mason,	Nov. 1, 1750
Ralph Wheelock & Experience Denison,	Jan. 24, 1750
William McKinstry & Mary Morse,	—— 31, 1750
Caleb Stacy & Abigail Bond,	June 6, 1751
Samuel Temple & Hannah Gleason,	Nov. 13, 1751
Jonathan Farr & Mary Wells,	June 5, 1751
Timothy Newton & Sarah Mirrick,	July 5, 1751
Simeon Walker & Judith Goss,	Oct. 10, 1751
Seth Lincoln & Lucy Page,	Oct. 10, 1751
John Green & Annah Bradish,	Dec. 7, 1751
Peter Gibbin & Sarah Green,	Dec. 7, 1751
Joseph Powers & Abigail Benjamin,	Dec. 25, 1751
John Auger of Framingham & Bethiah Lyscom of Southborough,	Feb. 22, 1752
Joseph Trumble, Jr., of Leicester & Susanna Richards of Dudley,	April 29, 1752
John Robert & Sarah Abbot,	April 1, 1752

George Page & Priscilla Whitcom, June 4, 1752
Thomas Denny of Leicester & Mrs. Tabitha Cutter
of Grafton, June 25, 1752
Andrew Oliphant of Dedham & Mrs. Elisabeth
Browning of Rutland, Nov. 22, 1752
John Beal (?) & Sarah Rood, March 30, 1752
Ephraim White & Abigail Upham, Dec. 21, 1752
Daniel Mathews and Huldah Putnam, Feb. 20, 1753
Benjamain Green & Mercy Taft, Oct. 2, 1753
Elias Parmenter & Bethial Tyler, March 22, 1753
✓ Joshua Wood & Rachel Hazeltine, May 9, 1754
ι Jonathan Jones & Mary Wood, May 29, 1754
Paul Hazeltine & Mary Rice, July 25, 1754
Elisha Taft & Experience Taft, July 21, 1754
Jonah Moore of Worcester & Elisabeth Bemis of
Spencer, July 10, 1755
William Thomson, Jr., of Leicester & Jane White
of New Braintree, Jan. 16, 1755
Obed Abbut— & Elizabeth Edmonds of Brookfield,
April 24, 1755
Joseph Barns & Susanna Cannon, Dec. 8, 1755
Dr. Joel Carpenter of Hardwicke & Mrs. Mary
Ruggles, Dec. 9, 1755
James Dudley & Mehitable Woodbury, both of
Concord, Dec. 25, 1755
Jos. Willard of Petersham & Lucretia Ward of
Westboro, Feb. 28, 1757
Noah Harris & Phebee Butler, Feb. 22, 1757
Jonathan Gale & Margaret Crawford, March 10, 1757
Silas Whitney & Jane Porson (?), April 25, 1758
Ezra Bemen (?) & Persis (?) Roys (?), June 1, 1758
Thomas Willard & Elizabeth Davenport, Jan. 10, 1759
Mathew Noble of Westfield & Lydia Eager of
Shrews, May 24, 1758
Anthony Clark & Jane Fairfield, July 31, 1759
Amos Spring & Phebe Porson (?), Oct. 11, 1759
William Goss & Elizabeth Pike, Nov. 8, 1759
David Child & Mehitabell Richardson, Nov. 29, 1759
Edward Newton & Sarah Winch, Feb. 7, 1760

WORCESTER.

Worcester was settled in 1674. October 15, 1684, " It was ordered that the plantation at Quansigamond be called Worcester and that the town brand mark be as illustrated in the record." Mass. Rec., Vol. V, p. 460. Incorporated June 14, 1722. A city, February 29, 1848. First (Congregational) Church organized 1716. Friends, 1735. Clergyman mentioned: Rev. Thaddeus Maccarty.

Josiah Holden & Abigail Bond of Watertown, Dec. 17, 1747
Nathaniel Tatman & Mary Rice, Dec. 17, 1747
Jonathan Eaton & Ruth Gleason, May 12, 1748
John Fisk & Azubah Moore, June 1, 1748
Joshua Child & Mary Hinds of Shrewsbury, June 2, 1748
Elisha Hubburd of Hatfield & Lucy Stearns, June 7, 1748
Solomon Gates & Mary Clark, Nov. 10, 1748
John Mower & Hannah Moore, Nov. 23, 1748
Thomas Cowden & Experience Gray, Nov. 24, 1748
John Osburn, Jr., of Hopkinton & Jane Gray, Nov. 29, 1748
William Little of Lunenburg & Elizabeth Wallis,
Dec. 1, 1748
James Forbush, Jr., & Margaret McFarland, Aug. 24, 1749
Robert Blair of Pelham & Margaret MacClewain,
Aug. 24, 1749
Matthias Stone & Susannah Chaddick, Nov. 16, 1749
John Chaddick & Lydia Gale, Nov. 16, 1749
William Harris of Holden & Patience Gleason,
Jan. 24, 1749–50
Duncan Campbell of Oxford & Elizabeth Stearns,
Jan. 27, 1749–50
Cornelius Stowell & Livilla Goulding, March 22, 1749–50
Cyrus Rice & Elizabeth Eaton, March 27, 1749–50
Samuel Randal & Ruth Bond of Bolton, Aug. 8, 1750
Asa Flagg & Lois Chaddick, Nov. 1, 1750
William Browning of Rutland & Rebekah McFar-
land, Nov. 22, 1750
Moses Bennet & Joanna Gleason, Dec. 19, 1750
Elisha Hedge, Jr., & Deliverance Stearns, Dec. 25, 1750
Henry Potter & Jane Rowlin, April 25, 1751
Joshua Hide of No. 6 & Rebekah Hubbard, May 2, 1751

Joseph Gleason & Lydia Whitney, May 9, 1751
James Smith of Leicester & Zaviah Hubburd, May 21, 1751
Isaac Stearns & Katherine Crosbey, Nov. 7, 1751
Daniel Biglo & Mary Bond, Nov. 21, 1751
Jno. Bond, Jr., & Silence King, Nov. 21, 1751
Jonas Rice (tertius) & Bathsheba Parmenter, Dec. 3, 1751
Henry Ward & Lydia Mower, Jan. 2, 1752
Samuel Lawrence of Pomfret & Hannah Tatman,
Jan. 2, 1752
Moses Peirce of Weston & Mehitabel Rice, Feb. 10, 1752
Palmer Goulding, Jr., & Abigail Heyward, Feb. 25, 1752
Phinehas Ward & Eunice Cutting, April 22, 1752
David Biglo & Sarah Eaton, May 21, 1752
Phinehas Gleason & Eunice Chaddick, June 23, 1752
Darius Bugbee of Woodstock & Mary Lovell, Jan. 10, 1753
Daniel Walker of Brookfield & Mary Lovell, Nov. 29, 1753
William Biglo of Pequiog & Margaret Gates, Nov. 29, 1753
Daniel Heyward, Jr., & Anna Wait, Nov. 29. 1753
John Waters and Kesia Holton, Dec. 13, 1753
Jabez Paine of Leicester & Elizabeth Hubbard, Feb. 19, 1754
Mathew Blair of Blanford & Jane Alexander, Feb. 21, 1754
Jonathan Moore & Sarah Gates, Feb. 27, 1754
Thaddeus Biglo & Rebeckah Warren, March 28, 1754
Samuel Wheelock of Shrewsbury & Dorcas Perry,
April 16, 1754
Daniel Greenwood, Jr., of Sutton & Jerusha Eaton,
Nov. 14, 1754
James Carlyle & Mary Mahan, Dec. 25, 1754
David Peirce of Waltham & Huldah Harrington,
Jan. 22, 1755
Solomon Bixby & Easthar Clark, April 3, 1755
Charles Davenport, Jr., & Mary Hart of Leicester,
April 16, 1755
Isaac Stearns & Elizabeth Roberts, April 30, 1755
Seth Russell of Cambridge and Dinah Harrington,
May 8, 1755
John Curtis, Jr., & Elizabeth Hawood, May 15, 1755
Timothy Green of Leicester & Sarah Cook, June 10, 1755
Samuel Moore & Grace Rice, Aug. 13, 1755

David Moore of Leicester & Elenor Rice,   Oct. 16, 1755
James Mcpheson & Sarah Calhoone,   Feb. 15, 1756
George Tracy & Elizabeth Hull,   April 9, 1756
William Ward & Elizabeth Moore,   April 15, 1756
Timothy Whiting of Lancaster & Sarah Osgood,
                                                 May 10, 1756
Reuben Hamilton of Brookfield & Lucretia Hub-
   burd,   June 8, 1756
John Kelso & Sarah Crawford,   Sept. 30, 1756
James Trowbridge & Mary Killey,   Jan. 10, 1757
Samuel Bridge & Mary Goodwin,   March 1, 1757
Samuel Curtis & Mary Ward,   March 30, 1757
John Green & Mary Osgood,   April 14, 1757
'Joseph Hastings & Mary Stearns,   June 13, 1757
John Crawford & Martha Smith,   July 28, 1757
David Cunningham & Elenor Wallis,   Aug. 10, 1757
John Anderson & Elizabeth McCrackin,   Oct. 25, 1757
Joseph Gray & Mary Thomas,   Nov. 17, 1757
David McClellan & Sarah Stevens,   Nov. 28, 1757
Absalom Cutting & Kesia Rice,   Jan. 10, 1758
Elijah Harrington & Azuba Rice,   Feb. 8, 1758
James Ball & Lydia Rice,   March 2, 1758
Ignatus Goulding & Elizabeth Goodwin,   March 9, 1758
Matthew Barber & Hannah Mcfarland,   March 16, 1758
Jacob Upham of Leicester & Zaviah Smith, March 22, 1758
Jonathan Chaddick & Hannah Saddler,   April 27, 1758
Joshua Johnson & Lydia Brown,   May 28, 1758
Alexander Calhoon of Leicester & Elenor Mcfar-
   land,   Dec. 28, 1758
Alexander Graham of Rutland & Martha Forbush,
                                                 Jan. 18, 1759
Micah Johnson & Phebe Moore,   May 8, 1754
William Taylor & Lois Whitney, both of Leices-
   ter,   Aug. 24, 1754
James Putnam & Elizabeth Chandler,   Sept. 20, 1754
Josiah Berry & Mrs. Jane Wright, Al* Doolittle,
                                                 March 16, 1756
Robert Earl of Leicester & Hepzebah Johnson,
                                                 March 23, 1756

wheeler

Abraham Wheeler & Elizabeth Millet of Mendon,
                                                July 13, 1756
Nathaniel Child & Abigail Adams of Sutton, Oct. 23, 1756
William Oak & Abigail Whitney,   Oct. 29, 1763
John Chaddick, Jr., & Sarah Johnson,   Nov. 8, 1756
William Bouttell of Leominster & Persis Hubburd,
                                                April 27, 1757
Thomas Lee & Sarah Verry,   Nov. 24, 1757
Peter Johnson & Abigail Parks,   Oct. 12, 1758
Hezekiah Stowell & Hepzibah Rice,   Nov. 24, 1758
Jonas Woodward, Jr., & Rachell Holms,   Jan. 16, 1759
John Green & Mrs. Azubah Ward,   Dec. 26, 1758
Amariah Parks & Elizabeth Holland, both of Sut-
    ton,   Feb. 8, 1759
Samuel Wiswall & Sarah Dyar,   July 18, 1759
David Richardson & Rebeca Nichols,   March 27, 1760
Timothy Bigelow & Mrs. Anna Andrews (in New
    Hampshire),   July 7, 1762
John Moore & Esthar Bigelow,   Sept. 11, 1760
Edward Newton & Sarah Winch, both of Shrews-
    bury,   Feb. 5, 1760
Jonathan Phillips of Oxford & Sarah Parker, March 6, 1760
Samuel Bemis, Jr., of Spencer & Mrs. Mehitabel
    Dannell of Sutton,   Aug. 11, 1760
Antipas Earl & Mary Stade, both of Leicester, April 9, 1761
Noah Mendall of New Brantree & Mrs. Mary Low
    of Rutland,   Dec. 22, 1762
John Child, Jr., of Holden & Mary Smith (minor),
    dau. of Elisha Smith, Jr.,   Feb. 18, 1762
Jonathan Sawin & Mary Whitney,   Feb. 15, 1759
Jonas Hubbard & Mary Stevens,   March 7, 1759
Alexander Mills & Mary Millet,   March 22, 1759
David Chaddick & Lydia Wait,   July 29, 1759
Jonathan Beaman of Shrewsbury & Sarah Seager,
                                                Oct. 3, 1759
Thomas Davenport & Abigail Wilder,   Oct. 25, 1759
Jonas Gray of Holden & Susannah Gray,   Nov. 22, 1759
George Waleup of Framingham & Jemima Very,
                                                Nov. 29, 1759

Increase Stearns & Deborah Hull,   Jan. 8, 1760
Adam Walker & Rosanna Mcfadden,   Jan. 31, 1760
James Hamilton of Rutland & Mary Knox,   Feb. 13, 1760
John Young of Pelham & Elisabeth Smith   Feb. 21, 1760
James Turner of Pelham & Susannah Thomas,
                                                  April 1, 1760
John Elder & Jennet Ross,   April 1, 1760
David McClellan & Elizabeth Harrington,   May 6, 1760
Samuel Sawin & Mary Wesson of Sudbury,   June 19, 1760
Samuel Johnson & Mary Spence,   Aug. 14, 1760
Samuel Smith & Margaret Crawford,   Nov. 19, 1760
Jacob Sanderson & Elizabeth Child,   Dec. 18, 1760
Nathan Patch of Ipswich & Eunice Adams,   Dec. 26, 1760
Jonathan Rice & Euice Whipple of Grafton,   Jan 14, 1761
Silas Moore & Mary Jennison,   Feb. 4, 1761
Ebenezer Millet & Mary Wheeler,   April 6, 1761
Jedediah Tucker of Shrewsbury & Elizabeth
    Lynds,   April 16, 1761
Eliot Gray of Pelham & Hannah Barber,   June 9, 1761
Samuel Herring of Dedham & Lucy Harthion, June 25, 1761
Peter Proctor of Littleton & Mary Ball,   June 25, 1761
James Hamilton & Margaret Mahan,   Aug. 20, 1761
Joseph Barber of Westfield & Martha Mcfarland,
                                                  Oct. 1, 1761
Jonathan Bullard of Rutland & Mary Barber,   Nov. 16, 1761
Isaac Miller of Westboro & Abigail Gleason, Dec. 30, 1761
Thomas Lovil of Sutton & Lydia Moore,   Jan. 13, 1762
Daniel Gleason & Patience Stow,   Jan. 27, 1762
Solomon Woodward & Priscilla Holms,   Feb. 3, 1762
John Woodward & Ruth Smith,   April 29, 1762
Samuel Heyden of Marlboro & Mary Harris,   June 1, 1762
Andrew Boyd & Molly Gray,   June 17, 1762
Nathaniel Tatman & Rachel Adams,   Dec. 2, 1762
John Duncan of Londonderry & Hannah Henry,
                                                  Dec. 16, 1762
Isaac Mitchel of Petersboro & Jemima Gray,   Feb. 24, 1763
Timothy Sullivan & Eleanor Rice,   June 6, 1763
Simon Oaks & Rhoda Knight,   Aug. 2, 1763
Nathaniel Water of Sutton & Eunice Bancroft, Oct. 13, 1763

Robert Oliver of Rutland & Mary Walker,   Oct. 13, 1763
James Nichols, Jr., & Jemima (?) Morris,   Oct. 18, 1763
Ephraim Curtis & Sarah Paine,   Dec. 4, 1763
Josiah Harrington, Jr., & Mary Jones,   Jan. 10, 1764
David Biglow & Deborah Heywood of Shrews-
    bury,   March 8, 1764
Elijah Davenport & Abigail Clark,   April 11, 1764
Asa Moore & Mary Cook,   April 12, 1764
Daniel Boyden, Jr., & Rebecca Barber,   June 7, 1764
Hezekiah Boyden & Elizabeth Green,   Sept. 13, 1764
Edward Knight & Tabitha Hair,   Sept. 21, 1764
William Gates & Joanna Stearns,   Nov. 7, 1764
Ebenezer Hamond of Charlton & Susanna Johnson,
    Feb. 6, 1765
John Gambell of Westboro & Elizabeth Elder, Feb. 21, 1765
Robert Henry of Leicester & Susanna Young,
    March 14, 1765
William Ward & Sarah Trowbridge,   Nov. 7, 1765
Volentine Harris & Priscilla Gleason,   April 16, 1765
Barzillai Rice & Silence Gould,   April 18, 1765
Edmund Hard & Sarah Willington,   June 20, 1765
Jonathan Stone & Mary Gates,   Oct. 29, 1765
Samuel Brown & Abigail Flagg,   Nov. 25, 1765
Thomas Beard & Mehitable Boyden,   April 10, 1766
Matthew Gray & Margaret Forbush,   May 5, 1766
Duncan Cameron & Mary Smith,   May 8, 1766
George Caldwell of Rutland & Elisabeth Hart, Jan. 22, 1767
Samuel Hutchinson of Lunenburg & Abigail Flagg,
    Jan. 29, 1767
Gardiner Earl of Leicester & Rebecca Brown, March 15, 1767
Michael Richmond of Killingly & Margaret Barber,
    April 2, 1767
Thomas Baker of Woodstock & Sarah Ward, April 14, 1767
John Smith & Sarah Doolittle,   July 5, 1767
Joseph Brooks & Agnes Walker,   Aug. 31, 1767
Aaron Farnsworth of Groton & Abigail Johnson,
    Sept. 21, 1767
Cumberland & Binah (negro servants to Gardiner
    Chandler, Esq.),   Nov. 29, 1767

2

Jonathan Gleason & Lucretia Moore,	Dec. 1, 1767
Rufus Flagg & Martha Chapman,	Dec. 3, 1767
Uriah Ward & Jemima Harrington,	Dec. 23, 1767
Samuel Ward of Lancaster & Dolly Chandler,	Dec. 26, 1767
Daniel Beard & Jane Smith,	Jan. 7, 1768
Nathan Hastings of Shrewsbury & Lois Rice,	Feb. 24, 1768
Josiah Ball & Esther Ward,	Feb. 26, 1768
John Moore & Percis Gates,	Aug. 18, 1768
Nathiel Stearns & Mary Rice	Oct. 13, 1768
Isaac Willard & Mary Dudley,	Oct. 27, 1768
John Barber, Jr., & Patience Gleason,	Dec. 1, 1768
Jonas Ward of Shrewsbury & Sarah Draper,	Dec. 1, 1768
Isaac Rice of Hardwick & Mehitable Stearns,	Dec. 1, 1768
Josiah Gale of Sutton & Elizabeth Rice,	Dec. 1, 1768
Stephen Gould & Esther Wilder,	Jan. 5, 1769
James Moore & Rebekah Jones,	Feb. 8, 1769
Samuel Foster & Elizabeth Boyden,	Feb. 23, 1769
Cyprian Stevens & Sarah Prince,	March 2, 1769
Jonathan Grout & Anna Harrington,	March 7, 1769
Thomas Mullens of Leominster & Elizabeth Rickey,	
	March 16, 1769
Josiah Knight & Anna Willington,	April 6, 1769
Eben Hearns & Martha Holbrook,	April 6, 1769
Jonathan Smith & Sarah Melvin,	June 1, 1769
Jacob Chamberlain & Anna Heywood,	July 4, 1769
John Ball & Lydia Ward,	Aug. 27, 1769
Peter Boyden & Hannah Nichols,	Aug. 31, 1769
Joseph Ball & Esther Mcfadin,	Nov. 16, 1769
Abraham Gale of Shrewsbury & Abigail Rice,	
	Nov. 28, 1769
Samuel Nichols of Templeton & Jane Wiley,	Dec. 7, 1769
Robert Cook & Elizabeth Parker,	Feb. 7, 1770
Asa Smith of Athol & Lydia Lynds,	March 7, 1770
Jonathan Hunt & Lucy How,	March 7, 1770
Lawrence Kelly & Mary Lovis,	March 12, 1770
Phineas Whitney of Leicester & Sarah Harrington,	
	May 20, 1770
Joel Wesson & Hannah Bigelow,	May 23, 1770
John Peirce & Lydia Jones,	Aug. 16, 1770

Joseph Howard of Holden & Sarah Chamberlain,
Sept. 13, 1770
Lewis Allen of Shrewsbury & Mary Adams, Sept. 26, 1770
William Barber & Margaret Knox, Sept. 27, 1770
Joel How & Molly Gates, Oct. 18, 1770
Nathan Hearsay of Leicester & Mary Brown,
Nov. 11, 1770
Rufus Chandler & Eleanor Putnam, Nov. 18, 1770
Moses Gray of Templeton & Sarah Miller, Nov. 27, 1771
Jonas Nichols & Hannah Boyden, Dec. 13, 1770
Josiah Gates & Silence Grout, in Hollis, N. H.,
Feb. 20, 1771
John Phelps of Lancaster & Anna Parker, Feb. 5, 1771
Elijah Harrington & (Mrs.) Mehetable Draper,
April 13, 1768
Asahel Warren & Margaret Spence, Jan. 21, 1771
Ebenezer Thurston of Fitchburg & Lydia Flagg,
Feb. 13, 1771
Holland Maynard of Bolton & Mary Moore, May 16, 1771
John Chamberlain & Mary Curtis, June 27, 1771
William Curtis & Sarah Tatman (or Tolman),
Aug. 25, 1771
William Bancroft & Mary Bancroft, Sept. 5, 1771
Peter Richardson of Shrewsbury & Mary Rice,
Sept. 11, 1771
Asa Ward & Hannah Heywood, Nov. 7, 1771
Ebenezer Willington, Jr., & Esther Boyden, Nov. 20, 1771
Cato (servant to Adam Walker) & Dido (servant to
John Chandler, Esq.), Nov. 24, 1771
Joseph Goodwin & Mary Rice, Dec. 26, 1771
Phineas Jones & Katherine Gates, April 21, 1772
Capt. Aaron Jones of Templeton & Meriam Brewer,
April 29, 1772
Simeon Stearns & Elizabeth Clark, May 6, 1772
Samuel Fullerton & Martha Rice, May 17, 1772
Nathaniel Stedman of Newfane & Ruth Morse of
Wor. Gore, Aug. 24, 1772
Ebenezer Bancroft & Phebe Bancroft, Sept. 17, 1772
Thomas Henly & Mary Temple, Sept. 21, 1772

Robert Gray, Jr., & Elizabeth How,   Oct. 8, 1772
Samuel Dunkin & Bettey Stearns,   Oct. 13, 1772
John Patrick of Western & Elizabeth Mcfarland,
                                                      Oct. 14, 1772
Ebenezer Bradish of Cambridge & Hannah Paine,
                                                      Oct. 22, 1772
Moses Miller & Sarah Gray,   Dec. 1, 1772
Thomas Mower of Leicester & Anna Brown,   Dec. 3, 1772
John Willard & Lucy Davis, both of Wor. Gore,
                                                      Jan. 19, 1773
John Woodward & Abigail Gates,   March 31, 1773
Reuben Gray & Lydia Mellet,   June 1, 1773
Matthew Gray, Jr., & Elizabeth Mcfarland,   Aug. 31, 1773
Abel Holbrook & Hannah Chaddick,   Sept. 28, 1773
Charles Stearns & Sarah Town,   Oct. 4, 1773
Edward Knight, Jr., & Elizabeth Flagg,   Nov. 2, 1773
Ezekiel How & Mary Young,   Dec. 21, 1773
Thomas Nichols & Rebecca Crosby,   Jan. 18, 1774
Alexander Graham of Rutland & Margaret Gray,
                                                      Nov. 25, 1773
Silas Harrington & Mindwell Wellington,   Nov. 25, 1773
Charles Leonard & Nancy Dillingworth,   Nov. 25, 1773
William Farr, Jr., of Chesterfield, N. H., & Lydia
        Trowbridge,   Dec. 6, 1773
Darius Borden & Levina Brown,   Dec. 16, 1773
Isaac Clark of Hardwick & Patience Stearns,   Jan. 5, 1774
Elisha Smith, Jr., & Persis Child of Holden,   Jan. 13, 1774
Thaddeus Chambelain & Judith Barnard,   Jan. 27, 1774
Shepard Gates & Hannah Moore,   Feb. 28, 1774
John Shepard of Acton & Naby Eaton,   March 8, 1774
James Kelly of Colchester, Conn., & Anna Hart,
                                                      March 17, 1774
Solomon Temple of Charlemont & Abigail Heyden,
                                                      May 2, 1774
William Greggs & Kathrine Stearns,   May 23, 1774
Moses Willey of Templeton & Phebe Fitts,   June 14, 1774
John Ward of Westminster & Mindwell Harrington,
                                                      July 10, 1774
Benjamin Chapin, Jr., & Dolly Moore,   Sept. 20, 1774

Caleb Lyman & Kathrine Swan, Oct. 25, 1774
Jonathan Gale of Warwick, N. H., & Mary Bancroft,
Feb. 14, (1755?) 1775
Jonathan Gray of Pelham & Elizabeth Willey,
March 8, 1774
Daniel Willington & Rebecca Putnam, Feb. 7, 1775
Thomas Knight & Sarah Hair, March 22, 1775
David Bigelow, Jr., & Hannah Willington, April 10, 1775
William Buxton & Mary Mahan, June 8, 1775
Joshua Harrington, Jr., & Sarah Bigelow, June 22, 1775
Isaac Gleason, Jr., & Prudence Smith, July 27, 1775
Caleb Ellis of Keene & Sarah Griggs, Aug. 11, 1775
William Stearns & Joanna Dunkin, Oct. 3, 1775
John Ephraim of Natick & Hannah Wisor (Indians),
Oct. 16, 1775
Daniel Gates of Fullam & Sarah Moore, Nov. 13, 1775

MENDON.

May 15, 1667, "Ordered that the name of Mendon be given to the Court's grant to Qun-stipauge, being the township of Qunshapage as it was laid out according to the grant of the General Court, and that Mendon be settled as a town." Mass. Rec., Vol. IV, Part. 2, p. 341. Town proceedings begin 1662. First church organized 1669 (Unitarian). Friends, 1727, now extinct. Clergyman mentioned: Rev. Joseph Willard.

Silvanus Holbrook of Uxbridge & Thankful Thayer,
Oct. 25, 1748
Aaron Legg & Experience Fish, Nov. 17, 1751
William Sprague & Margaret Cheeney, May —, 1748
Thomas White & Priscilla Bishop, July 27, 1748
John Lesure & Sarah White, March 16, 1749
Elijah Ward & Hannah Read, July 29, 1749
Amasa Frost of Mendon & Abigail Livermore of
Framingham, Feb. 1, 1749–50
John Rockwood & Deborah Thayer, March 21, 1750
Thomas Walker of Hopkington & Bethiah Chapin,
April 12, 1750
Joseph Damon & Hopestill Thayer, both of Belling-
ham, June 7, 1750

Oliver Brown of Hartford & Abigail Sheffield, Oct. 17, 1750
Thomas Albee of Mendon & Jemima Thompson of
 Bellingham,   Nov. 22, 1750
John Rockwood & Elisabeth Daniels,   March 18, 1751
Daniel Hayward of Mendon & Joanna Willson of
 Bellingham,   March 20, 1751
Joshua Chapin & Mary Haywood,   March 20, 1751
John Hayward & Margaret Albee,   April 4, 1751
Richard Poffer of Wrentham & Jemima Albee,
          April 11, 1751
Edward Gay of Wrentham & Margaret Rockwood,
          April 17, 1751
Uriah Thayer & Jemima Thayer,   May 8, 1751
William White & Elisabeth Brumil,   Nov. 16, 1749
Jephtha Chapin & Patience Haywood,   Nov. 5, 1749
—— Pratt of Grafton & Susanna Wood,   Aug. 24, 1749
Thomas Nelson & Sarah Pope, both of Upton, Nov. 28, 1749
Samuel Fisk of Upton & Comfort Thayer,   Nov. 1, 1750
Moses White of Uxbridge & Abigail Holbrook,
          Dec. 12, 1749
Thomas Darling & Rachel White,   Dec. 14, 1749
James Wood & Unity Gause (?),   Feb. 7, 1750
Daniel Hill & Elisabeth Pulcipher,   March 26, 1750
Gershom Whitney of Woodstock & Sarah Wood,
          March 21, 1751
Joseph White & Margery Aldrich,   April 11, 1751
Benjamin Carpenter of Ashford, Conn., & Joanna
 Hayward,   Nov. 7, 1751
Philip White & Rachel Green,   June 5, 1751
Elijah Lyon of Woodstock & Elizabeth Merriam,
          June 9, 1752
Benoni Benson & Abigail Staples,   Jan. 30, 1752
John Crooks & Abigail Burch,   March —, 1751
Seth Taft & Ann Taft,   Feb. 17, 1752
Jesse Wheelock & Mary Taft,   March 20, 1752
Aaron Aldrich & Mary Wheat,   May 1, 1753
Ebenezer Torry & Eunice Sturman (?) (Slueman) (?),
          Jan. 25, 1753
Israel Brown & Experience Thayer,   Feb. 15, 1753

Jesse Holbrook & Abigail Thayer, both of Bel-
    lingham, March 28, 1753
Job Warfield & Huldah Thayer, June 12, 1751
Joseph White of Mendon & Ann Colson of Holliston,
    Sept. 26, 1751
William Rexford of Medway & Hannah Thayer,
    Nov. 13, 1751
John Fisk & Deborah Ward, May 7, 1752
Isaac Tenny & Susanna Whitney, June 25, 1752
Joseph Torry & Deborah Holbrook, (old style) Sept. 6, 1752
Samuel Wight & Mary Thomson, both of Belling-
    ham, Oct. 18, 1752
Jesse Wheelock & Phebe White, Dec. 4, 1753
Aaron Legg & Mrs. Experience Fish (or Fisk), Nov. 7, 1751
Elisha Wait & Mrs. Susannah Thayer, June 1, 1752
Samuel White of Killingly & Mrs. Sarah Corbett,
    July 15, 1752
Luke Aldrich & Mrs. Anna French, June 28, 1753
Ebenezer Wheeler of Grafton & Mrs. Priscilla Hay-
    ward, Sept. 5, 1753
Noah Aldrich & Mrs. Rachel Thayer, Dec. 19, 1753
Jonathan Cook of Uxbridge & Mrs. Hannah Thayer,
    March 21, 1754
Henry Penniman & Mrs. Experience Wheelock,
    April 13, 1769
Ephraim Twitchell & Mrs. Lydia Parkhurst, April 13, 1769
Peter Albee & Mrs. Rhoda Penniman, June 8, 1769
Lieut. Josiah Chapin & widow Mary Corbett, Feb. 7, 1770
Barzillai Albee & Mary Marshall, March 21, 1770
Nathaniel Rawson & Elisabeth Nelson, March 24, 1768
Andrew Peters of Medfield & Beulah Lovitt, April 30, 1768
Phinehas Lovett, Jr., and Abigail Thayer, April 6, 1768
Moses Thayer, Jr., & Rachel Thayer, April 7, 1768
Caleb Boynton & widow Abigail Richardson of
    Medway, May 24, 1768
Ichabod Robinson & Abigail Smith of Weston, Oct. 6, 1768
Elijah Thayer & Sarah Robinson, Nov. —, 1768
Jacob Aldrich, Jr., & widow Sarah Steel, Nov. 3, 1768
Benjamin Thurston of Grafton & Dorcas Chapin,
    Nov. 24, 1768

Henry Aldrich & Elisabeth Hunt,	Nov. 24, 1768
Ebenezer Parkhurst & Mercy Hill,	Dec. 22, 1768
Laban Bates & Oliver Wheelock,	Dec. 28, 1768
David Cutler & widow Joanna Atwood,	Dec. 28, 1768
Ralph Haywood & Susanna Thayer,	Dec. 28, 1768
Ichabod Newton & Rhoda Chapin,	Jan. 12, 1769
Jonathan Heywood, Jr., & Mary Vickery,	Jan. 25, 1769
John Gleason of Princetown & Eunice French,	Feb. 2, 1769
Abraham Aldrich & Levina Taft of Uxbridge,	
	March 31, 1768
Nathaniel Taft & Abigail Holbrook of Uxbridge,	
	May 31, 1768
Seth Hayward & Marcy Whitman,	June 22, 1768
Obed Rutter & Mary Lesure,	Nov. 10, 1768
Abner Stanford & Jemima Green,	Nov. 24, 1768
William Foster of Upton & Abigail Chapin,	Dec. 1, 1768
Josiah White & Mary Green,	Jan. 26, 1769
Benjamin Benson & Martha McNammar, both of	
Uxbridge,	Feb. 15, 1769
Thomas Morey of Smithfield & Rhoda Aldrich of	
Uxbridge,	Sept. 14, 1769
John Clark of Westminster & Hannah Green,	Aug. 29, 1769
Ephraim Taft & Hannah Wheelock,	Nov. 16, 1769
Isaac Kent of Bellingham & Sarah Wheelock,	May 17, 1770
Jesse Rutter & Abigail Lesure,	July 9, 1770
Samuel Scarborough of Pomfret & Mary Amedown,	
	Oct. 23, 1770
Phillip Amedon & Silva Taft,	Nov. 15, 1770
David Daniel, Jr., & Olive Adams of Bellingham,	Jan. 15, 1771
Ebenezer Auldis of Wrentham & Hannah Penni-	
man,	June 5, 1771
Benoni Smith & Mehetable Staples,	July 25, 1771
Seva Pond and Silva White,	April 4, 1770
John Hunt & Deborah Darling,	Nov. 8, 1770
Benoni Bensan, Jr., & Ruth Holbrook,	Dec. 6, 1770
John Holbrook of Uxbridge & Rhoda (?) Thayer,	
	Dec. 6. 1770
Turner Ellis & Mary White,	March 16, 1769
Stephan Hilyard & Joanna Darling,	April 13, 1769

Elijah Darling & Sarah Washburn,   April 13, 1769
Job Burnham & Mary Obrian,   June 25, 1769
Silas Richardson & Silence Daniels,   Nov. 14, 1771
Levi Lesuer & Zibiah Rutter,   Feb. 26, 1772
David Stearns & Dinah Bullard,   May 31, 1770
Josiah Ball, Jr., & Sarah Palmer,   July 5, 1770
Simeon Fisher of Holliston & Hepzibah Albee, Dec. 6, 1770
William Cheeney & Hannah Bowher,   Dec. 6, 1770
Elijah Ball & Joanna French,   Dec. 19, 1770
James Dix & Submit Fairbank of Holliston, March 19, 1771
Levi Thayer & Hannah Parkhust,   April 25, 1771
Micah Bates & Urania Thayer,   May 22, 1771
Nathaniel Parkhust & Sarah Brown,   May 29, 1771
Andrew Adams of Grafton & widow Sarah Torrey,
                                                  May 30, 1771
Noah Keith of Uxbridge & Mary Legg,   June 13, 1771
Francis Clark & Anna Gould of Hopkinton,   Oct. 10, 1771
Nathaniel Legg of Upton & Abigail White,   Nov. 21, 1771
Priseved Baker of Wrentham & Elizabeth Daniels,
                                                  Jan. 30, 1772
Ebenezer Merriam & Margaret Jeppardson, April 22, 1771
Simeon Morey of Charlton & Rachel Taft,   May 27, 1772
David Hayward & Abigail Holland, both of North-
    bridge,   Nov. 26, 1771
Saul Ramsdell & Mary Balcom,   Jan. 8, 1773
William Nichols & Mary Smith,   April 1, 1773
Amariah Yeats of Smithfield, R. I., & Margaret
    Thayer,   April 1, 1773
Samuel Orel & Susanna Aldrich, both of Uxbridge,
                                                  April 12, 1773
Nicholas Berry & Mary Morgan, both of Upton,
                                                  April 22, 1773
Increase Daniels & Lona Thayer,   April 29, 1773
Increase Thayer & Leath Wheelock,   Nov. 20, 1771
Timothy Jones & Ann Scammell,   Dec. 3, 1771
Aaron Legg & Mrs. Jerusha Holbrook,   Jan. 16, 1772
Douglas Marsh & Rachel Merriam,   March 12, 1772
Ebenezer Scarbrough of Pomfret & Hannah Ami-
    down,   April 2, 1772

Silas Penniman of Bellingham & Huldah Daniels,
                                                April 22, 1772
Sherebiah Baker of Upton & Clotilda Daniels, June 25, 1772
James Sumner, Jr., & Melatiah Jones,   Oct. 29 1772
Jotham Taft of Dudley & Mary Wilson,   Dec. 2, 1772
John Wharfield & Lydia Taft,   Dec. 3, 1772
Joseph Sadler of Upton & Lydia Daniels,   Dec. 3, 1772
Samuel Wilbour Heath of Newport & Elizabeth
     Thayer,   May 26, 1772
Naham Clark of Holliston & Mary Stearns,   July 9, 1772
Joseph Fisk & Eunice Lathorne,   July 30, 1772
Jacob Hayward & Elizabeth Gibbs,   Oct. 29, 1772
Joseph Pasmore & Thankful Barns,   Nov. 5, 1772
Silas Wood & Asenath Stewart of Holliston,   Dec. 6, 1772
Job Barstow of Holliston & Silence Sumner,   Dec. 6, 1772
Barzillai Taft & Abigail Taft, both of Uxbridge, Dec. 17, 1772
Aaron Wood & Sarah Wood, both of Upton,   Sept. 2, 1773
Benjamin Ellis & Rosannah Thayer,   Sept. 6, 1773
Levi Rawson & Anna Nelson, both of Upton, Nov. 18, 1773
Rufus Chilson & Ruth Hill, both of Uxbridge, Dec. 23, 1773
Paul Lesuer & Susanna Tucker,   March 17, 1774

UXBRIDGE.

June 27, 1727, " Part of Mendon established as Uxbridge." Prov. Laws, Vol. II, p. 427.
First (Congregational) Church organized 1730. Unitarian, 1731. Friends, 1730.

Josiah Benson of Mendon & Susan Bolster,   April 16, 1754
Samuel Thayer, 3d, of Mendon & Sarah Farnum, May 9, 1754
Jonathan Cook of Uxbridge & Jane Dunsmore of
     Mendon,   Aug. 6, 1754
Elnathan Wight & Mrs. Abigail Blood, both of Bel-
     lingham,   Aug. 13, 1754
Jonathan Wood of Lunenburg & Rachel Wood, Oct. 10, 1754
Luke Emerson & Ruth Emerson,   April 30, 1755
John Burnap of Hopkinton & Anna Whoate (?), May 1, 1755
John Harwood & Margaret De le Marude (?),   Dec. 4, 1755
John Prentice of Uxbridge & Mary McClellan of
     Sutton,   July 29, 1756

Peter Harrwood (?) & Mary Webb, April 22, 1756
Thomas Rawson & Eunice Read, May 6, 1756
Cuff & Dinah (negro servants of Lieut. Draper),
March 6, 1760
Nicholas Baylies, Jr., & Abigail Wood, April 24, 1760
Benjamin Blake & Sarah Kimpton, May 8, 1760
Joseph Jackson of Mendon & Bathsheba Thayer,
May 8, 1760
Benjamin Murdock & Katherine Read, May 20, 1760
Levi Walker of Pomfret & Keziah Thompson,
June 12, 1760
Amariah Preston & Susanna Wood, Sept. 25, 1760
Jonas Prentice & Abigail Comings, Nov. 25, 1760
Dependence Hayward of Mendon & Esther Wood,
Nov. 27, 1760
Jonathan Allen & Ruth Newcomb, Dec. 11, 1760
Lieut. Obadiah Brown & Lucy Hall, March 5, 1761
Edmund Rawson & Mrs. Lydia Daniels of Holiston,
March 5, 1761
Joseph Tyler, Jr., & Ruth Read, April 2, 1761
David Leisure & Sarah Peirce, July 21, 1761
Ichabod Collie & Mary Brown, Oct. 8, 1761
Nathan Rawson & Mary White, Feb. 13, 1762
Stephen Powers & Rachell Winter, April 2, 1762
Benjamin Read & Comfort Taft of Mendon, May 27, 1762
Edward Leisure & Cloe Taft, July 1, 1762
Elijah Ward & Else Holbrook, Sept. 16, 1762
John Taft, Jr., & Mary Harwood, Nov. 25, 1762
Samuel Cumings & Lecia Taft, Dec. 9, 1762
Samul Morse & Deborah Hadlock, Dec. 16, 1762
Joel Rawson & Mary Hall, Feb. 17, 1763
Stephen Taft & Mercy Hazeltine, April 14, 1763
James Bardins & Tryphena White, May 5, 1763
Jesse Taft & Lydia Sibley, May 12, 1763
William Bancroft & Mary Daniels, Sept. 29, 1763
Jonathan Cook & Lydia Aldrich, Oct. 20, 1763
Jesse Penniman of Mendon & Lois Wood, Dec. 8, 1763
Thomas Read & Martha Parks, Dec. 14, 1763
Benjamin Fish & Sarah Wood, Feb. 16, 1764

Gershom Taft & Abigail Read,	May 22, 1764
Nathaniel Rawson & Mary Chase,	May 24, 1764
Jonathan Cook of Douglas & Jerusha Bardins,	June 4, 1764
Reuben Walker & Mary Read,	Nov. 28, 1764
John Hawkins of Providence, R. I., & Sarah Emerson,	Nov. 29, 1764
John Hylard & Mehitable Thompson,	Feb. 14, 1765
Benjamin Pike & Aby Keith,	Feb. 21, 1765
Barnabas Aldrich & Prudence Albee,	April 9, 1766
Benjamin Archer & widow Deborah Hull,	May 8, 1766
Elixander Aldrich & Abigail Clark,	Aug. 21, 1766
James Hull & Rebecca Draper,	Sept. 15, 1766
Stephens Williams & Lydia Hicks of Sutton,	Oct. 16, 1766
Edward Battles of Mendon & Ruth Kimpton,	Nov. 26, 1766
Peter White, Jr., & Cloe Farnum,	Dec. 4, 1766
Nathan Twitchel & Hannah Kimpton,	Dec. 18, 1766
Moses Keith & Mary Cumings,	Jan. 22, 1767
Joseph Rist & Rachal Keith,	Dec. 18, 1766
Ezekiel Powers & Hannah Hall,	Jan. 28, 1767
John Sanger & Eunice Davis of Mendon,	Jan. 28, 1767
Mahun Taft & Rachiel Albee,	Feb. 19, 1767
Asa Taft & Elizabeth Buckman,	March 5, 1767
Peter Taft, Jr., & Mary Arnold of Glocester, R. I.,	June 4, 1767
Eleazer Albee & Dorcas Daniels,	Aug. 27, 1767
Jesse Taft & Hannah Taft,	Sept. 10, 1767
Matthew Darling of Mendon & Hannah Emerson,	Oct. 29, 1767
Elisha Hale & Mary Brown,	Nov. 5, 1767
James Taft & Esther Taft,	Nov. 19, 1767
Samuel Amidown of Douglass & Ruth Wood,	March 3, 1768
Silas Rawson & Sarah Draper,	March 17, 1768
Uriah Thayer of Mendon & Mrs. Abigail White,	June 2, 1768
David Woodard & Molley Farnum,	June 23, 1768
Ebenezer Chase & Mary Friphel,	June 30, 1768
Gersham Ward of Grafton & Prudence Powers,	Sept. 1, 1768
Simeon Fish of Mendon & Tabatha Taft,	Nov. 10, 1768
Thomas Ellison & Dorothy Tampling,	Dec. 6, 1768

Thomas Reed, Jr., & Ruth Carryl of Sutton, Dec. 29, 1768
Roger Thompson of Smithfield, R. I., & Elizabeth
    Fish, Jan. 12, 1769
Nathaniel Fish & widow Mary Farnum, April 13, 1769
Levi Walker & Elizabeth Wallis, May 11, 1769
Aaron Taft, Jr., & Rhoda Rawson, June 1, 1769
Abijah Keyes & Jane Aldrich, June 8, 1769
Samuel Gage & Lydia Fish, June 8, 1769
Thomas Willson & Lydia Butler of Upton, Sept. 27, 1769
David Draper, Jr., & Martha Hull, Feb. 15, 1770
Joseph How of Sutton & Mehatable Darling, April 12, 1770
John Curtis of Dudley & Phebe Keith, April 19, 1770
Amos White & Azuba Taft, May 17, 1770
Joseph Cleaveland & Jermima White, May 24, 1770
Abel Fish & Thankful Brown, Sept. 6, 1770
Israel Salem & Bulah Albee, Sept. 27, 1770
Samuel Penniman of Mendon & widow Deborah
    Taft, Oct. 25, 1770
Daniel Taft & Mary Siblee, Nov. 22, 1770
Samuel Stoddard of Grafton & Eliza Dunn, Dec. 6, 1770
Timothy Taft & Priscilla Taft, Dec. 6, 1770
Robert Taft & Cloe Taft, Jan. 3, 1771
Adam White & Sarah Creighton of Douglass, Jan. 10, 1771
John Thwing of Conway & Ruth Holbrook, Oct. 6, 1771
John Hopkins & widow Sarah Benham, Oct. 13, 1771
Ezra Holbrook of Towsend & Mehitable Tyler, Nov. 18, 1771
Victorius Smith & Susanna Pasmore, Nov. 21, 1771
Paul White & Susanna Parcas, Dec. 5, 1771
Stephen Partridge of Midway & Esther Emerson,
    Feb. 27, 1772
Marvel Taft of Northbridge & Ruth Murdock, April 29, 1784
Josep Mosely of Sutton & Susanny Young, April 19, 1784
Paul Wheelock & Mrs. Deborah Morse, Aug. 30, 1784
John Smith of Sutton & Molly Chilson, Oct. 20, 1784
Col. Joseph Hammon, Esq., of Swanzey & Mrs.
    Mary Fish, Oct. 21, 1784
Daniel Holbrook & Joanna Benson of Mendon, Jan. 9, 1785
Joseph Morse & Olive White, Jan. 13, 1785
Ezekiel Morse of Sutton & Mary Tyler, Feb. 18, 1785

RUTLAND.

February 23, 1713, "Certain common lands," the name in general being "Naquag," "established as Rutland." First (Congregational) Church organized 1727.

Stephen Barret & widow Elizabeth Howe,	May 15, 1750
James Wheeler & Abigail Ball,	May 24, 1750
William Banks & Azubah M. (Mc) Maine,	June 7, 1750
Shears (?) Berry (?) of Rutland & Esther Woodward of Holdin,	June 15, 1750
David Bent & Lucy Moore,	April 3, 1751
Jacob Shaw of Leicester & Anna Fulton,	March 16, 1753
Abraham Black & Mary McIntier (?),	April 18, 1753
Thomas Gill & Margaret Haffron,	April 30, 1753
Daniel Davis, Jr., & Sarah Phelps,	May 3, 1753
Oliver Davis & Mary Read,	May 21, 1753
Phinehas Moore & Anna Rice,	June 14, 1753
Thomas Child & Anna Bullard,	Nov. 23, 1753
William Whitaker & Jane Cunningham,	Nov. 27, 1753
Mathew Caldwell & Mary Browning,	Jan. 31, 1754
George Dun & Rachell Harper,	Jan. 31, 1754
Peter Fletcher & Susanna Rice,	April 12, 1754
Aaron Holden & Anna Clarke,	April 20, 1758
Amos Marsh of Hardwick & Bulah Leonard,	Nov. 3, 1757
James Thompson of Leicester & Mrs. Mary Black,	May 26, 1757
Samuel Hunt of Hardwicke & Sarah Osgood,	Dec. 28, 1758
Edward Rice & Mary Stone,	May 10, 1758
Silas Rice & widow Abigail Stevens,	May 12, 1758
William Ball & Christian McFarland,	Sept. 13, 1759
George Duncan & Mary Slarrow (?),	May 9, 1760
Caleb Benjamin of Hardwick & Elizabeth Rice,	Nov. 18, 1760
John Black & Isabel Moore,	Nov. 27, 1760
Daniel Winch of Framingham & Rebecca Reed,	Feb. 18, 1761
Capt. Thomas Cowdin of Worcester & widow Hannah Craige,	Oct. 2, 1761
Michael Heffron & Mary Stevenson,	Oct. 29, 1761

Eleazor Rice & widow Lydia How,	Dec. 3, 1761
James Ames & Elisabeth Hall,	Dec. 8, 1761
Nathan Davis, Jr., & Mary Nurse,	Dec. 8, 1761
Elisha Mirick of Holden & Pursis Moore,	Jan. 6, 1762
Dr. Solomon Persons of Leicester & Mrs. Elizabeth Sweetser,	Jan. 7, 1762
Robert Clerk of Pelham & Mary Patrick,	March 2, 1762
Samuel Metcalf & Hannah Richardson,	March 11, 1762
Willard Moore & Elizabeth Hubbard,	March 18, 1762
John Stevenson & Sarah Gilbert of Brookfield,	May 18, 1762
Samuel Ball, of Roxbury, Canada (so-called) & Lucy Leonard,	July 9, 1761
David Clark & Sarah Bacon,	Oct. 29, 1761
Oliver Robinson & Elizabeth Hail (Thald),	Oct. 7, 1762
Samson Bixby & Mary Bullard,	Dec. 1, 1761
Theophilus Chandler of Petersham & Elizabeth Frink,	May 26, 1763
John Black & Sarah Work,	May 9, 1763
Adam Wheeler & Marcy Wheeler,	Nov. 17, 1763
Elijah Man & (Mrs.) Susanna Wilder,	June 7, 1764
Ephraim Heyden & Abigail Nurse,	July 11, 1764
Barnabas Sears of Hardwick & Mrs. Rachel Bullard,	Nov. 1, 1764
Aaron Smith & Mrs. Mary Akers (or Acres),	March 8, 1764
Joseph How & Hepzibah How, both of Princetown,	Jan. 24, 1765
John Sweeney & (Mrs.) Abigail Jackson,	Feb. 21, 1765
Samuel Leonard & Silence Ripley,	Nov. 21, 1765
Makepeace Gates & Kathrine Smith,	June 6, 1765
John Haskel of Hardwick & Hannah Rice,	Dec. 9, 1765
Samuel Bullard & Mrs. Sarah Barber,	March 13, 1766
Samuel Smith & (Mrs.) Sarah Fay,	April 22, 1766
Thomas Rice & (Mrs.) Hannah Wright,	May 15, 1766
Asahel Osgood & Mrs. Hannah Wilder,	Jan. 15, 1767
Jonas Permenter & Sarah Butrick,	July 25, 1765
Matthew How & Azubah Davis,	Oct. 8, 1767
Israel Stone & Lydia Barrel of Paxton,	July 12, 1768
John Fesinden & Elizabeth Wyman,	Nov. 23, 1769
Rev. John Strickland & Pattey Stone of Oakham,	Oct. 29, 1767

William Oliver of Athol & Anna Forbes,	Dec. 30, 1767
Solomon Robinson & Abigail Badger,	Dec. 31, 1767
Joel Bent & Mary Mason,	July 13, 1768
Capt. Benjamin Lee & Mehitable Jenkins,	July 28, 1768
Samuel Forbes & Jane Montor,	Nov. 30, 1768
James Berry, Jr., of Pelham & Margaret Smith,	
	Dec. 1, 1768
Nathaniel Jenison & Isabel Caldwell,	March 28, 1769
Jabez Upham & Hannah Burgess,	May 10, 1768
Ebenezer Johnson & Hannah Chandler,	July 20, 1769
Sheribiah Lee & Esther Miles,	July 20, 1769
John Jones of Princetown & Bettey Hapgood,	Oct. 19, 1769
Joshua Bartlet & Bettey Felton,	Oct. 26, 1769
James Morse & Hannah Smith,	Nov. 26, 1769

DUDLEY.

February 2, 1732, "Part of Oxford and certain common lands established as Dudley." Prov. Laws, Vol. II, p. 626. First (Congregational) Church organized 1732.

David Hall of Killingly & Sarah Robinson,	April 21, 1763
Eleazor Bellows of Oxford & Abigail Putney,	Oct. 27, 1763
Lemuel Corbin of Dudley & Rebecca Davis of Oxford,	Dec. 8, 1763
Jonathan Lyon of Woodstock & Rebecca Corbin,	
	Dec. 22, 1763
John Jefferds & Mary Sanger,	Feb. 20, 1764
Isiah Putney & Abigail Warrin,	Nov. 24, 1764
Joseph Upham, Jr., & Eunice Kidder,	April 16, 1764
Benjamin Newell & Lucy Dodge,	May 7, 1765
Thomas Taylor & Lucy Dexter,	July 8, 1765
Aaron Jewett of Sheffield & Hannah Curtis,	Jan. 23, 1766
John Hutchins & Olive Rood of Sturbridge,	Oct. 9, 1766
Isaac Lee, Jr., of Killingly & Abigail Jewett,	Dec. 4, 1766
Timothy Barton of Charlton & Amy Allen,	Jan. 20, 1767
Ichabod Chamberlain & Sarah Gale,	March 29, 1767
John Newell & Mary Willard,	Sept. 28, 1767
David Kidder & Susanna Upham,	Feb. 23, 1768

Amos Hooker & Hannah Foster, March 10, 1768
John Edmunds & Silence Emerson, May 19, 1768
Simon Stone of Killingsly & Hannah Robinson, May 19, 1768
Joseph Perrin of Woodstock & Dorothy Corbin, July 13, 1768
Samuel Pagon, Jr., & Sarah Pagon (Indians), July 21, 1768
Daniel Newell & Elisabeth Putnam, Dec. 1, 1768
Ebenezer Taylor & Mary Scott, Oct. 13, 1768
Jonas Fairbank & Mary Carter, Dec. 1, 1768
Isaac Humphrey, Jr., & Susana Libret, Dec. 22, 1768
Samuel Warren & Susanna Farrow, Jan. 4, 1769
John Morss & Eunice Bartholomew, Jan. 12, 1769
Samuel Newell & Rachel Ross, Feb. 23, 1769
Dr. Thomas Sterne & Sarah Gleason, March 5, 1769
Joseph Sabin, Jr., of Dudley & Susanna Adams of
     Killingsly, March 16, 1769
Asa Corbin & Patience Smith, Nov. 16, 1769
Jonathan Shattuck of Oxford & Huldah Curtis,
     Nov. 30, 1769
Elijah Converse of Killingsly & Experience Hibbard,
     Jan. 30, 1770
David Cutten & Dorothy Sabin, March 4, 1770
Ira Green & Elizabeth Dodge, April 5, 1770
John Polley of Charlton & Phebe Chamberlain,
     April 12, 1770
Daniel Bacon of No. Woodstock & Esther Jones,
     March 3, 1770
Henry Huker & Molley Edmund, July 12, 1770
Timothy Gay & Anna Bridges, Sept. 20, 1770
Edward Curtis & Lucy Chamberlain, Oct. 4, 1770
Richard Foster & Lydia Titus, Dec. 6, 1770
Edward Morris & Dorcas Corbin, March 23, 1771
Josiah Brown & Dinah Wetherill, Jan. 14, 1772
Jesse Sabin & Rhoda Waters, April 16, 1772
Jonathan Conant & Lucy Corbin, July 9, 1772
Moses Jewell & Jemima Corbin, July 23, 1772
Jedediah Corbin & Hannah Howe, Oct. 9, 1772
Thomas West & Mary Spear, Nov. 12, 1772
John Bacon & Mary Jewell, Nov. 19, 1772
Ezekial Hovey & Eunice Pease, Nov. 19, 1772

3

Aaron Barrett of Killingly & Mary Williams,   Dec. 3, 1772

Winthrop Chandler of Killingly & Mary Gleason,

                                      Feb. 16, 1773

Joseph Winter & Azubah Barton of Oxford,   Oct. 6, 1773

William Brewer & Lucy Davis,   Oct. 14, 1773

Josiah Hovey & Hannah May of Pomfret,   Nov. 25, 1773

Samuel May, Jr., & Amy Putnam,   Nov. 25, 1773

Eben White & Lydia Davis,   Dec. 16, 1773

Edward Coburn of Windham & Sarah Wyman, Jan. 20, 1774

Simeon Howard & Abigail Witherell,   April 14, 1774

Samuel Wright of Brookfield & Lois Corbin,   May 25, 1774

Dr. William Gleason & Mary Kidder,   May 31, 1774

Seth Perry of Sturbridge & Lois Jennings,   June 28, 1774

Leiut. Mark Elwell of Killingsly & Dorothy White,

                                      Aug. 29, 1774

Timothy Corbin & Abigail Vinton,   Oct. 20, 1774

William Brown & Mary Freeman of Killingly,

                                   March 25, 1779

Daniel Arnold & Nancy Brown,   March 25, 1779

Thomas Chafey of Woodstock & Mary May,   April 8, 1779

John White & Lucy Conant,   April 15, 1779

Josiah Barns & Rebecca Kidder,   Nov. 25, 1779

Lemuel Edmunds & Hannah ————,   Dec. 1, 1779

James Brown & Sarah Oaks,   Dec. 9, 1779

Joshua Atwood & Prudence Parker,   Feb. 29, 1780

John Bowers & Sarah Inman,   March 7, 1780

Benjamin Joslin of Killingly & Susannah Robin-

   son,   Nov. 16, 1774

Jacob Chambain, Jr., & Mary Vinton,   Nov. 22, 1774

Capt. Andrew Coburn of New Marlboro & widow

   Phebe Bacon,   Nov. 27, 1774

Daniel Hibberd & Esther Converse,   Jan. 5, 1775

Jacob Warren, Jr., & Lucy Fosket of Charlton, Jan. 17, 1775

Samuel Rogers of Sturbridge & Rachel Hibberd,

                                      Feb. 6, 1775

Elisha Corbin, Jr., & Experience Barns,   Feb. 27, 1775

Samuel Fosket of Charlton & Sarah Hunt,   March 29, 1775

Jacob Barrett of Roxbury School farms & widow

   Hannah Robinson,   April 13, 1775

Jesse Jewel & Zerviah Corbin,   June 1, 1775
Zebedee Appleby of Smithfield & Joanna Sly (?),
                                                 June 19, 1775
Joseph Inman & Lucy Sprague,   Aug. 17, 1775
Alexander Brown of Killingly & Hannah Kidder,
                                                 Aug. 17, 1775
Benjamin Edmunds & Eunice Parker,   Aug. 30, 1775
William Havens & widow Sarah Brock of Wood-
    stock,   Sept. 21, 1775
Philip Brown & Louis Upham,   Sept. 28, 1775
William Smith & Hannah Albee,   Nov. 8, 1775
Benjamin Kidder & Phebe Sabin,   Nov. 9, 1775
John Gore & Hannah Carpenter,   Nov. 23, 1775
John Bacon & widow Elizabeth Dodge,   Jan. 1, 1776
Joseph Edmunds, Jr., & Phebe Andrews of Pom-
    fret,   March 28, 1776
Samuel Curtis, Jr., of Charlton & Mary Putney,
                                                 April 3, 1776
Reuben Chamberlain & Rebecca Healey,   April 25, 1776
Ebener Edmunds & Molly Gail,   May 16, 1776
Jonathan Putney & Tamar Haskell,   May 29, 1776
Jonathan Webster & Martha Carpenter,   Nov. 17, 1776
John Edmunds & Hanna Graton,   Feb. 12, 1777
Jeremiah Haskell & Hannah Newell,   April 8, 1777
Jacob Willson of Pomfret & Molly Dodge,   April 22, 1777
Moses Dresser of Chesterfield & Abigail Blood of
    Charlton,   May 7, 1777
Benoni Adams & Susanna Chamberlain,   May 8, 1777
Joseph Keith & Sarah Mayo,   May 19, 1777
William Richards, Jr., of Killingly & Rebecca
    Jewell,   May 27, 1777
John Bayley of Killingly & Lydia Barstow,   Aug. 6, 1777
Daniel Barrett of Killingly & widow Mary Dodge,
                                                 Sept. 18, 1777
Richard Hunt & Elizabeth Warren,   Nov. 13, 1777
Amariah Preston of Uxbridge & widow Elizabeth
    Bacon,   Nov. 18, 1777
William Carter, Jr., & Hannah Mayo,   Dec. 18, 1777
Stephen Edmunds & Sarah Kidder,   Jan. 15, 1778

John Albee & Zerviah Sales,   Feb. 26, 1778
Shadrach Smith & Joanna Albee,   Feb. 26, 1778
David Lamb of Charlton & Judith Fitts,   March 12, 1778
Benjamin Dresser & Jemima Scott, both of Charl-
    ton,   April 8, 1778
Bezaleel Gould of Douglass & Bathsheba Robin-
    son,   April 9, 1778
John Applebee of Smithfield & Patience Sly, April 16, 1778
William Abbot of Pomfret & widow Hannah Ed-
    munds,   June 4, 1778
Luther Wakefield of Sutton & Mary Wakefield, June, 10, 1778
Nathan Fletcher & Huldah Clemens,   Aug. 2, 1778
James Town of Charlton & Lucy Bettiss,   Aug. 6, 1778
Elijah Humphrey of Killingly & Esther Brown,
                                                   Sept. 13, 1778
Deacon John Davis of Oxford & widow Susanna
    Kidder,   Oct. 1, 1778
Roger Williams of Glouster & Hannah Howard, Jan. 7, 1779
Eleazor May & Abigail Prince,   Sept. —, 1779
Amasa Marshall & Tamar Wilder,   March 20, 1780
John Healey & Elizabeth Dalrymple,   April 20, 1780
Moses Hill of Douglass & Dinah Robinson,   Sept. 20, 1780
Bradford Barnes & Sarah Howard,   Oct. 23, 1780
Philemon Parker & Susanna Stone,   Oct. 26, 1780
Elnathan McIntire of Charlton & Martha Thomp-
    son,   Dec. 7, 1780
Isaac Dresser of Charlton & Susanna Taft,   Dec. 20, 1780
Samuel Corbin, Jr., of Killingly & Lucy Larned,
                                                   Jan. 18, 1781
Wyman Ainsworth & Elizabeth How,   Jan. 31, 1781
Nathan Dennis & widow Rebecca Jewell,   Feb. 6, 1781
William Foster & Mary Brown,   Feb. 8, 1781
John Heath & Eunice Oaks,   Feb. 12, 1781
John Cleveland & Caty May,   March 15, 1781
Dr. John Eliot & widow Beriah Marcy,   April 12, 1781
Dan Warren & Mary Hayden,   May 3, 1781
Oliver Willard & Asenath Newell,   May 3, 1781
John Davisson & Rhoda Putney,   July 26, 1781
Joshua Corbin & Rhoda Wood,   Sept. 6, 1781

Ephraim Willard & Sylvia Albee,   Oct. 11, 1781
Thomas McClanathan of Rutland & Dolly Dal-
    rymple,   Nov. 22, 1781
Captain Joseph Albee & widow Phebe Turtelot of
    Killingly,   Nov. 29, 1781
John Larned, the 3rd, of Oxford & Martha Wake-
    field,   Dec. 6, 1781
Stephen Wood & Levina Newell,   Feb. 11, 1782
Henry Brown & Hannah Brown,   March 14, 1782
Jedediah Marcy, Jr., & Ruth Larned,   April 4, 1782
Charles Brown of Johnstone & Dinah Fenner,
                                              April 15, 1782
Timothy Stow Barton of Whitingham & Phebe
    Stone,   June 20, 1782
John Chamberlain & Mary Lee,   Sept. 19, 1782
Edward Pike & Mary Hibberd,   Sept. 19, 1782
Stephen Healy & Rhody Marcy,   Jan. 23, 1783
Melvin Cotton of Hartford, Vt., & Joanna Dennis,
                                              Jan. 30, 1783
Micaiah Robinson & Sarah Ballard of Oxford,
                                              May 29, 1783
John Ammidon of Charlton & Olive Sanger, June 19, 1783
Aaron Albee & Martha Willard,   Aug. 1, 1783
Benjamin Stone, Jr., & Elizabeth Wilcox,   Sept. 11, 1783
Ebenezer Plummer & Hannah Allen,   Sept. 25, 1783
Amos Wakefield & Polly Knowland, both of Gore,
                                              Oct. 10, 1783
Joshua Wetherell & widow Mary Winter of Killing-
    ley,   Oct. 23, 1783
Ezra Holbrook & Anna Hedges,   Nov. 6, 1783
Jared Curtis of Charlton & Phebe Putney,   Dec. 10, 1783
Thomas Davis of Killingley & Rebecca Bracket,
                                              Dec. 25, 1783
Jacob Larned of Oxford & Elizabeth Atwood, Jan. 8, 1784
Thomas Upham & Elizabeth Pratt of Oxford, Feb. 19, 1784
Joseph Sheffield of Killingly & Theody Carter,
                                              Feb. 19, 1784
John Streeter & Marcy Morse, both of Charlton,
                                              March 24, 1784

Thomas Morriss & Margaret Warren,	June 3, 1784
James Hascall & Elizabeth Vinton,	June 3, 1784
James McCallen, Jr., of Sutton & Beulah Bacon,	
	Nov. 23, 1784
Jabez Vinton & Ruth Putney,	Dec. 22, 1784
Jonathan Bacon & widow Sarah Kidder,	Feb. 3, 1785
Silas Hayden & Rebecca Morriss,	Feb. 10, 1785
Thomas Larned & Hannah Morriss,	May 12, 1785
Simon or Simeon Upham & Miriam Larned,	June 22, 1785
Stephen Haskell & Rachel Larned,	Sept. 15, 1785
William Larned, Jr., & Nancy Amidown,	Oct. 13, 1785
Asa Newell & Jerusha Ward,	Oct. 17, 1785
Nathan Smith, Jr., & Elisheba Atwood,	Feb. 2, 1786
Nathan Waldron & Mary Willard,	Dec. 15, 1785
Ebenezer Fitts, Jr., & Mary Mansfield,	Dec. 15, 1785
Amasa Winter & Rebekah Richard,	Jan. 19, 1786
William Cargill & Lucretia Carter, married in Bennington, Vt.,	March 3, 1786

STURBRIDGE.

June 24, 1738, "The tract of land called New Medfield established as Sturbridge." Prov. Laws., Vol. II, p. 946. First (Congregational) Church organized 1736. Baptist, 1749, at Fiskdale. The following marriages were performed largely by Rev. Joshua Paine.

Eliphalet Allen & Elisabeth Livermore,	Feb. 8, 1753
Eneas Adams & Marcy Rood,	Sept. 26, 1753
Aaron Lyon & Mary Mason,	Dec. 5, 1753
Jabez Harding & Merriam Weld,	June 3, 1754
Elijah Marcy & Sarah Stacy,	Feb. 19, 1754
Eliphalet Allen & Elizabeth Livermore,	Feb. 8, 1755
Eneas Adams & Mercy Rood,	Sept. 26, 1753
Aaron Lyon & Mary Mason,	Dec. 5, 1753
Jabez Harding & Merriam Ward,	Jan. 3, 1754
Elijah Marcy (?) & Sarah Stacy,	Feb. 4, 1754
Jonathan Bond & Lydia Allen,	April 18, 1754
Aaron Elwell & Abigail Wood,	May 23, 1754
Aaron Cromp (?) & Hepzibah Mason,	July 24, 1754
William Plympton & Prudence Marcy,	Nov. 28, 1754

Josiah Partridge & Sarah Martin,	July 30, 1755
David Smith & Mary Smith,	April 8, 1755
Joseph Sollne (?) & Susanna Johnson,	Feb. 12, 1756
Seth Hinds & Elisabeth Hale,	Feb. —, 1755
Methrop (?) Remington & Mary Marcy,	July 9, 1755
Jason Morse & Phebe Stacey,	March 16, 1759
Seth Bond & Martha Blunt,	April 28, 1762
Stephen Fay & Susen Fisk,	July 1, 1762
Joseph Morse & widow Sarah Stacey,	Oct. 20, 1762
Samuel Hamant & Kezia Baker,	Nov. 30, 1762
Adam Martin & Abigail Cheny,	Dec. 19, 1762
Abel Mason & Ruth Hobbs,	Dec. 30, 1762
James Johnson, Jr., & Hannah Harding,	June 13, 1763
Daniel Williams & Rachel Foster,	July 8, 1763
Joseph Lumbird & Lydia Leach,	July 21, 1763
Job Hamant & Jemima Baker,	Sept. 1, 1763
Thomas McKlure & Zilpah Leach,	Nov. 4, 1762
Philip Mahon & widow Ruth Rion,	Feb. 28, 1764
Asahel Corbin & Jerusha Morse,	Dec. 22, 1763
Arriel Blanchard & Abigail Mason,	Jan. 10, 1764
Aaron Allen, Jr., & Abigail Allen,	March 15, 1764
John Cheny, Jr., & Mary Shumway,	May 30, 1764
Moses Weld & Deborah Faulkner,	July 11, 1764
Aaron Clark & Katherine Ingraham,	May 11, 1765
Reuben Alexander & Sarah Foster,	Oct. 3, 1764
Abner Plympton & Esther Man,	Nov. 27, 1764
Asher Rice & Dinah Allen,	Dec. 13, 1764
William White & Mercy Dresser,	April 7, 1763
Josiah Blanchard & Elizabeth Hobbs,	April 7, 1763
Nicholas Harwood & Lucy Alexander,	Sept. 9, 1766
Ebenezer Lovell & Abigail Lyon,	March 14, 1765
Nathan Howard & Sibbel Marsh,	April 10, 1765
Asa Walker & Prudence Bond,	Jan. 10, 1765
John Graham & Mary Child,	April 17, 1765
Israel Ganes & Abigail Fay,	May 1, 1765
Abel Allen & Jerush Tarbill,	May 9, 1765
Zachariah Coburn & Dinah Hobbs,	Aug. 7, 1765
Rowland Taylor & widow Abigail Stacy,	Aug. 8, 1765
Nathan Abbot & Lydia Hatch,	Oct. 10, 1765

Elijah Carpenter & Hannah Corey,	Oct. 10, 1765
Aaron Martin & Olive Harding,	Jan. 9, 1766
Eliphlit Allen & widow Susanna Pollis (?),	July —, 1764
Joseph Smith, Jr., & Sarah Rice,	Dec. 13, 1764
Ebenezer Fay & Mary Mason,	Nov. 19, 1765
Joseph Chamberlain & Susanna Newell,	Jan. 16, 1766
John Streeter & Kezia Morse,	Feb. 12, 1766
Simeon Allen & Sarah Puffer,	June 4, 1766
Benjamin F–umiss (?) & widow Abigail Taylor,	
	Sept. 1, 1766
Jeremiah Twichell & Rhoda Clark,	Sept. 4. 1766
Samuel Freeman, Jr., & Elizabeth Cheney,	Sept. 25, 1766
John Lace & Mary Guest,	Nov. 6, 1766
Oliver Mason & Lucy Johnson,	Dec. 18, 1766
Silas Corbin & Anna Fisk,	Dec. 30, 1766
Timothy Newell & Miriam Marcy,	Jan. 1, 1767
Abijah Searls & Zilpah Sabin,	July 2, 1767
Silas Hedges & Rachel Freeman,	Sept. 23, 1767
Charles Dugen (?) & Sarah Chubb,	May 14, 1767
Eliphlit Allen & Sabra Lee,	March 12, 1767
Samuel Richardson & Mary Walker,	April 23, 1767
Jonas Pike & Mary Howard,	May 7, 1767
Ephraim Bacon & Hannah Chamberlain,	May 28, 1767
Benjamin Wiser & Abigail Thomas,	June 25, 1767
Daniel Hobbs & Elizabeth Chubb,	July 23, 1767
Samuel Hooker & Mary Pierce,	Oct. 15, 1767
Gideon Sabin & Truelove Serls,	Jan. 21, 1768
Daniel Marcy & Hannah Morris,	March 3, 1768
Nathan Smith & Sarah Pike,	Jan. 13, 1768
David Smith & widow Abigail Stacy,	April 19, 1768
Seth Hamant & Mehitabel Mix,	June 9, 1768
John Blanchard & Mary Stacy,	June 29, 1768
Abner Lyon & Elizabeth Martin,	Aug. 9, 1768
Joseph Morse, Jr., & Mary Martin,	Sept. 14, 1768
Timothy Allen & Mary Moffit,	Dec. 8, 1768
Eleazer Adams & Elizabeth Cory,	Jan. 12, 1769
John Dresser & Anna Clark,	March 23, 1769
Silas Hooker & Francis Tarbill,	April 13, 1769
Elijah Plimpton & Mary Cheny,	July 25, 1769

Isaac Upham & Hephzibah Shaply,   Oct. 10, 1769
—— Belknap & —— Stacy,   Jan. 25, 1770
Jedidiah Smith & Sarah Blanchard,   Jan. 25, 1770
Thomas Cheny, Jr., & Eunice Gleason,   May 18, 1779
Rufus Robbins & Sabra Whittell,   Dec. 7, 1769
Jonathan Newell & Mehitable Marcy,   May 12, 1771
Joshua Crosman & Sarah Weld,   Nov. 5, 1772
Moses Bliss & Mary Newell,   Nov. 26, 1772
Amos Broughton & Abigail Corbin,   Dec. 3, 1772
Jason Allen & Martha Johnson,   March 4, 1773
John Mason & Sarah Sabin,   April 20, 1773
Luke Harding and Lydia Marsh,   Oct. 19, 1773
Abel Bacon & Sarah McKinstry,   Sept. 19, 1773
Cyral Shumway & Sarah Harding,   Jan. 11, 1774
Jedidiah Ellis & Martha Freeman,   April 28, 1774
Henry Fisk, Jr., & Sarah Fisk,   May 5, 1774
Abel Mackentier & Hannah Mory,   June 9, 1774
Jared Freeman & Martha Marcy,   Dec. 22, 1774
Jacob Mason & Mary Johnson,   Jan. 31, 1775

√ LUNENBURG.

August 1, 1728, "The south part of Turkey Hills established as Lunenburg." Prov. Laws, Vol. II, p. 520. First (Congregational) Church organized 1835. A Unitarian Church became extinct there in 1860. Date of organization unknown. Officiating clergymen mentioned: Revs. David and Ebenezer Stearns, Rev. Zabdiel Adams.

William Barrow of Ashuelots & Isabella Larrabee,
    Sept. 28, 1752
Bradstreet Spafford of No. 4 & Mary Page,   Oct. 16, 1752
Joseph Hammond of Lower Ashuelots & Esther
    Gould,   Nov. 2, 1752
Joseph Platts of Rowley, Canada, & Deborah Page,
    Nov. 16, 1752
Benjamin Larrabee of Lunenberg & Margaret
    Williams of Groton,   Dec. 7, 1752
Aaron Taylor & Mercy Gould,   Dec. 21, 1752
Gershom Makepeace of Dunstable and Lipha
    Dodge,   Jan. 18, 1753

Joseph Brown of Cambridge & Abigail Foster, Jan. 18, 1753
Timothy Darling of Lunenburg & Joanna Blood
    of Groton,   Feb. 8, 1753
David Steel of Londonderry & Jennit Little,   Feb. 8, 1753
John White and Mary Whitney,   Feb. 22, 1753
Stephen Boynton & Elizabeth Lovejoy,   March 6, 1753
Zachariah Tarbell & Mary Gould,   March 27, 1753
William Henry, Jr., & Mary Harper,   Dec. 6, 1753
Abner Whitney of District of Shirley & Sarah
    Hilton,   June 21, 1753
John Smith of Peterborough & Mary Hark-
    ness,   Oct. 2, 1753
William Mahan, Jr., of Worcester & Mary Kennedy,
    Dec. 4, 1753
Benjamin Corey, Jr., of Lunenburg & Beulah
    Holden of District of Shirley,   Dec. 26, 1753
Benjamin Stearns & Anna Taylor,   Jan. 15, 1754
Thomas Putnam of Charlestown, N. H., & Rachel
    Wetherbee,   Jan. 24, 1754
Timothy Dorman of Boxford & Eunice Burnam,
    May 27, 1754
Moses Stearns of Narraganset No. 2 & Ruth
    Houghton,   July 29, 1754
Joseph Beman & Hannah Knight,   July 23, 1755
Jacob Peabody & Dorothy Foster, both of Leo-
    minster,   March 4, 1756
Alexander Swan & Lucy Foster,   March 7, 1756
Zimri Haywood & Jane Foster, both of Dorchester,
    Canada (so-called),   June 5, 1756
William Dodge & Elizabeth Salmon of Harvard,
    Jan. 28, 1755
John Simonds & Mary Page,   March 13, 1755
Henry Hopkins & Mary Dutton,   May 8, 1755
Solomon Steward, Jr., & Elizabeth Taylor,   May 28, 1755
Benony Wallace & Rebecca Brown of Lyn,   July 2, 1755
Jonathan Bennet of Groton & Going (?),   Oct. 2, 1755
Levi Stiles & Patience Smith,   Dec. 16, 1755
John Fuller & Prudence Gilson,   Dec. 18, 1755
Jonas Gilson & Sarah Divoll,   Jan. 29, 1756

Phineas Steward & Anne Ireland,   April 22, 1765
Nehemiah Fuller & Mary Conant,   May 4, 1756
Samuel Pool & Mary Potter,   Dec. 4, 1756
Samuel Pool & Sarah Potter,   Dec. 14, 1756
Nathaniel Souchee of Ipswich, Canada, & Eliz.
    Priest of Stow,   Jan. 13, 1757
William Braybrook of Lancaster & Thankful Dut-
    ton,   March 4, 1757
Thomas Dutton & Sarah Fitch,   Sept. 9, 1756
Nathaniel Carlton, Jr., & Olive Farwell,   Nov 1, 1756
Abner Jackman & Elizabeth Bayley,   Feb. 10, 1757
Daniel Steward & Mary Ireland,   March 14, 1757
Benjamin Redington & Ruth Stearns,   March 24, 1757
✔ Jonathan Wood & Sarah Gary,   April 19, 1757
Daniell Austin, Jr., & Pheebee Lovejoy,   April 26, 1757
Elijah Grout & Mary Willard,   July 17, 1757
Samuel Hodgskins & Rebeckah Rice,   Aug. 8, 1757
John Moors, Jr., of Bolton & Unity Willard,   Aug. 3, 1757
Timothy Bancroft & Mary Harriman,   Nov. 1, 1757
Joseph Davis & Elizabeth Forster,   Nov. 8, 1758
Barzillai Willard & Hepsabah Redington,   Nov. 18, 1757
Ephraim Stockwell & Sarah Grout, both of Peter-
    sham   Nov. 21, 1757
William Cowdin of Worcester & Mary Henry, Sept. 7, 1757
James Clark & Anne Freeman, both of Lancaster,
                                      Jan. 5, 1758
Joseph Houghton & Mary Wilson, both of Leo-
    minster,   Jan. 31, 1758
Abner Wheelock of Leominster & Mary Brown,
                                      April 12, 1758
John Richards & Elizabeth Mitchel,   Oct 17, 1758
Samuel Russel & Susannah Mitchel,   Nov. 28, 1757
Elisha Bigelow of Narraganset No. 2 & Sarah
    Goodridge,   Dec. 1, 1757
Moses Child & Sarah Stiles,   March 28, 1758
Thaddeus Harrington of Shirley & Thankful
    Dodge,   April 6, 1758
Wincal Wright of Dunstable & Sibbil Farewell,
                                      April 7, 1758

Samuel Hart & Mary Fuller,   April 20, 1758
Benjamin Bellows, Esq., of Walpole, N. H., & Mrs.
    Mary Jenison,   April 21, 1758
Ebenezer Hart & Sarah Poole,   May 4, 1758
Jonathan Stedman of Westminster & Tabitha
    Hart,   Sept. 8, 1761
Ebenezer Pratt & Lydia Stone of Groton,   Sept. 22, 1761
Josiah Dodges, Jr., & Hannah Conant of Leo-
    minster,   Nov. 8, 1761
David Poor of Ipswich, Canada, & Jane Martin, Dec. 2, 1761
James Carter & Sarah Gilson,   Dec. 3, 1761
Reuben Smith & Prudence Pierce,   Sept. 6, 1762
Henry Hodgkin of Ipswich, Canada, & Jemima
    Ball of Westminster,   Nov. 7, 1762
Francis Gardiner of Stow & Mrs. Sarah Gibson,
                                              Oct. 5, 1762
Josiah Bailey, Jr., & Sarah Carter,   Oct. 7, 1762
Jacob Wilson & Margaret Freeman, both of Leo-
    minster,   Dec. 6, 1762
Samuel McCracken of Worcester & Lettice Cor-
    lisle,   Dec. 8, 1762
Asa Carlton & Ruth Bailey,   Feb. 8, 1763
Silas Dutton & Sarah Whitney,   March 3, 1763
John Endicott of Danvers & Martha Putnam,
                                             April 19, 1763
Page Norcross & Elizabeth Bailey,   Feb. 15, 1763
Phinehas Divol & Abigail Stockwell,   June 6, 1763
Rev. Ebenezer Sparhawke of Templeton & Mrs.
    Abigail Stearns,   Sept. 1, 1763
James Bennet and Elizabeth Fuller,   Sept. 6, 1763
David Stearns & Mary Law,   Oct. 20, 1763
Samuel Hilton & Rebeccah Stickney,   Nov. 17, 1763
Phinehas Hutchins & Abigail Read,   Nov. 24, 1763
Eliphalet Goodridge & Rebeccah Snow,   Dec. 29, 1763
Eleazer Houghton & Susannah Holman   March 8, 1764
Ebenezer Bridge & Mehitabel Wood,   Nov. 3, 1763
Joseph Chaplain & Lois Hastings,   April 5, 1764
Jacob Gates of Harvard & Mrs. Elizabeth Gibson,
                                              May 9, 1764

Benjamin Gould of Rowley, Canada, N. H., &
   Sarah Foster,   May 14, 1764
Michal Wood & Lois Willson of Leominster,   Aug. 21, 1764
Joseph Bellows & Lois Whitney,   Oct. 3, 1764
Samuel Hazon of Stow & Elizabeth Little,   Nov. 20, 1764
Joseph Fuller & Rebecca Wyman,   Feb. 6, 1763
Thomas Carter, Jr., & Priscilla Reed, or Rud, Feb. 13, 1765
David Carlisle, Jr., & Sarah Cumming,   Feb. 11, 1765
Thomas Hartwell & Prudence Carter,   May 9, 1765
Timothy Farley of Fitchburg & Sarah Colburn,
                                                Nov. 19, 1765
Eli Dodge, Jr., & Mary Chaplain,   Jan. 21, 1766
Nathaniel Parkhill & Mary Holden, both of Leicester,
                                                May 30, 1766
William Moffatt of Winchenden & Mary Price (?)
   of Shirley,   Sept. 22, 1766
Daniel Goodridge of Winchendon & Mary Low, Oct. 30, 1766
Simeon Burnam & Mary Wanson, both of Shirley,
                                                May 30, 1765
Amos Davis of Westmoreland, N. H., & Patience
   Griffin,   June 11, 1765
Job Colman of Ashburnam & Elisabeth Martin, Feb. 20, 1766
Nathan Plats & Relief Austin,   May 27, 1766
Benjamin Darling & Mary Holt,   June 26, 1766
John Gibson & Hannah Martin, both of Fitchburg,
                                                Sept. 16, 1766
John Dunsmore, Jr., & Mary Kimball of Fitch-
   burg,   Sept. 30, 1766
Jacob Steward of Fitchburg & Elizabeth Pierce (?),
                                                Nov. 8, 1766
Moses Whitney of Petersham & Sarah Gray,   Nov. 20, 1766
Joshua Peirce of Leominster & Lydia Goodridge,
                                                Nov. 27, 1766
Nathan Heywood & Mrs. Susanna Divol,   Dec. 2, 1766
Joseph Snow & Joanna Jewet,   Dec. 4, 1766
John Buss of Fitchburg & Mary Wood,   Jan. 1, 1767
Benjamin Page & Susanna Russell,   Jan. 8, 1767
John Ireland & Lydia Farwell,   Jan. 12, 1767
Isaac Stevens of Hollis, N. H., & Martha Jewett,
                                                Jan. 15, 1767

Elijah Gould & Eunice Patch, Feb. 26, 1767
Abner Hale of Winchendon & Abigail Goodridge,
March 12, 1767
Oliver Stickney & Hannah Stiles, May 26, 1767
Barnabas Wood & Sarah Holt, Sept. 10, 1767
Williams Stewart of Petersboro, N. H., & Elisabeth
White, Nov. 3, 1767
James Grimes of Swansey, N. H., & Elisabeth Gilchrist, Nov. 5, 1767
John Wood & Sarah Thurston of Fitchburg, Nov. 24, 1767
Ebenezer Harrington & Martha Wott (?), both of
Fitchburg, Nov. 26, 1767
Thomas Dunster & Lydia Pain, both of Westminster, March 23, 1768
Mighill Davis & Mary Johnson, June 30, 1768
James Brophey of Peterboro, N. H., & Martha Holl,
Aug. 23, 1768
John Rugg of South Hadley & Martha Forbush,
Aug. 25, 1768
Ezekial Fowler of Fitchburg & Dorcas Bradstreet,
Oct. 25, 1768
Rev. Aaron Whitney of Petersham & Mrs. Ruth
Starns, Nov. 9, 1768
Edmund Stone of Templeton & Susanna Whitney,
Dec. 6, 1768
James Reed, Jr., of Monadnock, No. 4, & Mary
Dodge, Dec. 11, 1768
Joseph Downe of Fitchburg & Martha Wood, Dec. 22, 1768
Nathan Smith of Weston & Sarah Reed, Dec. 22, 1768
Jonathan Pierce, Jr., & Sarah Chaplin, Jan. 5, 1769
Jonathan Cumming & Hannah Fletcher, Jan. 5, 1769
John Farwell of Fitchburg & Sarah Hovey, March 16, 1769
Thomas Kimball & Sarah Martin, March 30, 1769
William Kendall & Sarah Bradstreet, Aug. 20, 1769
Amos Heald, Jr., of Townsend & Betty Davis, Oct. 2, 1769
Daniel Stearns of Leominster & Hannah Wetherbee, Jr., Oct. 26, 1769
Josiah Flagg of Wor. & Hannah Wetherbee, Nov. 26, 1769
John Wood of Littleton & Lucy Martin, Nov. 16, 1769

Josiah Peirce & Molly Foss,   Nov. 23, 1769
John Campbell & Hannah Nickless,   Nov. 23, 1769
Elijah Carter of Fitchburg & Jane Goodridge, Jan. 18, 1770
David Beeman of Leominster & Sarah Pierce, Feb. 6, 1770
James Allen & Sarah Charlton,   April 22, 1770
Edward Kendall of Monadnock, No. 4, N. H., &
    Prudence Hartwell,   Feb. 12, 1769
Josiah Greenwood of Westminster & Martha
    Symonds,   March 28, 1769
Stephen Bathrick & Jemima Dodge,   Aug. 15, 1769
Isaac Wood & Elizabeth Hartwell,   Jan. 11, 1770
Ezekiel Goodale of Templeton, N. H., & Eleoner
    Gill of Westminster,   May 29, 1770
John Everett & Elizabeth Gill, both of West-
    minster,   May 29, 1770
Josiah Hartwell & Rebecca Walker,   Dec. 27, 1770
John Joyner of Westminster & Susanna Rayley or
    Bayley of Hillsburg,   June 11, 1771
Samuel Davis & Margaret Down,   Nov. 12, 1771
Jacob Walton & Elizabeth Jenkins, both of West-
    minster,   Nov. 18, 1771
Silas Holt & Sarah Harrington,   Jan. 25, 1772
Aaron Colman of Ashby & Eleanor Boynton, Feb. 20, 1772
Dr. John Taylor & Mrs. Anna Pool, at Dunstable,
    N. H.,   July 16, 1772
John Steles (?) & Keziah Divol,   July 5, 1770
Stephen Boynton & Sarah Stiles,   Nov. 9, 1772
Silas Buss & Hannah Pierce,   July 23, 1770
Sewell Dodge & Martha Martin,   Sept. 5, 1770
Benjamin Wilson of Westminster & Mehitable
    Foster,   Sept. 25, 1770
Thomas Harkness & Elizabeth Putnam,   Dec. 6, 1770
Jonathan Boynton & Elizabeth Divol,   Jan. 1, 1771
Caleb Wilson of Leominster & Phebe Divol, Jan. 1, 1771
Jabez Norcross & Hannah Bayley,   March 27, 1771
Thomas Peabody & Hannah Ritter,   June 20, 1771
Timothy Gibson & Sarah Foster,   July 22, 1771
Benjamin Bayley & Olive Bradstreet,   Aug. 22, 1771
Joshua Martin & Phebe Bradstreet,   Aug. 22, 1771

Moses Ritter & Mary Goodridge,	Sept. 5, 1771
Stephen Boynton of Winchendon & Tabatha Foster,	Jan. 29, 1772
Jonathan Martin & Susanna Taylor,	Aug. 31, 1772
Ebenezer Allen, Jr., & Mary Henry,	Nov. 10, 1772
Henry Haskel of Shirley & Martha Little,	Dec. 1, 1772
Samuel Whiting & Ruth Goodridge,	Dec. 1, 1772
John Wilmon of Worcester & Mary Chaplin,	Dec. 2, 1772
Ephraim Wetherbee & Keziah Pierce,	Dec. 3, 1772
Thomas Houghton of Leominster & Ruth Kilbourn,	Dec. 9, 1772
Amos Page & Elizabeth Randell,	Dec. 10, 1772
Ephraim Pierce & Huldah Witherbee,	Jan. 12, 1773
Elisha Brown & Elizabeth Dodge,	Jan. 19, 1773
John Witherbee & Susanna Page,	Jan. 21, 1773
Samuel Kendall of Monadnock, No. 4, & Bettey Wetherbee,	Feb. 25, 1773
Samuel Tarbell & Beatrie Carter,	Feb. 25, 1773

BOLTON.

June 24, 1738, " Part of Lancaster established as Bolton. First (Unitarian) Church organized 1740. Friends, 1799. Officiating clergymen mentioned: Rev. Thomas Goss, Rev. John Walley.

Paul Gates & Submit How,	Nov. 18, 1746
Jonas Brooks & Dinah Pike,	Dec. 25, 1746
Nehemiah How of Marlboro & Beulah Wheler,	March 4, 1746-7
Josiah Houghton of Lancaster & Bethesda Brabrook (?),	April 16, 1747
Samuel Moore & Zeresh Houghton,	Aug. 19, 1747
Nathaniel Roberson & Patience Keyes,	Aug. 24, 1747
Jonas More & Dinah Whitcomb,	Nov. 24, 1747
Abraham Rice & Susannah Wild,	Dec. 18, 1747
Philip Goss of Lancaster & Hannah Ball,	May 12, 1748
Samuel Snow & Keziah Hought,	May 12, 1748
Benjamin Edward of Stow & Elizabeth Fairbanks,	Nov. 24, 1748

Peter Joslyn, Jr., of Lancaster & Elizabeth Green-
    leaf, Jan. 5, 1748
James Snow, Jr., & Persis Houghton, Jan. 5, 1748
Eleazer Whitcomb & Mary Putnam, Oct. 5, 1749
Benjamin Marble & Mary Goss, Oct. 5, 1749
John French of Shrewsbury & Mary Whitcomb, Aug. 1, 1749
William Sawyer & Sarah Sawtell, July 7, 1748
Zachariah Glazier & Martha Snow, Sept. 1, 1749
Jonas Whitcomb & Hannah Sawtell, May 17, 1753
Amariah Thought of Bolton & Jane Smith of Marl-
    boro, May 17, 1753
David Whitcomb & Hannah Priest, May 31, 1753
Micah Bush of Marlboro & Hepzibah Fairbanks,
    Aug. 28, 1753
Peter Mebrow (?) & Dinah Thomas, Sept. 12, 1754
Abraham Hough & Caroline Houghton, Nov. 24, 1754
Jonathan Nicholls & Mary McClewean, Jan. 16, 1755
George Pi——es & Sarah Mcfaden, Feb. 14, 1755
Nathaniel Longley & Bulah Fairbank, May 14, 1755
Israel Greenleaf & Prudence Whitcomb, Nov. 28, 1754
Daniel Nichols & Mary Houghton, Dec. 5, 1754
Robert Lingley (?) & Anna Whitcomb, May 17, 1756
Hezikiah Gibbs & Elizabeth Pratt, May 24, 1745
Ezra Wilder & Betty Welch, March 9, 1762
Elijah Wilson & Sarah Bruce,   Sept. 22, 1761
Amos Fuller of Marlboro & Mary Coolidge, March 25, 1762
Thaddeus Hager of Framingham & Lois Sawyer,
    Dec. 9, 1762
Thomas Sawyer & Mary Houghton, March 25, 1762
David Nurse & Rebekah Barratt, June 3, 1762
John Gregg of Lunenburg & Rosanna Oliver, Nov. 19, 1761
William Pollard & Hannah Whetcomb, Oct. 7, 1762
Daniel Priest of Leominster & Lydia Graves, April 5, 1762
Calvin Greenleaf & Becke Whetcomb, Nov. 17, 1762
John Wilder & Rebeckah Sawyer, May 24, 1763
Abner Sawyer of Templeton & Hannah Piper, May 26, 1763
Samuel Snow & Mrs. Prudence Houghton, Oct. 11, 1763
Phineas Houghton & Mrs. Eunice Rogers of Har-
    vard, Nov. 28, 1763

4

John Bounds Moulton of Brimfield, South District,
    & Mrs. Eliz. Fosket,   Dec. 7, 1763
James McBride & Lydia Willson,   Dec. 8, 1763
Samuel Harris & Phebe Goodell,   Dec. 13, 1763
Samuel Jones & Dorothy Whetcomb,   Dec. 14, 1763
Abel Moor & Mrs. Betty Whetcomb,   Jan. 11, 1764
William Sawyer, Jr., & Hannah Barret,   Jan. 18, 1764
Andrew McClewain & Rebecca C—— of Lancaster,
                       Feb. 1, 1764
Silas How of Lancaster & Abigail Moor,   Feb. 2, 1764
Andrew Darby, Jr., & Elizabeth Sawin, both of
    Westminster,   Dec. 20, 1763
Abraham Knowlton of Narragt. No. 6 & Comfort
    Holman,   Feb. 13, 1759
Micah Bush of Marlboro & Hannah Wilder, April 19, 1759
Thomas Osborn & Mary Whitcomb,   April 26, 1759
William Swan of Cambridge & Lucy Rolens, May 1, 1759
Paul Whitcomb & Rebeckah Whitney of Harvard,
                     Sept. 19, 1759
Robert Alexander of Cumberland & Mary Alexan-
    der,   March 19, 1759
Jonathan Houghton & Susannah Moore,   Nov. 24, 1759
Josiah Moore & Abigail Richardson,   May 10, 1759
David Goodell, Jr., & Elizabeth Hutchinson, April 10, 1764
Andrew Haskell & Hazediah McClewain, April 18, 1764
James Flood & Betty Whetcomb,   May 15, 1764
James Townsend & Hannah Merriam,   May 29, 1764
Thaddeus Russell & Elizabeth Pratt,   June 18, 1764
Tille Whitcomb & Rachel Whitcomb,   Feb. 26, 1766
David Stiles & —— Oak,   Dec. 11, 1765
Richard Roberts & Sibil Goodenough of Marlboro,
                     Feb. 7, 1765
Silas —— & Mary Miriam,   Dec. 20, 1766
John Barrus (?) of Western & Nanney Haskell,
                     April 4, 1765
Dr. Nathaniel Martyn of Harvard & Mrs. Anna
    Townsend,   Dec. 23, 1765
Nehemiah Parker of Shrewsbury & Mrs. Mary
    Richardson,   Dec. 5, 1765

Joshua Atherton of Petersham & Mrs. Abigail
    Goss, Jr.,   Oct. 27, 1765
Abraham Scott & Mary Kent of Harvard,   Oct. 2, 1764
Caleb Church of Templeton & Elizabeth Walker,
                                      Oct. 2, 1764
David Dickenson & Persis Wheeler, both of Ash-
    burnham,   July 16, 1767
Hooker Sawyer & Relief Whetcomb,   Oct. 2, 1766
Jacob Holmes, Jr., of Wor. & Elisabeth Gates of
    Harvard,   July 2, 1767
Josiah Willson, Jr., & Patience Foskett,   Nov. 12, 1766
Phineahas Ward of Marlboro & Dorothy Osgood,
                                     Sept. 2, 1766
Paul Faulkner & Hepzibah Powers,   Aug. 21, 1766
William Wilder, Jr., & Sarah Sawyer,   Oct. 16, 1766
John Katherin (?) of —llam (?) & Lois Moor, Sept. 11, 1766
William White & Lydia Goodell,   July 3, 1766
Rev. Josiah Winchop of Woolwich & Mrs. Judith
    Goss,   July 7, 1766
Robert Holden & Sarah Tuttle,   Nov. 25, 1766
Joseph Houghton & Mrs. Susanna Brook,   June 23, 1767
James White & Mrs. Hulday Goodale of Danvers,
                                      Oct. 6, 1768
Jonathan Moor, Jr., & Desire Bayley,   July 28, 1768
John Hastings & Submitt Russell,   Dec. 31, 1767
Elisha Houghton of Harvard & Mrs. Meriah Peirce,
                                   Nov. 30, 1768
Benjamin Gould & Mrs. Silence Atherton,   July 3, 1767
Eliakim Atherton & Mrs. Elisabeth Sawyer, May 13, 1767
Seth Dean & Mrs. Betty Bruce,   Sept. 28, 1768
William Sawyer, 3d, & Kezia Moor,   Dec. 22, 1768
Amos Miriam & Mrs. Elisabeth Nurse,   July 15, 1767
John Richardson of Templeton & Mrs. Rebecca Moore,
                                  April 21, 1768
Beriah Oak & Mrs. Tabatha Fosket,   Dec. 31, 1767
* Jeridiah (Jedediah) Woods of Warwick & Mrs.
    Mary Burt,   March 7, 1769
Moses Wooster & Sarah Wott, both of Harvard,
                                  Jan. 12, 1769

Phinehas Warner & Lydia Whitney,	Feb. 27, 1769
Aholiab Sawyer & Barshebah Barrett,	June 5, 1769
John McClewain & Mrs. Joanna Burge,	Nov. 2, 1769
John Hannah & Hannah Coolidge,	Dec. 18, 1769
Benjamin Bruce & Nanny McBride,	Dec. —, 1768
Jame (?) McWain & Mrs. Rebecca Whitcomb,	Oct. 10, 1769
Abner Moore & Elisabeth Hastings,	Nov. 16, 1769
William Whitcomb & Lucy Meriam,	Dec. 13, 1769
Abraham Crosby of Nobletown, N. Y., & Ruth	
Digins,	May 15, 1769
Abraham Moor, Jr., & Mrs. Sarah Johnson,	Dec. 7, 1769
Jacob Moor & Elisabeth Baley,	Nov. 30, 1769
Jonas Stratton of Stow & Anna Barnard,	Nov. 15, 1770
Lemuel Burnam & Hannah Peirce,	June 29, 1769
Elijah Foster & Elisabeth Knight,	Dec. 4, 1769
Abel Farwell & Hannah Russell, both of Harvard,	
	June 14, 1769
Thos. McBride & Sarah Snow,	April 19, 1769
Nathan Jones & Mrs. Mary Bruce,	Nov. —, 1767
Rufus Houghton & Elizabeth Whitcomb,	July 23, 1770
Stephen Wilder (or Wilber) of Lancaster & Betty	
Sawyer of Harvard,	Sept. 3, 1770
Fradrick Albert of Lancaster & Mary Blood,	Feb. 26, 1770
Aaron Parsons of Swansey & Mrs. Damaras Whit-	
comb,	Feb. 8, 1770
Able Piper & Sible Sawyér,	Jan. 19, 1769
John Brown of Marlboro & Phebe Fosket,	Dec. 17, 1764
John Bruce & Martha Moors,	Feb. 18, 1768
Moses Cutler (?) of Monadnock No. 5 & Mary	
Whetcomb,	Dec. 27, 1770
John Sawyer & Mary Moor, 3d,	Nov. 29, 1770
Phinehas Moor & Sarah Nurss,	Nov. 27, 1770
Simon Houghton & Martha Stearns,	Dec. 6, 1770
Thomas Holt & Molley Corey, both of Lancaster,	
	Dec. 13, 1770
Silas Rice of Northboro & Lois Pollard,	Sept. 20, 1770
Daniel Sabin of Putney & Mary Snow,	Dec. 26, 1770
Joseph Blood of Marlboro & Betty Bruce, Jr.,	June 27, 1770
John Whitney & Sarah Atherton, both of Har——,	
	Jan. 9, 1771

Josiah Whetcomb of Leominster & Marcy Blood,

Jan. 29, 1771

Joseph Amsden of Marlboro & Mary Edwards,

April 12, 1771

Jonathan Puffer & Jemima Taft, both of Westminster, March 12, 1771

Jeremiah Priest, Jr., of Harvard & Rebecca Houghton, March 14, 1771

Jonas Richardson & Mary Bailey, June 6, 1771

John Mahanay of Londonderry & Lydia Kelcey,

July 9, 1771

William Biglow & Hannah Robbins, Jan. 1, 1772

Jonathan Horton of Templetown & Ruth Knight,

Feb. 25, 1772

Calvin Sawyer & Abigail Barrett, Jan 7, 1772

Oliver Jewet & Bettey Houghton, Jan. 23, 1772

Oliver Fairbank of Lancaster & Susanne Gates of Littleton, March 3, 1772

Thomas Osborn & Sarah Whetcomb, March 10, 1772

Jonathan Whitcomb, Jr., & Achsah Fairbank, March 30, 1772

William McWain & Anna Stun (?), Nov. 3, 1772

John Sampson & Rachiel Whetcomb, Dec. 2, 1772

Josiah Sawyer & Bathsheba Moor of Putney, Aug. 6, 1770

Samuel Stearns & Sarah Witt of Paxton, March 31, 1773

William Lincoln of Leominster & Release Sawyer,

April 27, 1773

Silas Houghton & Sarah Wyman of Harvard, May 20, 1773

Jonathan Whetcomb & Releaf Fife (?), June 1, 1773

Nathaniel Oak, Jr., & Susanna Hastings, June 2, 1773

Joseph Priest & Tabatha Russell, July 15, 1773

Daniel Priest & Bettey Dupee, Aug. 16, 1773

Lemuel Butler & Abigail Houghton, Dec. 6, 1773

Israel Sawyer & Bulah Willson, Nov. 25, 1773

Elijah Whitney of Harvard & Sarah Stearns, April 14, 1772

James Wilder, Jr., of Lancaster & Jemima Johnson,

April 30, 1772

Josiah Cooledge, Jr., & Molley Houghton, May 22, 1772

Edmund Taylor of Monadnock, No. 7, & Hepzibah French, July 6, 1773

Stephen Winchet of the Little Nine Partners in
    the province of New York & Relief Glazier, Dec. 24, 1772
Elijah Whitney, Jr., & Lydia McWain,   Jan. 25, 1773
William Burges of Harvard & Elizabeth Richard-
    son, Jr,   March 24, 1774
Nathaniel Burnam, Jr., & Hepzibah Hutchins of
    Harvard,   Sept. 26, 1774
Eli Harrington of Westboro & Susannah Baker,
                            Nov. 3, 1774
Aaron Foster & Anna Knight,   March 14, 1775
Hezekiah Gibbs, Jr., & Miriam Powers,   May 4, 1775
John Priest & Anna Houghton,   June 4, 1775
Joseph Jones & Ruth Holden,   Aug. 17, 1775
Stephen Harris & Sarah Butler, both of Templeton,
                          Dec. 28, 1775
Robert Fife & Hepzibah Bush of Marlboro,   July 11, 1776
Benjamin Edwards & Sarah Stiles,   Nov. 23, 1775
Israel Whetcomb, Jr., & Eunice Willson,   Nov. 28, 1775
John McBride & Phebe Wheeler,   Sept. 17, 1776
Ebenezer Warren, Jr., of Harvard & Deborah Ball,
                          Sept. 30, 1776
Ephraim Whetcomb & Sarah Longley,   Jan. 14, 1777
Simeon Whetcomb of Jeffery & Bathsheba Combs,
                          June 17, 1777
Ebenezer Blood & Abigail Barnard,   Dec. 13, 1773
Thomas Pollard & Deborah Woods,   Dec. 16, 1773
Holman Priest & Prudence Sawyer,   April 28, 1774
John Priest of Jeffery & Mary Hemenway,   March 10, 1774
Josiah Rice, Jr., & Hannah Marble,   March 22, 1774
Josiah Sawyer, Jr., & Judith Ross,   Dec. 7, 1774
Jacob Davis of Harvard & Ruth Atherton,   Dec. 15, 1774
Job Priest of Harvard & Martha Butler,   Jan. 3, 1774
Oliver Barret, Jr., & Sarah Whetcomb,   March 6, 1775
David Whetcomb, Jr., and Sarah Whetcomb,   May 28, 1776
Ephraim Fairbank, Jr., & Prudence Wilder,   Nov. 21, 1774
Daniel Laughton & Lucy Dutton, both of Harvard,
                          Sept. 2, 1777
Peter Stanhope & Elizabeth Parmenter of Sudbury,
                          Nov. 30, 1775

Caleb Gates of Stow & Mindwell Oaks,   March 10, 1776
James Stone of Harvard & Susanna Fosgate,   Feb. 13, 1777
Simeon Hemenway & Mary Goss,   May 4, 1777
Joel Fosgate & Naomi Gilbert,   Dec. 11, 1777
Stephen Pratt & Eunice Barnard,   March 24, 1778
Benjamin Nurss & Sibel Bailey,   Nov. 6, 1777
Micajah Fay of Grafton & Susanna King,   Dec. 18, 1777
Abijah Pollard & Hannah Moor,   April 30, 1778
William Walker of Sudbury & Elizabeth Stanhope,
                             May 29, 1777
Gardner Moore & Abigail Whetcomb,   July 23, 1778
Simon Meriam & Phebe Lock of Harvard,   April 8, 1779
Philemon Fairbank & Sally Smith, both of Athol,
                            June 19, 1779
Nathaniel Southwick & Abigail Moore,   Aug. 17, 1778
Abel Wilder & Hannah Green,   March 28, 1779
Jesse Jewett & Hannah Johnson,   Dec. 10, 1778
William ———— & Mary Houghton, both of Shrews-
    bury,   May 19, 1778
Stephen Brooks of Stow & Prudence Whetcomb,
                            July 7, 1779
Levi Moor, Jr., & Parnel Parker, both of Lancaster,
                           Jan. 24, 1780
Timothy Henry Curtis & Hannah Sawyer, March 20, 1780
David Stearns & Loas Crouch, both of Harvard,
                          Dec. 24, 1777
Jabez Fairbank, Jr., & Lucy Bailey, Jr.,   Jan. 23, 1778
Edward Baker & Hepzibah ————, Jr.,   Oct. 13, 1778
Barnabas Sawyer & Unity Houghton,   Dec. 14, 1778
Ezra Smith of Sudbury & Phebe Walcott,   Jan. 12, 1779
Josiah Sawyer, 3d, & Percis Baker,   Feb. 10, 1779
Micah Ross & Molly Moor, both of Lancaster, April 4, 1780
Samuel Baker, Jr., & Hannah Bush, Jr., of Marlboro,
                          May 25, 1780
Abraham Brigham & Emma Robbins,   May 15, 1780
Cyrus Fairbank of Harvard & Marcy Hale of Stow,
                         Nov. 10, 1779
Asa Houghton, Jr., & Dorcas Moor, both of Harvard,
                          Dec. 9, 1779

Samuel Nichols & Abigail Pierce,   Dec. 26, 1779
John Pitt & Dinah Wood,   April 21, 1780
Abel Whetcomb & Elizabeth Townsend,   May 8, 1780
Samuel Goss & Lucretia How,   March 7, 1780
Oliver Jewett & Keziah Snow,   April 28, 1780
John Whetcomb, Jr., & Azubah Whetcomb,   May 31, 1780
Nathan Priest of Harvard & Mary Bacon of Bedford,
     July 5, 1780
Zaccheus Dudley & Mary Conant, both of Harvard,
     Aug. 28, 1780
Simon Whetcomb & Hepzibah Houghton,   Sept. 13, 1780
Abraham Holman & Prudence Hills of Leominster,
     Oct. 25, 1780
Richard Townsend, Jr., & Susanna Houghton, Jr., Oct. 2, 1780
Silas Whetcomb & Lydia Underwood,   Oct. 12, 1780
Silas How & Silence Moore, Jr.,   Nov. 2, 1780
Samuel Forbush & Mary Warner, both of Harvard,
     Jan. 11, 1781
John Warner, Jr., of Harvard & Susanna Barratt of
     Leominster,   Feb. 22, 1781
Nathaniel Longley & Keziah Fairbank, both of
     Harvard,   March 5, 1781
Thaddeus Pollard & Mary Fairbank, both of Harvard,
     March 5, 1781
Jonathan Atherton, Jr., & Phebe Nurse,   March 6, 1781
Timothy Bruce & Matilda Wheeler,   April 5, 1781
Jonas Houghton, Jr., & Eunice Houghton,   May 10, 1781
Benjamin Bruce, Jr., & Philadelphia Wheeler, May 10, 1781

UPTON.

June 14, 1735, "Parts of Hopkinton, Mendon, Sutton and Uxbridge established as Upton." Prov. Laws, Vol. II, p. 764. First (Congregational) Church organized 1735. Clergyman mentioned: Rev. Joseph Door of Mendon.

Thomas Lealand of Grafton & Margaret Wood, July 23, 1747
Henry Walker & Phenwell White,   Dec. 8, 1747
William Green & Hannah Tyler,   Jan. 10, 1744–5
Benjamin Wood & Sybel Perham,   May 4, 1762

Elijah Rice & Prudence Hardy,	Aug. 12, 1762
Phinehas Pratt & Susanna Palmer,	Nov. 25, 1762
Samuel Wright & Deborah Bacon,	Feb. 29, 1764
Alexander Gore & Elizabeth Wood,	June 28, 1764
David White & Mary Woods,	May 24, 1764
Edward Rawson & Sarah Sadler,	July 19, 1764
David Blatcheler & Lois Wood,	Feb. 9, 1764
Jonah Wood & Rachel Wood,	Nov. 29, 1764
Nathan Wood & Levice Morse,	March 14, 1765
Aaron Hayward & Hannah Severy,	April 25, 1765
Peter Hazeltine & Mary Sadler,	Jan. 9, 1766
Abraham Boyd & Hannah Hill,	June 24, 1766
Joshua Jenney & Olive ———,	Oct. 7, 1766
William Batchellor & Lydia Warren,	Oct. 9, 1766
Abner Palmer & Hannah ————,	Nov. 6, 1766
Jonas Butterfield & Jane Hazeltine,	Nov. 11, 1766
Peter Holbrook & Huldah Wood,	Dec. 3, 1766
John Spring & Hannah Crosby,	May 27, 1767
Francis Bowman & Jerusha Wood,	June 9, 1767
Jonathan Nelson & Sarah Warren,	June 30, 1767
Levi Legg & Mary Beels (?),	Dec. 3, 1767
Hezekiah Larnard & Lydia Perham (?),	Dec. 3, 1767
Samuel Fletcher & Mehitable Hazeltine,	April 14, 1768
Jonathan Cutler & Mary Rawson,	April 26, 1768
Thomas Forbush & Submitt Ball,	July 11, 1768
Benjamin How & Hannah Blanchard,	Aug. 19, 1768
Joseph Lesure & Percis Whitney,	Sept. 13, 1768
Robert Fisk & Mary Hall,	Nov. 17, 1768
Isaac Sheffield & Abigail Wood,	Nov. 24, 1768
Nathan Peck & Sarah Tenny,	Feb. 9, 1769
Josiah Ward & Molly Scott Wiswall,	April 12, 1770
Naham Ward & Anna Wood,	May 3, 1770
Benjamin Sadler & Bathsheba Wand,	May 3, 1770
Benjamin Fisk & Jemima Holbrook,	June 14, 1770
Jacob Perham & Susanna Sadler,	Oct. 4, 1770
Matthew Lackey & Mary Rice,	Oct. 11, 1770
James Tony & ——— White,	Jan. 8, 1771
Seth Wood & Lydia Sadler,	April 30, 1771
James Kidder & Deborah Wood,	July 18, 1771

James Morgan & Mary Giles,	Sept. 24, 1771
Caleb Hayward & Elizabeth Taft,	Nov. 7, 1771
Grindel Wood & Mary Nelson,	Dec. 5, 1771
James Fletcher & Margaret Wood,	Dec. 24, 1771
Jonathan Hayward & Lydia Wood,	Jan. 23, 1772
Asa Ober & Susanna Tenney,	Feb. 6, 1772
Timothy Fisher & Levice Wood,	March 30, 1773
Jonathan Wood & Sarah Bradish,	Oct. 26, 1773
Abel Munroe & Rebecca Sadler,	Nov. 23, 1773
Moses Wood, Jr., & Sarah Long of Hopkinton,	Dec. 9, 1773
Farnum White of Mendon & Lois Nelson,	Dec. 16, 1773
John Axtell (a transient person) & Lucy Flagg of Grafton,	Jan. 19, 1774
Daniel Fisher of Townshend, N. Y., & Hannah Sadler,	Feb. 1, 1774
Ebenezer Butler & Thankful Curtis,	Feb. 8, 1774
James Lackey & Charlotte Forbes,	April 6, 1780
Joseph Potter & Elizabeth Childs,	May 9, 1780
William Hall & Sarah Boyce,	May 25, 1780
John Haywood of Mendon & Mary Pease,	Jan. 11, 1781
Elisha Bradish & Hannah Taft,	May 4, 1779
Joseph Wood & Elizabeth Bradish,	Aug. 12, 1779
Timothy Taft of Uxbridge & Abigail Wright,	Oct. 24, 1779
Elijah Harrington of Shrewsbury & Mary Warren,	Jan. 31, 1781
Elisha Warren & Anna Marble,	May 28, 1776
Abiel Sadler & Elizabeth Warren,	May 28, 1776
John Morris of Northbridge & Molly Whitney,	June 27, 1776
Jonathan Wright & Eunice Walker,	July 11, 1776
William Ward of Mendon & Hannah Taft,	Nov. 28, 1776
Peter Forbush & Deborah Flagg,	May 6, 1777
Amos Wood & Sarah Sadler,	July 24, 1777
Thomas Nelson, Jr., & Hannah Brackett,	Sept. 11, 1777
Isaac Nelson & Hannah Fisk,	Jan. 27, 1778
Henderson Walkup & Sarah Drury,	Aug. 26, 1779
Daniel Wood, Jr., & Maribel Hayward,	Sept. 30, 1779
Thomas Ellison & Abigail Goldthwaid, both of Northbridge,	Oct. 28, 1779

Peter Thurston of Grafton & Elizabeth Holbrook,
Oct. 28, 1779

Artimas Rawson & Dorcas Bachellor of Grafton,
Nov. 25, 1779

Elijah Warren & Abigail Fish, April 26, 1781

Grindly Jackson & Elizabeth Peterson, May 24, 1781

Jonathan Nelson & Abiel French of Holliston, Nov. 1, 1781

Capt. Jonathan Wood of Spencer & Mrs. Rebecca
Warren, Dec. 19, 1781

Amos Whitney & Eunice Taft, Feb. 7, 1782

Joel Bolster & Betty Perham, March 8, 1781

Ezra Wood & Sarah Taft, May 1, 1781

John Whitney & Sarah Twitchel of Westboro, June 21, 1781

Josiah Torrey & Lydia Fisk, June 19, 1781

Elias Fisher & Sible Wood, Jan. 3, 1781

William Bowing, Jr., of Northbridge & Mary Hathaway, March 27, 1783

Nathan Aldridge of Northbridge & Lucy Clark,
May 28, 1783

Nahum Wheelock & Betty Steel, both of Mendon,
Dec. 9, 1783

Elias Brown of Alsted & Rebecca Kyes, Feb. 8, 1784

David Chillson of North Providence & Sarah
Uiall, Oct. 3, 1784

Ceasor Tonney, Jr., & Susanna Harry, Dec. 16, 1784

Henderson Walkup & Susanna Condon or Coudon,
Dec. 30, 1784

James Huzza & Susanna Tobe, Jan. 20, 1785

Elisha Wood & Mary Warren, May 26, 1778

Jonathan Warren & Elizabeth Woodward, May 27, 1778

Enoch Batchelor & Jemima Fisk, June 4, 1778

William Putnam & Submit Fisk, June 25, 1778

Thomas Hayden & Molley Fobes, Sept. 7, 1778

Ichabod Fisher & Rhoda Wood, Sept. 24, 1778

Nathaniel Paige of Hardwick & Martha Fish, Sept. 4, 1783

Ebenr. Walker, Jr., & Molley Wood, Nov. 6, 1783

Josiah Fisk & Elizabeth Gore, Nov. 16, 1783

Samuel Fisk, Jr., of Sheburn & Rebecca Fisk, Jan. 23, 1784

Stephen Temple, Jr., & Susannah Wood, Feb. 5, 1784

Ezra Whitney & Mary Forbush,	April 29, 1784
Asa Child & Rebecca Taft,	Oct. 29, 1784
David Forbush of Grafton & Sarah Temple,	Sept. 6, 1785
Samuel Hills of Sterlington (so called) & Abigail Child,	March 2, 1786
Abner Lazell & Lucretia Temple,	April 16, 1786
Elazar Flagg & Patty Parks,	April 20, 1786

✓ HARVARD.

June 29, 1732, "Parts of Groton, Lancaster and Stow established as Harvard." Prov. Laws, Vol. II, p. 644. First (Congregational) Church organized 1733. Unitarian, 1733. Baptist, 1776. Officiating clergymen mentioned : Rev. John Seecomb, Rev. Joseph Wheeler, Rev. Daniel Johnson.

Timothy Whitney of Lancaster & Alice Whitney,	May 20, 1752
Robert Powers of Littleton & Anna Wetherbee,	May 26, 1752
Aretas Houghton & Anna Rand,	June 24, 1752
John Davis, Jr., & Hannah Johnson,	Nov. 28, 1752
Oliver Whitney & Abigail Hutchins,	Nov. 16, 1752
Joseph Atherton & Sarah Hutchins,	Dec. 19, 1752
Stephen Gates & Dinah Meeds,	Feb. 5, 1753
Joseph Willard, Jr., & Elisabeth Hapgood,	Feb. 14, ——
Jonathan Symonds & Judith Cole,	June 14, 1753
Joseph Moffet of Ipswich, Canada, & Dorothy Preist of Stow,	Aug. 2, 1753
James Read & Ann Conn (?),	Aug. 8, 1754
James Burt & Bulah Mead,	Dec. 3, 1754
John Pratt & Mary Hall,	Oct. 24, 1754
Amos Stone & Adna Hale,	Feb. 27, 1754
David Whitney of Harvard & Sarah Hill of Lancaster,	Nov. 25, 1753
Samuel Harper & Mary Wheeler,	Dec. 16, 1755
Manassah Sawyer & Lydia Fairbank,	Feb. 18, 1756
Nathaniel Marble of Stow & Abigail Houghton,	March 31, 1756
Clark Brown & Lucy Davis of Westford,	March 9, 1757
Aaron Rand & Elizabeth Randall of Stow,	March 31, 1757

Benjamin Hutchins & Lucy Davis, April 5, 1757
Ephraim Read & Elizabeth Pierce of Groton, May 26, 1756
Peter Atherton, Jr., & Betty Atherton of Bolton,
May 26, 1756
George Pierce of Lincoln & Deborah Tarball, Jan. 17, 1757
Peter Edes of Charlestown & Mrs. Anna Haskell,
Nov. 26, 1762
Tilly White of Lancaster & Ketura Somes, Dec. 15, 1761
Jeremiah Bridge of Lexington & Sarah Buttrick,
March 31, 1761
Ephraim Houghton & Lois Rogers of Boxford, Dec. 31, 1761
John Farwell & Eunice Snow, Jan. 18, 1762
Oliver Wetherbee & Rachel Willard, March 11, 1762
Jonathan Oak & Abigail Read (?), April 26, 1762
Silas Parkhurst of Pepperel & Sarah Atherton, April 29, 1762
Silas Rand & Sarah Farwell of Groton, Feb. 22, 1763
Samuel Fellows, Jr., & Mary Blodget, March 24, 1763
Ephraim Davis & Sarah Farnsworth, Sept. 26, 1763
Joseph Kneeland of Harvard & Abigail Bigelow of
Stow, Oct. 26, 1763
Abel Farnsworth & Elizabeth Mcfarland, Dec. 6, 1763
Josiah Haskell & Mary Gates, Dec. 15, 1763
Joshua Whitney of Stow & Mrs. Rebecca Whitney,
Jan. 25, 1764
Isaac Gates & Submit Lawrence, Feb. 16, 1764
Paul Fletcher of Groton & Abigail Willard, March 1, 1764
Charles Taylor & Mercy Sterns of Littleton, March 29, 1764
Ephraim Farr of Westminster & Elizabeth Cob-
leigh of New Braintree, Sept. 8, 1762
Thomas Sawyer of Templeton & Prudence Carter
of Bolton, Sept. 13, 1762
Oliver Stone & Lucy Willard, Dec. 30, 1762
Elisha Jaickson & Bulah Taylor, both of Westmins-
ter, Dec. 20, 1763
Josiah Houghton & Abigail Goodfrey, both of Lan-
caster, Dec. 21, 1763
Samuel Hunt & Lydia Willard, Jan. 19, 1764
Joseph Hurd of Oxford & Mary Livermore of
Framingham, Dec. 15, 1763

Samuel Cleland of Greenwich & Hannah Hale,

Sept. 17, 1767

Lemuel Farnsworth & Hannah Daby,   Jan. 12, 1768

Jonathan Priest Houghton of Bolton & Sarah Priest,

March 23, 1768

Thomas Parks of Groton & Rosanna Conn,   May 3, 1768

Thomas Willard, Jr., & Sarah Farwell,   May 3, 1768

Joseph Russell of Hatfield & Sarah Russell, July 25, 1768

Moses Richards of Lunenburg & Ruth Willard,

Feb. 18, 1768

Ambrose Hale & Mary Daby,   July 25, 1768

Simon Whitney & Patience Hazeltine,   May 5, 1768

Thomas Gould of Lunenburg & Elisabeth Willard,

April 5, 1768

Timothy Phelps & Sarah Farnsworth,   June 28, 1768

Nahum Daby, Jr., & Susanna Worster,   Oct. 18, 1768

Richard Harris, Jr., & Lydia Atherton,   Dec. 1, 1768

Jonathan Page of Fitchburg & Esther Willard, Feb. 2, 1769

Ebenezer Burges, Jr., & Anna Fairbank,   April 11, 1769

William Miles & Sarah Sanderson,   Aug. 14, 1769

Josiah Wetherbee & Lucy Haskell,   Sept. 27, 1769

Josiah Willard & Eunice Farnsworth,   Nov. 16, 1769

Nathaniel Whittimore & Martha Farnsworth, Nov. 16, 1769

William Farmer & Hannah Holt,   Feb. 22, 1770

Leonard Proctor of Westford & Mary Keep,   Dec. 23, 1769

Abel Whitcomb & Sarah Whitney of Stow,   Dec. 23, 1769

Joshua Holden & Huldah Sampson,   Jan. 23, 1770

Thomas Holt of Lancaster & Dinah Cory,   March 8, 1770

Ezra Atherton & Ann Willard,   March 8, 1770

Nathaniel Hastings & Jemima Bennett,   April 23, 1770

Abram Carlton of Lunenburg & Eunice Willard,

April 30, 1770

Shadrach Hapgood, Jr., & Elizabeth Keep,   July 23, 1770

Samuel Worster & Nancy Wizel,   July 26, 1770

Simon Daby & Judith Lymonds,   July 29, 1770

John Keley, Jr., of Shirley & Molly Park,   Sept. 11, 1770

Oliver Sanderson & Elizabeth Wentworth,   Sept. 11, 1770

Nathan Knight of Stoneham & Susanna Putnam,

Sept. 13, 1770

Jonathan Couch, Jr., & Derothy Law,   Oct. 11, 1770
Ephraim Barnard & Hannah Fairbank,   Oct. 25, 1770
Gibson Willard & Mary Hall,   Oct 25, 1770
John Farwell & Lydia Taylor of Townsend,   Dec. 4, 1770
Daniel Zwear (?), Jr., of Lancaster & Abigail (?) Willard,   Dec. 6, 1771
Samuel Haskell & Ruth Safford,   Dec. 6, 1770
Reuben Wetherbee of Stow & Hannah Burges, Jan. 31, 1771
Phinehas Sawyer & Hannah Whitcombe,   Feb 14, 1771
George Leason of Bolton & Bettey Sanderson, Feb. 20, 1771
Joshua Kendal of Lancaster & Dorothy Warner,
     April 16, 1771
William Henry, Jr., of Lunenburgh & Mary Conn,
     Dec. 4, 1770
*John Farwell & Lydia Taylor of Townshend, Dec. 4, 1770
Daniel Levear (?), Jr., of Lancaster & Abigail Willard,
     Dec. 6, 1770
Samuel Haskell & Ruth Saffor,   Dec. 6, 1770
Reubin Wetherbe of Stow & Hannah Burges,   Jan. 31, 1770
Phinehas Sawyer & Hannah Whitcomb,   Feb. 14, 1770
George Leason of Bolton & Betty Sanderson, Feb. 20, 1771
*John Kendall of Lancaster & Dorothy Warner,
     April 16, 1771
John Mead & Sarah Whitney,   Aug. 26, 1771
Samuel Willard & Molley Stearns,   Aug. 26, 1771
Jonathan Pierce & Anna Hyle,   Sept. 10, 1771
Timothy Coburn of Campdon & Pegg Whittemore,
     Nov. 12, 1771
Joseph Atherton, Jr., & Hannah Farnsworth, Nov. 24, 1771
Colman Sanderson & Submit Adams,   Dec. 5, 1771
Elijah Wiles, Jr., of Shirley & Eunice Saffor, Dec. 26, 1771
Amos Lawrence & Sarah Wetherbe of Littleton, Jan. 22, 1772
John Priest, the 3rd, & Hannah Stow,   March 19, 1772
Samuel Garfield & Sarah Cole,   March 30, 1772
Israel Whitney & Hannah Mead,   May 14, 1772
John Park & Rhode Cooper,   May 14, 1772
Jacob Whitney & Lois Hapgood,   May 25, 1772
Levi Whitney of Concord & Sarah Lawrence, Sept. 17, 1772

---

* Record evidently repeated, but with slight alterations not explained.—ED.

Abner Sampson & Lucy Farnsworth,	Oct. 20, 1772
Richard Whitney, Jr., & Marcy Willard,	Dec. 15, 1772
Francis Wright of Middleton & Anna Harper,	Oct. 15, 1771
Nathan Agar of Lancaster & Dinah Sawyer,	Sept. 17, 1772
Isaac Holden & Sarah Hale,	June 7, 1773
Jonathan Puffer, Jr., & Abigail Fairbanks,	May 5, 1774
Hezikiah Whitney & Lucy Pollard,	May 5, 1774
Elisha Fullam & Mary Willard,	July 27, 1774
John Overlook & Molly Bigelow, both of Ashburnham,	Dec. 19, 1774
John Farnworth & Hannah White,	March 9, 1773
Samuel Finney & Sibel Wright,	March 15, 1773
Isaac Gibson of Fitchburg & Lois Sampson,	March 16, 1773
Edmund Farwell of Groton & Mary Russel,	July 15, 1773
Aaron Hodgkins of Fitchburg & Phebe Wintworth,	July 19, 1773
John Knight & Elizabeth Davis,	Aug. 26, 1773
John Richards of Lunenburg & Margaret Conn,	Oct. 20, 1773
David Farwell & Hannah Taylor,	Nov. 25, 1773
Capt. Josiah Whitney & Sarah Dwelly (?),	Feb. 3, 1774
Aaron Whitney & Sally Pollard,	April 21, 1774
Solomon Haskell & Betty Davis,	April 21, 1774
Ward Safford & Priscilla Randal of Stow,	April 26, 1774
Abel Whitcombe & Jemima Keepe,	April 28, 1774
Daniel Wetherbee of Stow & Mary Stone,	April 28, 1774
Michael Sawtel & Sarah Foster,	May 3, 1774
Isaac Whitney of Stow & Lucy Meads,	May 12, 1774
Samuel Cooper & Sarah Willard,	May 17, 1774
John Hall of Lunenburg & Sarah Willard,	July 5, 1774
Wetherbe Whitney & Abigail Warner,	July 7, 1774
James Willis & Molly Willard,	July 13, 1774
Zachariah Whitney of Fitchburg & Eliza. Wetherbe,	Aug. 18, 1774
Simeon Turner & Anna Bridge,	Oct. 6, 1774
Benjamin Robbins & Lydia Hale,	Oct. 13, 1774
Thomas Atherton of Bolton & Betty Whitney,	Dec. 15, 1774
Francis Dickerson of Shelburn & Mary Fairbank,	March 13, 1776

James Willis & Alice Adams, March 14, 1776
Reuben Willard & Catherine Parkhurst, Jan. 3, 1775
John Burges & Betty Wetherbee of Stow, March 22, 1775
Elijah Willard & Mary Atherton, March 30, 1775
Abraham Munroe & Lydia Hapgood, April 4, 1775
Oliver Gates, Jr., of Stow & Patience Meriam, Oct. 25, 1775
Joseph Chandler & Elizabeth Dopson, Nov. 19, 1775
Prince Turner & Rebecca Keep, Dec. 5, 1775
Thomas Chamberlain & Anna Brown, Dec. 19, 1775
Josiah Whitney, Jr., & Anna Scollay, Jan. 10, 1776
Matthias Farnsworth of Groton & Azuba Farnsworth,
Feb. 21, 1776
Philimon Priest & Lois Hartwell, March 21, 1776
Moses Hale & Molly Hale of Groton, April 10, 1776
Reuben Grafield & Lydia Symonds, April 23, 1776
Aaron Warner & Mary Stow, April 30, 1776
Samuel Barrett, Jr., of Lancaster & Abigail Hough-
ton, Aug. 7, 1776
Jonathan Adams & Ruth Whitney, Feb. 19, 1776
Jonathan Davis & Alice Whitney, Aug. 10, 1777
Francis Farr & Abigail Haskell, Sept. 14, 1777
Joshua Bowers & Mary Whitney, Sept. 14, 1777
James Farmer & Deborah Stone, Nov. 20, 1777
Lemuel Stone & Martha Fullom, Nov. 20, 1777
Marlbroa Kingman & Sybil Haskell, Sept. 23, 1777
Gideon Sanderson & Hannah Dodge, Jan. 11, 1778
Jonathan Symonds & Hannah Clark, Jan. 23, 1778
Harbour Farnsworth of Groton & Lucy Haild,
March 12, 1778
Phineas Taylor, Jr., of Stow & Sarah Haseltine,
March 19, 1778
Barzillia Willard & Silva Kingman, March 31, 1778

√ LEICESTER.

Feb. 15, 1713. Resolve. The petition of those who purchased lands at a place called Towtaid, near Worcester, confirmed, "the town to be named Leicester." First (Congregational) Church organized 1718. Baptist, 1737, at Greenville. Officiating clergymen mentioned: Rev. Benjamin Forster, Rev. Benjamin Conklin.

Joseph Wilson of Leicester & Grace Harrington of
    Brookfield,   Oct. 8, 1745
Ebenezer Tolman & Ann Wilson,   April 24, 1746
William Breckendridge of Kingston & Agnes Tink-
    ler,   Dec. 11, 1746
Benjamin Willson & Mary Stowers,   July 17, 1748
Benjamin Baldwin & Winified Green,   April 6, 1749
James Graton & Hannah Baldwin,   April 27, 1749
Arther Forbus of Rutland & Ruth Lamon, June 30, 1749
Oliver Seagur & Lydia Clark,   July 12, 1749
Asa Baldwin & Abigail White,   March 7, 1749
Pliny Lawton & Lucretia Sargent,   June 18, 1750
William Bemis & Rebecah White,   July 5, 1750
Samuel Lynde & Dorcas Smith,   July 5, 1750
Samuel Garfield, Jr., & Phebe Worster,   Aug. 9, 1750
Nathaniel Garfield & Tobitha Newhall,   Aug. 9, 1750
Abell Woodward & Mary Worster,   Dec. 20, 1750
Jonathan Sargeant, Jr., & Mary Earl,   Jan. 24, 1750
Nathan Rice & Mehitabel Baldwin,   April 23, 1751
David Allen & Sarah Barton,   June 6, 1751
Daniel Lynd & Sara Bemus,   June 10, 1751
Benjamin Ellis & Dorcas Smith,   Aug. 1, 1751
John Lamb & Abigail Smith,   April 15, 1752
Daniel Gray of Pelham & Elisabeth Lammond,
                                  Aug. 18, 1752
Benjamin Garfield & Eunice Cooley,   April 2, 1752
John Taylor & Susanna Parsons,   May 28, 1752
George Smith of Rutland & Jane McClewain, June 9, 1752
Solomon Parsons & Elisabeth Taylor,   Sept. 5, 1752
William Campbell of Volentown & Sarah Barns,
                                   Oct. 1, 1752

Robert Paul of Union & Elisabeth Watson,   Nov. 23, 175–
John Cumings & Rachell Snow,   Dec. 14, 1752
Nathaniel Bemis of Leicester & Ruth Harrington
    of Brookfield,   Jan. 10, 1753
Nathaniel Sergeant & Ann Garfield,   Nov. 15, 1753
Joseph Merrit & Mary Farnsworth,   June 25, 1754
Francis Dodge & Deborah Sylvester,   Oct. 16, 1754
Oldham Gates & Patience Bartlet, both of Spencer,
    Nov. 20, 1754
Benjamin Green of Leicester & Lucy Marston, of
    Spencer,   Dec. 10, 1754
Ephraim Brown of Spencer & Hannah Edmunds
    of Oxford,   Feb. 21, 1755
John Lynde & Rebecca Denny,   Feb. 4, 1755
Richard Paley of Sudbury & Grace Rice (?),   April 16, 1755
Daniel Newell of Leicester & Elizabeth Stebbins
    of Spencer,   April 7, 1755
James Harrod & Martha Barney,   May 21, 1755
Alexander Kathan & Margaret Beard,   Dec. 4, 1755
James Browning of Rutland & Rebecca Scott,   Jan. 15, 1756
James Baldwin & Tamah Vinten,   Jan. 22, 1756
Thomas Newell, Jr., & Deborah Sargent,   July 1, 1756
Nathaniel Wait & Pheebee Read,   March 18, 1756
Joseph Bigelow of Framingham & Sarah Stebins,
    April 30, 1756
William Tucker & Anna Thompson, both of Gore.
    Sept. 1, 1756
John Thomas & Susanna Farnsworth,   Sept. 16, 1756
Thomas Snow & Thankful Bellows,   Oct. 19, 1756
Thomas Parker of Gore & Susanna Thompson of
    Maldin,   Dec. 2, 1756
James Call & Hannah Masters,   March 8, 1757
Abiather Vinton & Rhoda Wheelock of Gore,   April 14, 1757
William Thompson of Holden & Anna Thompson,
    June 23, 1757
John Brown, Jr., & Rebecca Baldwin,   July 21, 1757
Elias Bowker & Sarah Harwood,   Sept. 13, 1757
William Gillhay (?) & Elisabeth Barns,   Sept. 15, 1757
James Carlile of Worcester & Lydia Jackson,   Sept. 27, 1757

Samuel Denny & Elizabeth Henshaw (?),	Sept. 29, 1757
Jonathan Stoddard of Spencer & Mary May,	Oct. 25, 1757
Thomas Denny & Mary Storer of Pomfret,	Oct. 21, 1755
Elisha Pratt & Lucy Fletcher,	Feb. 10, 1757
Caleb Dodge & Merriaim Gilbert,	April 4, 1757
Ephraim Rice & Thankful Walker,	April 14, 1757
Jabez Crosby & Mary Hamilton,	June 16, 1757
Israel Richardson & Susanna Forbush,	Nov. 10, 1757
Benjamin Griffen & Hannah Wedge,	Nov. 29, 1757
John Pike & Mehitabel Heyward,	Dec. 11, 1757
Daniel Rolf & Mary Adams,	Nov. 3, 1757
John Hayward & Elizabeth Brooks,	Dec. 29, 1757
Jonas Bemis & Dorothy Wood,	Jan. 5, 1758
Charles Rice & Leah Jenings,	Jan. 6, 1758
Timothy Brooks & Mary Gilbert,	Jan. 12, 1758
Benjamin Merrit & Sarah Blanchard,	Jan. 28, 1758
Joseph Trumble & Lydia Hayward,	June 14, 1758
David Wicker & Ann Davis,	May 1, 1761
Jonas Livermore & Sarah Ward,	Nov. 10, 1761
Benjamin Sanderson, Jr., & Rachell Merritt,	Nov. 12, 1761
Samuel Babbitt of Killingsley & Abigail Goodspeed,	
	Dec. 3, 1761
James Whitemore & Dorothy Green,	Dec. 31, 1761
Abijah Stowers & Tabitha Hasey,	Jan. 14, 1762
William Hinshaw & Ruth Sergeant,	Feb. 4, 1762
Israel Spraige & Pheebee Hasey,	March 25, 1762
Perley Brow & Elizabeth Wilson,	April 20, 1761
Matthew Watson & Mary Taylor,	April 27, 1762
David Newton of Rutland & Meriam Smith,	May 13, 1762
Amos Wheeler of Worcester & Mary Belcher Henshaw,	May 20, 1762
Robert Converse & Sarah Newton,	May 24, 1762
Richard Southgate, Jr., & Sarah Sprague of Spencer,	June 2, 1762
Joktan Green & Esther Newhall,	May 27, 1762
William Drewry & Mary Shaw, both of Spencer,	
	June 22, 1762
Benjamin Parsons of Palmer & Elizabeth Stone,	
	Oct. 26, 1762

Benjamin Baldwin, Jr., & Mary Whitemore, Nov. 10, 1762
Jabez Lewis of Spencer & Rachel Wallis of
 Oxford, Jan. 29, 1763
Daniel Hill & Mary Clark, Sept. 28, 1769
Asa Waite & Zerviah Smith, Oct. 10, 1771
Phinehas Sargeant & Abigail Dunbar, March 20, 1772
William Frink & Sarah Eaton, May 3, 1772
Nathaniel Stearns & Phebe Upham, May 3, 1772
James Blair & Molley Watson, June 2, 1772
Ashbael Johnson & Jael Porter, Oct. 15, 1772
Daniel Lynds & Sarah Newhall, Dec. 3, 1772
Ebenezer Kent, Jr., & Esther Stone, Oct. 29, 1772
Gad Chapin & Sarah Brown, Dec. 31, 1772
Thomas Sawin & Hannah Merritt, Jan. 7, 1773
Ephraim Seager & Katey Sprowl, March 10, 1773
Asa Sprague & Martha Wilson, March 11, 1773
———— Gilbert & Abigail Nickols, both of Brookfield,
 Nov. 10, 1772
Ezra Parker & Mary Cook, both of Worcester,
 Jan. 30, 1768
Thomas Jones & Mary Bemus (?), both of Paxton,
 Nov. 2, 1769
Samuel Mower, Jr., & Nancy Leach, both of
 Worcester, Dec. 30, 1770
Benjamin Dix of Sturbridge & Hannah Sanderson,
 March 11, 1772
John Goodwin & Martha Mower, both of Worcester,
 Feb. 11, 1773
Demon Sheffield & Esther How, both of Worcester,
 March 5, 1773
David Henshaw & Mary Sargeant, Feb. 17, 1774
Frederich Balies & Hannah Brown, April 29, 1773
Richard Gleason & Bulah Swan, Sept. 23, 1773
Jonas Gleason & Lucy Harwood, July 8, 1773
Michael Hatch & Martha Rice, Oct. 13, 1773
David Dunbar & Hannah Hammond, Nov. 16, 1773
Ebenezer Baldwin & Phebe Baldwin, Nov. 26, 1773
Daniel Tenny & Mrs. Molly Bond, March 28, 1781
Francis Choat & Mrs. Betsy Lyon, July 29, 1781

Josiah Blake & Mrs. Judith Lyon,	Sept. 27, 1781
Thomas Waite & Mrs. Hannah Allen,	Oct. 8, 1782
John Green and Mrs. Phebe Brown,	Dec. 15, 1782
George Rogers & Dolle Livermore,	May 23, 1780
Hezikiah Sanderson & Elizabeth Pain,	Aug. 24, 1780
Andrew Scott & Sarah Hinshaw,	Nov. 23, 1780
Nathan Kingsly & Sarah Watson,	March 1, 1781
Livy Chilson & Hannah Warrin,	April 5, 1781
Samuel Sargent & Mary Washburn,	Oct. 11, 1781
Matthew Jackson & Elizabeth Work,	May 3, 1781
Peter Gun & Clove Rod. Revera,	Oct. 24, 1781
Daniel Newell & Esther Warrin,	Jan. 17, 1782
Ebenezer Hastings & Marriah Porter,	Jan. 24, 1782
John Alden & Elizabeth Gleason,	Feb. 27, 1782
James Greaton & Lydia Brown,	Nov. 21, 1782
Thomas Walker Ward & Elizabeth Denny,	Nov. 28, 1782
Thomas Warters & Rachall Commins,	May 28, 1782
Francis Pike & Keziah Morse,	May 30, 1782
Jacob March & Eleanor Moore,	July 4, 1781
Joel Earll & Percis Witt—,	Nov. 28, 1782
James Snow & Lydia Moore,	Jan. 2, 1783
Barnabas Aldrich & Betty Newhall,	March 6, 1783

◁ SPENCER.

April 12, 1753, part of Leicester established as the district of Spencer. Prov. Laws, Vol. III. p. 653. First (Congregational) Church organized 1744. Baptist, 1819, which became extinct 1877.

Joshua Bemis & Sarah White,	Sept. 18, 1755
Samuel Garfield & Abigail Peine of Holden,	May 27, 1756
James Blanchard & Hannah Tucker, both of County Gore,	Dec. 28, 1756
Thomas White & Abigail Muzzy,	Dec. 30, 1756
Jonathan Stoddard & Elizabeth Baldwin of Leicester,	April 10, 1760
Israel Ball & Percis Stone,	April 17, 1760
John Worster, Jr., & Mary Muzzy,	Nov. 20, 1760
David Lamb & Mary How of Rutland,	Dec. 25, 1760

Adam Prouty & Dorothy How of Rutland,   Jan. 19, 1761
George Lovell of Sutton & Hannah Roberts,   Jan. 21, 1761
Jonathan Lamb & Rebecca Warrin,   March 23, 1761
Reuben Morey & Sarah Eustice, both of Charlton,
                         April 14, 1761
Phineas Slayton of Brookfield & Eleanor Morey of
    Charlton,   May 14, 1761
Josiah White & Sarah McClure of Brookfield, June 4, 1761
Isaac Bridges & Mary Mixer,   Nov. 5, 1761
David Prouty, Jr., & Hannah Ball,   Nov. 24, 1761
John Muzzy, Jr., & Mary Ball,   Nov. 26, 1761
Richard Bears, Jr., & Hannah Sloper,   Feb. 4, 1762
Joseph Gibbs of Brookfield & Anna Clark,   June 3, 1762
David Barnes of Leicester & Rebecca Clark, Dec. 23, 1762
James Capen & Sarah Sawen,   Dec. 30, 1762
Nathan Hamilton, Jr., of Brookfield & Mary Bemis,
                        April 21, 1763
John Worster, Jr., & Rebecca White,   April 28, 1763
Peter Hawood of Brookfield & Phebe Prouty, May 25, 1763
David Baldwin, Jr., & Sibilah White,   June 9, 1763
Obediah Man & Marcy Fisher,   July 14, 1763
Robert Morgan, Jr., & Mary Woodard,   July 14, 1763
William Patterson of Litchfield & Lydia Thompson
    of Leicester,   Aug. 30, 1773
Isaac Morgan & Abigail Tucker of Leicester, Sept. 29, 1763
Benjamin Clemens of Charlton & Deborah Woodard,
                        Jan. 5, 1764
David May & Mary Stoddard of Leicester, April 5, 1764
John Bisco & Deborah Prouty,   May 10, 1764
John Stebbins & Olive Muzzy,   Oct. 11, 1764
Caleb Bridges, Jr., & Lucy Tucker of Leicester,
                        Nov. 14, 1764
John Ball & Bulah Whitney,   April 14, 1765
David Hammond of Charlton & Rebecca Ormes,
                        April 23, 1765
Silas Stevens of Brookfield & Lydia Prouty, June 20, 1765
James Prouty & Mary Dunsmore,   June 25, 1765
Allen Newhall & Rebecca Bemis,   July 2, 1765
Amos Adams & Mary Lynds of Leicester, Feb. 25, 1766

Daniel Henderson of Rutland & Sarah McIntyer,
Aug. 25, 1766
Robert Nickols of Berkle & Grissel Nickols of Paxton,
Oct. 23, 1766
Johnson Lynds & Abigail White, May 21, 1767
David Lamb, Jr., & Sarah Clark, Sept. 9, 1767
Ebenezer Smith of Leicester & Anna Rice, Dec. 2, 1767
William Watson & Phebe Garfield, Jan. 14, 1768
Jason Right & Elizabeth Muzzy, Jan. 21, 1768
Thomas Bridge, Jr., & Elizabeth Jones, April 21, 1768
William White & Esther Lynds, May 12, 1768
Benjamin Bemis, Jr., & Rebecca Draper, Nov. 17, 1768
Jeduthen Green & Ruth Slayton of Brookfield,
Dec. 1, 1768
James Draper, Jr., & Mary Prouty, May 31, 1769
Rev. Benjamin Conklin & Lucretia Lawton, July 26, 1769
Asa Thayer & Martha Morgan, Aug. 28, 1769
James Ormes, Jr., & Sarah Harrington of Brookfield,
Aug. 31, 1769
Shadrach Pierce & Anna Bridges, Oct. 19, 1769
Jonathan Monrow & Ruth Prouty, Oct. 19, 1769
Ebenezer White, Jr., of Charlton & Christian Adams,
Feb. 22, 1770
Eleazer Coller & Bulah Smith, March 19, 1770
Israel Morgan & Sarah Jackson, May 24, 1770
David Cranson & Bathsheba Brigs, Dec. 20, 1770
John Draper & Rebecca Muzzy, Dec. 24, 1770
Isaac Rice, Jr., of Sudbury & Sarah Lamb, Jan. 14, 1771
Jonas Muzzy & Sarah Draper, May 2, 1771
Ezekiel Willis & Lucy Woodard, June 17, 1771
Jude Adams of Brookfield & Jemima Adams, Aug. 29, 1771
Zebedee Edminster of Oakham & Mary Bemis,
Sept. 12, 1771
John Prouty, Jr., & Lucy Gleason, Oct. 13, 1771
Moses Bowen of Sturbridge & Martha Ball, Nov. 21, 1771
Simeon Woods & Mary Muzzy, Dec. 24, 1771
Isaac Prouty, Jr., & Anna Dunnell, Jan. 20, 1772
Daniel Ball, Jr., of Brookfield & Elizabeth Prouty,
Feb. 6, 1772

Samuel Watson, Jr., of Leicester & Ruth Baldwin,
Jan. 28, 1773
Ephraim Eddy of Brookfield & Esther Smith, Oct. 19, 1773
Thomas Dunbar of Leicester & Lucretia Smith,
Oct. 24, 1773
N. David Lamb & Jemima Rice, Nov. 6, 1773
John Knap & Asenath Green of Leicester, Nov. 25, 1773
John Prouty & Anna Livermore, April 5, 1774
Thomas Sprague & Thankful Hatch, May 3, 1774
William Knight & Beulah Prouty, July 7, 1774
Timothy Green & Ruth Bemis, Aug. 25, 1774
Ezra Wilson & Lucy Wilson, Aug. 30, 1774
Jabez Lamb of Leicester & Sarah Wilson, Aug. 30, 1774
David Baldwin of Leicester & Sarah Tucker, Sept. 22, 1774
Jacob Prouty, Jr., & Rachel Eddy, Sept. 29, 1774
Samuel Garfield, Jr., & Phebe Rice, Oct. 4, 1774
John Dunn of Northbridge & Elizabeth Sinclair,
Oct. 6, 1774
Benjamin Hayward of Holden & Sarah Prouty,
Dec. 29, 1774
Jonathan Warren of Leicester & Martha Bemis, Jan. 3, 1775
Benjamin Prouty & Sarah Green, Jan. 10, 1775
Asa Whittemore & Lucy Muzzy, March 2, 1775
David Bent of Rutland & Phebe Whittemore of
Paxton, April 26, 1775
James Lamb & Sarah Knap, May 4, 1775
Ephraim Morey of Charlton & Katharine Munye,
Feb. 1, 1776
Nathaniel Thomas Loving & Sarah Watson of
Leicester, Aug. 8, 1776
John Southgate & Eleanor Sargent, both of Leicester,
Oct. 10, 1776
Reuben Bemis & Abigail Smith of Charlton, Dec. 26, 1776
Abel Wheeler & Lydia Wilson, Jan. 2, 1777
Elijah Blood & Eunice Haman, Jan. 3, 1777
Amasa Bemis & Persis Bemis, Aug. 19, 1777
Luther Rich of Brookfield & Mary Jones, Nov. 9, 1777
Ebenezer Sanderson of Leicester & Abigal Upham,
Dec. 4, 1777

Samuel Newton of Winchendon & Martha David-
son of Charlton, Dec. 22, 1777
Jonathan Curtis of Charlton & Dolly Wilson, Jan. 15, 1778
Charles Morey & Phebe Blanchard, both of Charl-
ton, Jan. 29, 1778
Saul & Dinah, (negro servants belonging to John
Sumner, Esq.), Feb. 19, 1778
Deacon John Muzzy & Eleaner Snow, May 15, 1778
Edmund Bridges & Ruth Parks, May 15, 1778
Jones Muzzy & Abigail Lamb, June 9, 1778
Samuel Ryan & Mary Stoddard, June 18, 1778
Reuben Bemis & Sibbilah Bemis, Aug. 27, 1778
Jabez Hamilton of Brookfield & Abigail Willson, Oct. 1, 1778
Barnard Bemis & Sarah Whittemore, Nov. 10, 1778
Peter Rice & Olive Baldwin, Nov. 12, 1778
Isaac Prouty, 3d, & Molly Watson of Leicester,
Dec. 10, 1778
Reuben Whittemore & Abigail Watson, March 2, 1779
Abial Hatch of Hanover & Deborah Parker, April 1, 1779
James Sprague & Chloe Baldwin, May 4, 1779
Jethro Kinney of Murryfield & Ruth Jackson, May 26. 1779
Joseph Wheet & Anna Mercy, Oct. 21, 1779
Nathan Wright & Mary Whittemore, Oct. 26, 1779
Noah Furbush of Brookfield & Mehitabel Draper,
Nov. 9, 1779
Noah Woodward & Betty Jackson, Dec. 9, 1779
Ebenezer Warran of Leicester & Pheba Garfield,
March 30, 1780
John Graham & Olive Prouty, May 30, 1780
Jesse Smith of Charlton & Sarah Bemis, June 8, 1780
Sylvanus Gats & Elizabeth Graham, April 4, 1780
Elisha Whitney & Esther Clark, Feb. 20, 1783
Isaac Morgan, Jr., & Sarah Cowel, Feb. 27, 1783
Simeon Perry of Fitzwilliam & Hannah Barns,
April 20, 1783
Isaac Cutler of Brookfield & Susanna Watson, June 17, 1783
Eli Whittemore & Lucy Prouty, July 24, 1783
David Corey of Sturbridge & Abigail Adams, Nov, 20, 1783
Nathaniel Lamb & Rebecca Prouty, Nov. 20, 1783

James Biglow & Mary Graham, Dec. 18, 1783
Nathan Esterbrooks of Putney & Mary Upham,
Dec. 25, 1783
John Smith of Paxton & Persis Hunt, Jan. 8, 1784
Kerly How & Abiah Howland. Jan. 15, 1784
William Hiscock of Westfield & Susanna Whitney,
Feb. 5, 1784
Alexander Dean of Oakham & Sage Prouty, March 18, 1784
Buckminster White & Mercy Prouty, April 8, 1784
David Stow & Sarah Prouty, both of Ward, April 12, 1784
John Woodard, 3d, & Sarah Drury, May 5, 1784
John Lamb, Jr., & Abigail Prouty, July 1, 1784
Nathan Prouty & Patience Convers, Sept. 30, 1784
Isaac Coman & Dinah Rice, Nov. 22, 1784
Abner Snow of Leicester & Hannah Watson of
Brookfield, Nov. 25, 1784
Benjamin Gleason & Sarah Underwood, Feb. 24, 1785
Jesse Graham & Anna Parker, May 12, 1785
Hezekiah Saunderson of Westminster & Lucy
Upham, May 26, 1785
Ephraim Adams of Brookfield & Sibillah Bemiss.
June 26, 1785
Silvester Bemiss of Brookfield & Molly Bemiss,
June 26, 1785
Benja. Green & Martha Watson, June 26, 1785
Asa Draper & Routh Whittemore, July 7. 1785
Joseph Chadwick of Oakham & Elizabeth Willson
of Berri, July 19, 1785
John Pike & Ruth Bemiss, both of Paxton, April 7, 1785
James Capen & Susannah Drury of Brookfield, May 5, 1785

⸫ HOLDEN.

Jan. 9, 1741, part of Worcester, called North Worcester, established as Holden. Prov. Laws, Vol. II, p. 1043. First (Congregational) Church organized 1742. Baptist, 1806. Officiating clergyman mentioned : Rev. Joseph Avery.

Nathan Whitney of Stow & Tabitha Bennet of
 Holden,   Jan. 22, 1752
Thomas Stevens & Martha Rogers, March 24, 1753
Samuel Nichols & Anne Stevens,   Feb. 5, 1755
David Lynde of Leicester & Jerusha Peirce, Feb. 6, 1755
Jonathan Lovell of Holden & Mrs. Rachel How of
 Worcester,   May 18, 1756
Thomas Dryden & Lydia Ward,   June 17, 1756
Jonathan Wheeler, Jr., & Lydia Fletcher, April 13, 1763
John Willington of Worcester & Priscilla Heard, June 2, 1763
Elijah Demons of Brookfield & Lucy How of Rut-
 land,   Sept. 8, 1763
Thomas Perkins of Middleboro & Esther Thomp-
 son,   Jan. 17, 1764
Isaac Cutting & Abigail Flagg,   Sept. 1, 1764
Ebenezer Belknap & Silence Winch of Shrews-
 bury,   Oct. 27, 1764
Samuel Bigelo & Elizabeth Hubburd, Jan. 1, 1765
Ephraim Smith of Worcester & Ruth How, Jan. 17, 1765
Wm. Hartwell of Rutland & Mary Lovell, July 4, 1765
Josiah Stratton of Brookfield & Mary Davis, Oct. 31, 1765
Israel Davis, Jr., & Rebecca Hubbard, Jan. 16, 1766
John Stone, Esq., of Rutland & Mrs. Mary Brown,
           Dec. 4, 1766
Bartholomew Sterns of Worcester & Mary Ray-
 mond,   Feb. 25, 1767
Nathaniel Felch & Hannah How of Northboro, June 24, 1767
William Boyd of Grafton & Dinah Marshall, April 26, 1770
Elisha Hubbard & Mercy Hubbard, Dec. 3, 1767
William Dods & Annah Child,   April 10, 1768
William Raymond, Jr., & Eunice Glazier of Shrews-
 bury,   April 19, 1768

Jonathan Lovell, Jr., & Marcy Raymond,   Aug. 25, 1768
Dr. Isaac Chenery & Mrs. Susannah Peirce of Wor-
    cester,   Sept. 15, 1768
Joseph Morss & Lucy Whittemore,   Sept. 27, 1768
James Winch & Sarah Greenwood,   Oct. 10, 1769
John Black & Hannah Davis,   Dec. 21, 1769
Ephraim Miller of Worcester & Mary Flagg,   Feb. 20, 1770
Paul Goodale & Eunice Lovell,   March 20, 1770
John Wheaton of Leicester & Phebe Hubbard, June 14, 1770
Jotham How of Worcester & Dorothy Smith,   July 2, 1770
Willoughby Prescott of Concord & Elizabeth Hay-
    wood,   Oct. 11, 1770
Isaiah Brown & Phebe How of Princetown,   Nov. 8, 1770
David Livermore of Leicester & Anna Howard,
                                           March 14, 1771
Micah Sprout & Lydia Warner,   Oct. 10, 1771
Martin Holt & Abigail Wheeler.   Feb. 13, 1772
Moses Wheeler, Jr., & Anna Fisk,   Jan. 31, 1775
Josiah Cheney, Jr., & Lydia Gleason,   April 4, 1775
Dr. David Fisk & Elizabeth Chickering,   May 11, 1775
Hezekiah Walker & Lucy Raymond,   May 16, 1775
Jacob Black & Mrs. (?) Abigail Flagg,   Sept. 22, 1776
Joshua Gale & Mrs. (?) Molly Hubbard,   Oct. 10, 1776
Paul Davis & Lydia Black,   Nov. 14, 1776
Simeon Stickney & Zerviah Rice,   Dec. 12, 1776
John Dodds & Hannah Morse,   Feb. 6, 1777
John McMullen & Mary Smith,   March 5, 1777
James Davis & Eunice Newton of Paxton,   April 25, 1777
Aaron Glazier & Orpha Cutting, both of Lancaster,
                                            Dec. 25, 1776
Simeon Snow & Esther Smith of Lexington,   Jan. 8, 1777
Moses Ball & Vasliti Oaks,   March 6, 1777
Valentine Harris & Sarah Heywood,   Sept. 17, 1777
Joseph Fletcher & Mary Crosby,   Jan. 15, 1778
Nathan Wheeler & Rachel Flagg,   March 10, 1778
Ebenezer Barber & Mary Fletcher,   April 9, 1778
Edmund Davis & Eunice Hubbard,   June 2, 1778
Hosia Brigham & Cate Davis,   Sept. 17, 1778
Jabez Metcalf & Hannah Marshal,   Feb. 4, 1779

John Foster & Lydia Harrington,	March 11, 1779
James Lamb & Hannah Heywood,	June 13, 1779
Robert Earll & Abigail Harr—ton,	June 22, 1779
Thomas Craige & Katharine Bennett,	July 13, 1779
Abiel Buttrick & Mrs. Eunice Heywood,	Aug. 19, 1779
Jonathan Fisk & Mrs. Zerviah How,	March 12, 1778
Ephraim Bayley & Mrs. Sopha Glazier,	May 6, 1778
John Bennet of Shrewsbury & Mrs. Lucretia Rice of Lancaster,	May 7, 1778
Zedikiah Belknap of Worcester & Elizabeth Wait of Ward,	Sept. 8, 1778
Abel Biglow & Martha Biglow, both of Shrewsbury,	Oct. 1, 1778
Oliver Hale of Marlboro & Dorcas Bennet of Shrewsbury,	Oct. 1, 1778
Silas Cutting & Lucy Cutting, both of Shrewsbury,	May 20, 1779
Ebenezer Glazier & Martha Potter,	June 2, 1779
Zachriah Partridge & Marcy Whitney,	Aug. 4, 1779
Luke Reed & Martha Floyd, both of Shrewsbury,	Aug. 11, 1779
John Mellen & Lucy Kendal, both of Lancaster,	July 13, 1780
Benjamin Rice & Abigail Smith, both of Barre,	Aug. 31, 1780
Gardner Godard of Oakham & Sophia Rice of Rutland,	Dec. 11, 1782
Solomon Davis & Dorcas Glezen,	Nov. 24, 1779
Samuel Chaffin, Jr., & Abigail Hemmenway,	Dec. 9, 1779
Daniel Sergeant & Mary Lycett,	Feb. 10, 1780
Daniel Black, Jr., & Esther Davis,	Feb. 24, 1780
William Parker of Winchendon & Mary Gale,	June 1, 1780
Judah Mayo & Sarah Fuller,	Aug. 3, 1780
Jacob Gray of Pelham & Jennet Smith,	Sept. 26, 1780
Paul Raymond, Jr., & Sarah Gale,	Nov. 21, 1780
John Perry, Jr., & Tabitha Raymond,	Jan. 16, 1781
John Blair of Rutland & Eunie Harrington,	Nov. 30, 1780
John Forbes of Rutland & Elizabeth Heywood,	Jan 28, 1781
Artemas Dryden & Susannah Perry,	April 5, 1781

Gershom Stow of Northboro & Levinah Bartlett,
Sept. 24, 1781

Jonathan Moore & Patty Goulding, Oct. 2, 1781
Joshua Hemenway & Miliscent Eaton, Dec. 7, 1781
William McMullen of Pelham & Hannah Smith,
May 15, 1782
Jude Williams & Dorothy Davis, Aug. 14, 1782
Lemuel Heywood & Lucy Heywood, March 7, 1782
William Flagg, Jr., & Abigail Black, May 2, 1782
Timothy Marshal & Lucy Robinson, May 9, 1782
John How of Paxton & Lucy Hubbard, June 13, 1782
Thomas Davis & Lettice Rice, July 18, 1782
David Fisk, Jr., & Naomi Winch, July 11, 1782
John Williams & Sarah Davis, Sept. 2, 1782
Abner Rogers & Dorothy Nichols, Sept. 29, 1782
Jonathan Lovel & Hopestill Taft of Mendon, Jan. 1, 1783
William Heard & Betsey Dix, Jan. 16, 1783
Samuel Rowe & Submit Rice, Feb. 13, 1783
David Gray of White Creek & Sarah Smith, Feb. 27, 1783
Israel Johnstone Mills of Groton & Mary Frost of
Rutland. March 27, 1783
Charles Rozer of Rutland & Mary Smith, April 7, 1783
Sol. Clark Chany & Molly Estabrooks, May 6, 1783
Abel Marshal & Lydia Driden, May 15, 1783
Isaac Smith of Westmoreland, N. H., & Prudence Cut-
ting of Shrewsbury, Nov. 20, 1783
Samuel Herring and Ruth Stratton, Jan. 18, 1784
James Young & Mary Moore, April 21, 1785
Phinehas Bartlett & Rosinah Harris, both of Worces-
ter, Nov. 22, 1785
Reuben Knight & Hannah Allen, both of Worcester,
Nov. 24, 1785
Jonathan Flagg & Mitty Gay, May 29, 1783
Rufus Forbush of Westboro & Mary Brown, June 12, 1783
Ezra Rice & Rebecca Gardener, July 24, 1783
Robert Blair of Worcester & Betsey Harrington,
Dec. 11, 1783
Jonas Reed of Rutland & Elizabeth Wilson, Jan. 8, 1784
Nathan Turner of Walpole & Lucy Johnstone, Jan. 14, 1784

Tilla Hubbard & Anna Joslyn,	Jan. 15, 1784
Simon Davis of Princetown & Lucretia Davis,	March 25, 1784
Samuel Heyward, Jr., & Ruth Melvin,	April 22, 1784
Noah Harrington, Jr., & Elizabeth Davis,	April 29, 1784
John Rice Goulding & Ruth Webb,	June 10, 1784
Samuel Hubbard, Jr., & Lucy Wheeler,	Aug. 5, 1784
Thomas White, Jr., of Spencer & Hannah Estabrook,	Sept. 2, 1784
Ebenezer Glazier of Sterling & Lois Edgel,	Sept. 2, 1784
Abel Hubbard & Lucy Tainter of Hubbardston,	Dec. 28, 1784
Benjamin Andrews & Sarah Blair, both of Worcester,	Feb. 10, 1785
Jonathan Rogers & Phebe Sheppard,	May 12, 1785
Nahum Fisk & Sally Gay,	July 7, 1784
Thomas Wheeler & Hannah Grant,	Nov. 24, 1784
John Rice & Elizabeth Flagg,	Dec. 13, 1784
Jason Glezen & Elizabeth Goulding,	Dec. 15, 1784
Tilla Chaffin & Hannah Mirick,	Dec. 15, 1784
Moses Smith & Dorcas Gould, both of Worcester,	June 2, 1784
James Blake & Rebecca Cunningham, both of Worcester,	July 14, 1784
Joel Flagg & Betta Smith, both of Worcester,	Nov. 17, 1784
Aaron Smith of Worcester & Huldah Webb,	Nov. 25, 1784
Nicholas Powers & Sarah Knight,	Feb. 11, 1787
Stephen Cree & Mrs. Hannah Smith,	Feb. 27, 1787

SOUTHBOROUGH.

July 6, 1727, part of Marlborough established as Southborough. Prov. Laws, Vol. II, p. 428. First (Baptist) Church organized at Fayville 1825. Congregational, 1831. An old Unitarian church extinct. Officiating clergyman mentioned: Rev. Nathan Stone.

Joel Mathews & Abigail ——,	Nov. 22, 1752
Joseph Morse & Joannah Newton,	Jan. 3, 1753
Abraham Bond & Submitt Joslin,	April 5, 1753
Benoni Shertliff & Submit Pike,	July 23, 1753
Thomas Whitney & Ann Gould,	April 3, 1753

Ebenezer Dunton & Lydia Bellows,	Aug. 6, 1753
Ebenezer Walker & Sarah Fisk,	Dec. 17, 1754
Francis Nelson & Hannah Tyler,	Feb. 4, 1755
⸭ Daniel Wood & Rachel Aldrich,	April 1, 1755
Nathan Bridges & Sarah Parker,	Feb. 4, 1755
Timothy Peine & Abigail Knap,	March 27, 1755
Benjamin Parker & Thankful Fay,	May 27, 1755
John Hyscom (?) & Rachell Hudson,	Nov. 27, 1755
Robert Spaulding & Hasadiak Johnson,	June 4, 1755
Edward Newton & Silence (?) Bartlet,	June 5, 1755
Benjamin Mixer & Dinah Newton,	July 8, 1755
David Newton & Abigail Lawrence,	July 30, 1755
Aaron Fay & Eunice Farr,	Oct. 8, 1755
Jona Clemens & Hannah More,	Oct. 13, 1755
Hannaniah Parker & Abigail Ward,	Dec. 2, 1755
Edward Bingham & Sarah Lyscom,	Nov. 2, 1757
Nehemiah Newton & Elizabeth Morse,	Feb. 2, 1758
Josiah Fay & Mary Bent,	March 22, 1758
Reuben Cumings & Elizabeth Butler,	Nov. 30, 1756
Ebenezer Chamberlain & Joana Morse,	Dec. 23, 1756
Amos Newton & Phebee Johnson,	Dec. 29, 1756
Joseph Newton & Experience Drury,	Dec. 29, 1756
Nathan Newton & Lydia Hagor,	Jan. 13, 1757
William Richards & Sarah Bixby,	Feb. 16, 1757
Nathan Bridge & Tamar Hutson (?),	March 23, 1757
Thomas Witherbee & Anna Berry,	April 14, 1757
Edmund Brigham & Sarah Lyscom,	Nov. 2, 1757
Nehemiah Newton & Mary Morss,	Feb. 2, 1758
Joshua Fay & Mary Bent,	March 22, 1758
Daniel Newhall & Sarah Mixor,	Feb. 3, 1761
Joshua Newton & Mary Bellows,	March 11, 1761
Henry Balcom & Kezia Stow,	April 29, 1761
Elisha Bruce & Easther Buck,	May 4, 1762
Robert Fay & Anna Harrington,	May 19, 1761
Joel (?) Newton & Lydia Beary,	June 3, 1762
Charles Newton and Eunice Bellows,	July 22, 1762
Jonas Bali & Molle Taylor,	Dec. 6, 1762
Daniel Gregory & Pierces Newton,	Jan. 6, 1763
Peter Joslyn & Thankfull Mathew,	April 18, 1763

6

Aaron Hardy & Lydia Ward,	May 4, 1763
Jonathan Cliford & Mary Bridges,	Nov. 26, 1778
Bezaleel Walker & Huldah Newton,	Dec. 3, 1778
John Phillips & Huldah Amsden,	April 6, 1778
Ezek'l Newton & Sarah Whiteing,	May 19, 1779
David Newton, Jr., & Elizabeth Newton,	Dec. 7, 1779
Timothy Chase & Sarah Newton,	March 2, 1780
Jona. Nurse & Thankful Newton,	July 6, 1780
Jotham Bellows & Abigail Bellows,	July 27, 1780
Peter Fay & Eunice Matthews,	Oct. 31, 1780
Timothy Bellows & Hannah Bellows,	Nov. 15, 1780
Silas Ball & Katharine Newton,	Feb. 1, 1781
William Onthank, Jr., & Mitle (?) Newton,	Feb. 14, 1781
Andrew Adams & Molly Morse,	Jan. 4, 1780
Francis Fay & Lovisa Ball,	Feb. 22, 1781
Daniel Graves & Rhoda Fay,	May 31, 1781
Isaac Newton & Molly Bruce,	Sept. 20, 1781
James Onthank & Elizabeth Newton,	Oct. 18, 1781
Sylvanus Reed & Caroline Taylor,	Oct. 31, 1781
James Onthank & Elizabeth Newton,	Oct. 18, 1781
Sylvanus Reed & Caroline Taylor,	Oct. 31, 1781
Hezekiah Johnson & Rebecca Newton,	March 19, 1782
Joel Lee & Molly Newton,	March 21, 1782
Peter Stone & Batsee Eastabrook,	May 26, 1782
David Gardner & Lovina Wetherbee,	May 1, 1782
Joseph Graves & Zerviah Williams,	June 7, 1782
Silas Newton & Lovina Newton,	Aug. 15, 1782
Luke Newton & Sally Hayden,	Nov. 21, 1782
Benjamin Collins & Rebecca More,	Nov. 28, 1782
Elijah Snow & Abigail Hopping,	Dec. 17, 1782
Erasmus Ward & Hannah Chamberlain,	Dec. 24, 1782
Seth Newton & Patience Hervey,	Feb. 6, 1783

GRAFTON.

April 18, 1735, the plantation of Hassanamisco established as Grafton. Prov. Laws, Vol II, p. 743. First (Congregational) Church organized 1731. Baptist, 1830. An old Baptist church extinct. Officiating clergyman mentioned : Rev. Aaron Hutchinson.

Joshua Winchester & Mary Whipple,	Dec. 6, 1750
Moses Haven of Framingham & Anna Stow,	May 23, 1751
Samuel Chase, Jr., of Sutton & Silence Stow,	May 29, 1751
Eliphalet Wood of Littleton & Abigail Child,	Nov. 7, 1751
Peter Brooks & Rebekah Ball,	Jan. 8, 1752
Jacob Steven & Martha Sherman,	Feb. 16, 1752
Phinehas Leland & Sarah Warren,	May 12, 1750
Thomas Deny (?) of Leicester & Tabitha Cuttler,	June 25, 1752
William Anthony (negro) & Abigail Abraham (Indian),	Nov. 14, 1752
William Gibson of Pelham & Martha Ware,	Dec. 19, 1752
Joshua Biglow of Sutton & Elis Stimpson (?),	June 28, 1753
Jonathan Marble & Anna Sheapcott,	Oct. 4, 1753
Daniel Axtell of Hopkinton & Elisabeth Whitmore,	Nov. 12, 1754
Sampson Abram & Elisabeth Abram,	May 30, 1756
Fortune Barun (?) (negro) & Abigail Anthony (Indian),	Jan. 27, 1757
Benjamin Wheelock of Mendon & Hannah Chapin,	June 4, 1752
John Gould & Lucy Brooks,	Feb. 22, 1753
Aaron Kimball & Mary Brooks,	April 5, 1753
William Holbrook & Sarah Batchellor,	May 15, 1753
Nathan Whitney of Spencer & Abigail Marstass (?),	Feb. 20, 1754
David Haron of Framingham & Jerusha Whiple,	Nov. 28, 1754
Deacon Joseph Meriam & Hannah Wadsworth,	Dec. 26, 1754
Josiah Child & Elisabeth Ball,	April 24, 1755

John Stow & Hannah Ball,   May 22, 1755
Joseph Arnold & Abigail Newton,   Oct. 9, 1755
Joseph Winchester & Lucy Harrington,   April 15, 1756
Mark Collins of Southboro & Hepzibah Hardy,
                                                   July 6, 1756
Joseph Temple (?) & Mary Whitmore,   Oct. 28, 1756
Daniel Godard of Shrewsbury & Mary Willard,
                                                   Nov. 17, 1756
Elisha Brigham & Sarah Roberts,   Dec. 30, 1756
John Wesson & Rebona Davis,   Aug. 24, 1757
Isaac Harrington, Jr., & Hannah Whiple,   Aug. 25, 1757
Jonathan Hall & Mary Stow,   Jan. 19, 1758
James McClallan of Sutton & Sarah Axtell,   Feb. 2, 1758
Ebenezer Maynard of Westboro & Sarah Brigham,
                                                   March 19, 1776
Samuel Abbee of Catham, Conn., & Sarah Leland,
                                                   April 4, 1776
Thomas Griggs of Sutton & Mary Goddard,   July 4, 1776
Daniel Whipple & Martha Adams,   August 7, 1776
William Collens & Lydia David, both of New Brain-
    tree,   Oct. 27, 1776
Simon Willard & Hannah Willard,   Nov. 29, 1776
Livi Leland & Anna How,   March 13, 1777
Elijah Stanton & Hannah Leland,   March 13, 1777
Jonah Goulding & Grace Knowlton of Shrewsbury,
                                                   April, 1777
Thomas Axtell, Jr., & Deborah Jones,   June 10, 1777
Eleazer Leland of Croyden & Elizabeth Sherman,
                                                   June 30, 1777
William Town of Royalston & Sarah Sherman, Oct. 13, 1777
Jonathan Melven of Conway & Beulah Leland,
                                                   Nov. 12, 1777
Joseph Wood, Jr., & Martha Willard,   Dec. 25, 1777
Jonathan Robinson & Sarah Taylor,   Jan 29, 1778
Elijah Bruce & Eunice Rice,   Jan. 30, 1778
Jonathan Wheeler & Marcy Rawson,   Feb. 12, 1778
James Wheeler & Vashti Biglow,   Feb. 26, 1778
David Forbush, Jr., & Deliverance Goodell, March 20, 1778
Philemon Stacey & Mary Fairbanks,   June 2, 1778

William Walker & Lucy Sadler,   June 8, 1778
Ebenezer Leland & Molly Lyon,   June 25, 1778
Abner Stow, Jr., & Eunice Gooldsbury of Warwick,
                  July 2, 1778
Forten Burnee (negro man) & Phillis (a negro
    woman) of Mendon,   July 31, 1778
Thomas Leland of Sutton & Anna Bachellor Rawson,
                Aug. 21, 1778
Ephraim Whitney, Jr., of Upton & Jemima Whipple,
                Oct. 1, 1778
Nathaniel Batchelor & Betty Wait,   Oct. 8, 1778
Gershom Chapin of Uxbridge & Mary Sherman,
                Nov. 5, 1778
David W. Leland & Mary Rawson,   Jan. 21, 1779
Ebenezer Lyon & Matilda Boon,   March 30, 1779
Reuben Hoit of New Braintree & Lucy Stow, June 20, 1779
Daniel Prentice & Abigail Stanley of Medford, July 18, 1779
Rev. Joseph Farrer & Mrs. Mary Brooks,   July 20, 1779
Joel Brooks & widow Mary Hall,   Aug. 23, 1779
John Carlyl & Eunice Willard,   Oct. 3, 1779
Daniel Robbins of Westboro & Martha Miller, Nov. 25, 1779
Samuel Richards of Watertown & Phebe Willard,
                March 9, 1780
Thaddeus Reed of Uxbridge & Hannah Taylor,
                May 24, 1780
John Robert & Tabitha Leland,   July 6, 1780
Enoch Forbush of Upton & Mary Batchelor, Sept. 14, 1780
Cyrus French & Susannah Harrington,   Oct. 4, 1780
Thomas Leland & Lydia Sherman.   Oct. 11, 1780
Jonathan Hall & Mary Kimball,   Oct. 12, 1780
Levi Leland & Sarah Wooddy of Sutton,   Oct. 12, 1780
Simon Wait & Marcy Flagg,   Nov. 28, 1780
Paul Warfield & Elizabeth Taylor,   Dec 11, 1780
James Putnam & Elizabeth Willard,   Dec. 28, 1780
Benjamin White & Hadassah Esther Prentice,
                March 5, 1781
Daniel Rand & Abigail Rockwood,   June 21, 1781
Eliphalet Smith & Beriah Leland,   June 28, 1781
Nathaniel Balch Dexter & Lucy Willard,   July 26, 1781

Joshua Turner & Lydia Drury,	Aug. 22, 1781
Comfort Chaffee & Lucy Hoit,	Sept. 25, 1781
Benjamin Perham of Upton & Azubah Sadler,	Oct. 4, 1781
Truman Clark & Anna Braman,	Oct. 8, 1781
Aaron Kimball, Jr., & Molly Goulding,	Oct. 18, 1781
Christian Ehlich & Meriam Flagg,	Oct. 22, 1781
Forten Burnee & Sarah Hector of Sutton (negroes),	Nov. 8, 1781
David Temple of Marlboro & Rebecca Brooks,	March 14, 1782
Thomas Fay of Westboro & Mime Garfield,	March 29, 1782
Zebulon Daniels & Sarah Brigham,	April 18, 1782
Moses Harrington, Jr., & Hannah Prentice,	May 7, 1782
Isaiah Fairbanks & Molly Goodell,	Nov. 28, 1782
Eliphalet Smith & Betty Brown,	April 14, 1783
Elijah Brooks & Mary Hall,	Dec. 25, 1783
Robert Taft of Upton & Rhoda Rockwood,	Jan. 8, 1784
Ezekiel Brigham, Jr., & Patience Gowing,	Feb. 5, 1784
Nathaniel Adams & Mary Harrington,	Feb. 8, 1784
Josiah Holbrook & Mary Sherman,	Feb. 26, 1784
Jonathan Furbush & Betty Hayden,	Nov. 5, 1782
Noah B. Kimball & Molly Chase,	Dec. 12, 1782
Moses Marsh & Betty Lyon,	Dec. 12, 1783

✓ SHREWSBURY.

Dec. 6, 1720. Resolve. A committee is paid for "running the lines of Whitehall Farm and Shrewsbury," which service they performed in July, 1717. First (Congregational) Church organized 1723. An old Baptist church extinct. Officiating clergymen mentioned : Rev. Ebenezer Morse, Rev. Job Cushing, Rev. Joseph Sumner.

Jonathan Keyes, Jr., & Sarah Taylor,	Jan. 23, 1752
Micah Pratt & Dinah Cutting,	May 18, 1752
Samuel Stearns of Grafton & Jemima Hoyt,	Aug. 19, 1752
Ephraim Pratt, Jr., & Abiel Leland,	Oct. 10, 1752
Jotham How & Priscilla Rice,	Jan. 3, 1753
Abiel Bragg & Abigail Wilson,	Jan. 29, 1753
Samuel Hibbert & Mary Collar,	Feb. 6, 1753
Asa Bouker & Hannah Crosby,	Jan. 3, 1753

Jason Parmenter of Neshawagg & Abigail Frissell,

                                            March 7, 1753

Daniel Hastings, Jr., & Priscilla Keyes,   Aug. 16, 1753

Jonathan Wheelock & Anna Drury,   June 20, 1753

Nathaniel Whittemore & Sarah Rice,   Aug. 17, 1753

Stephen Choat & Bathsheba Newton,   March 27, 1754

John Baker, Jr., & Persis Wheeler,   June 11, 1754

Bezaleel Maynard & Elizabeth Keyes,   Feb. 28, 1754

William Chestnut & Huldah Maynard,   Nov. 4, 1754

Benjamin Wilson of Gardiners Farm & Sarah Sawyer,

                                            July 4, 1754

Isaac Drury & Lois Muzzy,   Dec. 25, 1754

Jasper Stone & Grace Goddard,   April 17, 1755

Aaron Smith & Dinah Wheeler,   Aug. 4, 1757

Stephen Hastings & Martha Walker,   June 16, 1757

Ephraim Allen of Rutland & Huldah Chestnuts,

                                        July 12, 1757

Samuel Hastings & Anna Biglo,   Oct. 26, 1757

William Crawford of S. & Mary Dunsmore of Lan-

    caster,   Feb. 26, 1758

Ep. Temple & Mary (?) Frarrow (?),   March 7, 1758

Ebenezer Pike of S. & Lydia Glaris (?) of Lancaster,

                                      March 21, 1758

Cyprian Roys (?), Jr., & Martha Bush,   Jan. 27, 1756

Jonas Temple & Olive Keyes,   March 22, 1756

Jacob Hind & Triphena Roys (?),   Nov. 24, 1756

Josiah Wood of Upton & Ziporah Wheelock of Mendon.

                                        Feb. 3, 1757

Solomon Biglo & Sarah Newton,   March 4, 1762

Levi Goodanow & Melicent Keyes,   June 8, 1762

Seth Heyward and Martha Temple,   Aug. 24, 1762

Joseph Arnold & Lydia Fay,   Dec. 10, 1762

Eli Keyes, Jr., & Hannah How,   April 1, 1762

John Britain & Esthar Newton,   April 14, 1762

Solomon Newton & Hannah Hastings,   May 18, 1762

John Hastings & Betty How,   May 25, 1762

Artemas Maynard & Miriam Keyes,   May 27, 1762

Asaph Sherman & Lucy Whitney,   July 14, 1762

Constantine Hardy & Jemima Brigham,   Jan. 25, 1763

Timothy Newton & Huldah Wheelock,	Feb. 10, 1763
Silas Cook of Norton & Elizabeth Nixon,	April 1, 1763
Elisha Ward & Mary Baldwin,	April 7, 1763
Ezra Baker & Hannah Warrin, both of Westboro,	
	June 23, 1763
James Goodnough & Elizabeth Crosset,	July 4, 1763
Asa Rice & Miriam Wheeler,	July 25, 1763
Lemuel Rice & Abigail Lynds,	Sept. 15, 1763
Paul Johnson & Hannah Olds, both of Westboro,	
	Dec. 7, 1763
Jedidiah Tucker & Lucy Mixer,	Oct. 4, 1763
Charles Adams, Jr., of Worcester & Abigail Drury,	
	Feb. 8, 1764
Amos Rice of Northboro and Sarah Graves,	May 8, 1766
Benjamin Hinds & Tabatha Holland,	July 1, 1766
Abiel Stone of Lancaster & Mary Bradstreat,	Dec. 25, 1766
Jonas Goodenough of Princetown & Mary Davenport,	Jan. 29, 1767
Thaddeus Pollard & Submit Maynard,	March 24, 1767
Joshua Randall & Patte Wright of Rutland,	April 17, 1767
Ephraim Smith of Grafton & Sarah Bigelow,	June 8, 1767
James Goddard of Athol & Betty Goddard,	June 24, 1767
Thomas Miles & Rachel Keyes,	Oct. 29, 1767
William Brittan of Rutland & Lydia Whitney,	Nov. 3, 1767
David Cutting & Mary Keyes,	Nov. 10, 1767
Thomas Baker & Mary Newton,	Feb. 22, 1768
William Drury & Elizabeth Drury,	March 10, 1768
John Keyes Wetherbee & Levinah Rand,	May 3, 1768
Jonathan Peirce & Jemima Miles,	May 3, 1768
Israel Allen & Thankful Greenwood,	July 26, 1768
Isaac Moor of Bolton & Mary Bigelow,	June 2, 1768
Samuel Brittan of Rutland & Ruth Parker,	Oct. 4, 1768
John Bellows of Southboro' & Susanna Whitney,	
	Oct. 4, 1768
Daniel Hemenway & Mrs. Elisabeth Johnson,	Dec. 1, 1768
Seth Swan of Paxton & Dorcas Biglo,	Dec. 1, 1768
Ebenezer Drury of Temple, N. H., & Meriam Goodale,	Dec. 2, 1768
Timothy Whitney & Katharine Davenport,	Dec. 8, 1768

Jotham Flagg & Rebecca Kimball,   Aug. 15, 1765
David Brigham & Mercy Maynard,   March 21, 1765
Thomas Keyes of Westminster & Mary Temple,
                          April 14, 1765
Zebulon Throop & Lucy Wheeler,   May 27, 1765
John Glazier & Sarah Temple,   Oct. 21, 1765
Abel Holt & Eunice Keyes,   Oct. 21, 1765
John Wright & Jane Crosett of Templeton, April 30, 1765
Isaac Stone & Rachel Fisk,   May 3, 1765
Archelus Anderson of Chesterfield & Meriam Biglo,
                          May 30, 1765
Aaron Temple & Elizabeth Smith,   June 4, 1765
Simeon Keyes & Lucy Temple,   Dec. 5, 1765
Rev. Asaph Rice of Westminster & Mary Morse,
                          Dec. 26, 1765
Abel Osgood of Rutland & Eunice Holland, Feb. 13, 1766
James Mahoney & Jemima Temple,   Feb. 20, 1766
Samuel Lee of Rutland & Bulah Child,   Feb. 27, 1766
Josiah Boyden & Lydia Whitney, both of Worcester,
                          April, 1766
Francis Temple & Elizabeth Holland,   Dec. 18, 1766
Jonathan Wheeler of Grafton & Anna Rand, April 2, 1765
Elijah Stone of Framingham & Elizabeth Lynd,
                          April 4, 1765
Nathaniel Watt of Leicester & Joanna Tucker,
                          April 25, 1765
Josiah Bowker, Jr., of Westboro' & Sarah Muzzy,
                          May 23, 1765
Daniel Drury, Jr., & Sarah Knowlton,   May 28, 1765
Jacob Hapgood & Abigail Stone,   June 20, 1765
Rev. William Goddard of Westmoreland & Mrs.
    Rachel Goddard,   Aug. 14, 1765
Jonathan Newton & Sibbilah Harrington of Grafton,
                         Sept. 25, 1765
Phinehas Byam of Templeton & Mary Miles, Oct. 7, 1765
Rev. Nathan Stone of Yarmoth and Mrs. Mary
    Cushing,   Oct. 17, 1765
Asa Mixer & Mary Newton,   Nov. 26, 1765
Joseph Sherman, Jr., & Abigail Muzzy,   Feb. 4, 1766

James Simonds of Templeton & Sarah Knowlton,

Feb. 19, 1766

Daniel Holden of Leicester & Jemima Tucker, Aug. 20, 1766

Daniel Knight, Jr., of Worcester & Mehitable Bancroft,   Dec. 4, 1766

William Johnson of Southboro' & Zerviah Bragg,

Jan. 1, 1767

Ebenezer Hatshorn of Athol & Eunice Hapgood,

April 20, 1767

Michael Martyn & Zilpah Eager, both of Northboro',

May 11, 1767

Simon Phelps of Rutland & Tabitha Maynard, June 24, 1767

Robert Smith of Worcester & Elizabeth Goodale,

Dec. 16, 1767

—— Brown & Lydia Robertson,   Nov. 24, 1768

Jacob Ellis & Relief Bennett,   Feb. 10, 1769

Ephraim Wheeler & widow Elisabeth Temple,

March 22, 1769

Edward Goodenow of Westminster & Lois Rice,

June 17, 1770

Solomon Biglo, Jr., & Mary Damon,   April 6, 1769

Nathan Pike & Abigail Holland,   May 10, 1769

John Morse & Elisabeth Andrews,   May 11, 1769

Joseph Bixbee & Miriam Briant of Lancaster, July 13, 1769

Nathan Banister of Brookfield & Sarah Whitney,

Dec. 17, 1769

Joshua Blanchard of Wilton & Elisabeth Keys, Feb. 6, 1770

Nathaniel Whitney of New Marlboro & Molly Houghton of Lancaster,   Jan. 21, 1771

Oliver Barns of Northboro & Dinah Bennitt, Dec. 24, 1770

Richard Barns, Jr., & Anna Bathrick, both of Westboro,   Jan. 1, 1772

Amsden Gale of Westboro & Elizabeth Henderson,

March 17, 1772

Simeon Allen & Candice How,   July 20, 1772

Phinehas Heywood, Jr., & Kezia Snow of Westboro,

Nov. 19, 1772

Peter Hubbard & Phebe Brigham, both of Holden,

Aug. 12, 1773

Jonas Bennett & Mary Williams, Jan. 10, 1773
David Bennett & Persis Cutting of Lancaster, Feb. 14, 1773
Joshua Morse & Levinah Holland, April 29, 1773
Caleb Kendel & Priscilla Townsend, Dec. 8, 1773
Samuel Richardson of N. Fain & widow Sarah
    Holland, Feb. 6, 1774
Jonathan Stone, Jr., & Hannah Gates of Worcester,
    July 7, 1769
Thomas Drury of Temple & Martha Knowlton,
    Sept. 11, 1769
Rev. Edward Goddard of Swansey & Miss Lois How,
    Nov. 1, 1769
Samuel Biglo & Abigail Hastings, May 7, 1770
James Curtis of Worcester & Sarah Eager, May 24, 1770
Joseph Jeseph of Worcester and Jemima Bozworth,
    July 10, 1770
Daniel Hemingway, Jr., & Mary Carryl, Aug. 1, 1770
Abijah Kendal of Templeton & Millesent Miles,
    March 26, 1771
Edward Goddard, Jr., & Margaret How, May 23, 1771
Jonah How & Prudence Bouker, July 4, 1771
Solomon Wheeler & Zipporah Harrington of Grafton,
    Aug. 26, 1771
Joseph Ballard of Andover & Molly Smith, Sept. 10, 1771
Thomas Johnson & Elizabeth Smith, Sept. 24, 1771
Jonathan Heywood, Jr., of Concord & Zerviah Baldwin,
    Nov. 7, 1771
Jonas Wyman of Lancaster & Hannah Smith, May 27, 1772
Joseph Stone & Lydia Rice, Nov. 18, 1772
Ebenezer Kint of Leicester & Sarah Stone, Nov. 19, 1772
Joseph Holland & Elizabeth Gleason of Worcester,
    Dec. 29, 1772
Thaddeus Easterbrook of Rutland & Sarah Wyman,
    Dec. 31, 1772
Jonas Whitney & Tamar Houghton of Lancaster,
    Jan. 11, 1773
Jonathan Thurstin & Lois Wheeler, May 5, 1773
Nathan Wait of Leicester & Hannah Pierks, May 20, 1773
Jacob Kent of Leicester & Mary Tucker, May 23, 1773

Abner Miles & Deborah Underwood of Westford,
June 24, 1773
Rev. Isaac Stone of Douglass & Susan Goddard,
Oct. 27, 1773
Elnathan Allen, Jr., & Lydia Pratt, Nov. 24, 1773
Stephen Wheelock & Lucretia Newton, Jan. 18, 1774
Joseph Hastings, Jr., & Katherine Joslin, Nov. 15, 1770
Elijah Southgate of Leicester & Patty Hastings,
Jan. 19, 1774
Joseph Curtis of Worcester & Eleaner Flint, Aug. 1, 1774
Jotham Bush & Mary Taylor of Northboro, June 23, 1781
John Wright & Deliverance Houghton, Sept. 26, 1781
William Raa of Greenwich & Patience Wyman, Nov. 5, 1782
Asa Fay of Grafton & Mary Robins of Westboro,
April 13, 1780
Samuel Andrews & Judith Flagg, July 10, 1777
John Keyes of Wilton & Lucy Hale, Sept. 11, 1777
Jacob Wheelor of Petersham & Huldah Maynard,
March 5, 1778
Daniel Ball & Lydia Smith, Sept. 8, 1778
Francis Biglow of Boston & Levinah Beaman, Oct. 29, 1778
Jonas Rice of Ashburnham & Zilphar Townsend,
May 10, 1779
Ebenezer Ingolsbee, Jr., & Phebe Easterbrooks, Nov. 20, 1779
Charles Henny & Happy Tompson (negroes), March 3, 1780
Joseph Morse & Sophia Biglow, May 4, 1780
John Parker & Olive Temple, May 25, 1780

WESTMINSTER.

Oct. 20, 1759, the plantation called Narragansett Number Two established as the district of Westminster. Prov. Laws, Vol. IV, p. 265. Made a town April 26, 1770. Prov. Laws, Vol. V, p. 50. First (Congregational) Church organized 1742. Clergymen mentioned: Rev. Asaph Rice, Rev. Elisha Fish.

Nathan Peirce & Mary Cottingham, Oct. 31, 1765
Daniel Munjoy & Katey Randall of Stow, Feb., 1766
Abel Lawrence & Deborah Gordan, March 26, 1767
Josiah Wilder & Luce Graves, May 24, 1767

Silas Kendall & Eunice Conant,	Dec. 24, 1767
Joseph Miller, Jr., & Luce Walker,	Jan. 12, 1768
Solomon Harvey & Mary Woodward,	Feb. 5, 1768
John Matthews & Patience Graves,	April 14, 1768
Peter Graves and Susanah Hagar,	Feb. 10, 1768
Moses Thurston & Easter Bigelow,	April 21, 1768
Thomas Newhall & Sarah Dwight,	March 1, 1770
Charles Richardson & Susannah Taylor,	March 21, 1770
Christopher Wheaton & Abigail Brewer,	July 26, 1770
Ezekiel Fosgate & Hannah Harrington,	Sept. 30, 1770
Edward Goddard & Ruth Shaw,	Jan. 17, 1770
Jonathan Evens & Lydia Clemons,	March 28, 1769
Jonathan Batchelor & Thankful Whitney,	April 6, 1769
Eleazer Ball & Mary Bradish,	April 7, 1769
James Watkins & Sarah Whitney,	Nov. 16, 1769
Jonas Warren, the 3d, & Mary Ober,	Feb. 1, 1770
Phillip Ardenay & Anna Brown,	May 15, 1768
Ephraim Miller & Bulah Wheeler,	Nov. 6, 1768
Asa Taylor & Sarah Williams,	Jan. 5, 1769
James How & Mary Sherman,	June 19, 1769
Hubbard Dunster & Ruth Bayley,	Aug. 31, 1769
Elijah Gibbs & Mary Whitney,	Nov. 9, 1769
David Merium & Martha Conont,	Nov. 30, 1769
Francis Wheeler & Huldah Stedman,	Dec. 26, 1769
Joshua Mostman & Sarah Barnard,	April 10, 1770
Abner Whitney & Elizabeth Glazier,	May 14, 1770
Ephraim Weatherbee & Hannah Woodward,	Dec. 11, 1770
Dorcas Sawyer & Sarah Garey,	March 26, 1771
Jeremiah Gayer & Ruth Walker,	May 29, 1771
Samuel Sawine & Martha Miller,	Nov. 6, 1771
Paul Walker & Rebecca Haines,	Nov. 6, 1771
Thomas Wheeler & Mary Child,	Jan. 2, 1772
Nathan Kezer & Hannah Morse,	May 27, 1772
Dudley Bayley & Reuhamah Dunster,	Oct. 26, 1772
William Bemis & Abigail Annis,	Nov. 12, 1772
Elijah Simons & Abigail Roff,	April 20, 1773
Edmund Bernard & Elizabeth Holden,	Nov. 25, 1773
Silas Whitney & Sarah Withinton,	Jan. 27, 1774
Jonas Baker & Elizabeth Adams,	Feb. 27, 1774

Jonathan Kezer & Abigail Snow,	Feb. 24, 1774
Samuel Warren & Anne Merium,	March 3, 1774
Joshua Fletcher & Ruth Holden,	June 30, 1772
William Wicker of Hardwicke & Susanna Parker	
of Paxton,	June 4, 1772
John Whitney & Polly Jones,	Feb., 1781
James Bowers & Abigail Herrington,	May 14, 1782
Elisha Whitney & Eunice Sever,	Dec. 27, 1781
Thomas Amory & Polly Sawin,	Nov. 15, 1—
Livi Brooks & Bettsa Flint,	Feb. 20, 1784
James Fosgate & Sarah Emmorson,	Dec. 18, 1783
Samuel Wood & Anna Calef,	June 8, 1784
Samuel Jones & Marthy Willard,	Jan. 22, 1783
Abner Holden, Jr., & Elizabeth Howard,	Feb. 9, 1785
Stephen Hoar & Hannah Wood,	June 22, 1780
Barth Senior & Mary Stebings,	1780
Aaron Saunders & Sarah Hosley,	April 12, 1774
Aaron Bolton & Dorcas Winship,	April 12, 1774
Isaac Williams & Hannah Walker,	Nov. 3, 1774
Jonathan Brooks & Mary Winship,	Dec. 13, 1774
Joseph Cummins & Hannah Bride,	Aug. 15, 1775
Samuel Miller & Lydia Cutting,	Oct. 23, 1775
Jonathan Goodale & Mary Hadley,	Jan. 26, 1776
John White & Ruth Fletcher,	April 10, 1776
Thomas Farnsworth & Relief Holden,	April 29, 1776
Elias Stearns & Sarah Keyes,	Dec. 21, 1776
John Bemas & Abigail Stevens,	Dec. 30, 1776
Joseph Flint & Mary Hartwell,	Feb. 20, 1777
Joseph Hapgood & Ruth Jackson,	June 4, 1778
Zachariah Rand & Jerusha Sawyer,	June 23, 1778
Nehemiah Bowers & Sarah Sawin,	June, 1777
Sibes Jackson & Elizabeth Watten,	March 16, 1778
Abner Bemis & Catherine Deering,	July 6, 1778
Thomas Farnsworth & Anna Estherbrooks,	Nov. 26, 1778
Jude Sawyer & Phebe Keyes,	Nov. 26, 1778
Joseph Holden & Rebeckah Hoar,	March 18, 1779
Abner Whitney & Levinah Ward,	April 22, 1779
George Taylor & Abigail Sever,	July 13, 1779
Edmon Bemas & Phebe Spring,	July 22, 1779

Nathan Heward & Rebeckah Wood, Oct. 27, 1779
Abijah Wood & Dorothy Wheeler, Dec. 9, 1779
Isaac Miller & Sarah Bennett, Dec. 9, 1779
Thomas Noe & Anna Miles, Feb., 1780
Zeeb. Green & Sarah Cowee, May 9, 1780
John Woodward & Rebeckah Stowell, May 18, 1780
Stephen Holden & Elizabeth Miller, June 8, 1780
Jonathan Phillips & Elizabeth Bemas, Nov., 1780
Abel Wood & Phebe Holden, Nov. 21, 1780
Eli Smith & Sarah Holden, Dec. 21, 1780
Joel Miles & Mary Ester Brooks, Dec. 26, 1780
Levi Graves & Rebeccah Wood, Dec. 26, 1780
Amos Shed & Tripheny Hadley, Jan. 4, 1781
Stephen Miles & Sarah Hoar,
William Pennyman & Sarah Bigelow, Dec. 18, 1782
Ezra Pennyman & Lovisa Eagur, Nov., 1782
Peter Prescott & Mary Wilson, Feb., 1783
James Cowee & Susannah Baldwin, Feb., 1783
Joseph Hadley & Naomi Perse, Jan., 1784
Elias Holden & Olive Smith, Jan., 1784
John Chandler & Mary Jackson, 1782
Samuel Taylor & Prudence Winship, 1782
David Weld & Abigail Osgood, Feb., 1783
David Wiman & Sarah Stedman, Feb., 1784
Shadrach Newton & Mary Dike, April, 1784
James (or Jaines) Richardson & Sarah Jackson, June, 1784
Nicholas Dike & Joanna Baker, Jan., 1785
Samuel Miriam & Elizabeth Fessenden, Jan., 1785
Pelatiah Everett & Mary Cutting, Jan., 1785
William Mills & Sarah Bowman, Jan., 1785
Nathan Wood & Mehitabel Cohe, March, 1781
Oliver Jackson & Mary Pierce, 1780
Jonas Winship & Mary Jackson, Sept., 1781
Samuel Brown & Abigail Darby, Nov., 1782
Josiah Conant & Annes Darby, Nov., 1784
Thomas Conant, Jr., & Ruth Rice, Dec. 21, 1784
Joel Hail & Jana Ramor, April 26, 1785

↓ NORTHBOROUGH.

June 24, 1766, part of Westborough established as the district of Northborough. Prov.
Laws, Vol. IV, p. 839. District of Northborough made a town August 23, 1775. Prov. Laws,
Vol. V, p. 419. First (Unitarian) Church organized 1746. Clergyman mentioned: Rev.
Peter Whitney.

Joseph Eager & Elizabeth Green,	March 28, 1768
Joseph Sawyer & Sarah Townsend,	April 28, 1768
Nathan Green & Abigail Williams,	July 26, 1768
Aaron Davis of Harvard & Ruth Rice,	Dec. 1, 1768
Zackeus Cutler of Amherst & Hasadiah Eager,	
	Oct. 6, 1771
Silvanus Oak & Abigail Ball,	Nov. 21, 1771
Jonathan Hastings of Lancaster & Mary Fay, Feb. 21, 1771	
Nathaniel Bragg of Shrewsbury & Sarah Wilson,	
	March 14, 1771
Zephaniah Briggs & Margaret Lambert,	June 25, 1772
Jonas Badcock & Miriam Hudson,	Nov. 30, 1772
William Kelley of Shrewsbury & Lucy Carruth,	
	Oct. 14, 1772
Jonathan Bruce, Jr., & Anna Barnes,	June 13, 1775
William Winslow & Martha Hayward,	June 17, 1775
Timothy Hall of Wilton, N. H., & Sarah Keyes,	
	Aug. 15, 1775
Daniel Allen of Shrewsbury & Martha Maynard,	
	Sept. 20, 1775
Dr. Jonathan Livermore & Jane Dunlap,	Nov. 16, 1775
Adam Fay & Lydia Badcock, Jr.,	Jan. 18, 1776
Abel Tenney & Anna Rice,	Feb. 12, 1776
Isaac Stow (or How?) & Hannah Fay,	May 16, 1776
Breek Parkman of Westboro' & Susannah Brigham,	
	Jan. 9, 1777
Silas Hastings & Hannah Reed,	April 23, 1777
Asa Rice & Betty Taylor,	May 20, 1777
Reuben Gaschet & Cate Witt,	June 19, 1777
Robert Baylies & Patience Haiden,	Aug. 16, 1777
Daniel Gaschet & Hannah Wilson,	Aug. 21, 1777

Major Joseph Mixtor of Shrewsbury & Elizabeth
    Ball,   Sept. 3, 1777
William Parmenter, Jr., of Sudbury & Submit
    Fairbanks,   May 25, 1780
Zadock Bartlett & Hannah Severs,   1780
Edward Johnson, Jr., & Relief Johnson, both of
    Bolton,   Feb. 14, 1781
John Hosmer of Marlboro & Anna Fosgate of Bolton,
        June 21, 1781
Nathan Johnson of Bolton & Beulah Wood,   Dec. 13, 1781
Eliab Wheelock & Mary Gaschet,   Jan. 2, 1782
Elisha Rice of Westboro & Ruth Rice,   April 4, 1782
Gershom Brigham of Marlboro & Sarah Allen,
        May 23, 1782
Lemuel Munroe & Anna Toozer,   June 13, 1782
Eliphalet Wood of Harvard & Mary Badcock, Sept. 1, 1782
Jesse Brigham, Jr., & Elizabeth Henderson,   Dec. 15, 1782
Daniel Harris of Bolton & Abigail Reed,   Jan. 1, 1783
Daniel Brigham of Westboro (physician) & Anna
    Munroe,   Nov. 9, 1783
Dean Wyman & Betty Rice,   Nov. 30, 1783
James Longley of Shrewsbury & Molly Bartlett,
        Jan. 15, 1784
Ephraim Wilson & Persis Daschet,   Jan. 18, 1784
Samuel Mahan & Grace Harrington of Shrews-
    bury,   Feb. 18, 1784
Caleb Seager & Hannah Goodenow,   Feb. 23, 1784
Jonathan Gage & Mary Brigham,   March 28, 1784
Jonathan Conn & Mary Wilder,   Sept. 19, 1784
John Ward of Westminster & Copia Rice,   Oct. 14, 1784
Israel Saunderson of Putney, Vt., & Relief Rice,
        Nov. 9, 1784
Levi Bush of Sterling & Patty Ball,   Nov. 23, 1784
Silas Rice & Mehitable Goodenow,   Dec. 3, 1784

MARRIACES.

LEOMINSTER.

June 23, 1740, part of Lancaster established as Leominster. Prov. Laws, Vol. II, p. 1023. First (Unitarian) Church records begin 1743. Clergyman mentioned: Rev. John Rogers.

Elisha Coolidge & Sarah Boutell,	June 4, 1754
Jonathan Harris & Abigail Phillips,	Dec. 31, 1759
Thomas Wilder & Abigail Carter,	Feb. 12, 1760
Nathaniel Carter, Jr., & Dorothy Joslin,	June 26, 1760
Joseph Daby & Elizabeth Wheelock,	May 11, 1761
William Warner & Mary Wilder,	Jan. 4, 1762
Caleb Sawyer, Jr., & Sarah Rogers,	Aug. 1, 1762
Philip Sweetser & Mary Parmenter,	Nov. 5, 1762
Abel Wilder of Winchendon & Anna Butler (?),	June 27, 1764
Thomas Gowing & Esther Richardson,	Jan. 17, 1763
Henry Sweetser & Lucy Johnson,	Oct. 5, 1763
Joseph Joslin & Sarah Tarbell,	Oct. 20, 1763
Josiah White, Jr., & Tabitha Carter,	May 15, 1764
Gideon Ellis of Keen & Lucy Osgood,	June 6, 1764
Jonathan Priest Whitcomb of Swansey & Dorothy Carter,	Sept. 5, 1764
Thomas Mears & Mary Stewart,	Sept. 19, 1764
Elisha Whitcomb of Swansey & Joanna Whitcomb,	Oct. 7, 1764
Benjamin Rogers and Susanna Battles,	Jan. 17, 1764
Abraham Houghton of Bolton & Sarah Divol,	Oct. 8, 1764
Daniel Peirce & Marcy Gates,	Dec. 11, 1766
Josiah Swan, Jr., & Elizabeth White,	Dec. 11, 1766
James Joslin & Mary Daby,	Jan. 8, 1767
William Lincoln & Prudence Buss,	May 27, 1767
John Beaman & Mary Fuller,	Aug. 6, 1767
Enos Jones of Ashburnham & Mary Whitmore,	Jan. 20, 1768
David Wilder & Lucy Joslin,	Jan. 24, 1768
Joseph Witherbe of Stow & Sarah Gates,	Jan. 27, 1768
Ephraim Hale & Hannah Spofford of Lancaster,	May 22, 1768

Jeramiah Wilson of Bolton & Eunice Whetcomb, Dec. 1, 1768
Elisha Davis & Rebecca Wyman, Jan. 31, 1770
Samuel Wilson of Swansey, N. H., & Susanna Divoll,
April 17, 1770
David Wilson & Dorcas Osgood of Lancaster, Dec. 6, 1770
James Gray & Rebecca How, both of Lancaster, Dec. 20, 1770
Reuben Pierce & Mary Wood, Jan. 1, 1771
James White of Charlemont & Ruth Ballard of Lancaster, Feb. 4, 1771
Amos Brown & Marcy Gates, May 30, 1771
Nathan Colburn & Betty Fuller, May 10, 1769
Nathaniel —— & Elizabeth Symonds, Feb. 8, 1770
Elias Gates of Westmoreland & Mary Beamon, Feb. 26, 1770
Ephraim Carter & Joanna Wheelock, April 2, 1770
Nathaniel Beamon of Lancaster & Thankful Farnsworth, April 10, 1770
Josiah Carter & Elizabeth Graves, April 22, 1770
Jonathan Thayer of Charlemont & widow Dinah Stearns, Nov. 1, 1770
John Woods & Elizabeth Nickols, Dec. 4, 1770
David Kendall & Annise Johnson, Jan. 17, 1771
Josiah Richardson & Rebecca Beaman, Feb. 17, 1771
Elijah Garfield of Petersham & Jenny Nickols, May 29, 1771
Nathaniel Brown & Priscilla Robins, Dec. 25, 1771
Samuel Buss & Lydia Lincoln, June 18, 1772
Reuben Kendall & Priscilla Beaman, Dec. 25, 1771

DOUGLAS.

June 5, 1746, the district or precinct of New Sherburn to be called by the name of Douglas. August 23, 1775, district of Douglas made a town. Prov. Laws, Vol. V, p. 419. First (Congregational) Church organized 1747. Clergymen mentioned: Rev. William Phips, Rev. Isaac Stone.

Caleb Whitney & Hannah Southwath of Sutton,
March 20, 1760
Ward Nye of Rochester & Mary Chase, by Rev. David Hall, Jan. 28, 1768
Elisha Smith & Luce Balkom, April 21, 1772

Joseph Titas, Jr., & Mary Biglow,   June 11, 1772
Nathan Lackey of Sutton & Susanna Nye,   Sept. 3, 1772
Seth Fish & Louis (Louise?) Cummings, both of
 Uxbridge,   Dec. 10, 1772
Abel Aldrich & Olive Lovell,   Jan. 7, 1773
William Robins & Mellison Hill,   April 8, 1772
Peter Reed & Olive Marsh,   Dec. 3, 1772
Caleb Hill, Jr., & Elizabeth Whitney,   Dec. 3, 1772
Jesse Aldrich of New Salem & Rachel Brown of
 Uxbridge,   Dec. 3, 1772
Jonathan Mansfield of Waltham & Martha Hayward,
             Dec. 3, 1772
Aaron Herendeen & Bulah Cook,   Dec. 3, 1772
Thomas Biglow & Hannah Chase,   March 3, 1774
James Hayword of Upton & Rebecca Aldrich,
             March 27, 1774
David Parker & Susanna Atcenson (?) of Sutton,
             Sept. 14, 1775
Aaron Hill & Mary Whitney,   May 5, 1775
Lu^t Samuel Jonesen & Neomi Enirdon,   Dec. 7, 1775
Nathaniel Davidson & Sarah Reed,   Sept. 29, 1774
David Elixander & Sarah Whitney,   Oct. 23, 1774
George Linton of Uxbridge & Deliverance Nye,
             March 13, 1775
Amiriah Holbrook of Uxbridge & Keziah Nye,
             Nov. 20, 1777
Jacob Perun of Woodstock & Abigail Woodward,
             Feb. 10, 1778
Amos Marsh & Elizabeth Jeperson,   April 22, 1778
Bezeliel Balcom & Jemima Morse,   May 13, 1778
Benjamin Duelley & Mercy Walles,   Aug. 18, 1778
Elijah Crosman of Sutton & Rebecce Mersh, May 22, 1757
Stephen Streeter of Oxford & Sarah Chamberlin,
             Sept. 10, 1778
Asa Blake of Uxbridge & Jonna Nye,   Dec. 10, 1778
Aaron Benson & Lydia Fairbanks,   Dec. 30, 1778
Samuel Davidson (?) & Hannah Rich of Sutton,
             April 22, 1778
James Wallis & Chloe Humes,   March 15, 1781

David White & Huldah Marsh, April 19, 1781
Samuel Whitney & Azubah Hill, Dec. 13, 1781
Daniel Whitney of Chesterfield & Eunice Marsh, Jan. 3, 1782
Solomon Stockwell & Mary Howell, Feb. 20, 1782
Richard Lee & Bethiah Gould, Feb. 21, 1782
Josiah Reed, A. M., of Uxbridge & Elizabeth Taylor,
April 21, 1782
Edward Corbitt & Mary Rutter, May 22, 1782
Alexander Wilson of Mendon & Patience Nye, Nov. 7, 1782
Jacob Staples of Pomfret & Molly Sears, Nov. 17, 1782
Eli Stockwell & Eunice Hill, Nov. 20, 1782
Gideon Gould & Hannah Marsh, both of Sutton, Dec. 5, 1782
Denies Darling of Mendon & Deborah Bolkcom,
Dec. 24, 1782
Peter Sherman & Hannah Ross, June 30, 1783

NEW BRAINTREE.

Jan. 31, 1751. Resolve. "The precinct consisting of the lands called New Braintree and part of the town of Hardwick is erected into a district." Aug. 23, 1775, the above district made a town. Prov. Laws, Vol. V, p. 419. First (Congregational) Church organized 1754.

Beriah Haws & Mrs. Dorothy Joslyn, Nov. 10, 1762
Lott Whitcomb of Hardwick & Lydia Nye, Dec. 9, 1762
John Cannon & Abigail Messer, Jan. 13, 1763
George Nye & Mrs. Jane Timton, April 26, 1764
Dr. Percival Hall & Margaret Ware, May 10, 1764
Joseph Little & Elizabeth Willson, May 29, 1764
Jonathan Force (?) & Mary Woods, June 28, 1764
Moses Gilbert of Brookfield & Merriam Bains, Jan. 24, 1765
Silas Mathews of Brookfield & Priscilla Woods,
Sept. 10, 1765
Joseph Parker, Jr., & Zerviah Lincoln, Feb. 6, 1766
John Steal & Sarah Culveson (?), May 8, 1766
Alevander Woolson & Huldah Gilbert, June 5, 1766
John Woods & Lydia Woods, Feb. 5, 1767
Daniel Eldridge of Hardwick & Prudence Warner,
Feb. 10, 1767

James Barr & Deborah Nye,	April 16, 1767
Bille Hancock & Percis Woods,	May 9, 1767
Reuben Fay of Hardwick & Elizabeth Perkins, June 11, 1767	
Joseph Johnson & Sarah Hunter,	Feb. 4, 1768
David Ayres & Mary Perkins,	March 17, 1768
Ebenezer Nye & Thankfull Dean,	July 7, 1768
Nathaniel Weeks & Marcy Richmond,	Feb. 16, 1769
Joseph Finton & Sarah Steel,	Feb. 23, 1769
Samuel Warren & Unity Ware,	April 11, 1769
James Hunter & Sarah Hall,	April 13, 1769
James Washburn & Ruth Rice,	Sept. 7, 1769
George Barr & Eunice Woods,	Sept. 21, 1769
Thomas Rainger of Brookfield & Marcy Woods, Jan. 9, 1770	
Benjamin Woods & Sarah Adams,	March 8, 1770
Jonathan Ware & Sarah Woods,	April 26, 1770
James Blair & Sarah Joslin,	April 26, 1770
John Cunningham, Jr., of Spencer & Anna Thomson,	
	May 31, 1770
Isaac Patrick of Western & Jane Anderson,	Nov. 1, 1770
Nathan Thomson & Mary Haws,	Nov. 15, 1770
Samuel Ruggles & Elizabeth Fisher,	Dec. 11, 1770
Isaiah Butler of Hardwick & Abigail Thrasher, Feb. 7, 1771	
George Caswell & Wealthy Richmond,	March 28, 1771
Elias Hall & Judith Walker,	May 26, 1771
Henry Chase of Petersham & Rachel Lincoln, July 11, 1771	
Silvester Richmond & Lucy Weston,	Aug. 8, 1771
Jonathan Cunningham of Oakham & Bethyah	
Thrasher,	Sept. 13, 1770
Jonathan Witherby & Mehitable Fisher,	Oct. 21, 1771
Nathan Upham of Brookfield & Eleaner Gilbert, Feb. 27, 1772	
Dr. Gershom Gilbert & Mary Hall,	April 2, 1772
James Steal & Sarah Willson,	April 21, 1772
William Gilcrest & Agnis Thomson,	Sept. 8, 1772
John Fenton & Joanna Torrence,	Nov. 19, 1772
Simeon Cannon & Mary Nickols,	Jan. 21, 1773
John Hunter & Elizabeth Matthews,	Jan. 28, 1773
George Cannon & Abigail Craigue,	Feb. 28, 1773
Stephen Thrasher & Anna Cutter (or Cutler), March 11, 1773	
Thomas Steal & Anna Downing of Ware,	April 1, 1773

✓ FITCHBURG.

Feb. 3, 1764, part of Lunenburg established as Fitchburg. Prov. Laws, Vol. IV, p. 685. First (Congregational) Church organized 1768. Unitarian, 1768. Clergyman mentioned : Rev. John Payson.

Jonathan Dix (?) of New Ipswich & Anna Kimball,
Oct. 20, 1767
James Litch and Rebecca Upton, Feb. 9, 1768
Mordacai Moors & Lucy Buncraft (?), April 6, 1769
Jonathan Ware & Hannah Battles of Leominster,
April 11, 1769
Joseph Gibson of Lunenburg & Esther Pierce,
July 3, 1769
Matthew Brooks & Dolley Kimball, June 19, 1770
Samuel Downes & Eunice Wentworth, Jan. 1, 1771
Daniel Melven of Holliston & Mrs. Susannah Farwell,
Jan. 21, 1771
Jacob Gibson & Mary Polley, Feb. 20, 1772
William Small & Miriam Thurston, May 10, 1772
Joshua Billings of Ashburnham & Lois Gibson,
June 13, 1772
Benjamin Frost & Rachael Kimball, Dec. 3, 1772
Silas Gibson of Lunenburg & Damaras Bennett,
Feb. 20, 1772
Joseph Baldwine & Elisabeth Danforth, May 2, 1782
John Thurston & Esther Wood, Aug. 20, 1782
John Polley & Abigel Kimball, Nov. 4, 1782
Elijah Phelps & Keziah Gibson, Feb. 10, 1783
Thomas Gibson & Relefe Hartwell, April 1, 1783
Benjamin Hawks of Leominster & Mrs. Mary Boutell,
April 22, 1783
Thomas Gibson & Lucy Marten of Westminster,
May 7, 1783
John Upton & Abigel Low, Oct. 20, 1783
Dr. Samuel Lock & Hannah Cowdin, Dec. 30, 1783

◊ WINCHENDON.

June 24, 1764, the plantation called Ipswich-Canada established as Winchendon. Prov.
Laws, Vol. IV, p. 721. First (Congregational) Church organized 1762. Methodist Episcopal,
1796. Advent Baptist, 1798. Clergyman mentioned: Rev. Daniel Stimpson.

Thomas Sweetland & Abigail Puslia (?), both of
    Ipswich-Canada, N. H.,   Jan. 4, 1763
Bartholomew Pearsons of Ipswich-Canada & Lydia
    Kendall of Lunenburg,   Nov. 3, 1763
Aaron Hodgkins & Eunice Bixby, both of Ipswich-
    Canada,   Jan. 24, 1764
Henry Poor of Royalshire & Kezia Foster,   Sept. 11, 1764
James Mansfield & Lois Darling,   March 4, 1766
Isaac Stimson & Elizabeth Bixby,   March 26, 1767
Richard Pearsons & Kezia Bixby,   July 6, 1767
Daniel Gould & Mary Porter,   Feb. 15, 1770
John Torner & Jerusha Bixby,   July 5, 1770
John Day & Elizabeth Joslin,   Jan. 10, 1771
David Goodridge & Silence Joslin,   Aug. 20, 1772
Abijah Stimson & Lois Bixby,   Sept. 28, 1772
Ephraim Sawyer & Peggy Fisher,   Dec. 3, 1772
Job Boynton & Mary Joslin,   March 18, 1773
Samuel Steel & Rachel Putnam,   Nov. 4, 1773
Nathan Green & Lucy Gardner,   March 20, 1774

√ TEMPLETON.

March 6, 1762, the plantation called Narragansett Number Six established as Templeton. Prov. Laws, Vol. IV, p. 533. First (Unitarian) Church organized 1733. Baptist, 1782.
Clergyman mentioned: Rev. Ebenezer Sparhawk.

Joel Fletcher & Ruth Church,   May 31, 1764
Ezra Hudson of Petersham & Relief Atherton,
            July 23, 1764
Uriah Witherbee & Mary Nichols,   Oct. 9, 1764
Richard Stewart & Eunice Stewart,   Oct. 11, 1764
Joshua Wright & Olive Church,   Nov. 29, 1764

Jonathan Holman & Olive Farce, June 3, 1765
Israel Lamb & Lucy Wheeler, Oct. 31, 1765
David Thurston & Eunice Whitney, April 16, 1766
Samuel Treadwell & Sarah Nickless, June 18, 1766
Hezekiah Sprague & Rachel Byam, Aug. 13, 1767
William Crosiel & Susanna Jackson, Jan. 7, 1768
Henry Sawtell, Jr., & Joshua Hudson, April 4, 1768
Oliver Holman & Olive Reed, Nov. 30, 1768
George Nickless, Jr., & Betty Sawyer, Feb. 9, 1769
Aaron Whitney & Hannah Wait of Petersham,
July 20, 1769
James Caruth & Lucy Gary of Lancaster, Oct. 5, 1769
Josiah Willis Seaver (?) & Sarah Whitcomb, Dec. 28, 1769
Simon Stone & Hannah Whittemore, Feb. 27, 1770

√ SUTTON.

Oct. 28, 1714. Resolve. "Voted a concurrence with the Representatives approving and confirming a survey and plat of the laying out of the township of Sutton." First (Congregational) Church organized 1720. First Baptist, 1785. Officiating clergymen mentioned: Rev. David Hall, Rev. James Wellman, Rev. Ebenezer Chaplain, Rev. Jeremiah Barstow.

Benjamin Fitts & Sarah Rich, Oct. 31, 1749
Follensbee Chase & Hannah Marsh, Jan. 2, 1749–50
Jonathan Marsh, Jr., & Hannah Holt, July 20, 1749
Thomas Fuller of Uxbridge & Sarah Wheeler, Feb. 6, 1749–50
Enoch Marble & Abigail Holland, Jan. 9, 1749–50
John Severy & Hannah Holman, March 8, 1749
Nathaniel Fairfield & Priscilla Wilkins, March 13, 1749–50
William Ellis of Medway & Mary Walker, May 10, 1750
Joshua Carter & Elizabeth Lovell, July 25, 1750
Rev. Ezekiel Dodge of Abington & Mrs. Mary Goddard, Sept. 27, 1750
Joseph Moseley & Sybella Dudley, Oct. 18, 1750
Robert Dunklee of Brimfield & Martha Singlebury
(or Singletury), Oct. 22, 1750
Samuel Clark of Chester, N. H., & Mary Town, Nov. 30, 1750
Amos Gould & Desire King, Oct. 31, 1749

Arthur Dagget & Mehetabell Marsh,	Jan. 28, 1750–51
Caleb Gould & Sarah Adams,	Dec. 13, 1750
Timothy Claflin & Mary Gould,	Jan. 16, 1750–51
Jonathan Dunil, Jr., & Mary Gould,	Dec. 13, 1750
Amos Mullicken of Bradford & Mehetibell Dodge,	
	Feb. 28, 1750–51
Samuel Bixby & Lydia Bond,	March 13, 1750–51
Benjamin Davis & Mary Whitemore,	April 29, 1751
Rev. James Wellman & Mrs. Sarah Barnard,	Nov. 8, 1750
Daniel Kinny, Jr., of Sutton & Abigail Davis of	
Western,	April 29, 1751
Henry Harbach & Rebeckah Stockwell,	Sept. 5, 1751
Dr. Thomas Chase & Mrs. Mary Whipple,	Sept. 26, 1751
Josiah White, Jr., & Lucy Whipple,	Nov. 28, 1751
James Richardson of Leicester & Elizabeth Chase,	
	Nov. 7, 1751
Elijah Sibly & Mary Carril,	Dec. 12, 1751
Jeremiah Stockwell & Mary Cutler,	Nov. 27, 1751
Stephen Holman & Ruth Putnam,	Nov. 5, 1751
Samuel How & Rebekah Gould,	Dec. 3, 1751
David Bates & Lydia Gale,	March 4, 1752
Moses Chase & Hannah Brown,	April 15, 1752
Daniel Day & Susannah Hutchinson,	May 14, 1752
Ichabod Town & Jemima Stockwell,	Dec. 5, 1751
Eliphalet Rowell & Sarah King,	Dec. 26, 1751
Timothy Bacon & Lydia Rice,	Aug. 6, 1752
David Harwood, ye 3d, of Sutton & Rebekah Twist	
of Oxford,	April 30, 1752
Joshua Woodbury & Dorcas Park,	July 6, 1752
William Kinny & Sarah Stockwell,	Aug. 13, 1752
Richard Bartlet, Jr., & Hannah Bucknam,	Oct. 19, 1752
Nathaniel Carril & Jane Dwight,	Oct. 10, 1752
Daniel Gleason of Oxford & Martha Bartlet,	April 26, 1753
Jonathan Stockwell, Jr., & Mary Kinny,	May 10, 1753
Eleazer Hawes & Ruth Comings, ·	May 1, 1753
Daniel Allen & Mary Holman,	May 30, 1753
Fuller Putnam & Mary Comings,	Dec. 4, 1752
Ebenezer Whitney & Lydia Goodale,	Feb. 6, 1753
Cornelius Putnam, Jr., & Elisabeth Perkins,	Aug. 2, 1753

Stephen Southworth & Hannah Sibley,	Sept. 27, 1753
Timothy Sibley & Ann Wait,	Oct. 16, 1753
Rogers Chase & Sarah Walker,	Feb. 6, 1754
John Harbach & Hannah Greenwood,	Dec. 4, 1753
Benjamin Sibley & Lucy Park,	Feb. 6, 1754
Dr. Benjamin Morss & Mrs. Abigail Dudley,	May 25, 1735
Jonathan Dudley & Hannah Putnam,	Aug. 18, 1736
Ebenezer Whiple & Prudence Dudley,	March 25, 1736
Abell Chase & Judith Gale,	Jan. 3, 1754
John Feling (?) of Pomfret & Mary Keyes,	March 20, 1754
Edward Holman of Sutton & Rebekah Gale of Oxford,	May 7, 1754
Jona Wheeler, Jr., of Sutton & Ann Davenport of Douglas,	May 2, 1754
James Caldwell & Elisabeth Hicks,	Aug. 15, 1754
Stephen Bartlett & Elisabeth Whitney,	Feb. 27, 1754
Dr. John Hale of Hollis & Mrs. Elisabeth Hale,	Sept. 5, 1754
Joshua Barnard & Abigail Hazeltine,	Sept. 5, 1744
Samuel Buck, Jr., & Sarah Fisk (or Fish),	Sept. 18, 1754
Thomas Hall & Mrs. Huldah Park,	June 24, 1758
Asa Kenney & Mehetabel Stockwell,	July 24, 1762
Moses Tyler Dodge & Lydia Gibbs,	Feb. 11, 1762
Jonathan Sibley, Jr., & Eunis Perkins,	April 26, 1762
Benjamin Rich & Rebeccah Dagget,	July 15, 1762
John Daniels of Mendon & Lydia Putnam,	May 26, 1762
Ralph Richardson & Sarah Bartlett,	March 5, 1762
Comfort Streater & Bethiah Rich,	June 24, 1762
Jonathan Bartlett & Mahetabel Hull of Worcester,	Oct. 6, 1762
Joseph Aldrich of Bellingham & Experience Stockwell of Oxford,	Dec. 9, 1764
Daniel Gould & Mary Putnam,	Dec. 9, 1762
Josiah Bond & Sarah Mellady,	Jan. 28, 1762
Israel Richardson of Woburn & Elisabeth Hutchinson,	Aug. 13, 1762
Jonas Gale & Tamer Marsh,	Dec. 23, 1762
Richard Mower & Margaret Burnham,	Feb. 10, 1763
David Lillie, Jr., & Elizabeth Gibbs,	Sept. 23, 1762

Deacon Jonathan Newell of Dudley & Mrs. Eliz.
    Putnam,   Nov. 17, 1762
Ephraim Fletcher of Grafton & Sarah Davenport,
                                          Dec. 7, 1762
Thomas Nichols & Kezia Fitts,   Dec. 9, 1762
Archibald Campbell of Oxford & Mrs. Hannah
    Barnard,   Nov. 15, 1762
Stephan Stockwell and Mehitable Holman,   Dec. 14, 1762
Jonathan Dudley, Jr., & Mary Garfield,   Feb. 1, 1763
Bartholomew Woodbury & Ruth Greenwood,   May 5, 1763
Bradford Chase & Abigale Sibley,   June 21, 1763
Elisha Sibley & Lydia Carriel (?),   July 14, 1763
Joseph Buxton, Jr., & Lydia Rice,   July 28, 1763
Nathaniel Stockwell & Abigail Dodge,   March 31, 1763
Francis Kidder, Jr., & Mary Chase,   April 21, 1763
Bartholmew Hutchinson & Ruth Haven,   Aug. 4, 1763
Moses Chase & Susanna Lillie,   Oct. 6, 1763
Theophilus Kenney & Abigail Gibbs,   Oct. 13, 1763
Nathaniel Whitemore & Elizabeth Marsh,   Feb. 9, 1764
Francis Temple of Shrewsbury & Anna March,
                                          Nov. 16, 1763
Jonathan Pierce & Mary Goodell,   Feb. 2, 1764
John Eliot & Hannah Dudley,   Jan. 19, 1764
David Harwood, 3d, & Mary Streeter,   Feb. 6, 1764
Abraham Fitts & Mary Holman,   April 14, 1767
Reuben Town & Sarah Dodge,   July 7, 1767
Nathaniel Gibbs & Sarah Holton,   July 9, 1767
Nathaniel Stone & Abigail Town,   Aug. 2, 1767
Jacob Leland & Anne Taylor,   Aug. 2, 1767
Aaron Eliot & Lydia Taylor,   Oct. 13, 1767
John Burdon, Jr., & Lucy Sibley,   Oct. 19, 1767
Willis Hall, Jr., & Rebecca Parsons,   Dec. 3, 1767
Ebenezer Waters & Mary Adams of Grafton, Dec. 10, 1767
Asa Curtis of Dudley & Hannah Carriel (?), Dec. 25, 1767
James Giles & Martha Gould,   Feb. 11, 1768
Jonathan Sibley & Hannah Burnap,   Dec. 3, 1739
Jonathan Waters, Jr., & Hannah Trask,   Nov. 27, 1766
Caleb White and Rebecca Marsh,   Feb. 26, 1767
Elisha Gale & Mary Singletary,   April 8, 1767

Andrew Eliot & Anne Carter,   May 7, 1767
Robert Fitts & Lydia Town,   June 2, 1767
David Bacon & Tabitha Wakefield,   Dec. 17, 1767
Joseph Harwood, Jr., & Mary Pratt,   Jan. 7, 1768
Reuben Swan of Leicester & Rachel Butnam, Feb. 25, 1768
Edward Holman & Sarah Kenney,   March 22, 1763
Richard Bartlet, Jr., & Ruth Holman,   July 7, 1763
Daniel Knap & Hannah Lyon,   April 22, 1763
Solomon Holman, 3d, & Sarah Goold,   Dec. 22, 1763
Andrew Putnam of Winchester & Lucy Park, Jan. 10, 1764
Thomas Gleason of Oxford & Hannah Walker,
                                               March 29, 1764
Timothy Child & Lydia Kidder,   Jan. 17, 1764
Asa Roberts & Ruhamah Brown,   March 22, 1764
Simeon Gleason of Petersham & Martha Dudley,
                                               June 2, 1764
Thomas McKnight of Oxford & Abigail Goold,
                                               March 1, 1764
Asa Waters & Sarah Goodale,   June 14, 1764
Lot Hutchinson & Hannah Morss,   Sept. 25, 1764
Solomon Lealand & Lois Haven,   Nov. 27, 1764
Asa Walker of Hopkinston & Sarah Burbank, Dec. 13, 1764
Capt. Caleb Hill of Douglas & Ruth Hicks,   Jan. 10, 1765
John Corban of Dudley & Abigail Harback,   Jan. 30, 1765
Reuben Sibley & Ruth Sibley,   Jan. 30, 1765
Benjamin Garfield of Grafton & Lucy Case,   Nov. 15, 1764
William Foster of Oxford & Hannah Richards, Dec. 3, 1764
William Sibley & Hannah Stockwell,   Jan. 24, 1765
Elisha Putnam & Abigail Chamberlain,   April 2, 1763
John Harwood, Jr., & Lydia Holman,   Aug. 13, 1763
Joseph Pearse & Abigail Carriel,   Oct. 10, 176--
Joel Stevens of Charlton & Rebeckah Marble, Nov. 19, 1765
Joel Wheeler of Petersham & Mary Dudley,   Dec. 19, 1765
John Blanchard & Sarah Carriel,   Dec. 19, 1765
Dr. Ephraim Woolson of Weston & Mrs. Mary Rich-
    ardson,   July 30, 1765
Samuel Bouttell, Jr., & Hannah Barton,   Oct. 29, 1765
John Hicks & Margaret Burbank,   April 10, 1765
Benjamin Marsh, ye 4th, & Melleson Davenport, May 8, 1765

John Howard & Huldah Sibley,	June 26, 1765
Jacob Nelson & Annabel Harback,	July 4, 1765
Archelaus Putnam & Sarah Putnam,	Oct. 10, 1765
David Keith of Uxbridge & Ruth Bacon,	Nov. 5, 1765
Josiah White of Uxbridge & Hannah Gould,	Nov. 14, 1765
John Carriel & Tamar King,	Dec. 12, 1765
Jacob Cummings, Jr., & Bridget Lilley,	Dec. 19, 1765
Ebenezer Putnam & Hannah Dike,	Jan. 16, 1766
Thomas Chase & Deborah Killum,	Feb. 20, 1766
Jeremiah Stockwell of Chesterfield & Sarah Stockwell,	Feb. 27, 1766
Obadiah Brown of Uxbridge & Mary Barton,	April 3, 1766
Joshua Weatherell of Dudley & Hannah William,	April 17, 1766
Asa Grosvenor of Pomfret & Hannah Hall,	April 24, 1766
Benjamin Hicks & Mary Woodbury,	Sept. 4, 1766
Adonijah Putnam & Mary Wilkins,	Nov. 27, 1766
Bartholomew Town, Jr., & Betty Rice,	Jan. 22, 1767
John Barnard & Sarah Fisk,	Oct. 30, 1766
Samuel Holman & Hannah Commings,	Dec. 18, 1766
Edward Goddard of Shrewsbury & Eunice Walker,	June 11, 1764
Ebenezer Marsh & Mary Bullen,	Jan. 29, 1765
Thomas Moor of Brookfield & Priscilla Holland,	Sept. 25, 1766
John Singletary & Sarah Jennison,	April 15, 1767
Jonathan Gale of Oxford & Violetty Kinny of Brookfield,	April 21, 1768
John Adams, Jr., of Uxbridge & Elisabeth Newton,	Nov. 28, 1768
Joseph Gleason, Jr., & Marcy Streater, both of Oxford,	Feb. 10, 1769
Samuel Woodward of Worcester & Submit Hagar,	Feb. 8, 1769
Joel Johnson & Elanor Park, both of Hardwick,	Sept. 27, 1768
Reuben Park & Molly Barton,	Sept. 27, 1768
Elisha Holman & Jerusha Snow,	May 21, 1767
Jedidiah Bugbee of the Union & Molly Hiscock,	Oct. 29, 1767

Timothy Carter, Jr., & Sarah Walker,   May 29, 1768
Daniel Bucknam, Jr., & Rebecca Boyden,   June 11, 1768
Asa Taft & Molly Stone,   Nov. 24, 1768
Ebenezer Gould & Tabitha Kinny,   Feb. 25, 1768
Joseph Bullen & Phebe Garfield,   June 20, 1768
Bartholomew Carriel (?) & Rebecca Harbach, Aug. 11, 1768
Abel Chase, the 3d, & Elisabeth Eliot,   Nov. 30, 1768
Joseph Newell of Thompson & Elisabeth Ames,
                                              Sept. 1, 1768
Solomon Cook & Keziah Holton,   Nov. 29, 1768
Stephen Sibley & Eleanor Lillie,   Dec. 29, 1768
Joshua Lillie & Betty Cummings,   April 28, 1768
Ambrose Stone & Mary Everdan,   May 22, 1768
Stephen Rice & Ruth Stone,   May 12, 1768
Samuel Wakefield & Mary Davenport,   May 25, 1768
Asa Hazeltine of Upton & Mary Woodward, May 26, 1768
John Dudley & Molly Morss,   Oct. 13, 1768
David Fisk & Sarah Goodale,   June 24, 1769
Peter Jennison & Mehitable Singletary,   March 31, 1769
William Brown & Grace Wadsworth,   Jan. 22, 1769
Moses Huse of Methuen & Elisabeth Barton,
                                              April 20, 1769
John Gould of Lyndesboro & Susanna Chase, Oct. 31, 1769
Ezra (?) Harwood & Lydia Hiscock,   Feb. 16, 1769
Joseph Lillie & Prudence Kinny, both of Charlton,
                                              Oct. 12, 1769
Levi Newton & Elisabeth Woodward, both of Wor-
    cester,   Oct. 26, 1769
Abner Gleason & Abigail Rich of Oxford,   Jan. 18, 1770
Simon Chase & Hannah Chase,   May 11, 1769
John Gould & Mary Gould,   Aug. 17, 1769
Malachi Willson of Wrentham & Hannah Burdon,
                                              Aug. 22, 1769
David Sibley & Phebe Lillie,   Jan. 25, 1770
Samuel Goddard & Elizabeth King,   May 25, 1769
William Dike (?) & Abigail Jennison,   Sept. 21, 1769
Abraham Taylor & Mary Leland,   Sept. 21, 1769
John Burley of the Union & Percis Harwood, Oct. 28, 1769
Benjamin Hutchinson & Judith Lillie,   Nov. 2, 1769

Simonds Whipple & Mary Sibley,   Nov. 16, 1769
Noah Stockwell & Mercy Wright,   Dec. 12, 1769
Benjamin Swinnerton & Elisabeth Hall,   Dec. 21, 1769
Daniel Stone, Jr., & Hannah Gould,   Jan. 9, 1770
Gershom Biglo, Jr., & Lydia Stockwell,   Jan. 11, 1770

[*Sutton continued p. 144*].

⟍ LANCASTER.

May 18, 1653, "Nashaway" to be a township to be called Lancaster. Mass. Rec., Vol. IV,
Part. I, p. 139.   First (Unitarian) Church organized 1653.   Officiating clergymen mentioned:
Rev. Timothy Harrington, Rev. John Mellen, Rev. Samuel Harrington.

Ebenezer Taylor & Mary Houghton,   March 9, 1749
Nathaniel White & Lydia Phelps,   Nov. 9, 1749
Rev. John Mellen & Rebeckah Prentice,   March 27, 1749
John Rogers of Leominster & Relief Prentice,
                                              March 27, 1750
Jotham Biglow of Holden & Mary Richardson,
                                                May 23, 1750
David Taylor of Lunenburg & Elizabeth Houghton,
                                               Nov. 29, 1750
Rev. John Rogers of Leominster & Mrs. Releafe
    Prentice,   March 27, 1750
Gershom Flagg & Mary Willard,   Dec. 6, 1750
William Phelps & Mary Nichols,   April 25, 1751
Jonas Fletcher of Groton & Ruth Fletcher,   May 23, 1751
John Beaman & widow Sarah Page,   May 22, 1751
David Wilder & (Mrs.) Martha White,   Dec. 4, 1751
Josiah Cutting of Shrewsbury & Orpah Houghton,
                                                Jan. 2, 1752
Joseph Kilbourn & Mary Sawyer,   Jan. 22, 1752
George Mcfarling of Lunenburg & Margaret Terrance,
                                              April 16, 1752
David Baldwin of Billevica & Keziah Bennet, June 18, 1752
Reuben Lipunwell & Anna Wyman,   June 18, 1752
Primas Law & Ross Canterbery (negroes),   Oct. 18, 1752
Enoch Hill & Sarah Rugg,   Oct. 24, 1752
Abijah Willard & Anna Prentice,   Nov. 15, 1752

Nathaniel Joslin & Martha Fairbanks,   Nov. 30, 1752
James Richardson of Leominster & Hannah House,
                                               Jan. 10, 1753
Asa Harris & Abigail Bennet,   Jan. 10, 1753
Phinehas Houghton & Ruth Osgood,   Jan. 6, 1753
Thomas Heywood of Lunenburg & Elizabeth Rich-
    ardson,   July 11, 1753
William Smith (Townsend) & Martha Dunsmore,
                                               Nov. 27, 1753
Joshua Read of Lexington & Susannah Houghton,
                                               Nov. 27, 1753
Benjamin Osgood, Jr., & Mary Carter,   Dec. 5, 1753
John Divol & Elizabeth Beman,   Dec. 26, 1753
Aaron Osgood, Jr., & Hannah Warner,   March 6, 1754
Dr. William Dunsmore & Hannah Sumner of Kil-
    lingsly,   Jan. 7, 1754
Amos Sawyer, Jr., & Mary Rugg,   Jan. 9, 1755
Tyrus Houghton & Rachel Honn (?),   Jan., 1755
Samuel Prentice & Prudence Osgood,   Feb. 13, 1755
William Tucker & Mary Kendall,   Feb. 20, 1755
Nathaniel Wilder, Jr., & Lydia Kendall,   Feb. 27, 1755
George Parkhurst & Keziah Whitcomb of Bolton,
                                               March 13, 1755
Converse Richardson & Mercy Nichols,   March 27, 1755
David Thomas of Pelham & Elizabeth Harper, Nov. 18, 1755
Ephraim Wilder (Terts) & Lucretia Lock,   April 3, 1755
Jabez Fairbank & widow Naomi Dupee,   Jan. 22, 1756
Benjamin Shead of Lunenburg & Elizabeth Bloors (?),
                                               July 19, 1756
Isaac Eveleth of Brookfield & Eunice Hudson, Sept. 2, 1756
William Deputron of Lancaster & Sarah Rice of
    Shirley,   Oct. 12, 1756
Rev. Elisha Marsh of No. 2 & Susannah Willard,
                                               July 25, 1757
William Kendall & Mary Lipinwell,   Aug. 15, 1757
Samuel Gamble & Eunice Dunsmore,   Oct. 11, 1757
Mark Lincoln & Mary Carter,   Oct. 20, 1757
Josiah Whitcomb of Bolton & Dorothy Osgood,
                                               Oct. 24, 1757

S

Joseph Woods & Lucy Butler,   Nov. 30, 1757
Elijah Woods & Mary Goodfree,   Feb. 2, 1758
Jonathan Wheelock of Leominster & Thankful Has-
  kell,   Dec. 27, 1757
Phineas Carter & Mary Sawyer,   Feb. 22, 1758
Philemon Houghton & Rebeckah Gates,   Feb. 23, 1758
Paul Sawyer & Lois Houghton,   March 7, 1758
John Brooks & Katherine Dunsmore,   March 8, 1758
Ephraim Sawyer & Susanna Richardson,   June 11, 1752
Ezekiel Kendall & Mary May,   Dec. 21, 1752
Josiah Bayley & Lydia Parker,   Feb. 13, 1753
Nathan Burpee, Jr., & Azubah Sawyer,   March 14, 1753
Nathan Burpee & Azubah Osgood,   Jan. 24, 1754
Josiah Jackson & Mary Darby of Narraganset No. 2,
                                               Jan. 30, 1755
Oliver (Hoar) & Silence Houghton,   Feb. 28, 1754
Levi Moore & Rebeckah Sawyer,   March 7, 1754
Samuel Rice & Mary Bennet,   April 10, 1754
Aaron Sawyer & Abigail (Sawyer),   April 25, 1754
Dorchester & Pegg (negroes) married in hay time,   1754
Asa Wilder & Lydia Rugg,   Dec. 12, 1754
Jonathan Fairbank & Ruth Houghton,   Feb. 3, 1754
Joseph Stuart & Mary Snow,   Aug. 28, 1755
John Curtis & Elizabeth Robbins,   Nov. 13, 1755
Josiah Houghton & Grace Whitney,   Jan. 6, 1756
Israel Moore & Abigail How,   Jan. 15, 1756
Joseph Osgood & Katherine Sawyer,   Jan. 29, 1756
Elisha Sawyer & Susanna Husk,   March 8, 1756
Thomas Gary, Jr., & Jane Wilder,   April 22, 1756
Samuel Burpee, Jr., & Martha Brocklebank,   June 10, 1756
Charles Morris & Elizabeth Lagget,   Sept. 5, 1756
Jabez Brooks & Lucy Sawyer,   Jan. 27, 1757
James Cowey & Mary Parsons,   March 3, 1757
Christian Angell & Hannah Bennet,   April 14, 1757
John May, Jr., & Keziah Sawyer,   June 1, 1757
Benjamin Houghton (Tert[s]) & Priscilla Wilder,
                                               Nov. 17, 1757
Tilly Littlejohns & Hannah Brooks,   Dec. 1, 1757
John Benney & Dinah Beman,   Dec. 26, 1757

David Nelson & Hannah Bailey,	Dec. 29, 1757
John Farrar & Ann Chandler,	Jan. 11, 1758
Lemuel Houghton & Dinah Osgood,	May 1, 1758
Thomas Ross, Jr., & Priscilla Cooper,	June 8, 1758
Nathaniel Houghton & Mary Richardson,	June 29, 1758
Lewis Conguerett & Abigail Wheeler,	July 23, 1758
Daniel Rice & Keziah Snow,	Nov. 2, 1758
Barzillai Holt & Lois Allerd,	Feb. 22, 1759
David Osgood, Jr., & Sarah Bailey,	April 12, 1759
Samuel Snow & Sarah Bernett (?),	July 19, 1759
Jonathan Bailey & Eunice Houghton,	Jan. 16, 1760
Elisha Wilder & Mehitabel Dresser,	Jan. 17, 1760
Jonathan Osgood & Joanna Bearnon,	Jan. 17, 1760
Israel Moore & Katherine Sawyer,	Oct. 9, 1760
Josiah Kendall, Jr., & Esthar Sawyer,	Mar. 26, 1760
Samuel Ross & Katherine Gary,	Nov. 27, 1760
Ezra Sawyer & Keziah Sawyer,	Dec. 11, 1760
Joseph Sawyer & Agnes Dunsmore.	Aug. 20, 1761
Roger Ross & Molly Rugg,	Sept. 3, 1761
Jonathan Whitcomb & Tamar Ross,	Sept. 3, 1761
John Boynton & Elizabeth Jewitt,	Nov. 26, 1761
Peter Goodenow & Ann Mosemon,	Dec. 17, 1761
Asa Whitcomb & Bettey Sawyer,	Jan. 26, 1762
Joseph Houghton & Martha Snow,	March 11, 1762
Richard Proutee & Ephe Smith,	May 6, 1762
Nathaniel Jones & Phebe Burpee,	May 11, 1762
Josiah Wilder & Abigail Osgood,	June 3, 1762
Phinehas Wilder & Lois Brown,	Sept. 8, 1756
Jonathan Osgood, Jr., & Abigail Whitcomb,	June 20, 1758
Jonathan Coborne & Sarah Harvey,	April, 1759
Peter Snow & Eunice Goodfree,	Dec. 19, 1754
Henry Haskel, Jr., & Rebeccah Willard,	Jan. 6, 1757
Jacob Williams & Abigail Wyman,	Nov. 29, 1759
James Willard & Sarah Longley,	March 31, 1761
James Ballard & Mary Robbins,	May 11, 1756
Ebenezer Maynard & Sarah Knight, both of Westboro,	July 16, 1756
Phinehas Willard & Rebeckah Willard, both of Harvard,	Jan. 5, 1758

Sherebiah Hunt & Deborah Wilder,   April 2, 1758
Luke Richardson & Demarius Carter, both of Leo-
    minster,   Sept. 7, 1758
Daniel Knight & Elizabeth Houghton,   May 12, 1758
Levi Nichols & Elizabeth Sawyer,   Nov. 29, 1759
Gardner Wilder & Martha Wilder,   Nov. 13, 1760
John Heywood of Lunenburg & Silence White,
                                                Dec. 31, 1761
Benjamin Priest & Hannah Johnson,   Jan. 20, 1761
Joshua Johnson, Jr., & Hannah Avery of Groton,
                                                Jan. 20, 1761
Mitchel Richards of Shirley & Esthar Mitchel of
    Lunenburg,   July 2, 1761
Timothy Kendall & Anna Houghton, both of Leo-
    minster,   Jan. 20, 1762
James Lock & Rebeckah Wilder,   Feb. 2, 1762
John Gibbs & Elizabeth Kendall,   Sept. 3, 1760
Samuel Titus of Ipswich-Canada, N. H., & Ann Big-
    low of Westminster,   Sept. 11, 1760
Samuel Osgood of Naraganset No. 6 & Thankfull
    Mathews,   Sept. 18, 1760
Seth Harrington of Westminster & Priscillai
    Houghton,   Nov. 13, 1760
Josiah Osgood & Jane Boynton,   Dec. 9, 1760
Zaccheus Bemis & Elizabeth Lyon, both of West-
    minster,   Feb. 10, 1761
Joel Houghton & Sarah Parson of Shrewsbury, Feb. 25, 1761
Gideon Smith & Mary Biglow, both of Westminster,
                                                April 16, 1761
Jeremiah Stewart of Leominster & Hannah Stewart,
                                                Feb. 4, 1762
Samuel Bixby of Princetown & Hannah Powers,
                                                March 4, 1762
George Peterson & Margaret Dorchester,   Feb. 26, 1762
William Gibbs & Joanna Gleason, both of Prince-
    town,   April 14, 1762
James Houghton (tert[s]) & Ann Eveleth,   Sept. 10, 1762
John Boynton of Shrewsbury & Elisabeth Bemon,
                                                Jan. 13, 1763

Josiah Jackson & Mary Darby, both of Narraganset
    No. 2,   Jan. 30, 1755
Warren Snow of Leicester & Anna Harvey,   Oct. 25, 1759
Edward Houghton & Lucretia Richardson,   Oct. 16, 1760
William Phelps & Mary Flagg,   Sept. 17, 1761
Dr. Nathan Raymond of Littleton & Rebeckah Rich-
    ardson,   Dec. 1, 1762
Thomas Gates & Abigail Wilder,   April 23, 1761
Nathaniel Turner & Anna Goss,   Sept. 12, 1758
Simon Willard & Elizabeth Willard of Harvard, Oct. 5, 1758
Richard Baker of Narraganset No. 2 & Mary Sawyer,
                                  Nov. 16, 1758
Elijah Beaman & Thankful Nichols,   April 16, 1759
Edward Parmenter of Sudbury & Sarah Beaman,
                                  June 5, 1759
Hooker Osgood, Jr., & Susanna Sawyer,   June 29, 1759
Thomas Page of Leominster and Mary Knight,
                                 Aug. 16, 1759
John Cobley of Narraganset No. 6 & Mary Wilder,
                                 Nov. 18, 1759
Thomas Grant & Hannah Churchill,   Feb. 7, 1760
Edmund Larkin & Abigail Albert,   May 21, 1760
Elijah Osgood & Mary Wallingsford,   Nov. 19, 1760
Joseph Wilson of Petersham & Hannah Osgood, Jan. 1, 1761
Josiah Fairbank & Abigail Carter,   Jan. 22, 1761
John Ball of Westboro & Abigail Wilder,   Jan. 22, 1791
John McCarty & Margaret Mcfarling,   March 16, 1761
Fortunatus Eager & Thamar Houghton,   June 18, 1761
Peter Thurston & Dorothy Gates,   Dec. 3, 1761
Matthew Knight of Leominster & Dinah Carter,
                              March 18, 1762
Nath. Wilder & Lucy Knight,   April 17, 1762
John Phelps & Elizabeth Walker,   May 12, 1762
Joel Phelps & Prudence Brown,   May 26, 1762
Stanton Carter & Peninnah Albert,   May 27, 1762
Ens. Tilly Moore & Mrs. Zilpah Whiting, Aug. 26, 1762
Ebenr Hills of Swansey, N. H., & Abigail Nichols,
                                Oct. 19, 1762
Cyrus Fairbanks & Lucy Wilder,   Dec. 9, 1762

Stephan Smith & Lucy Kendall,	July 8, 1762
Enoch Dole & Eunice Richardson,	Oct. 26, 1762
Oliver Dresser & Olive Osgood,	Nov. 4, 1762
Daniel Greenleaf & Dorothy Richardson,	Nov. 18, 1762
Moses Sawyer & Mary Sawyer,	April 27, 1763
David Moors & Elizabeth Whitcomb,	Aug. 11, 1763
William Brown & Elizabeth Houghton,	Oct. 20, 1763
Nathaniel Hastings & Elizabeth Goodenow,	
	March 8, 1764
Nathan Gary & Hepsibeth Wilder,	April 11, 1764
Elijah Houghton & Mary Allen,	Oct. 3, 1764
Peter Hilt of Worcester & Margaret Z——red (?),	
	Feb. 7, 1763
William Willard of Petersham & Katherine Wilder,	
	Nov. 22, 1763
Josiah Locke & Esther Kitteridge of Tewksbury,	
	Feb. 29, 1764
Robert Phelps & Rachel Richardson of Billerica,	
	Jan. 24, 1765
Dr. Stephen Ball of Westboro & Mary Fairbank,	
	May 23, 1765
James Goodwin & Bathsheba Robbins,	May 28, 1765
Daniel Warner & Susanna Rugg,	Oct. 30, 1765
Jonathan Whitney & Mary Wyman,	Oct. 31, 1765
Daniel Rugg, Jr., & Elizabeth Divoll,	Oct. 31, 1765
Paul Dickinson of Groton & Damaris Knight,	
	March 10, 1766
Joseph Wheeler & Mrs. Sarah Allen,	Aug. 14, 1766
William Kendall & Mary Knight,	Sept. 18, 1766
James Godfry & Mrs. Mary Pratt of Harvard,	May 19, 1767
Ephraim Carter, Jr., & Abigail Carter, Jr.,	Dec. 3, 1767
David Nims, Jr., of Keene, N. H., & Jemima Carter,	
	Jan. 12, 1768
Silas Carter & Lucy Sawyer,	Jan. 12, 1768
Jonathan Kendall, 4th, & Hannah Johnson,	Feb. 9, 1768
Capt. Samuel Wilder of Ashburnham & Mrs. Dorothy	
Carter,	Feb. 18, 1768
Benjamin Warren of Littleton & Elizabeth Haywood,	
	Sept. 19, 1764

Zach. Harvey, Jr., & Mary Norcross, both of Prince-
  town,   Nov. 15, 1764
Samuel Hancock of Harvard & Abigail Snow,
                                         July 21, 1763
Levi Houghton & Ame Richardson,   Nov. 21, 1763
Jonathan Townsend & Hulda Newton, both of West-
  minster,   March 24, 1765
Jotham Rice of Rutland & Hannah Snow,   Feb. 11, 1767
William Williams of Marlboro & Zilpah Wilder,
                                         Feb. 12, 1767
Kendall Boutell (or Routell) of Lunenburg & Mary
  Wilder of Leominster,   April 1, 1762
Sol. Shed & Elizabeth Boynton, both of Lunenburg,
                                         May 24, 1763
Benjamin Houghton & Achah Whetcomb,   Oct. 14, 1763
Josiah Sawyer of Bolton & Mary Tooker,   Jan. 14, 1764
Joseph Russ & Susanna Priest,   July 1, 1764
Gardener Wilder & Dorothy Richardson,   March 8, 1765
John Lock & Lucy Wilder,   March 8, 1765
Jacob Bennet & Anna Boynton,   Dec. 11, 1763
Enoch Jewett of Templeton & Mary Moore of Shrews-
  bury,   March 8, 1764
Jedediah Woods of Warwick & Mary Bixby, Jan. 11, 1765
Hannaniah Rand of Westminster & Martha Osgood,
                                         Dec. 20, 1765
Josh. Church & Kezia Goss,   Feb. 21, 1765
Manassah Bixby of Shrewsbury & Elizabeth Duns-
  moor,   Nov. 12, 1765
Amos Powers & Molly Parmenter, both of Prince-
  town,   Jan. 21, 1766
Aaron Stearns of Princetown & Esther Glazier of
  Westminster,   Feb. 16, 1766
Joseph Houghton, Jr., & Lois Ross, both of Bolton,
                                         Nov. 29, 1770
Ethan Kendall & Thankfull Moor,   July 4, 1771
Jonathan Carter of Leominster & Damarius Whit-
  comb,   April 3, 1765
Ephraim Robins of Petersham & Joanna Holden
  of Harvard,   July 25, 1765

Elkenah Woodcock of Swansey & Susanna Nichols,
Sept. 24, 1765
Wyat Gun of Swanzey & Martha Houghton, Feb. 25, 1766
Daniel Spooner of Petersham & Bethia Nichols.
Sept. 3, 1767
Samuel Joslin & Abigail Wilder, Oct. 1, 1767
William Alexander, Jr., of Lunenburg & Ruth Put-
nam of Harvard, May 31, 1759
James Digens & Lydia Hale, both of Leominster,
June 1, 1769
Abisha Phelps & Katharine Richardson, April 22, 1770
Jonathan Carter of Sudbury & Deborah Hunt, Oct. 25, 1771
Silas Church & Mary Osgood of Templeton, Nov. 25, 1771
John Wilder & Abigail Kendall, Dec. 1, 1771
Thomas Meriam & Sarah Wilder, both of West-
minster, Nov. 24, 1762
Robert Crawford of Worcester & Elizabeth Leitch
of Lunenburg, Jan. 13, 1763
Levi Woods of Petersham & Tamar Houghton of
Leominster, April 20, 1763
Nathaniel Willard & Eunice Farwell of Stow, May 25, 1763
William Longley of Shirley & Lydia Wallingsford,
Aug. 8, 1763
Robert Proctor & Ruth Fowl, Oct. 7, 1764
David Hastings & Dinah Williams, both of Shrews-
bury, May 25, 1763
John Richardson of Petersham & Eunice Green,
Dec. 18, 1765
Thomas Bennett & Lydia Longley, Dec. 29, 1765
Samuel Norcross & Rachel Harvey, both of Prince-
town, May 2, 1766
Moses Russell of Littleton & Sarah Phelps, Nov. 27, 1767
Andrew Poor & Esther Snow, Nov. 1, 1767
John Hammond & Lucy Powers, Nov. 3, 1768
Andrew Haskell & Lois Bullin, Aug. 10, 1769
Joseph Moor, Jr., & Hepzibeh Bush of Shrewsbury,
Oct. 26, 1769
Moses Smith & Abigail Green, Jan. 24, 1771
Timothy Blodget & Lydia Walker, June 3, 1771

Eliphalet Rogers of Princetown & Eunice Bennet,
Aug. 14, 1771
William Tinney & Mehitable Jones, both of Bolton,
Oct. 15, 1771
Jedidiah Boynton & Elizabeth Holt,   Feb. 10, 1772
Nathaniel Wright, Jr., & Ruth Richardson,   May 22, 1770
William Thompson & Elizabeth Jewett,   May 30, 1770
Joshua Piper & Betty Proctor,   June 11, 1770
Thomas Rugg & Mehitabell Houghton,   July 26, 1770
Daniel Norcross & Thankful Sawyer,   Oct. 9, 1770
Elijah Ball & Rebecca Moors,   Oct. 18, 1770
Solomon Goodale & Persis Bayley,   Oct. 30, 1770
Ephraim Willard, Jr., & Lois Geary,   Nov. 29, 1770
Rev. Caleb Prentice & Pamela Mellen,   Jan. 1, 1771
Stephen Haywood & Ruth Dunsmoor,   March 6, 1771
Joseph Whitaker & Mary Whitney,   April 25, 1771
Jonathan Buss & widow Mary Stewart,   July 4, 1771
David Holt & Hannah Kendall,   Sept. 25, 1771
Jonas Johnson & Damaris Rugg,   Oct. 17, 1771
Samuel Gerrish & Abigail Moor,   Dec. 26, 1771
Asa Smith & Sarah Stewart,   March 29, 1772
David Goodale & Dorothy Newton,   April 8, 1772
Giles Wills & Relief Wilder,   May 5, 1772
Ezra Hale & widow Thankful Brabrook,   June 23, 1772
Jonathan Butterick & Hannah Wilder Sawyer, July 2, 1772
Joseph Seaver & Abigail Sawyer,   July 7, 1772
Jonathan Moor & Elizabeth Richardson,   July 8, 1772
Luther Graves & Phebe Jewett,   Aug. 13, 1772
Samuel Mason & Sarah Whitney,   Oct. 8, 1772
Obadiah Gross & Lucy Houghton,   April 1, 1773
Lemuel Beman & Prudence Rowe,   May 19, 1773
Elias Farnsworth & Lois Willard,   Nov. 25, 1773
Abner Farrington & Joanna Kilburn,   Dec. 7, 1773
Joseph Lewis & Martha Lock,   Dec. 14, 1773
Moses Newhall & Hannah Robbins,   Dec. 16, 1773
Levi Carter & Silence Beman,   Jan. 20, 1774
Nathaniel Brown & Esther Smith,   Feb. 1, 1774
John Phelps & Lois Davis,   Feb. 10, 1774
Silas Fairbanks & Mrs. Lydia Prouty,   March 17, 1768

Jacob Bennet of Leominster & Mrs. Elizabeth
    Wilder,   April 7, 1768
Joseph Page & Mrs. Eunice White,   July 21, 1768
Samuel Wilder & Mrs. Sarah Ballard,   Aug. 1, 1768
Timothy Temple & Mrs. Deborah Ball,   Aug. 31, 1768
James Crosman of Monadnock & Mrs. Mary Preist,
                                             Oct. 17, 1768
Abel Shead of Groton & Mrs. Ruth Haskell,   Nov. 29, 1768
Francis Eager of Paxton & Sarah Frairbank,   Dec. 1, 1768
Paul Richardson of Winchester, N. H., & Mrs. Euse-
    bius Harrington,   Jan. 5, 1769
Joseph House & Mrs. Alice Houghton,   Jan. 31, 1769
Joseph Carter & Mrs. Bulah Carter,   Feb. 22, 1769
Deacon Israel Houghton & Mrs. Elizabeth Wilder,
                                            March 14, 1769
John Wilder & Mrs. Catherine Sawyer of Bolton,
                                             June 1, 1769
John Jonus (?) of Colrain & Mrs. Abigail Atherton,
                                             July 12, 1769
William Shaw of Peterboro & Mrs. Barbara Zwier (?),
                                             July 20, 1769
William Heywood of Lunenburg & Mrs. Rebecca
    Kendell,   Oct. 12, 1769
Edward Poor of Worc. & Mrs. Eunice Goodridge,
                                             Nov. 11, 1769
James Pratt & Mrs. Zerniah (?) Rugg,   Nov. 16, 1779
Sampson Ayner & Lucy Lew of Littleton (free
    negroes),   Dec. 14, 1769
Joseph Goodridge of Lunenburg & Mrs. Elizabeth
    Phelps,   Dec. 28, 1769
James Elder of Worcester & Mrs. Sarah Gates, Jan. 16, 1770
James Foster of New Ipswich & Hannah Priest, April 10, 1770
Joseph Brown & Mrs. Annice Knight,   May 29, 1770
John Priest, Jr., & Mrs. Mary Longley,   May 5, 1770
William Grimes, Jr., of Swanzey, N. H., & Mrs.
    Mary Willard,   May 31, 1770
John Townsend of Bolton & Mrs. Eunice Fairbank,
                                             July 25, 1770

ED.—The title " Mrs." applied evidently to maidens as well as widows, but no distinction
on the Record.

Salmon Goodfrey & Mrs. Rebecca Phelps,   Aug. 20, 1770

John Brown of Charlemont & Mrs. Lucy Rugg, Oct. 1, 1770

Nathaniel Joslyn & Mrs. Mary Bennet,   Sept. 5, 1770

Micah Brian & Mrs. Rebecca Ball,   Nov. 27, 1770

Jonas Fairbank & Mrs. Elizabeth Wilder,   Dec. 6, 1770

Thomas Stearns of Fitchburg & Mrs. Molley White,
    Jan. 9, 1771

Joshua Smith of Southboro & Mrs. Abigail Wilder,
    Jan. 31, 1771

John Bennett & Mrs. Lucy Phelps,   Feb. 7. 1771

Jacob Zwier (?) & Mrs. Abigail Priest,   March 21, 1771

Daniel Bigelow of Worcester & Mrs. Mary Ballard,
    May 2, 1771

Antipas Bartlet of Northboro & Mrs. Lois White,
    June 13, 1771

Aaron Kendall of Leominster & Mrs. Katherine
    Wyman,   Nov. 21, 1771

John Robbins & Mrs. Lydia Haskell,   Nov. 27, 1771

Lemuel Haskell of Harvard & Mrs. Lucy Green,
    Nov. 28, 1771

Daniel Goss & Mrs. Eunice Wilder,   Dec. 20, 1771

Samuel Wilder & Mrs. Martha Rugg,   Jan. 15, 1772

Samuel Crosby of Billerica & Mrs. Abigail Bailey,
    Feb. 6, 1772

Joshua Whitcomb of Templeton & Mrs. Eunice
    Prescott,   Feb. 26, 1772

William Locke & Mrs. Mary Fowle,   June 18, 1772

Jonathan Bosworth & Mrs. Mary Holt,   Aug. 6, 1772

Moses Wilder & Mrs. Eunice Furbush,   Aug. 26, 1772

Dr. Israel Atherton & Mrs. Rebecca Prentice, Sept. 6, 1772

Elijah Rice of Holden & Mrs. Leafy Williams of
    Princetown,   Nov. 10, 1772

Samuel Kilbourn of Lunenburg & Mrs. Sarah Cook,
    Dec. 7, 1772

John Locke of Templeton & Mrs. Henrietta Har-
    rington,   Dec. 23, 1772

Titus Wilder & Mrs. Mary Allen,   April 21, 1773

Jotham Woods & Mrs. Mehatable Aldis,   Aug. 19, 1773

Moses Russell & Mrs. Hannah Kendall,   Aug. 21, 1773

William Brooks & Mrs. Bulah Wilder,   Nov. 10, 1773
Reuben Geary & Mrs. Lucy Cutter Brooks,   Nov. 17, 1773
Timothy Knight, Jr., & Mrs. Lydia Wilder,   Nov. 18, 1773
Dr. Abraham Haskell of Lunenburg & Mrs. Sarah
     Green,   Nov. 25, 1773
Lemuel Fairbank & Mrs. Phebe Winn, .   Dec. 9, 1773
Joseph Wilder, Jr., of Leominster & Mrs. Susanna
     Phelps,   Dec. 16, 1773
Benjamin Turner & Mrs. Sarah Lypenwell,   Dec. 22, 1773
Phinehas Sawyer, Jr., of Fitchburg & Mrs. Mary
     Prescott,   Jan. 4, 1774
Joel Osgood & Mrs. Lois Rugg,   Jan. 6, 1774
Jeremiah Sackwell & Mrs. Hannah Ross,   March 2, 1774
John Abbott & Lois Burnett,   March 22, 1775
Moses Mosman of Sudbury & Mary Willard,   April 2, 1775
Ephraim Kendall & Elizabeth Knight,   May 30, 1775
Joseph Joslyn & Dorothy Osgood,   July 20, 1775
Lemuel Sawyer & Anna Pratt,   Sept. 10, 1775
Eleazer Brown of Swansey, N. H., & Susanna Rugg,
                                             Oct. 5, 1775
John Prescott, Jr., & Mary Ballard,   Oct. 25, 1775
Nathaniel Haskell & Abigail Sawyer,   Oct. 31, 1775
Rev. Jacob Biglow of Sudbury & Elizabeth Wells,
                                             Nov. 23, 1775
Capt. Israel Jennison of Worcester & Margaret
     Coolidge of Boston, resident in Lancaster, Dec. 26, 1775
Colonel Joseph Wilder & Rebecca Lock,   Dec. 27, 1775
Samuel Moor & Abigail Hasting,   Jan. 6, 1776
Jonathan Osgood & Rebecca Divoll,   Jan. 11, 1776
Capt. Samuel Mower of Wor. & Esther Lock,   Jan. 18, 1776
John Hoar of Westminster & Abigail White,   Feb. 21, 1776
John Chandler & Katy Holman,   Feb. 29, 1776
Henry Willard (farmer) & Sybal Knights,   July 16, 1776
Daniel Knights & Mary Woods,   Feb. 27, 1777
Luther Fairbank & Thankful Wheelock,   March 5, 1777
Moses Sawyer & Betty Larkin,   April 23, 1777
Samuel Adams & Mrs. Elizabeth Nowell,   May 1, 1777
Josiah Sawyer & Mrs. Susanna Green,   May 8, 1777
Joseph Willson of Keene & Mrs. Sarah Wilder, June 2, 1777

Samuel Dickerson & Mrs. Lois Willard,   June 19, 1777
Mr. Israel Butler & Mrs. Anna Phillips,   June 26, 1777
Deacon Cyrus Fairbank & Mrs. Elizabeth Wynne,
           July 2. 1777
Zebediah Wyman of Woburn & Mrs. Eunice Wyman,
           Aug. 6, 1777
William Wilder & Mrs. Relief Carter,   Dec. 18, 1777
Ephraim Munrow & Mrs. Mary Atherton, both of
    Harvard,   June 12, 1778
Samuel Thompson & Mrs. Eunice Dole,   April 1. 1778
Joseph Farnsworth & Mrs. Mary Hersey,   April 8, 1778
Abel Phelps & Mrs. Lois Willard,   May 7, 1778
Jonathan White & Mrs. Rebeccah Haskell,   May 28, 1778
Thomas Cummings & Mrs. Dolly Case,   Sept. 7, 1778
Nathaniel Eaton & Mrs. Lucy Bennett,   Dec. 30, 1778
Dr. R. P. Bridge & Mrs. Anna Harrington.   Jan. 24, 1772
Jacob Fowle & Mrs. Elizabeth Abbott,   Jan. 31, 1772
Jonathan Wallas of South Brimfield & Mrs. Eliza-
    beth Osgood,   March 4, 1772
Jeremiah Ballard & Mrs. Rebecca Joslyn,   March 4, 1772
Dr. Jonas Prescott of Rindge & Mrs. Susanna Wilder,
           March 31, 1772

HARDWICK.

Jan. 10, 1739, the plantation of Lambstown established as Hardwick. Prov. Laws, Vol. II, p. 971. First (Congregational) Church organized 1736. Officiating clergyman mentioned: Rev. David White.

Elisha Field & Betty Pratt,   Jan. 11, 1753
John Haskell & Elizabeth Lawrence,   March 4, 1753
Jacob Gibbs & Bethiah Bacon,   March 13, 1753
Gideon Carpenter & Jemima Jennis,   May 31, 1753
Samuel Atwood & Peace Steward,   Aug. 30, 1753
Joseph Safford & Martha Powers,   Oct. 26, 1753
Benjamin Stearns & Mary Warren,   Nov. 12, 1753
Solomon Emmons & Mary Marsh,   Jan. 31, 1754
Jacob Pepper & Abigail Foster,   Feb. 28, 1754
Elisha Temple & Abigail Thompson,   Feb. 3, 1755

Nathaniel Merrick & Susanna Lawrence,	Feb. 13, 1755
James Bacon & Abigail Aikens,	June 5, 1755
Nathaniel Whitcomb & Margaret Aikens,	June 19, 1755
Ichabod Stratton & Hannah Goodenow,	July 1, 1755
Chellis (?) Safford & Rebekah Winslow,	July 10, 1755
Zeru Shaddai (?) Doty & Mary Warner,	Dec. 4, 1755
Phillip Spooner & Elizabeth Winslow,	Dec. 25, 1756
Joseph McMichaell & Thankful Olmstead,	Jan. 21, 1756
James Fay, Jr., & Mary Winslow,	March 18, 1756
Timothy Pratt & Ruth Abbott,	Oct. 14, 1756
Zebu. (?) Johnson & Ellis Mirick,	Nov. 25, 1756
Israel Olmstead & Anna Safford,	Nov. 25, 1756
Jonathan Farr & Mercy Winslow,	Jan. 19, 1757
Nathan Billing & Lydia Wells,	Feb. 24, 1757
Jeremiah Anderson & Isabell Partrick,	Nov. 15, 1757
Isaac Morgan & Lucretia Downing,	Dec. 6, 1757
Daniel Billing & Mary Rugles,	Feb. 23, 1758
Stephen Ghoram & Sarah Freeman,	March 16, 1758
David Gilbert & Esther Ginne,	March 23, 1758
Moses Whiple & Katherine Forbush,	May 20, 1758
Noah Emmonds & Mary Farr,	May 20, 1758
Daniel Warner & Mary Wright,	May 31, 1758
Stephen Fisk & Anna Green,	June 29, 1758
Lieutenant Nathaniel Kellog & Martha Hamond,	
	July 19, 1758
Lenard Robinson & Rebecca Billing,	Aug. 31, 1758
Abell Benjamin & Susanna Carpenter,	May 22, 1759
Thodorus Doty & Jane Dunsmore,	May 30, 1759
Daniel Fay & Mary Crosby,	March 10, 1757
Ebenezer Safford & Abigail Higgins,	Nov. 24, 1759
Samuel Dexter & Thankfull Freemon,	Nov. 25, 1759
Dr. Chilles Safford & Lydia Warner,	Feb. 8, 1760
Capt. Jonathan Fletcher & Mary Sears,	May 1, 1760
Ensign Jonas Fay & Sarah Fasset,	May 1, 1760
Isaac Abbot & Elizabeth Goodenow,	Aug. 14, 1760
Benjamin Rogers & Mehitable Fay,	Sept. 10, 1760
Benjamin Winchester & Sarah Allen,	Feb. 19, 1761
Wilson Freeman & Dorcas Fish,	Feb. 28, 1761
Simon Giffen & Abigail Higgens,	March 24, 1761

Elkanah Slevant (?) & Lydia Cobb,	Sept. 7, 1761
Freemon Sears & Mehitabel Haskel,	Oct. 22, 1761
Rev. Lamuel Hedge & Mrs. Sarah White,	Nov. 5, 1761
David Allen & Elisabeth Fisk,	Nov. 12, 1761
Edward Clafford & Abigail Winslow,	Nov. 30, 1761
Israel Johnson & Abial Safford,	Dec. 29, 1761
Edward Foster & Deborah Bangs,	Jan. 13, 1762
Elijah Warner & Submitt Wells,	Jan. 14, 1762
Ebenezer Chipman & Susanna Ruggles,	March 4, 1762
Abijah Edson & Hannah Ruggles,	June 10, 1762
Azariah Wright & Mary Safford,	June 29, 1762
Nathan Wheeler & Hannah Hunt,	July 1, 1762
Jacob Hastings & Mary Bangs,	July 22, 1762
Thomas Wheeler & Sarah Warner,	Sept. 8, 1762
Lieut. John Granger & Rebecca Hascall, both of New Brantree,	June 16, 1763
Noah Houghton of Palmer & Rachel Thompson of New Brantree,	Sept. 7, 1763
Ebenezer Lawrence & Lydia Richmond of New Brantree,	Dec. 18, 1763
Moses Whitcomb & Sarah Powers,	Nov. 4, 1762
Solomon Johnson & Sarah Dexter,	Dec. 28. 1762
Benjamin Rogers & Temperance Finney,	April 5, 1763
Jonathan Farr, Jr., & Lucy Fay,	Oct. 27, 1763
Enoch Babcock & Katherine Densmore,	Dec. 15, 1763
Solomon Green & Elizabeth Page,	Dec. 29, 1763
Benjamin Robarts & Martha Abbot,	Feb. 29, 1764
Abraham Knolton & Susanna Jorden,	March 12, 1764
Henry Gilbert & Patience Marsh,	April 5, 1764
Samuel Billings & Buelah Fay,	June 28, 1764
John Cobb & Thankfull Sears,	July 19, 1764
Benjamin Green & Hannah Robinson,	Aug. 31, 1764
Ebenezer Lyscomb & Mary Hooker,	Oct. 8, 1764
Edward Higgins & Thankful Rice,	Oct. 17, 1764
Edward Goodspeed & Judith Winslow,	Oct. 19, 1764
Nathaniel Dickinson & Elizabeth Fisk,	Nov. 7, 1764
Stephan Belding & Martha Johnson,	Nov. 7, 1764
Joseph Warner & Mary Whipple,	Nov. 13, 1764
Isaac Fay & Keziah Doan,	Nov. 22, 1764

Joseph Nye & Sarah Bradish,	Dec. 27, 1764
John Dunsmore & Elizabeth ———,	April 15, 1765
John Burt of Springfield & Bathsheba Warner,	June 4, 1765
David Aken & Hannah Simons of Ware,	July 18, 1765
Aaron Hunt & Sarah Robinson,	Oct. 24, 1765
William Thomas & Abiel Collins,	Aug. 23, 1765
John Tufts & Martha Ruggles,	Nov. 11, 1765
Abel Harwood & Sarah Ruggles,	Nov. 27, 1765
Lemuel Cobb & Lydia Allen,	Oct. 10, 1765
John Hunt & Patience Wright,	Dec. 25, 1765
David Glazier & Sarah Pratt,	Feb. 6, 1766
Asa Hatch & Lucy Warner,	Jan. 23, 1766
Samuel Hunt & Abigail Fisk,	Feb. 20, 1766
Jonathan Warner & Hannah Mandell,	Feb. 5, 1766
John Tufts & Martha Ruggles,	Nov. 11, 1763
Leonard Robinson & Mercy Newton,	March 13, 1766
James Wright & Mary Hunt,	June 18, 1766
Job Dexter & Mary Hinkley,	July 17, 1766
William Sherman & Hannah Steward,	Sept. 10, 1766
Shearjashub Goodspeed & Elizabeth Ruggles,	Nov. 20, 1766
Benj. Ruggles, 3d, & Elizabeth Fay,	Nov. 26, 1766
Sol. Bush & Content Whetcomb,	Nov. 27, 1766
Asa Curtis & Lois Goss,	Nov. 27, 1766
Silas Johnson & Patience Walker,	Nov. 27, 1766
Silas Nye & Patience Carpenter,	Nov. 27, 1766
Philip Washburn & Sarah Carpenter,	Jan. 8, 1767
Abiel Stetson & Ruth Bonny,	Feb. 24, 1767
Eli Freeman & Mary Rice,	March 26, 1767
Zachariah Harwood & Levina Rice,	April 30, 1767
Samuel Beak & Abigail Thomas,	July 30, 1767
Samuel Billing & Sarah Crosby,	Nov. 26, 1767
William Fuller & Mercy Powers,	Dec. 3, 1767
Aaron Power & Hannah Goodenow,	March 10, 1768
Abner Marble of Petersham & Zerniah Rice,	April 19, 1768
John Stone & Susanna Mundell,	May 12, 1768
Stephen Warner & Lois Goss,	May 25, 1768
Timothy Moore & Mary Warner,	May 25, 1768
Joseph Smith & Jane Smith of Petersham,	Aug. 26, 1768
Daniel Steward & Eunice Allen,	Sept. 5, 1768

William Page, Jr., & Mercy Raymond,	Oct. 6, 1768
James Page, Jr., & Thankfull Raymond,	Oct. 6, 1768
John Foster of ——chester & Rebecca Page,	Oct. 6, 1768
Benjamin Robinson of New Braintree & Hannah Nye,	
	Nov. 2, 1768
Henry Higgins & Mary Fisk,	Nov. 9, 1768
Elisha Gilbert of Oakham & Submit Glaizer,	Nov. 16, 1768
Nathaniel Rice of Rutland & Elisabeth Lawrence,	
	Nov. 24, 1768
Silas Dean & Elisabeth Randell of Greenwich,	Nov. 30, 1768
Luke Brown, Jr., & Mary Adams, both of Worcester,	
	Jan. 26, 1769
Reuben Snow & Mercy Sears,	May 11, 1769
Eleazer Packard & Mary Woodbury,	June 9, 1769
John Griffin & Mary Weeks,	Sept. 7, 1769
Eliphalet Washburn & Anna Benjamin,	Sept. 19, 1769
Paul Knowlton & Lucy Forbush,	Nov. 8, 1769
David White & Bathsheba Crowell,	Nov. 23, 1769
Experience Luce & Anna Lawrence,	Nov. 30, 1769
Jabez Elwell & Thankfull Clark.	Dec. 21, 1769
Ebenezer Chiles & Abigail Wellis,	Dec. 16, 1769
Nathan Billing & Relience (?) Bangs,	Dec. 26, 1769
Jonathan Fisk & Hannah Rice,	Jan. 18, 1770
John Raymond & Mercy Jordan,	March 7, 1771
Lemuel Willis & Rebecca Berry,	May 27, 1771
Daniel Munden & Rebecca Wheeler,	Aug. 8, 1771
Daniel Clarke & Lydia Carpenter,	July 3, 1771
Elisha Sears & Hannah Sears,	Oct. 31, 1771
Stephen Warner & Damaris Church,	Nov. 13, 1771
Richard Waite & Submit Thomas,	Nov. 14, 1771
Richard Sears & Mary Lee,	Dec. 19, 1771
Ezra Alden & Sarah Harwood,	Jan. 2, 1772
John Hamilton & Isabel Burnet,	Feb. 27 (?), 1772
Edward Ruggles, Jr., & Anna Dean,	March 25, 1772
Elias Walker & Sarah Aiken,	Feb. 25, 1772
Silvanus Cobb & Elizabeth Warren,	March 9, 1772
Samuel Linds & Deborah Perkins,	March 19, 1772
Joseph Clawland & Betty Wheeler,	May 4, 1772
Roger Haskell & Joanna Haskell,	May 28, 1772

9

Joanna Flint & Marcy Leonard,	June 18, 1772
James Wing & Rebecca Willis,	Aug. 13, 1772
Benjamin Stebbins & Marcy Aikens,	Sept. 24, 1772
Luke Bonney & Marcy Thomas,	Nov. 5, 1772
Benajah Putnam & Eliz[a] Livermore,	Nov. 19, 1772
Robert McIntyre & Rhoda Warner,	Nov. 26, 1772
John Amidown & Mercy Allen,	Feb. 14, 1771
John Nims & Betty Rice,	Feb. 14, 1771
John Hunt & Elizabeth Webster,	Dec. 23, 1772
Benjamin Ruggles & Jerusha Aikens,	Feb. 11, 1773
David Leonard & Hannah Whipple,	Feb. 15, 1773
John Bradish & Hannah Warner,	March 4, 1773
Stewart Southgate & Deborah Rayment,	July 22, 1773
Ezra Conant & Anna Fisk,	March 21, 1770
Thomas Wheet & Abigail Hearns,	March 22, 1770
Jonathan Danforth & Susanna White,	April 19, 1770
Benjamin Fisk & Hannah Winslow,	Aug. 15, 1770
Stephen Rice & Thankful Gleazer,	Oct. 23, 1770
James Page & Anna Warren,	Oct. 25, 1770
Elisha Cobb & Elisabeth Burnet,	Nov. 8, 1770
Southworth Jenkins & Hulda Wright,	Nov. 15, 1770
Ephraim Cleveland & Lydia Whipple,	Nov. 15, 1770
Isaac Nye & Hannah Walker,	Nov. 29, 1770
Amos Thomas & Eunice Bangs,	Dec. 20, 1770
Ephraim Titus & Hannah Cobb,	Dec. 20, 1770
James Lawton & Mary Rayment,	Jan. 3, 1771
Nathaniel Leason & Sarah Johnson,	Jan. 14, 1771
Gideon Wheeler & Sarah Forbush,	Jan. 14, 1771
Nathan Carpenter & Anna Cox,	March 15, 1773
Joseph Robinson & Sarah Clark,	Sept. 30, 1773
Paul Dean & Elizabeth Ruggles,	Sept. 19, 1773
Timothy Nichols & Joanna Dean,	Jan. 13, 1774
Edward Taylor & Lydia Haskell,	Nov. 23, 1775
William Johnson & Hannah Johnson,	Jan. 25, 1776
James Hawkes & Olive Willis,	March 7, 1776
Thomas Robinson, Jr., & Rebecca Paige,	April 11, 1776
Joseph Chamberlain & Deborah Nye,	April 18, 1776
Calvin Fairbanks & Jenney Ayres,	June 20, 1776
Dudley Jordan & Bathsheba Rice,	Aug. 8, 1776

Jesse Kinney & Hannah Stearns,	Aug. 11, 1776
Jabez Cobb & Content Clark,	Dec. 8, 1776
Paul Mandell, Jr., & Mary Briggs,	Nov. 28, 1776
Thomas Martin Wright & Elizabeth Newton,	Dec. 19, 1776
Jesse Byam & Sarah Chamberlain,	Jan. 30, 1777
Edmund Willis & Mary Fuller,	Feb. 23, 1777
Rufus Carpenter & Olive Whitcomb,	Feb. 27, 1777
Lemuel Cobb & Abigail Ammidown,	March 27, 1777
Stephen Woodward & Molly Sibley,	May 13, 1777
Moses Mandell & Mary Wheeler,	May 28, 1777
Judah Simonds & Thankful Allis,	May 28, 1777
Nathaniel Graves & Marcy Paige,	May 29, 1777
John Ruggles & Mary Caldwell,	May 29, 1777
Andrew Haskell & Susannah Paine,	July 10, 1777
John Perkins & Sarah White,	July 23, 1777
James Thompson & Polly Sellon,	Aug. 20, 1777
John Hedge & Mary Haskell,	Sept. 7, 1777
Hon. Jonas Fay, Esq., of Bennington, Vt., & Mrs. Lydia Safford,	Nov. 20, 1777
Thomas Shaw & Elizabeth Finney of Petersham,	Jan. 7, 1778
Jonathan Lynds of Petersham & Mrs. Rhoda McIntyer,	April 26, 1778
Pauz (?) Rice & Chloe Lincoln,	April 8, 1779
Lieut. John Hastings & Mehitable Berry,	April 11, 1779
Capt. Edward Clark of Hubbardston & Susanna Rice,	April 22, 1779
Seth Babbit & Betty Blanchard,	April 22, 1779
Martin Rice of Charlemont & Lucy Rice,	July 6, 1779
John Dotey & Mary Mandell,	Sept. 19, 1779
Ephraim Hodges & Katharine Johnson,	Nov. 25, 1779
Atwood Aiken & Hannah Willis,	Dec. 9, 1779
Benjamin Ruggles, 4th, & Betty Parks,	Dec. 15, 1779
Levi Babbit of Norton & Betty Babbit,	Dec. 21, 1779
Daniel Ruggles & Lucy Paige,	Dec. 30, 1779
Moses Haskell, Jr., & Priscilla Hinkley,	Jan. 12, 1780
Benjamin Holmes of Princeton & Elizabeth Weeks,	Feb. 10, 1780
Joseph Robinson of New Braintree & Lucy Ruggles of Barre,	Feb., 1780

Asa Hodge & Meriam Dexter,   May 31, 1780
Peter Ford & Mary Fothergill,   June 25, 1780
Seth Woodward of Petersham & Ruth Ayres, Aug. 25, 1778
Jonathan Richardson of Barre & Temperence Nye
  of Oakham,   Nov. 12, 1778
Samuel Hopkins & Elizabeth Hastings,   Dec. 17, 1778
Silvanus Nye of Barre & Mary Banks of Keene, N. H.,
    March 2, 1779
Timothy Newton, Jr., late of Hardwick, & Abigail
  Earl,   March 4, 1779
Aaron Hudson & Sarah Webster,   Nov. 3, 1777
Jacob Whipple & Edna Furbush,   Dec. 30, 1777
Elijah Washburn & Mary Winchester,   Jan. 1, 1778
Jonathan Child & Deliverance Freeman,   Jan. 15, 1778
John Newton & Lydia Freeman,   Jan. 15, 1778
Daniel Fay, Jr., & Mary Paige,   Aug. 23, 1778
Asa Hull of Montague & Martha Furbush,   Oct. 12, 1778
Jedidiah Fay & Jerusha Aiken,   Nov. 12, 1778
Thomas Fuller & Lydia Paige,   Nov. 26, 1778
Moses Hunt & Esther Jinney,   Dec. 10, 1778
Jonathan Gilbert of New Braintree & Sarah Ammi-
  don,   Jan. 5, 1779
Benjamin Stetson & Mary Johnson,   Aug. 24, 1780
Joseph Hews of Lime & Mary Rice,   Oct. 5, 1780
Ebenezer Cobb & Martha Hastings,   Oct. 5, 1780
David Prat & Hannah Hammond of Petersham, Oct. 12, 1780
Deacon Daniel Spooner of Petersham & Mrs. Mary
  Dean,   Oct. 16, 1780
Theodoras Forbes & Elizabeth Winchester,   Jan. 22, 1781
James Biram & Elizabeth Cox,   Feb. 8, 1781
Henry Rixforth & widow Sarah Stanford,   Feb. 2, 1781
Nathaniel Harriman of Chesterfield & Bethany Snow,
    March 14, 1781
Oliver Harris & Mehitable Shaw,   April 4, 1781
Ephraim Hunt, Jr., of Greenwich & Rhod Furbush,
    April 5, 1781
Robert Sprout & Betsey Lincoln,   Sept. 17, 1781
Isaac Parmeter & Lydia Furnas, both of Oakham,
    Oct. 4, 1781

Antipas How of Swanzey, N. H., & Joanna Larrance,

Jan. 20, 1782

Gamaliel Ellis & Jemima Nye,   Feb. 21, 1782

John Rice of Charlemont & Ruth Rice,   March 6, 1782

George Haskell & Comfort Knowlton,   April 25, 1782

Seth Hinckley, Jr., & Lydia Berry,   May 12, 1782

Stephen Chandler & Meribah Nye,   May 23, 1782

Moses Cheney, Jr., of Warwick & Lucy Dexter, July 4, 1782

Samuel Haskins, Jr., & Percis Johnson,   Sept. 5, 1782

John Terry, Jr., & Sarah Ramsdel,   Sept. 26, 1782

John Keith & Lerviah Willis,   Oct. 21, 1782

William Nye & Molly Purrington,   Dec. 26, 1782

Tilly Foster & Abigail Hammond, both of Petersham,

Dec. 29, 1782

Benjamin Woodward & Molly Woodward,   Jan. 17, 1783

Solomon Mason, Jr., of Greenwich & Margaret Harris,

Jan. 30, 1783

Edward Allen of New Windsor & Sarah Snow,

Jan. 30, 1783

Noah Patch & Jemima Cox,   Feb. 4, 1783

David Barnard of Shelburne & Rhoda Allen, March 4, 1783

Ephraim Ruggles & Olive Powers,   March 20, 1783

Nathan Rozer of Rutland & Abigail Mead of Hubbardston,   April 5, 1783

David Weeks & Betsey Robinson,   May 22, 1783

John Giffin & Kezia Smith,   July 22, 1783

Phinehas Meigs of Sunderland & Susanna Winslow,

Aug. 3, 1783

Silvanus Brimhall of Barre & Triphena Johnson,

Sept. 14, 1783

Nathaniel Johnson, Jr., & Mary Nye,   Sept. 5, 1783

Peter Rainheart of Greenwich & Polly Crose, Nov. 2, 1783

Henry Butterfield of Greenwich & Rachel Thayer,

Nov. 20, 1783

David Basset & Phebe Terry,   Dec. 11, 1783

Ebenezer Sprout & Mary Thayer of Petersham,

Dec. 11, 1783

Joseph Parks of Norwich & Dorothy Bartlett,

Dec. 11, 1783

Asa Brigham of Barnard & Sarah Newton,	Dec. 25, 1783
Elijah Carpenter & Sarah Wing,	Feb. 1, 1784
Eleazar Dexter & Abigail Dexter,	April 8, 1784
Nathan Paige & Hanna Cobb,	April 25, 1784
John Gorham & Polly Dexter,	June 3, 1784
Frederick Wicker & Susanna Newton,	June 24, 1784
Lot Jenny of Hartland & Olive Hatch,	Aug. 4, 1784
Israel Lawton & Dolly Billing,	Aug. 26, 1784
Timothy Hathaway & Rhoda Clark,	Sept. 23, 1784
Israel Aiken of Windsor & Susanna Smith,	Sept. 23, 1784
John Hunt & Sarah Fay,	Oct. 1, 1784
Silas Gorham & Cynthia Hanmer,	Nov. 14, 1784
Robert Dean of Barnard & Unice Billing,	Dec. 23, 1784
Foster Paige & Amittia Page,	Jan. 6, 1785
Moses Forbush & Patty Marble of Petersham,	Jan. 9, 1785
Samuel Warden of Petersham & Betsey Sibley,	
	June 30, 1785
Simon Oliver of Barre & Mary Morgan,	July 24, 1785
Abijah Sibley & Patty Korey,	Sept. 29, 1785
John Earl & Unice Allen,	Oct. 2, 1785
Abel White & Abigail Babbit, both of Barre,	Oct. 5, 1785
James Pierce & Susanna Mirick,	Nov. 20, 1785
James Bailey & Silence Humphrey of Sheutesbury,	
	Nov. 24, 1785
Judah Hinckley & Sally Ruggles,	Dec. 15, 1785
Silas Johnson, Jr., & Hanna Nye,	Dec. 15, 1785
John Jameson & Rhoda Smith of Petersham,	Dec. 15, 1785
Thomas Spooner & Martha Smith,	Dec. 15, 1785
Abraham Bell of New Braintree & Elizabeth Joslyn,	
	Dec, 29, 1785
Joseph Bowman, Jr., of Barnard & Fanny Spooner,	
	Jan. 26, 1786
Joseph Harvey & Polly Arnold,	Feb. 2, 1786

OXFORD.

May 31, 1693, "Daniel Allen is recorded as Representative from Oxford." Mass. Archives, Vol. VI, p. 278. First (Congregational) Church organized 1721. Officiating clergymen mentioned: Rev. Jonathan Campbell, Rev. John Campbell, Rev. Joseph Bowman.

Oliver Shumway of Oxford & Elisabeth Holman of
    Sutton,   April 15, 1747
Elias Tenison & Hannah Twist, both of Sutton,
                                          June 16, 1748
John Eddy & Patience Town,   June 18, 1747
Ebenezer Merriam & Elisath Lock, both of County
    Gore,   Sept. 17, 1747
Joseph Robbins of Douglass & Mary Chamberlain,
                                          Nov. 3, 1748
Ebenezer Learned & Jerusha Baker,   Oct. 5, 1749
Job Mackintire & Abigail Mackintire,   May 29, 1750
John Boyle & Mary Hunkins,   June 7, 1750
John Thomas of Worcester & Elizabeth Wiley,
                                          Nov. 12, 1747
Caleb Barton of Oxford & Susannah March of Sutton,
                                          Jan. 13, 1747
Ichabod Stockwell of Sutton & Experience Gleason,
                                          Feb. 2, 1747-8
Nehemiah Stone & Hannah Lock, both of County
    Gore,   Dec. 1, 1748
Ebenezer Barton & Hannah Barton, both of Dudley,
                                          Jan. 24, 1748-9
Samuel Curtis of County Gore & Mary Town,
                                          Sept. 19, 1751
Tabez Holden & Rebekah Ward,   Oct. 3, 1751
James Town & Ann Blood,   Dec. 10, 1747
Samuel Robinson of Dudley & Hannah Learned,
                                          Aug. 25, 1748
Jonathan Streeter & Olive Gleason,   March 3, 1748-9
Samuel Mower of Worcester & Comfort Learned,
                                          May 18, 1749

Thomas Read & Experience Shumway,	Aug. 2, 1749
John Wilson & Lois Town,	Sept. 7, 1749
Elnathan Beers (?) of Leicester & Bulah Pratt,	Nov. 24, 1749
Jonathan Wart of Sutton & Mrs. Mercy Gleason,	
	—— 19, 1749
Joseph Pratt & Katherine Read,	7 mo. 27 da., 1750
Jonathan Fuller & Mary Whiple,	Oct. 5, 1750
John Learned & Miriam Smith,	Jan. 31, 1750
Samuel Edward & Prudence Miriam of Gore,	June 25, 1751
Elisha Davis & Mary Harris,	July 11, 1751
John Jones & Mary Rockett,	Oct. 17, 1751
Alexander Nickoll & Joan Hart of Leicester,	Oct. 30, 1751
Josiah Wolcott & Mrs. Isebell Campbell,	Feb. 13, 1751–2
Thomas Town & Hannah Ballad (?),	Feb. 13. ——
Phinehas Ward & Sarah Rockett,	April 1. 1752
Levi Shumway & Priscilla Gleason,	Sept. 3, 1752
Joseph McIntyre & Rebonah Harwood,	Sept. 3, 1752
Solomon Harwood & Sarah Taylor,	Dec. 4, 1752
Samuel Lamb & Sarah Dana,	April 5, 1753
John Rocket & Hannah Frost,	June 4, 1753
John Stone of Palmer & Estor Spencer (?),	June 19, 1753
Jonathan Phillips of County Gore & Rachel	
Humphy (?),	Oct. 4, 1753
Nathan Shumway & Judith Whitney,	Feb. 7, 1754
John Adams of Brookfield & Mary Brown,	Oct. 3, 1754
Joseph Lafflin (?) & Martha Cumins (?),	Nov. 21, 1754
William Learned of Killingly & Mrs. Elizabeth	
Maya (?),	Dec. (?) 12, 1754
Ephraim Ballard & Martha Moore,	Dec. 29, 1754
Nathaniel Gleason & Susanna Streeter,	Jan. 2, 1755
Hezekiah Meriam of County Gore & Sarah Cla-	
flin (?),	April 3, 1755
David Town & Kezia (?) Shumway,	Aug. 26, 1755
John Marvin & Rebona Ballard,	Oct. 23, 1755
Abijah Kingsbury & Mary Chamberlain,	Oct. 23, 1756
Joseph Phillips & Lydia Wilson,	Nov., 1756
John Wyman & Experience Read,	April 23, 1752
John Wyley & Rachell Curtis,	June 18, 1752
Samuel Harris & Margaret Robins,	Aug. 27, 1752

William Lamb & Rebecca Hovey,   Feb. 12, 1753
Joseph Lafflin & Phebie Wilson,   July 12, 1753
Job Welds & Eunice Thayer, both of County Gore,
                                                 May 23, 1754
John Nickolls & Jerusha Moore,   May 15, 1755
Jonathan Ballard & Ellis Moore,   July 15, 1755
Joseph Twiss, Jr., & Esther Frost, both of Charlton,
                                                 July 24, 1755
Josiah Town & Susanna Rich, both of Charlton,
                                                 Aug. 13, 1756
Edmund Town & Hannah Sparhawk,   Aug. 13, 1756
Edward Davis & Abigail Learned,   Nov. 11, 1756
Southwick Hebberd of Dudley & Abigail Coller (?)
    of Shrewsbury,   March 24, 1757
Samuel Learnard & Mehitable Town,   June 12, 1760
Zebulon Streeter & Tabitha Hovey,   July 16, 1760
Thaddus Rich & Abial Frost, both of Charlton, Aug. 19, 1760
Abel Levins & Esthar Muneil,   Aug. 28, 1760
Israel Phillips & Huldah Town,   Sept. 18, 1760
David Pratt, Jr., & Sarah Shumway,   Oct. 23, 1760
Joseph Phillips & Mrs. Bethsheba Town,   Dec. 10, 1760
Noah Dodge of Dudley & Mary Wiley,   March 12, 1761
John Town, Jr., & Dorothy Pratt,   April 9, 1761
Ebenezer Humphrey & Ruth Shumway,   April 9, 1761
Deacon Jonathan Town & Mrs. Martha Rogers,
                                                 April 28, 1761
Southwick Hibberd of Dudley & Abigail Coller of
    Shrewsbury,   March 21, 1757
Noah Hall of Killingsley & Lydia Brown,   April 24, 1759
William Simpson & Susannah McKnight,   Oct. 3, 1759
Nehimiah Houghton of Sturbridge & Eunice Curtis
    of Gore,   Dec. 19, 1759
Isaac Putnam & Rachel Pratt,   May 28, 1760
Abijah Harris & Sarah Lamb,   Dec. 18, 1760
Asa Conant & Sarah Edwards,   March 30, 1761
Jacob Peirce of Township No. 1 & Abigail Meriam
    of said township,   June 18, 1761
Reuben Barton & Katherine Learnard,   June 29, 1761
Isaac Barton & Sarah Covel,   July 29, 1761

Jabez Tatman & Mary Dudley, both of Worcester,

Sept. 23, 1761

Isaac Mophit of Dudley & Sarah Learnard of Oxford,

Nov., 1761

John Dana & Hannah Humphrey,   Dec. 15, 1761
Thomas Eddy and Hannah Eddy,   May 10, 1762
Richard Moore, 3d, & Mary Eddy,   Aug. 19, 1761
John Crowl (?) of Leicester & Sarah Meriam,   Jan. 13, 1763
Benjamin Fitts & Mary Cook, both of Sutton,   Oct. 19, 1762
Andrew Crowl of Leicester & Mary Claflin,   Dec. 9, 1762
Samuel Moore & Zeriah Levins,   Dec. 16, 1762
Joseph Gleason of Sandisfield & Sarah Eddy,   Dec. 20, 1762
Ebenezer Robbins & Susanna Kingsbery,   Jan. 12, 1763
Edward Davis, Jr., & Elizabeth Davis,   Jan. 19, 1763
William Davis, Jr., & Sibbel Davis,   July 5, 1764
Jacob Davis of Charlton & Rebecca Davis,   Jan. 9, 1765
James Gray & Molley Lamson of Gore,   Jan. 24, 1765
Henry Burnet & Ruth Merriam of County Gore,

March 26, 1765

Reuben Lamb of Leicester & Rebecca Nichols,

April 4, 1765

Henry King & Abigail Timsdell, both of Sutton,

Oct. 24, 1765

Jonah Titus & Thankfull Parker, both of Douglas,

Oct. 29, 1765

Jacob Kingsbery & Hannah Parker of Douglas,

March 10, 1766

Abel Sibley & Abigail Nickols, both of Sutton,

May 22, 1766

Abner Sibley & Betty Lilley, both of Sutton,   May 28, 1766
Samuel Lamb of Spencer & Elizabeth Davis,   April 16, 1766
Nathaniel Davis & Sarah Stone,   May 13, 1765
Stephen Barton & Mrs. Dorothy Moore, Jr.,   May 28, 1765
Jedidah Barton & Mrs. Mary Rackit,   May 29, 1765
James Freeland of Brimfield & Mrs. Elizabeth Thomas,

Sept. 5, 1765

Jonathan Baldwin of Spencer & Mary Hunt,   Oct. 28, 1766
John Ballard & Mrs. Mary Marsh of Douglas,   Dec. 18, 1766
William Burnit & Lucy Gleason,   Jan. 22, 1766

Nathaniel Rich of Royalston & Phebe Putnam of
    Sutton,   Sept. 25, 1766
Paul Sibley & Sarah Putnam, both of Sutton,   Dec. 2, 1766
Nathaniel Cummings & Molly Robins, both of
    Douglas,   Dec. 11, 1766
Noah Amidown & Abigail Putney,   Feb. 19, 1767
Benjamin Keyes of Shrewsbury & Lucy Miriam,
                                    April 13, 1767
Daniel Hood & Sarah Hovey,   April 22, 1767
Isnath (?) Pratt, Jr., & Abigail Davis, Jr.,   April 30, 1767
John Darby & Hannah Earcy (?),   May 1, 1766
John Rand & Mrs. Tabitha Stedman,   June 5, 1766
Jacob Emerson & Sarah Dole (?),   July 3, 1766
Joseph Hosley, Jr., & Abigail Kendall,   July 24, 1766
Jeremiah ——— & Elizabeth Warren,   Sept. 7, 1766
Elijah ——— & Bethnia Hosley,   June 1, 1767
Samuel Davis, Jr., & Mary Rich of Sutton, Aug. 17, 1767
Stephin Bullen & Elizabeth Rich,   Sept. 3, 1767
Jonathan Day of Needham & Mary Mayo, May 21, 1767
Thomas Fisk & Naomi Mixter of Sutton, June 25, 1767
Elias Pratt & Lydia Holl,   Aug. 6, 1767
Isaac Burnitt of Warwick & Esther Meriam of
    County Gore,   Oct. 15, 1767
Elijah Moore, Jr., & Jemima Kingsbury,   Oct. 29, 1767
John Campbell & Elizabeth Stone of Gore, Nov. 26, 1767
James Brown & Mary Shumway,   Feb. 16, 1768
David Gleason & Lydia Meriam of County Gore,
                                 March 17, 1767
John Learned, Jr., & Abigail Davis,   Sept. 29, 1768
Josiah Blood of Charlton & Mrs. Thamazin Hudson,
                                   Nov. 9, 1768
Ebenezer Coburn, Jr., & Dorcas Shumway, Nov. 10, 1768
Joseph Pratt, the 3d, & Mary Hudson,   Sept. 29, 1768
Nathan Prat & Mary Pratt of Gore,   Oct. 23, 1768
Jason Collar & Mary Bogle,   Nov. 24, 1768
Jonathan Stone of Dudley & Elizabeth Gros,
                                   Nov. 29, 1768
James Hill of Douglas & Dorothy Learned, Feb. 16, 1769
Samuel Town & Tabatha Eddy,   March 9, 1769

Jeremiah Ammedown & Elizabeth Martin of Douglas,
                              Feb. 23, 1769
Micah Pratt & Lucy Shumway,   Feb. 23, 1769
Bartholomew Putnam & Molly Putnam, both of
      Sutton,   March 1, 1769
Uriah Stone, Jr., of ye Country Gore & Lois Stone,
                              July 25, 1769
Asa Pratt & Susanna Bemis of Charlton,   Sept. 6, 1769
Philip Amidown & Eunice Shumway,   Nov. 2, 1769
Jacob Peirce & Mrs. Abigail Shumway,   Nov 7, 1769
Joshua Meriam & Mrs. Hannah Lovell,   Nov. 14, 1769
Isaac Shumway & Rebecca Gros of Douglas, Nov. 14, 1769
Jonathan Smith of Warwick & Elisabeth Harbridge
      of Dudley,   Nov. 30, 1769
Aaron Wakefield & Olive Wright of ye Country Gore,
                              Nov. 16, 1769
Collins Moor & Hannah Town,   March 26, 1770
Abner Shumway of Sutton & Lucy How,   April 19, 1770
Benjamin Tewel of Warwick & Elizabeth Merriam,
                              May 30, 1770
Jonas Pratt, Jr., & Jenny Foster,   July 5, 1770
Ichabod Stockwell & Mary Snow,   Sept. 17, 1770
Benjamin (or Benajah) Putnam & Mrs. Sarah Fitts,
      both of Sutton,   Dec. 13, 1770
John Allen & Mrs. Kezia Amidown,   Jan. 16, 1771
Aaron Grant of Royalston & Mrs. Mary Town of
      Sutton,   Feb. 20, 1771
Joseph Davis & Hannah Lamb,   Jan. 15, 1771
Benjamin Jewell of Warwick & Eliza Merriam of ye
      County Gore,   May 30, 1770
Ichabod Stockwell & Mary Snow,   Sept. 17, 1770
Samuel Robertson of Sutton & Hannah Shumway,
                              Nov. 25, 1771
William Mills, Jr., of Needham & Eunice Eddy,
                              March 4, 1772
Joseph Pratt, the 3d, & Esther Blood of Charlton,
                              May 29, 1772
Salem Town of Charlton & Elizabeth Mayo, July 11, 1771
Reuben Robinson of Dudley & Rebecca White, Aug. 29, 1771

Daniel Whitney of Shrewsbury & Katy Stone of
  Gore, Sept. 26, 1771
Moses Fay of New Rutland & Eliz[a] Learned, Nov. 7, 1771
Craft Davis & Katherine Streeter, Jan. 16, 1772
Gideon Sibley & Tamar Fitts, April 28, 1772
Edmund Eddy & Phebe Nichols, Oct. 15, 1772
Gideon Smith of Springfield & Mrs. Mary Freeland,
  Nov. 4, 1772
Daniel Fisk & Mrs. Susanna Thurston, Nov. 10, 1772
Ephraim Amidown, Jr., & Jane Robins, Dec. 17, 1772
Douglass Robins of Dudley & Esther Kingsbury,
  May 4, 1772
Joseph Sparhawk & Patience Lamson, May 12, 1772
James Gleason, Jr., & Huldah Wite of the Gore,
  May 28, 1772
Stephen Pratt & Phebe Meriam of the Country Gore,
  Nov. 26, 1772
John Ives & Eunice Collar, Dec. 1, 1772
Reuben Davis of Charlton & Sarah Moore, March 3, 1772
Amasa Allen & Esther Fish, June 23, 1773
Ezekiel Gleason & Esther Streeter, Oct. 5, 1773
William Watson & Mrs. Abigail Peirce, June 8, 1773
Jacob Shumway, Jr., & Cloe Hancock, June 16, 1773
Capt. Isaac Hartwell & Mrs. Phebe Brewer, both
  of Gore, July 14, 1773
Reuben Eddy & Sibbele Moore, Nov. 25, 1773
Jonathan Underwood & Thamazin Hudson, Feb. 17, 1774
Charles Hart of Worcester & Olive Fish, March 10, 1774
Salem Town of Charlton & Ruth Moore, April 11, 1774
William Nichols, the 3d, & Lydia Town, May 5, 1774
Samuel Campbell & Ruth Nichols, Dec. 15, 1774
Anthony Dike of Sutton & Ann Jennison, Jan. 16, 1775
George Robinson & Deborah Learned, Feb. 7, 1775
Solomon Cook & Sarah Hancock, March 29, 1775
Silvanus Town & Margaret Watson, March 29, 1775
Levi Davis & Deborah Moore, April 3, 1775
Ephraim Meriam & Ruth Gleason, both of Country
  Gore, April 10, 1775
Joseph Read & Hannah Learned, May 7, 1775

William Hudson, Jr., & Ruth Shumway, June 28, 1775
John Hart of Leicester & Sarah Singletarry, Oct. 26, 1775
John Barton & Persis Eddy, April 3, 1776
Curtis Dixon & Lydia Wight of the Gore, April 4, 1776
Deacon Edward Davis of Dudley & widow Abi-
 gail Watson, April 22, 1776
Asa Learned & Mary Child, May 7, 1776
Frost Rockwood & Sarah Pratt, May 16, 1776
Thomas Pratt & Lydia Phillips, May 28, 1776
Elihu Thurston & Deborah Stevens of Worcester,
 Aug. 14, 1776
Obadiah Allen & Mehitable Amidown, Sept. 19, 1776
Smith Johnson & widow Abigail Amidown, Nov. 5, 1776
Ambrose Stone & Mercy Hovey, Dec. 12, 1776
Israel Stone & Tryphena Boyden of Worcester, July 4, 1776
David Stone & Sarah Treadwell of Sutton, July 25, 1776
Joshua Rawson of Upton & Rebecca Griffeth, Oct. 23, 1776
William Talle & Jemima Eddy, both of Leicester,
 Aug. 20, 1776
Edward Gros & Joanna Nichols, Nov. 15, 1774
John Harwood, Jr., & Lydia Sibley, both of Sutton,
 Aug. 28, 1777
Ebenezer Farr of Chesterfield & Mary Titus of
 Douglass, Feb. 6, 1777
Timothy Sparhawk & Mary Conant, Feb. 4, 1778
Moses Rowel of Oxford & Elizabeth Baker of Charlton,
 March 19, 1778
Robert Fitts, Jr., & Phebe Patch, Aug. 25, 1778
Jedidiah Barton & Sarah Miller, Oct. 7, 1778
Jeremiah Davis & Hannah Davis, Nov. 19, 1778
Benjamin Upham of Dudley & Hepzibah Learned,
 Nov. 26, 1778
William Smith & Esther Delaney of Ward, Dec. 30, 1778
Samuel Carriel of Sutton & Elizabeth Shumway,
 Dec. 31, 1778
David Dana Town & Elizabeth Breed of Sutton,
 Dec. 31, 1778
Nathan Taft of Northbridge & Judith Sibley of
 Sutton, Oct. 1, 1778

Daniel Carriel & Betty Gould, both of Sutton, Dec. 3, 1778
Daniel Sibley & Phebe Prince, both of Sutton, April 14, 1779
Jonas Collar & Elizabeth Parsons of Spencer, March 4, 1779
Sampson Marven & Ruth Miriam, March 16, 1779
Moses Nelson & Sarah Hovey, Aug. 19, 1779
Jesse Merriam & Deborah Pratt, Nov. 3, 1779
Joseph Rockwood & Martha Shumway, Nov. 11, 1779
John Pratt & Anna Davis, Dec. 9, 1779
Tarrant Sibley & Hannah Putnam, April 22, 1779
Samuel Webster of Upton & Lucy Warren of Dudley,
May 24, 1779
Benjamin Cogswell of Uxbridge, now of Grafton,
& Susanna Holton of Sutton, Aug. 29, 1779
Henry Harback & Sarah Prince, both of Sutton,
July 20, 1780
Stephen Ward & Patience Cook, both of Charlton,
Nov. 4, 1780
Lieut. David Putnam, Jr., & Martha Waters, both
of Sutton, Jan. 15, 1781
Moses Twiss of Charlton & Sarah Nichols, Jan. 18, 1781
Joseph Davis, Jr., & Jemima Davis, March 28, 1780
Caleb Fitts of Dudley & Rachel Patch, Aug. 24, 1780
Nathaniel Carriel of Killingly & Mary Ballard,
March 15, 1781
Jonathan Harris & Huldah Town, June 14, 1781
Phinehas Kimball of Killingly & Rebeccah Marven,
Oct. 9, 1781
William Smith & Rachel Lewis, Oct. 11, 1781
Jonathan Corbin of Woodstock & Abigail Wight
of Gore, Dec. 24, 1781
Daniel Rawson & Jemima Utter (?), both of Gore,
Jan. 27, 1782
Ebenezer Brown & Bathsheba Conant, both of
Charlton, Feb. 11, 1782
George Pike & Mary Sever, both of Charlton, Feb. 27, 1782
Samuel Brown and Hannah Marsh, both of Sutton,
Jan. 2, 1782
Elijah McIntire & Hannah Wilson, both of Charlton,
June 6, 1782

Josiah Wakefield & Molly Putnam, both of Sutton,
                                    Dec. 31, 1782
Elisha Blandin & Molly Wakefield,   June 3, 1783
Thomas Barrett of Woodstock & Elizabeth Smith
     of South Gore,   Feb. 13, 1782
Levi Wight, Jr., & Sarah Corbin, both of South Gore,
                                    Oct. 24, 1782
Jonathan Bixby of Dudley & widow Kezia Allen
     of So. Gore,   June 3, 1784
Eleazer Allen & Margaret Harwood, both of Sutton,
                                    Jan. 21, 1784
Jonathan Harwood & Apphya Woodbury, both of
     Sutton,   March 23, 1784
David Coburn of Woodstock & Experience Wyman,
                                    March 31, 1784
Simeon Fuller & Mary Harwood of Sutton,   May 10, 1784
Aaron Carriel & Sally Woodbury, both of Sutton,
                                    May 11, 1784

CHARLTON.

Nov. 21, 1754, part of Oxford established as the district of Charlton. Prov. Laws, Vol. III, p. 781. A town Aug. 23, 1775. First (Congregational) Church organized 1761. Officiating clergyman mentioned: Rev. Caleb Curtis.

Reuben Comings & Mary Parker,   Dec. 2, 1762
John Wymon of Oxford & Anna Town,   Dec. 9, 1762
David Allen of Sturbridge & Experience Streeter,
                                    March 10, 1763
Josiah Blanchard & Elizabeth Hobbs,   April 7, 1763
William White & Mary Dressor,   April 7, 1763
Elisha Hamilton of Brookfield & Mary Smith, March 3, 1763
Nathaniel Mcintier & Debora Mcintier,   April 21, 1763
Ebenezer Lamson & Ruth Phillips,   April 28, 1763
Abijah Lamb & Betty Wheelock,   Aug. 24, 1763
David Twiss & Esther Town,   Oct. 20, 1763
Lemuel Lyon & Hannah Dresser,   Nov. 10, 1763
Josiah Robinson & Sarah Twiss,   Nov. 17, 1763
Asa Wheelock & Rachel Drury,   Dec. 8, 1763

Benjamin Merrit & Elizabeth Smith,	April 19, 1764
Thomas Holland & Hannah Thompson,	Feb. 3, 1764
Joseph Putney & Mary Wakefield,	May 8, 1764
Jonathan Clemons & Hannah Woodard,	Nov. 29, 1764
Benjamin Allton & Susanna Blood,	June 6, 1765
Robert Manning & Abigaill Eustis,	July 11, 1765
Ebenezer Shumway & Comfort White,	Sept. 24, 1765
Amosa Turner & Experience Streeter,	Feb. 27, 1766
Peter Delvey & Lucy Town,	July 10, 1766
Levi Eddy & Sarah Smith,	Sept. 24, 1766
Daniel Elexander & Mehitable McIntire,	Oct. 10, 1766
Lenex Tituss & Rosanna Mory,	Nov. 25, 1766
Lemuel Comes & Rachel Stevens,	Nov. 27, 1766
David Thayer & Joanna Wild,	Feb. 5, 1797
Joseph Streeter & Hannah Dennes,	Feb. 19, 1767
Ebenezer Twist & —— Clemons,	June 5, 1767
Samuel Eustis & Sarah Eustis,	Oct. 14, 1767
Stephen Weld & Elizabeth Thayer,	Oct. 21, 1767
David Hammond & Delight Marit,	Nov. 19, 1767
Richard Blood, Jr., & Mary Thomson,	Nov. 26, 1767
Danield Wild, Jr., & Hannah Swmerton (?),	Jan. 14, 1768
Philip Corban & Mary How,	June 9, 1768
Isaac Taylor & Phebe McIntire,	June 9, 1768
Richard Coburn & Sarah Edwards,	June 16, 1768
Benjamin Wheelock & Elizabeth Thompson,	June 30, 1768
Jonathan Tucker, Jr., & Mary Humphrey,	Sept. 29, 1768
Joseph Thomson & Sarah Wheelock,	Oct. 13, 1768
Nathan McIntire, Jr., & Jemima Ames,	Nov. 25, 1768
Samuel Robinson & Mary Hammond,	Dec. 1, 1768
Jesse McIntire & Martha Lamb,	Dec. 13, 1768
Ebenezer Town & Huldah Wheelock,	Dec. 15, 1768
Jonas Ward & Persis Stow,	March 16, 1769
Samuel Pike & Abigail D——miss (?),	April 4, 1769
Benjamin Goddard of Shrewsbury & Hannah Williams,	Nov. 14, 1769
Jacob Comens & Phebe Converse,	Sept. 14, 1769
Nathan Taylor & Huldah Curtis,	Sept. 14, 1769
Job Marit & Hannah Thomson,	Oct. 18, 1769
Thomas Hall & Anne Milens,	Oct. 26, 1769

10

Nehemiah Stone & Martha Daggot,	Nov. 16, 1769
Asa Town & Abigail Morey,	Nov. 28, 1769
Elisha Thomson & Abigail Dresser,	Jan. 25, 1770
Thomas Fenton & Charity Dennis,	Dec. 28, 1769
William Polley & Serviah Mower,	March 29, 1770
Zedikiah Drury & Mary Wheelock,	April 17, 1770
Peter Wheelock & Olive Wheelock,	May 24, 1770
Enoch Bigelow & Betty Clemons,	Aug. 28, 1770
Clement Coborn & Dorothy Edwards,	Dec. 26, 1770
Jonas Eddy & Lucy Oak,	Dec. 26, 1770
Ebenezer Harwood & Rebecca Amesbury,	Jan. 3, 1771
Asa Dressier & Abigail Wheelock,	Jan. 10, 1771
Abner Millen & Mary Marith,	May 15, 1771
Isaac Southgate & Eunice White,	June 20, 1771
Joseph Whitemore & Mary Mellen,	Sept. 5, 1771
Stephen Twiss & Mary Needham,	Sept., 1771
Joshua Woodward & Sarah Clemons,	Oct. 24, 1771
John Streeter & Anna Robinson,	Dec. 12, 1771
Eleazer Wheelock & Betty Woodward,	Dec. 12, 1771
Demenicus Davidson & Hannah Twiss,	Aug. 13, 1772
Levi Ward & Hannah Maritt,	Sept. 3, 1772
Elijah Blood & Annis Ward,	Oct. 29, 1772
Jethniel Rich & Elizabeth Davidson,	Nov. 25, 1772
Seth Jones & Mary Dogget,	Feb. 23, 1773
Thomas Lessure & Anna Hall,	April 20, 1773
John Thomson, Jr., & Catherine Town,	July 20, 1773
Jonathan Stow & Mary Twiss,	Aug. 19, 1774
John Dagget & Sarah Jones,	Oct. 19, 1773
Edward Drury & Experience Goodell,	Oct. 20, 1773
Josiah Blanchard & Mary Lamb,	Jan. 26, 1774
Gardner McIntier & Meriam McIntier,	April 9, 1778
John Birchard of Granby & Abigail Curtis,	Jan. 28, 1779
Nathaniel Burden of Sutton & Susanna Sanders,	
	March 4, 1779
Benjamin Green of Spencer & Mary Streeter,	
	March 16, 1779
Levi Hicks of Glocester & Hannah Smith,	Oct. 28, 1779
Stephen Goodell & Margaret Evard,	May 7, 1778
Aaron Maret & Prudence Coock,	June 29, 1778

Daniel Convers & Mary Drury,	Sept. 5, 1778
Thomas Stephens & Esther Tucker,	Oct. 13, 1778
Joseph Woodworth & Elizabeth Morey,	Oct. 29, 1778
Nathaniel Green & Esther Bun,	Nov. 13, 1778
John Edwards & Sabra Curtis,	Dec. 30, 1778
Moses Axdel & Tamer Curtis,	March 30, 1779
David Brown & Sarah Duggen,	May 20, 1779
Samuel Streeter & Bathsheba Barton,	July 8, 1779
Paul Wheelock & Beulah Johnson,	Sept. 30, 1779
Jonathan Weld & Ruth Taft,	Dec. 9, 1779
Seth Tucker & Louis Learned,	Dec. 17, 1779
David Dresser & Serviah Polly,	Jan. 13, 1780
Richard Dresser, Jr., & Huldah Taylor,	April 13, 1780
David Daggett & Azubah Wheelock,	June 30, 1774
Elijah Leavens & Rachel Blood,	June 16, 1774
Moses Morey & Persis Baldwin,	Aug. 25, 1774
Eleazer Gleason & Esther Fesley (?),	Dec. 8, 1774
David Powers & Miriam Ward,	Dec. 15, 1774
Joseph Capen Baker & Susanna Foskett,	June 15, 1774
George Needham & Lucy Edward,	Dec. 20, 1774
Isaac Putney & Dorcas McIntire,	March 30, 1775
Nathaniel Blood & Bathsheba Upham,	May 4, 1775
John Dagget & Mary Stephens,	Aug. 22, 1775
John Fitts & Rebecca Dresser,	Oct. 12, 1775
John Stephens & Jerusha Nichols,	Nov. 23, 1775
Abijah Conant & Bathsheba Nickols,	Nov. 29, 1775
Daniel Duggan & Sarah Leath,	Jan. 30, 1776
Elijah Ward & Rachel Nichols,	April 2, 1776
David Rich & Polly Edwards,	May 2, 1776
Capt. Jonathan Tucker & Lucy Livermore,	June 18, 1776
Abijah Clemons & Elizabeth McIntire,	June 18, 1776
Isaiah Blood, Jr., & Martha Upham,	June 27, 1776
Edward Wheelock & Martha Dagget,	July 4, 1776
Caleb McIntire & Elizabeth Herwood,	July 11, 1776
Israil Holton & Isabel Town,	July 23, 1776
William Stodard & Ruth Needham,	Sept. 5, 1776
Reuben Moor & Else Nichols,	Oct. 17, 1776
Ephraim McIntire & Mary Edwards,	June 24, 1777
Jonathan McIntire & Joanna Wiman,	July 10, 1777

Caleb Blood & Sarah Hill of Spencer,	Sept. 2, 1777
David Goodell & Mary Baker,	Oct. 9, 1777
Joseph Grigs of Sturbridge & Presiler Baker,	
	Nov. 25, 1777
Joseph Chamberlain & Esther Twiss,	Feb. 9, 1778
Thomas Edwards & Susanna Town,	March 5, 1782
Eli Wheelock & Hannah Streeter,	March 14, 1782
Jonathan Clemons & Mary Hopkin,	March 14, 1782
Elisha Ward & Thankful Cook,	April 15, 1782
Rufus Bacon & Eleanor Edward,	April 17, 1782
Daniel Bacon, Jr., & Anna Fay,	May 16, 1782
Samuel Green & Hannah Kenny, both of Leicester,	
	April 4, 1779
Ithamar Smith & Sarah Wheeler, both of Grafton,	
	Oct. 7, 1779
Alpheus Coburn & Joanna Edwards,	May 27, 1780
Joseph Blood & Mary Johnson,	May 27, 1780
Eliakim Chamberlain & Anna Stow,	June 18, 1780
Abner Wheelock & Elizabeth Blanchard,	March 26, 1780
Elias Twiss & Lydia Needham,	June 30, 1780
Abel Wheelock of Spencer & Sarah Wyman,	
	Dec. 19, 1780
Aaron Tucker & Tamenson Stacey,	Dec. 13, 1781
Benjamin Edwards & Marcy Wells,	Dec. 12, 1781
Elijah Thompson & Damaris Wheeler,	March 20, 1781
Bennona Mercy & Huldah Brown,	Jan. 25, 1781
Jonathan Mower, Jr., & Sarah Stephens,	June 17, 1781
John Mower & Elizabeth Edwards,	May 29, 1782
James Lamb, Jr., & Abigail Moore,	May 29, 1782
John Rich & Susannah Putney,	May 29, 1782
Benjamin Dennis, Jr., & Esther Alexander,	May 29, 1782
Jonathan Blanden & Submit Cook, both of Oxford,	
	Feb. 6, 1783
William Sleeman & Huldah Kinney,	Oct. 9, 1783
David Fisk of Sturbridge & Elenner Jones,	Nov. 13, 1783
Nehemiah Stone, Jr., & Mrs. Lucy Bartlett,	Jan. 15, 1783
Dr. Abel Waters & Mrs. Sarah Davis,	Jan. 15, 1783
Moses Hammond & Mrs. Dorothy Dresser,	April 2, 1783
Ebenezer Stone & Mrs. Esther Lamb,	April 15, 1783

Samuel Lamb, the 3d, & Mrs. Assenah Marsh of
    Brookfield,   April 15, 1783
James Dresser & Mrs. Irena Hewin,   May 7, 1783
Ezra McIntier, Jr., & Mrs. Mary Hatfield,   May 8, 1783
Ebenezer Wellington & Mrs. Rebecca Leavens,

                                 May 29, 1783
Thomas Wedge, Jr., of Brookfield & Mrs. Margaret
    Ryan,   June 5, 1783
Jeremiah Barton of Leicester & Mrs. Susannah
    Dennis,   Oct. 14, 1783
Ebenezer Twiss, Jr., & Mrs. Mary Nichols of Ox-
    ford,   Nov. 19, 1783
Josiah Eddy & Mrs. Sarah Dennis,   Jan. 2, 1784
Abijah Oakes & Mrs. Hannah Clemons,   Jan. 22, 1784
John Fargue, a Frenchman, & Mrs. Elizabeth Chubb,

                                 Jan. 22, 1784
Joseph Chubb & Mrs. Mary Freeman,   Feb. 10, 1784
Jonathan Shumway of Belchertown & Mrs. Dorothy
    Wyman,   March 3, 1784
Robart Edwards & Mrs. Mehitabel Clemons,   April 7, 1784
Aaron Hammond & Mrs. Sarah Bartlett,   May 25, 1784
Nathaniel Wellington & Mrs. Pegge Taft,   June 15, 1784
William O'brine & Mrs. Anna Albee,   June 17, 1784
Thomas Dyer & Mrs. Sibbel Marcy,   July 8, 1784
Solomon Laflin & Mrs. Abijah Woodard,   July 8, 1784
Ripley Merrill & Susannah Gleason,   Nov. 13, 1783
Thomas Wiseman & Abigeal McIntire,   Dec. 11, 1783
Ebenezer Slaton & Rebeckah Hamilton of Brookfield,

                                 Jan. 22, 1784
Peter Wheelock & Lydia Green,   Jan. 22, 1784
Jonathan Harwood & Mrs. Damaris Clemons, Aug. 18, 1784
Isaiah McIntier & Deborah McIntier,   April 14, 1784
Seth Wheelock & Elizabeth Weld,   April 8, 1784
Israel Morey & Sarah Follett,   April 13, 1785
Adams Wheelock & Lucy Lamb,   April 28, 1785

RUTLAND.

[CONTINUED FROM P. 24.]

Joel Pollard & Mary Maynard,	March 8, 1770
Abraham Wheeler & Jemima Walker,	Aug. 22, 1770
Steven Stone & Marcy Muroe (?),	Aug. 30, 1770
Eli Clark & Lois Stone,	Aug. 30, 1770
Joseph Temple of Dummenston & Lois Hubbard,	
	Dec. 4, 1770
David Stoel of Guilford & Mary Larrabee,	Dec. 6, 1770
Samuel Dunkan, Jr., & Betty Nurse,	Dec. 11, 1770
Eliphalet White & Dinah McIntyre,	Feb. 28, 1771
Elijah Stone & Eunice Savage,	April 18, 1771
Benjamin Hoit of Hubbardston & widow Stevens,	
	April 21, 1771
Jonah Smith of Shrewsbury & Elizabeth Browning,	
	Oct. 15, 1771
Phillip Boyns & Mary McClanathan,	March 6, 1772
William Smith, Jr., & Elizabeth Ames,	Sept. 1, 1772
Thomas Elder of Murryfield & Margaret Moor,	
	Nov. 26, 1772
Joseph Knap of Spencer & Martha McClanathan,	
	Dec. 1, 1772
Benjamin Nurse & Marcy Stevens,	Dec. 14, 1772
Eben Lee of Conway & Bethiah Jenkins,	Jan. 11, 1770
Jonas Leonard of Warwick & Sarah Mason,	
	Feb. 22, 1770
Jonathan Gates & Catey Morse,	May 4, 1770
Elijah Gregory & Jane Carruth,	June 7, 1770
Jonas Carruth of Petersham & Mary Carruth,	
	June 14, 1770
James Rice & Susanna Cutting,	Sept. 25, 1770
Benjamin Holden & Abigail Bacon,	Nov. 1, 1770
Joseph Wilson of Petersham & Hannah Stone,	
	Dec. 6, 1770

Ebenezer Bodfish of Barnstable & Hannah Child,

Dec. 27, 1770

Timothy Jenkins & Mary Cunningham,	Jan. 24, 1771
Seth Clark of Keen & Meriam Metcalf,	May 29, 1771
Abijah Jenison & Mary Robinson,	Dec. 5, 1771

Amos Parker of Hubbardston & Lucy Robinson,

Jan. 2, 1772

Daniel Buxton & Lucy Allen,	Jan 2, 1772
Samuel Carruth & Mary Hamilton,	Jan. 30, 1772

James Laughton of Hardwicke & —— Fuller,

June 17, 1772

Nathaniel Smith & Sarah Jennison,	March 11, 1772
Abel Davis & Sarah Mendall,	June 18, 1772
Isaac Balcom & Ruth Bacon,	July 9, 1772
Ezra Jones, Jr., & Susanna Stone,	Oct. 15, 1772
Lemuel Osgood & Lydia Merryfield,	Nov. 12, 1772
James Holden & Hannah Bacon,	Nov. 12, 1772
Thomas Richardson & Lois Perry,	Dec. 17, 1772
Jonathan Davis & Hannah Dogget,	Dec. 17, 1772
William Elder of Wor. & Sara Crawford,	Dec. 30, 1772
Enoch Curtis & Sarah Felton,	Jan. 7, 1772
Jeduthan Stone & Elizabeth How of Paxton,	Jan. 11, 1773
Caleb Harrington & Anna Laughton,	Jan. 12, 1773
Charles Man & Elizabeth McCobb,	Jan. 24, 1773
Abijah Perry & Grace Locke,	March 18, 1773
John Partridge & Phebe Boyden,	Oct. 7, 1773
Hampton & Kate, (blacks) of Capt. E. Jones,	Nov. 4, 1772
John Caldwell & Sarah Caldwell,	Dec. 16, 1773
Hopstill Jenison & Relief Fletcher,	Dec. 16, 1773

Jonathan Hemingway & Martha Resign Wilder of
 Petersham,   April 7, 1774

Thomas Oliver & Hannah Northgate (free blacks),

May 15, 1774

Noah Leonard & Bethiah Witherel,   May 27, 1772

Nimrod Quameus (negro) & Elizabeth Harris (Indian),   May 17, 1774

Phinehas Perry & (Mrs.) Esther Gates,	May 17, 1774
Barnaba Sears & Rachel Bullard,	May 17, 1774
Micah Boyden & (Mrs.) Phebe Sears,	May 17, 1774

William Choate & (Mrs.) Susanna Church,   May 17, 1774
Elijah Robinson & Sarah Blake,   May 17, 1774
Stephen Johnson of Hardwick & Abigail Rice,
                                             May 31, 1774
Thaddeus Ames & Mercy Rice,   June 2, 1774
John Wit & Priscilla Moxtor,   June 9, 1774
John Chamberlain & Sarah Winslow,   June 16, 1774
Nathan Swift of Rut. District & Mary Willis of
    Hardwick,   Sept 8, 1774
Thomas Rice & Sarah Nurse,   Nov. 17, 1774

√ SUTTON.

[CONTINUED FROM P. 104.]

Jonathan Hale & Silence Goddard,   Nov. 22, 1769
Jonathan Kidder & Susannah Dwinel (?) (or Durnel ?),
                                              Jan. 30, 1770
Jonathan Gould & Hannah Singletary,   Jan. 30, 1770
James Leland, Jr., of Grafton & Anne Gale,   Feb. 22, 1770
Capt. Palmer Goulding & Mrs. Rebekah Richardson,
    both of Worcester,   Oct. 31, 1770
Thomas Eaton of Reading & Abigail Bancroft of
    Wor.,   Oct. 24, 1770
Joseph Blanchard, Jr., & Mehetable Putnam,   April 10, 1770
Lot Marsh & Abigail Blanchard,   July 5, 1770
Richard Davenport & Anne Buxton,   July 5, 1770
John Woodbury & Mary Chase,   Oct. 17, 1770
Jonathan Robertson & Mary Wood,   Oct. 24, 1770
Moses Park & Hannah Barton,   Oct. 29, 1770
Moses Sibley & Elizabeth Rich,   April 19, 1770
Jonas Jackson & Lucy Cole,   Dec. 5, 1770
David Putnam & Elisabeth Woodbury,   April 12, 1770
Richard Dodge, Jr., & Lois Town,   July 19, 1770
John Safford & Ruth Hayden, both of Worcester,
                                              Dec. 6, 1770
John Kitts & Rebekah Stockwell,   Jan. 15, 1771

John Kidder & Sarah Dodge,	Feb. 25, 1771
Reuben Barton & Olive Jennison,	June 1, 1770
Reuben Eaton & Abigail Lovell,	Dec. 6, 1770
Samuel Melody of Guilford & Sarah Gale,	Dec. 6, 1770
John Waters & Phebe Goodale,	May 28, 1771
Levi Wesson & Olive Locke,	July 9, 1771
Stephen Harwood & Abigail Streater,	Dec. 10, 1770
Thomas Holman, Jr., & Lydia Bates,	Oct. 17, 1771
Ebenezer Freeman & Mary Frazier of Providence,	Nov. 13, 1771
Francis Dudley & Elizabeth Whipple,	May 21, 1771
Jonathan Elliot, Jr., & Sarah Chase of Uxbridge,	Oct. 17, 1771
Aaron Sibley & Lucy Newell,	Jan. 9, 1772
Isaac Dodge, Jr., & Abigail Morss,	March 19, 1771
John Fuller & Susanna Putnam,	March 26, 1771
Absolom Forbes & Martha Hall,	July 25, 1771
Benjamin Hall & Elizabeth Mossley,	Aug. 22, 1771
Jesse Cummings & Mary Fitts,	Aug. 29, 1771
Stephen Rice & Mary Batchellor,	Sept. 18, 1771
Benjamin Nichols & Lucy Fitts,	Feb. 28, 1772
Ebenezer Sibley & Mary Chase,	Oct. 24, 1771
Samuel Small & Molley Waters,	Jan. 2, 1772
David Sprague of Killingly & Rebecca Wadsworth,	Jan. 2, 1772
Joseph Allen, Jr., of Hardwick & Greely Singletary,	Jan. 15, 1772
Simon Tenney & Sarah Trask,	Jan. 23, 1772
John Bartlett & Rebecca Chase,	Jan. 23, 1772
Jotham Stearns & Mary Roberts,	May 27, 1772
John Davidson & Anna Gould,	Jan. 16, 1772
Isaac Chase, Jr., & Betty Yeates,	Oct. 1, 1772
Daniel Buchnam & Phebe Nichols,	July 1, 1771
Samuel Meriman, Jr., of Northfield & Eunice Severy,	June 11, 1772
Eleazer Stockwell & Ruth Algar, both of Oxford,	Nov. 3, 1772
James Willard of Worcester & Abigail Hayward,	Jan. 5, 1773

Samuel Woodward & Eunice Biglow,	Sept. 8, 1772
Joshua Badger & Ruth Waite,	Sept. 29, 1772
Abijah Tainter & Sarah Small,	Dec. 3, 1772
Abraham Waters & Mehetable Waters,	Dec. 3, 1772
John Waite, Jr., of Worcester & Rachel Case,	Dec. 24, 1772
Samuel Trask, Jr., & Ruth Tenney,	Jan. 21, 1773
Samuel Titus & Martha Steans,	May 14, 1772
Henry King, Jr., & Prudence Dudley,	June 18, 1772
Ezekiel Goldthwait & Anna Adams,	Dec. 3, 1772
Adam Brown, Jr., of Ipswich & Priscilla Putnam,	
	Dec. 3, 1772
Arthur Dagget, Jr., & Lucy Cutler,	Dec. 10, 1772
Solomon Parsons, Jr., of Glocester & Prudence Dodge,	
	Dec. 18, 1772
Isaiah Wakefield & Eunice Burdon,	Dec. 24, 1772
Nathaniel Carriel & Bridget Prime,	Dec. 29, 1772
Isaac Hamond of Swanzey, N. H., & Mehitable Prime,	
	Feb. 16, 1773
Elijah Davis of Oxford & Hannah Rich,	Oct. 29, 1772
Abraham Brown of Salem & Elizabeth Putnam,	
	March 2, 1773
Hezekiah Hayden & Lois Hayden,	March 4, 1773
Daniel Hayden & Submit Flagg, both of Grafton,	
	June 9, 1773
Benjamin Carlton & Elizabeth Smith,	June 7, 1773
Samuel Paine of Lebanon, N. H., & Lucy Hall,	Sept. 6, 1773
John Nelson & Elizabeth Kidder,	Oct. 13, 1773
William Chase & Molley Elliot,	Oct. 14, 1773
Joseph Bullen, Jr., & Hannah Morse,	Feb. 11, 1773
Isaac Platts, Jr., of Bradford & Rachel Chase,	Sept. 21, 1773
Jonathan Willard of Worcester & Hannah Putnam,	
	Nov. 25, 1773
Andrus Waters & Bettey Goodale,	Nov. 25, 1773
David Dudley, Jr., & Lois Whitney,	Dec. 16, 1773
David Grover & Mary Kenney,	Feb. 2, 1774
Thomas Lovell, Jr., & Hannah Gould,	Feb. 9, 1774
John Marble & Lucretia Richardson,	Feb. 24, 1774
Moses Bancroft, Jr., & Sarah Taylor,	Feb. 24, 1774
James Allen of Westboro & Phebe Tenny,	April 21, 1774

Jedidiah Barton & Lydia Peirce,   March 23, 1774
Daniel Bucknam & Abigail Pratt,   April 19, 1774
David Chase & Judith Holman,   April 18, 1774
James Merriam of Country Gore & Eunice Lovel,
                                                    May 25, 1774
Anthony Sigourney & Ruth Chase,   June 23, 1774
Jacob Chase & Mary Ingerson,   March 17, 1774
Moody Moorss, Jr., & Abigail Leland,   March 31, 1774
Isaac Gleason & Abigail Dudley,   April 12, 1774
Nathaniel Fry Morss & Hannah Gibbs,   May 18, 1774
Benjamin Stiles & Elizabeth Cutler,   May 22, 1774
Micah Putnam & Anna Carriel,   May 26, 1774
Free Cummings & Ruth Stockwell,   June 16, 1774
Jonathan Rich & Mehetable Dagget,   July 7, 1774
Alpheus Marble & Anna Dudley,   Dec. 15, 1774
Abraham Batchellor, Jr., & Rebecca Dwight,   Dec. 28, 1774
Enos Buxton, Jr., & Mary Dodge,   Jan. 3, 1775
Gideon Woodbury & Abigail Burbank,   Jan. 10, 1775
David Stockwell of Croyden, N. H., & Abial Giles,
                                                    Jan. 23, 1775
Timothy Leland & Mary Sibley,   Feb. 9, 1775
Samuel Harwood & Lydia Kenney,   Jan. 5, 1775
Joseph Waters & Elizabeth Dwight,   Feb. 28, 1776
Rev. Daniel Grosvenor of Grafton & Mrs. Deborah
    Hall,   May 9, 1776
Joshua Willard of Grafton & Phebe Porter,   June 13, 1776
David Putnam, Jr., & Phebe Woodbury,   July 3, 1776
John Couse & Rebecca Sibley,   July 11, 1776
Caleb Putnam & Judith Sibley,   Aug. 21, 1776
Stephen Marble & Betty Putnam,   Nov. 14, 1776
Free Cumming & Alice Gould,   Nov. 14, 1776
John Hall & Dolly Ward,   Jan. 2, 1777
Matthew Lackey & Dorcas Woodbury,   Jan. 28, 1777
Aaron Adams & Sarah Dodge,   Jan. 29, 1777
John Meriam of Concord & Martha Putnam,   Feb. 6, 1777
Samuel Hardy & Judith Garfield,   March 14, 1776
Charles Richardson, Jr., & Susannah Taylor, March 28, 1776
Samuel Eaton & Joanna Waite,   April 11, 1776
Israel Waters of Charlton & Elizabeth Bartlet, June 27, 1776

Abel Rowe & Beulah Potter of Upton,	July 8, 1776
Josiah Stiles & Lydia Gale,	July 11, 1776
Jonathan Gould, Jr., & Lydia Jennison,	July 11, 1776
Joshua Waite & Mary Burnap,	Sept. 19, 1776
Ezra Lovell & Mary Jennison,	Sept. 24, 1776
Jacob Snow, Jr., & Betty Marble,	Dec. 18, 1776
Andrew Dodge of Dudley & Jane Carriel,	May 8, 1777
Jonathan Cutler of Oxford & Betty Lillie,	May 8, 1777
Jotham Meriam of Warwick & Sarah Burnap,	July 8, 1777
Moses Hovey & Phebe Jenney,	Aug. 14, 1777
Stephen Fuller & Lydia Putnam,	Nov. 7, 1777
John Bancroft & Anna Waters,	Dec. 1, 1777
John Mellody & Sarah Eastey,	Jan. 20, 1778
Daniel Gould & Mary Gould,	Jan. 22, 1778
Elijah Sibley & Abigail Stone,	Feb. 9, 1778
Daniel Jennison of Oxford & Molly Putnam,	Jan. 29, 1778
Thomas Harbarch & Abigail Gould,	July 8, 1777
Deacon Thomas Holman & Mary Palmer of Mendon,	
	Feb. 4, 1778
John Childs & Susanna Gould,	March 12, 1778
Daniel Fitts & Chloe White,	April 9, 1778
Benjamin Carter, Jr., & Mary Gale,	March 13, 1777
William Snow & Judith Holman,	Oct. 21, 1777
Timothy Morse of Holden & Hannah Mixer,	Nov. 5, 1777
Joshua Carter & Abigail Nickolas,	Nov. 19, 1777
David Prina Chase & Sarah Greenwood,	Dec. 2, 1777
Jonathan Stone & Chloe Hazeltine,	Dec. 23, 1777
Timothy Sibley, Jr., & Mary Barstow,	Nov. 5, 1778
John Shepard Delyrample of Northbridge & Hannah	
Elliot,	Dec. 16, 1778
Eli Putnam of Western & Elizabeth Harback,	
	March 12, 1778
Ebenezer Waters & Susanna Thurston,	May 5, 1778
Samuel Wallis & Sarah Town,	May 7, 1778
Elias Parkman of Braintree & Apphia Putnam,	
	May 25, 1778
Archelaus Dwinel & Olive Hall,	May 26, 1778
Artemas How of Braintree & Ruth Putnam,	July 4, 1778
Stephen Holman & Mary Jenny (or Tenny),	July 30, 1778

Jacob Winslow & Elizabeth Knap, both of North-
    bridge,   Sept. 28, 1778

John Sellen, Jr., of Hardwick & Martha Mosely,
                                         Nov. 26, 1778

Samuel Sibley, Jr., & Sarah Leland,   Dec. 10, 1778
Nehemiah Chase & Oashti (?) Batchellor,   Dec. 17, 1778
Nathaniel Chenney & Mary Harris,   Dec. 31, 1778
Benjamin Snow & Rebecca Gould,   Jan. 7, 1779
Thomas Green & Mary Jacobs,   Jan. 26, 1779
Daniel Tenny, Jr., & Martha Morss,   Jan. 29, 1779
Asa Dodge & Lydia Buxton,   Feb. 9, 1779
Samuel Pain Jones & Rachel Cole,   June 15, 1779
Ezra Mixer & Azubah Haven,   June 21, 1779
William Duncan of Oxford & Sarah Day,   June 22, 1779
Moses Putnam & Mary Allen,   June 24, 1779
Stephen Humes & Mary Hovey,   July 15, 1779
Noah Stockwell & Jemima Town,   July 15, 1779
Bezeleel Gleason & Sarah King,   Nov. 4, 1779
Simeon Blake of Uxbridge & Sarah Wheller, Nov. 4, 1779
Stephen Sibley & Sarah Collins,   Dec. 9, 1779
Josiah Prime of Swansey, N. H., & Rachel Carriel,
                                         Feb. 20, 1780
William (?) Sarvey (?) & Elizabeth Ward,   March 16, 1780
David Town & Elizabeth Southworth,   March 23, 1780
David Gibson of Fitchburg & Anna Barton, April 24, 1778
David Copland of Royalston & Martha Putnam,
                                         Sept. 1, 1778
Samuel Leland of Grafton & Abigail Gale,   Dec. 10, 1778
Moses Park & Lydia Bixby,   May 19, 1779
Elias Jenison & Battey Gage,   July 1, 1779
John Cook & Martha Pierce,   July 13, 1779
Eli Whitney of Westboro & Judith Hazeltine, July 15, 1779
Gershom Wait & Persis Chase,   Sept. 15, 1779
Abel Chase, Jr., & Hannah Bond,   Sept. 29, 1779
Abner Sibley & Mary Studley,   Dec. 9, 1779
Francis Adams & Abigail Taft,   April 11, 1780
Lazarus Le Baron & Mrs. Molly Chase, March 21, 1786 (?)

BROOKFIELD.

Oct. 15, 1673, Quobauge to be the town of "Brookfield" when forty or fifty families shall have settled there. Mass. Rec., Vol. IV, Part 2, p. 568. A town Nov. 12, 1718. First (Unitarian) Church organized 1754. Congregational, 1756. Baptist, at East Brookfield, 1818. Clergymen mentioned: Rev. Joseph Parsons, Rev. Eli Forbes, Rev. N. Fisk.

Samuel Leach & Rebecca Harris,	June 2, 1755
William Hencher & Ruth Wolcott,	Nov. 6, 1755
Moses Bragg & Sarah Barns,	Oct. 21, 1755
Ebenezer Wright & Thankful Goss,	Dec. 4, 1755
Ez^l (or Er^e) Woodbury & Mary Barns,	Aug. 19, 1755
John Gilburt & Priscilla Walker,	Dec. 23, 1755
Ithamer Wright & Elisabeth Walker,	Feb. 26, 1756
John Peesa (?) & Hannah Ranger,	April 3, 1756
David Bridges of Spencer & Betty Rice,	April 27, 1756
David Brewer & Elizabeth Smith,	May 8, 1763
Jediah Gilbert & Margaret Walter,	Sept. 19, 1764
Nathan Abbott & Mercy Banister,	Nov. 29, 1764
Thomas Brown & Judith Gilbert,	Feb. 7, 1765
James Smith & Sarah Burnet,	March 21, 1765
Beushy Tottle & Priscilla Partridge,	May 30, 1765
Samuel White & Thankful Gilbert,	Aug. 20, 1766
Abraham Patch & Anna Banister,	March 12, 1766
Benjamin Wait & Lois Gilbert,	Jan. 11, 1767
Moses Hamilton & Hannah Felton,	Jan. 15, 1767
John Watt & Martha Brewer,	Feb. 23, 1767
William Dean, Jr., & Lydia Kindrick,	Nov. 8, 1767
Benjamin Felton & Jenna Doroty (?),	Dec. 24, 1767
Abraham Cutler & Huldah Batchellor,	May 25, 1768
Jesse Gilbert & Lucy Barns,	June 30, 1768
James Cunningham & Mary Tuft,	June 9, 1768
Jonathan Bartlett & Anna Mixer,	Dec. 18, 1768
John Bacon, Jr., & widow Mary Olds,	March 25, 1763
Ezra Hamilton & Abigail Crosby,	June 30, 1763
Ephraim Green & Mary Rogers,	Dec. 8, 1763
Martin Ainsworth & Hannah Streeter,	Dec. 13, 1763

Nathan Richardson & Tamyson Upham,	Feb. 16, 1764
Ephraim Cooley & Lois (?) Walker,	Jan. 23, 1765
Jesse Abbott & Sarah Wakefield,	Dec. 4, 1765
Nathan Hobbs & Lydia Warren,	Feb. 26, 1766
Oliver Wilson of New Braintree & Susannah Walker,	
	Feb. 27, 1766
John Gilbert. 3d, & Sarah Rich,	March 6, 1766
Josiah Olds & Dorothy Smith,	May 25, 1766
Abraham Walker & Jemima Lovell,	July 17, 1766
Jonas Newton & Mary Woods,	Nov. 19, 1767
Obadiah Cooley, Jr., & Eunice Walker,	Nov. 26, 1767
Benjamin Aldrich & Dorothy Hamilton,	Nov. 27, 1767
Ebenezer Newell & Sarah Banister,	Dec. 3, 1767
Samuel Allen of Wrentham & Hannah Vorce,	Jan. 4, 1768
Jacob Shaw & Mary Hill,	May 6, 1767
William Ayres, 2d, & Rachel Barnes,	May 3, 1753
Obadiah Bartlet & Rebecca Adams,	May 9, 1753
Andrew Kimball & Rebecca Watson,	June 19, 1753
David Barnes & Elizabeth Paterson,	Dec. 11, 1753
Daniel Gilbert & Lucy Barnes,	June 6, 1754
Jer^h Gould & Hannah Bartlet,	June 5, 1755
Josiah Converse & Mercy Gilbert,	Nov. 18,1755
Thomas Barnes & Elisabeth Dodge,	Feb. 24, 1756
Rufus Dodge & Elisabeth Dodge,	Dec. 15, 1756
John Germings & Rachel Davis,	June 2, 1757
Josiah Holfield & Hulda Bacon,	July 4, 1757
Timothy Hill & Alice Hinds,	Sept. 26, 1757
Abner How & Sarah Lane,	Sept. 29, 1757
Nathan Gould & Martha Gilbert,	Oct. 31, 1757
Josiah Dwight, Esq., & Elisabeth Buckminster,	
	Nov. 2, 1757
Samuel Barnes & Mary Bartlet,	Dec. 19, 1757
Jonas Brewer & Mary Jennings,	April 20, 1758
Jonas Hayward & Martha Gilbert,	May 25, 1758
John Lamson & Mary Weeks,	Nov., 1758
Levi Walker & Sarah How,	March 12, 1759
Moses Ayers & Anna Goodale,	Dec. 6, 1759
Gideon Rugg & Dinah Hinds,	July 1, 1760
Jer^h Gould & Hannah Stevens,	Aug. 21, 1760

Joseph Lane & Rebecca Wit,	June 23, 1760
Asa Bacon & Rhoda Dunkan,	July 3, 1760
Jer[h] How & Lucy Gilbert,	Oct. 30, 1760
Jos. Wolcott & Rebecca Jones,	March 26, 1761
John Watson of Rutland & Thankful Watson,	
	Nov. 2, 1761
Joseph Gilbert & Hannah Gott,	Dec. 13, 1761
Joshua Draper & Sarah Wright,	May 28, 1762
James Brown & Mary Beacon,	Oct. 7, 1762
Isaac Green & Rachel How,	April 7, 1763
Dan. Wyman & Betty Stone,	Sept. 15, 1763
Jona. Barnes & Dorothy Stow,	Nov. 13, 1763
Reuben Gilbert & Persis Denny,	Dec. 8, 1763
Jesse Barnes & Patience Gilbert,	Dec. 8, 1763
Micajah Ayres & Mary Barnes,	March 14, 1769
Dr. Jos. Stow & Sarah Adams,	May 22, 1765
Rediat Stewart & Lucy Adams,	May 22, 1765
Daniel Bullard & Olive Partridge,	May 29, 1766
Solomon Goodale & Mary Hale,	Nov. 4, 1766
Robert Richmond & Martha Hind,	Nov. 4, 1766
S. Mixter & Betty Bigelow,	May 21, 1767
Henry Spring & Mercy Hamilton,	July 3, 1767
John Berry & Elizabeth Shindle,	Nov. 30, 1769
Phillip Gilbert & Martha Lambson,	Jan. 11, 1770
John Gilbert, 4th, & Bettey Manning,	Oct. 8, 1770
John Cutler & Dorothy Converse,	Nov. 8, 1770
Aaron Willard & Hannah Hamilton,	April 24, 1769
William Gilbert & Rachel Barns,	Dec. 21, 1769
Daniel Watson & Anna Saterley,	March 15, 1770
John Hamilton & Sarah Stone,	March 29, 1770
John Lynds & Sarah Warner,	April 19, 1770
Thomas Cowen & Hannah Rich,	July 23, 1770
Daniel Thomas & Marcy Bartlett,	Aug. 30, 1770
Isaac Robinson & Hannah Collins,	Aug. 30, 1770
Lemuel Gilbert & Ruth Gilbert,	Dec. 6, 1770
Asa Gilbert & Hannah Cutler,	Jan. 3, 1771
Emerson Woolcott & Mary Adams,	Dec. 2, 1767
Samuel Grimes & Mary Hinckley,	May 8, 1768
Abijah Bruce & Hannah Barns,	Aug. 3, 1768

Malacha Maynard & Elizabeth Hinds,	Sept. 6, 1768
John Stevens & Ruth Moor,	Oct. 27, 1768
Jacob McCombs & Anna Richmond,	Dec. 7, 1768
Joseph Belknap & Sarah Walker,	Feb. 15, 1769
Noah Hardy & Hannah Forbes,	March 7, 1769
Daniel Forbes & Sarah Hinckley,	March 22, 1769
William Bowman & Susanna Hinds,	May 23, 1769
Charles Knowlton & Eunice Packard,	Oct. 25, 1769
Eli Gould & Lydia Jennings,	Dec. 21, 1769
John Hamilton & Sarah Stone,	March 29, 1770
James Homer & Mary Stevens,	May 2, 1770
Aaron Putnam & Patience Potter,	June 6, 1770
Samuel Sever & Lucy Biglow,	June 7, 1770
Nathan Bartlett & Ester Child,	June 14, 1770
Thomas Moor, Jr., & Rebecca Harrington,	July 26, 1770
Roger Stevens & Mary Smith,	Dec. 6, 1770
Aaron Bowen & Mary How,	March 20, 1770
Obediah Rice, Jr., & Hannah Hill,	March 21, 1770
John Berry & Elizabeth Kendal,	Nov. 30, 1769
Phillips Gilbert & Martha Lamson,	Jan. 11, 1770
John Gilbert, 4th, & Bettey Manning,	Oct. 8, 1770
John Cutler & Dorothy Converse,	Nov. 8, 1770
Aaron Willard & Hannah Hamilton,	April 24, 1769
William Gilbert & Rachel Barns,	Dec. 21, 1769
Daniel Watson & Anna Saterly,	March 15, 1771
John Lynds & Sarah Warner,	April 19, 1771
Thomas Cowen & Hannah Rich,	July 23, 1771
Daniel Thomas & Marcy Bartlett,	Aug. 30, 1771
Isaac Robinson & Hannah Collins,	Aug. 30, 1771
Lemuel Gilbert & Ruth Gilbert,	Dec. 6, 1771
Asa Gilbert & Hannah Cutler,	Jan. 3, 1771
Emerson Woolcott & Mary Adams,	Dec. 2, 1767
Samuel Grimes & Mary Hinckley,	May 8, 1768
Abijah Bruce & Hannah Barns,	Aug. 3, 1768
Malacha Mainard & Elizabeth Hinds,	Sept. 6, 1768
John Stevans & Ruth Moor,	Oct. 27, 1768
Jacob McCombs & Anna Richmond,	Dec. 7, 1768
John Belnap & Sarah Walker,	Feb. 15, 1769
Noah Hardy & Hannah Forbes,	March 7, 1769

11

Daniel Forbes & Sarah Hincher (or Hinchen),

	March 22, 1769
William Bowman & Susanna Hinds,	May 23, 1769
Charles Knowlton & Eunice Packard,	Oct. 25, 1769
Eli Gould & Lydia Jenings,	Dec. 21, 1769
James Homes & Mary Stevens,	May 2, 1770
Aaron Putnam & Patience Potter,	June 6, 1770
Samuel Chevers & Lucy Biglow,	June 7, 1770
Nathan Bartlett & Esther Childs,	June 14, 1770
Thomas Moor, Jr., & Rebecca Herrington,	July 26, 1770
Roger Stevens & Mary Smith,	Dec. 6, 1770
Aaron Bowen & Mary Howe,	March 20, 1771
Obediah Rice & Hannah Hill,	March 21, 1771
Jason Hamilton & Lydia Hill,	June 27, 1771
Jude Hamilton & Sarah Hoyt,	Oct. 31, 1771
Daniel Brown & Darius (?) Barns,	July 10, 1771
Samuel Palmer & Sarah White,	Sept. 24, 1771
Aaron Barns & Elizabeth Gilbert,	Oct. 3, 1771
Asa Barns & Persis Ross,	Dec. 5, 1771
Peter Lovejoy & Silence Bartlett,	Dec. 25, 1771
Charles Elsworth & Rachel Makepeace,	May 29, 1771
Benjamin Sumner & Martha Clark,	Aug. 29, 1771
William Parke & Mary Leech,	Feb. 6, 1772
Francis Foxcraft & Sarah Upham,	May 5, 1768

Josiah Adams & Nancy Samson of Sturbridge,

	July 21, 1768
James Shay & Thankful Walker,	Sept. 21, 1768
Ebenezer How & Sarah Rice,	Sept. 29, 1768
John Marble & Hannah Olds,	Nov. 30, 1768
Reuben Lamb of Spencer & Patience Adams,	Dec. 1, 1768
Elias Brown of Lincoln & Abigail Hobbs,	Feb. 23, 1769
John Nale & Anna Elwell,	May 18, 1769
Abner Cutler & Hannah Peters,	Oct. 24, 1769
Joseph Richardson & Hannah Stevens,	Dec. 7, 1769
Benjamin Bruce & Damaris Gilbert,	March 8, 1770
Nathan Rood & Rachel Streeter,	Aug. 20, 1770
Daniel Ralph & Priscilla Beals,	Aug. 20, 1770
Gideon Gilbert & Lois Crowfoot,	Aug. 30, 1770
Joshua Slayton & Desire Felton,	Aug. 30, 1770

Samuel Barnard, Jr., of Dearfield & Abigail Upham,

	Oct. 3, 1770
Moses Hitchcock & Hannah Wilson,	Nov. 28, 1770
Samuel Wood & Abigail Moore,	Dec. 5, 1770
Thomas Wood, Jr., & Abigail Banister,	Dec. 6, 1770
Uriah Fa–e & Hephsibah Dodge,	Dec. 13, 1770
Nathan Hamilton & Abigail Omstead,	Jan. 1, 1771
Simeon Olds & Salley Wright,	Jan. 1, 1771
Benjamin Lynds & Hannah Phips,	Jan. 3, 1771
Benjamin Felton & Ruth Hamilton,	Feb. 3, 1771
William Olds, Jr., & Abigail Hewes,	March 7, 1771
Richard Wait & Susanna Allen,	May 9, 1771
John Rich & Elizabeth Chickley,	April 10, 1771

Thomas Danforth of Tyringham & Lydia Abbot,

	May 26, 1771
Josiah Hamilton & Mary Barrows,	June 25, 1771

Jonathan Nutting of Brimfield & Abigail Banister,

	June 27, 1771
Simeon Rockwood & Damaris Olds,	July 11, 1771
Solomon Walker & Mary Gilbert,	April 9, 1772
Isaac Barron & Bathsheba Rich,	April 30, 1772
Timothy Wolcot & Miriam Walker,	Dec. 10, 1772
Simeon Olds & Elizabeth Banister,	April 1, 1773
George Bridge & Abigail Williams,	April 9, 1772
John Hinds & Lydia Seager of Spencer,	May 24, 1772

Samuel Parker of Amherst & Sarah Rood of Sturbridge,

	July 9, 1772
Jonathan Gilbert & Hannah Converse,	May 27, 1772
Elisha Drake & Mary Richmond,	July 1, 1773
Daniel Edson & Betty Fullen (?),	Aug. 10, 1773
Joseph Draper, Jr., & Mary Pratt of Spencer,	Aug. 12, 1773
John Howland & Bulah Bemiss of Spencer,	Aug. 29, 1773
Carley Ward & Caty Graham of Spencer,	Sept. 28, 1773
Ezra Hamilton & Esther Watson,	Dec. 2, 1773
Thomas Dodge, Jr., & Molley Allen,	Dec. 30, 1772

William Terrence of Betshire Town & Hepssibah Batchellor,

	Jan. 11, 1774
John Reed, Jr., & Martha Richmond,	May 11, 1772
Josiah Partridge & Experience Morse,	Dec. 22, 1772

Isaac Warner & Bulah Hobbs,	Dec. 9, 1772
Zechariah Reddy & Rebecca Warren,	April 7, 1774
Joshua Allen & Susanna Sprague of New Braintree,	
	April 20, 1774
George Blake & Bethiah Allen of Oakham,	May 19, 1774
Bryant Foster & Thankful Blackwell,	Nov. 21, 1771
Witt Taylor & Lucy Bruce,	Jan. 9, 1772
Moses Rainger & Hannah Ball,	1772
William Dean & Eunice Harrington,	Oct. 15, 1772
Luther How & Elizabeth Watson,	Nov. 19, 1772
William Ayres, Esq., & Mary Woolcott,	Dec. 23, 1772
Thomas Hill & Eleoner Bartlett,	Dec. 24, 1772
John Hill & Rachel Rice,	Feb. 25, 1773
Eli How & Elizabeth Smith,	April 8, 1773
Nathan Gilbert & Jemima Kindrick,	Oct. 14, 1773
Simeon Stone & Dorothy Harwood,	June 2, 1773
Ebenezer Goodell & Anna Newton,	Sept. 3, 1773
Eli Bartlett & Mary Hill,	Nov. 25, 1773
Moses Keep & Hannah Woodbury,	Dec. 2, 1773
Ezra Tucker & Abigail Moulton,	Dec. 9, 1773
Benjamin Adams & Eunice Hale,	Dec. 16, 1773
Moses Woods & Elizabeth Capen,	Dec. 30, 1773
Abel Wilson & Abigail Foster,	Feb. 14, 1774
Thomas Ball & Sarah Woodbury,	Feb. 20, 1774
John Furbush & Kathrine Harper, both of Oakham,	
	Nov. 22, 1774
Joseph Barns of New Braintree & Merriam Ayers,	
	March 29, 1775
Samuel Hamilton of Northfield & Molly Tyler,	
	May 9, 1775
Enoch Bothwell & Sarah Bacon,	June 29, 1775
Samuel Blair & Ann Brown of Westboro,	June 9, 1775
John Bemis & Patience Slayton,	July 4, 1775
Eph. Potter & Susannah Rice,	June 21, 1774
John Burk (?) & Rachel Hair,	Jan. 19, 1775
Thomas Bacon & Hepzibah Boutell,	Feb. 3, 1775
Silas Potter & Tabitha Hersey,	Feb. 3, 1775
Reuben Hendrick & Hannah Jennings,	Feb. 16, 1775
John Whitney & Anna Hamilton,	Feb. 2, 1775

John Wilder of Dummerston & Mary Rice, April 4, 1775
Isaac Beal of Mendon & Prudence Abbot, April 12, 1775
Caleb Rice & Sarah Abbott, June 8, 1775
Thomas Taylor & Dorcas Davis, June 8, 1775
Robert Stevenson of Oakham & Mary Adams,
Jan. 18, 1776
Benjamin Richardson & Alice McCluer, Feb. 15, 1776
John Boyden of Sturbridge & Abigail Brown, Feb. 26, 1776
George Watkins of Sturbridge & Hannah Hobbs,
Feb. 26, 1776
Jonathan Sampson of Belchertown & Sarah Stearns,
March 12, 1776
Asahel Peters & widow Hannah Bartlett, March 14, 1776
Nicholas McCluer & Thankful Kingsbury, May 16, 1776
James Miller, Jr., of Westboro & Mercy Livermore,
June 18, 1776
John Sargeant of Stockbridge & Mary Codner, Jr.,
June 26, 1776
Thomas Draper & Hannah Potter, July 11, 1776
John Hebbert & Dorothy Walker, Nov. 21, 1776
Eli Hitchcock of Weston & Abigail Olds, Dec. 20, 1776
Ezra Torrey & Zilpah Jennings, Jan. 9, 1777
Isaac Lackey of Spencer & Patience Staten, Feb. 15, 1776
Peter Washburn & Sarah Ayres, April 8, 1776
Oliver Hinds & Mary Capen of Spencer, May 2, 1776
Ebenezer Parkman & Sarah Lyscomb, June 6, 1776
Jabez Leath of Grafton & Betty Hall, Nov. 8, 1776
Silvanus Curtis & Mary Phillips of Sturbridge,
Nov. 14, 1776
Moses Ayres & Lucy Cutting, Jan. 1, 1777
Benjamin Higgins & Mary Drury, both of Spencer,
Jan. 14, 1777
Thomas Harbach & Kathrine Beamis, both of Sutton,
Jan. 15, 1777

√ BARRE.

June 17, 1774, Rutland district established as Hutchinson. Prov. Laws, Vol. V, p. 162.
Nov. 7, 1776, the name of the town of Hutchinson changed to Barre. Prov. Laws, Vol. V, p.
592. First (Unitarian) Church organized 1756. Congregational, 1827. Baptist, 1832.

Stepney (servant of George Caldwell) & Mary War-
      bon,   May 8, 1775
Skelton Felton of Northampton & Silence Pratt,
                                          Aug. 23, 1775
Obadiah Walker & Agnes McCullough,   Aug. 24, 1775
Jacob Wetherel & Ruth Rice,   Oct. 4, 1775
John Lenard & Betty Nurse,   Nov. 15, 1775
Caleb Allen of Conway & Sarah Jenkins,   Nov. 16, 1775
Joseph Farrar & Lydia Stone,   Nov. 23, 1775
Amos Richardson & Martha Dennis,   Nov. 30, 1775
Silas Smith & Eunice Eaton,   Dec. 14, 1775
Doctor Oliver Stickland of Templeton & Mary Low,
                                          May 2, 1776
Jonathan Little & Lydia Nye,   May 2, 1776
Elisha Marsh & Esther Berry,   Aug. 1, 1776
Aaron Ball & Rachel Cheever,   Sept. 26, 1776
Ebenezer Tatman & Dorothy Woodberry,   Nov. 7, 1786
Peter Ripley of Warwick & Abigail Smith, Dec. 12, 1776
Josiah Bacon of Hutchinson & Polly Tileston (?) of
      Boston,   Jan. 2, 1777
Joseph Myrick & Ruth Swift,   Jan. 5, 1777
Robert Perkins of Hutchinson & Silence Leach of
      Pelham,   Jan. 7, 1777
Doctor John Williams of Lebanon & Abigail Jones,
                                          Jan. 23, 1777
Moses Caldwell & Mary Ruggles,   Jan. 29, 1777
James Kennedy of Colrain & Margaret Thompson,
                                          March 18, 1777
Dr. Daniel Rood & Dorothy Robinson,   March 27, 1777
Josiah Parker & Martha Goodell,   April 10, 1777
Reuben Tatman & Margaret English,   June 5, 1777

Andrew Thompson & Hannah Carruth,   Sept. 18, 1777
David Richardson & Susannah Bacon,   Oct. 2, 1777
Aaron Holden & Rachel Richardson,   Oct. 30, 1777
Solomon Bacon & Margaret Forbes,   Nov. 13, 1777
Richard Kelley & Hannah Caldwell,   Nov. 20, 1777
Thomas Spooner of Hardwick & Mary Haven, Nov. 20, 1777
Jotham Rice, Jr., & Elizabeth Sullen,   Jan. 15, 1778
Alexander Thompson of Colrain & Bathsheba Burnet,
                                                            Jan. 28, 1778
William Chamberlain & Elizabeth Winslow,   Feb. 24, 1778
Nathaniel Babbet of Athol & Mary Mandell, March 3, 1778
David Hagar & Levinah Holden,   March 12, 1778

MILFORD.

April 11, 1780, part of Mendon established as Milford. First (Congregational) Church
organized 1741. Clergyman mentioned: Rev. Amariah Frost.

John Kilburn of Mendon (now Milford) & Abigail
     Littlefield of Holliston,   June 15, 1780
Joshua Thayer & Sarah Curtis of Holliston,   June 15, 1780
Aaron Bullard of Holliston & Lovice Godfrey, Sept. 21, 1780
John Dewing & Patience Sumner,   Sept. 21, 1780
John Bullard & Rachel Boynton,   Oct. 13, 1780
John Beall & Silence Atwood (?),   Oct. 19, 1780
Luther Wheelock & Mary Sumner,   Nov. 8, 1780
Richard Hiscock & Sarah Cody,   Nov. 16, 1780
Jonathan Hayward & Mary Ballard,   Dec. 21, 1780
Artemas Cheeney & Rachel Albee,   Feb. 8, 1781
Ebenezer Nelson & Patience Twitchel,   March 8, 1781
Nathan Nelson & Jerusha Chapin,   March 8, 1781
Jonathan Kimball & Mary Cheeney,   July 7, 1781
Isaac Chapin & Rachel Wheeten,   Oct. 18, 1781
John Foristell, Jr., of Warwick & Lydia Tenney,
                                                            Nov. 8, 1781
Abner Adams of Northbridge & Ruth Wood, Jan. 16, 1782
John Bowker of Hopkinton & Esther Wedge, March 7, 1782
Stephen Kilburn & Hannah Wight,   March 31, 1782

Adam Hayward & Judith Ballard, April 18, 1782
Joshua Bullard of Bellingham & Bethiah Taft,
April 18, 1782
Ezekiel Jones & Mary Wight, May 9, 1782
Boyce Kimbell, Jr., & Mary Pike of Bellingham, May 2, 1782
Ebenezer Peck & Rachel Lesure, Dec. 7, 1780
Thomas Hiscock & Mary Cody, June 7, 1782
Ziba Holbrook & Rebecca Kimball, Nov. 7, 1782
Nathaniel Flagg of Upton & Mehitabel Cutler, Nov. 13, 1781
John Scammell & Hannah Jones, Nov. 24, 1782
Thomas Twitchel of Westboro & Phebe Pond, Nov. 27, 1782
John Nelson & Bettee Brown, Nov. 28, 1782
Daniel Thompson & Margaret Davison, Dec. 8, 1782
Joseph Johnson & Hannah Albee, Dec. 12, 1782
Asa Jones & Hannah Nelson, Feb. 13, 1783
Jonathan Stearns & Hannah Thayer, May 1, 1783
Stephen Thompson & Phebe Chapin, May 4, 1783
Samuel Hart of Chesterfield & Jemima Warren,
June 29, 1783
James Hiscock of Hopkinton & Anna Cody, Nov. 13, 1783
Paul Davis & Rachel Chapin, Nov. 29, 1783
Abijah Warfield & Lydia Wheelock, Dec. 11, 1783
Smith Phillips of Holliston & Mary Saunders, Dec. 28, 1783
David Chapin & Martha Bates of Mendon, Feb. 12, 1784
Darius Sumner & Anna Daniels of Mendon, Feb. 19, 1784
Ebenezer Thompson & Abigail Davison, March 11, 1784
Joel Thayer & Susanna Cheeney, April 15, 1784
➤ Nathan Wood & Experience Thayer, April 22, 1784
Oliver Chapin & Mary Jones, April 29, 1784
➤ Abel Albee & Annah Wood, April 29, 1784
Enos Beall & Relief Cheeney, June 25, 1784
James Sumner, Jr., & Mary Jones, July 7, 1784
Jotham Thayer & Bathsheba Wheelock, Aug. 29, 1784
Samuel Thayer & Rachel Nelson, Dec. 9, 1784
Ebenezer Cheeney, Jr., of Warwick & Anna Nelson,
Feb. 17, 1785
Dick Brattle of Bellingham & Rose Lucy (Africans
or negroes), May 3, 1785
James Luther & Mary Parkhurst, March 16, 1783

ᐯ ATHOL.

March 6, 1762, the plantation called Payquage established as Athol. Prov. Laws, Vol. IV, p. 534. First (Congregational) Church organized 1750. Unitarian, 1750. Baptist, 1813.

Elijah Flagg & Elizabeth Comming, both of Templeton,	April 26, 1781
Zaccheus Hasey & Abigail Sergeant, both of Hubbardstown,	May 30, 1781
John Allen & Dolly Dalrymple, both of Northbridge,	July 5, 1781
Zaccheus Rich, Jr., & Lydia Brown,	Nov. 7, 1781
Alpheus Ward & Molly Raymond,	March 7, 1782
Jesse Stockwell & Anna Grought of Templeton,	April 3, 1782
Samuel Duncan & Patience Choat, both of Warwick,	April 13, 1779
David Biglow & Lois Taylor,	June 3, 1779
Willard Varnum & Patty Tompson,	Sept. 9, 1779
Moses Hutchins & Susanna Thayer,	Sept. 9, 1779
Isaac Train & Elizabeth Cummins,	Sept. 14, 1779
Asa Goddard & Lucy Goddard,	Nov. 2, 1779
Daniel Benjamin & Tamason Felton,	Nov. 10, 1779
Charles Baker, Jr., & Anna Jackson,	Nov. 25, 1779
William Young & Keziah Haven,	Jan. 18, 1780
William Straten & Elizabeth Smith,	March 2, 1780
John Fairbank, Jr., & Fanny Kilton,	July 16, 1780
Uriah Rice & Unice Church,	Sept. 7, 1780
Jesse Kendall, Jr., & Elizabeth Raymond,	Oct. 12, 1780
Ruggles Ward & Isabel Oliver,	Nov. 2, 1780
Moses Oliver & Lois Wiswell Humphrey,	Nov. 23, 1780
Solomon Smith & Tabitha Briggs,	Dec. 27, 1780
Willard Varnum & Hannah Walkup,	Feb. 15, 1781
William Raymond & Lydia Ward,	July 6, 1781
Obadiah Janes & Mary Oliver,	Aug. 2, 1781
Elisha Sibley & Elizabeth Twitchel,	Nov. 1, 1781
Levi Fletcher & Jerusha Morton,	March 13, 1783

Asahel Sanders & Afia (?) Rich,   May 26, 1783

Thomas Canless (?) & Abigail Sawtell, both of Templeton,   Aug. 16, 1783

Edward Raymond, Jr., & Jane Oliver Kindall,
                                              Oct. 30, 1783

John Haven & Nabbe Fay,   Feb. 10, 1784

John Coalman, Jr., & Susa Shute, of Templeton,
                                         March 18, 1784

Thomas Stratton & Thankful Rich,   April 5, 1784

Francis Mazrow of Petersham & Anna Frederick,
                                          April 12, 1784

Nathaniel Phillips & Mary Baley,   April 29, 1784

Ephraham Capron & Sarah Fairbank,   May 18, 1784

John Piper & Sarah Willington, both of Templeton,
                                            Aug. 1, 1784

David Young & Hannah Lumbard,   Sept. 30, 1774

Caleb Thompson of New Salem & Mehitabel Knowles,
                                            Nov. 7, 1784

Edward Goddard, Jr., & Ann Death,   Nov. 11, 1784

Earll Cutting & Lydia Kendall,   Dec. 10, 1784

Asa Lord & Lydia Humphrey,   Aug. 15, 1785

Thaddeus Bates (?) & Polly Shattuck, both of Templeton,   Sept. 1, 1785

George ———— Felton of Petersham & Hannah Oliver,
                                           Sept. 12, 1785

Ebenezer Knight, Jr., & Esther Sprague,   Jan. 5, 1786

Chester Bingham of Chesterfield & Deborah Rich,
                                           Sept. 23, 1786

Levi Kendall & Sally Newell,   Oct. 22, 1786

David Pike & Joanne Cheeney,   Oct. 26, 1786

Benjamin Powers of Petersham & Anna Raymond,
                                            Nov. 1, 1786

NORTHBRIDGE.

July 14, 1772, part of Uxbridge established as the district of Northbridge. A town Aug. 23, 1775. Prov. Laws, Vol. V, p. 419. Friends Society organized 1730. Congregational, 1782. Clergyman mentioned: Rev. John Crane.

Benjamin Powers & Lydia Melandy,	April 16, 1777
Lemuel Powers & Abigail Newland,	April 16, 1777
Lieut. William Park & Mrs. Sally Potter,	Oct. 5, 1780
Abijah Thayr (?) of Douglass & Mrs. Betty Thayr (?),	Aug. 22, 1780
Joel White & Martha Fobes,	Nov. 21, 1780
William Winter & Anna Chamberlain of Grafton,	April 19, 1781
Samuel Cooper & Anna Straight,	May 10, 1781
Jonathan Bacon, Jr., & Molly Adams,	Dec. 13, 1781
Samuel Allbe & Hannah Pratt,	Dec. 20, 1781
Ruben Randal of Richmond & Molly Aldrich,	Aug. 13, 1782
David Winter & Anna Cooper,	Aug. 29, 1782
Nathaniel Fish & Miriam Hamlinton,	April 28, 1783
Enoch Child & Elizabeth Tafts of Smithfield,	July 2, 1783
Israel Thayer & Dolly Hayward,	March 22, 1784
Joshua Slocomb of Franklin & Lucy Dunn,	Nov. 25, 1784
Samuel Lincoln & Mehitabel Thayer,	Jan. 5, 1785
David Batchellor, Jr., & Pattee Hills of Sutton,	Jan. 26, 1785
Wheelock Wood & Lydia Murdock,	March 31, 1785
Jacob Goldthwait & Rachel —— Axtel (?),	April 14, 1785
Samuel Aldrich, Jr., & Sarah Brown,	May 5, 1785
Amos Wheeler of Worcester & Martha Reed,	June 2, 1785
George Aldrich, Jr., of Mendon & Polly Brown,	June 30, 1785
Stephen Trask of Uxbridge & Juda Hunt,	June 13, 1786

ROYALSTON.

Feb. 19, 1765, the tract of land called Royalshire established as Royalston. Prov. Laws, Vol. IV, p. 738. First (Congregational) Church organized 1766. Baptist, at West Royalston, 1768. Clergyman mentioned: Rev. Joseph Lee.

Thomas Thompson & Elizabeth Fry,	March 29, 1769
Abner Ball & Mary Poor,	May 25, 1767
Daniel Brown & Eunice Heminway,	June 28, 1770
Jonathan Woodward & Hepsebah Goddard,	June 19, 1770
Peletiah Metcalf & Lydia Estey,	June 28, 1770
John Wilson of New Braintree & widow Mary Graham,	
	Oct. 10, 1770
Ezra Prat & Susanna Barton,	Nov. 21, 1771
Jacob Easty & Sarah Chamberlain,	March 19, 1772
James Work & Martha Pierce,	April 28, 1772

BERLIN.

March 16, 1784, part of Bolton and Marlborough established as the district of Berlin. A town Feb. 6, 1812. First (Congregational) Church organized 1779.

James Goddard, Jr., & Keziah Fairbank,	July 28, 1785
Manassah Fairbank & Abigail How of Shrewsbury,	
	Nov. 3, 1785
Jonathan Fairbank & Perny (?) How,	Jan. 12, 1786
Caleb Fairbank & Moley Goddard,	Nov. 10, 1785
Nahum Houghton & Leovitia How,	Sept. 26, 1786

PAXTON.

Feb. 12, 1765, parts of Leicester and Rutland established as the district of Paxton. Prov. Laws, Vol. IV, p. 734. A town Aug. 23, 1775. First (Congregational) Church organized 1767.

James Sproute & Molly Whittemore,	July 11, 1784
Aaron Morse & Relief Moore,	July 11, 1784
John Pike, Jr., of Sturbridge & Beulah Davis,	Nov. 11, 1784
Samuel Bridgham & Phebe Davis,	Jan. 18, 1785

✓ PRINCETON.

Oct. 20, 1759, part of Rutland and certain common lands adjacent established as the district of "Princetown." Prov. Laws, Vol. IV, p. 266. A town April 24, 1771. First (Congregational) Church organized 1764.

David Averet & Mrs. Susanna Ralf,   Oct. 27, 1767

✓ WORCESTER.

[CONTINUED FROM P. 13.]

Nathan Gleason of Oxford & Rachel Nichols, Jan. 11, 1776
Isaac Knights & Rebecca Cree of Shrewsbury, Jan. 24, 1776
William Stearns, A. M., of Lunenburg & Mary Dana,
                                                    Feb. 26, 1776
John Moore & Mary Gurney,   April 24, 1776
Nathaniel Harrington & Ruth Stone,   July 2, 1776
John Warren of Sudbury & Elizabeth Carson, July 24, 1776
Simon Glasco & Prudence Jone (negroes),   Aug. 1, 1776
John Walker & Mary Willard,   Aug. 7, 1776
Tyler Curtis & Lydia Chamberlain,   Sept. 5, 1776
Micah Johnson, Jr., & Sarah Willard,   Nov. 13, 1776
William Johnson of Westboro & Marcy Taylor, Nov. 25, 1776
Daniel Heywood & Molly Pierce,   Nov. 25, 1776
William Trowbridge & Sarah Rice,   Dec. 12, 1776
Joel Doolittle of Petersham & Tabitha Goodwin,
                                                    Dec. 12, 1776
John Campbell of Oxford & Martha Stevens,   Jan. 16, 1777
Phinehas Smith & Eunice Gleason,   Jan. 22, 1777
Paul Gates & Phebe Mahon,   Jan. 23, 1777
Jonathan Stone, Jr., & Mary Harrington,   Feb. 13, 1777
Ebenezer Smith of Sturbridge & Rebecca Knight,
                                                  March 25, 1777
Josiah Perry & Lydia Flagg,   April 3, 1777
Phineas Flagg & Rhoda Stone,   May 25, 1777

Charles White of Peterboro' & Sarah Gray, June 10, 1777
Moses Coolidge of Watertown & Hannah Stowell,
                                          Sept. 25, 1777
Dr. William Walker & Molly Chaddick,   Oct. 8, 1777
Daniel Stone of Charlton & Abigail Jones,   Nov. 5, 1777
John Hair & Elizabeth Bigelow,   Nov. 20, 1777
Vernon Gleason & Lucy Smith,   Dec. 25, 1777
Solomon Willard & Lydia Johnson,   Dec. 25, 1777
James Mcfarland, Jr., & Betty Moore,   Jan. 5, 1778
William Quigley & Thankful Moore,   Jan. 16, 1778
Gideon Griggs & Patty Stevens,   Feb. 10, 1778
Samuel Wiswell & Sally Ward,   Feb. 12, 1778
Cato Walker & Prudence Williams (negroes), Feb. 26, 1778
Noah Bigelow of Shutesbury (?) & Elizabeth Gould-
    ing,   March 18, 1778
Henry Gale & Lucy Knight,   March 19, 1778
Anthony Haswell (?) & Lydia Baldwin,   April 23, 1778
Nathaniel Heywood & Hannah Heywood,   April 23, 1778
David Richards & Rebekah Gates,   May 5, 1778
Samuel Howlet, Jr., & Lucretia Richardson, May 6, 1778
Silas Henry & Relief Knights,   May 16, 1778
William Cunningham of Spencer & Rebeckah Mc-
    Farland,   June 4, 1778
Elisha Clark & Mary Bigelow,   June 7, 1778
Elisha Johnson of Southboro' & Sarah Perry, June 9, 1778
Samuel Whitney & Mary Whitney,   June 24, 1778
David Pierce & Kezia Packard,   July 2, 1778
Ellis Blake & Jane Cook,   Aug. 23, 1778
Josiah Rice & Betty Trowbridge,   Sept. 1, 1778
Samuel Hunt of Charlemont & Eunice Gleason,
                                            Oct. 4, 1778
John Williams of Boston & Hannah Chandler, Nov. 10, 1778
James Blair of Rutland & Martha Young,   Nov. 24, 1778
Thomas Rice, Jr., & Lydia Totman,   Nov. 26, 1778
Juba Williams & Hagar Eveleth (negroes),   Dec. 1, 1778
Nathan White of Uxbridge & Eunice Chapin, Jan. 14, 1779
John Hamilton & Katharine Quigley,   Jan. 27, 1779
Dr. Benjamin Green & Sarah Salisbury,   Feb. 1, 1779
Jonathan Osland & Parnel White,   Feb. 18, 1779

Phineas Gleason & Margaret Keko, March 31, 1779
Alvin How of Shrewsbury & Mary Willington,
                                        April 21, 1779
Isaiah Thomas & Mary Fowle of Londonderry
    (mar. Boston), May 26, 1779
James Trowbridge & Lydia Ward, June 22, 1779
Samuel Sturtevant & Susannah Packard, July 6, 1779
Daniel Chaddick & Elizabeth Fisk, Sept. 26, 1779
William Jones of Westminster & Sarah Curtis, Oct. 5, 1779
William Brown & Mary Cowden, Oct. 21, 1779
John Prentice of Ward & Rebeckah Richardson,
                                        Nov. 9, 1779
John Gambel of Northboro & Jane Hambleton, Nov. 11, 1779
Thomas Pollard of Boston & Betsey Carbet, Nov. 14, 1779
Thomas Follansbe of Newbury-port & Eunice Stearns,
                                        Dec. 5, 1779
Simeon Dunkin, Jr., & Mary Blair, April 11, 1780
Abel Heywood & Abigail Chamberlain, April 27, 1780
John Mahan & Sally Hemingway, April 27, 1780
Calvin Glazier of North Shrewsbury & Lydia Pierce,
                                        May 18, 1780
Thaddeus Chapin & Lucy Whitney, June 29, 1780
Josiah Perry & Prudence Harrington, July 6, 1780
Isaac Flagg & Abigail Baldwin, Sept. 13, 1780
John Stanton & Sarah Chandler, Sept. 14, 1780
Joseph Ball & Lucretia Stearns, Oct. 12, 1780
Joseph Gray & Hannah Millet, Nov. 2, 1780
Elijah Flagg & Sarah Moore, Nov. 23, 1780
William Brown, Jr., & Mary Cowdin, Nov. 29, 1780
Benjamin West, Esq., of Charlestown, N. H., & Mary
    Maccarty, Jan. 18, 1781
Jonathan Thayer of Charlemont & Azuba Gleason,
                                        Jan. 31, 1781
James Campbell of Sutton & Anna Gleason, Feb. 7, 1781
Henry Patch & Hannah Moore, Feb. 8, 1781
William Johnson & Sarah Baldwin, Oct 11, 1770
John Taylor & Elizabeth Young, April 13, 1775
Nathan Lovell of Holden & Anna Inglesbee of
    Shrewsbury, April 1, 1781

Noah Jones & Debroah Holbrook,	April 25, 1780
Stephen Taylor & Susanna Gates,	Sept. 4, 1781
Jacob Holmes & Anne Harrington,	April 5, 1781
Amos Singletary, Jr., of Sutton & Mrs. Betty John-son,	Jan. 27, 1777
Archibald McDonald of Chester, Vt., & Mary Moore,	Feb. 4, 1785
William Seaver, Jr., of Kingston & Polly Chandler,	Oct. 29, 1785
Nathaniel Paine & Elizabeth Chandler,	Dec. 18, 1785
Joseph Trumbell of Petersham & Elizabeth Paine,	Feb. 14, 1786
John Johnson & Lydia Johnson,	March 8, 1786
Alpheus Eaton & Sarah Johnson,	April 6, 1786
John Brown & Polly Goulding,	Oct. 6, 1786
Benjamin Butman & Susannah Chamberlain,	Oct. 22, 1786
Nathaniel Coolidge & Katharine Baldwin,	Nov. 14, 1786
Ebenezer Putnam of St. John, N. B., Canada, & Elizabeth Chandler,	Dec. 2, 1786
Abraham Lincoln & Nancy Bigelow,	Jan. 7, 1787

INDEX.

13

Early Massachusetts Marriages

Prior to 1800.

As found on the official records of

Plymouth County.

Second Book.

Edited by

The Rev. Frederic W. Bailey, B.D.,

Official copyist of parochial archives, diocese of Connecticut; editor "Early Con-
necticut Marriages;" designer Bailey's photo-ancestral record, "The Record
of my Ancestry;" member New England Genealogical and Biographical
Society; Connecticut Historical Society; New Haven Colony
Historical Society; Sons of the American
Revolution (Massachusetts).

Published by the

Frederic W. Bailey, Mgr.
P. O. Box 587. New Haven, Conn.

PREFACE.

EARLY MASSACHUSETTS MARRIAGES.

PLYMOUTH COUNTY.

Grateful for the continued interest and patronage that has marked the successive issues of our five books of early Connecticut and Massachusetts marriages, and more than ever deeply impressed with a sense of the real worthiness and increasing popularity of this cause, it is our pleasure now to present still another contribution to genealogical research which we also feel to be our crowning effort.

While in the search for Connecticut ancestry it would have been but natural for us to turn Eastward in the direction of old Plymouth, so many of our early settlers having come from there, still the more has it an abiding attraction because of all localities here in New England deserving historic precedence and honor, this name in the minds of our best people reserves to itself an unmatched dignity and superiority. Of course there could have been but one first place for the Pilgrims to land and but one Plymouth Rock; and that place would ever have possessed its own unique charm whatever inherent value it may have had. But it is interesting to us all to feel that while other localities have, because of modern needs and industrial activities, seen great and sometimes unsatisfactory changes, this section of country, with its precious records, exists almost monumental in its sameness. Commercially of little importance, with a sparse rural community backed by vast stretches of wild wood, a beautiful and picturesque harbor, though shallow and bare with each receding tide, it derives its chief inspiration from its tablets, its monuments and its antiquities everywhere conspicuous. And yet to us all and everywhere old Plymouth lives as an ideal country, whose thrifty, God-fearing people years ago dwelt in exceeding virtue which a real, genuine faith had made even more transparent and pure. Famous men have written much about her and her aims. Our best poets have portrayed some of her leaders. Favorite novelists have woven from her inner life their fascinating tales. There is little more to add except such facts as are here given, whereby to reveal all her people at the most interesting period of their lives. Sufficient be it here said that in and about the Mayflower precious memories will ever linger, apt tradition survive as fact, sturdy manhood under the enchantment of distance grow heroic; and more than all, as old Father Time sweeps us along amidst new scenes and newer situations, we shall still love to think of that contented world of mortals wherein the immortal principles of truth and right and duty had so thoroughly transfixed human thought and action. As well indeed, if it be possible, to find in scenes as tranquil some better anchorage for our own harried lives.

We are confident, therefore, that in the publication of this book containing the Plymouth County marriages there will be opened up a new source of gratification for a worthy ambition, in affording ready access to the oft sought records of these peculiar people. We shall see for ourselves just who and when they married, where they lived, if surely of Pilgrim origin, and perhaps by them trace out our own family lines clearly to the Mayflower itself.

Our effort, however, has not been unattended by some obvious diffi-
culties which only such as have thoroughly examined these ancient
records may fully appreciate.   To copy a writing seems easy enough if
it be of our own people, language. time and place.   Trouble begins as
soon as we deviate from this standard, increasing rapidly with the
changed conditions.   The well nigh hundred years covered by these
books, dating back some two hundred years for a beginning, saw a number of different penmen engaged thereon. each with his own peculiar
style of chirography, as well as his own estimate of the value of such
record in determining the amount of care to be bestowed upon the
transcription.   That, however, has been on the whole the least difficult
task, in that, as a rule, they wrote with remarkable clearness, which the
many years of service has not greatly obscured.

Allowing for the individual traits of each writer, the severest part of
the problem consisted in the varied spelling of surnames during the
changing years and the changing clerks.   While really not their fault
if they truly copied in exact form the reports sent from time to time
by town officials, they did serve as the instrument of their transmission
as we ourselves do now; and must together share any blame for error
and inaccuracy.   Instances have been met with where persons prepar-
ing legal documents of their own did not themselves know just how to
spell their own name; and so, in order to make sure of covering the case
it was made to appear on the same page in two or more ways.   Under
such circumstances it could hardly be expected that the scribe would
do else than increase the complication by some little originality.
Unfamiliar names were often spelled as they were pronounced, some-
what after the phonetic method, and even those well known were in the
different localities slightly changed.   In this way much of the variation
may be accounted for.   And yet Plymouth County, away off there by
itself, seems to have been given to much originality in this particular, as ,
an examination of our carefully prepared Index will bear us out in say-
ing; or else, as the only alternative, their pronunciation in the several
townships considerably at fault.

It seems, therefore. but fair to our readers, as just to ourselves, while
confessing to no infallibility of judgment in such work any more than
others under similar conditions may have possessed, to call attention to
this frequent diversity.   It certainly would be impossible in a labor of
this sort to avoid some error due to the uncertain lines of the original.

Our only fear is that our readers may forget that the original itself
bears these marks of seeming error, which, according to our ideas of duty,
did not devolve upon us even to attempt to correct.   Our one aim has
been to secure, as best we could, an exact copy of the record, in no
case to seemingly improve upon or to modernize.   In other words to
place before our readers just what they would see were they to exam-
ine the old books for themselves.

Now to us there seems great need of placing especial stress upon this
phase of the subject.   For so rapidly has the interest in genealogical
research increased to-day, and as a result so much coming into print,
that there is great danger, not only of propagating errors and inaccu-
racies, but of emphasizing a source of authority which ought seldom, if
ever, to be employed.   It should always be remembered that we deal
altogether with facts—not inferences—facts, too, capable of the most
absolute proof, and of little value to others without the proof.   And yet,
how oft do we see published, genealogies, the evidence for the truth-
fulness of which lie altogether in the recesses of the compiler's brain,
or in some private papers, which, in his book, he makes no reference
to.   The bare, bald statements proved. borrowed or invented we
know not; they are all there equally interesting, upon the simple

authority of the unknown compiler whom we are obliged to implicitly trust. How thorough he has been, how much he has accepted the statements of others without further proof, how correctly he may have drawn his conclusions, how much, to save labor and expense, he has employed that ready substitute—personal opinion—we cannot know. He has constructed in a short time an elaborate and beautiful structure, he, alone, knowing just where the weak beams and buttresses are.

We repeat that it is not quite fair, nor does it add to the reputation of genealogy in general, to expect others to accept the statements of the compiler merely because he is supposed to know just what he writes about. In every difficult question at least proof should be given or reference made, so that in matters of dispute at any time thereafter to arise, it may be possible to consult and review for ourselves. The apostolic injunction to " Prove all things and hold fast that which is good," does very well for the individual searcher ; but when sending the results of genealogical study abroad for permanent service, justice demands that the authorities to some extent be furnished therewith.

We have been led to make this digression partly by our endeavor to prepare these records for others' benefit. It has been exceedingly hard to deal with these many instances of shaded spellings without some interpretation of our own in which, opinion, would necessarily have entered. This we have sought to avoid, especially in the Index, wherein no great amount of classification has been attempted, preferring to leave such vexed questions to those who have their own particular problems to solve.

With reference to the subject-matter herein contained, much that is said in the Preface of the First Book will apply. The officials of the County seem to have carefully conformed to the law of the Commonwealth with reference to the recording of marriages in the various towns. It was, perhaps, a question of strict economy which led to their being kept in the same books with the court proceedings. But there they are, scattered about in five volumes to be found in the vault of the Clerk of the Courts in Plymouth. For convenience the order of the successive books has been followed, so that in any disputed case the particular record may be the more readily located.

The particular volumes are these:

Record Common Pleas, No. II, from 1693–1694.

Record of General Sessions, Book I, from 1730.

Record of General Sessions Book II, from 1749.

Record of General Sessions, Book III, from 1760.

Record of General Sessions, Book IV, from 1782.

FREDERIC W. BAILEY.

New Haven, Conn., October 1, 1900.

CONTENTS.

PLYMOUTH.

The first mention of the name of Plymouth in the records is in "Plimouth's great Book of Deeds of Lands enrolled" under the date of 1620. First (Congregational) Church (Pilgrimage) organized, 1606. Unitarian Church, 1620. Second (Congregational) Church (South Plymouth), 1738.

John Dotey, Jr., & Mehetabel Nelson,	Feb. 2, 1692-3
Joseph Finney & Mary Bryant,	June 14, 1693
John Nelson & Patience Morton,	May 4, 1693
Joseph Burland & Deborah Barrow,	Oct. 17, 1693
Jeduthan Robbins & Hannah Platt,	Jan. 11, 1693-4
Samuel Dunham & widow Sarah Watson,	Jan. 15, 1693-4
Hugh Cole, Sr., & widow Mary Morton,	Jan. 30, 1693-4
John Dotey, Sr., & Sarah Jones,	Nov. 22, 1694
George Barrow & Patience Simons,	Feb. 14, 1694-5
Lemuel Doten & Jean Fish,	March 24, 1748
Thomas Hinkley & Elisabeth Decoster,	March 31, 1748
James Crandon & Sarah Delano,	May 29, 1749
Reuben Chandler of Duxboro & Hannah Tillson,	July 4, 1749
William Serjant & Mary Rider,	Oct. 26, 1749
Paul Doten & Ruth Rider,	Nov. 2, 1749
Benjamin Smith & Sarah Tincom,	Nov. 13, 1749-50
Isaac Harlow (Hartow?) & Jerusha Finney,	Jan. 4, 1749-50
Jabez Gibs of Sandwich & Susanna Cornish,	Feb. 8, 1749-50
Robert Harlow, Jr., & Jean West,	March 27, 1749-50
Seth Swift, Jr., & Desire Tincom,	March 29, 1749-50
Thomas Silvester & Martha Tinkom,	April 23, 1749-50
James Wood & Deborah Fish,	Jan. 21, 1735
Simeon Totman & Sarah Little John,	June 13, 1738
William Clarke & Experience Doty,	June 13, 1738
Edward Doten & Phebe Phinney,	Aug. 3, 1738
William Harlow & Hannah Bartlett,	Aug. 3, 1738
Joshua Swift of Sandwich & Jane Faunce,	March 21, 1738-9
David Morton & Rebecca Finney,	May 8, 1738-9
John Jones & Sarah Barnes,	Aug. 18, 1740
Edward Sparrow & Jerusha Bradford,	April 16, 1741

Mr. Ezra Whitmarsh & Mrs. Dorothy Gardner, June 30, 1741
Jonathan Sanders of Warham & Elizabeth Tinkam,
                                           July 3, 1741
William Wood & Elizabeth Finney,   May 13, 1742
Ephraim Holmes & Sarah Finney,   May 19, 1742
Peleg West & Lydia Keen, both of Kingston, March 3, 1742-3
Gideon Gifford of Rochester & Lois Jackson,
                                  March 14, 1742-3
Silvanus Bartlett & Martha Waite,   July 7, 1742-3
Cornelius Holmes & Mary Doten,   June 7, 1743
Benjamin Barnes & Experience Rider,   June 14, 1742
Mr. Samuel Veazie (?) of Duxboro & Mrs. Deborah
    Samson of Kingston,   Aug. 6, 1742
Barzilla Stetson & Ruth Kempton,   Sept. 6, 1742
Robert Shattuck & Ruhama Cooke,   Sept. 9, 1742
Theodore Cotten & Martha Sanders,   Oct. 29, 1742
Lemuel Bartlett & Mary Dotey,   Nov. 25, 1742
Henry Saunders, Jr., of Warham & Mary Hambleton,
                                  Dec. 13, 1742
Joseph Shurtleff & Sarah Cob,   Dec. 9, 1742
Joseph Ruggles of Hardwich & Hanah Cushman,
                                Jan. 13, 1742-3
Thomas Faunce, 4th, & Sarah Bartlett,   Jan. 20, 1742-3
Job Hammond (negro) & Hannah Quay (Indian),
                                Feb. 17, 1742-3
Noah Bradford & Hannah Clarke,   March 10, 1742-3
William Keen & Ruth Sergeant,   March 17, 1742-3
Dr. Lazarus Lebaron & Mrs. Lydia Cushman, May 2, 1743
Jonah Whetemore of Charlestown & Mary Hatch,
                                  May 26, 1743
Francis Perriss & Mary Thomas (Indian),   May 30, 1743
David Curtice of Scituate & Hannah Ward, Sept. 22, 1743
John Bradford of Plymton & Elizabeth Holmes,
                                  Nov. 10, 1743
Mr. John Greenleaf of Boston & Mrs. Priscilla Brown,
                                  Dec. 8, 1743
Peter Daniel & Sarah Waterman (Indians), Dec. 18, 1743
Amos Donham & Ann Muckleroy,   Feb. 13, 1743-4

Ephraim Ward & Sarah Donham,   Feb. 14, 1743-4
Gideon White of Marshfield & Joanna Howland,
  Feb. 23, 1743-4
Ebenezer Harlow & Meriah Morey,   Aug. 24, 1740
Nathaniel Morton & Mary Elles,   Nov. 16, 1740
Jonathan Tobey of Sandwich & Deborah Swift, Feb. 19, 1740
Thomas Clarke & Ruth Morton,   March 18, 1742
Jonathan Harlow & Sarah Holmes,   April 22, 1742
Joseph Morton, 3d, & Experience Morton,   Aug. 11, 1743
Edward Tinkham of Kingston & Lydia Rider, Sept. 29, 1743
Eleazer Holmes, Jr., & Esther Ellis,   Dec. 14, 1743
Joseph Croswell of Groton & Jerusha Bartlet, March 11, 1744
Joslyn Sepit & Joanna Sepit (Indians),   Nov. 29, 1744
Ebenezer Holmes, 3d, & Susanna Holmes,   April 11, 1745
William Fish & Mary Morey,   Aug. 5, 1744
Joseph Fulgham & Rebecca Young,   March 1, 1744-5
Jacob Deco—er & Elizabeth Cole,   Sept. 26, 1745
Elkanah Shaw of Middleboro & Joannah King, April 11, 1745
Ebenezer Donham of Plimton & Phebe Lucas, April 25, 1745
Jire Fish of Sandwich & Hannah Finney,   July 28, 1745
Caleb Sherman & Rebecca Rider,   Aug. 15, 1745
Azariah Whiten of Plimton & Rebecca Holmes, Sept. 10, 1745
Joseph Churchel & Meriah Rider,   —— 23, 1745-6
Stephen Doten & Hannah Bartlett,   Feb. 10, 1745-6
Benjamin Delano of Duxboro & Lydia Jackson,
  March 6, 1745-6
Daniel Robins & Sarah Sanders (Indians),   Oct. 3, 1745
Thomas Ling & Elizabeth Mackfun,   Oct. 4, 1745
Amaziah Churchel & Elizabeth Silvester,   Oct. 31, 1745
Thomas Burge & Patience Dotey,   Feb. 23, 1745-6
Peleg Sprague & —— Chandler, both of Duxboro, 1745-6
Samuel Winsor & Rhoda Delano, both of Duxboro, 1745-6
Lemuel Holmes & Abigail Rider,   April 28, 1746
John Howard & Unice Curtice,   June 19, 1746
Jabez Mendall of Plimton & Mariah Churchell, July 3, 1746
James Watkins & Jerusha Rider,   July 29, 1746
William —erman & Elenor Thomas,   Aug. 28, 1746
Benjamin Eaton of Kingston & Mary Tinkam, Oct. 28, 1746

2

Josiah Bradford & Hannah Rider,	Nov. 6, 1746
Nathaniel Bradford & Sarah Spooner,	Nov. 24, 1746
James Howard, Jr., & Thankful Branch,	Dec. 11, 1746
Samuel Harlow & Mercy Bradford,	Dec. 15, 1746
Nathaniel Goodwin & Lydia Lebaron,	Dec. 25, 1746-7
Thomas Paterson & Susannah Beale,	Jan. 1, 1746-7
Josiah Carver, Jr., & Jerusha Sparrow,	Jan. 22, 1746-7
Edward Wright & Eliza Decoster,	Jan. 27, 1746-7
Isaac Morton & Meriah Lewen,	March 19, 1746-7
Thomas Swift, Jr., & Rebecca Clarke,	Oct. 21, 1746
Benjamin Churchell & Ruth Dellano,	Nov. 3, 1746
Perez Tilson & Elizabeth Doty,	Nov. 20, 1746
Doughty Randall of Scituate & Elizabeth Tillson,	Jan. 8, 1746
Jacob Tinkam & Lydia Donham,	Feb. 5, 1746
Nathaniel Hatch & Ruth Rider,	May 5, 1746
Amaziah Harlow & Lois Doten,	May 30, 1746
Ezekiel Morton & Abigail Morton,	July 24, 1746
Joshua Benson & Sarah Shurtleff, both of Middle-boro,	April 7, 1746
Thomas MaComber & Mercy Tilden,	May 9, 1745
John Sherman & Mercy Lucas,	Dec. 3, 1745
Seth Vinal of Scituate & Hannah Tilden,	Jan. 9, 1745-6
William Clift, Jr., of P—— & Bethiah Hatch of Scituate,	April 17, 1746
John Hall, Jr., & Zilpha Crooker,	Sept. 1, 1746
Israel Smith of Scituate & Abigail Foord,	Oct. 24, 1746
Joshua Brimhall of Hingham & Katharine Hall,	July 30, 1747
Deacon Samuel Hatch of Scituate & widow Mary Silvester,	Oct. 27, 1747
Amos Steward & Hannah Moses,	Oct. 27, 1747
Mr. Joseph Lebaron & Mrs. Sarah Leonard,	April 23, 1747
Mr. Nathaniel Torrey & Mrs. Ann Leonard,	May 14, 1747
Edward Stephens, Jr., & Phebe Harlow,	July 16, 1747
Jonathan Samson & Sarah Drew,	Sept. 24, 1747
Eleazer Stephens & Sarah Silver,	Oct. 29, 1747
Mr. Thomas Foster, Jr., & Mrs. Mary Wethrel,	Nov. 5, 1747
Job Morton & Mary Barnes,	Nov. 12, 1747
Samuel Morton & Ruth Rogers,	Nov. 16, 1747

Josiah Johnson & Patience Faunce,   Nov. 16, 1747
Ebenezer Churchell & Mercy Branch,   Nov. 23, 1747
Guiney & Hagar (negroes),   Dec. 10, 1747
Mr. William Greenleaf of Boston & Mrs. Mary Brown,
    June 3, 1747
Lemuel Churchell & Lidia Silvester,   Oct. 13, 1747
Joseph Branhall & Sarah Tilson,   Nov. 26, 1747
Elkanah Churchell, Jr., & Susanna Bartlett,   March 8, 1747
James Doten & Ruth Finney,   April 24, 1750
Reuben Bisbey & Lydia Faunce,   April 26, 1750
Solomon Bartlett & Joanna Holmes,   April 26, 1750
James Barnes & Sarah Nash,   June 11, 1750
Dennis —irmy (?) & Elisabeth Cook,   June 28, 1750
Thomas Warren & Lydia Barnaba,   Sept. 25, 1750
James Weston of Middleboro & Abigail Donham,
    Feb. 9, 1748
Daniel Beak & Rhoda Beal,   July 13, 1748
Zephaniah Morton & Jerusha Donham,   April 19, 1747
David Stockbridge of Hanover & Mrs. Jean Reed,
    April 21, 1747
Benjamin Lothrop of Kingston & Mrs. Deborah Thomas,
    May 5, 1747
Mr. Isaac Thomas & Mrs. Mary Hatch,   May 12, 1747
Joseph Pierce & Rebecca Eames,   June 30, 1747
Timothy Fales, Esq., of Bristol & Mrs. Elisabeth
    Thomas,   July 11, 1747
John Richard & Bashuba Morton,   July 14, 1747
Samuel Marshall, Jr., & Susanna Bartlett,   Oct. 10, 1747
Solomon Atwood & Lydia Cushman,   Oct. 13, 1747
Ichabod Holmes & Rebecca Elles,   Oct. 25, 1747
James Donham & Elisabeth Wood,   Oct. 31, 1747
Silas Morton & Martha Morton,   Nov. 3, 1747
Samuel Bartlett, Esq., & Mrs. Elisabeth Wetherell,
    Nov. 24, 1747
Moses Barrowes, Jr., of Plimpton & Deborah Tottman,
    Nov. 29, 1747
Ebenezer Dogget & Elisabeth Brace,   Jan. 5, 1748
Stephen Sampson & Abigail Morton,   Jan. 19, 1748

William Foster & Joana Lanmon,	March 15, 1748
Martin Wright & Sarah Beal,	March 20, 1748
Jonathan Darling & Martha Bramhall,	March 21, 1748
John Churchell & Sarah Cole,	Sept. 14, 1748
Jonathan Morton & Rebecka Wetherell,	Oct. 5, 1748
Jerimiah Holmes & Phebe Crymbel,	Oct. 12, 1748
Scipo (negro of Deacon Terry) & Hager (negro of Dr. Lebaron),	——
John Harlow & Lydia Holmes,	Oct. 26, 1748
Ebenezer Bartlett & Abigail Finey,	Jan., 1749-50
Simon Moses & Sarah Adams (Indians),	Jan. 11, 1749-50
Thomas Sawyer & Margaret Cotten,	Sept. 14, 1749
John Thomas, Jr., & Abigail Clark,	Nov. 11, 1746
William Churchell & Susana Clark,	Aug. 7, 1748
James Clark, Jr., & Hannah Swift,	Aug. 6, 1748
Samuel Churchell of Plimton & Mary Elles,	April 12, 1748
Jonathan Parker of Plimton & Mrs. Lydia Bartlett,	July 5, 1748
Abner Silvester & Jedidiah Harlow,	Nov. 10, 1748
Thomas Edder of Barnstable & Lydia Harlow,	March 30, 1749
Benjamin Ryder & Betty Bartlett,	May 6, ——
Robert Harlow & Remembrance Wethered,	Sept. 15, ——
Zac. Mendal of Sandwich & Mary Swift,	Oct. 26, ——
Ichabod Bartlett, Jr., & Hannah Rogers,	Nov. 15, 1753
William Weston of Plimpton & Mary Weston,	1754
Samuel Jackson & Experience Atwood,	Jan. 3, 1754
Rev. Elijah Packard & Mrs. Mary Rider,	March 14, 1754
Arthur Shepard (resident) & Mrs. Mary Morton,	May 30, 1754
Samuel Torrey of Boston & Deborah Torrey,	June 20, 1754
Zaccheus Churchill & Mary Trask,	Sept. 16, 1754
E—— Waterman & Mary West,	Oct. 16, 1754
Ephraim Dexter of Rochester & Martha Wait,	Nov. 28, 1754
Nathaniel Holmes & Lydia Churchill,	Dec. 5, 1754
Ebenezer Nelson & Ruth Jackson,	Dec. 12, 1754
George Peckam of Providence & Jerusha Bartlett,	Jan. (?), 1755

William Carver, ye 3d, of Marshfield & Margaret
    Kempton,   Feb. 13, 1755
John Washburn, Jr., & Lydia Prince,   April 10, 1755
Corban Barnes & Rebecka Atwood,   May 1, 1755
Ebenezer Churchill, Jr., & Jean Fisher,   May 19, 1755
Jacob Taylor & Jemima Sampson,   June 5, 1755
William Barns & Mercy Lemote,   June 24, 1755
John Marshall & Jerusha Watkins,   Aug. 5, 1755
Charles Boult (?) & Lydia Curtis,   Nov. 13, 1755
James Coal of Plimton & Deborah Devenport, Dec. 1, 1755
Benjamin Linkon of Taunton & Mercy Carver, Jan. 21, 1756
John Cornwich & Lydia Shurtleff,   April 8, 1756
John Bartlett, Jr., & Sarah Bartlet,   April 15, 1756
Micah Sepit & Mary Sepit (Indians),   April 25, 1756
David Turner & Rebecca Warren,   June 1, 1756
James Carver & Hope Doten,   July 6, 1756
William Chambers & Susanah Lemote (?), July 13, 1756
Joshua Totman & Elisabeth Rogers,   Aug. 10, 1756
Lazarus Lebaron & Mary Lothrop,   Oct. 18, 1756
Peleg Faunce & Marcy Faunce,   Nov. 16, 1756
Nathaniel Washburn & Mary Rider,   Nov. 18, 1756
John Mackeel & Susanna Sampson,   Nov. 23, 1756
Snow Keel of Pembroke & Rebecca Burbank, Nov. 25, 1756
James Bunker of Sherburn & Hannah Shurtleff, Jan. 6, 1757
William Morton & Mary Warren,   May 10, 1750
Ebenezer Doten of Plimton & Mercy Whitton, June 12, 1750
Jacob Albertson & Margaret Nicholson,   July 19, 1750
Richard Durfey of Freetown & Rebeckah Cole, Aug. 30, 1750
Benjamin King of P—— & Bettey Lovell of Kings-
    ton,   Oct. 16, 1750
Samuel Rogers & Hannah Bartlett,   Oct. 25, 1750
Samuel Sherman & Experience Branch,   Nov. 8, 1750
Jabez Gorham of Barnstable & Mary Burbank, Nov. 15, 1750
Jabez Cobb & Sarah Bartlett,   Nov. 16, 1750
Edward Curtiss of Stoughton & Sarah Freeman,
                          Jan. 31, 1750-1
William Bradford of Warren, R. I., & Mary Lebaron,
                       March 22, 1750-1

James Drew & Mary Churchill,	April 4, 1750-1
Joseph Freebles & Sarah Haward,	April 4, 1750-1
William Sutton & Lydia Rider,	April 11, 1750-1
Lemuel Barns & Sarah Lebaron,	April 17, 1751
John King, Jr., of Plimton & Hannah Pierce,	April 25, 1751
Benjamin Bagnall & Hannah Jackson,	April 29, 1751
Thomas Jackson, Jr., & Sarah Taylor,	May 20, 1751
Abraham Hicks & Basheba Dunham,	July 1, 1751
David Gorham & Abigail Jackson,	July 11, 1751
John Lewin (?) & Sarah Holmes,	Oct. 25, 1751
Thomas Rogers, Jr., & Elizabeth Ward,	Oct. 31, 1751
Lemuel Drew & Priscilla Warren,	Nov. 4, 1751
Walter Rich & Experience Totman,	Nov. 19, 1751
Moses Suchamus & Sarah Numoch (Indians),	Nov. 28, 1751
Francis Howard & Elizabeth Curtis,	—— 17, 1751
James Haward of P—— & Mercy Warren of Middleboro,	April 15, 1752
William Gamons & Fear Curtis,	June 13, 1752
Joshua Totman & Joanna Scarrit,	July 14, 1752
Abijah Fisher of Norton & Mary Washburn,	July 23, 1752
Silvanus Morton & Mary Stephens,	Oct. 18, 1752
Jabez Harlow & Experience Churchill,	Oct. 19, 1752
Joseph Rider of Provincetown & Thankful Poland,	July 13, 1752
Zachariah Bartlett & Margaret Barns,	April 12, 1753
Thomas Hinkley, Jr., of Barnstable & Phebe Holmes,	Nov. 9, 1753
Thomas Davis & Mercy Hedge,	May 24, 1753
Ebenezer Ransom of Plimton & Rebekah Harlow,	May 24, 1753
Joseph Fulgham & Lurany Clark,	Aug. 13, 1753
Benjamin Morton & Hannah Faunce,	Sept. 20, 1753
Archippus Fuller of Plimton & Mary Churchill,	Sept. 26, 1753
Nathaniel Morton, Jr., & Rebeckah Jackson,	Nov. 13, 1753
John Morrey & Jerusha Swift,	Oct. 17, 1751
Cornelius Morrey & Sarah Johnson,	Oct. 17, 1751
John Swift of Sandwich & Desire Swift,	Sept. 21, 1752
John Phillips & Lydia Morton the 2d,	Oct. 8, 1752

William Bundick Peterson & Phebe Holmnes,
March 30, 1753
Samuel Ransom of Plimton & Content Meryfield,
Oct. 2, 1753
Alpheus Whiton of Plimton & Ruth Grafton,   Nov. 5, 1753
Samuel Crow of Providence, R. I., & Hannah Rider,
May 28, 1755
Quosh (negro servant to Dr. Lazarus Lebaron) &
    Phills (negro servant to Capt. Theophilus Cotton),
Sept. 2, 1756
Thomas Crandon & Ruth Howland,   June 20, 1751
Benjamin Bartlet, Jr., & Jean Ellis,   June 27, 1751
Daniel Diamond & Elizabeth Morton,   Oct. 21, 1751
William Davis & Sarah Doget,   Feb. 20, 1750-1
Nathaniel Crosman of Taunton & Ester Hatch, April 3, 1752
Josiah Gibs of Sandwich & Mary Cornish,   April 16, 1752
Isaac Tinkam & Remembrance Cooper,   May 4, 1752
William Bartlett & Mary Bartlett,   July 26, 1752
Samuel Churchill & Abigail Rider,   Nov. 23, 1752
Thomas Cornish & Elizabeth Burton,   Dec. 7, 1752
James Doten & Basheba Delino,   April 26, 1753
Simon Mahomman & Phebe Robins (Indians), April 3, 1754
Zacheus Holmnes of P—— & Ruth Bryant (resident
    of P——),   April 11, 1754
Seth Barnes, Jr., & Elizabeth Rider,   June 11, 1754
Job Brewster of Duxbro & Elizabeth Ellis,   Sept. 1, 1754
Thomas Cornish & Ann Bates,   May 20, 1756
Samuel Doten & Mary Cook,   June 28, 1753
David Turner, Jr., & Deborah Lothrop,   Oct. 18, 1753
Nathan Simons of Kingston & Lydia Holmnes, Oct. 24, 1753
Abner Silvester & Abigail Washburn,   Oct. 29, 1753
Samuel West & Elisabeth Rich,   Oct. 30, 1753
Cornelius Holmes, Jr., & Lydia Drew,   Nov. 8, 1753
Robert Roberts & Margaret Decoster,   Nov. 29, 1753
Zedekiah Tinkam & Mercy Tinkam,   Dec. 6, 1753
Robert Perrigo & Susana Holmnes,   June 17, 1754
Thomas Morton & Mary Morton,   July 11, 1754
Jesse Rider & Bethiah Thomas,   Oct. 10, 1754

Lemuel Fish & Hannah Doten,	Oct. 15, 1754
James Wade of Bridgewater & Ann Clark,	Nov. 14, 1754
John Wall of Greenwich, R. I., & Ruth Leeds (?),	
	Dec. 17, 1754
Thomas Bailey (resident in Plimouth) & Sarah Langlee,	
	Dec. 22, 1754
William Hudson & Elizabeth Waite,	March 18, 1755
Alexander Anderson (resident in Plimouth) & Jeane	
Seller?	March 21, 1755
Joseph Silvester & Susannah Cobb,	April 3, 1755
Nathaniel Little of Tiverton & Keziah Adams,	April 14, 1755
Andrew Thompson & Elizabeth Murdock,	July 14, 1755
John Donham & Mary Thomas,	Nov. 13, 1755
Mr. William Sever of Kingston & Mrs. Sarah Warren,	
	Dec. 2, 1755
Joshua Holmnes & Hannah Doten,	Dec. 4, 1755
Nathan Delano & Sarah Cobb,	Dec. 11, 1755
Samuel Donham & Susannah Thomas,	Dec. 15, 1755
William Keen & Margaret Drew,	Dec. 28, 1755
Thomas Mitchell & Elizabeth Totman	March 28, 1756
Ebenezer Donham, Jr., & Hannah Morton,	April 2, 1756
Samuel Dogget & Deborah Foster,	May 6, 1756
Benjamin Holmnes & Rebecca Drew,	July 1, 1756
Nathaniel Bartlett, Jr., & Lydia Barnes,	July 1, 1756
Terret Lester & Sarah Little,	July 8, 1756
John Jones & Lydia Tinkam,	July 12, 1756
Thomas Robinson & Ruth Hatch,	Aug. 3, 1756
John Wetherell & Sarah Crandon,	Nov. 11, 1756
Ebenezer Holmnes & Hannah Nelson,	Nov. 15, 1756
Joseph Waterman & Fear Tinkam,	Dec. 9, 1756
Branch Blackmer & Sarah Waite,	Dec. 28, 1756
Isaac Churchill & Sarah Cobb,	Dec. 30, 1756
John French of Hampton, N. H., & Rhoda Peek,	
	Jan. 18, 1751
Nicholas Spinks & Sarah Goddard,	Feb. 8, 1760
Nathaniel Holmes & Cloe Sears,	April 17, 1760
Francis Crapoo of Rochester & Margaret Beals,	
	April 24, 1760

James Thomas & Hannah Barnes,	April 27,	1760
Hezadiah Job & Betty Sepitt (Indians),	Oct. 16,	1760
James (negro) & Pese (Indian),	Dec. 4,	1760
Samuel Calderwood & Priscella Bartlett,	Dec. 11,	1760
Patrick Morris & Mary Vincent,	Jan. 1,	1761
Thomas Trask & Hannah Waterman,	Feb. 25,	1761
John Harlow, ye 3d, & Rebecca Ho—es,	March 26,	1761
Nathaniel Tupper & Susannah Blackmer,	April 23,	1761
Samuel Sherman & Betty Sears,	April 23,	1761
Nathaniel Leonard & Bethiah Rider,	May 24,	1761
Samuel Kempton, Jr., & Elisabeth Samson,	Aug. 13,	1761
Ebenezer Fuller & Hannah Rider,	Oct. 21,	1761
Adam Allen (negro) & Susannah Sachemus (Indian),		
	Nov. 2,	1761
Seth Morton & Mercy Samson,	Nov. 12,	1761
Samuel Gray of Kingston & Eunice Delano,	Nov. 13,	1761
Isaac Cole & Martha Harlow	Nov. 26,	1761
Faunce Hammond of Rochester & Mary Holmes,		
	Dec. 3,	1761
Benjamin Willis, Jr., of Bridgewater & Sarah Bradford,		
	Dec. 17,	1761
Thomas Davie & Hannah Rogers,	Dec. 31,	1761
Silvanus Bramhall & Mercy Warren,	Jan. 7,	1762
Samuel Pearce of Bristol & Elisabeth Hearsey,	Jan. 21,	1762
Joseph Bartlett, Jr., & Lidia Cobb,	Feb. 4,	1762
John Rogers & Mary Holmes,	Feb. 25,	1762
Jesse Harlow & Elisabeth Samson,	April 22,	1762
Bartlett LeBaron & Mary Easdell,	April 25,	1762
Rev. Ammi Ruhamah Robins of Norfolk, Conn., &		
Mrs. Elisabeth LeBaron,	May 3,	1762
Brittain Hammond of Marshfield (negro) & Hannah		
(negro),	June 3,	1762
Lemuel Goddard & Nancy Kingston,	July 1,	1762
William Richard & Martha Tilley,	Aug. 26,	1762
Seth Ewer of Barnstable & Lidia Holmes,	Sept. 16,	1762
Matthew Claghorn of Chilmark & Jane Bartlett.	Oct. 4,	1759
Daniel Pratt of Plimton & Lidia Cobb,	Nov. 23,	1759
Benjamin Bartlett, Jr., & Jemima Holmes,	Dec. 13,	1759

Solomon Holmes & Abigail Bartlett,   Jan. 3, 1760
Jabez Dogget of Middleboro & Rebecca Rich,   Jan. 24, 1760
Joseph Mitchel & Mary Tinkham,   Feb. 3, 1760
Daniel Finn (resident of Plimouth) & Mary Samson,
                                                 March 20, 1760
Peleg Stevens (resident of Plimouth) & Sarah Wright,
                                                 March 27, 1760
William Cunnet & Mary Squib (Indians),   April 17, 1760
Joseph Barnes & Hannah Rider,   May 1, 1760
Thomas Finney of Bristol & Elisabeth Clark,   June 5, 1760
Richard Cooper & Hannah Samson,   Jan. 22, 1761
Thomas Holmes, Jr., & Mercy Bartlett,   March 3, 1761
William Bartlett, Jr., & Rebeccah Trask,   Sept. 10, 1761
James Poland & Elisabeth Beal,   Sept 13, 1761
Cesar (negro slave of Mr. Elka. Watson) & Hester
        (negro slave of Edward Winslow, Esq.),   Oct. 27, 1761
Elnathan Holmes & Bathsheba Holmes,   Nov. 5, 1761
William Polden & Susannah Lee,   Feb. 21, 1762
Benjamin Barnes & Elisabeth Holmes,   March 18, 1762
Gershom Holmes of Taunton & Deborah Delano,
                                                  May 27, 1762
Richard Kimbal & Susannah Dorham,   Nov. 18, 1762
Samuel Brattles & Alice Barnes,   Dec. 30, 1763
Seth Harlow & Sarah Warren,   March 3, 1763
Samuel Eddy of Middleborough & Anna Morton,
                                                 March 10, 1763
Col. Stephen Miller & Hannah Dyer,   April 20, 1763
George Atwood & Joannah Bartlett,   June 9, 1763
Andrew Crosswell, Jr., of Boston & Mary Clarke,
                                                 June 23, 1763
John Hampton, Jr., & Mary Hatch,   Dec. 4, 1763
James Bartlett & Elisabeth Bates,   Dec. 8, 1763
Ephraim Spooner & Elisabeth Shurtleff,   Feb. 2, 1764
Seth Holmes & Mary Holmes,   Oct. 28, 1762
Ezekiel Ryder & Lidia Attwood,   Nov. 7, 1762
Ezra Burbank & Priscilla Savory,   Nov. 11, 1762
John Bartlett, 3d, & Mercy Ellis,   Dec. 2, 1762
Stephen Smith of Sandwich & Deborah Ellis, Dec. 23, 1762

James Holmes, Jr., & Remember Wetherhead, Jan. 27, 1763
Elijah Morey & Rebecca West, March 24, 1763
Josiah Finney, Jr., & Alice Barnes, April 28, 1763
Joseph Warren & Mercy Jorrey or Torrey, Sept. 15, 1763
Rufus Ripley of Kingston & Mary Shurtleff, Oct. 20, 1763
Joseph Holmes & Phebe Bartlett, Oct. 27, 1763
Amos Jeffery of Plimpton & Phebe Sepit, Nov. 10, 1763
Judah Bartlett & Love Sprague, Nov. 13, 1763
Isaac Jackson of Plimouth & Lidia Barrows, Feb. 14, 1764
Nathaniel Donham & Hannah King, Oct. 13, 1753
Benjamin Smith & Sarah Doten, Oct. 4, 1756
Benjamin Goodwin of Boston & Hannah Le Baron,
Nov. 17, 1757
Joseph Kempton of Dartmouth & Mary Lathrop,
Oct. 24, 1759
Elisha Morton & Elisabeth Mitchel, Sept. 24, 1760
Joseph Lovel of Barnstable & Elisabeth Harlow, Oct. 1, 1761
James Coade & Hannah Ward, Nov. 18, 1762
Zepheniah Holmes, Jr., & Mercy Wetherhead, Sept. 29, 1763
Samuel Harlow & Mary Morton, Oct. 9, 1763
Isaac Mackey & Sarah Harlow, April 7, 1763
George Lemote & Catharine Nicholson, July 12, 1764
William Harlow, Jr., & Sarah Harlow, Aug. 5, 1764
Joseph Tolman & Elisabeth Curtis, Aug. 30, 1764
Eleazer Churchell, Jr., & Jane Rider, Sept. 27, 1764
William Warren & Rebecca Easdell, Oct. 18, 1764
Ellis Churchell & Patience Churchell Oct. 18, 1764
John King & Thankful Holmes, Nov. 7, 1764
William Donham & Abigail Thomas, Nov. 8, 1764
James Doten & Elisabeth Kempton, Nov. 8, 1764
Neg (servant of Madam Thacher of Middleboro) &
Betty Cunnit (Indian), Nov. 11, 1764
Jonathan Bartlett, Jr., & Mary Doten, Nov. 22, 1764
Josiah Doten & Deborah Rider, Nov. 28, 1764
George Holmes & Anna Rich, Dec. 2, 1764
Nathaniel Carver & Sarah Churchell, Dec. 6, 1764
William Barnes & Mary Rider, Dec. 6, 1764
Capt. Ebenezer Gorham, Jr., of Barnstable & Hope
Carver, Dec. 6, 1764

Andrew Bartlett & Lidia Churchell,   Dec. 6, 1764
John Bates of Hanover & Hannah Sylvester,   Dec. 14, 1764
Perez Tillson & Sarah Wethrell,   June 7, 1764
Ebenezer Ward & Lidia Polden,   July 22, 1765
Elkanah Barnes & Hannah Bartlet,   Aug. 1, 1765
Bartlet Holmes & Lucy Bartlet,   Oct. 31, 1765
Ebenezer Harlow, Jr., & Lidia Doten,   Feb. 6, 1766
Richard Holmes & Mercy Barnes,   April 26, 1764
Daniel Hill of Black Point in Casco Bay & Elizabeth
    Holmes,   July 8, 1764
Ezra Corban of Killingsley & Hannah Barnes, April 20, 1765
Jonathan Polden & Mary Ward,   April 24, 1765
e Joshua Shaw & Margaret Atwood,   Oct. 14, 1765
Silas Donham & Bethiah Bartlet,   Jan. 10, 1765
e John Atwood & Lidia Holmes,   June 2, 1765
John Otis & Hannah Churchel,   June 20, 1765
Zacheus Bartlet & Hannah Curtis,   Sept. 22, 1765
Ansel Churchel & Bethiah Holmes,   Oct. 17, 1765
Nathaniel Doten & Mercy Rider,   Oct. 20, 1765
Seth Washburn of P. & Fear Howard of Kingston,
                                                           Oct. 31, 1765
Charles Churchel & Sarah Churchel,   Oct. 31, 1765
Abraham Tisdale of Taunton & Experience Tolman,
                                                           Nov. 7, 1765
Thomas Bartlet & Betty Bartlet,   Dec. 5, 1765
Robert Finney & Lidia Clark,   Dec. 12, 1765
Corban Barnes & Mary Finney,   Dec. 26, 1765
Eleazer Stevens & Susannah Silvester,   Feb. 9, 1766
Nathaniel Ripley & Elisabeth Bartlet,   April 13, 1766
Isaac Morton & Ruth Tinkham,   April 13, 1766
Moses Redding & Sarah Jones,   April 17, 1766
Nathaniel Barnes & Jerusha Blackmer,   June 12, 1766
Stephen Churchel & Lucy Burbank,   July 10, 1766
Samuel Bartlet, Jr., & Elisabeth Jackson,   Aug. 7, 1766
Andrew Hill (resident in P.) & Elisabeth Burges, Oct. 2, 1766
Isaac Bartlet & Lois Harlow,   Oct. 16, 1766
Barnabas Donham & Lidia Cole,   Nov. 13, 1766
Robert Davee & Elisabeth Churchel,   Nov. 13, 1766

Alexander Dow & Lidia Eames, Dec. 4, 1766
Elijah Harlow & Patience Drew, Dec. 8, 1766
William Saverey & Lidia Holmes, Dec. 18, 1766
Benjamin Goddard & Mary Morton, Dec. 25, 1766
Isaac Morse of Middleboro & Jemima Pratt, Jan. 8, 1767
William Clark, Jr., & Sarah Howard, April 16, 1767
William Dewee & Rebecca Cole, 2d, Aug. 6, 1767
Oliver Kempton of Duxboro & Experience Ripley,
Sept. 6, 1767
Jonathan Oliver & Mehitable Stetson, Sept. 13, 1767
John Bishop & Abigail Holmes, Sept. 18, 1767
Zacheus Morton & Sylvester Aken, Oct. 29, 1767
Joseph Rider, Jr., & Abigail Atwood, Oct. 29, 1767
Jonas Clark of Boston & Martha Richard, Oct. 29, 1767
Robert Donham & Ruth Hatch, Nov. 1, 1767
Peter Shurtleff of Plimton & Rebecca Holmes, Nov. 5, 1767
John Foster & Elisabeth Rider, Nov. 12, 1767
Reuben Washburn & Meriah Holmes, Nov. 19, 1767
Thomas Faunce, Jr., & Mary Curtis, Nov. 26, 1767
Seth Nickerson & Lidia Holmes, Dec. 10, 1767
Philip Leonard & Hannah Warren, March 20, 1766
Gamaliel Arnold of Duxboro & Hannah Wait, April 17, 1766
Jonathan Watkin (resident in P.) & Lucy Donham,
July 6, 1766
Thomas Silvester & Elisabeth Donham, July 24, 1766
Lemuel Leach & Sarah Holmes, Sept. 25, 1766
Prince Wadsworth of Duxboro & Zilpah Ellis, Nov. 11, 1766
James Cobb of Kingston & Melatiah Holmes, Nov. 13, 1766
Ezra Harlow & Susannah Warren, April 9, 1767
Stephen Mason & Lidia Simmons, Oct. 20, 1767
Thomas Ellis & Jerusha Clark, Dec. 10, 1767
Consider Drew of Duxboro & Jenne Ellis, Jan. 4, 1768
Lemuel Drew & Elisabeth Rider, Feb. 25, 1768
Benjamin Cornish, Jr., & Rhoda Swift, Oct. 22, 1760 (1750?)
Robert Gamble (resident in P.) & Rebecca Poland,
Jan. 25, 1762
James Seller & Rebecca Cobb, April 25, 1765
Rev. Samuel West of Dartmouth & Mrs. Experience
Howland, March 7, 1768

William Campbell (resident in P.) & Rebecca Gamble,
          April 18, 1768
Daniel Gifford of Sandwich & Sarah Vallur (?), April 25, 1768
Ellis Holmes & Content Howland,   Nov. 18, 1768
Ezra Harlow of Middleboro & Betty Ellis, Nov. 24, 1768
Silvenus Finney & Mary Morton,   Dec. 1, 1768
Isaac Howland & Sarah Doten,   Dec. 14, 1768
Caleb Rider & Hannah McFarland,   Dec. 15, 1768
Ezra Finney & Hannah Luce,   Jan. 12, 1769
William Bassett (resident in P.) & Abigail Lee, Jan. 19, 1769
James Harlow & Hannah Delano,   Oct. 25, 1770
William King & Susannah Harlow,   Oct. 30, 1770
Miles Long & Thankful Clarke,   Nov. 1, 1770
Joseph Bartlett, Jr., & Molly Bartlett, Dec. 13, 1770
Nathaniel Churchell, Jr., & Betty Rider, Dec. 25, 1770
John Barnes & Margaret Rider,   April 14, 1771
Cornelius Morey & Ruth Holmes,   Aug. 15, 1771
Enoch Randall & Phebe Tinkham,   May 4, 1766
Joseph Burbank & Joanna Holmes,   April 10, 1767
George Bramhall & Zilpah Richmond, July 12, 1767
Samuel Harlow & Remembrance Holmes, May 19, 1768
William Bolt & Joannah Ward,   June 27, 1768
Thomas Diman of Bristol, R. I., & Salomi Foster,
          Dec. 4, 1768
Thomas Watson (now resident in P.) & Sarah Lester,
          Dec. 12, 1768
Barnabas Holmes & Mercy Holmes, Dec. 15, 1768
John Cornish & Sarah Bartlett,   Jan. 5, 1769
Benjamin Boyston (now resident in P.) & Mercy
  Bartlett,   Sept. 21, 1769
John Randall (now resident in P.) & Lurama Bearse,
          Sept. 22, 1769
William Straffen (now resident in P.) & Susanna Kimber,
          Sept. 24, 1769
Joseph Bartlett, 4th, & Lucy Holmes, March 8, 1770
James Waterman of P. & Joanna Wood of Plimton,
          March 26, 1770
Thomas Hayward & Ruth Holmes, Jan. 5, 1768

John Sampson & Hannah Sherman,	Feb. 11,	1768
Cuff (negro servant to George Watson, Esq.) &		
Nanne (negro servant to Samuel Bartlett, Esq.),		
	March 24,	1768
Nathaniel Cornish & Abigail Swift,	March 12,	1768
Thomas Davee, Jr., & Jane Holmes,	March 14,	1768
Lemuel Harlow of Plimton & Joanna Holmes,		
	March 18,	1768
Samuel Rider & Jane Swift,	March 12,	1768
Daniel Whitman & Mary Doten,	July 21,	1768
Daniel Hosea & Hannah Bartlett,	July 31,	1768
Ephraim Darling & Rebecca Bartlett,	Aug. 18,	1768
John Bartlett, 3d, & Dorothy Carver,	Sept. 29,	1768
Ephraim Holmes, Jr., & Lucy Barries (?),	Oct. 1,	1768
John Allen & Esther Savery,	Oct. 6,	1768
William Davee & Lydia Harlow,	Oct. 20,	1768
Samuel Hollis (now resident in P.) & Abigail Drew,		
	Oct. 25,	1768
William Loring of Plimton & Lucy Rider,	Oct. 25.	1768
Henry Highton (?) (now resident in Plymouth) &		
Elizabeth Polden,	Oct. 27,	1768
Elkanah Bartlett & Sarah Atwood,	Oct. 27,	1768
Thomas Fanner (?) & Susannah Tinkam,	Oct. 30,	1768
Solomon Holmes & Mary Delano,	Nov. 7,	1768
Ichabod Bearse of Pembroke & Esther Holmes,		
	Nov. 10,	1768
William Curtis of Pembroke & Hannah Tinkam,		
	Nov. 17,	1768
Elisha Doten & Mercy Harlow,	Nov. 24,	1768
Nathaniel Jackson & Elizabeth Foster,	Nov. 24,	1768
Gilbert Holmes & Mercy Holmes,	Nov. 27,	1768
Thomas Wethrell & Anna May,	Dec. 8,	1768
John Cooper & Sarah Sampson,	Jan. 19,	1769
Thomas Doten & Jerusha Howes,	Jan. 26,	1769
Ephraim Luce & Ruth Morton,	Feb. 16,	1769
John Richard, Jr., of Plimton & Lydia King,	Feb. 23,	1769
Silvenus Holmes, Jr., & Rebecca Churchil,	March 26,	1769
John Watson & Lucia Marston,	May 4,	1769

Nathaniel Goodwin, Jr., & Molley Jackson,   June 22, 1769
Amos Dunham & Abigail Faunce,   July 16, 1769
Robert Roberts (now resident in P.) & Sarah Weston,
    Aug. 27, 1769
Nathaniel Sherman & Meriah Clark,   Oct. 19, 1769
William Smith (now resident in P.) & Sarah Stetson
    Oct. 20, 1769
Nathan Cobb & Jerusha Harlow,   Nov. 2, 1769
Nicholas Drew, Jr., & Mercy Holmes,   Nov. 12, 1769
Lothrop Holmes & Mary Bartlett,   Nov. 16, 1769
Richard Babb & Meriah Bartlett,   Nov. 16, 1769
Joseph Holmes & Rebecca Eames,   Nov. 26, 1769
Joseph Sylvester & Susannah Tupper,   Dec. 10, 1769
Edward Clark of Boston & Elizabeth Watson, Dec. 10, 1769
Jonah (or Josiah) Bisbee, Jr., of Pembroke & Ruth
    Sherman,   Dec. 28, 1769
Robert Bartlett & Jenna Spooner,   Feb. 22, 1770
Jonathan Harlow & Betty Blackmer,   March 8, 1770
Samuel Sherman & Jerusha Morton,   March 18, 1770
Isaac Harlow & Martha Swinnerton,   March 18, 1770
William Donham of P. & Mercy Raymond of Middleboro,
    March 11, 1770
Nicholas Smith & Susanna Churchil,   April 12, 1770
David Lothrop & Bathsheba May,   July 12, 1770
Thomas Sears & Rebecca Ryder,   Oct. 23, 1770
William Williams & Thankful Ryder,   Oct. 28, 1770
Richard Durfee & Elizabeth West,   Nov. 23, 1770
Benjamin Eaton & Hannah Holmes,   Jan. 3, 1771
George Dunham (now resident in P.) & Anna Dunham,
    Jan. 3, 1771
Lemuel Cobb & Hannah Kempton,   Feb. 14, 1771
Thomas Covington & Sarah Treble,   April 4, 1771
John Atwood, Jr., & Deborah Doten,   April 7, 1771
John Edwards & Lydia Lamson,   April 18, 1771
Ichabod Thomas & Hannah Morton,   April 21, 1771
Samuel Morton & Joanna Totman,   April 28, 1771
Thomas Lanman & Rebecca Kempton,   May 30, 1771
James Hovey, Esq., & Mary Harlow,   June 2, 1771

William Breek of Boston & Margaret Thomas, July 11, 1771
Cornelius Brimhall of Falmouth, Casco Bay, & Mercy
    Torrey,   Aug. 22, 1771
Thomas Hatch Whitemore & Thankful Holmes, Oct. 9, 1771
Rev. Joseph Penniman of Bedford & Hannah Jackson,
                                    Oct. 10, 1771
Ansel Holmes & Martha Hayward,   Oct. 14, 1771
John Churchil, 3d, & Elisabeth Eames,   Oct. 27, 1771
Thomas Hackman & Lydia Sutton (?),   Nov. 10, 1771
James Wadlins (?) & Ruth Dunham, daughter of
    Cornelius,   Nov. 26, 1771
Joseph Brimhall & Remember Robbins,   Nov. 28, 1771

PLYMPTON.

June 4, 1707. "Part of Plymouth established as Plympton." First Congregational Church organized 1698.

Robert Avery & Anna Cushman,   Feb. 23, 1741
Isaac Lobdel & Ruth Clarke,   Feb. 24, 1741
Thomas Loring & Sarah Lobdel,   Feb. 24, 1741
Philemon Samson & Rachel Standish,   May 12, 1742
David Darling & Ruth Faunce,   June 9, 1742
Asa Cook & Susanna Bryant,   Nov. 10, 1742
Ichabod Churchel & Rebecca Curtis,   Nov. 11, 1742
Benjamin Shaw & Mary Attwood,   Nov. 1, 1742
Ephraim Paddock & Sarah Bradford,   Nov. 25, 1742
Robert Cook & Hannah Bisbee,   Nov. 25, 1742
Elkanah Cushman & Hannah Standish,   April 7, 1743
John Holmes & Joanna Adams,   Aug. 12, 1743
Eleazer Richard & Martha King,   Oct. 6, 1743
Simeon Holmes & Abiah Stertevant,   Dec. 1, 1743
James Whiten, Jr., & Molly Lucas,   Jan. 19, 1743
Ephraim Tilson & Deborah Ransom,   July 31, 1744
Abraham Jackson of Plimouth & Bethiah Whitin,
                                Sept. 25, 1744

Samuel Thomas of Middleboro & Mehitable Barows,
Jan. 4, 1744

Mr. John Doten of P. & Hannah Sherman of Plimouth,
April 25, 1745

James Cole & Merriah Richard, Feb. 14, 1749

James Thomas & Abigail Waterman, Aug. 4, 1750

Capt. Nehemiah Cushing & Mrs. Hannah Thomas,
Sept. 5, 1750

Richard Everson & A. Standish, Oct. 30, 1750

Edward Wright & Desire Weston, Oct. 31, 1750

David Churchell & Jane Ellis, Feb. 20, 1751

Jabez Prier & Abigail Samson, June 5, 1751

Jonathan Samson & Deborah Bradford, Oct. 27, 1751

Simeon Boney & Thankful Whiten, Nov. 21, 1751

Abel Stetson & Lydia Washburne, Dec. 26, 1751

Zebediah (Zahdiel?) Samson & Abiah Whitmarsh,
Aug. 27, 1752

Samuel Wright, Jr., & Abigail Standish, Sept. 1, 1752

Jacob Wright & Deborah Torrey, Nov. 20, 1752

Isaac Thayer & Jael Whitin, March 28, 1753

Josiah Perkins & Deborah Sole, April 26, 1753

Jeremiah Kille & Rebecca Samson, July 3, 1753

John Bishop & Ruth Parker, Oct. 18, 1753

Josiah Cushman & Sarah Ring, Nov. 1, 1753

William Bennitt of Middleboro & Tabathe Briant,
Nov. 26, 1753

Isaac Little & Hannah Soule, Jan. 10, 1754

Samuel Hayford & Rebecca Waterman, Jan. 31, 1754

John Bridgham & Joanna Comer, Feb. 28, 1754

Adam Wright & Ruth Samson, Feb. 28, 1754

Eseker Fuller & Elisabeth Doten, June 29, 1747

George Stertevant & Jerusha Cushman, May 11, 1748

Ebenezer Donham & Lydia Fuller, May 12, 1748

Ebenezer Thomas & Mary Wright, July 13, 1748

Theophilus Richard & Hannah Harlow, April 18, 1749

James Harlow & Mehetable Finney, June 22, 1749

Josiah Cushman, Jr., & Sarah Standish, July 10, 1749

Mr. William Hunt & Mrs. Sarah Bradford, Sept. 7, 1749

Josiah Marshel & Sarah Churchell,	Nov. 16, 1749
Jacob Staples & Mary Vought,	Nov. 16, 1749
Edward Doten & Joanna Whitten,	Nov. 16, 1749
Lemuel Richard & Parceus Shaw,	Feb. 3, 1749
Joshua Perkins & Hannah Samson,	Feb. 8, 1749
John Shaw, Jr., & Elizabeth Lucas,	Jan. 31, 1750
John Barrows & Lidia Shaw,	Feb. 27, 1750
James Dunham & Rebecca Holmes,	May 2, 1751
Elijah Percy (or Perrey) & Sarah Crocker,	Aug. 1, 1751
Joshua Perrey & Patience Lucas,	Aug. 21, 1751
Consider Benson & Elizabeth Washburn,	Dec. 3, 1751
John Perkins & Mehitable Shaw,	April 2, 1752
Jonathan Ransom & Mary Shaw,	April 23, 1752
James Palmer & Marebe Nye,	July 2, 1752
Benony Lucas & Elizabeth Wilkinson,	Nov. 16, 1753
Elisha Lucas, Jr., & Rebecca Barrow,	June 16, 1753
Robert Wilkinson & Susana Barrow,	June 27, 1754
Rev. Roland Thacher & Mrs. Hannah Ferren,	Sept. 15, 1754
Simeon Bradford & Phebe Whiton,	Jan. 23, 1755
Noah Pratt & Mercy Cole,	March 18, 1755
Benjamin Lucas & Lidia Crocker,	April 3, 1755
Joseph Barrow & Sarah Atwood,	April 3, 1755
Joseph Lathrop & Deborah Perkins,	May 22, 1755
John Russel & Elizabeth Bridgham,	June 4, 1756
Abiel Shurtlef & Molley Lebaron,	Jan. 4, 1756
Melatiah Washburn & Zilpha Shaw,	March 16, 1756
John Sturtevant & Faith Shaw,	Nov. 12, 1756
Abner Barrow & Basheba Faunce,	Nov. 12, 1756
Lieut. Samuel Darling & Margret Cushing,	Nov. 25, 1756
George Barrow, ye 3d, & Patience Cobb,	Nov. 29, 1756
Amos Fuller & Rachel Samson,	Oct. 25, 1759
Simeon Samson & Deborah Cushing,	Nov. 1, 1759
William Churchell & Sarah Rider,	Nov. 29, 1759
John Rider & Susannah Bryant,	May 15, 1760
Elisha Howard & Mercy Whiten,	July 10, 1760
David Weston & Abigail Soul,	July 11, 1760
Samuel Ellis & Lidia Chandler,	Jan. 20, 1761
Isaac Wright & Faith Chandler,	July 2, 1761

Joel Dean & Hannah Weston,	Sept. 10, 1761
Thomas Harlow & Anna Fuller,	May 3, 1762
Seth Waterman & Hannah Perkins,	Nov. 11, 1762
⚬ Ebenezer Atwood & Leah Churchell,	Nov. 25, 1762
Thomas Waterman, Jr., & Priscilla Perkins,	Dec. 2, 1762
Isaac Sprague & Sarah Blossom,	Jan. 6, 1763
Eleazer Fuller & Margaret Holmes,	Jan. 6, 1763
John Stetson & Joannah Doten,	Feb. 3, 1763
George Bryant & Sarah Lobdell,	Dec. 15, 1763
Zephaniah Perkins & Patience Ripley,	Dec. 22, 1763
Isaac Churchell, 3d, & Eunice Ripley,	Jan. 26, 1764
Ebenezer Doten & Mary Richard,	Feb. 23, 1764
Ebenezer Bonney & Deborah Drew,	March 22, 1764
Joseph Chamberlain & Susannah Pratt,	April 10, 1764
Abner Hall & Mehitable Chamberlain,	June 24, 1764
Nathaniel Cole & Hezediah Samson,	Nov. 20, 1760
Edward Cole & Deborah Cobb,	Jan. 8, 1761
Timothy Tillson & Silence Whiten,	Feb. 5, 1761
Zebedee Chandler & Repentance Bennet,	Aug. 6, 1761
William Cobb & Mary Pyncheon,	Dec. 3, 1761
Perez Shaw & Patience Donham,	Dec. 31, 1761
Ichabod Shurtleff & Elisabeth Pratt,	March 4, 1762
William Tillson & Mary Ransom,	April 1, 1762
Francis Pumroy, Jr., & Sarah Nye,	Aug. 26, 1762
Eleazer Robins & Priscilla Lucas,	Dec. 7, 1762
Zephaniah Doten & Rebecca Donham,	Dec. 14, 1762
John Samson & Elisabeth Cobb,	May 19, 1763
Joseph Ransom & Lidia Thomas,	Dec. 1, 1763
John Atwood & Keziah Harlow,	Dec. 8, 1763
Jacob Cushman & Hannah Cobb,	May 10, 1764
Zebedee Churchell & Sarah Cushman,	May 24, 1764
Job Tucker & Hannah Barrows,	May 24, 1764
David Fearing & Huldah Cushman,	Dec. 23, 1756
Pero & Hannah (servants to ——— Bartlett),	Feb. 18, 1757
Rowland Hammond & Mary Southworth,	May 5, 1757
⚬ Samuel Cobb & Lidia Atwood,	March 17, 1757
Benjamin Barrows & Hannah Atwood,	June 5, 1757
William Stertevant & Jemima Shaw,	Nov. 14, 1757

Joseph Cushman & Elisabeth Samson,	Jan. 5, 1758
Rowland Cobb & Hannah Stetson,	Nov. 16, 1758
Ephraim Cole & Bethiah Samson,	Jan. 2, 1759
Ebenezer Shurtleff & Mary Pratt,	March 22, 1759
Amos Bryant & Margaret Pratt,	April 3, 1759
Consider Chase & Eunice Tillson,	June 7, 1759
Ephraim Soul & Rebecca Whitmarsh,	Feb. 10, 1757
Luke Perkins & Elisabeth Churchell,	March 27, 1757
Benjamin Soul & Mehitable Bonney,	May 5, 1757
Abner Harlow & Rachel Richard,	June 2, 1757
Edward Lanman & Abiah Bryant,	Feb. 2, 1758
Matthew Whiten & Sarah Thear (?),	Feb. 7, 1758
Elkanah Cushman & Patience Perkins,	March 16, 1758
Josiah Cushman & Deborah Ring,	July 20, 1758
Jonathan Waterman & Hannah Soul,	Oct. 27, 1758
Benjamin Bryant & Sarah Tinkham,	Feb. 1, 1759
Nathaniel Bryant, Jr., & Joannah Cole,	Feb. 21, 1759
Consider Fuller & Lidia Bryant,	Feb. 21, 1759
James Whiten & Mercy Soul,	Oct. 4, 1759
Ebenezer Churchell & Luce Palmer,	July 17, 1764
Elephes Ring & Rebecca Weston,	Sept. 20, 1764
Jacob Jonson of Plymouth & Eunice Cushman,	Oct. 9, 1764
Levy Bradford & Elisabeth Luice,	Nov. 15, 1764
Benjamin Drew & Elisabeth Doged,	Nov. 22, 1764
Tymothy Rypley, Jr., & Hannah Waterman,	Feb. 14, 1765
Isaac Churchell, Jr., & Maletiah Bradford,	Aug. 1, 1765
Joel Ellis, Jr., & Annes Pratt,	Sept. 26, 1765
Seth Bryant & Deborah Lobbdil,	Oct. 24, 1765
Ephraim Holmes & Zerniah Bryant,	Oct. 30, 1765
James Churchil & Priscilla Soul,	Oct. 31, 1765
Silas Tillson & Joanah Churchell,	Nov. 28, 1765
Jonathan Parker, Jr., & Abigail Loring,	Dec. 5, 1765
Levy Bradford & Elisabeth Lewis,	Nov. 15, 1764
Moses Shaw & Mary Pratt,	Aug. 16, 1764
Simeon Barrows & Mary Shaw,	Nov. 29, 1764
Israel Dunham & Hannah Whitin,	Dec. 13, 1764
Robert Sturtevant & Deborah Murdock,	Feb. 28, 1765
Micah Foster & Hazediah Crocker,	March 7, 1765

Ezekiel Samson & Sarah Fance,	April 4, 1765
Tymothy Cobb & Deborah Churchell,	April 16, 1765
Hezekiah Cole & Elisabeth Shurtliff,	July 8, 1765
John Gamon & Hannah Cole,	Sept. 3, 1765
George Williams & Kesiah Attwood,	Sept. 11, 1765
Joseph Attwood & Elisabeth Shaw,	Oct. 17, 1765
Thomas Savery & Hannah Bennet,	Oct. 24, 1765
Jabez Muxam & Anna Shurtleff,	Oct. 30, 1765
Thomas Miller & Mary Boney,	April 17, 1766
John Cobb & Priscilla Lucas,	Sept. 17, 1766
James Morton & Mary Holmes,	Oct. 9, 1766
Jobb Weston & Hannah Bisbee,	Oct. 23, 1766
Cornelius Sturtevant & Sarah Bozworth,	Dec. 16, 1766
Nathaniel Churchil & Lidia Samson,	March 30, 1766
Jabez Fuller & Ruth Wright,	April 24, 1766
Isechar Bisbe & Mary Harlow,	April 28, 1766
Nathaniel Boney, Jr., & Hannah Bearce,	Nov. 27, 1766
Hopestill Bisbe, Jr., & Abigail Churchill,	Sept. 4, 1766
Josiah Sears & Lidia Boney,	Feb. 5, 1767
Ephraim Anequit & Lydia Jeffery,	Feb. 15, 1767
Freeman Ellis & Sarah Bradford,	March 19, 1767
James Wright, Jr., & Mercy Richard,	Dec. 15, 1768
Stephen Attwood & Jennet Murdock,	May 11, 1769
Stephen Tillson, Jr., & Hopestill Shaw,	May 18, 1769
John Lucas & Lydia Fuller,	Nov. 16, 1769
John Bennet, Jr., & Keziah Shaw,	Nov. 30, 1769
Thadeus Ripply & Abigail Ransom,	Feb. 8, 1770
Ichabod Attwood & Hannah Shaw,	Feb. 19, 1770
Jabez Pratt & Sarah Chamberlain,	Oct. 9, 1770
David Wood, Jr., & Elisabeth Doten,	Dec. 6, 1770
Seth Barrows & Abigail Attwood,	Dec. 20, 1770
Thomas Edward Barrows & Elisabeth Rogers,	Jan. 15, 1771
Isaac Perkins & Molly Shurtliff,	April 18, 1771
Gideon Perkins & Desire Dunham,	May 23, 1771
Deacon Thomas Savory & Mary Crocker,	May 30, 1771
Andrew Barrows & Sarah Perkins,	Aug. 1, 1771
Jonathan Cobb & Mariah Cole,	Aug. 6, 1771
Isaac Holmes & Ruth Ransom,	Oct. 27, 1768

Judah Washburn & Priscilla Samson,   Feb. 23, 1769
John Rayment, 2d, & Elizabeth Norcutt,   March 2, 1769
Silas Tinkham & Lydia Smith, both of Middleboro,
                                             Dec. 20, 1771
Joseph Fance & Hannah Winslow, both of Middleboro,
                                             Aug. 11, 1772
Samuel Cobb of Middleboro & Sarah Churchil of
    Wareham,   Sept. 24, 1772
Edward Wood, Jr., & Elce Fance, both of Middleboro,
                                             Jan. 7, 1773
Elisha Whitton & Jedidah Whitton,   April 13, 1767
Samuel Nichols & Sarah Soule,   May 21, 1767
Francis Holmes & Lidia Samson,   Dec. 3, 1767
Joshua Churchill & Elisabeth Bonney,   Feb. 4, 1768
Francis Ring & Molly Weston,   April 28, 1768
James Magoun & Elisabeth Bradford,   May 19, 1768
Benjamin Bryant & Sarah Harlow,   Sept. 13, 1768
Patrick Colen & Molly Mackfarland,   Oct. 27, 1768
Austin Bearce & Mary Bradford,   Dec. 1, 1768
Nathaniel Hayward & Hannah Soule,   March 24, 1769
Abner Richard & Susanna Wright,   March 23, 1769
Benjamin Blossom & Molly Ripley,   April 13, 1769
Isaac Cushman & Sarah Ellis,   Nov. 16, 1769
Job Randall & Hannah Lobdell,   Feb. 15, 1770
Zebulon Robinson & Lydia Sears,   March 15, 1770
Nathaniel Fuller & Lydia Holmes,   March 29, 1770
Jonathan Barrows & Lydia Perkins,   April 4, 1770
Ezekiel Powers & Abigail Bonney,   April 12, 1770
Elkanah Cushman & Hannah Churchill,   May 17, 1770
Ichabod Phinney & Deborah Churchill   ·   Nov. 1, 1770
Nathaniel Churchill, Jr., & Deborah Wright, Dec. 27, 1770
Dependance Sturtevant & Abigail Smith,   Jan. 17, 1771
John Churchill & Molly Bradford,   April 4, 1771
Ebenezer Cushman & Rebecca Churchill.   April 4, 1771
Shadrach Standish & Molly Churchill,   April 25, 1771
Joshua Austin & Sarah Faunce,   May 14, 1771
Nathaniel Pratt, Jr., & Content Richard,   Oct. 23, 1771
Jabez Bryant & Hannah Pratt,   Oct. 30, 1771

Josiah Chandler & Rachel Magoun,	Nov. 14, 1771
Joseph Bennet & Molly Blossom,	Dec. 5, 1771
Silvanus Samson & Molly Wright,	Feb. 20, 1772
Nathaniel Rider & Priscilla Bradford,	Nov. 5, 1772
Caleb Coomes & Hannah Bisbe, Jr.,	Nov. 5, 1772
Silvanus Bartlett & Sarah Loring,	Nov. 19, 1772
David Ripley & Jane Churchill,	Dec. 3, 1772
James Harlow & Sarah Bryant,	March 18, 1773
Obed Barlow & Rebekah Churchill,	March 25, 1773
George Bisbe & Grace Ripley,	April 8, 1773
Adam Wright & Sarah Tinkham,	June 1, 1773
Samuel Everson & Sarah Bearce,	Oct. 14, 1773
Josiah Cushman, Jr., & Patience Perkins,	Nov. 25, 1773
Ephraim Washburn & Sarah Bisbe,	Dec. 9, 1773
Elijah Bisbe, Jr., & Susanna Ripley,	Dec. 16, 1773
Joseph Vaughan & Hannah Cobb,	Nov. 21, 1771
John Tilson & Ruth Barrows,	Dec. 19, 1771
Ephraim Cole & Mary Holmes,	Jan. 23, 1772
Silvanus Donham & Lydia Shaw,	Feb. 27, 1772
John Shurtleff & Mary Goward,	April 2, 1772
William Jackson & Elisabeth Vaughan,	June 4, 1772
Willard Sears & Sarah Robbins,	Nov. 3, 1772
James Bosworth & Mehitable Shaw,	Feb. 2, 1773
Caleb Samson & Hopestill Barrows,	Feb. 4, 1773
Gideon Cushman & Ruth Shaw,	Feb. 25, 1773
Silas Donham & Molly Tilson,	April 8, 1773
Joseph Ellis & Hannah Shurtleff,	May 20, 1773
George Ellis & Phebe Stephens,	May 23, 1773
Lucas Donham & Rebekah Wood,	Oct. 1, 1773
Nehemiah Cobb & Mehitable Richard,	Nov. 4, 1773
Bartlett Murdock, Jr., & Deborah Perkins,	Nov. 11, 1773
Ebenezer Blossom & Hannah Murdock,	Nov. 11, 1773
Daniel Shaw & Mary Barrows,	Aug. 6, 1778
John Butterworth & Elisabeth Boult,	Sept. 27, 1778
Peres Churchill, Jr., & Priscilla Wood,	Oct. 1, 1778
George Donham & Phebe Lucas,	Oct. 15, 1778
John Applin & Mary Donham,	Oct. 22, 1778
Isaac Shaw Lucas & Martha Shaw,	Oct. 29, 1778

Reuben Mackfarland & Margaret Crocker,	Nov. 26,	1778
Zurishaddai Palmer & Susanna Cobb,	Dec. 21,	1778
Elijah Lucas & Sarah Shaw,	April 17,	1779
Joseph Robbins & Elisabeth Stephens,	June 6,	1779
Perkins Gurney & Patience Tinkham,	Sept. 9,	1779
Silvanus Stephens & Sylvia Fuller,	Nov. 4,	1779
Barnabas Raymond & Bethial Jackson,	Nov. 5,	1779
Samuel Bradford & Susanna Vaughan,	Nov. 11,	1779
William Bridgham & Anna Hammond,	Nov. 15,	1779
Silvanus Bennet & Hannah Raymond,	Dec. 16,	1779
Elias Nye & Ruth Shaw,	Feb. 3,	1780
William Bump & Hannah Barrows,	Feb. 10,	1780
Morris Bump & Huldah Bump,	Feb. 10,	1780
Zabdiel Tomson & Clara Sturtevant,	Feb. 23,	1780
Ephraim Pratt & Kezia Wood,	March 16,	1780
Stoddard Totman & Rebekah Cobb,	March 16,	1780
Jabez Churchill & Lovisa Lucas,	May 11,	1780
William Barrows & Sarah Donham,	June 8,	1780
Benjamin Crocker & Deborah Vaughan,	July 6,	1780
Zenas Atwood & Mary Perry,	Aug. 6,	1780
Silvanus Shaw & Rebekah Donham,	Aug. 15,	1780
Joseph Perkins & Sarah Cushman,	Oct. 5,	1780
James Donham & Elisabeth Robbins,	Oct. 19,	1780
James Cobb & Deliverance Shaw,	Nov. 9,	1780
James Murdock, Jr., & Lydia Hamond,	Nov. 9,	1780
Job Cole & Mary Savery,	Nov. 30,	1780
Solomon Bolton & Elizabeth Pratt,	Dec. 7,	1780
Peter Thayer & Ruth Sturtevant,	June 28,	1775
Jonathan Whitman & Ruth Churchill,	Sept. 21,	1775
John Barden & Hannah Chamberlain,	Sept. 28,	1775
Caleb Tomson & Molly Perkins,	Nov. 23,	1775
Edward Stranger & Deborah Richard,	Dec. 15,	1775
Beza Soule & Zerviah Cushman,	Jan. 18,	1776
Ebenezer Wright & Deliverance Churchill,	Feb. 7,	1776
Samuel Ripley & Phebe Samson,	April 5,	1776
Jabez Weston & Lydia Billington,	Oct. 12,	1776
Isaac Lobdell & Polly Stetson,	Dec. 21,	1776
John Bradford & Annie Loring,	Dec. 26,	1776

Thomas Gannett & Susanna Loring,	Jan. 10, 1777
John Bartlett & Molly Bonney,	April 17, 1777
Holmes Thomas & Susanna Churchill,	July 9, 1777
Zenas Byrant & Molly Ruggles,	Oct. 2, 1777
Levi Bryant & Lydia Bryant,	Dec. 24, 1777
Gideon Bradford & Abigail Samson,	Jan. 8, 1778
Joshua Loring & Hannah Campbell,	Jan. 22, 1778
Noah Bisbe & Jane Bradford,	Feb. 12, 1778

KINGSTON.

June 16, 1726. "Part of Plymouth established as Kingston." First Church (Unitarian) organized 1717. Baptist, 1805.

Joshua Sherman & Deborah Croade,	Oct. 2, 1735
Joshua Bradford & Hannah Bradford,	Feb. 17, 1736
Jonathan Tilson & Martha Washburne,	Jan. 11, 1737
Cornelius White & Sarah Ford,	Feb. 22, 1742
Elisha Stetson, Jr., & Sarah Adams,	April 26, 1742
Thomas Phillips & Mary Mitchel,	Sept. 14, 1743
Timothy Morton & Mary Wilson,	Dec. 15, 1737
Ebenezer Chandler & Anna, his wife,	Feb. 23, 1737
Charles Cooke & Hannah Faunce,	May 30, 1738
Andrew Samson & Sarah Phillips,	June 12, 1738
Peter Tinkham & Mary, his wife,	Jan. 6, 1736
James Claghorn & Elisabeth Ring,	June 26, 1736
John Simmons & Hopestil Stutson,	Oct. 21, 1736
Zachariah Chandler & Zeriah Holmes,	Oct. 21, 1736
Nathan Wright & Hannah Cook,	Dec. 7, 1736
Edmund Hodges & Mercy Cook,	Jan. 31, 1736
John Wright & Mercy Coomer,	Aug. 18, 1736
Samuel Wade & Mary Curtiss,	Aug. 30, 1737
Abner Hall of K. & Sarah Hatch of Pembroke,	Dec. 30, 1742
Benjamin Eaton & Mary Tilson,	Jan. 27, 1742
John Finney of K. & Betty Lovel of Abington,	April 5, 1743
Ebenezer Morton & Susanna Holmes,	May 5, 1743

Ichabod Brodford & Mary Johnson, Nov. 25, 1743
David Eaton & Deborah Fuller, 1744
Ignatius Cushing of Halifax & Tabitha Fish, June 27, 1744
Mr. James Reed of Camebridge & Mrs. Hannah Stacey,
Sept. 27, 1744
Mr. Jacob Gould of Hull & Mrs. Deborah Samson,
Oct. 4, 1744
Deacon John Washburne of K. & Mrs. Mehitable
Wright of Plimton, Dec. 13, 1744
Mr. Amos Corbis of Scituate & Mrs. Mary Faunce,
Jan. 8, 1744
Mr. Isaiah Thomas of Newport & Mrs. Keziah Holmes,
Oct. 3, 1745
Isaac Holmes & Mary Atherton, June 16, 1746
Thomas Hall & Hannah Edgarton, July 14, 1746
Timothy Briggs of Taunton & Bersheba Mitchel,
Aug. 14, 1746
Joseph Tilden, Jr., of Scituate & Mrs. Sarah Foster,
Feb. 2, 1762
Joshua Bryant & Susanah Randal, Sept. 4, 1766
Ebenezer Adams & Lidia Cook, Nov. 3, 1766
Mr. Gersham Cob & Mrs. Sarah Cook, Nov. 19, 1766
Joseph Adams & Eleanor Came, Nov. 20, 1766
Capt. Joseph Bartlet, Jr., & Mrs. Lurania Drew,
Nov. 27, 1766
Thaddeus Ransom & Martha Drew, Dec. 27, 1766
Job Andrew & Thankful Delano Prince, May 21, 1767
Nehemiah Drew & Ruth Putnam, June 11, 1767
Nathaniel King of Plimton & Rebecca Everson, Oct. 1, 1767
Cephas Wadsworth of Duxboro & Molly Cook, Nov. 5, 1767
Enos West & Sarah Ripley, March 14, 1768
Josiah Cook & Lidia Faunce, March 31, 1768
Mr. Ebenezer Fuller, Jr., of Halifax & Mrs. Deborah
Eaton, April 7, 1768
Mr. Uriah Bartlett & Mrs. Susannah Cook, Aug. 25, 1768
Capt. Theophilus Stetson & Mrs. Abigail Prince,
Nov. 24, 1768
Mr John Adams, Jr., & Mrs. Sarah Drew, Feb. 9, 1769

Mr. Paul Bailey of Scituate & Mrs. Ann Holmes,
March 8, 1769
Josiah Holmes, Jr., & Hazadiah Sturtevant, July 6, 1769
Mr. Joseph Shurtleff & Mrs. Olive Ripley, July 6, 1769
Mr. Josiah Waterman, Jr., & Mrs. Lidia Everson,
July 27, 1769
Mr. Elijah Chandler & Mrs. Eunice Washburne, Feb. 8, 1770
Mr. Levi Holmes & Mrs. Lidia Bradford, April 19, 1770
Mr. Consider Orcutt & Mrs. Lidia Bradford, May 17, 1770
Mr. Benjamin Sampson & Mrs. Esther Weston,
Sept. 16, 1770
Mr. Nathaniel Cook & Mrs. Keziah Thomas, Sept. 27, 1770
Mr. Ebenezer Everson & Mrs. Betty King, Nov. 28, 1770
Mr. Joseph Holmes & Mrs. Jemima Adams, Nov. 29, 1770
Mr. John Phinney & Mrs. Ruth Ring, Dec. 25, 1770
Mr. Melatiah Holmes & Mrs. Elisabeth Bradford,
Jan. 31, 1771
Asa Whitten of Plimpton & Lydia Cook, May 8, 1771
John Bartlett & Bathsheba Shurtleff, May 16, 1771
Silvanus Everson & Thankful Fuller, Oct. 24, 1771
Josiah Ripley of Plimpton & Sarah Cushman, Oct. 30, 1771
Stetson Bradford & Lurana Holmes, Oct. 31, 1771
Elnathan Fish, Jr., of Pembroke & Hannah Wright,
Nov. 7, 1771
David Lucas & Lydia Wright, Nov. 14, 1771
Nathaniel Gilbert & Hannah Hanks, Jan. 29, 1772
Joshua Ripley, Jr., of K. & Lydia Bartlett of Duxboro,
May 7, 1772
Lot Eaton & Elisabeth Everson, July 23, 1772
Josiah Fuller, Jr., & Elisabeth Holmes, Nov. 12, 1772
Seth Drew & Hannah Brewster, Dec. 3, 1772
Robert Thomas & Betty Robinson, Dec. 20, 1772
Jedediah Holmes & Sarah Adams, Jan. 31, 1773
Ezekiel Loring of Plimpton & Hannah Stetson, July 1, 1773
Zephaniah Mayhew of Chilmark & ———— Wadsworth,
Nov. 24, 1773
William Curtis of Hanover & Rebecca Gilbert, April 21, 1774
James Lincoln of Scituate & Hannah Everson, June 13 1774

Samuel Drew & widow Hannah Cooke,   July 13, 1774
Seth Randall of Pembroke & Sarah Weston,   July 14, 1774
Ephraim Everson & Susanna Bradford,   Aug. 4, 1774
Joseph Hall of Marshfield & Susanna Randal, Sept. 15, 1774
Capt. Joseph ——and & Sarah Bartlett,   Sept. 22, 1774
Robert Cook & Lydia Adams,   Dec. 1, 1774
Calvin Ripley & Pegg Bradford,   Dec. 8, 1774
Benjamin Fuller of Plimton & Abigail King,   Dec. 15, 1774
Capt. John Gray & Desire Cushman,   Jan. 26, 1775
Solomon Whitten of Hingham & Asenath Cook,
    Feb. 22, 1775
Ebenezer Cushman & Susannah Holmes,   March 23, 1775
Abner Holmes & Sarah Kent,   June 8, 1775
Jacob Fish & Sarah Keen,   Oct. 5, 1775
William Lincoln of Scituate & Lydia Cook,   Nov. 1, 1775
Ichabod Bradford & Rachel Wright,   Nov. 2, 1775
David Carver of Marshfield & Sarah Holmes, Nov. 23, 1775
Ebenezer Daws & Priscilla Bassett,   Dec. 14, 1775
Samuel Stetson & Huldah Brewster,   Jan. 25, 1776
Nathaniel Hanley & Allice Ripley,   Feb. 29, 1776
Nathan Bradford & Sarah Sturtevant,   March 19, 1776
Barnabas Winslow of New Gloucester & Deborah
    Bradford,   June 13, 1776
Capt. Josiah Thatcher, Jr., of Yarmouth & Elisabeth
    Lathrop,   Nov. 12, 1776
Peter West & Tabathy Wright,   Jan. 1, 1777
Perez Bradford of Plimpton & Sarah Prince, March 13, 1777
Abijah Drew & Betty Stetson,   May 19, 1777
Joseph McLaughlen of Duxboro & Jenny West, July 24, 1777
Capt. William Barker of Scituate & Sarah Lathrop,
    Dec. 12, 1777
Jesse Fuller & Ruth Prince,   June 11, 1778
Isaac Cook & Rebecca Bradford,   Aug. 13, 1778
Capt. Thomas Stetson & Elisabeth Cook,   Sept. 3, 1778
Adam Fish of Duxboro & Mary Hunt,   Nov. 23, 1778
John Cook of Plimpton & Molly Faunce,   Jan. 14, 1779
Ichabod Bradford & Ruth Fuller,   Oct. 19, 1780
Amos Cooke & Lydia Stetson,   Oct. 24, 1780

Elisha Washburn & Deborah Prince,	Oct. 26,	1780
Sylvanus Cooke & widow Mary Adams,	Jan. 22,	1781
David Beal & Lydia Prince,	May 7,	1781
Cornelius Drew & Sarah Stetson,	Nov. 12,	1781
Seth Delano of Winthrop in Lincoln Co. & Rebecca		
Fish,	Feb. 7,	1782
Capt. Robert Bradford, Jr., & Keziah Little,	Feb. 19,	1782
James Foord of Pembroke & Lydia Bradford,	June 20,	1782
Levi Bradford & Polly Ripley,	Aug. 22,	1782
William Samson of Duxboro & Deborah Randal,		
	Sept. 26,	1782
Oliver Samson of Duxboro & Sarah McLaughlin,		
	Nov. 21,	1782
Zachariah Cushman of Plymton & Sabra Adams,		
	Dec. 2,	1782
Thomas Jackson of Plymouth & Lucy Samson,	Jan. 8,	1783
Abner Hall & Mercy Gibbs,	Dec. 18,	1783
Dr. Jonathan Crane of Bridgewater & Lydia Adams,		
	Dec. 23,	1783
Benjamin Snow of Duxboro & Betty Simmons,	Jan. 5,	1784
John Perkins, Jr., of Plimton & Sarah Adams,	May 20,	1784
Thomas Russell, Esq., of Boston & Sarah Sever,		
	Aug. 22,	1784
Jeremiah Sampson of Middleboro & Sarah Washburn,		
	April 24,	1780
Elisha Cushman & Lydia Fuller,	May 15,	1780
Benjamin Bearce & Lydia Bisbee,		1784
Bildad Washburn & Lucy Adams,		1784
Elnathan Holmes & Deborah Brewster,	Sept. 11,	1784
Melatiah Cobb & Rebecca Brewster,	Sept. 11,	1784
Francis Adams & Mercy Adams,	Nov. 30,	1784
Luther Bryant of Plimton & Priscilla Washburn,		
	Jan. 30,	1785
Barnabas Faunce & Polly Doten,	April 20,	1785
Seth Washburn & Anna Fullerton,	April 20,	1785
Israel Bradford & Hannah Everson,	Dec. 15,	1785
Abel Wanner of Hardwick & Sarah Cook,	Feb. 15,	1786
Elijah Faunce & Lydia Waterman,	March 30,	1786

Martin Brewster & Sally Drew, April 23, 1786
Lewis Bradford of Duxboro & Priscilla Tupper, July 6, 1786
Barzillai Fuller & Mary Cushman, July 20, 1786
Joseph Chandler of Duxboro & Saba Ripley, Nov. 9, 1786
Elkanah Washburn & Mercy Foster, Nov. 16, 1786
Peter Winsor of Duxboro & Charlotte Delano, Oct. 31, 1786
Samuel Randall & Lydia Everson, Nov. 1, 1786

✓ MARSHFIELD.

March 1, 1642. "Marshfield is mentioned as one of the towns for which officers are chosen." March 7, 1643. Bounds were established. First (Congregational) Church organized 1632. Friends, 1692. Second Church (Unitarian), 1738. Baptist, 1788.

Thomas Tilden, Jr., & Hannah Mendall, Dec. 20, 1692
Elnathan Fish of Kingston & Lydia Adams, Dec. 12, 1739
Thomas Ford & Jane Thomas, Jan. 2, 1739-40
Michael Harry (?) & Gail Rogers, Jan. 14, 1739-40
Michael Samson of Kingston & Deborah Gardner,
Feb., 1739-40
Seth Ewell & Jane Eames, Feb. 21, 1739-40
Job Winslow & Elisabeth Macumber, March 20, 1740
Samuel Silvester & Sarah Mori, May 8, 1740
Benjamin Hatch, Jr., of Scituate & Mercy Phillips,
June 25, 1740
Robert Shareman & widow Mary Eames, Sept. 23, 1740
Mathew Simonton of Falmouth & Mary Oakman,
March 12, 1741
Benjamin Hatch of Scituate & Jerusha Phillips, April 7, 1741
Thomas Silvester & Hannah Harris, April 16, 1741
Elisha Kent & Susannah Ford, June 11, 1741
Elisha Rogers & Margaret Mackfarland, Dec. 2, 1741
John Tilden, 3d, & Rachel Hall, March 4, 1741
Derby Fits Patrick & Joanna Rogers, May 1, 1742
James Sprague, Jr., & Patience Ford, Feb. 24, 1742-3
John Baker & Ruth Barker, Feb. 24, 1742-3

Benjamin White & Hannah Decro,	April 3, 1743
Joseph Stetson of Scituate & Mary Eames,	Sept. 15, 1743
James Rogers & Lydia Rogers,	Dec. 1, 1743
Ignatius Vinall of Scituate & Mary Tilden,	Dec. 15, 1743
Joseph Bruster of Duxboro & Jedidah White,	Nov. 26, 1740
Ezekiel Kent & Susanna Winslow,	Dec. 22, 1740
John Tilden & Lydia Holmes,	Feb. 12, 1740
Nehemiah Thomas & Bial Winslow,	July 6, 1741
Joseph Soul, Jr., of Duxboro & Mary Fullerton,	
	March 18, 1742
Thomas Eames & Margaret Dugles,	June 10, 1742
William Winslow of Middleboro & Hannah Loe,	
	Nov. 11, 1742
Snow Winslow & Lydia Crooker,	Nov. 24, 1742
John Tilden of Hanover & Sybel Thomas,	Dec. 2, 1742
Robert Booth of Norwich & Lydia Hewett,	March 21, 1743
Benjamin Phillips & Else Thomas,	Nov. 15, 1743
Jedediah Bourn & Sarah Thomas,	Oct. 24, 1743
Thomas Ford of Marshfield & Hannah Turner of	
Pembroke,	Sept. 8, 1743
Ames Ford & Lillis Turner,	Jan. 3, 1743-4
Thomas Little & Abigail Howland,	March 9, 1742
Jabez Whittemore & Elisabeth Howland,	Sept. 26, 1743
Thomas Phillips, Jr., of Duxboro & Lydia Carver,	
	Jan. 24, 1744-5
Joseph Kent & Lydia Thomas,	Feb. 28, 1743
Jonathan King of Plimouth & Deborah Carver,	
	Feb. 21, 1744-5
Benjamin Barnes & Mary Gullifer,	Sept. 16, 1745
Mr. Anthony Thomas of M. & Mrs. Abigail Allden of	
Duxboro,	Jan. 23, 1745-6
John Fullerton of M. & Rebecca Dellano of Dux-	
boro,	April 17, 1746
Anthony Sherman & Silence Foord,	April 17, 1746
Joshua Cushman of Duxborough & Deborah Ford,	
	March 5, 1752
Thomas Hartly of Boston & Sarah Phillips,	March 5, 1752
Benjamin Phipils (?) of Boston & Elisabeth Burn,	
	Sept. 10, 1752

Ebenezer Totman of M. & Grace Turner of Scituate,
Nov. 27, 1752
David Freeman & Sarah Hall, Dec. 2, 1752
Thomas Oldham & Jane Rogers, Dec. 10, 1752
Jedediah Eames & Bethiah Tilden, Feb. 7, 1753
Rev. Joseph Green & Mrs. Hannah Lewis, April 4, 1753
Elijah Ford & Elianor Thomas, May 7, 1753
John Sha—man & Elisabeth Dingley, Aug. 21, 1746
Phillip Hammon of Boston & Anna Bourn, Aug. 15, 1747
William Thomas of Plimouth & Susanna Howland,
Nov. 26, 1747
Ebenezer Cobb of Kingston & Joanna Williamson,
Dec. 14, 1747
Israel Rogers & Bethiah Thomas, Dec. 31, 1747
Benjamin White & Mercy Thomas, Dec. 29, 1748
Jacob Dingley, Jr., of Duxborough & Desire Phillips,
Feb. 2, 1748
James Wallis of Pembroke & Sarah Shaw, Feb. 23, 1748
Aaron Simmes of Duxborough & Sarah Holmes,
Jan. 14, 1749
Comfort Bates of Pembroke & Mellason Carver,
Sept. 24, 1749
Thomas Lapham & Abiah Joyce, Feb. 22, 1749
William Foord & Patience Dilly March 6, 1749
Samuel Thomas, Jr., & Mary Cushing, July 10, 1750
Arther Howland & Jerusha Foord, Dec. 27, 1750
Jeremiah Crooker of M. & Lydia Barker of Pembroke,
Feb. 20, 1750
Isaiah Walker & Bathsheba Sherman, April 5, 1750
Lemuel Eames & Ruth Porter, May 16, 1750
Joshua Tilden & Phebe Wales, June 29, 1750
James Sylvester of Hanover & Lydia Clift, Nov. 29, 1750
Cornelius Cook of Truro & Abigail Hatch, March 26, 1751
Timothy Sylvester & Lydia Joyce, April 10, 1751
Simeon Turner of Scituate & Bethier Foord, April 11, 1751
Simeon Keen of Pembroke & Lydia Stephens, May 16, 1751
John Tilden & widow Mary Trewant, Sept. 4, 1751
Kenelin Backer, Jr., & Tabitha Hewett, May 29, 1753

4

Joseph Farmer of M. & Elanor Samson of Duxborough,
July 5, 1753
Elijah Damon & Anna Oldes, May 17, 1753
John Steavens & Eleanor Jarm (?), Dec. 6, 1753
Abraham Walker of M. & Bette Simmons of Duxboro,
April 11, 1751
Adam Hall, Jr., & Keziah Foord, April 7, 1752
Joseph Tolman of Scituate & Bette Rogers, April 11, 1754
Peleg Rogers & Hannah Stephens, April 26, 1754
John Lapham of Rochester & Bathsheba Eames,
Oct. 31, 1754
Joseph Silvester & Bradbury Hatch, Feb. 14, 1755
Joseph Percy & Abigail Tillden, Aug. 14, 1755
Timothy Rogers, Jr., & Desire Sylvester, Aug. 28, 1755
Gideon Ramsdell of Abington & Abiail Eame, Sept. 3, 1755
John James, ye 3d, of Scituate & Sarah Tilden, Dec. 3, 1755
Nathaniel Foord & Eunice Rogers, Feb. 12, 1755
Caleb Carver, Jr., & Abigail Dammond, March 25, 1756
Jabez Washburn of Kingston & Mary Sherman, May 14, 1756
William Thomas of M. & Abiah Thomas of Duxboro,
April 11, 1754
James Thomas of Duxboro & Priscilla Winslow, Sept. 8, 1754
Ebenezer Joice & Allathea Fullerton, April 11, 1754
Joseph Thomas, Jr., of M. & Eleanor Baker of Duxboro,
Nov. 7, 1754
Jabez Washbourne of Kingston & Deborah Thomas,
Dec. 5, 1754
Abner Foord & Bethiah Lamson, Dec. 5, 1754
Joshua Eames of M. & Deborah Dotey of Duxboro,
Aug. 28, 1755
Asa Thomas & Jemima Jones, Dec. 18, 1755
Josiah Foster & Elizabeth Carver, Feb. 10, 1756
John Joice, Jr., & Faith Stevens, Sept. 9, 1756
Nathan Thomas & Sarah Bourn, Dec. 21, 1756
Thomas Dingley & Anna Philips, Jan. 20, 1757
Jeremiah Low & Sarah Thomas, April 19, 1757
Joseph Sherman & Alice Shurtleff, Oct. 23, 1760
David Thomas, Jr., & Mercy Macumber, Jan. 8, 1761

William Stevens, Jr., & Bethiah Oakman,   Jan. 22, 1761
Josiah Eames & Betty Eames,   March 4, 1761
John Turner, Jr., of Pembroke & Mary Little, Feb. 26, 1761
Noah Thomas & Keziah Eames,   April 16, 1761
Peter Ripley of Hingham & widow Elizabeth Howard,
    June 22, 1761
Jonathan Joyce & Abigail Holmes,   July 7, 1761
Abner Crooker of M. & Jerusha Hatch of Scituate,
    Oct. 1, 1761
Stephen Lapham & Ruth Rogers,   Nov. 12, 1761
William Delano of Scituate & Eleanor Stephens,
    Nov. 19, 1761
Japhet Allen of Bridgewater & Betty Thomas, Nov. 26, 1761
John Trouant & Elisabeth Church,   Dec. 31, 1761
Blaney Phillips of Duxboro & Mary Trouant, April 8, 1762
John Carver, Jr., & Lucinda Thomas,   April 18, 1762
Daniel Lapham & Sarah Sherman,   Nov. 25, 1762
Rev. Thomas Brown & Mrs. Lidia Howard,   Feb. 22, 1763
Puffer Loudon & Alice Barnet,   Feb. 10, 1763
John Sherman & Lucy Rogers,   April 2, 1763
Joseph Webb, Jr., of Boston & Penelope Phillips,
    Nov. 13, 1759
Anthony Waterman & Deborah Foster,   March 27, 1760
Moses Soul of Pembroke & Eleanor Williams, May 7, 1761
Carpus White of M. & Anna Delano of Duxboro,
    July 8, 1761
Abijah Thomas of M. & Deborah Samson of Duxboro,
    Dec. 24, 1761
Lemuel Delano & Mary Eames,   April 20, 1762
Daniel Fisher of Duxboro & Lucy Barker,   Dec. 9, 1762
Abner Dingley of Duxboro & Ruth Bryant,   Jan. 4, 1759
Simeon Curtis of Hanover & Lucy Macomber,   Jan. 9, 1759
John Hyland of Scituate & Rebecca White,   Nov. 1, 1759
Levi Foord & Penelope Rogers,   Nov. 29, 1759
Elisha Foord & Elisabeth Tilden,   Dec. 6, 1759
Samuel Holmes & Zerviah Simons,   Nov. 16, 1757
Jacob Pilsborough of Abington & Ann Dingley,
    May 25, 1758

John Allen of Pembroke & Alice Adams,	Sept. 28,	1758
John Bourn & Lucy Dingley,	May 25,	1758
Jabez Dingley & Rebecca Phillips,	March 20,	1763
Benjamin Faunce of Kingston & Lidia Trouant,		
	April 13,	1763
Luke Hall of Boston, now of Scituate, & Jane Hatch,		
	April 26,	1763
Zatter Cushing of Menduncook & Bethiah Thomas,		
	Oct. 13,	1763
Joshua Chase of Scituate & Rebecca Eames,	Oct. 13,	1763
Samuel Tilden, Jr., of M. & Mercy Hatch of Scituate,		
	Nov. 10,	1763
Thomas Eames & Rebecca Harnice (?),	Jan. 9,	1764
Joseph Clift of M. & Mary Hatch of Scituate,	Jan. 12,	1764
Nathaniel Joyce of M. & Elisabeth Curtis of Scituate,		
	Jan. 18,	1764
Edward Hatch of M. & Hannah Lapham of Scituate,		
	April 23,	1764
Benjamin Tolman, Jr., of Scituate & Mercy Thomas,		
	April 23,	1764
John Phillips of Duxboro & Rhoda Hall,	April 26,	1764
Jedediah Ewell & Elisabeth Tilden,	Dec. 6,	1764
Thomas Turner of Pembroke & Joanna Philips,	Dec. 18,	1765
Silvester Prince (mulatto) & Susanna Rider (Indian),		
	Dec. 25,	1765
Wonyst Prince (negro) & Jane Patience (Indian),		
	Feb. 14,	1766
Levi Simmons of Duxboro & Lidia Lewis,	Oct. 10,	1765
Simeon Rogers & Sarah Clift,	Jan. 29,	1767
Noah Hatch & Alice Little,	Feb. 5,	1767
Thomas Macumber, Jr., & Leah Tilden,	July 12,	1767
Asa Lapham & Betty Rogers,	Dec. 10,	1767
Rouse Bourn & Lucy Cushing,	Feb. 13,	1767
Abner Eames & Patience Foord,	Feb. 26,	1767
Samuel Perry of Pembroke & Alice Baker,	March 26,	1767
Ezra Cushman & Ruth Winslow,	Dec. 10,	1767
Josiah Winslow & Penelope Kent,	Dec. 15,	1767
Abraham Samson, Jr., of Duxboro & Huldah Carver,		
	Dec. 29,	1767

Joseph Drew of Duxboro & Alathea Thomas, Dec. 31, 1767
Samuel Smith of Great Partners, N. Y. Province, &
    Hannah Baker of Duxboro,   June 29, 1767
John Wing, Jr., of Sandwich & Elisabeth Rogers,
                        Feb. 17, 1768
Daniel Lewis of Pembroke & Mercy Winslow, Jan. 21, 1768
Charles Baker of Duxboro & Deborah Williamson,
                        Jan. 21, 1768
Abraham Petenon of Duxboro & Patience Baker,
                      March 3, 1768
Joseph Lapham of Scituate & Lucy Shurtleff,
                    March 16, 1768
John Magoun of Pembroke & Hulda Shurtleff, Nov. 30, 1768
Charles Samson of Duxboro & Sarah Dingley, Jan. 12, 1769
Manuel Freeman & Lucy Sprague,   Jan. 19, 1769
Jabez Studley of Hanover & Katurah Simmons,
                    March 30, 1769
Lott Keen of Pembroke & Joanna Sprague,   Aug. 17, 1769
Mark Eames & Priscilla Howland,   Oct. 12, 1769
Ezekial Reed of Abington & Mary Rogers,   June 16, 1768
Thomas Macumber, 3d, & Prudence Stetson,   July 28, 1768
Job Mitchell & Sarah Brewster,   Feb. 1, 1769
Seth Deuone (?) (Derrow?) & Elisabeth Sylvester,
                    March 29, 1769
William Turner of Scituate & Betsey Oakman, April 27, 1769
Job Ewell of M. & Elisabeth Mitchell of Scituate,
                    June 1, 1769
Amos Eames & Hannah Deuone (?) (Derrow?), July 19, 1769
Jedediah Hammon & Molly Stetson,   Feb. 14, 1770
Thomas Magoun of Pembroke & Mary Wales, April 24, 1770
Jonathan Hatch & Betsey Jones,   March 1, 1770
Amos Jones of Scituate & Abigail Carver,   Aug. 28, 1770
James Hall of M. & Hannah Keen of Pembroke,
                    Nov. 19, 1770
Timothy Silvester & Luce Eames,   Nov. 26, 1770
Frederick Lewis & Phebe Tilden,   Dec. 2, 1770
Mark Hatch of Scituate & Abigail Joyce,   Dec. 29, 1770
Edmund Silvester of Scituate & Mary Hall,   Jan. 22, 1771

Joshua Tilden, Jr., & Sarah Jewel,	April 25,	1771
John Hatch of Scituate & Deborah Oakman,	Oct. 10,	1771
Samuel Jones & Thankful Hatch,	Jan. 16,	1772
Gideon Harlow of Duxboro & Patience Eames,	Jan. 4,	1770
Silvester Prince & Rhoda Ceser,	Jan. 4,	1770
Joseph Brown & Margaret Royal,	Jan. 22,	1770
Abijah Waterman & Mary Thomas,	April 26,	1770
William Fisk of Duxboro & Mary Sprague,	June 31,	1771

George James Yeats of Bristol in Broad Bay & Nancy
    Richards, Nov. 26, 1772

Caleb Taylor of Pembroke & Sarah Tilden,	June 3,	1773
Benjamin Ames, Jr., & Ruth Porter,	Oct. 28,	1773
Calvin Turner of Pembroke & Sarah Barker,	Nov. 4,	1773
Enoch Curtis of Scituate & Martha Sherman,	Dec. 7,	1773

Thomas McDoniel of Hanover & Desire Sherman,
May 2, 1774

Joseph Hatch of Scituate & widow Phebe Lewis,
May 26, 1774

Joseph Fish of Pembroke & Thankful Lapham of
    Scituate, Dec. 8, 1774

Thomas Macghlan of Duxborough & Sabra Eames,
March 2, 1775

Samuel Boo—— & Martha Lowden,	May 23,	1776
Daniel Wright & Sarah Porter,	May 9,	1777
Ezekiel Jones of Scituate & Hulda Sherman,	Nov. 20,	1777
Jeremiah Hatch, Jr., & Lydia Porter,	Nov. 22,	1778
Nathaniel Rogers & Bethiah Clift,	June 24,	1779
Seth Hatch of Pembroke & Molly Hatch,	Nov. 12,	1779
Melzar Turner Oakman & Persis Rogers,	Dec. 2,	1779
Absel (?) Sherman & Lucy Sylvester,	Feb. 4,	1781

Simeon Granderson of M. & Charity Thomas of
    Bridgewater, April 23, 1781

Thomas Ruggles of Scituate & Eunice Oakman, May 10, 1781

Thomas Rogers, 3d, of M. & Egatha Hatch of Scituate,
Aug. 16, 1781

Joseph Tilden & Seabury Silvester,	Feb. 27,	1783
James Wright & Rebecca Rogers,	Oct. 24,	1781
Asa Rogers & Abiah Oakman,	Dec. 13,	1781

Anthony Eames Hatch of Scituate & Bethiah Rogers,
Feb. 28, 1782
John Man of Scituate & Patience Rogers, March 12, 1782
Mathew Tower & Jerusha Hatch of Scituate, June 1, 1782
Jesse Hodges of Norton & Olive White, Dec. 1, 1782
John Hatch & Agatha Rogers, Nov. 12, 1782
William Bryant, a transient man, & Remembrance
Curtis, Dec. 25, 1782
Joshua Vinal & Lucy Little, Dec. 25, 1782
Willis Clift & Rachel Belden, Oct. 2, 1783
Arunah Daman & Deborah Silvester, Oct. 8, 1783
William Clift & Mary Eames, Oct. 15, 1783
Ichabod Sherman & Sarah Joyce, Dec. 10, 1783
Constant Fobes Oakman of M. & Rachel Hatch of
Scituate, Dec. 11, 1783
David Joyce & Rebecca Sprague, Nov. 25, 1784
Wales Tilden & Abigail Little, April 1, 1784
John Porter & Ruth Stevens, Dec. 2, 1784
Peleg Rogers, Jr., & Jemima Eames, Dec. 9, 1784
Benjamin Hatch, 3d, of Scituate & Sarah Wales, Jan. 13, 1785
Zacheus Rogers, Jr., & Ruth Oakman, May 9, 1785
Briggs Thomas & Abigail Thomas, March 18, 1779
Jedediah Burnum of Norwich, Ct., & Lydia Kent,
April 27, 1779
Gersham Sherman & Elizabeth Howland, July 27, 1779
Joshua Crooker of Pembroke & Ruth Joyce, Nov. 4, 1779
Benjamin White, Jr., & Susanna Howland, Dec. 1, 1779
Joseph Delano of Duxboro & Mary Thomas, Jan. 13, 1780
Charles Kent & Ruth Baker, Jan. 27, 1780
Melzar Samson of Duxboro & Sarah Kent, March 2, 1780
Nathaniel Foord, Jr., & Abigail Foord, Nov. 6, 1780
Prince Withrill of Pembroke & Zina Holmes, Dec. 7, 1780
John Hatch of M. & Judith Delano of Duxboro, Feb. 22, 1781
William Thomas, Jr., & Abigail Sherman, April 12, 1781
Charles Samson of Waldoborough, Co. of Lincoln, &
Elisabeth Sprague, July 12, 1781
Peleg Foord & Olive Samson, Oct. 4, 1781
Jesse Simmons of Duxboro & Lucy Weston, Oct. 17, 1781

Jesse Wright & Hannah Foord,   Nov. 8, 1781
Judah Thomas & Hannah Thomas,   July 11, 1782
Peleg Thomas & Bethiah Walker,   Oct. 6, 1782
Jacob Dingley of Duxboro & widow Alethea Joyce,
                                                     Oct. 24, 1782
Abner Dingley, Jr., of Duxboro & Bu——y Weston,
                                                     Nov. 28, 1782
Prince Hatch of Scituate & Hannah Phillips,   Nov. 13, 1783
Samuel Taylor of Pembroke & Hannah Low,   Feb. 15, 1784
Daniel Walker & Experience Tuels,   Aug. 6, 1784
William Weston & Keziah Dingley,   Dec. 21, 1784
Edmond Silvester & Deborah Cushman,   Dec. 23, 1784
Robert Cushman & Persis Phillips,   April 7, 1785
Matthew Pettingill & Bethiah Foord,   —— 22, 1785
Nathan Sherman & Bethiah Thomas,   Aug. 16, 1785
Bela Lewis & Mercy Lapham,   Oct. 4, 1785
Constant Southworth & Lucy Foord,   Oct. 27, 1785
Levi Walker & Ruth Cushman,   Jan. 15, 1786
James Silvester & Sarah Osborn,   Jan. 26, 1786
Thomas Weston of Duxboro & Abiah Fish,   Feb. 7, 1786
John Thomas & Lucy Baker,   March 30, 1786
Samuel Holmes of M. & Anna White of Duxboro,
                                                     June 15, 1786
Thomas Sampson of Duxboro & Lucy Thomas, Dec. 28, 1786
Amos Oakman & Silvina Thomas,   Feb. 1, 1787
Josiah Hatch & Martha Keen,   Feb. 22, 1787
Charles Hatch of Scituate & Joanna Winslow, Feb. 27, 1787
Joseph Phillips & Ruth Macomber,   April 19, 1785
William Foord & Lydia Rogers,   Sept. 15, 1785
John Pemberton of Long Island, Co. of Lincoln, &
    Betsey Rogers,   Dec. 26, 1785
Lemuel Hatch Silvester & Zintha Tilden,   Jan. 5, 1786
Samuel Rogers & Patience Little,   Jan. 12, 1786
Calvin Lewis & Penelope Little,   Feb. 24, 1786
John Tilden, Jr., & Mary Ewell,   Feb. 15, 1787
Marlborough Foord & Mary Tilden,   March 1, 1787
Isaac Johnson of Bridgewater & Polly Wright, Jan. 17, 1787
William Henry Little of Bristol, R. I., & Rhoda
    Trouant,   Sept. 2, 1787

Joshua Josselyn of Hanover & Sarah Chapman, Dec. 1, 1787
Obadiah Damon & Sarah Thomas, Dec. 27, 1787
Charles Rogers & Lydia Healy, May 5, 1787
Seth Magoun & Abigail Eames, Sept. 6, 1787
Isaac Lapham & Phebe Rogers, Oct. 28, 1787
Jabez Wright & Elisabeth Bourn, Dec. 27, 1787
Ichabod Weston & Eleanor Barker, Jan. 8, 1788
John Hyland of Scituate & Deborah Sherman, Feb. 21, 1788
John Kent & Betty Walker, March 6, 1788
Rev. Kilborn Whitman of Pembroke & Elizabeth
    Winslow, June 5, 1788
Adam Lapham & Tabitha Baker, July 10, 1788
Nathaniel Waterman of Scituate & Lydia Phillips,
    Oct. 15, 1788
Joseph Warrick & Dinah Osgood, transient blacks,
    May 8, 1788
Ebenezer Rogers of M. & Hannah Cole of Scituate,
    Nov. 23, 1788
Winsor (negro) of M. & Silvia (negro) of Scituate,
    Feb. 23, 1789

√ WAREHAM.

July 10, 1733. "Part of Rochester and a plantation in Plymouth called Agawam established as Wareham." First Church (Congregational) organized 1793. Church records begin 1739.

Gershom Morss of Middleboro & Elizabeth Swift,
    Sept. 6, 1741
Josiah Swift & Mary Besse, Nov. 19, 1741
Jonathan Dillano of Rochester & Rachel Bump, Dec. 9, 1741
Josiah Man of Scituate & Mary Chubbuck, March 15, 1741-2
Daniel Raymond & Elizabeth Doty, March 21, 1741-2
Hezekiah Bourne, aged 65, & Mehitable Hinckley,
    aged 25, Oct. 22, 1742
Joseph Landers, Jr., & Sarah Lovell, Nov. 4, 1742
Jonathan Earle & Hannah Dotey, Nov. 3, 1743

Joshua Besse & Lydia Landers,   Dec. 22, 1743
John Bump, 3d, & Alice English,   May 20, 1744
Adonijah Muxum of Sharon & Keziah Benson, Oct. 31, 1744
Nathan Leonard of Bridgewater & Thankful Besse,
                                              Nov. 22, 1744
Jeremiah Bump, Jr., & Judith Randal,   Dec. 20, 1744-5
Peleg Landers & Elizabeth Bishup,   Jan. 24, 1744-5
Nathan Briggs of Rochester & Sarah Perry, Feb. 28, 1744-5
Nathaniel White of Rochester & Mary Raymont,
                                              May 20, 1745
Rowland Swift & Mary Dexter,   Dec. 5, 1745
John Gibbs & Sylvia Hunter,   Oct. 9, 1746
Samuel Briggs, Jr., of Rochester & Elizabeth Besse,
                                              Oct. 9, 1746
Phillip Bump & Mary Burge (?),   Dec. 18, 1746
Joseph Perry & Rhoda Bump,   May 5, 1747
Barnabas Batts & Phebe Gibbs,   Sept. 17, 1747
Ebenezer Burn & Anna Bump,   Oct. 1, 1747
Jonathan Pratt & Abigail Lovell,   Oct. 22, 1747
Noah Bump & Hannah Bump,   Nov. 19, 1747
Nathaniel Blackwell, Jr., of Dartmouth & Lydia
    Landers,   Feb. 4, 1747-8
Joseph Doten, Jr., & Elisabeth Lander,   March 3, 1747-8
Silas Doten & Susannah Bump,   April 7, 1748
William Basset of Rochester & widow Susanah Bumpas,
                                              April 21, 1748
Edward Raymond & Hannah Bishop,   Dec. 5, 1751
Salathiel Bump & Lydia Ellis,   Jan. 2, 1752
Jabez Benson of W. & Susana Gurney of Rochester,
                                              July 26, 1752
Jabez Bass & Margaret Norris,   Sept. 28, 1752
Zepheniah Bump & Thankful Gibbs,   March 22, 1753
Samuel Leonard & Lydia Basse,   July 7, 1748
Nehemiah Basse & Sarah Perry,   Oct. 25, 1748
Samuel Perry & Elisabeth Omens,   Nov. 7, 1748
John Gibbs & Deborah Doten,   March 9, 1748-9
Joshua Bump & Mary Bates,   March 16, 1748-9
Edward Bump & Meriah Benson,   Nov. 24, 1748

Joseph Dotey & Phebe Bump, Feb. 26, 1756
Ephraim Griffeth of Rochester & Mary Ellis, Feb. 10, 1756
Joseph Stertevant (?) & Mary Gibbs, March 3, 1757
James Burge & Sarah Stertevant, March 20, 1760
Ebenezer Thomson, Jr., of Hallifax & Elizabeth Bessee,
May 1, 1760
David Lincoln, Jr., of Hingham & Elizabeth Fearing,
Sept. 16, 1760
Benjamin Norris, Jr., & Mary Bump, March 12, 1761
John Millard of Freetown & Huldah Fearing, Nov. 12, 1761
Rowland Benson & Mary Swift, July 2, 1761
Elnathan Benson & Sarah Gibbs, Dec. 3, 1761
Nathan Muxam of Rochester & Martha Chubbuck,
Jan. 15, 1761
Thomas ———— of Rochester & Mary Baker of Dart-
mouth, Feb. 17, 1762
Jirah Smith, Jr., of Dartmouth & Elizabeth Haskell of
Rochester, Jan. 6, 1763
Elnathan Samson & Abigail Burge, Aug. 17, 1762
Benjamin Briggs & Elizabeth Landers, Nov. 25, 1762
Thomas Samson & Marcy Bates, Dec. 8, 1762
Nathaniel Howland of Barnstable & Martha Thacher,
Dec. 15, 1762
John Gibbs of Sandwich & Jerusha Thacher, Jan. 11, 1763
Simeon Bates of Rochester & Martha Swift, Feb. 10, 1763
Joshua Griffeth & Mercy Briggs, March 3, 1757
Enoch Swift & Esther Samson, July 21, 1757
Stephen Washburn of Plimton & Hannah Norris,
May 11, 1757
David Perry & Mary Bump, Aug. 28, 1757
Ebenezer Haskel of Rochester & Anne Fearing, Nov. 20, 1757
Consider Sturtevant & Anne Bessee, Dec. 7, 1758
William Washburn of Plimton & Sarah Bates, Nov. 8, 1759
Jabez Bessee, Jr., & Ruth Bessee, Nov. 29, 1759
Joseph Edwards of Rochester & Mary Swift, Feb. 14, 1760
David Bessee, Jr., & Jedidah Burge, May 12, 1763
Nathan Lincoln of Hingham & Martha Fearing, Oct. 13, 1763
Noah Bumpas & Elisabeth Perry, Aug. 24, 1763

John Whetten & Abigal Morse,   May 17, 1764
Josiah Stephens, Jr., & Abigail Nye,   July 22, 1764
Thomas Whetten, Jr., & Chloe Bump,   Nov. 22, 1764
John Bessee of W. & Hannah Cushman of Plimton,
                                           Nov. 29, 1764
Joshua Benson, Jr., of Middleboro & Sarah Ellis,
                                           Nov. 29, 1764
Edward Sparrow & Rhoda Bump,   Feb. 21, 1765
Asa Swift & Lucy Briggs,   March 7, 1765
Freeman Snow of Rochester & Sarah Fuller, March 27, 1765
Robert Whetten & Joanna Morse,   April 7, 1765
Barnabas Swift of W. & Lois Benson of Middleboro,
                                           March 28, 1765
James Holmes of Middleboro & Rhoda Muxom,
                                           Aug. 15, 1766
William Peirce of W. & Lidia Lovel, 2d, of Middleboro,
                                           Nov. 5, 1766
John Briggs, Jr., & Bulah Hammond, both of Rochester,
                                           April 7, 1767
Edward Drake & Elisabeth Bump,   Oct. 24, 1765
Elijah Caswel of Rochester & Mary Chubbuck,
                                           April 27, 1766
Thomas Norris & Elisabeth Morse,   July 13, 1766
Joseph Benson, Jr., of Middleboro & Hannah Swift,
                                           Jan. 22, 1767
David Muxom of Rochester & Rebeccah Bessee,
                                           March 8, 1767
Zebulon Morse of Rochester & Mary Norris, April 19, 1767
Ebenezer Clarke of Hallifax & Mehitable Savery,
                                           April 21, 1767
John Muxom, Jr., of Plimton & Martha Norris, July 29, 1767
Zephaniah Thomas of Middleboro & Mary Savery,
                                           Nov. 1, 1767
Samuel Briggs & Sarah Blackmer,   Jan. 14, 1768
Jabez Nye & Molly Fuller,   Feb. 18, 1768
William Conit (?) & Bethiah Lothrop,   March 31, 1768
Thomas Lavery of W. & Elisabeth Randall of Rochester,
                                           July 31, 1768

Joshua Allen of Rochester & Mehitable Norris, Nov. 27, 1768
Alvan Crocker of Barnstable & Silvia Thatcher, Nov. 30, 1768
Willard Swift & Zepha Hamblen, Dec. 1, 1768
John Keen & Mary Clifton, both of Rochester, Jan. 14, 1768
John Jspet (?) of Plimton & Mary Francis of Rochester,
Feb. 11, 1768
Benjamin Easterbrooks of Dartmouth & Deborah
Edwards of Rochester, Oct. 23, 1768
Thomas Muxum & Jerusha Lions, both of Rochester,
Dec. 1, 1768
Elisha Burgs & Desire Blackwel, Jan. 26, 1769
Benjamin Chubbuck, Jr., & Ruth Bump, March 28, 1769
Richard Sears of Rochester & Sarah Bump, Nov. 9, 1769
Barzillai Besse & Lucy Barrows, Nov. 16, 1769
Enos Hayward of Bridgewater & Mary Samson,
Nov. 16, 1769
Barzillai Swift & Sarah Fearing, Dec. 21, 1769
Willis Barrowes & Lucy Chubbock, Dec. 28, 1769
David Sanders of this town & Lydia Gifford of Sand-
wich, March 15, 1770
Joseph Briggs & Mary Hammond, March 29, 1770
John Lothrop & Alice Chubbuck, March 29, 1770
William Whetten & Thankful Morss, May 2, 1770
Barnabas Bump & Elisabeth Barrows, May 20, 1770
Andrew Mackie & Charity Fearing, Dec. 6, 1770
Samuel Sauerey, Jr., & Ruth Gibbs, Dec. 13, 1770
Elijah Bates of Rochester & Lydia Briggs, Jan. 3, 1771
Samuel Burge, Jr., & Hannah Stertevant, Jan. 8, 1771
David Nye & Desire Thacher, March 7, 1771
Benjamin Richard of Pembroke & Lydia Chubbuck,
June 10, 1771
Jeremiah Bump, Jr., & Elisabeth Sauerey, Nov. 7, 1771
Charles Blankinship of Rochester & Betty Bates,
Nov. 21, 1771
John Carver & Patience Bates, Nov. 21, 1771
Silvester Bates of Rochester & Sarah Landen, Feb. 13, 1772
Jonathan Sanden & Mercy Chubbuck, March 5, 1772

DUXBURY.

June 7, 1637. "Ducksburrow" made "a towneship and to have the privileges of a towne."
March 2, 1641. Bounds were established. First Church (Unitarian) organized 1632. Friends,
1702.

James Thomas & Mary Tilden,	Jan. 3, 1692-3
Richard Waste & Mary Samson,	Oct. 26, 1693
James Soul & Lidia Tomson,	Dec. 14, 1693
Samuel Hill & Phebe Leonard,	Nov. 6, 1694
Elisha Wadsworth & Elisabeth Wisewall,	Dec. 9, 1694
Samuel Samson & Assadiah (?) Eedey,	May 29, 1695
James Bonney & Abigail Bishop,	June 14, 1695
Robert Samson & Else Samson,	Dec. 19, 1734
Hartale Jaffere (?) & Betty Tom (?), both of Plymouth,	
	Dec. 23, 1734
John Wadsworth, Jr., & Mary Allden,	Dec. 31, 1734
Nathaniel Phillips & Joanna White, both of Mansfield,	
	Jan. 16, 1734
James Arnold & Joannah Sprague,	Feb. 19, 1734
Ichabod Brewster of D. & Lidiah Barton of Pembroke,	
	June 3, 1735
Seth Bartlet & Charity Cullifer,	Feb. 27, 1735-6
Nathaniel Dunham of Plymouth & Anne Peterson,	
	April 7, 1735
Joseph Morgan of Preston, Ct., & Ruth Brewster,	
	May 8, 1735
John Pryer & Mary Dellano,	Oct. 14, 1735
Mr. Jonathan Trumble of Lebanon, Ct., & Mrs. Faith Robinson,	Dec. 9, 1735
Ichabod Wadsworth, Jr., & Anne Hunt,	Nov. 25, 1736
Asa Hunt & Sarah Partridge,	Dec. 2, 1736
Ichabod Wormwell & Lydia Dellano,	Dec. 13, 1736
Samuel Drew, Jr., of Kingston & Anna White,	Dec. 28, 1736
Sylvanus Curtiss of Plymouth & Dorothy Dellano,	
	Nov. 26, 1734

John Hanks & Mary Delano,   Jan. 16, 1734-5
Allerton Cushman of Plymton & Allathea Sole,

                                    Jan. 30, 1734-5
Samuel Wormwel & Mary Forest,   Jan. 27, 1736-7
Isaac Simmons & Elisabeth Sams (?),   May 11, 1736-7
Seth Bartlet & Martha Baun,   Nov. 23, 1736-7
Experience Holmes of Dartmouth & Hannah Samson
    of Rochester,   Dec. 13, 1737
Caleb Jenney of Dartmouth & Patience Standish,

                                   April 6, 1738
Eliakim Willis of Dartmouth & Lydia Fish,   July 20, 1738
Jethro Sprague & Patience Bartlett,   Dec. 12, 1738
Miles Standish, Jr., of D. & Mehitable Robins of
    Plymouth,   Dec. 13, 1738
Hezekiah Herrington & Hannan Southworth, both of
    Marshfield,   March 1, 1738-9
Nathaniel Simmons & Mercy Simmons,   June 12, 1739
Isaac Tinkam of Plymouth & Keziah Wormall, July 20, 1739
William Wilson of Scituate & Hannah Bourne of
    Marshfield,   Nov. 28, 1739
Hezekiah Ripley & Abigail Hunt,   Dec. 3, 1739
Eleazer Harlow of D. & Abigail Thomas of Marshfield,

                                  March 1739-40
Nathaniel Blackmer of Dartmouth & Rebecca Samson,

                                  May 22, 1740
William Tolman of Scituate & Abigail Williamson of
    Marshfield,   June 23, 1740
Jedediah Soule & Tabitha Bishop,   Nov. 4, 1741
Samuel Sprague, Jr., & Sarah Oldham,   July 8, 1742
Benjamin Howland of Pembroke & Experience
    Edgerton of Halifax,   Feb. 10, 1742-3
Thomas Gullifer & Keturah Samson,   Oct. 26, 1743
John Chandler, 3d, & Sarah Weston,   Nov. 4, 1743
David Delano & Abigail Chandler,   May 28, 1740
Micah Soule & Mercy Southworth,   May 31, 1740
Joseph Russel & Abigail Wadsworth,   Dec. 31, 1740
Abisha Sole & Abigail Delano,   May 14, 1741
Lemuel Delano & Lidia Bartlett,   July 7, 1741

Charles Rider of Plymouth & Rebecca Bartlett, Oct. 8, 1741
Briggs Allden & Mercy Wadsworth, Nov. 19, 1741
Simeon Curtis of Scituate & Aseneth Sprague, April 20, 1742
Nathaniel Bartlett & Zenobe Wadsworth, June 20, 1742
Jonathan Crooker of Pembroke & Bettrice Lowden,
Jan. 14, 1742-3
Nero (negro) & Patience (Indian), March 17, 1743
John Sprague & widow Deborah Simmons, Dec. 5, 1744
John Goold of Hull & Huldah Brewster, June 13, 1745
Eleazer Harlow of D. & Abigail Clarke of Plymouth,
Sept. 11, 1745
Ichabod Simmons & Lydia Soule, Dec. 8, 1743
Thomas Prince of Kingston & Lydia Delano, Dec. 8, 1743
Jabez Cole & Grace Keen, Aug. 23, 1744
Amos Samson & Deborah Samson, Oct. 19, 1744
Ebenezer Delano & Lydia Wormall, May 16, 1745
Joshua Thomas of D. & Marcy Berstow of Pembroke,
Dec. 13, 1747
Andrew Samson & Abigail Bisbee, Feb. 1, 1747
Joseph Bartlett & Sarah Simmons, July 11, 1749
Abner Samson & Sarah Samson, Oct. 12, 1749
James Robins & Ruth Pirce, March 20, 1749
Ezekiel Bradford & Betty Chandler, July 21, 1750
Jedediah Simmons & Lydia Soule, Aug. 23, 1750
John Simmons & Joanna Doten, Sept. 13, 1750
Elnathan Weston & Jemima Bisbee, Nov. 8, 1750
John Oldham & Hannah Soule, Nov. 8, 1750
Joseph Freeman, Jr., & Caroline Chandler, Nov. 21, 1752
Eliphat Bradford of Plymouth & Hannah ——— of
Duxboro, Aug. 8, 1751
James Robinson & Jerusha Bartlett, Oct. 31, 1751
Jonathan Chandler & Rebecca Packard, *Nov. 27, 1751
Jonathan Chandler & Rebecca Packard, *Nov. 27, 1755
Jacob Weston & Deborah Simmons, Dec. 5, 1756
Simeon Cook & Mary Dingley, Jan. 13, 1756
Abner Samson & Deborah Bisbee, April 20, 1756

* As written.

John Soul & Patience Wormall,	Jan. 11, 1759
Ichabod Delano & Hulda Samson,	Feb. 15, 1759
Caleb House & Elisabeth Randall,	July 12, 1759
Nathaniel Sylvester & Silvinia Sprague,	Dec. 6, 1759
Seth Bradford & Lidia Southworth,	Feb. 7, 1760
Jacob Barstow & Desire Brattles,	March 13, 1760
Oliver Seabury & Alice Allden,	May 7, 1760
William Weston & Ruby Chandler,	Oct. 21, 1760
Michael Lowden & Eunice Prior,	Nov. 25, 1760
Thomas Frazier & Rebecca Alden,	Nov. 27, 1760
Henry Perry & Bethiah Baker,	Dec. 25, 1760
Bezaleel Merrick & Ruth Lowden,	Dec. 28, 1760
Elijah Samson & Ruth Bradford,	Sept. 3, 1761
Cornelius Delano & Sarah Peterson,	June 24, 1762
Joshua Cushman & Mercy Wadsworth,	Nov. 17, 1763
Nehemiah Peterson & Prince Dillingham,	Dec. 13, 1764
Jasher Southworth & Raimah Southworth,	May 5, 1763
Asa Chandler & Martha Delano,	June 30, 1763
John McClathlen, Jr., & Jedidah Samson,	June 7, 1763
Joshua Cushing & Mary Freeman,	Sept. 27, 1763
Silas Freeman & Mary Brewster,	Dec. 8, 1763
John Hunt, Jr., & Mary Simmons,	April 24, 1764
Benjamin Clap of Scituate & Hannah Seabury,	Sept. 6, 1764
Benjamin Goodwin of Pembroke & Jemima Delano,	
	Oct. 11, 1764
Peleg Oldham & Anna Simmons,	Nov. 29, 1764
Silvanus Delano & Huldah Woodcock,	Dec. 3, 1764
Judah Hunt & Betty Oldham,	Dec. 18, 1764
Enoch Freeman & Abigail Weston,	Dec. 20, 1764
Abner Russel & Susana Phillips,	Dec. 24, 1764
Benjamin Prior, Jr., & Sarah Soul,	Jan. 8, 1765
Henry Segar of Kingston & Lenity Wadsworth,	Feb. 7, 1765
Zenas Thomas of Marshfield & Abigail Peterson,	
	Feb. 14, 1765
Joshua Soul, Jr., & Mary Cushman,	Feb. 14, 1765
Elijah Peterson of D. & Abigail Whetemore of Mansfield,	Oct. 24, 1765
Job Peterson of D. & Sarah Hewit of Marshfield,	
	Sept. 30, 1765

Lemuel Delano of Hanover & Rachel Gurnett, or Gumett, of Abington,	Nov. 1, 1768
Edward Southworth & Mercy Thomas,	Jan. 18, 1769
Thomas Simmons & Bethiah Sprague,	Feb. 8, 1769
Zebediel Weston & Hannah Curtis,	Feb. 22, 1769
Israel Damon & Zerviah Walles,	March 8, 1769
Joseph Prior & Bethiah Peterson,	April 18, 1769
Noah Simmons & Silvia Southworth,	July 2, 1769
Samuel Samson & Jenny McClathlen,	Aug. 22, 1769
John Gulliver & Betty Delano,	Aug. 31, 1769
Asa Phillips & Cynthia Southworth,	Oct. 5, 1769
Israel Perry & Abigail Baker,	Oct. 15, 1769
Joshua Winslow & Hannah Delano,	Dec. 3, 1772
Oliver Winslow & Sarah Bryant,	Nov. 9, 1786
Joseph Barstow & Lydia Soule,	Nov. 16, 1786
Bisbee Chandler & Abigail Bradford,	Dec. 21, 1786
Nathaniel Hodges & Mercy Delano,	Dec. 28, 1786
Joshua Brewster & Ruth Chandler,	Feb. 2, 1787
Job Samson & Betsey Winsor,	June 15, 1787
Azira Chandler & Molly Fish,	Sept. 9, 1787
Dura Wadsworth & Lydya Bradford,	Jan. 17, 1788
Alden Church & Lucy Faunce,	Feb. 7, 1788
Zachariah Silvester & Lucy Bradford,	Feb. 24, 1788

PEMBROKE.

March 21, 1712. "Part of Duxbury called Mattakeeset, a tract of land known as the Major's Purchase and the land called Marshfield Upper Lands at Mattakeeset established as Pembroke." Society of Friends organized 1708. First Unitarian Church, 1712.

Jacob Ellis of Herwick & Elisabeth Foster,	Aug. 20, 1724
Ichabod Bonney & Elizabeth Howland,	Oct. 29, 1724
Samuel Parris & Ruth Bonney,	Jan. 21, 1725
Isaac Sole & Egatha Parry,	March 11, 1725
Josiah Foster, Jr., & Mary Bonney,	July 29, 1725
Thomas Holloway & Rebecca Tubs,	Sept. 14, 1725

John MackFarland, Jr., & Mary Foster,   March 28, 1726
Benjamin Hanks & Mary Ripley of Bridgewater,

     March 23, 1727
Anthony Peane & Keturah Newland,   April 27, 1727
Jacob Norton of Chilmark & Mrs. Hannah Barker,

     June 8, 1727
Andrew Miller & Jane Macklucas (?),   Dec. 19, 1727
Joseph Stetson, Jr., & Abigail Hatch,   Dec. 26, 1727
Ezekiel Turner of Scituate & Batheba Stockbridge,

     Dec. 27, 1727
Joseph Parry & Rebecca Joslyn, both of Hanover,

     April 24, 1728
Thomas Partin & Margaret Gorden,   May 30, 1728
John Franckley of Reboboth & Hannah Record, Oct. 16, 1728
John Lambert, Jr., & Sarah Staples, both of Hanover,

     Nov. 4, 1728
Anthony Winslow of Marshfield & Deborah Barker,

     June 7, 1729
Ebenezer Bonney & Elizabeth Parriss,   Oct. 16, 1729
Joseph Chandler & Deborah Bonney,   Nov. 27, 1729
Rouse Howland & Ann Bonney,   Nov. 27, 1729
Elisha Bonney & Elizabeth Lincoln,   Dec. 10, 1729
Joseph Tubs, Jr., & Elizabeth Randall,   Dec. 11, 1729
James Hayes & Abigail Knapp,   Feb. 25, 1730
Joshua Baker & Sarah Cushing,   Sept. 30, 1730
Lott Thacher of Barnstable & Rebecca Keen, Sept. 29, 1730
Benjamin Thomas of Mansfield & Jennet Stetson,

     Nov. 5, 1730
Solomon Beals, Jr., & Ann Howland,   Nov. 10, 1730
Isaac Wadsworth & Susanna Nichols,   Dec. 16, 1730
Joshua Turner & Sarah Winslow, of Scituate, Jan. 28, 1731
Abraham Howland, Jr., & Sarah Simmons of Plymton,

     March 11, 1731
Zechariah Simmons of Duxboro & Deborah Bishop,

     May 27, 1731
Nicholas Webster & Content Bishop,   Sept. 7, 1731
Nehemiah Peane & Elizabeth Hanks,   Oct. 27, 1731
Isaac Oldham, Jr., & Mary Stetson,   Nov. 11, 1731

Isaac Mackfarland & Sarah Foster,	Dec. 8, 1731
Isaac Foster & Frances Joslyn of Hanover,	Jan. 6, 1732
Thomas Elmour of Hanover & Elizabeth Russel,	
	March 16, 1732
Barnabas Perry & Alce Sole of Duxboro,	March 30, 1732
Isaac Little, Esq., & Mrs. Abigail Thomas,	Nov. 29, 1732
George Russell & Hannah Mackfarland,	Dec. 18, 1732
Andrew Linsey & Jane Curbe,	April 5, 1733
Job Bonney & Ruth Bisbe,	May 9, 1733
Daniel Hayford & Deliverance Boles,	May 24, 1733
Thomas Tracy & Lidia Bantow of Hanover,	May 28, 1733
John Bisbe, Jr., & Aliah Bonney,	Sept. 6, 1733
Jesse Foord & Mary Crooker	Oct. 17, 1733
Aaron Sole, Jr., & Lidia Peterson of Duxboro,	Dec. 26, 1733
Thomas Hayford & Susanna Perry,	Sept. 23, 1734
Samuel Parry & Unice Wethrel of Hanover,	Sept. 24, 1734
William Mackfarland & Sarah Peterson of Duxboro,	
	Nov. 18, 1734
John Stetson & Abigail Crooker,	Nov. 28, 1734
Ezekiel Bonney & Hannah Bryant,	Dec. 26, 1734
Joseph Foord, Jr., & Hannah Nichols,	March 6, 1735
Joseph Stetson & widow Mary Parry,	March 1, 1736
Job Randall & Mary Jennings,	March 4, 1736
Daniel Crooker & Mary Ramsdell,	April 28, 1736
Elijah Cushing & Hannah Barker of Hanover,	May 3, 1736
Jedediah Lincoln of Hingham & widow Mary Barker,	
	June 10, 1736
Daniel Lewis, Jr., & Sarah Bisbee, Jr.,	Sept. 30, 1736
Austin Beane of Hallifax & Hannah Stetson,	Oct. 21, 1736
Joseph Osyer & Mercy Thomas,	Dec. 8, 1736
Josiah Bishop & Sarah Crooker,	Dec. 16, 1736
Samuel Keen & Margaret Reddin of Scituate,	Jan. 4, 1737
Benjamin Jacob of Scituate & Mary Thomas,	May 12, 1737
James Randall & Ruth Magoon,	June 15, 1737
Elijah Bonney & Susanna Tubbs,	June 27, 1737
Deacon Joseph Foord & widow Sarah Dogget of	
Mansfield,	Sept. 7, 1737
Jedediah Beals & Deborah Boles,	April 5, 1738

James Johnson of Scotland, Great Britain, & Bethia
    Barker, Jr.,   July 31, 1738
Jonah Bisbe & Ruth Briant,   Aug. 24, 1738
William Richards of P. & Hannah Simmons of Dux-
    boro,   Sept. 7, 1738
Richard Bordman of Duxboro & Ester Samson, Oct. 17, 1738
Samuel Howland & Sarah Joy,   Oct. 13, 1738
William Curtis & Martha Macfarland, Jr.,   Nov. 14, 1738
Henry Munroe of Swansey & Hannah Joslyn, Jr.,
                                Nov. 16, 1738
Robert Stetson, Jr., of Scituate & Hannah Turner,
                                Nov. 23, 1738
Isaac Crooker & Desire Bates, Jr.,   Nov. 23, 1738
Elisha Barker & Elizabeth Bowen,   Jan. 25, 1738
Gideon Soule & Mercy Silvester,   March 5, 1738-9
Caleb Turner, Jr., of Scituate & Ruth Briggs, May 1, 1739
Francis Keen & Margaret Hunt,   Nov. 1, 1739
Richard Tellah (mulatto) & Peg (negro servant of
    Mr. Josiah Cushing),   Dec. 11, 1739
Solomon Russel & Dorothy Tubs,   Dec. 27, 1739
John Orcut of Bridgewater & Mary Webster, March 31, 1740
John Jordan of Scituate & Mercy Damon,   Dec. 23, 1740
Nathaniel Baker & Susannah Lincoln, Jr.,   Dec. 29, 1740
John Lincoln, Jr., of P. & Content Turner of Hanover,
                                Feb. 25, 1740
John Allen of Bridgewater & Bethia Crooker, March 5, 1740
Hutson Bishop & Eliza Keen,   Sept. 3, 1741
Nehemiah Cushing, Jr., & Sarah Humphreys, Nov. 18, 1741
Abraham Joslyn & Mary Soule,   Dec. 16, 1741
John Wallis of P. & Elizabeth Patterson of Hanover,
                              Dec. 29, 1741
Joseph Ramsdell, Jr., of P. & Mary Daws of Bridge-
    water,   Dec. 30, 1741
Elisha Palmer of Hanover & Jerusha Stetson, Dec. 31, 1741
William Page & Agatha Stetson,   May 31, 1742
Joshua Briggs & Zervia Dellano,   June 3, 1742
Gideon Bisbee & Rebecca Turner,   Sept. 7, 1742
Shubal Munroe & Mary Joslyn,   Nov. 10, 1742

Benjamin Tailer of Hanover & Mary Russel,	Dec. 23, 1742
Samuel Peine & Rachel Cordwell,	June 12, 1742
Recompence Magoune & Ruth Crooker,	July 20, 1742
John Ransom of Kingston & Desire Bishop,	Oct. 11, 1742
Job Simmons of Plimton & Abigail Pains,	Oct. 20, 1742
Job Crooker & Abigail Winslow,	Dec. 15, 1742
Nathaniel Croade & Elizabeth Carter, both of Plymouth,	Dec. 29, 1742
Israel Claylie & Phebe Shurtleff,	May 10, 1743
David Hearsey, Jr., & Susannah Ramsdell,	May 20, 1743
Josiah Smith & Dorithy Dun,	Oct. 1, 1743
Evens Skinner & Sarah Stacey,	Nov. 5, 1743
Samuel Gardner & Hannah Russell,	Dec. 29, 1743
Jonathan Peterson & Jael Dillingham,	June 21, 1744
Rouse Howland & Lydia Bowles,	July 23, 1744
David Weston of Duxboro & Susanna Churchell,	Oct. 22, 1744
Amos Foord & Sarah Bisbe, Jr.,	Aug. 2, 1745
Job Barstow & Susanna Tuels,	June 3, 1743
Benjamin Ramsdell & Luranna Bishop,	Dec. 8, 1743
Nathaniel Chamberlain & Sarah Foster,	Dec. 15, 1743
Isaac Tubs & Lois Jennings,	Dec. 29, 1743
John Delano of Duxboro & Ruth Cox,	May 22, 1758
George Turner of Bridgewater & Jane Linsey,	Nov. 9, 1758
Benjamin Bonney & Silence White,	April 3, 1759
Saul Job—— & Experience Samson (blacks),	Sept. 2, 1759
John Leavitt & Ruth Keen,	Oct. 25, 1759
Benjamin Bates of Hanover & Betty Crooker,	Nov. 29, 1759
William Phillips, Jr., & Hannah Prior,	Jan. 10, 1760
Webster Hayford & Mary Bonney,	Jan. 17, 1760
Ephraim Linsey & Anna Howland,	May 22, 1760
Pomp —— & Ruth Wampey (blacks),	Aug. 21, 1760
Jabez Bolton of Halifax & Hannah Bisbee,	Nov. 7, 1760
Daniel Teague & Alice Peterson,	March 19, 1761
Noah Cole of Plimton & Hannah Russell,	May 19, 1761
Increase Robinson, Jr., & Rebecca Bourse,	June 18, 1761
Edward Cox & Abigail Hanks,	Oct. 14, 1761
Simeon Jones & Deborah Beals,	Dec. 24, 1761

Benjamin Taylor of P. & Abiah Phillips of Bridge-
    water,   Jan. 7, 1762
Josiah Thomas & Rachel Thomas,   Jan. 21, 1762
William Cox, Jr., & Mary Josselyn, Jr.,   Jan. 21, 1762
Urban Lewis of Hingham & Abigail Jones,   Feb. 4, 1762
David Foster & Deborah Peterson,   April 8, 1762
John Thomson of Bridgewater & Elizabeth Bisbe,
                                April 13, 1762
Job Stetson of Hanover & Hannah Munroe,   July 8, 1762
Mark Phillips of Bridgewater & Mercy Phillips, Oct. 7, 1762
Joseph Bates, Jr., of Hanover & Phebe Buker, Oct. 28, 1762
Rev. Daniel Shute of Hingham & Mrs. Deborah Cushing,
                                Jan. 6, 1763
James Hatch & Mary Moore,   Jan. 27, 1763
Philips Chandler of Duxboro & Christian Philips,
                                Dec. 15, 1763
William Phillips & Sarah Crooker,   April 3, 1764
Scipo of Bridgewater & Peggy (blacks),   June 8, 1764
Isaac Lane of Hingham & Sarah Hatch,   Oct. 1, 1759
Edward King of Boston & Alice Perry,   July 30, 1759
John Chubbuck of Abington & Lidia Crooker, Nov. 12, 1759
Capt. John Church of Scituate & Mrs. Huldah Soul,
                                Feb. 24, 1760
Josiah Smith & Mary Barker,   June 15, 1760
Charles Josselyn & Rebecca Keen, 3d,   July 10, 1760
Ichabod Bonney, Jr., & Mary Turner,   Sept. 14, 1760
Isaac Little & Lidia Hatch,   Oct. 27, 1760
William Hersey of Abington & Patience Bisbee, Oct. 15, 1760
Asa Bearce of Hallifax & Mary Randall, 3d, Nov. 27, 1760
Freedom Chamberlin, Jr., & Deborah Turner, Jan. 8, 1760
Ichabod Thomas & Ruth Turner,   Jan. 22, 1760
Matthew Stetson of Scituate & Mary Randall, 2d,
                                Feb. 5, 1761
Ebenezer Barker & Priscilla Loring,   April 2, 1761
Joseph Taylor of P. & Thankful Clark of Tiverton,
                              April 15, 1761
Poole Spear of Boston & Christiana Turner, May 10, 1761
Joshua Turner, Jr., & Betty Buker,   June 22, 1761

Thomas Randall & Deborah Barker,	Sept. 10,	1761
Nathaniel Cushing & Lucy Turner,	Sept. 24,	1761
Isaac Foord of Marshfield & Lucy Josselyn,	Oct. 1,	1761
Perez Samson of Duxboro & Mary Taylor,	Oct. 1,	1761
Lemuel Bonney & Lucy Bonney,	Dec. 3,	1761
Nathaniel Stetson & Sarah Bishop,	Dec. 3,	1761
Joseph Dwelly & Mary Magoun,	Jan. 7,	1762
Asa Keen & Zilpha Hatch,	Feb. 18,	1762
William Haylord & Betty Bonney, Jr.,	March 11,	1762
Caleb Howland & Deborah Oldham,	May 2,	1762
Jesse Lapham of Scituate & Mercy Randall,	Nov. 15,	1762
Jedediah Dwelly of Scituate & Lidia Soul, Jr.,	Feb. 24,	1763
Diamond Perry & Nabby Cushing,	April 28,	1763
John Mitchell, Jr., of Scituate & Zilpha Richards,	June 2,	1763
Robert McCathen & Mary Keen,	Oct. 13,	1763
Adam Turner & Chloe Bonney,	Oct. 18,	1763
Isaac Hatch & Sarah Cushing,	Nov. 28,	1763
Daniel Tubbs & Hannah West,	Dec. 6,	1763
William Standish & Abigail Stetson,	Dec. 8,	1763
Jonathan Turner & Hannah Ford, Jr.,	Feb. 22,	1764
Seth Fuller & Deborah Ford,	March 8,	1764
Silvanus Cook of Kingston & Sarah Barstow,	March 22,	1764
Jehiel Simmons of Duxboro & Deborah Loring,	Oct. 22,	1761
Abisha Stetson & Sarah Crooker, Jr.,	April 2,	1761
Simeon Hall of Kingston & Mary Bearce of Hallifax,		
	Feb. 16,	1762
Thomas Corleu of Scituate & Mary Russell,	July 18,	1764
Abel Russel & Lydia Garnet,	May 7,	1765
Abner Magean (or Magoan) & Ruth Briggs,	Oct. 14,	1765
Ezra Larraince of Abington & Mary Jeffery,	Sept. 26,	1765
Nathaniel Winslow & Sarah Hatch,	Nov. 21,	1765
Thomas Lincoln & Lydia Randal,	Feb. 13,	1766
John Jordin & Cloe Tubbs,	Feb. 23,	1766
Daniel Bonney & Elisabeth Barten, Jr.,	May 15,	1766
Robert Page & Susanna Bennet,	May 26,	1766
Elish Hatch of Scituate & Betty Howland,	Aug. 7,	1766
Rev. Isaiah Dunster of Harwich & Mrs. Mary Smith,		
	Nov. 13,	1766

Amaziah Goodwin & Thankful Russell,   Dec. 8, 1766
Thomas Barker & Olive Foord,   Jan. 8, 1767
Ichabod Bearce & Eanis Witherell,   Jan. 29, 1767
Stephen Richerson of Bridgewater & Mary D—ing,
    April 7, 1767
Jonathan Turner & Mary Bonney,   March 8, 1768
Hezekiah Bearse & Mehetabel Gibbins,   Oct. 24, 1768
Zeleck Bassett of Kingston & Huldah Garnet, Oct. 29, 1767
Lemuel Church of Scituate & Susanna Baker,   Dec. 10, 1767
Samuel Jennings & Keziah Bearce,   Dec. 24, 1767
Appolus Cushman of Duxboro & Eleanor Keen,
    March 1, 1768
Amos Witherell & Ruth Stetson,   Dec. 24, 1767
Japhat Crooker & Lidia Turner,   March 10, 1768
Joseph Turner of P. & Elisabeth Crooker of Dux-
    boro,   March 16, 1768
Nathaniel Turner of Sunderland & Sarah Rogers,
    June 14, 1768
James Glover & Rachel Bonney, .   July 7, 1768
Stockbridge Joselyn & Olive Standish,   Nov. 24, 1768
Joseph Peirce & Olif Fish,   May 23, 1769
Daniel Oldham & Desire Ransom,   June 15, 1769
Ebenezer Baerce & Lydia Jennings,   Nov. 16, 1769
Hezekiah Bryant of Halifax & Deborah Crooker,
    Sept. 28, 1769
Joshua Witherell & Mary Standish, Jr.,   Dec. 25, 1769
Simeon Nash of Dartmouth & Huldah Bates, Jan. 18, 1770
Joseph Ramsdell, Jr., of Hanover & Elisabeth Barber,
    Feb. 1, 1770
Thomas Crooker & Nabby Ramsdell,   Feb. 1, 1770
Thomas Cook of Hanover & Hannah Lincoln,
    March 26, 1770
James Cox & Ruth Magoun,   Feb. 15, 1770
John Thomas & Sarah Loring,   June 10, 1770
Zadock Reed & Luce Garnet,   Sept. 16, 1770
Shubel Buttler of Tisbury & Hannah Garnet, Oct. 22, 1770
Caleb Baston & Si—— Magoan,   Nov. 22, 1770
Nathaniel Sprague & Hannah Foord,   July 19, 1770

Samuel Hill & Lydia Ramsdell,	Feb. 24, 1768
Benjamin Ramsdell, Jr., & Hannah Ladd,	Dec. 6, 1770
Lieut. Elijah Cushing & Anne Thomas,	May 2, 1765
Isaiah Cushing of Hingham & Betty Cushing,	Sept. 26, 1765
Seth Cooks & Elisabeth Josselyn,	Dec. 19, 1765
Thomas Nash of Scituate & Eunice Stetson,	Feb. 13, 1766
Elijah Crooker & Elisabeth Ramsdell,	Sept. 18, 1766
David Beals & Alice Phillips,	Nov. 19, 1767
Ephraim Briggs of Hallifax & Lettice Hill,	Oct. 19, 1765
Joseph Howland & Lydia Bearce,	Nov. 8, 1768
John Walker & Deborah Record,	Nov. 8, 1768
Reuben Clark of Hanover & Deborah Josselyn,	Dec. 23, 1768
Elijah Crooker & Deliverance Howland,	Jan. 12, 1769
Hawks Cushing of Scituate & Ruth Cushing,	Sept. 28, 1769
Daniel Gardner & Hannah Sherman,	Nov. 3, 1769
Jacob Gurney of Abington & Elizabeth Keen,	Dec. 14, 1769
Samuel Bonney & Mary Soper, Jr.,	Dec. 24, 1769
Joshua Pratt, Jr., & Mercy Sherman,	Dec. 28, 1769
John Stetson, Jr., & Hannah Cushing, Jr.,	June 25, 1770
Samuel Howland & Lydia Robinson,	Dec. 6, 1770
John Jackson & Betty Wade,	Feb. 8, 1771
Amos Turner of Hanover & Betty Perry,	Feb. 14, 1771
Robert White of H. & Mary Crooker, Jr.,	April 25, 1771
Daniel Child & Ruth Record,	May 9, 1771
Jacob Bearce & Mary Munro,	Sept. 12, 1771
Henry Munro, Jr., & Mary Millar,	Sept. 12, 1771
Joseph Nichols & Lydia Bisbee,	April 12, 1772
Nathan Cushing, Esq., of Scituate & Abigail Tilden,	
	July 11, 1772
Noah Perry & Jane Hobart,	Oct. 1, 1772
Robert Holmes of Kingston & Abigail Howland,	
	Nov. 5, 1772
Ebenezer Drake of Bridgewater & Susanna Leavitt,	
	Feb. 18, 1773
Thomas Record & Deborah Phillips,	March 11, 1773
David Cudworth of Scituate & Deborah Soul,	June 3, 1773
Nathan Bryant of Plimpton & Betty Bearce,	June 24, 1773
Joshua Berstow of Hanover & Margaret Bonney,	
	Sept. 28, 1773

West Cole & Margaret Robinson, March 6, 1774
Matthew Whitten, Jr., of P. & Althea Bearce of Kingston,
 July 10, 1774
Gideon Walker of Marshfield & Ruth Oldham, July 28, 1774
Nathaniel Jennings & Mary Barnes, Nov. 14, 1774
Lindes Tower of Hanover & Rebecca Barker, Nov. 24, 1774
Gersham Ramsdell & Mary Garey, Jan. 12, 1775
James White Cushing & Sarah Turner, 3d, Feb. 16, 1775
Gain Robinson, Jr., & Lydia Garnet, March 30, 1775
Christopher Phillips & Priscilla Cushing, May 25, 1775
Barnabas Jackson, transient, & Lydia Oldham, Oct. 19, 1775
Edward Hayford & Abigail Ramsdell, Dec. 28, 1775
Isaac Wade & Lucy Harding, May 23, 1776
Daniel Ramsdell of Bridgewater & Betty Soul, Aug. 22, 1776
Alexander Soper, Jr., & Lucy Stetson, Nov. 14, 1776
Daniel Crooker of P. & Hannah White of Hanover,
 Dec. 19, 1776
Samuel Ramsdell, Jr., & Betty Soper, Dec. 26, 1776
Seth Phillips & Betty Hamlen, Feb. 27, 1777
Jonathan Gannett & Sarah Record, April 9, 1777
Dr. Daniel Child & Rebecca Howland, April 20, 1777
Seth Briggs, Jr., & Deborah Barker, July 30, 1777
Enos Briggs & Sarah Thomas, Oct. 16, 1777
Enoch Hall of Kingston & Bethiah Crooker, May 7, 1778
William White of Middleboro & Hannah Stetson,
 July 30, 1778
Andrew Leach of Middleboro & Hannah Hobart,
 Aug. 9, 1778
Joseph Hearssy, Jr., of Abington & Pamela Record,
 Aug. 13, 1778
Samuel Jacobs, Jr., & Mary Hatch, Jr., Oct. 13, 1778
William Whitman of Bridgewater & Content Cole,
 Jan. 7, 1779
Lot Phillips & Diana Howland, May 20, 1779
John Allan & Cynthia Phillips, Sept. 9, 1779
Hezekiah Stetson & Elisabeth Tillson, Jan. 20, 1780
Reuben Harding & Betty Pynchon, Feb. 9, 1780
Abel Bourn & Deborah Bourn, June 5, 1780

Isaiah Keen & Lydia Bourn,	April 16, 1781
Isaac Bonney & Abigail Robinson,	May 24, 1781
David Record & Abigail Damon,	Sept. 9, 1781
Francis Josselyn of Hanover & Mary Hill, Jr.,	Feb. 17, 1782
George Osborn, Jr., & Jerusha Fish,	March 14, 1782
Isaac Moore of P. & Hannah Studley of Hanover,	
	March 18, 1782
Samuel Wade of P. & Patience Niles of Bridgewater,	
	April 7, 1782
Joseph Barstow & Mary Hatch, 3d,	April 11, 1782
Joshua Barker & Sarah Palmer of Hanover,	April 21, 1782
Eleazer Litchfield of Scituate & Deborah Wetherell of	
Hanover,	July 15, 1782
Seth Ewells of Marshfield & Sarah Dwelly,	Nov. 10, 1782
Benjamin Studley, Jr., of Hanover & Silvester Bonney,	
	Nov. 28, 1782
Eleazer Josselyn & Elizabeth Bourn,	Jan. 9, 1783
James Bourn, Jr., & Tamer Josselyn,	Feb. 13, 1783
Joseph Gannett, Jr., of Bridgewater & Anna Hobart,	
	Oct. 23, 1783
Ichabod Chandler of Duxboro & Olive Fish,	Jan. 29, 1784
Capt. James Hatch & Sarah Cushing,	Jan. 29, 1784
Calvin Gardner & Desire McDaniel,	March 11, 1784
Jeremiah Stetson, Jr., & Lydia Bonney,	Aug. 5, 1784
Eleazer Briggs of Worthington & Abigail Josselyn,	
	Sept. 23, 1784
James Vaughan of Plimpton & Lydia Stetson,	Nov. 2, 1784
Ichabod Samson of Duxboro & Deborah Jones, Jr.,	
	Nov. 5, 1784
Thomas Wales of Braintree & Mary Hobart,	Nov. 25, 1784
Joshua Winslow of Duxboro & Ruth Walker,	Dec. 9, 1784
Hugh Osborn & Zuba Wade,	Jan. 13, 1785
Joseph Torrey & Phebe Hatch,	March 7. 1785
Nathan Sprague & Celia Josselyn,	March 31, 1785
Nehemiah Thayer of Braintree & Sarah Hobart,	
	June 23, 1785
Richard Joel & Betty Humphrey,	July 7, 1785
Edward Blake of Hanover & Susanna Thomas,	Aug. 18, 1785

Joseph Josselyn, Jr., of P. & Deborah Hatch of
    Bridgewater,   Aug. 23, 1785
Isaac Thomas & Nancy Cushing,   Feb. 5, 1786
Benjamin Bates of Hanover & Martha Stetson,

                         March 3, 1786
John Swift & Lydia Robinson,   March 12, 1786
Puffer Lowdon of Marshfield & Violet Osgood,

                         March 16, 1786
Samuel Briggs of Hallifax & Mercy Daman,   May 28, 1786
William Collamore & Charlotte Hatch,   Jan. 1, 1787
Benjamin Beuker & Jemima Hill,   Jan. 14, 1787
George Cushman of Duxboro & Anna Perry, Feb. 1, 1787
Jacob Bryant & Joanna Bisbee,   Feb. 1, 1787
Cornelius White of Hanover & Sarah Lindsey Hill,

                         May 21, 1787
Barnabas Holmes of Plymouth & Anne Damon,

                         Nov. 29, 1787
Josiah Barker & Penelope Hatch,   Dec. 9, 1787
Richard Lowden, Jr., of P. & Betsy Hatch,   Jan. 9, 1788
Isaac Beals & Lydia Stetson, 3d,   March 16, 1788
William Delano & Deborah Heals (?),   April 28, 1788
Rowland Cushman of Attleboro & Mary White Cushing,

                         July 7, 1788
Rev. Levi Whitman of Wellsfleet & Sarah Thomas,

                         Dec. 13, 1787
Seth Josselyn of Hanover & Priscilla Standish, Dec. 19, 1787
Isaac Little of P. & Worthy Winsor of Duxboro,

                         Jan. 15, 1788
Jacob Tracy & Hannah Foord,   Feb. 24, 1788

MIDDLEBOROUGH.

June 1, 1669. "Namassakett shall be a township and to be called by the name of Middleberry." Sept. 28, 1680. "Certain lands at Assowamsett Neck and places adjacent granted to Middleborough." First (Congregational) Church organized 1694. North Middleboro Congregational, 1748. First Baptist, 1756. Third Baptist, 1761.

James Wood & Experience Fuller, April 12, 1693
Jacob Tomson & Abigail Wadsworth, Dec. 28, 1693
Samuel Eaton & Elisabeth Fuller, May 24, 1694
Stephen Donham of M. & Lydia Taylor of Taunton,
May 10, 1743
Nathaniel Holloway of M. & Mehitable Bassett of
Bridgewater, June 20, 1733
James Bumpas & Rachell Hawks, March 14, 1732-3
Benjamin Wood & Priscilla Richard, both of Plymton,
April 12, 1733
Francis Eaton & Lydia Fuller, June 12, 1733
ZacheriahWhitman of Bridgewater & Elinor Bennet,
Nov. 1, 1733
Ebenezer Hayford of M. & Mary Brooman of Taunton,
March 20, 1733-4
Caleb Cowing of Rochester & Anna Richmond, May 3, 1734
William Smith & Elisabeth Renolds, July 4, 1734
Ephraim Pratt of Seabrooke & Beulah Williamson,
July 30, 1734
Benjamin Waldron of Dighton & Hannah Hackett,
Nov. 7, 1734
John Montgomery & Mary Strawbridge, Jan. 30, 1734-5
Edward Weston & Elizabeth Smith, March 20, 1734-5
Thomas Tupper & Rebecca Bumpas, June 19, 1735
Isaac Peine (or Reine), Jr., & Deliverance Holloway,
May 5, 1735
William Redding & Bennett Eddy, Feb. 7, 1733-4
Nathan Cobb of Plymouth & Joanna Bennet, April 2, 1734
Samuel Warren, Jr., & Rebecca Donham, June 13, 1734
Joseph Jennings & Hannah Thomas, Aug. 6, 1734

Ephraim Tompson of Halifax & Joanna Thomas,
Nov. 6, 1734
John Cannady & Anna Hathaway, Nov. 7, 1734
Nathaniel Foster of Plymouth & Mercy Thacher,
Feb. 6, 1734-5
Moses Eddy & Jedediah Wood, March 25, 1735
Elnathan Wood & Patience Cushman, April 23, 1735
Nathan Thomas & Abigail Allden, May 1, 1735
Silvanus Brimhom (?) of Plymouth & Mary Bennet,
July 13, 1735
Daniel Vaughn & Sarah Cushman, Aug. 12, 1735
John Jackson & Joanna Bate, Aug. 19, 1735
Peter Bennet, Jr., & Sarah Stevens, Sept. 11, 1735
Hezekiah Purrington of Truro & Mercy Bate, Oct. 7, 1735
John Miller & Priscilla Bennet, Oct. 3, 1735
Simeon Leonard & Abijah Morss, Nov. 6, 1735
William Cushman & Susanna Samson, Dec. 25, 1735
Nathaniel Macomber of Taunton & Priscilla South-
worth, Nov. 13, 1735
Benjamin Renolds & Sarah Smith, March 10, 1737
William Holloway of Middleboro & Sarah Walker,
May 12, 1737
Robert Spout & Hannah Samson, Feb. 2, 1737-8
Benjamin Samson, Jr., of Plymton & Mary Williamson,
May 1, 1738
Daniel Taylor, Jr., & Mary Russell, Sept. 20, 1738
George Williamson, Jr., & Fear Eddy, Nov. 2, 1738
Samuel Holloway & Rebecca Treuant, July 7, 1737
Shadrack Peine of M. & Abigail Hoskins of Taunton,
Aug. 16, 1737
James Keith of Bridgewater & Deborah Bennet, Oct. 25, 1737
Charles West & Deborah Williamson, Nov. 17, 1737
Phillip Leonard & Mary Richmond, Jan. 6, 1737-8
John Hayford of Freetown & Thankful Finney,
Nov. 23, 1738
Ephraim Keen of Freetown & Mercy Allen, Jan. 4, 1738-9
John Hodson (?) & Sarah Renals, March 2, 1738-9
Ephraim Renolds & Alice Braley, Aug. 16, 1739

Josiah Holloway & Hannah Parris,   Nov. 29, 1739
Mark Haskell of Rochester & Mrs. Abiah Nelson,
                                              June 18, 1740
William Nelson & Elizabeth Howland,   Oct. 2, 1740
* Josiah Wood & Mary Holmes,   Jan. 29, 1735-6
John Smith & Deborah Bardin,   Feb. 20, 1735-6
John Warren & Ann Reed,   July 27, 1737
Jonathan Smith, Jr., & Experience Cushman,   Sept. 6, 1737
Seth Howland & Lydia Cobb,   Jan. 25, 1738-9
Nathan Caswell & Hannah Shaw,   May 4, 1739
Gersham Cobb, Jr., & Meriam Thomas, Jr.,   Feb. 28, 1739-40
Nathaniel Washburne of Bridgewater & Mary Pratt,
                                           Feb. 28, 1739-40
Manasah Donham of Plymouth & Sarah Hanks,
                                              Aug. 11, 1740
William Lyon & Martha Knowlton,   Aug. 26, 1740
Benjamin Washburn, 3d, & Zerviah Packard, both of
   Bridgewater,   Sept. 1, 1740
William Roach & Mary Kingman, both of Bridge-
   water.   Sept. 1, 1740
William Reed & Sarah Warren,   June 2, 1740
Samuel Pratt, 3d, & Wibray (?) Bumpas,   March 18, 1740-1
Phineas Pratt & Sarah White,   Nov. 5, 1741
Ephraim Donham & Mercy Tinkham,   Dec. 30, 1741
Benjamin Warren & Jedidah Tupper,   Dec. 31, 1741
Joseph Bumpas & Mehetable Tupper,   Jan. 28, 1741
Joseph Alden of M. & Hannah Hall of Bridgewater,
                                              April 1, 1742
Jacob Barden & Elinor Rackett,   April 1, 1742
Joshua Lazel & Elisabeth Ames,   May 24, 1742
Samuel Thurber of Swanzey & Egatha Bryant, Oct. 14, 1742
Israel Thomas & Phebe Lyon,   Oct. 28, 1742
Peter Walker of Taunton & Sarah Samson,   Nov. 11, 1742
* Simon Lazel & Joanna Wood.   Dec. 20, 1742
John Tinkham, Jr., & Jerusha Vaughn,   Jan. 27, 1742-3
John Harris & Marcy Torrey,   Feb. 9, 1742-3
Jedediah Lyon & Mary Cushman,   Nov. 24, 1743
John Thurber, Jr., of Swansey & Ann Bryant, Dec. 19, 1743

Ichabod Wood & Thankful Cobb,   Feb. 16, 1743-4
Barnabas Eaton & Elisabeth Clemons,   Feb. 21, 1743
Jesse Bryant & Susanna Winslow,   April 10, 1744
Isaac Reynolds, Jr., & Mercy Niles,   Aug. 10, 1743
Josiah Richmond of Taunton & Elisabeth Smith, June 9, 1743
Joseph Richmond, Jr., of Taunton & Elisabeth Hacket,
  Oct. 6, 1743
Mallachy Howland & Hopestill Dwelley,   Nov. 4, 1743
Nathaniel Sprout & Esther Thrasher,   Feb. 16, 1743-4
Nathan Bennet & Jemima Samson,   Dec. 5, 1745
Ebenezer Briggs of Taunton & Margery Leonard,
  Feb. 6, 1745-6
John Hall & Lydia Hacket,   Dec. 13, 1745
Mr. Samuel Southworth & Mrs. Elizabeth Caswell, Jr.,
  Jan. 2, 1745
Josiah Richmond & Lidia Crocker,   Feb. 6, 1745-6
Joseph Peirce of M. & Phebe Smith of Taunton,
  Feb. 19, 1745-6
Aaron Sekins & Hannah Westcoat,   April 17, 1746
Jacob Caswell of M. & Deliverance Caswell of Taunton,
  May 8, 1746
Caleb Jenne of Dartmouth & Silence House,   May 29, 1746
Samuel Allen, Jr., & Betty Willis,   June 20, 1746
Joseph Phinney of M. & Phebe Cole of Berkley,
  Sept. 18, 1746
Ithamer Hoskins of M. & Mercy Fry, Jr., of Taunton,
  Sept. 23, 1746
John Macumber & Elisabeth Phinney,   Jan. 27, 1767
Thomas Richmond of M. & Mary Dodson of Fretown,
  Feb. 12, 1767
John Richmond, Jr., & Hannah Paddock,   March 5, 1767
Phillip Wapquish & Abiah Hoswit (Indians),   Nov. 4, 1746
Mr. Moses Redding & Mrs. Joanah Vaughn,   April 1, 1745
Mr. Samuel Tinkham, 3d, & Mrs. Hope Cobb, April 5, 1745
Mr. William Parker & Mrs. Martha Lebaron,   May 15, 1745
Mr. John Perkins & Mrs. Patience Paddock,   Oct. 23, 1745
Mr. David Delano, Jr., of M. & Mrs. Deborah Holmes
  of Plimton,   March 17, 1745

6

Silas Richard of Pomfret & Elisabeth Raymond,
March 11, 1745

Ezekiel Raymond & Hannah Hoskins, March 21, 1745-6

Joseph Tomson & Mary Cox, April 25, 1746

Thomas Raymond, Jr., & Elisabeth Hall, Jr., June 11, 1746

Josiah Hathaway of Berkley & Sarah Ransom, Aug. 13, 1746

Benjamin Raymond & Thankful Wood, Sept. 18, 1746

John Cox, Jr., & Lydia Redding, Jan. 6, 1746

John Cushman, Jr., of Plimton & Deborah Raymond,
Feb. 3, 1746

Eleazer Thomas & Mary Shaw, Jr., Feb. 20, 1746

Josiah Warren & Joanna Spooner, April 5, 1747

Ebenezer Vaughan & Rachel Soule, Jan. 6, 1744

Joshua Sprague & Elizebeth Keen, both of Abington,
Aug. 21, 1744

James Kith & Lydia Perkins, both of Bridgewater,
Nov. 8, 1744

Jabez Fuller & Hannah Pratt, Dec. 27, 1744

Manassah Clap & Rebekah Cushman, Jan. 14, 1744

Jeremiah Howland & Betty Vaughan, Jan. 24, 1744

Noah Allden & Joanna Vaughn, March 4, 1744

George White of Raynham & Hannah Bryant, June 4, 1745

Benjamin White, Jr., & Bette Pratt, Oct. 15, 1745

Jabez Soul of Hallifax & Abigail Bennet, Oct. 17, 1745

Benjamin Shelley, Jr., of Rainham & Lydia Wood, Jr.,
Jan. 23, 1745

Seth Simmons of Freton & Prissiella ———, Feb. 3, 1745

Joseph Leonard, Jr., & Ruth White, March 27, 1746

Samuel Rickard & Sarah Joslin, both of Pembrooke,
March 3, 1746

Elisha Vaugn & Ester Tinkham, April 4, 1746

Jacob Green & Sarah Jackson, June 17, 1746

Nathan Trevant & Leah Hoskins of Tanton, ·Aug. 21, 1746

Jedidiah Holmes & Ruth Barnes, Dec. 12, 1746

Uriah Samson & Ann White, Dec. 25, 1746

Isreal Felix (an Inden man) & Deliverance Cowit of
Barnstabl (Inden woman), Dec. 26, 1746

Zebulun Thayer of Brantry & Sarah Bennet, Jan. 8, 1746

Jonathan Snow & Ruth Bennet, Jan. 22, 1746
Joshua White & Abithier Bryant, Nov. 12, 1747
Samuel Thacher & Deborah Bennet, Sept. 24, 1747
Prince (a negro man and servant to Capt. Ebenezer
    Morton) & Jenny (a negro woman and servant to
    Capt. Peter Bennet), Oct. 1, 1747
William Winslow & Patience Cobb, Nov. 26, 1746
John Morton & Elizaboth Bennat, Jan. 21, 1747
Josiah Tom & Naomi Peirce, Jr., April 22, 1747
Alexander Degley of Dighton & Mary Wascoat,
    May 22, 1747
Gershom Richmond & Phebe Richmond, July 30, 1747
John Parris & Lydia Samson of Tanton, June 16, 1747
Benjamin Hacket & Marcy Richmond, Dec. 3, 1747
Nathan Prat & Margaret Samson, Dec. 3, 1747
Daved Shaw & Abigail Richmond, Nov. 2, 1748
William Marshallor Macfall & Elizaboth Dugglass,
    Feb. 21, 1748-9
Captain Josiah Winslow of Freetown & Mrs. Hannah
    Booth, March 2, 1749
Ebenezer Sproutt & Bathsheba Wood, June 8, 1749
Gideon Hacket & Bettey Samson, Aug. 3, 1749
Nathaniel Fuller of Hallifax & Mary Parlow, Sept. 19, 1749
Ichabod Morton of Sandwish & Deborah Parlow,
    Oct. 16, 1749
Joseph Bates, Jr., & Eunice Tinkham, Nov. 16, 1749
Nelson Finney & Martha Simmons, Dec. 7, 1749
Jacob Lazell & Elizabeth Devenport of Bridgewater,
    Dec. 20, 1749
Christopher Thresher of Taunton & Thankfule Thomas,
    May 14, 1747
Abraham Barden & Susannah Durfey of Taunton,
    Sept. 22, 1748
Jedediah Thomas, Jr., & Keziah Churchel, Dec. 28, 1749
Nathan Holloway, Jr., & Sarah Booth, May 22, 1749
Auro (Mrs. Samuel Williams' negro man of Taunton)
    & Pegg (Captain Nathaniel Southworth's woman),
    June 2, 1749

Elnathan Wood, Jr., & Susannah Horskins,   Sept. 1, 1749
Joseph Allen & Hannah Willes,   Sept. 12, 1749
George Willimson & Deborah Clark,   Nov. 13, 1749
Benjamin Deen of Tanton & Marcey Barrows, Nov. 16, 1749
William Southworth & Mrs. Bathsheba Smith, Dec. 21, 1749
Lemuell Thomas & Mehitebal Weston,   April 19, 1750
Benjamin Phill of Easton & Hannah Cox,   Jan. 17, 1749
John Soule & Mary Leach,   April 12, 1750
Elkanah Elmes & Sarah Lazile,   May 10, 1750
James Fame & Abigail Rickerd,   Nov. 26, 1747
Thomas Paddock & Hannah Thomas,   Dec. 3, 1747
James Lebaron of M. & Hannah Turner of Rochester,
    Feb. 4, 1747
Robert Mackfun & Jemima Samson,   Feb. 18, 1747
Joseph Barden, Jr., & Marcy Vaught,   March 3, 1747
Moses Stertivant, Jr., & Elisabeth Thomas,   April 26, 1748
Abisha Warshborn of Bridgewater & Mrs. Hannah
    Morton,   Aug. 11, 1748
Nathaniel Southworth, Jr., & Susannah Smith, Feb. 16, 1748
Ephraim Bryant of Plimton & Abigail Samson, Dec. 19, 1748
John Lebaron & Mary Raymond,   Feb. 23, 1748
Mad—m (?) Thacher of M. & Martha Chummuch of
    Scituate,   Feb. 23, 1748
David Shaw & Abigail Richmond,   Nov. 24, 1748
William Macsall & Elisabeth Dugglass,   Feb. 21, 1748-9
Capt. Josiah Winslow of Freetown & Mrs. Hannah
    Booth,   March 2, 1748-9
Zephamiah Deirow & Jain Thomas,   June 17, 1748
Thomas Holmes & Lidia White,   Oct. 12, 1748
Ensign David Hayward of Bridgewater & widow
    Elisabeth Oakeman,   Oct. 19, 1748
Capt. John Littels (negro) & Mary Wille,   July 6, 1749
William Roggers & Susanna Rogers,   Nov. 13, 1749
John Gorham & Mary Torry,   Nov. 16, 1749
Nicholas Porter & Sarah Deirow,   Dec. 27, 1749
Ebenezer Sherman, Jr., & Elisabeth Wormall,   Jan. 1, 1749
Jabez Hatch & Hannah Manlon,   Feb. 8, 1749
Caleb Tilden & Mary Carver,   March 5, 1749

Samuel Thurber of Warren & Alice Wood, May 23, 1750
Seth Haskeol of Rochester & Abiah Nelson, Aug. 13, 1749
John Alden & Rebeckah Weston, July 12, 1750
George Shaw, Jr., & Marcy Thomas, July 20, 1750
Samuel Leach, Jr., of Bridgewater & Phebe Richards,
Aug. 30, 1750
Joseph Eaton & Hannah Crossman, Nov. 22, 1750
———— ———— & Abigail Turner, Nov. 22, 1750
Consider Samson of M. & Rachel ——— of Rochester,
Dec. 13, 1750
Nathaniel Fry of Tanton & Lydia Caswell, Dec. 28, 1750
Joseph Cole of Plimton & Ruth Samson, Jan. 3, 1750
Joshua Dean of Tanton & Kaziah Paddock,
March 13, 1749-50
George Smith & Hannah Hoar, July 14, 1750
Gideon Brayles & Patience Mago (Mayo), July 5, 1750
Jonathan Reed & Joanna Tinkham, Oct. 11, 1750
Job Howland & Jamima Booth, Oct. 25, 1750
Deacon Edward Richmond of Tanton & Mrs. Elisa-
beth Samson, Nov., 1750
Christopher Richmond & Susanna Barden, Nov. 15, 1750
Israel Dean of Tanton, called ye 3d, & ——— Barrows
of M., Jan. 1, 1750-1
Abeel Edson of Bridgewater & Martha Thomas, May 2, 1751
Seth Barrows of Plimton & Mary Lovell, March 14, 1750
William Cushman & Priscilla Cobb, April 11, 1751
Jachob Cushman & Patience Mackfun, April 29, 1751
Samuel Thurber & Alice Wood, May 23, 1750
Seth Haskel & Biah Nellson, Aug. 31, 1749
John Alden & Rebecca Weston, July 12, 1750
George Shaw, Jr., & Marcy Thomas, July 26, 1750
Samuel Leach, Jr., & Phebe Richard, Aug. 30, 1750
Joseph Eaton & Hannah Crosman, Nov. 22, 1750
Noah Benson & Abigail Turner, Dec. 13, 1750
Consider Samson & Rachell Randall, Dec. 13, 1750
Nathaniel Fry & Lydia Caswell, Dec. 28, 1750
Joseph Cole & Ruth Samson, Jan. 3, 1750
Joshua Dean & Keziah Paddock, March 13, 1749-50

Gideon Braily & Patience May,	July 5, 1750
Jonathan Reed & Joanna Tinkham,	Oct. 11, 1750
Job Howland & Jemima Booth,	Oct. 25, 1750
Edward Richmond & Elisabeth Tomson,	Nov. 6, 1750
Christopher Richmond & Susanna Barden,	Nov. 15, 1750
Israel Dean the 3d & Hannah Barrow,	Jan. 1, 1750-1
Obed Edson & Martha Thomas,	May 2, 1751
Seth Barrows & Mary Lovel,	March 14, 1750
William Cushman & Priscilla Cob,	April 11, 1751
Ichabod Cushman & Patience McCarland,	April 29, 1751
Daniel Thrasher & Abiah Richmond,	March 28, 1750-1
Jonathan Cobb, Jr., & Patience Benson,	April 4, 1751
Peter Vaughan & Joanna Barrow,	April 25, 1751
Robert Richmond & Hannah Ramsden,	May 3, 1751
Rev. Nathan Stone & Mrs. Mary Thacher, Jr.,	May 16, 1751
Jonathan Washburne, Jr., & Judah Wood,	May 23, 1751
Jacob Bennet & Hope Nellson,	March 22, 1750-1
Elkanah Leonard, Jr., & Deliverance Smith,	Sept. 26, 1751
Gershom Cobb, Jr., & Elisabeth Corbet,	Dec. 12, 1751
Nathaniel Bumpas & Abijah (?) Vaughan,	Feb. 6, 1752
Silas Cobb & Priscilla Cobb,	Nov. 24, 1752
Ebenezer Morton & Sarah Cobb,	July 23, 1753
William Canada & Charity Leonard,	Dec. 6, 1753
Samuel Thrasher & Susanna Pratt,	June 27, 1751
John Ruggles & Mary Braily,	July 27, 1751
John Booth & Lydia Richmond,	March 12, 1752
Thomas Perkins & Abigail Brigs,	April 9, 1752
Joseph Leonard & Abigail Raymond,	M——, 1752
Joseph Dowing & Dorothy Niles,	June 5, 1752
Jonathan Donham & Ann ———,	Sept. 24, 1752
Jedediah Wood & Keziah Samson,	Sept. 26, 1752
Josiah Smith, Jr., & Priscilla Pratt,	Nov. 30, 1752
John Perkins & Ruth Cushing,	Dec. 21, 1752
William Sprague & Sarah Wescoat,	Jan. 5, 1753
William Snow & Priscilla Richmond,	Jan. 11, 1753
James Perkins & Margaret Strawbridge,	Aug. 20, 1753
Abraham Shaw & Sarah Barrows,	Nov. 1, 1753
Benjamin Horskins & Hannah Duggless,	Dec. 26, 1753

George Smith & Hannah Hoar, July 4, 1753
William Ellis & Elisabeth Lazell, Jan. 16, 1753
Nathan Landers & Ruth Benson, Jan. 25, 1753
John Bent & Bethia Morse, May 16, 1753
Col. George Watson & Mrs. Elisabeth Oliver, June 14, 1753
Robert Hoar & Judath Tinkham, Oct. 4, 1753
Abraham Washburne & Mary Weston, Oct. 18, 1753
Gideon Tinkham & Marcy Thomas, Nov. 1, 1753
Thomas Wood & Sarah Thomas, Nov. 17, 1753
David Alden & Lucy Thomas, Nov. 1, 1753
Samuel Eaton & Patience Tinkham, Nov. 8, 1753
Nathan Cobb & Abijah Tinkham, Nov. 29, 1753
Abial Smith & Lydia Potter, Jan. 10, 1754
Nathaniel Billington & Mary Donham, Jan. 21, 1754
William Briant & Hannah Cobb, April 11, 1754
Joseph Booth & Sarah Hoskins, Dec. 21, 1754
Abiel Smith & Lydia Potter, Jan. 10, 1755
Nathaniel Billington & Marah Donham, Jan. 17, 1755
William Bryant, Jr., & Hannah Cobb, April 11, 1755
Lawrence Kits & Mrs. Abigail Thayer, Nov. 12, 1754
John Norcut (?) & Mary Hayford, Nov. 21, 1754
John Cole, Jr., of Plimton & Hasadiah Lewis, Feb. 12, 1755
Samuel Niler & Elisabeth Raynolds, March 21, 1755
Elisha Benson & Mariah Bump, Feb. 4, 1754
Jabez Burge & Hannah Lothrop, May 3, 1754
Benjamin Besse, Jr., & Margaret Chubock, Jr., June 27, 1754
Samuel Burge & Deborah Bessee, Nov. 7, 1754
Benjamin Besse of Plimton & Eloner Winslow, Dec. 12, 1754
Ebenezer Churchell & Mary Burge, Dec. 12, 1754
Willard Clark of Rochester & Jane Landers, Jan. 16, 1755
Aron Stertevant & Elisabeth English, Jan. 26, 1755
Ebenezer Holmes of Rochester & Ruth Bump, April 13, 1755
Nathaniel Wing of Sandwich & Thankful Swift, May 22, 1755
Nathaniel Gibbs of Sandwich & Joanna Norris, June 26, 1755
John Watts & Elisabeth McNeal, July 15, 1761
Perez Cobb & Abiah Richmond, May 3, 1759
Edward Sherman of M. & Lucia Hathaway of Freetown,
Sept. 21, 1759

Stephen Smith & Judah Reynolds,	Dec. 20, 1760
George Douglas & Prudence Casswell,	Jan. 3, 1760
John Haskings & Meriam Casswell,	April 3, 1760
James Hathaway of Taunton & Abigail Peirce,	April 16, 1760
Job Hunt, resident in Middleboro, & Abiah Allen,	
	April 20, 1760
Levy Rounsevell & Betty Howland,	April 28, 1760
John Harlow & Mrs. Joanna Thomas,	July 24, 1760
John Nellson of M. & Mrs. Hope Rounsevell of	
Freetown,	Nov. 6, 1760
Levi Peirce & Bathsheba Babbit,	Feb. 11, 1761
Jacob Samson & Alice Clark,	Feb. 12, 1761
Joseph Bennet & Mercy Winslow,	Feb. 26, 1761
Joseph Drake of Taunton & Lidia Frye,	July 24, 1760
Job Peirce & Elisabeth Rounsevell,	May 28, 1761
Abiah Nichols of Killingly & Lidia Wood,	Oct. 8, 1761
Seth Tinkham of M. & Eunice Soul of Hallifax,	Oct. 22, 1761
Micàh Turner of Raynham & Mary Eaton,	Oct. 1, 1761
Moses Wood of M. & Lidia Waterman of Hallifax,	
	Jan. 12, 1762
William Fuller & Deborah Rider,	Jan. 14, 1762
Abraham Peirce & Mrs. Priscilla Reed,	Aug. 6, 1761
Job Simmons & Mrs. Elizabeth Howland,	Sept. 1, 1761
Robert Hoar & Mrs. Rachel Haskings,	Nov. 26, 1761
David Vaughn of M. & Phebe Washburn of Plimton,	
	March 22, 1762
David Bryant & Lucy Bryant,	Jan. 14, 1762
David Niles & Mrs. Mary Caswell,	March 4, 1762
Gibbons Sharp (?) & Thankful Hayford,	Sept. 8, 1762
Dick, alias Richard Goal (negro servant of Lt. Jacob Tomson) & Betty Hammond (mulatto) of Pembroke,	Dec. 2, 1762
Thomas Raymond, resident in Middleboro, & Sarah Haskings,	Dec. 9, 1762
James Littlejohn & Mrs. Sarah Thomas, 2d,	Feb. 10, 1763
Jessee Pratt & Lidia Ramsden,	Nov. 20, 1762
Paul Handy of Dartmouth & Mrs. Anne Sherman,	
	Oct. 20, 1762

Benjamin Smith & Elizabeth Finney,   Dec. 9, 1762

John Howland & Mrs. Lidia Peirce,   Jan. 10, 1763

Samuel Richmond & Mrs. Rhoda Mayo,   Jan. 17, 1763

Jonathan Hoar, Jr., & Anna Smith,   Dec. 22, 1761

Cephas Briggs of Berkley & Hopewill Allen,   Feb. 11, 1762

Samuel Rigges of Rutland & Mrs. Bathsheba South-
    worth,   May 26, 1762

Nathaniel Hooper, Jr., of Bridgewater & Elisabeth
    Byrant,   March 31, 1763

Benjamin Haskell & Sarah Sherman,   May 3, 1760

Benjamin ———, Jr., & Phebe Shaw,   June 30. 1763

John Reed & Lidia Booth,   June 9, 1763

Jabez Vaughn, Jr., of M. & Lois Soul of Hallifax,
      Aug. 25, 1763

Benjamin Hall, Jr., & Abigail Burge,   Sept. 22, 1763

George Hamas (?) of Bridgewater & Hannah Lyon,
      Oct. 27, 1763

Ebenezer Allden of M. & Ruth Fobes of Bridgewater,
      Dec. 22, 1763

Ebenezer Hacket & Betty Cannedy,   Jan. 2, 1764

Thomas Blackmore, resident in M., & Sarah Ransom,
      July 28, 1757

George Peirce & Sarah Peine,   Sept. 14, 1757

Samuel Raymond & Dinah Wood,   Sept. 16, 1757

Joseph Turner & Mercy French,   Oct. 5, 1757

Mr. Joseph Haskell of Rochester & Mrs. Judah Thomas,
      Nov. 15, 1757

Nathan Eddy & Eunice Samson,   Nov. 17, 1757

John Eddy & Ruth Hayfords,   Dec. 6, 1757

John Whitaker of Rehoboth & Mary Casswell, March 8, 1758

John Leonard & Susanna Jackson,   Aug. 10, 1758

Jacob Tillson & Elisabeth Barden,   Nov. 23, 1758

Jabez Eaton of M. & Elizabeth Williams of Taunton,
      Jan. 4, 1759

Thomas Hooper of Bridgewater & Abigail White,
      March 15, 1759

Thomas Cole, Jr., & Abiah Bryan,   May 4, 1759

Mr. Elkanah Leonard & Mrs. Sarah Leonard, June 21, 1759

John Leach & Betty Vaughn,   July 19, 1759
Simeon Dogget & Abigail Pratt,   Feb. 28, 1760
Barnabas Samson & Mercy Clark,   March 28, 1760
Joshua Casswell & Zilpha Ransom,   March 28, 1760
John Eddy, Jr., & Hannah Pumroy,   May 29, 1760
Philip Dean of Taunton & Abigail Shaw, Oct. 2, 1760
Archippus Cole & Dresilla Howland,   Nov. 19, 1761
Job Richmond & Jenny Washburn,   Feb. 11, 1762
Isaac Richmond of Taunton & Mehitable Richmond,
                          Feb. 11, 1762
Jesse Curtis of M. & Esther Herrington of Raynham,
                          Dec. 27, 1762
Isaac Thomas & Phebe Thomas,   June 3, 1762
Samuel Barrow & Sarah Thomas, 3d,   Aug. 5, 1762
Isaac Shaw & Betty Beal,   April 21, 1763
Zebedee Pratt of M. & Dordana Keith (?) of Bridge-
    water,   Dec. 8, 1763
Isaac Samson & Mary Casswell,   Nov. 10, 1763
Nathaniel Mayo & Dorothy Smith,   Nov. 21, 1763
David Peirce of Rochester & Martha Canady, Dec. 1, 1763
Nathaniel Cobb, Jr., of Plimton & Penelope Standish
    of Bridgewater,   March 19, 1764
Hugh Canady of M. & Bathsheba Baker of Rochester, ——
Abner Wood of M. & Deborah Bearce of Hallifax,
                       May 10, 1764
Jonathan Woods, Jr., & Keziah Keith of Bridgewater
                       May 3, 1764
John Richard & Ruth Pratt,   May 24, 1764
Job Thrasher & Lidia Smith,   March 24, 1763
Edward Richmond of Taunton & Abigail Wood,
                     April 26, 1763
Archelaus Leonard & Lidia Casswell,   July 28, 1763
John House of Dartmouth & Eleanor Barden, Aug. 10, 1763
George Fish of Dighton & Thankful Reynolds, Nov. 24, 1763
David Sherman of M. & Lidia Staples of Taunton,
                       Dec. 1, 1763
George Leonard of Taunton & Charity Nelson, Jan. 5, 1764
Ephraim Hacket & Elizabeth Paddock, May 14, 1764

Robert Simon & Sarah Thomas (Indians),   March 26, 1764
Caleb Tinkham & Deborah Babbish,   May 27, 1764
Isaac Barker of M. & Abigail Robins of Rochester,
                                           June 14, 1764
Thomas Simmons & Rebecca Peirce,   July 26, 1764
Samuel Bennet & Ann Bennet,   July 24, 1764
Caleb Williamson & Mary Jackson,   Aug. 23, 1764
Calvin Delano of Dartmouth & Mary Alden,   Aug. 30, 1764
William Peirce of Taunton & Joanna Doggett, Sept. 13, 1764
John Randal & Jemima Washburn,   Oct. 11, 1764
Mr. Batchelor Bennet & Mary Samson,   Nov. 1, 1764
Zebulon Vaughan & Mercy Pratt,   Jan. 3, 1765
Mr. Seth Billington & Betty Washburn,   Jan. 15, 1765
William Smith, 3d, & Keziah Hinds,   Oct. 18, 1764
Benny Spooner, Jr., & Mary Pearce,   Oct. 19, 1764
Nathaniel Smith, 4th, & Anna Dillingham,   Dec. 18, 1764
Elijah Thomas & Martha Pratt,   Dec. 20, 1764
Woodward Tucker of Bridgewater & Mary Tinkham,
                                           April 8, 1756
Jacob Tomson of Hallifax & Waitstill Miller, April 15, 1756
John Elmes & Lidia Rider,   April 22, 1756
Jonah Washburn & Huldah Sears,   July 7, 1756
Manassah Wood & Sarah Pomroy,   July 27, 1756
Nathaniel Billington & Eleanor Warren,   Aug. 5, 1756
Lemuel Ransom of Freetown & Mary Richard, Nov. 17, 1756
Silas Stertevant of Plimton & Elizabeth Samson,
                                           Nov. 18, 1756
—shia Thomas & Lucy Vaughan,   Nov. 25, 1756
Ebenezer Fuller of Plimouth & Lois Rider, Dec. 1, 1756
Ensign Charles Ellis of M. & Bathsheba Fuller of
     Hallifax,   Dec. 13, 1756
Samuel Shaw & Fear Thomas,   Dec. 16, 1756
Seth Billington & Deborah Smith,   Dec. 30, 1756
Simeon Freeman of Rochester & Patience Wood,
                                           Jan. 13, 1757
Isaac Bennet & Zilpha Peterson,   Jan. 13, 1757
Thomas Darling, Jr., & Ruth Howland,   Jan. 26, 1757
John Smith, Jr., & Betty Tucker,   March 1, 1757

John Weston, Jr., & Elisabeth Leonard,	April 4,	1757
Bristol & Dinah (negro servants of Mr. Caleb Tomson),	April 14,	1757
Jesse Snow & Mary Eaton,	May 19,	1757
Nathan Wood & Betty Shaw,	July 18,	1757
Nehemiah Briant & Hannah Tolman,	Aug. 9,	1757
Ebenezer Hacket of Raynham & Abigail Thomas,	Aug. 23,	1757
Abiel Cole & Anna Pearce,	Aug. 25,	1757
Josiah Vaughan & Lidia Thomas,	Sept. 22,	1757
John Benson & Priscilla Tinkham,	Dec. 15,	1757
Barzilla Thomas & Elizabeth Cox,	Dec. 15,	1757
Nehemiah Allen & Abiah Thomas,	March 23,	1758
Capt. Joel Ellis & Jemima Bennet,	March 27,	1758
John Thomas, Jr., & Elizabeth Shaw,	March 29,	1758
Philip (negro servant Peter Oliver, Esq.), & Violet (negro servant L. Phineas Pratt),	April 13,	1758
Jesse Vaughn & Margaret Shaw,	April 17,	1758
Moses Thomas & Deborah Shaw,	Sept. 5,	1758
Mr. Seth Samson & Mrs. Thankful Bennet,	Oct. 9,	1758
Ichabod Billington of M. & Betty Peck of Bridgewater,	Oct. 26,	1758
James Willis & Mary Thomas,	Jan. 11,	1759
Abner Samson of M. & Hannah Drew of Hallifax,	Feb. 15,	1759
Joseph Darling & Huldah Thomas,	Jan. 10,	1760
Andrew Cobb & Experience Samson,	Jan. 10,	1760
Joseph Porter of Taunton & Martha Rider,	March 11,	1760
Dr. Stephen Powers & Lidia Drew,	March 20,	1760
Benjamin Tucker, Jr., & Mary Thomas, Jr.,	April 17,	1760
William Soul & Sarah Briggs,	Oct. 30,	1760
Samuel Tinkham, Jr., & Patience Simmons,	Nov. 6,	1760
Ebenezer Donham & Patience Clap,	Nov. 20,	1760
Joseph Silvester of Duxboro & Lucy Samson,	Nov. 20,	1760
Samuel Bishop of Bolton & Patience Cox,	Dec. 17,	1760
Seth Thomas & Mary Barrows,	Dec. 18,	1760
John Lambert of Taunton & Lidia Miller,	Jan. 1,	1761
Jeremiah Thomas, Jr., & Susanna Thomas, 2d,	Jan. 15,	1761

William Tupper & Susanna Clap,   Jan. 22, 1761

✏ Amos Wood & Mary Thomas,   April 23, 1761

Jonathan Porter of Taunton & Mercy Redding, May 12, 1761

Ephraim Hacket & Abiah Leonard,   June 18, 1761

David Miller, Jr., & Sarah Tomson,   Aug. 27, 1761

John Norris, Jr., of Wareham & Jemima Benson,

    Sept. 17, 1761

Ebenezer Samson, Jr., of Plymouth & Priscilla Pratt,

    Oct. 29, 1761

Ebenezer Thomas, Jr., & Joannah Cushman,   Nov. 5, 1761

Gideon Cobb & Mehitable Warren,   Nov. 12, 1761

Joseph Tupper & Joannah Cole,   Nov. 26, 1761

Eliakim Barlow & Mary Billington,   Dec. 3, 1761

Silvanus Thomas & Susanna Tomson,   Dec. 3, 1761

Jacob Soul & Sarah Shaw,   Jan. 21, 1762

William Cushman, Jr., & Susanna Pratt,   March 4, 1762

John Thomas, Jr., & Faith Benson,   March 18, 1762

Benney Cob & Azuba Shaw,   March 25, 1762

Samuel Turner & Lucy Pratt,   April 29, 1762

Samuel Bonney of Plimton & Lidia Smith,   Jan. 13, 1763

James Weston, Jr., & Betty Warren,   Jan. 13, 1763

John Briggs & Abigail Morse,   July 5, 1763

Israel Smith & Mary Bates,   July 21, 1763

Moses Robins of M. & Abigail Barrow of Plimton,

    Sept. 22, 1763

Robert Tucker, Jr., of Norton & Martha Willis, Oct. 3, 1763

John Eddy of Norton & Elisabeth Clap,   Oct. 3, 1763

Samuel Snow & Jedidah Bumpas,   Dec. 8, 1763

Zadock Bozworth of Hallifax & Elizabeth Smith, Dec. 8, 1763

Paul Pratt & Jael Bennet,   Feb. 9, 1764

Consider Brannock & Desire Simmons,   March 8, 1764

John Murdock of Plimton & Sarah Samson,   March 29, 1764

John Standish of Hallifax & Rebecca Ellis,   June 21, 1764

John Miller, 3d, & Zilpha Tinkham,   Sept. 6, 1764

John Alden & Lucy Spooner,   Sept. 27, 1764

John Severy, Jr., & Thankful Cob,   Oct. 25, 1764

Peter Tinkham & Molly Tomson,   Nov. 15, 1764

John Smith, Jr., of M. & Bethiah Chipman of Halli-

    fax,   Nov. 22, 1764

Joseph Smith & Abigail Bent,	Nov. 22,	1764
Eliakim Briggs of Abington & Lois Thomas,	Dec. 6,	1764
Abraham Vaughn of M. & Anna Russel of Pembroke,	Dec. 20,	1764
John Bradford of Kingston & Hannah Eddy,	Feb. 7,	1765
Nathan Barden of Freetown & Hannah Pratt,	March 28,	1765
Elijah Macomber & Mehitable Johnson,	July 14,	1766
Mr. Daniel Smith & Mrs. Hannah Bates,	Aug. 1,	1765
John Cole of Plimton & Elisabeth Proute (?),	Feb. 28,	1765
Roger Haskel & Judith Nelson,	Feb. 28,	1765
Joseph Haskins & Mary Smith,	July 19,	1765
Edward Washburne, Jr., & Hannah Jones,	Oct. 29,	1765
Simeon Wood & Sarah Weston,	Dec. 12,	1765
Abiel Wood & Betty Tinkham,	Dec. 19,	1765
Mr. James Smith & Mrs. Patience Wood,	Jan. 2,	1766
Obediah Covel & Lidia Thomas,	Feb. 27,	1766
James Bartlett, Jr., of Plymouth & Zerviah Knolton,	March 27,	1766
Josiah Thomas & Elisabeth Robins,	May 6,	1766
Lot Eaton & Martha Cobb,	May 22,	1766
John Clark, residing in M., & Miriam Bryant,	June 3,	1766
Elijah Macomber & Mehitable Johnson,	July 14,	1766
Nathaniel Jackson, Jr., & Rebecca Holloway,	April 13,	1766
Henry Evens of Berkley & Rachel Rennels,	April 15,	1766
Nathaniel Barrows & Hannah Jones,	July 17,	1766
Simeon Vaughan & Naomi Jones,	Aug. 14,	1766
John Jacob, a transient person, & Abigail Faunce,	Sept. 30,	1766
Benjamin Jones, resident in M., & Abiah Cole,	Dec. 11,	1766
John Eaton of Bridgewater & Patience Shelly of Raynham,	Sept. 23,	1764
John Townsell, Jr., & Hannah Curtis,	Nov. 29,	1764
Abel Richmond of M. & Bathesheba Richmond of Taunton,	Sept. 19,	1765
Mr. Zepheniah Leonard of Raynham & Mrs. Abigail Alden,	Oct. 13,	1765
Thomas Cobb & Phebe Shaw,	Feb. 6,	1766
Zadock Leonard of M. & Deborah Keith of Bridgewater,	June 10,	1766

John French, Jr., & Hayden Shaw,   July 24, 1764
Amos Howard & Mary Ripley, both of Bridgewater,
                                                    Nov. 6, 1766
Samuel Keith & Zilpah Conant, both of Bridgewater,
                                                    Dec. 2, 1766
Henry Leonard, Jr., & Silence Alden,   March 19, 1767
Joel Reynolds & Hannah Fry,   Jan. 16, 1766
John House of Dartmouth & Eunice Pratt,   Jan. 29, 1767
Stephen Hathaway of Freetown & Hopestil Peirce,
                                                    Feb. 11, 1767
Joseph Alden &'Deborah Williamson,   Sept. 3, 1767
William Rounsevel of Freetown & Rebecca Hoar,
                                                    July 30, 1767
Isaac Reynolds & Huldah Reynolds,   Dec. 3, 1767
Simeon Sherman & Thankful Hall,   Dec. 18, 1767
Robert Hoar, Jr., & Sarah Reed, 2d,   Jan. 17, 1768
Zebedee Booth & Mary Holloway,   March 16, 1768
John Edminster of Freetown & Mary Howland,
                                               March 17, 1768
Henry Peirce of Freetown & Salomi Hinds,   March 31, 1768
Samuel King of Taunton & Margaret Montgomery,
                                                    Sept. 26, 1765
Asa French & Anna Smith,   Oct. 24, 1765
Eleazer Richmond & Deborah Barrows,   Dec. 5, 1765
Nathan Alden & Priscilla Miller,   Oct. 16, 1766
John Barrow of Taunton & Jemima Johnson,   Nov. 26, 1766
Nathaniel Faunce of Dartmouth & Abigail Sherman,
                                                    Dec. 18, 1766
James Ashly of Taunton & Anna Caswel,   Feb. 17, 1767
Jonathan Harvey, Jr., & Abigail Hoskins, both of
      Taunton,   May 5, 1767
Ezra Tilson & Anna Barna,   July 23, 1767
Nathaniel Tomson, resident in M., & Phebe Jones,
                                                    Sept. 1, 1767
Joshua Crapoo of Rochester & Jane Horkin (or Hoskin),
                                                    Nov. 5, 1767
Andrew Ritchie, resident in Freetown, & Isabella
      Montgomery,   Nov. 10, 1767

Mr. Seth Cooper of Taunton & Mrs. Susanna Miller, 2d,	May 26, 1767
Nathaniel Wilder & Priscilla Samson,	May 29, 1768
Jesse Bryant & Mary Shaw, 2d,	June 2, 1768
Nathan Bennet of M. & Patience Peterson of Scituate, R. I.,	April 4, 1765
Abiel Leach, Jr., & Lucy Wood,	Aug. 29, 1765
Nathan Howland & Priscilla Drew,	May 2, 1765
Job Thomas & Molly Pratt,	Aug. 29, 1765
Silvanus Cobb & Molly Ellis,	Oct. 24, 1765
David Thomas, Jr., & Rebecca Tinkham,	Oct. 31, 1765
Lemuel Wood & Rebecca Tupper,	Dec. 12, 1765
Ebenezer Elmes & Hannah Pratt,	Jan. 26, 1766
Seth Wood & Lidia Randall,	Feb. 13, 1766
Abner Barrow & Rachel Thomas,	April 13. 1766
Joshua Willis & Phebe Leach,	Sept. 4, 1766
Shubael Tomson of M. & Ruth Hall of Bridgewater,	Oct. 9, 1766
Josiah Clark of Plymouth & Hannah Hall,	Dec. 25, 1766
William Smith & Remembrance Thomas,	Jan. 8, 1767
Benjamin Patty, a transient, & Mercy Fuller,	Feb. 12, 1767
Bani Teague of Hanover & Joanna Darling,	March 5, 1767
Nathan Vaughan & Priscilla Barrow,	April 2, 1767
John Strong & Deborah Tinkham,	April 9, 1767
Ebenezer Cobb, Jr., Joanna Cushman,	June 7, 1767
Isaac Bryant & Esther Samson,	June 25, 1767
James Rider of Rochester & Hannah Cushman,	Aug. 13, 1767
Nathaniel Tucker & Jedidah Warren,	Aug. 18, 1767
Joshua Briggs of Wareham & Hope Benson,	Sept. 3, 1767
Jabez Smith & Lidia Savery,	Nov. 26, 1767
Benjamin Miller & Esther Clap,	Dec. 3, 1767
John Cobb & Jael Tinkham,	Dec. 10, 1767
Nathan Hollis & Susanna Briggs,	Dec. 17, 1767
Samuel Smith & Susannah Wood,	Dec. 24, 1767
Levi Bearse & Barsheba Wood,	Feb. 22, 1768
Lemuel Bryant & Joanna Barrow,	April 28, 1768
Nathan Darling & Martha Bennet,	June 9, 1768
John Cavender & Joanna Shaw,	June 21, 1768

Mr. John Vaughan, 2d, & Mrs. Experience Miller,
Oct. 27, 1768

Abner Pratt & Ruth Bryant, 2d, Dec. 1, 1768
Asa Seton & Ann Stephens, Dec. 29, 1768
Stephen Richmond & Hannah Beals, April 16, 1767
Ezra Washburn, Jr., & Lucy Fuller, Nov. 3, 1767
Jabez Eddy of Bridgewater & Mehitable Barrow,
Jan. 21, 1768
Robert Howard & Hannah Keith, both of Bridgewater,
Sept. 28, 1768
William White & Betty Barden, Dec. 15, 1768
Jonathan Lyon & Abiah Shaw, Feb. 16, 1769
David Hooper of Bridgewater & Martha Shaw,
March 23, 1769
John Spooner of Dartmouth & Lidia Alden, March 25, 1769
Samuel Rider & Patience Weston, Sept. 7, 1769
Mr. George Leonard of Taunton & Mrs. Charity Nel-
son, Jan. 17, 1764
Mr. Ephraim Hacket & Mrs. Elisabeth Paddock,
May 14, 1764
Mr. Eber Mirick of Berkley & Mrs. Elisabeth Hos-
kins of Taunton, June 26, 1764
Mr. John Miller, Jr., & Mrs. Elisabeth Reed, Nov. 29, 1764
Jeremiah Jones, Jr., & Isabella Casswell, Nov. 29, 1764
Mr. Joshua Waterman & Mrs. Bethiah Reed, Dec. 27, 1764
Mr. Isaac Wood & Mrs. Lurania Southworth, June 14, 1768
Mr. William Reed, 3d, & Mrs. Alice Richard, Sept. 22, 1768
Mr. Benjamin Reed & Mrs. Abiah Macomber, Oct. 23, 1768
Jonathan Morse, Jr., & Priscilla Darling, Nov. 10, 1768
Perez Richmond of Berkley & Phebe Hathaway, Dec. 8, 1768
Mr. Seth Randall of Rochester & Mrs. Hannah Hef-
ford, Jan. 5, 1769
Mr. Gideon Briggs of Berkley & Mrs. Keturah Allen,
Jan. 17, 1769
Mr. Seth Jones & Mrs. Priscilla Miller, Feb. 23, 1769
Mr. Andrew Oliver & Mrs. Phebe Spooner, Feb. 23, 1769
Rowland Gavern of Berkley & Hopestil French,
April 27, 1769

7

Mr. Daniel Diman of Plymouth & Mrs. Susanah
    Southworth, May 4, 1769
Ezra Clark & Mary Hoar, Aug. 11, 1768
Isaac Hathaway of Freetown & Judah Hoar, Aug. 16, 1768
Luke Perkins of Freetown & Margaret Peirce, Dec. 6, 1768
John Demeranvelle of Dartmouth & Mary Peirce, 2d,
     Dec. 22, 1768
Justus Barden of Freetown & Nancy Simmons, Jan. 12, 1769
Isaac Cannady & Deborah Benson, 2d, April 30, 1769
Amos Nelson & Eunice Peirce, May 25, 1769
John Perkins of Freetown & Rachel Pearse, Sept. 25, 1769
Foxel Thomas & Martha Holmes, March 22, 1770
Peregrine White of Freetown & Mary Howland, May 3, 1770
Lot Hathaway of Dartmouth & Abigail Howland,
     May 10, 1770
Ebenezer Nelson & Joana Holmes, May 24, 1770
Manasseh Tucker & Lidia Pratt, April 19, 1770
Michail Kennidy, transient, & Mary Hooper, May 31, 1770
Benjamin Leneord & Hannah Pratt, 2d, Dec. 11, 1770
John Shaw of Reinham & Hannah Keith, Dec. 27, 1770
Joseph Churchell & Sarah Cobb, March 21, 1770
Michail Mosher & Zilpha Peirce, Oct. 30, 1770
Seth Hathaway of Taunton & Wealthy Howland,
     Jan. 31, 1771
Samuel Allen of Dartmouth & Rebecca Pein, April 7, 1771
Edmund Muxham, Jr., & Rebecca Fance, both of
    Plimton, Nov. 7, 1771
Thomas Harlow & Jerushah Pratt, Jan. 1, 1772
Mr. Caleb Muxham & Mrs. Lidia Bumpas, April 16, 1772
Mr. Ezra Harris of M. & Mrs. Charity Griffith of
    Rochester, Dec. 24, 1772
Reuben Muxham of M. & Jemima Russel of Wareham,
     Dec. 25, 1771
Jedadiah Bennet & Cloe Miller, Feb. 27, 1772
Ebenezer Norcutt (?) & Elisabeth Benson, March 10, 1772
Mr. Nathaniel Shaw, Jr., of Plymton & Miss Deborah
    Samson, Sept. 21, 1769
Seth Peine & Huldy Samson, Nov. 9, 1769

Seth Peirce & Huldy Samson, Nov. 9, 1769
Ebenezer Blackman & Lidia Thrasher, Nov. 9, 1769
Cornielious Warren & Patience Hoar, March 1, 1770
Josiah Warren & Susanah Makepeace, March 29, 1770
Joseph Dunham & Sarah Jonson, July 12, 1770
Micah Briant, Jr., & Margaret Paddock,. Nov. 22, 1770
Eliezar Washburn of Brookfield & Sarah Southworth,
         May 9, 1771
Joshua Spooner & Huldah Harden, May 9, 1771
John Smith, 3d, & Eleanor Warren, May 23, 1771
William Richmond of M. & Susannah Richmond of
 Taunton, June 9, 1771
Moses Cain, Jr., & Febe Briggs, both of Taunton,
         June 27, 1771
Robert Sprout, Jr., & Hannah Leonard, 3d, Nov. 21, 1771
Paul Dean of Taunton & Rebecca Jones, Nov. 21, 1771
Simeon Macomber of M. & Lidia Richmond of Taunton,
         Dec. 26, 1771
Seth Barden & Mary Smith, Jan. 9, 1772
Thomas Jonson & Deborah Ellis, Jan. 15, 1772
Jedediah Miller & Bethy Howland, Feb. 15, 1772
Timothy Barden of Freetown & Miribah Simmons,
         June 27, 1771
Silas Pein of M. & Amy Hathaway of Taunton, Oct. 31, 1771
Ellis Luther of Swansey & Bathsheba Simmons, May 3, 1772
Enoch Thomas & Mary Howland, Oct. 1, 1772
Josiah Allen & Elisabeth Thrasher, Dec. 10, 1772
Jonathan Drown of Bristol & Rhoda Dillis, June 14, 1772
William Pratt & Mary King, July 2, 1772
¶ Ephraim Wood, 2d, of M. & Sarah French of Bridge-
 water, Jan. 13, 1773
Joseph Lincoln, resident in M., & Mary Morse, Oct. 4, 1768
Josiah Howard & Dinah Muxham, Sept. 22, 1768
Joseph Cushman & Deborah Barrows, Nov. 3, 1768
John Smith of Rochester & Lucy Jackson, Nov. 15, 1768
George Simmons & Thankful Howland, Dec. 1, 1768
Samuel Benson & Agness Tinkham, May 22, 1769
Noah Cushman & Mary Soule, May 25, 1769

Ebenezer Livy Bennet & Patience Bennet,   Oct. 8, 1769
Ebenezer Bennet & Elisabeth Ellis,   Oct. 19, 1769
Ebenezer Briggs, 4th, & Silence Redding,   Oct. 29, 1769
Jacob Soule, 2d, of Halifax & Hannah Thomas, Nov. 16, 1769
William Shurtleff, Jr., of Plymton & Ruth Shaw,
                                               Nov. 16, 1769
John Barrows, Jr., & Sarah Morton, 2d,   Nov. 16, 1769
William Raymond & Febe Thomas, 4th,   Nov. 30, 1769
Francis Tomson & Mary Bumpas,   Dec. 17, 1769
James Pratt of M. & Isaac Elliot of Taunton,   Jan. 8, 1770
Thomas Ling & Theodate Bennet,   March 29, 1770
John Faunce of Plymouth & Jane Paddock,   April 12, 1770
Caleb Wood & Ruth Thomas,   April 26, 1770
Joseph Thomas, Jr., & Deborah Thomas, 3d,   Oct. 4, 1770
Thomas Giffords of Sandwich & Lidia Thomson,
                                               Nov. 14, 1770
Zachariah Weston & Sarah Wood,   Dec. 6, 1770
Zebedee Tinkham & Lucy Thomas,   Dec. 6, 1770
James Tinkham & Sarah Redding, 2d,   Dec. 20, 1770
Soloman Hall & Hepzibah Allen,   Jan. 10, 1771
Jacob Thomas & Content Johnson,   March 28, 1771
Seth Miller & Abigail Tomson,   Oct. 17, 1771
Nathaniel Wood, Jr., & Desire Shaw,   Nov. 21, 1771
Jacob Miller & Deborah Soule, 2d,   Nov. 21, 1771
Israel Wood & Priscilla Vaughan,   Feb. 27, 1772
Abraham Powers, resident at M., & Deborah Simmons,
                                             March 26, 1772
Elisha Hutchinson, Esq., of Boston & Mrs. Mary
    Watson,   June 5, 1772
John Perkins & Hannah Garner,   Aug. 28, 1772
John Soule, 2d, & Priscilla Simmons,   Oct. 8, 1772
Joseph Haskol of Rochester & Thankful Samson,
                                               Oct. 14, 1772
Isaac Soule & Lidia Wood, 4th,   Nov. 12, 1772
Joseph Purinton & Lucy Allen,   Nov. 26, 1772
Daniel Tomson of Halifax & Fear Lion,   Dec. 3, 1772
Joshua Reed & Ruth Snow, 2d,   Dec. 3, 1772
Samuel Wood & Molly Leonard,   Dec. 10, 1772

Abiel Caswell & Joanna Warren, both of Taunton,
Aug. 27, 1772
Israel Thomas, Jr., & Mrs. Abigail Phinney, Nov. 19, 1772
Thomas Blackmer & Mrs. Rebekah Finney, Nov. 19, 1772
Amos Briggs of Berkley & Mrs. Welthy Hoskins of
Taunton, Nov. 26, 1772
Ichabod Cushman & Mrs. Hope White, Dec. 22, 1772
Gideon Southworth, Jr., & Mary Haskell, Dec. 24, 1772
Moses Samson & Mrs. Lucy Churchell, Dec. 24, 1772
Zebulon Thomas & Mrs. Lidia Tinkham, Jan. 7, 1773
Thomas Blackmar & Mrs. Lydia Drake, April 29, 1773
Jacob Green, Jr., & Mrs. Sarah Richard, June 24, 1773
George Caswell & Charity Makepeace, July 6, 1773
John Stephens of Dighton & Mrs. Elisabeth Hacket, 2d,
Sept. 28, 1773
Jeremiah Tinkham, Jr., & Mrs. Zerviah Richmond (?),
Nov. 2, 1773
Cornelius Tinkham & Mrs. Mercy Barrows, Nov. 25, 1773
Charles Reynolds of M. & Sarah Smith, transient,
March 31, 1774
Nathaniel Holmes, 2d, & Mrs. Mary Richard, July 11, 1774
Benjamin Cain of Taunton & Sarah Aldrich, Nov. 8, 1774
Joseph Deane of Taunton & Mrs. Anna Arobridge,
Dec. 1, 1774
Joseph Caswell & Mrs. Silence Richmond, both of
Taunton, Dec. 15, 1774
David Caswell & Mrs. Anna Donham, Feb. 9, 1775
Zebulon Caswell of Rainham & Mehitabel Raymond,
Feb. 13, 1775
William Elmes of M. & Lucy Poole of Dighton, Sept. 8, 1775
Joseph Vaughan & Lois Booth, Dec. 25, 1775
Capt. Amos Wade of M. & Mrs. Mary Richmond of
Taunton, Feb. 6, 1776
Ezra Reynolds & Sarah Hayfords, April 1, 1776
Ebenezer Paul, Jr., of Berkley & Mrs. Hannah Staples
of Taunton, June 27, 1776
John Perkins & Mrs. Abigail Washburn, Jan. 9, 1777
Seth Hoar & Mrs. Mary Holmes, March 4, 1777

Silvanus Warren & Peirce Booth,	Oct. 2, 1774
Lewis Hall of Raynham & Fear Alden,	Feb. 23, 1775
Thomas Shaw & Joanna Vaughan,	Jan. 29, 1775
Henry Evans & Sarah Fry,	March 14, 1775
Ebenezer Hinds, Jr., & Charity Canedy,	April 30, 1775
Joseph Richmond, 2d, & Judith Howland,	July 2, 1775
John Peirce & Lucy Ashley,	Aug. 31, 1775
Rufus Howland & Bathsheba Canedy,	Sept. 14, 1775
Joshua Caswell & Alice Reynolds,	Nov. 10, 1775
Samuel French of Berkley & Lucy Peirce.	Nov. 30, 1775
Nathan Vaughan, Jr., & Mary Fry,	Dec. 11, 1775
Josiah Jones, 2d, & Betty Vaughan.	Feb. 8, 1776
Ephraim Reynolds & Elisabeth Duglas.	March 17, 1776
Noah Clark & Anna Hoar,	March 28, 1776
Samuel Parker of Freetown & Hannah Fuller,	April 4, 1776
Ebenezer Hayfords & Priscilla Booth,	May 12, 1776
Samuel Wood & Abiah Peirce,	May 23, 1776
Daniel Braman & Eunice Howland,	May 28, 1776
Richard Peirce, Jr., & Lydia Booth,	Aug. 29, 1776
Seth Hathaway of Rochester & Abigail Evans,	Oct. 6, 1776
Benjamin Hill of Dartmouth & Ruth Hoskins,	Oct. 3, 1776
Job Smith of M. & Diadema Booth of Taunton,	Jan. 9, 1777
Abiel Chase & Hannah Holloway,	Jan. 12, 1777
Joseph Peirce of Rochester & Rhoda Clark,	Jan. 23, 1777
Isaac Parris & Phebe Peirce,	June 24, 1777
Philip Rounsevel & Mercy Cole, both of Freetown,	
	Nov. 9, 1775
Joseph Perry, Jr., of Rochester & Susanna Tupper,	
	March 18, 1773
Levi Wood & Joanna Finney,	Oct. 7, 1773
George Hammond of Plimpton & Betty Thomas,	
	Nov. 25, 1773
Consider Barden of M. & Bethiah Edson of Bridgewater,	
	Nov. 25, 1773
Ebenezer Elmes & Lidia Nichols,	Jan. 12, 1774
Benjamin Gilbert of Kingston & Deborah Torrey,	
	March 3, 1774
Joshua Waterman & Hannah Washburn,	March 8, 1774

Cornelius Ellis & Jerusha Bryant, March 13, 1774
David Bates & Thankful Savery, Oct. 20, 1774
Gersham Curtis of Hanover & Tabitha Briggs, Oct. 20, 1774
Perez Thomas & Sarah Wood, Oct. 30, 1774
Daniel Downing & Lidia Nye, Nov. 17, 1774
Amos Wood of M. & Rebecca Barrows of Plymouth,
Nov. 24, 1774
Elisha Rider & Rebecca Weston, Dec. 15, 1774
Joseph Bumpas & Mary Barden, Feb. 9, 1775
John Tomson of Lime, N. H., & Abigail Tomson,
Feb. 16, 1775
William Smith of New Salem & Priscilla Thomas,
Feb. 23, 1775
Abiel Edson of Bridgewater & Hannah Norton,
March 15, 1775
Ebenezer Briggs, Jr., & Betty Ellis, March 16, 1775
Ichabod Wood, Jr., & Sarah Tinkham, 2d, July 6, 1775
Isaiah Washburn & Priscilla Wood, July 20, 1775
Jonathan Fuller & Lucy Eddy, Aug. 1, 1775
Daniel Leonard of Bridgewater & Hope Clap, Oct. 15, 1775
Nathaniel Tomson & Hannah Thomas, Nov. 1, 1775
Jabez Thomas, Jr., & Judith Thomas, Nov. 9, 1775
Nathaniel Munham of Rochester & Mehitable Thomas,
Nov. 9, 1775
Elkanah Bennet & Mary Bryant, Nov. 23, 1775
James Bumpus & Mercy Sherman, Dec. 27, 1775
James Cobb & Sarah Simmons, Jan. 4, 1776
Elijah Hacket & Weltha Eaton, Jan. 24, 1776
Jesse Tinkham & Betty Tucker, April 24, 1776
Joseph Shaw & Lidia Shaw, April 25, 1776
Silvanus Raymond & Sila— Thomas, May 23, 1776
Joseph Hathaway & Hannah Warren, May 23, 1776
Ebenezer Barrows, Jr., & Susanna Cushman, May 30, 1776
Samuel Eaton, Jr., & Susanna Barden, June 11, 1776
John Hacket, 2d, & Sarah Wood, 3d, June 13, 1776
John Weston & Priscilla Sturtevant, Dec. 6, 1776
Joseph Pratt & Susanna Cobb, Dec. 12, 1776
Henry Brightman of Hopkinton, R. I., & Hannah
Paddock, Jan. 7, 1777

Seth Thomas & Hannah Thomas,	March 13,	1777
Consider Fuller & Ruth Elmes,	March 20,	1777
Phineas Thomas & Mary Thomas,	March 27,	1777
Ichabod Wood & Priscilla Thomas,	March 27,	1777
John Hacket & Elisabeth Raymond,	April 27,	1777
John Raymond & Sarah Cox,	July 6,	1777
Eliphalet Elmes & Chloe Leonard,	July 31,	1777
Joseph Jackson & Rebecca Green,	Oct. 2,	1777
Thomas Leach & Elizabeth Thomas,	Oct. 9,	1777
Elisha Thomas & Rachel Weston,	Oct. 31,	1777
Rufus Weston of M. & Sarah Whitman of Bridge-water,	Oct. 31,	1777
Isaac Fuller of Plimpton & Lydia Ellis,	Nov. 20,	1777
Nathaniel Wilder & Sarah Tinkham,	Nov. 23,	1777
Stephen Drew of Plymouth & Jerusha Bryant,	Nov. 27,	1777
James Thomas & Martha Thomas,	Nov. 27,	1777
George Leonard, 2d, & Mary Allen,	Nov. 27,	1777
Benjamin Dunbar of Bridgewater & Wealthy Washburn,	June 17,	1774
Joel Edson & Lucy Leonard,	Dec. 29,	1774
William Nelson of Norton & Sarah Reed,	Jan. 12,	1775
Gamaliel Bisbe of Pembroke & Ruth Shaw,	March 30,	1775
Solomon Fobes & Keziah Fobes, both of Bridgewater,	April 11,	1776
Levi Pratt of Bridgewater & Mary Hathaway,	March 20,	1777
Abraham Perkins & Fear Tomson,	Oct. 23,	1777
Benjamin Washburn & Allice Shaw,	Aug. 6,	1777
Moses Leonard & Lois Shaw,	Aug. 6,	1777
Joseph Leonard, 4th, & Rebeckah Lion,	Nov. 20,	1777
Ebenezer Ellis & Hannah Wood,	Nov. 20,	1777
Polycarpus Edson of Bridgewater & Lucy Eaton,	Dec. 3,	1777
Elias Miller, Jr., & Theodate Ling,	Jan. 11,	1778
Elias Thomas of Woodstock & Silva Tomson,	Feb. 5,	1778
Caleb Edson & Silvia Walker,	March 11,	1778
George Wilbour & Betty Packard,	Dec. 8,	1778
Samuel Eaton, Jr., & Hannah Clap,	Feb. 18,	1779
Robert Green & Susana Leonard,	June 24,	1779

Elijah Reed & Lucy Washburn,	July 3, 1779
Joshua Wood & Silva Fry,	Oct. 12, 1779
Rufus Weston & Abigail Knowlton,	Oct. 27, 1779
Joseph Aldredge, Jr., & Hannah Shaw,	Nov. 4, 1779
Stephen Robertson & Rebeckah Leonard,	Nov. 22, 1779
Luther Hooper & Phebe Washburn of Bridgewater,	Nov. 25, 1779
Dr. Joseph Clark & Rebecca Jacoks,	Dec. 14, 1779
John Darling & Mary Wood,	Jan. 27, 1780
Dan Shaw of Bridgewater & Joanna Perkins,	March 30, 1780
John Eaton of M. & widow Sarah Fobes of Bridgewater,	May 15, 1780
Samuel Bourn of Falmouth & Diadama Leonard,	May 16, 1780
Jairus Shaw of Raynham & Polly Pratt,	July 25, 1780
Rodolphus Edson of Bridgewater & Lydia Crane of Berkley,	Aug. 14, 1780
Daniel Thomas & Mary Jacocks,	Aug. 17, 1780
William Cobb & Sarah Bates,	Oct. 19, 1780
Jabez Bennet of Woodstock & Abigail Thomas,	Oct. 24, 1780
Ichabod Tupper & Rebecca Ripley,	Oct. 31, 1780
Ebenezer Cox & Zilla Darling,	Dec. 7, 1780
Robert Cushman & Lucy Thomas,	Dec. 28, 1780
Isaac Tribou of Bridgewater & Molly Lyon,	March 6, 1781
Holden Wilbour of Bridgewater & Ruth Tisdale of Taunton,	July 5, 1781
Thomas Sherman of Brookfield & Betty Keith,	July 27, 1781
Daniel White & Hannah Reed,	Oct. 4, 1781
Pelatiah Finney & Hannah Curtis,	July 1, 1781
John Fobes, 2d, of Bridgewater & Rosinda Alden,	March 12, 1783
Ziba Leonard of Bridgewater & Chloe Shaw,	May 5, 1783
Andrew White & Betty Edson,	July 22, 1784
Israel Leach, a transient, & Sarah Simmons,	Aug. 16, 1784
Stephen Ellis of Sandwich & Agness Benson,	Sept. 7, 1779
Jacob Bennet, Jr., & Mercy Porter,	Oct. 5, 1780
Eleazer Thomas & Arispey (?) Bryant,	April 26, 1781
Joseph Lovell, Jr., & Jerusha Sparrow,	Sept. 16, 1783

Ebenezer Smith & Lucy Leach,	July 22, 1784
Benjamin Perkins & Abiah Haskell,	Dec. 16, 1784
Henry Ha—kell & Deborah Gibbs,	Dec. 30, 1784
James McFarling & Olive Elmes,	July 11, 1784
Abraham Shaw & Hannah Miller,	Sept. 16, 1784
Ephraim Wood of Brookfield & Sarah Wood, 3d,	
	Jan. 20, 1774
Lewis Hall of Raynham & Fear Alden,	Feb. 23, 1775
Zephaniah Shaw & Hannah Pratt,	March 24, 1776
Joshua Ellis of Rochester & Azubah Jackson,	Dec. 22, 1776
David Weston, Jr., & Kezia Eaton,	Jan. 6, 1779
Samuel Reed & Rebecca Knowlton,	Jan. 19, 1779
Ezra Richmond & Molly Reading,	Aug. 16, 1780
Zenas Warren & Susanna Weston,	March 1, 1781
Andrus Murdock of Plympton & Meribah Eaton,	
	March 12, 1782
Francis Billington & Jedidah Wood,	April 11, 1782
Calvin Rickard of Bridgewater & Huldah Leonard,	
	Oct. 29, 1782
Jonathan Leonard of M. & Phebe Williams of Raynham,	Oct. 29, 1782
Israel Butler of Bridgewater & Huldah Alden,	Feb. 20, 1783
Phillip Knap of Raynham & Lydia Richmond,	Aug. 25, 1779
William Strobridge & Susanna Hinds,	Sept. 25, 1779
Zebedee Booth & Katherine Reynolds,	Oct. 7, 1779
Stephen Clark & Olive Smith,	Nov. 4, 1779
Henry Admi—ster (?) & Robe Howland,	Jan. 13, 1780
Abner Pits of Taunton & Robe Peirce,	March 14, 1780
Benjamin Allen & Olive Booth,	April 4, 1780
Benjamin Reynolds of M. & Mary Demeranvele (?) of Dartmouth,	Sept. 1, 1780
Samuel Parish of M. & Rebecca Rusell of Wareham,	Dec. 6, 1780
Bartlett Hinds & Ruth Pickins,	Dec. 7, 1780
Seth Ramsden of M. & Seviah Payn of Freetown,	June 5, 1781
John Allen & Abiah Holloway,	July 1, 1781
Zo—eth (?) Tobey of Dartmouth & Abigail Keen,	Jan. 10, 1782

Silas Townsend & Hope Hasken,   March 14, 1782
Peter Hoar & Mercy Peirce,   Oct. 4, 1782
Andrew Cole & Abigail Nelson,   Dec. 19, 1782
Abraham Peirce & Mary Russell,   June 5, 1783
Benjamin Lawrence of Freetown & Mercy Lewis,
                                                              Sept. 1, 1783
Edward Gesby, transient, & Deborah Elmes,   Jan. 21, 1776
Isaac Tinkham, 3d, & Sylva Sturtevant,   May 2, 1776
Nathan Pratt, Jr., & Betty Howland, 2d,   Oct. 17, 1776
Samuel Torrey & Mary Finney,   Nov. 20, 1777
Capt. Samuel Thatcher & Katherine Stevens,   May 6, 1779
Willard Thomas & Susanna Bennet,   Oct. 18, 1779
Archippas Leonard & Arseveth Cobb,   Jan. 6, 1780
James Perry & Esther Tinkham,   Feb. 3, 1780
Samuel Bates of Wareham & Susanna Mcfarlin, Feb. 10, 1780
Israel Samson & Thankful Martin,   March 31, 1780
Ephraim Cushman & Mary Hacket,   Dec. 24, 1780
Ebenezer White & Betty Leonard,   March 15, 1781
Peter Miller & Keziah Besse,   March 21, 1781
Sylvanus Warren of M. & Sarah Washburn of Rochester,
                                                              Aug. 1, 1782
Seth Tinkham, 2d, & Lydia Wood,   Aug. 15, 1782
Elijah Caswell of M. & Mercy Sekens of Raynham,
                                                              Jan. 25, 1776
Samuel Howe of Westmorland & Mehitable Hacket,
                                                              June 9, 1776
Joel White & Margaret Shaw,   June 21, 1776
Nathan Hall, Jr., of Raynham & Sarah Snow of Bridge-
     water,   Aug. 1, 1776
Abraham Jones of Raynham & Waitstil Lee of Bridge-
     water,   May 28, 1777
Thomas Delano of Dartmouth & Mary Warren of
     Bridgewater,   July 20, 1777
Daniel Faunce of Plimpton & Ruth Alden of Bridge-
     water,   Aug. 24, 1777
Samuel Tucker & Hannah Dunbar,   Nov. 13, 1777
Nathaniel Bolton & Jane Tomson, both of Bridgewater,
                                                              Dec. 18, 1777

Asa Shaw of Raynham & Sarah Alden of Bridgewater,
Jan. 14, 1778
Elisha Freeman & Mercy Eddy, 2d, Feb. 26, 1778
Cyral Keith & Bathsheba Sprout, 2d, July 22, 1778
Josiah Hambelton & Mary Newcomb, both of Bridge-
water, Oct. 22, 1778
Silas White & Bethiah Washburn, Nov. 12, 1778
John Eliot of Taunton & Sarah Ransom, Nov. 26, 1778
Samuel Parris of Hallifax & Sarah Pratt, Jan. 21, 1779
Elijah Alden of M. & Molly Alden of Bridgewater,
March 25, 1779
Salmon Keith & Cloe Wilbore, March 25, 1779
Elnathan Wood & Sarah Hayford, May 18, 1779
Joseph Bumpas, 2d, & Abiah Leonard, May 20, 1779
George Caswell & Betty Blackman, July 8, 1779
Nathan Richmond & Hepsebath Crossman, Dec. 7, 1779
John Shaw, 3d, & Polly Eaton, Dec. 15, 1779
Seth Eddy & Jerusha Barden, March 16, 1780
John Norcut, Jr., & Susanna Winslow, May 18, 1780
George Richmond & Olive Richmond, July 20, 1780
Joseph Eliot (?) of Taunton & Mercy Hacket, Nov. 5, 1780
Israel Eaton & Allice Richmond, Aug. 2, 1781
Francis Keen (?) of Pembroke & Sarah Keith, Oct. 2, 1781
Jotham Willmoth & Hannah Richard of Bridgewater,
Nov. 4, 1781
Ebenezer Leach, Jr., of Killingly, Ct., & Hepzibah
Leach of Bridgewater, Nov. 11, 1781
Ezra Clark, 2d, & Huldah Richmond, Dec. 6, 1781
Lemuel Macomber & Sarah Hooper, both of Bridge-
water, Feb. 28, 1782
Josiah Kingman of M. & Cloe Fobes of Bridgewater,
March 1, 1782
Daniel Tucker & Susanna Tomson, May 30, 1782
Solomon Ames & Eunice Sprague, both of Bridgewater,
July 18, 1782
Ephraim Dunham & Joanna Lyon, Aug. 10, 1782
William Drake & Abigail Shaw, Jan. 8, 1783
Jabez Dagget & Jale (?) Caswell, Oct. 20, 1783

Amasa Wood & Mehitable Eaton,   Nov. 27, 1783
William Caswell & Hannah Richard,   Dec. 27, 1783
Absel Dean of Taunton & Abthier White, 2d,   July 11, 1784
Joshua Richmond of Taunton & Sarah Snow of
    Bridgewater,   Sept. 30, 1784
Jonathan Snow & Huldah Snow, both of Bridgewater,
                                           Nov. 18, 1784
Caleb Leach & Molly Adams,   Dec. 5, 1784
Stephen Cornish of Taunton & Keziah Richmon,
                                           Dec. 26, 1784
Edward Richmond of Taunton & Mary King of Bridge-
    water,   Jan. 20, 1785
Joseph Churchel & Alice Drake,   March 8, 1785
Job Hathaway of Taunton & Deborah Rickard,
                                           March 29, 1785
Silas Sprague & Polly Leonard,   May 19, 1785
Uiab (?) Alden & Polly Hatheway,   May 26, 1785
Marshall Harvey & Orpah Edson,   Aug. 23, 1785
Asa Pease of Rochester & Martha Perkens,   Jan. 20, 1780
Isaiah Tinkham of Hallifax & Susanna Ellis,   Feb. 3, 1780
Nehemiah Bennet & Sarah Howland,   Feb. 16, 1780
Josiah Harlow & Mary Wood,   March 30, 1780
Benjamin Rayment, Jr., of M. & Betsy Andrews of
    Taunton,   April 7, 1780
Joseph Vaughan & Sarah Thomas,   May 2, 1780
Samuel Perkins & Matilda Briggs,   May 25, 1780
Levi Thomas & Hannah Weston,   July 20, 1780
Dr. Samuel Montgomery of M. & Katherine Wales of
    Taunton,   Oct. 5, 1780
Capt. Lemuel Bishop of Rehoboth & Sarah Foster,
                                           Oct. 8, 1780
Joshua Smith of Claremont & Abigail Perkins,   Nov. 2, 1780
John Smith, 4th, & Molly Bourn,   Nov. 12, 1780
Rev. John Read of Bridgewater & Hannah Samson,
                                           Nov. 16, 1780
Seth Haskell & Elisabeth King,   Dec. 7, 1780
Samuel Ransom & Sarah Gaven (?),   Dec. 7, 1780
Noah Ashly of Freetown & Abigail Hoar,   Dec. 19, 1780

John Skiff of Dartmouth & Wealthy Makepeace of
 Taunton,   Jan. 4, 1781
Benjamin Paddock & Phebe Leonard, Jan. 23, 1781
Thomas Brown, Jr., & Hannah Lovell, Jan. 25, 1781
Nathan Andrews of Taunton & Arubah Raymond,
            March 8, 1781
Samuel Miller & Rhoda Richmond, May 3, 1781
Joseph Pratt, 2d, & Lucy Simmons, June 28, 1781
Andrew Perry & Lydia Reed,   July 3, 1781
Abner Dean & Hannah Seekens, both of Taunton,
            Sept. 6, 1781
Barzillar Thomas, Jr., & Mercy Thomas, Sept. 13, 1781
Benjamin Shaw, Jr., of M. & Sarah Richmond of
 Taunton,   Sept. 27, 1781
Noah Allen of East Windsor, Ct., & Elisabeth Stro-
 bridge,   Oct. 4, 1781
Joshua Staple of Taunton & Hope Peirce, Oct. 11, 1781
Elisha Bennet & Lucy Raymond,   Oct. 18, 1781
Capt. Josiah King of Taunton & Sarah Samson, Oct. 18, 1781
Israel Richard & Voadica Weston, Nov. 22, 1781
Absal Terry of Freetown & Hannah Foster, Nov. 26, 1781
Dr. Samuel Shaw of Bridgewater & Olive Leonard,
            Dec. 4, 1781
Barnabas Caswell & Rachel Briggs, both of Taunton,
            Dec. 6, 1781
Gershom Foster & Jenny Montgomery, Jan. 21, 1782
Samuel Perkens & Lydia Cole,   Feb. 14, 1782
Joseph Keen & Annah Smith,   March 3, 1782
John Holmes & Experience Samson, March 21, 1782
Ebenezer Robinson & Anna Richmond, both of Taun-
 ton,   Sept. 10, 1782
Gideon Leonard & Hannah Sprout, Sept. 19, 1782
Dr. Isaac Barker (Indian) & Sarah Mun, Oct. 14, 1782
Elijah Smith & Molly Southworth, March 20, 1783
Jedediah Caswell & Susanna Barrows, June 3, 1783
Joshua Lincoln & Elisabeth Seekens (?), both of Taun-
 ton,   June 5, 1783
Edward Dean & Robey Shaw,   July 23, 1783

Seth Richmond & Phebe Richmond, Dec. 2, 1783
Luther Crane of Berkley & Sarah Strobridge, Dec. 11, 1783
Abner Williams of Taunton & Jael Southworth, Feb. 15, 1784
Seth Macomber & Katherine Pratt, Feb. 17, 1784
Barnabas Clark & Judah Hoar, April 29, 1784
Benjamin Spooner & Triphany Booth, May 9, 1784
Perez Simmons & Abiah Leonard, July 14, 1784
Jonathan Curtice of Raynham & Mary Jones, Sept. 2, 1784
James Harvey & Bethse—a Hoskins, both of Taunton,
Nov. 8, 1784
Gideon Dean & Achsa Richmond, Nov. 30, 1784
Benjamin Combs of Rochester & Priscilla Benson,
Oct. 22, 1772
John Le Baron, Jr., & Repentance Lucas, Dec. 3, 1772
Luther Hall & Zilpha Randall, May 17, 1773
Zebulon Le Baron & Elisabeth Lucas, Nov. 2, 1773
Japhet Le Baron & Sarah Holmes, Nov. 25, 1773
Daniel Tinkham & Martha Le Baron, Dec. 30, 1773
Jonathan Peterson & Lois Sturtevant, March 10, 1774
George Howland & Deborah Shaw, Dec. 15, 1774
Asa Barrows & Content Benson, Dec. 18, 1774
Reuben Bisbee of Kingston & Eunice House, March 18, 1775
Israel Holmes & Margaret Purrington, May 20, 1776
Eleazer Robbins of Plympton & Sarah Robbins, Oct. 31, 1776
David Delano & Phebe Leach, Jan. 1, 1777
Elisha Clark & Lucy Tinkham, Jan. 9, 1777
Judah Hall of M. & Hannah Pratt of Plimpton, April 20, 1777
Thomas Eskridge of Dartmouth & Mary Allen, May 15, 1777
Samuel Muxham & Margaret Lucas, May 17, 1777
James Shaw & Thankful Vaughan, Oct. 9, 1777
John Willis & Patience Jackson, Jan. 15, 1778
Elisha Donham of Plimpton & Eunice Thomas, April 2, 1778
Ebenezer Willis of M. & Thankful Smith of Rochester,
Aug. 22, 1778
George Thomas & Hope Thomas, Sept. 17, 1778
Ichabod Tillson of Plimton Azubah Thomas, Dec. 24, 1778
Daniel Sherman of M. & Phebe Baker of Rochester,
Jan. 21, 1779

Isaac Churchell & Elisabeth Raymond,	Jan. 21,	1779
Isaac Shaw of Plimpton & Hannah Muxham,	Feb. 23,	1779
Samuel Raymond & Elisabeth Bumpas,	Feb. 25,	1779
Samuel Macomber of M. & Phebe Peirce of Rochester,		
	March 17,	1779
Jonathan Shaw of Plimpton & Patience Benson,	July 15,	1779
Ellis Muxham of Plimpton & Anna Raymond,	April 5,	1780
Jacob Shaw & Molly Benson,	June 18,	1780
Edward Raymond, Jr., & Mary Bishop,	July 14,	1780
Francis Wood & Joanna Hall,	April 12,	1781
Benjamin Gurney of Rochester & Thankful Ellis,		
	Aug. 23,	1781
A—ds (?) Peirce of M. & Jemima Caswell of Rochester,		
	Nov. 11,	1781
Isaac Jackson & Sa—a Pratt,	Dec. 13,	1781
James Le Baron & Elisabeth Washburn,	May 9,	1781
Simeon Combes of M. & Experience Millerd of		
Rochester,	June 13,	1782
Daniel Cary & Phebe Doty,	Aug. 1,	1782
Thomas Jeffers & Sarah Sepit,	Aug. 25,	1782
Benjamin Haskins of Rochester & Rachel Ellis,	Aug. 29,	1782
John Maxham of Rochester & Mella Whiting,	Nov. 24,	1782
Chipman Shaw & Deborah Bishop,	Dec. 25,	1782
Alexander Perkins & Remember Raymond,	Jan. 23,	1783
Eliphalet Peirce & Tabitha Bryant,	Feb. 4,	1783
William Le Baron & Lureany Bennet,	April 10,	1783
Timothy Shurtleff of Plimpton & Eunice Le Baron,		
	June 12,	1783
Ezra Muxham & Abigail Harlow,	Sept. 4,	1783
Caleb Atherton of Stoughton & Joanna Holmes,		
	Dec. 10,	1783
Noah Haskell & Sarah Weston,	Feb. 10,	1784
William Thomas & Martha Lucas,	July 27,	1783
Josiah Leonard of Buckland & Lureany Keith,	May 13,	1784
James Thompson & Jane Hutchinson,	June 22,	1784
Samuel Gibbs of Sandwich & Mary Weston,	Sept. 6,	1784
David Babcock, transient, & Sarah Faunce,	Oct. 21,	1784
Pollipus Hammond of Rochester & Meriah Benson,		
	Nov. 7,	1784

Joseph Williams, transient, & Experience Sherman,

	Nov. 18, 1784
William Hall & Priscilla Raymond,	Nov. 25, 1784
David Sears & Hannah Weston,	Dec. 20, 1781
Joseph Redding & Mehitable Richmond,	Dec. 20, 1781

Andrew Thomas of Woodstock & Ruth Thomas,

	Feb. 12, 1782
Benjamin Bryant & Elisabeth Bates,	March 21, 1782
Micah Leach & Lucy Pratt,	April 1, 1782
Samuel Leonard & Susanna Ripley,	April 28, 1782
Elkanah Elmes & Lucretia Cole,	May 9, 1782
Dr. John Samson & Deborah Perry,	Sept. 1, 1782
Samuel Wood & Phebe Morton,	Nov. 14, 1782
Ichabod Cushman & Molly Morton,	Nov. 28, 1782
Ephraim Norcutt & Molly Kitts,	Dec. 12, 1782
Seth Tinkham, 3d, & Sarah Nichols,	Dec. 19, 1782

Isaiah Shaw, transient, & Abijah (?) Tinkham,

	Jan. 9, 1783
Ebenezer Levi Bennet & Betty Shaw,	Jan. 23, 1783
Jonah Washburn, Jr., & Sally Eddy,	April 3, 1783
Amasa Bryant & Lavinia Parker,	April 3, 1783
Zenas Norcutt & Comfort Davis,	April 6, 1783
Silas Hall of Raynham & Hannah Warren,	May 22, 1783
Ephraim Samson & Elisabeth Barden,	July 27, 1783
Zenas Thomas & May Vaughan,	Aug. 20, 1783
John King of Plimpton & Elisabeth Bennet,	Oct. 15, 1783
Seth Morton, Jr., & Rosamond Finney,	Nov. 20, 1783

William Chamberlain of Plimpton & Lorania Dagget,

	Dec. 4, 1783
Nehemiah Shaw & Sarah Bryant,	Dec. 7, 1783
Joshua Thomas & Phebe Thomas,	Dec. 11, 1783
⸸ Thomas Wood, 3d, & Lois Pratt,	Jan. 8, 1784

Oliver Williams of Woodstock & Urania Thomas,

	Jan. 25, 1784
William Torrey of Pembroke & Mary Sproutt,	Feb. 1, 1784
Daniel King & Susanna Wood,	March 7, 1784
Hazail Tinkham & Susanna Pratt, 2d,	April 1, 1784
⸸ Nichols Wood & Hope Barrows,	April 13, 1784

8

Israel Eaton & Kezia Sears,   June 10, 1784
Josiah Washburn & Phebe Cushman,   Aug. 26, 1784
Zebedee Hacket & Sarah Wood,   Nov. 4, 1784
Eliphalet Cushman & Joanna Wood,   Nov. 25, 1784
Samuel Eddy & Sally Paddock,   Nov. 25, 1784
Ebenezer Jones of Barre & Mercy Reed,   Dec. 5, 1784
Zenas Tinkham of Hallifax & Rachell Warren,   Dec. 9, 1784
John Oxenbridge Thatcher & Lucy Richmond, Dec. 14, 1784
Nathaniel Johnson & Bithiah Niles,   Jan. 25, 1785
Roger Nash & Susanna Howland,   Feb. 14, 1785
Daniel Caswell & Abigail Jones, both of Taunton,
                                                     March 17, 1785
Joshua Russell of Dartmouth & Abiah Smith,   April 10, 1785
David Smith & Freelove Smith, both of Taunton,
                                                     Aug. 1, 1785
John Cavender Stephens, transient, & Deliverance
     Peirce,   Aug. 1, 1785
Samuel Niles of M. & Abigail Andrews of Taunton,
                                                     Aug. 31, 1785
John Martin of Providence & Betsey Foster,   Sept. 19, 1785
John Rouse, 2d, of Dartmouth & Susanna Raymond,
                                                     Oct. 25, 1785
Capt. Robert Sprout & Mercy Smith,   Oct. 27, 1785
Silvanus Tillson & Hannah Southworth,   Dec. 15, 1785
Ephraim Farrington & Polly Dean, both of Taunton,
                                                     March 23, 1786
John Cain of Taunton & Annah Barrows,   May 4, 1786
Hugh Montgomery & Anna Samson,   June 25, 1786
Thomas Wood, 2d, & Lydia Vaughan,   Sept. 5, 1786
Abijah Hathaway, Jr., of Berkley & Polly Tinkham,
                                                     Sept. 8, 1786
Seth Haskell & Mary Eskridge,   Nov. 14, 1786
Solomon Padelford of Taunton & Sally Cushing, Dec. 9, 1786
Ebenezer Howland & Hope Allen,   Jan. 18, 1787
Nathan White & Elisabeth Sprout,   Feb. 25, 1787
Abner Elmes & Anna Thomas,   April 19, 1787
George Barrows of Taunton & Rachel Nash of Free-
     town,   May 24, 1787

Richard Winslow of Freetown & Jane McCully, Aug. 4, 1787
John Morton & Elizabeth Leonard,   Nov. 27, 1787
Noah Leonard of M. & Mehitable Richmond of Taun-
    ton,   Dec. 13, 1787

√ HALIFAX.

July 4, 1734. "Parts of Middleborough, Pembroke and Plympton established as Hallifax." First (Congregational) Church organized 1734.

Ebenezer Bennett, Jr., of Middleboro & Esther Tomson,
                                             Oct. 25, 1737
Samuel Waterman & Mary Tomson,   March 16, 1737
Isaac Jennings, Jr., of Pembroke & Elisabeth Simmeons,
                                        March 17, 1737
Jonathan Sears & Hannah Brigs,   April 18, 1738
Noah Cushing & Hannah Cushing,   Nov. 9, 1738
Caleb Stertevant & Patience Cushman,   July 23, 1739
Joshua Palmer of Scituate & Lydia Waterman, Jr.,
                                          Aug. 7, 1740
Edward Atwood of Abington & Elisabeth May, Nov. 20, 1740
Peter Johnson of H. & Hannah Bolton of Bridgewater,
                                        March 18, 1740
James Ba—se, Jr. (Barse ?) of H. & Mary Bumpass
    of Middleboro,   April 2, 1741
John Tomson of Middleboro & Lydia Wood,   June 4, 1741
James Pratt of Plimton & Abigail Pitts, Sept. 23, 1741
Elisha Cook of Kingston & Rebecca Egerton, Nov. 5, 1741
Joseph Bozworth & Ruth Fuller,   Nov. 6, 1741
Samuel Fuller & Elisabeth Tomson,   Sept. 30, 1743
Joseph Bearse & Hannah Holmes,   Nov. 17, 1743
Benjamin Hathaway of Bridgewater & Abigail Eddy,
                                         Nov. 22, 1743
Barnabas Brigs of H. & Lois Briant of Plimpton,
                                         Nov. 23, 1743
Eleazer Waterman & Alice Bozworth,   Dec. 15, 1743
John Fuller, Jr., & Joanna Tillson,   Dec. 27, 1743

Amasa Thomson of H. & Lydia Cobb of Middleboro,

Feb. 23, 1743-4

Ephraim Holmes & Jane Holmes,   June 26, 1744

Josiah Stertevant & Priscella Croade,   Aug. 7, 1744

Stephen Leach of Bridgewater & Lydia Flowy, Jan. 24, 1744-5

Perez Randall of Scituate & Susanna Stertevant,

Jan. 30, 1744-5

George Barrows, Jr., of Plimton & Mary Ransom,

June 10, 1745

Caleb Eddy of H. & Phebe Bobbet of Barkley, July 11, 1745

Joseph Works of Ashford, Ct., & widow Joanna Tomson,

Oct. 23, 1745

Zebeda Tomson & Zerviah Standish,   Dec. 5, 1745

Abner Cushman & Mary Tilson,   Feb. 6, 1745-6

Ebenezer Brigs of H. & Abigail Bryant of Plimton,

Dec. 9, 1746

Rev. John Cotton & Mrs. Hannah Stertevant,   Dec. 9, 1746

Peleg Bradford of Kingston & Lydia Stertevant,

March 9, 1746

Zacheus Fish of Kingston & Lydia Barse,   July 9, 1747

John Leach & Betty Eddy,   July 9, 1747

Benjamin Washburn, 3d, of Bridgewater & Mary Cush-

man, Jr.,   April 5, 1748

Solomon Leavitt of Pembroke & Susanna Harden,

May 16, 1749

John May of Plimouth & Anna King,   Oct. 25, 1749

Joseph Waterman of Middleborough & widow Joanna

Fuller,   Jan. 3, 1749

Jonathan Shurtleff of Plimton & Elisabeth Leach,

Nov. 1, 1750

Francis Stertevant of H. & widow Orcutt of Bridge-

water,   Nov. 14, 1750

Gideon Bearse & Abigail Ripley,   June 13, 1751

John Tillson & Marcy Stertevant,   Nov. 11, 1751

Ephraim Churchell of Bridgewater & Jemima Briant,

Nov. 28, 1751

Zachariah Weston & Rebecca Standish,   May 12, 1752

Silas Bese of Bridgewater & Bredged Samson, June 16, 1752

Hezekiah Bearse & Deborah Stertevant,   July 23, 1752

Moses Parish of Middleboro & Sarah May,
                              Nov. 1, 1752 (N. S.)

Peter Drew & Zerviah Wood,   Dec. 14, 1752

Ephraim Tillson & Marcy Sears,   Dec. 25, 1752

Benjamin Cushman (Cushing ?) of Hingham & Ruth
     Croade,   July 18, 1753

Silvanus Bryant of Plimpton & Sarah Sears,   Jan. 17, 1754

Benjamin Smith & Silence Keith, both of Bridgewater,
                                 Aug. 2, 1739

Ruben Tomson & Mary Tomson,   Nov. 8, 1739

Ebenezer Standish, Jr., & Averick Churchell, both of
     Plimton,   Dec. 27, 1739

John Waterman, Jr., & Fear Stertevant, Jr.,   May 15, 1740

Barnabas Phinney of Barnstable & Mehitable Morton
     of Plimton,   Aug. 14, 1745

Nathan Tinkham of H. & Sarah Soule of Plimton,
                                 Dec. 10, 1746

Ebenezer Fuller, Jr., & Lydia Chapman,   Jan. 6, 1746

William Stertevant & widow Joanna Tillson,   Jan. 25, 1747

John Holmes, Jr., of H. & Elisabeth Leavitt of Pem-
     broke,   Feb. 14, 1748

Isaac Tinkham of Middleboro & Hannah Robins,
                                 June 14, 1753

Elisha Bates of Hingham & Content Hathaway,
                                March 16, 1754

Benjamin Darling of Middleboro & Hannah Harris,
                                 July 29, 1756

Jonathan Heydon of Bridgewater & Hannah Cush-
     man,   June 25, 1754

Nehemiah Stetson, Jr., & widow Elisabeth Pearce,
                                 July 30, 1754

David Hatch & Desire Standish,   Jan. 16, 1755

William Sturtevant & Joana Waterman,   Nov. 6, 1755

Samuel Waterman & Mary Fuller,   Sept. 14, 1756

Ebenezer Washburn of Kingston & Sarah Waterman,
                                 Nov. 17, 1757

Moses Ingly & Hannah Ransom,   Nov. 10, 1757

Ephraim Tinkham of Middleboro & Sarah Standish,
Jan. 5, 1758
Abiel Lucas of Plimton & Desire Sturtevant,　Feb. 21, 1758
Daniel Dunbar & Rebecca Ripley,　May 21, 1758
George Hammond of Plimton & Lucy Stertevant,
Nov. 26, 1759
Jeptha Harden of Pembroke & Mary Leach,　July 14, 1757
Francis Tomson & Rebecca Snow,　May 19, 1761
Nathan Tomson & Mary Harlow,　Oct. 27, 1761
Ebenezer Cole, Jr., of Kingston & Hannah Bryant, Jr.,
Feb. 11, 1762
Elkanah Cowen & Elisabeth Atwood,　Feb. 18, 1762
Jabez Hall & Deborah Stetson,　April 12, 1762
John Fuller of H. & Lidia Eddy of Middleborough,
April 27, 1762
Benjamin Washburne, 3d, of Bridgewater & Desire
Sears (?),　April 29, 1762
Francis Perkins of Bridgewater & Susannah Water-
man,　Dec. 14, 1762
Peter Tomson & Rebecca Thomas,　June 14, 1763
Micah Allen of Middleboro & Hannah Cushing, Jr.,
Nov. 3, 1763
Gideon Soule of H. & Ruth Harden of Pembroke,
Dec. 22, 1763
Jonathan Porter of Bridgewater & Mary Chipman,
Feb. 16, 1764
Jabez Stertevant & Azubah Wood,　March 8, 1764
Stephen Bryant & Rebecca Bearce,　April 19, 1764
Thomas Mansfield of Volentown & Experience Cortis
(Curtis ?),　Aug. 4, 1762
Joseph Packard, 2d, of Bridgewater & Ruth Bozworth,
Sept. 27, 1759
Seth Jackson of Plymouth & Ann May,　Nov. 6, 1760
Nathan Hartwell & Bettee Cushman,　Aug. 20, 1761
Thomas Hooker, Jr., of Bridgewater & Deborah Cush-
man,　March 4, 1762
Joseph Dunbar & Mary Cushman,　Oct. 26, 1767
Jesse Stertevant & Susanna Bozworth,　Nov. 10, 1767

Peleg Bryant of Plimton & Elice Stertevant, Nov. 11, 1767
Mesheck Leonard of Middlesex & Patience Water-
man, Nov. 17, 1767
Zadock Fuller & Elice Porter, Dec. 3, 1767
Barnabas Briggs, Jr., & Zenoba Bartlett, April 12, 1768
Ephraim Tinkham & Eunice Cushman, Aug. 18, 1768
Micah Reed of Abington & Deborah Tomson, Oct. 24, 1768
Ezekiel Bryant of Plimton & Lucy Beane, Oct. 31, 1768
David Dunbar, Jr., of Bridgewater & Joanna Dunbar,
Dec. 1, 1768
Noah Tomson of H. & Priscilla Holmes of Middleboro,
Dec. 27, 1768
Charles Cushing of Hingham & Hannah Croade,
Feb. 23, 1769
Thomas Fuller & Hannah Ripley, May 25, 1769
Caleb Stertevant & Abigail Beane, May 31, 1770
William Perry of H. & Lucy Holmes of Middleboro,
Aug. 30, 1770
William Tomson of Middleboro & Deborah Stertevant,
Nov. 16, 1770
Benjamin Curtis & Ruth Cushing, Nov. 29, 1770
Reuben Tomson of H. & Sarah Tomson of Middleboro,
Jan. 22, 1771
Elijah Leach, Jr., & Ruth Fuller, July 10, 1771
Ichabod Churchell of Middleboro & Sarah Tinkham,
Nov. 7, 1771
Stephen Ellis of Plimton & Susanna Tomson, Nov. 14, 1771
Samuel Lucas, Jr., of Plimton & Abigail Draw (?), Jr.,
Dec. 10, 1771
Isaac Tomson & Huldah Stertevant, Dec. 5, 1771
Silvanus Leach & Rebecca Cushman, Feb. 27, 1772
Benjamin Dunbar & Ruth Pratt, March 4, 1772
Nathaniel Stertevant & Zerviah Dunbar, March 5, 1772
Ephraim Fuller & Zerviah Tomson, July 9, 1772
John Dye, resident of H., & Susanna Leach, Dec. 5, 1772
Gamaliel Bryant & Sarah Stetson, Nov. 20, 1772
David Briggs & Hannah Briggs, Oct. 21, 1773
Obadiah Lyon & Lydia Cushman, Oct. 28, 1773

Ezra Drew & Betty Holmes,   Jan. 6, 1774
Benjamin Parris of Bridgewater & Sarah Parris, Feb. 3, 1774
Giles Leach & Deborah Jackson,   June 4, 1774
Isaac Tompson of Middleboro & Lucy Sturtevant,
                                             June 19, 1774
Josiah Whitman of Bridgewater & Sarah Sturtevant,
                                             Nov. 27, 1774
Samuel Stafford Sturtevant & Priscilla Palmer, Jan. 22, 1775
Joshua Curtis & Phebe Waterman,   Feb. 16, 1775
Peleg Barrows of Plimton & Jemima Drew,   May 4, 1775
Joseph Dunbar & Hannah Ripley,   Dec. 6, 1775
Benjamin Dunbar & Hannah Hatheway,   Dec. 29, 1775
Dr. William Batchelor of Milton & Joanna Wakeman,
                                             Jan. 1, 1776
David Mahurin of Easton & Ruth Dunbar,   Jan. 12, 1776
Oliver Holmes & Lydia Tompson,   Feb. 7, 1776
Samuel Hayfords of Hardwich & Bathsheba Tinkham,
                                             March 1, 1776
Thomas Drew & Lucy Tomson,   May 2, 1776
Asael Lyon of Plimpton & Fear Cushman,   Oct. 10, 1776
Samuel Whitman of Bridgewater & Sarah Waterman,
                                             Nov. 7, 1776
Ignatius Loring of Plimton & Abigail Soul,   Nov. 27, 1776
Thomas Sturtevant of Middleboro & Sarah Soul,
                                             April 10, 1777
James Faunce & Mary Cushman,   July 17, 1777
Levi Everson of Kingston & Eunice Briggs,   July 17, 1777
Charles Sturtevant, Jr., of Rochester & Ruth Bearse,
                                             Aug. 13, 1777
Jonathan Curtis & Molly Faxon,   Sept. 15, 1777
Abraham Whitten & Abijah (?) Wood,   Nov. 20, 1777
Adam Tomson & Molly Tomson,   Dec. 18, 1777
Nehemiah Besse & Priscella Perry,   Feb. 26, 1778
Nehemiah Sturtevant of Plimton & Huldah Fuller,
                                             May 28, 1778
George Osbourn of Pembroke & Deborah Taylor,
                                             Aug. 9, 1778
Job Hall of Raynham & Abigail Leach,   Feb. 11, 1779

Elias Haskell of Greenwich & Mercy Tilson,   June 22, 1779
William Wood of Middleboro & Susanna Fuller,

             Oct. 21, 1779
Sylvanus Bradford of Kingston & Jane Briggs, Dec. 16, 1779
Ichabod Tomson & Lydia Hall,   Dec. 17, 1779
Nathan Perkins & Hannah Sturtevant,   Jan. 6, 1780
James Crooker of Pembroke & Joanna Cushman,

             Jan. 20, 1780
Richard Bozworth & Hannah Chipman,   Feb. 10, 1780
Ezekiel Palmer & Polly Walles,   Feb. 23, 1780
Matthew Parris & Mercy Tomson,   Feb. 24, 1780
Isaac Hobert of Pembroke & Lydia Hatch,   March 17, 1780
Noah Waterman & Esther Ellis,   April 4, 1780
Leonard Hill of Pembroke & Lois Briggs,   June 15, 1780
Nathan Tinkham, Jr., & Abigail Perry,   Sept. 21, 1780
Samuel Brown of Abington & Tabatha Porter, Dec. 21, 1780
Jonathan Records of Pembroke & Remember Briggs,

             Feb. 8, 1781
Elisha Mitchell of Bridgewater & Hannah Tomson,

             Feb. 21, 1781
Eliab Knapp of Raynham & Lois Tomson,   March 12, 1781
Holmes Sears & Mercy Cushing,   March 18, 1781
Francis Cook & Ruth Bearce,   April 27, 1781
Barnabas Snell of Bridgewater & Hannah Holmes,

             May 25, 1781
David Rogers of Greenwich & Rebecca Jackson, June 7, 1781
Ezra Tompson & Sarah Whitton,   Oct. 5, 1781
Zebadiah Tomson & Phebe Curtis,   Feb. 13, 1782
Timothy Briggs of Norton & Hannah Waterman,

             Sept. 20, 1782
Mark Andrews of Berkley & Ruth Parris,   Feb. 16, 1783
Jonah Benson of Bridgewater & Martha Tomson,

             March 6, 1783
David Hatch & Lucy Samson,   Jan. 15, 1784
Seth Sturtevant & Abigail Cushing,   March 23, 1784
Jacob Loring of Plimpton & Lydia Tilson,   Sept. 27, 1784
Edward Murdock of Plimpton & Betty Ripley, Dec. 3, 1784
Asa Soule & Ruth Howland Stetson,   Dec. 27, 1784

John Fuller of Medfield & Martha Fuller,   Dec. 30, 1784
Sherebiah Corthel of Hingham & Lidia Whitton,
                                                  Oct. 3, 1784
Ebenezer Vaughan of Middleboro & Lucy Pratt, Jan. 13, 1779
Robert Layman & Meriam Forest,   Jan. 27, 1780
John Phinny of Bridgewater & Sarah Tomson, April 16, 1780
Jonathan Pratt of Middleboro & Martha Palmer,
                                                  Feb. 13, 1783
Benjamin Bozworth & Hannah Samson,   April 10, 1785
 ♦ Judah Wood & Tabitha Holmes,   Oct. 24, 1785
Levi Tomson & Betty Snell,   Dec. 3, 1785
Waterman Bozworth & Mercy Tillson, 3d,   Dec. 11, 1785
Elijah Howard of Bridgewater & Mary Tomson, 3d,
                                                  Jan. 5, 1786
David Sturtevant & Mercy Parris, Jr.,   April 11, 1786
James Soul, 3d, of Middleboro & Eunice Tomson,
                                                  April 20, 1786
Thaddeus Tomson & Ruth Tillson,   Sept. 14, 1786
John Hayford of Pembroke & Betty Hall,   Jan. 18, 1787
Joshua Palmer, Jr., & Lois Sturtevant,   Feb. 1, 1787
Cornelius Pratt & Martha Leonard, both of Bridgewater,
                                                  Feb. 7, 1787
Azor How & Lydia Pratt, both of Bridgewater, Feb. 15, 1787
David Bozworth & Abigail Inglee,   Sept. 23, 1787
Benjamin Faxon of Bridgewater & Ruth Bryant,
                                                  Dec. 20, 1787
John Putnam of Middleboro & Elisabeth Bozworth,
                                                  Dec. 11, 1787
Joseph Tilson of H. & Molly Loring of Plimpton,
                                                  April 24, 1788
Allen Hatch of Bridgewater & Sarah Standish,   May 8, 1788
Ephraim Tinkham & Huldah Tomson, Jr.,   April 5, 1788

√ BRIDGEWATER.

June 3, 1656. "Duxborrow New Plantation established as Bridgewater." First Church (Unitarian) organized 1716. Protestant Episcopal (Trinity), 1747.

James Harris & Elisabeth Bayley,	Feb. 14, 1692-3
Richard Holt & Lidia Wormwood,	May 10, 1693
James Washburn & Mary Bowden,	Dec. 20, 1693
John Whitemore & Ruth Bassett,	Dec. 22, 1692
Benjamin Snow & Elisabeth Alden,	Dec. 12, 1693
John Emerson & Elisabeth Leech (?) widow,	Dec. 27, 1693
David Whitman & Susanna Hayward,	July 13, 1738
Josiah Hayward & Sarah More,	Oct. 11, 1738
Eleanor Washburn & Anna Alden,	Nov. 22, 1738
Ephraim Cary & Susanna Alden,	Nov. 22, 1738
Ebenezer Byram & Abigail Alden,	Nov. 22, 1738
Benajah Smith of Easton & Mary Hill,	Nov. 22, 1738
Seth Mitchell & Ann Latham,	Dec. 21, 1738
James Radsford & Margaret Bells,	Dec. 26, 1738
Jonathan Allen of Braintry & widow Alice Latham,	
	March 27, 1739
Samuel Harden & Elisabeth Wade,	May 16, 1739
Bridgewater & Cate (Col. Homan's negroes),	Nov. 20, 1739
Charles Cushman & Mary Harvey,	Dec. 10, 1739
Benjamin Vickory & Mary Kingman,	Dec. 21, 1739
John Pain & Hannah Pool,	Jan. 4, 1738
Caleb Orcutt & Mehetable Harvey,	Jan. 24, 1738
Soloman Leach of B. & Jerusha Bryant of Plimton,	
	April 19, 1739
Jeremiah Conant & Mary Packard,	April 26, 1739
John Freelove of Freetown & Abigail Washburn,	
	May 10, 1739
Lieut. Daniel Hudson & widow Abigail Fobes,	
	May 23, 1739
Moses Orcutt & Mercy Allen,	May 30, 1739
Thomas Drew of Hallifax & Abigail Harris,	Aug. 16, 1739

Ebenezer Leach of B. & Lydia Tillson of Plymton,

	Nov. 27,	1739
Joseph Whesley & Jean Gillmore,	Nov. 27,	1739
Seth Alden & Mehetable Carver,	Jan. 1,	1739
Israel Washburn & Leah Fobes,	Jan. 3,	1739
Benjamin Leach & Hannah Keith,	Jan. 10,	1739
Josiah Leonard & Jemimah Washburn,	Jan. 24,	1739
Joseph Bolton & Deliverance Washburne,	Feb. 6,	1739
Josiah Fobes & Freelove Edson,	March 5,	1739
Robert Washburn & Mary Fobes,	March 6,	1739
Nathaniel Bolton & widow Deborah Ripley,	March 24,	1739
Joshua Fobes & Esther Porter,	May 29,	1740
Elisha Hayward & Elisabeth Washburne,	Oct. 7,	1740

Abraham Hardin of B. & Ruth Perry of Scituate,

	Oct. 22,	1740
Jonathan Benson & Martha Snell,	Nov. 7,	1740
Jonathan Pratt & Elisabeth French,	Nov. 11,	1740
Henry Chamberlain & Susanna Hinds,	Dec. 7,	1740
Irael Keith & Betty Chandler,	Feb. 17,	1740

Ephraim Holmes of Halifax & Margaret Washburn,

	Feb. 19,	1740

Nehemiah Bryant of Middleboro & Bethiah Washburne,

	Feb. 24,	1740
Robert Keith & Tabitha Leach,	March 4,	1740
Jabez Cowing & Susanna Bolton,	March 23,	1740
Samuel Edson, 3d, & Martha Perkins,	Sept. 26,	1738
Nathan Edson & Mary Sprague,	Feb. 27,	1738
John Cary & Mary Harden,	May 13,	1741
Daniel Rickards & Mary Packard,	Sept. 16,	1740
William Packard & Sarah Rickards,	Sept. 16,	1740
Josiah Allen & Sarah Orcut,	April 28,	1741
Arthur Harris & Bethiah Hayward,	May 20,	1741
Seth Whitman & Ruth Reed,	June 23,	1741
Jonathan Bass & Susanna Byram,	Nov. 11,	1741
Ichabod Cary & Hannah Gannett,	Dec. 3,	1741
Benjamin Hayward & Sarah Cary,	Jan. 6,	1741
Daniel Cary & Martha Cary,	Jan 28,	1741
Jonathan Mahurin & widow Mary Packard,	July 9,	1740

Ebenezer Kingman & Content Turner,	Aug. 15, 1740
Abisha Willis & Zerviah Willis,	April 2, 1741
Thomas Willis & Susanna Ames,	Nov. 11, 1741
Benjamin Parterson of Easton & Hannah Perry,	
	Nov. 19, 1741
Joseph Peterson of Duxboro & Lydia Howell,	Dec. 19, 1742
Jesse Byram & Abigail Thurston,	June 4, 1742
Hugh Or & Mary Bass,	Aug. 4, 1742
Eleazer Whitman & Abigail Alden,	Nov. 4, 1742
James Allen & Ann Pryer,	Nov. 10, 1742
Zachariah Cary & Susanna Bass,	Nov. 11, 1742
Japhet Byram & Sarah Allen,	Dec. 13, 1742
Joseph Alden & Susanna Packard,	Dec. 16, 1742
John Whitman & Hannah Snow,	Dec. 16, 1742
Nathan Allen & Rebecca Reed,	Nov. 30, 1743
Daniel Howell & Deliverance Latham,	Jan. 18, 1743
John Edson & Mary Gannet,	Feb. 7, 1743
Isaac Lathroop & Patience Alger,	April 13, 1743
Thomas Wade & Elizabeth Hanmer,	May 5, 1743
David Johnson & Susannah Willis,	May 26, 1743
Daniel Lathroop & Rhoda Willis,	April 19, 1744
Elijah Edson & Ann Packard,	April 21, 1741
James Clansey & Ruth Ballaney,	May 4, 1741
Ebenezer Leach of B. & Mary Wilbore of Raynham,	
	May 26, 1741
Benamiel Leach & Betty Perkins,	1741
Ruben Hall & Ruth Gilbert,	July 29, 1741
Stoughton Willis & Hannah Harlow,	Aug. 11, 1741
William Leach & Mary Cohoone,	Oct. 12, 1741
Mr. Eliab Byram & Mrs. Phebe Leonard,	Dec. 3, 1741
Joseph Wilbore of Raynham & Susanna Harris,	Dec. 22, 1741
Benjamin Pratt & Lydia Harlow,	1741
Josiah Hayward & Mary Perkins,	Feb. 11, 1741
James Wickett & Betty Moses (Indians),	March 5, 1741
James Perkins & Bethial Dunham,	May 5, 1742
Jonathan Allen of Brantry & Mary Latham,	June 3, 1742
Ezra Washburn & Susanna Leach,	July 20, 1742
William Gilmore & Margaret Stewart,	Aug. 5, 1742

Samuel Bolton of B. & Rebecca Simmons of Halifax,

Oct. 25, 1742

Nathaniel Hayward of B. & Elizabeth Curtiss of Halifax,

April 5, 1743

Jabez Carver & Sarah Perkins,   Sept. 29, 1743
Abraham Perkins & Mary Carver,   1743
Benjamin Price & Silence Hayward,   Oct. 17, 1743
Benjamin Peine of Scituate & Charity Hayward, Nov. 3, 1743
William Snow & Hannah Hill,   Nov. 7, 1743
Isaac Pool & Sarah Leonard,   Dec. 10, 1743
Arthur Bennett of Middleboro & Keziah Keith, June 12, 1743
Jonathan Allden & Experience Hayward,   June 24, 1743
Lot Conant of B. & Betty Homes of Middleboro,

Feb. 17, 1743

✓ Robert Hoar of Middleboro & Sarah Willis,   March 8, 1743
Joseph Hayward of Raynham & Mary Cohoone,

April 10, 1744

Daniel Keith & Elisabeth Conant,   June 14, 1744
Joseph Bosworth of Halifax & Sarah Cobb,   Sept. 20, 1744
Abiezer Edson & Mary Packard,   Nov. 15, 1744
Joseph Cowing of Scituate & Jean Keith,   Nov. 24, 1744
Nathan Kingsley of Easton & Betty Dunbar,   Dec. 10, 1744
Joab Willis & Martha Bolton,   March 4, 1774
Joel Edy & Rachel Vorse,   March 1, 1741
Jacob Hayward & Tabitha Hayward,   Nov. 11, 1742
James Stacy of Easton & Mehitable Willis,   April 21, 1743
Thomas Willis of Taunton & Bethiah Hayward, July 19, 1743
William Hall & Ann Charta (?) (Chasta ?),   Aug. 26, 1743
Benoni Hayward & Hannah Page,   Oct. 13, 1743
Seth Thayer & Hannah Pray,   June 14, 1744
Oliver Cheney of Pomphret & Hannah Hayward,

Nov. 22, 1744

James Linsey & Hannah Turner,   Dec. 3, 1744
Robert Dawes & Lydia Harden,   May 28, 1744
Joseph Gannet & Betty Latham,   June 7, 1744
Naphtali Byram & Hannah Pratt,   Sept. 27, 1744
Nathan Pratt & Sarah Harlow,   Oct. 15, 1745
Benjamin Benson & Keziah Snell,   Oct. 30, 1745

Thomas Thomson & Jane Washburne,	Oct. 31, 1745
Thomas Conant & Mary Wood,	Oct. 29, 1745
Nathaniel Pratt & Hannah Conant,	Nov. 5, 1745
Eleazer Cary & Betty Fobes,	Nov. 12, 1745
Elijah Leach & Jemima Snow,	Dec. 4, 1745
James Dunbar & Hannah Benson,	Jan. 22, 1745
Josiah Washburne & Abigail Curtis,	Jan. 29, 1745
Eleazer Carver, Jr., & Hepsiba Perkins,	April 3, 1746
John Sprague & Susanna Cob,	June 20, 1746
Joseph Lathrop & Content Washburne,	Oct. 24, 1746
Jonathan Carver & Sarah Thomas,	Oct. 13, 1746
John Hooper & Sarah Carver,	Dec. 1, 1746
Joseph Clap & Sarah Carver,	Dec. 23, 1746
Joseph Carver & Sarah Hartwell,	Dec. 25, 1746
Charles Snell & Susanna Packard,	March 26, 1745
Jonathan Chandler & Alethea Wade,	May 23, 1745
George Haward & Abigail Copeland,	Aug. 29, 1745
Samuel Dunbar & Mary Haward,	Feb. 11, 1745
Nathaniel White & Susanna Cronnan (?),	May 27, 1745
Benanuel Leach & Elizabeth Edson,	June 6, 1745
Thomas Lindsey & Elizabeth Turner,	Oct. 3, 1745
John Whitman & Margarett Willis,	Dec. 11, 1745
Edward Wentworth Stoughton & Sarah Winslow,	
	Jan. 22, 1745-6
Terah Whitman of Easton & Anna Willis,	Feb. 4, 1745-6
John Conant & Abigail Pratt,	——
William Shurtleff & Sarah Kingman,	Feb. 7, 1745
Isaac Allen & Joanna Packard,	Feb. 20, 1745
Joseph Pettingail & Mary Edson,	Feb. 25, 1745
John Alden & Rebecca Nightingail,	March 15, 1745
Peter Edson & Sarah Southworth,	March 28, 1745
Isaac Packard & Abigail Porter,	March 28, 1745
Amos Cordner & Abigail Colley (mulattoes),	April 18, 1745
David Edson & Susanna Ganett,	Jan. 1, 1746
Ebenezer Packard & Sarah Perkins,	Feb. 25, 1746
Samuel Beals & Elizabeth Blackmer,	Oct. 17, 1745
Elisha Allen & Rebecca Pratt,	Oct. 24, 1745
Joseph Byram & Mary Bowditch,	Dec. 17, 1745

Dr. Isaac Otiss & Mehitable Bass,	June 30, 1746
Joseph Keith, Jr., & Ann Turner,	Oct. 7, 1746
Stephen Leach & Sarah Hooper,	Feb. 7, 1749
Theodore Byram & Elisabeth Beal,	April 27, 1749
Henry Carey & Martha Byram,	May 3, 1749
James Edson & Esther Allen,	May 11, 1749
John Smith & Mary Hanmer,	Oct. 5, 1749
Zebulon Carry & Lydia Phillips,	Nov. 28, 1749
Nathan Alen & Mary Hudson,	Jan. 16, 1749-50
Simeon Whitman & Martha Snow,	March 16, 1749-50
Daniel Beal & Mehitable Byram,	April 3, 1749-50
Mathew Jennett & Martha Byram,	April 9, 1749-50
Ignatius Loring & Bathshabe Bass,	Aug. 22, 1749-50
William Holmes & Elisabeth Hamblen,	Nov. 5, 1749-50
Benjamin Jennett & Mary Clap,	Dec. 20, 1749-50
* Elisabeth Hayward & Silence Snell,	Feb. 14, 1750-1
Samuel Bisbe of Pembroke & Martha Snell,	May 2, 1750-1
John Prett of Pembroke & Sarah Perce,	Aug. 28, 1750-1
John Wade & Hannah Kingman,	Sept. 19, 1751
John Richards & Keziah Bailey,	Nov. 27, 1751
Benjamin Harris & Sarah Shaw,	Dec. 18, 1751
William Barrill & Sarah Carry,	Dec. 19, 1751
Ezra Warren & Mary Phillips,	Jan. 13, 1752
Peter Whitman & Susanah Keith,	June 18, 1752
Eleazer Hamblen & Lydia Bonny,	June 30, 1752
David Kingman, Jr., & Abigail Hall,	Aug. 5, 1752
James Keith & Sarah Holman,	Oct. 26, 1752
John Orcut, Jr., & Jerusha Hanmer,	Nov. 3, 1752
John Young & Eunice Bass,	Nov. 22, 1752
John Howard, Jr., & Abigail Hudson,	Dec. 28, 1752
Nathaniel Ramsdell & Mary Pratt,	Jan. 10, 1753
Jesse Washburn & Silence Washburn,	Dec. 29, 1748
James Thurston & Phebe Perkins,	Feb. 10, 1748
Ebenezer Edson & Jean Grissin (?),	March 14, 1748
Joseph Hervey, the 3d, & Betty Keith,	March 16, 1748
Ruben Washburn & Betty Dilley,	May 11, 1749

---

* So reads.

John Cooper & Sarah Edson,	July 21, 1749
Benamin Shelley, Jr., of Rainham & Mary Turner,	
	Dec. 21, 1749
John Foster of Kingston & Mary Dilley,	Nov. 1, 1750
William Lincoln of Taunton & Hannah Wade,	
	March 20, 1751
Seth Harris & Abiah Alden,	Nov. 26, 1751
John Mitchel & Sarah Makurian,	Nov. 28, 1751
Daniel Washburn & Experience Harlow,	June 4, 1752
Daniel Leonard & Mary Dunbar,	Nov. 1, 1750
Nathan Ames & Elisabeth Snow,	Dec. 31, 1750
Ebenezer Perkins & Experience Holmes of Middleboro,	
	Feb. 28, 1750-1
David Leach & Hannah Newcomb of Plimouth,	
	June 20, 1751
Benjamin Leach & Joanna Miller of Rainham,	
	July 15, 1751
John Edson & Hannah Allen,	July 15, 1751
James Hayward, Jr., & Sarah Harris,	Aug. 13, 1751
Nathaniel Rickard & Jerusha Dunber,	Aug. 23, 1751
John Bolton, Jr., & Elisabeth Hayward,	Sept. 20, 1751
David Johnson, Jr., & Parnel Packard,	Oct. 2, 1751
Isaac Lee & Waitstill Ripley,	Dec. 15, 1751
Ebenezer Hinds & Lydia Bartlett,	Dec. 26, 1751
Robert Wallis of Pembroke & Anna Hooper,	Jan. 30, 1752
David Manley of Easton & Joanna Turner,	April 8, 1752
Jonathan Perkins, Jr., & Abigail Packard,	July 21, 1752
Abiah Cobb & Sarah Lad, both of Hanover,	Nov. 2, 1752
Jonathan Wellis & Judath Packard,	Nov. 2, 1752
William Wood & Annie Mear,	Jan. 2, 1753
Edward Powers & Phillis Bartlett,	Jan. 30, 1753
Jonathan Randall & Abigail Allen,	July 27, 1749
Luke Perkins & Rebecca Packard,	Aug. 24, 1749
Ebenezer Hayward of Braintree & Elisabeth Hanoner,	
	Dec. 13, 1750
Edward Southworth & Abiah Packard,	Dec. 15, 1750
David Howard, Jr., & Keziah Ames,	Feb. 5, 1751
Noah Tinkham & Sarah Porter,	June 16, 1751

David French & Abigail Owen,	July 4, 1751
Ebenezer Edson & Lucy Packard,	Nov. 17, 1751
Elias Monk & Elisabeth Wright,	May 27, 1751
John Kinsley & Thankful Washburne,	Feb. 19, 1746-7
Cornelius White & Susanna Howell,	Oct. 14, 1747
Nathan Washburne & Mary Mehurine,	April 20, 1748
Israel Hill & Beriah Latham,	June 27, 1748
Seth Hayward & Tabitha Pratt,	Sept. 6, 1748
John Muxam & Silence Pratt,	Sept. 15, 1748
Ebenezer (Eleazar ?) Alden & Sarah Whitman,	Nov. 22, 1748
Isaac Swift & Susanna Ames,	Jan. 26, 1748-9
Joseph Pratt, 2d, & Alice Hayward,	April 5, 1749
James Hayward & Bethia Willis,	June 1, 1749
John Harden & Anna Harden,	Sept. 7, 1749
Benjamin Mahurine & Mehitable Williams,	Sept. 25, 1749
Phineas Conant & Joanna Pratt,	Sept. 26, 1749
Ezekiel Washbourn & Experience Curtis,	Oct. 4, 1749
Joseph Harvey, 2d, & Keziah Washburn,	Oct. 10, 1749
Benjamin Keith & Abigail Leach,	Nov. 9, 1749
Francis Cook & Sarah Briant,	Sept. 24, 1750
John Lazell & Mary Byram,	Oct. 24, 1750
Obadiah Edy & Sarah Lawrence,	Oct. 31, 1750
Jonathan Beal & Abigail Harlow,	July 11, 1751
Ebenezer Leach & Deborah Samson,	Oct. 10, 1751
Joseph Orcutt & Deborah Pratt,	Dec. 10, 1751
Nathan Perkins & Sarah Pratt,	April 2, 1752
James Shaw & Margaret Murry,	Aug. 10, 1752
Joseph Crossman & Elisabeth Washburne,	Aug. 20, 1752
Eleazer Carry & Mary Washburne,	March 7, 1753
Jabez King & Mary Washburne,	April 12, 1753
Seth Pratt & Hannah Washburne,	April 24, 1753
Josiah Washburne & Phebe Hayward,	May 3, 1753
Nathan Conant & Hannah Lazall,	June 14, 1753
Isaac Washburne & Deborah Conant,	Sept. 11, 1753
Josiah Aldrich & Sarah Baker,	Oct. 18, 1753
Timothy Perkins & Zipporah Washbourne,	Oct. 7, 1753
Jonathan Cary & Lois Hooper,	March 7, 1754
Jeremiah Washburn & Charity Pratt,	April 24, 1754

Nathan Mitchell & Ann Cary,	April 25, 1754
John Heiford & Sarah Conant,	Oct. 10, 1754
Captain Josiah Edson & Abigail Dean,	April 3, 1755
William Hack & Experience Phinney,	May 22, 1755
Seth Lathrop & Martha Conant,	Sept. 11, 1755
Joseph Washburn & Mary Washburn,	Sept. 23, 1755
Josiah Washburn & Huldah Leonard,	Oct. 15, 1755
Nathaniel Latham & Mercy Leach,	March 11, 1756
Joseph Warren & Mercy Perkins,	Aug. 3, 1756
Solomon Leonard, Jr., & Joanna Washburn,	Oct. 5, 1756
Joseph Bassett & Phebe Cushman,	Dec. 2, 1756
Charles Besswick & Tracy Hubbard,	Jan. 6, 1757
Jonathan Washburn & Rebecca Perkins,	Jan. 18, 1757
Job Pratt & Mary Washburne,	Feb. 1, 1757
Ichabod Packard & Ruth Allen,	May 3, 1757
Nehemiah Latham & Lucy Harris,	May 26, 1757
John Allen & Sarah Campbell,	July 12, 1753
Zachariah Gurney & Mary Ames,	Jan. 9, 1754
Jesse Edson & Lydia Packard,	March 26, 1754
Isaac Perkins & Joanna Edson,	May 2, 1754
Simeon Cary & Mary Hayward,	June 27, 1754
William Edson & Martha Hayward,	Nov. 27, 1754
John McBride & Jane Willson,	Jan. 16, 1755
Daniel Pettingell & Sarah Gannet,	April 9, 1755
Barnabas Hayward & Mehitable Packard,	July 2, 1755
Josiah Perkins & Abigail Edson,	Aug. 17, 1755
Mathew Kingman & Jane Packard,	Nov. 6, 1755
John Alden, Jr., & Martha Packard,	Nov. 6, 1755
Jacob Dunbar & Hannah Randall,	July 8, 1756
Nathaniel Tillden & Susanna Brett,	Nov. 11, 1756
Andrew Gamel & Betty Tomson,	Oct. 27, 1756
Joshua Packard, Jr., & Martha Hartwell,	Oct. 28, 1756
David Edson & Sarah Edson,	Dec. 8, 1756
Thomas West & Martha Packard,	Dec. 9, 1756
Edward Soper & Eunice Curtiss,	Dec. 30, 1756
Robert Hayward, Jr., & Abigail Snell,	May 5, 1757
Daniel Snell & Abigail Packard,	Nov. 27, 1753
Joseph Eames & Ruth Packard,	Jan. 30, 1754

Jonathan Bur & Martha Cudworth,	May 22, 1754
Zepheniah Willis & Bethiah Haward,	Nov. 28, 1754
Ephraim Burr & Susanna Alger,	Sept. 5, 1755
Alexander Kingman & Sarah Lathrop,	Oct. 16, 1755
Jeremiah Belcher & Annie Haward,	Feb. 26, 1756
Jonathan Haward & Phebe Ames,	March 1, 1756
Ezra Alden & Rebecca Keith,	April 4, 1756
David Wade & Mary Littlefield,	Sept. 9, 1756
Jeremiah Thayer & Tabitha Levit,	Nov. 11, 1756
Caleb Washburn & Mehitable Allen,	May 27, 1756
Solloman Allden & Sarah Hall,	1755
John Alger & Abihail Johnson,	March 4, 1754
Jonathan Bozworth & Abihail Alger,	Jan. 6, 1756
Samuel Waters & Jane Kennedy,	Feb. 26, 1754 (?)
Ezra Edson & Rebecca Johnson,	Nov. 18, ——
Isaiah Johnson & Ruth ——,	Jan. 23, 1757
David Harvy & Content Byram,	Oct. 12, 1756
Daniel Willis (?) & Keziah Willis,	Nov. 11, 1756
Josiah Haward & Mercy D—ch,	March 16, ——
John Shaw & Hannah Willis,	Nov. 30, 1756
Elez. Snow, Jr., & Mary Wood,	Jan. 13, 1757
Simeon Haward & Mary Besse,	March 17, 1757
Samuel Bartlett & Susannah Dunbar,	May 12, 1757
Samuel Whitman & Elizabeth Bonney,	July 27, 1757
William Tolman of Stoughton & Bethe Ames,	
	Sept. 29, 1757
James Dunbar & Martha Conant,	Oct. 5, 1757
Ezra Hayward & Lidia Lee,	Oct. 11, 1757
Philip Briant & Silence Haward,	Oct. 13, 1757
Elisha Dunbar & Rebecca Wade,	Nov. 24, 1757
Samuel Packard, 4th, & Elizabeth Carver,	Dec. 13, 1757
James Snow, Jr., & Mary Edson,	Jan. 10, 1758
Ebenezer Edson & Hannah Leach,	April 27, 1758
Solomon Ripley & Miriam Briggs,	May 18, 1758
Nathan Packard & Lidia Jackson,	Oct. 10, 1758
Nathaniel Packard & Anna Stone,	Oct. 17, 1758
Josiah Dunbar & Silence Packard,	Dec. 12, 1758
Seth Morton & Hepsibah Packard,	Sept. 12, 1757

Nathaniel Morton & Lucy Washburn,	Sept. 13,	1757
Seth Richards & Susannah Perkins,	Sept. 15,	1757
Hezekiah Porter of Windsor & Sarah Carver,	Sept. 25,	1757
Ephraim Allen & Bethe Woods,	March 16,	1758
Nathan Alden & Lidia Richards,	July 7,	1757
Jonathan Ames & Keziah Tinkham,	Nov. 17,	1757
Christopher Dyer & Sarah Bassett,	Nov. 17,	1757
Josiah Keith & Susannah Williams,	Feb. 28,	1758
Thomas Ames, Jr., & Deborah Brett,	March 28,	1758
Ebenezer Wade & Mehitable Kingman,	March 1,	1759
Jonathan Kingman, Jr., & Hannah Copeland,	March 29,	1759
Richard Bartlett & Mary Robinson,	Nov. 17,	1757
Judah Wood of Halifax & Hannah Porter,	Dec. 15,	1757
Samuel Allen & Hannah Pratt,	Nov. 16,	1758
Joseph Snow & Ruth Shaw,	Feb. 7,	1759
James Bradley & Catherine Moore,	Feb. 21,	1759
Nathaniel Edson & Joanna Snow,	March 29,	1759
Ichabod Orcut & Susannah Davenport,	Nov. 29,	1757
Seth Alden & Joel Hayward,	April 19,	1758
Jonathan Leonard & Martha Washburn,	April 25,	1758
Samuel Dunbar & Mary Snow,	May 11,	1758
Hezekiah Hooper & Elisabeth Leonard,	Oct. 11,	1758
John Hayward & Bethiah Harvey,	Jan. 1,	1759
Edward Curtis & Abigail Pratt,	Jan. 9,	1759
Amasa Richard & Deliverance Pratt,	March 12,	1759
Amos Snell & Experience Washburne,	March 13,	1759
Lemuel Southworth & Patience West,	Nov. 6,	1757
Joseph Cole & Betty Southworth,	Dec. 8,	1757
Simon Griffen & Gennit Brown,	Jan. 5,	1758
Ephraim Willis & Elisabeth Gernsey,	April 13,	1758
Frederick Pope & Mary Cole,	June 8,	1758
Abiah Packard & Phebe Paine,	Nov. 30,	1758
Ichabod Edson & Jemima Packard,	July 19,	1759
Joseph Keith & Chloe Packard,	May 31,	1759
Jonathan Conant & Jane Latham,	June 12,	1759
Joseph Robinson & Hannah Snow,	Oct. 25,	1759
Seth Mitchell & Mary Wade,	Feb. 21,	1760
Benjamin Byram & Rachel Bailey,	April 10,	1760

Eleazer Keith & Elizabeth Mitchell,	Sept. 11,	1760
John Hanmer & Martha Pryer,	Oct. 9,	1760
Solomon Packard, Jr., & Hannah Bailey,	Nov. 20,	1760
Jeptha Byram of Mendham, N. J., & Susannah Wash-		
burne,	Feb. 19,	1761
Nathan Whitman & Betty Allen,	March 19,	1761
John Ames & Susanna Haward,	July 12,	1759
Eliab Fobes & Mehitable Ames,	July 12,	1759
Isaac Willis, Jr., & Rebecca Haward,	Oct. 9,	1759
Eliakim Haward & Mary Haward,	Dec. 20,	1759
Elijah Snell & Susannah Haward,	May 29,	1760
Uriah Brett & Charity Kingman,	June 4,	1760
Mr. Richard Perkins & Mrs. Mary Hancock,	Oct. 9,	1760
George Packard & Abigail Eastee,	Nov. 27,	1760
Jacob Edson & Betty Packard,	May 4,	1759
Adam Haward & Mary Keith,	June 25,	1759
Reuben Packard & Anna Perkins,	Oct. 1,	1759
Jonathan Orcutt & Experience Washburne,	Nov. 5,	1759
Levi Keith & Jemima Perkins,	Nov. 8,	1759
Elisha Gurney (or Gumey) & Jane Kingman,	March 13,	1760
Adam Kingman & Ruth White,	March 27,	1760
Solomon Packard & Dorothy Perkins,	Oct. 5,	1760
Edward Pettingale & Sarah Curstis,	Jan. 15,	1761
Robert Morrison & Mary McIntire,	Jan. 22,	1761
Ezekiel Southworth & Mary Newman,	April 7,	1761
Zebedee Snell & Martha Haward,	April 9,	1761
Beriah Willis & Abigail Haward,	Oct. 10,	1759
Ebenezer Keith & Hepsibah Carver,	Nov. 6,	1759
William Fobes, Jr., & Hannah Willis,	Nov. 6,	1759
Solomon Perkins & Sarah Edson,	Jan. 31,	1760
Jacob Johnson of Stoughton, Mass., & Mercy Snow,		
	Feb. 28,	1760
Edward Haward of Easton & Zilpha Leach,	June 19,	1760
Joshua Warren & Rebecca Leach,	July 8,	1760
Hezekiah Mahurrin & Abigail Dickerman,	Aug. 7,	1760
Ebenezer Pratt & Bula Washburn,	Aug. 8,	1760
Israel Bailey & Martha Allden,	Aug. 18,	1760
Joseph Knap of Norton & Susannah Packard,	Aug. 28,	1760

Silas Williams of Easton & Susannah Richard, Oct. 18, 1760
John Shaw of Raynham & Dinah Leach, Jan. 8, 1761
Uriah Richard & Zilpha White, June 2, 1761
Benjamin Perkins of B. & Hepsibah Washburn of Middleboro, July 28, 1761
Joseph Perkins & Martha Haward, both of Middleboro, Aug. 11, 1761
Seth Bolton of Hallifax & Ann Wade of Pembroke, Aug. 13, 1761
Daniel Haward & Abigail Davenport, Aug. 14, 1761
Ebenezer Hooper & Relief Bartlett, Aug. 25, 1761
Ebenezer Alger & Ruth Willis, Oct. 22, 1761
Ezra Allen & Phebe Cary, April 23, 1761
William Whitman & Mary Studley, May 26, 1761
Consider Bearce of Hallifax & Elizabeth Perkins, Sept. 17, 1761
Archibald Tomson & Martha Robinson, Oct. 15, 1761
Jonathan Snow & Bettie Packard, Dec. 8, 1761
Ephraim Groves & Bathsheba Bowditch, Feb. 17, 1762
Simeon Packard & Mary Perkins, July 6, 1761
Zechariah Watkins & Abigail Keith, Sept. 1, 1761
Seth Dunbar & Deborah Belcher, Dec. 3, 1761
Daniel Littlefield, Jr., & Catherine Cole, Feb. 11, 1762
Solomon Smith of Easton & Elisabeth Cole, Feb. 11, 1762
Ephraim Graves & Bathsheba Bowditch, Feb. 17, 1762
John Keith & Alice Mitchell, June 16, 1763
Joseph Keith & widow Keziah Bailey, Oct. 26, 1763
Lot Dwelly of Hanover & Sarah Allen, Dec. 8, 1763
Zebulon Packard & Rebecca Richardson, March 15, 1764
Prince Cowing & Margaret —arkings, March 30, 1762
Tom Drew & Ann Colley (negroes), Nov. 25, 1762
Nathaniel Howard, Jr., & Mary Packard, March 5, 1762
Charles Perkins & Abigail Waterman, March 11, 1762
Benjamin Sprague & Eunice Holmes, Aug. 12, 1762
Timothy Manley of Easton & Susanna Packard, April 1, 1762
Nathan Hartwell & Sarah Bonney, June 19, 1762
Abner Sears of Middleboro & Lidia Perkins, July 15, 1762
John Carver & Bathsheba Edson, Oct. 18, 1762

Jonathan Hayward of Easton & Sarah Leach,	Nov. 11,	1762
Nicholas Wade, Jr., & Betty Thomson,	Nov. 25,	1762
David Lathrop & Mary Howard,	Dec. 2,	1762
David Dunbar & Mercy Soul,	April 21,	1763
Luke Washburn & Desire Packard,	Aug. 30,	1763
Abner Lewis of Middleboro & Mercy Hall,	Sept. 25,	1763
Isaac Leach of Westmoreland, N. H., & Jerusha		
Leach,	Oct. 10,	1763
Amasa Soper & Ruth Dwelly,	Oct. 11,	1763
Jesse Haward of Hallifax & Mary Harden of Pembroke,		
	Oct. 27,	1763
Jonathan Leach & Abigail Leach,	Nov. 30,	1763
Zadock Leach of B. & Susannah Washburn of Mid-		
dleboro,	Dec. 6,	1763
Robert Keith & Silence Hartwell,	Dec. 6,	1763
Benjamin Leach & Abigail Bassett,	Feb. 2,	1764
Josiah Snell, Jr., & Ruhamah Hartwell,	May 26,	1763
Ebenezer Ames & Jane Haward,	June 2,	1763
Jesse Edson & Rebecca Belcher,	Jan. 5,	1764
Daniel Copeland & Susannah Ames,	March 13,	1764
Elisha Washburne & Charity Snell,	Dec. 8,	1763
Joseph Muxam & Ann Conant,	March 8,	1764
Ebenezer Soul of Plimton & Silence Hudson,	April 3,	1764
Ebenezer Campbel & Hannah Pratt,	May 15,	1764
Daniel Snow & Hannah Dunbar,	April 19,	1764
James Wood & Achsa Phinney,	June 5,	1764
Prince Robbin (negro) & Margaret Curtis, alias Pegge		
Wampee,	Sept. 15,	1764
Stephen Pettingail & Abigail Ripley,	Sept. 20,	1764
Benjamin Leach & Mary Keith,	Oct. 2,	1764
Abijah Dyer & Rhoda Bolton,	Oct. 7,	1764
Daniel Lathrop, Jr., & Hannah Haward,	Oct. 23,	1764
Edward Keith of Easton & Susannah Littlewater,		
	Jan. 10,	1765
Isaac Fuller, Jr., & Mary Alden,	Jan. 24,	1765
John Freelove & Sarah Fuller,	Jan. 24,	1765
Seth Packard, Jr., & Lois Leach,	March 7,	1765
James Leach & Hatadiah Leach,	April 4,	1765

Jonathan Lathrop & Chloe Dickerman,	April 30, 1765
Jacob Staples of Taunton & Lois Edson,	May 24, 1765
Simeon Ames & Experience Standish,	May 28, 1765
Gideon Washburne, Jr., & Ruth Whitman,	Sept. 24, 1765
Ephraim Jackson & Bathsheba Trask,	Sept. 26, 1765
Jedediah Leach & Phebe Keith,	Oct. 3, 1765
Calvin Edson & Lidia Conant,	Feb. 6, 1766
Levi Wade of Pembroke & Deborah Phillips,	Feb. 20, 1766
Zepheniah Perkins of B. & Mary Foard of Easton,	
	Feb. 25, 1766
Nathaniel Harvey, Jr., & Betty Hayward,	March 20, 1766
Nathan Edson & Mary Hall,	Sept. 2, 1766
Josiah Byram & Sarah Hall,	Sept. 11, 1766
John Hooper & Sarah Pool,	Sept. 25, 1766
Daniel Keith & Millicent Hooper,	Oct. 30, 1766
Jonathan Alden & Experience Washburne,	Nov. 20, 1766
John Wood, Jr., of Easton & Rachel Barrow,	Nov. 27, 1766
William French & Lidia Keyser,	Jan. 13, 1767
Joseph Chamberlain & Mary Wethrel,	Feb. 12, 1767
Jabez Washburne of Middleboro & Zilpha Hooper,	
	Feb. 17, 1767
Israel Keith & Abigail Leonard,	March 4, 1767
Nathaniel Lowden of Duxboro & Experience Pratt,	
	April 29, 1762
Obediah Bates & Ruth Pratt,	May 27, 1762
Edward Mitchell, Jr., & Jane Latham,	Sept. 30, 1762
Jacob Allen & Abigail Bailey,	Dec. 7, 1762
Jacob Mitchell & Rebecca Loring,	Jan. 26, 1763
Winslow Richardson & Rhoda Johnson,	March 24, 1763
Abner Pratt & Martha Cary,	Aug. 28, 1764
Samuel Darby & Sarah Atwood,	Sept. 13, 1764
Amos Whitman & Anna Washburne,	Nov. 22, 1764
Seth Keith & Abigail Holman,	Dec. 27, 1764
Zachariah Whitmarsh of Weymouth & Mary Pinkney,	
	Jan. 10, 1765
Cushing Mitchel & Jennit Orr,	Sept. 26, 1765
Arthur Latham & Margaret Bearse,	Oct. 17, 1765
James Thomson & Abigail Allen,	Nov. 14, 1765

John Hubbard of Abington & Mary Allen,	Dec. 5, 1765
Samuel Staples of Hanover & Betty Washburne,	
	Dec. 9, 1765
Joseph Noyes of Abington & Mercy Hatch,	Jan. 9, 1766
William Bonney & Phebe Allen,	April 4, 1766
Amos Foard of Duxboro & Sarah Pettingail,	May 29, 1766
William Britton, Jr., of Raynham & Mary Latham,	
	June 5, 1766
Nathaniel Southworth & Catherine Haward,	Aug. 27, 1762
Benjamin Packard & Ruth Leach,	Dec. 23, 1762
Eliphalet Phillips & Mary Haward,	March 3, 1763
Benjamin Southworth & Mary Smith,	March 3, 1763
Josiah Hayden & Silence Haward,	March 15, 1763
John Packard & Sarah Hammond,	March 17, 1763
Simeon Alden & Mary Packard,	May 23, 1763
John Benson & Sarah Williams,	Sept. 24, 1765
Abram Washburne & Rebeccah Lennard,	Oct. 28, 1765
Oliver Alden & Experience Lennard,	Nov. 21, 1765
Newland Samson of Hallifax & Lucy Waterman,	
	Aug. 28, 1766
John Harden & Eunice Benson,	Nov. 13, 1766
William Keith & Eunice Leach,	Feb. 11, 1767
Azael Edson & Olive Edson,	Feb. 12, 1767
John Whitman & Lydia Snow,	Nov. 11, 1764
Elijah Copeland & Rhoda Snell,	Oct. 31, 1765
Isaiah Keith & Sarah Burr,	Oct. 13, 1767
William Hudson, Jr., & Lucy Kingman,	Nov. 5, 1767
Elijah Snow & Sarah Dunbar,	Dec. 9, 1767
Ezra Whitman & Rhoda Snow,	Sept. 1, 1768
Silvenus Ames & Huldah Jonson,	Sept. 20, 1768
John Hayward & Mercy Fobes,	Oct. 6, 1768
Benjamin Marshall & Mary Hayward,	Dec. 29, 1768
Ephraim Fobes, Jr., & Bethiah Ames,	Feb. 9, 1769
Samuel Briggs & Rhoda Juyce (?),	Sept. 1, 1763
Joseph Pettingail, Jr., & Hepbzibah Townsell,	Feb. 20, 1764
Ebenezer Snell & Sarah Packard,	April 5, 1764
Job Briant & Mary Turner,	May 3, 1764
Samuel Porter & Ruth Read,	May 31, 1764

Bennet O (?) Bellen & Abigail Cordner (negroes),

	Nov. 8, 1764
Pompey & Mehitable Colly (negroes),	Nov. 8, 1764
Plato & Rachel Colley (negroes),	Nov. 8, 1764
Mark Foard & Hannah Brett,	Nov. 22, 1764
Levi French & Annie Packard,	Nov. 29, 1764
David Packard, Jr., & Joanna Jackson,	Dec. 27, 1764
Isaac Brett & Priscella Jackson,	Jan. 7, 1765
Dependence French & Rebecca Hammond,	Feb. 7, 1765
Seth Briant & Elisabeth French,	Feb. 7, 1765
Micah Gurney & Hopestill Jackson,	April 25, 1765
Jonathan Lawrence & Rachel Smith,	May 22, 1765
Enoch Thayer & Rebecca Curtis,	July 4, 1765
Daniel Packard & Hannah Perkins,	July 14, 1765
Daniel Edson & Olive Fuller,	Oct. 21, 1765
Philip Reynolds & Hannah Packard,	Oct. 29, 1765
Simeon Leach & Betty Curtis,	Dec. 31, 1765
Theophilus Curtis & Mehitable Keith,	Feb. 13, 1766
George Packard & Abigail Packard,	May 15, 1766
John Morrison & Elisabeth Giffen,	Oct. 27, 1766
Robert Fulton & Agnis Thomson,	July 23, 1767
Hosea (?) Dunbar & Jennet Hendry,	Oct. 22, 1767
David Packard & Dorothy Bassett,	Dec. 31, 1767
Jeremiah Beal & Mary French,	June 20, 1768
Dominus Records & Martha Dailey,	Aug. 19, 1768
Lemuel Leach & Rebecca Washburn,	Oct. 12, 1767
John Sprague & Rebecca Alden,	Oct. 12, 1767
Mr. Ephraim Hyde & Mrs. Mary Angier,	Oct. 16, 1767
Nathan Hudson & Betty Gannett,	Nov. 26, 1767
Winslow Richardson & Elisabeth Byram,	April 27, 1768
Elijah Dean & Susannah Bass,	April 28, 1768
Zadock Hayward & Experience Bearse,	May 12, 1768
Asaph Sole & Mary Hudson,	May 20, 1767
Solomon Pratt & Abial Hooper,	June 11, 1767
Calvin Peirce & Huldah Hayward,	Dec. 2, 1767
Seth Alden & Mary Carver,	Dec. 3, 1767
Benjamin Mahurin & Hannah Snow,	Dec. 3, 1767
Nathan Richard & Mary Snell,	Dec. 3, 1767

John Porter, Jr., & Martha Perkins,	July 14,	1768
John Dyer & Bathsheba Monk,	Aug. 23,	1768
Eli Bozworth & Hannah Cox,	March 19,	1767
Samuel Edson, 4th, & Ann Hall,	April 30,	1767
Levi Hooper & Susannah Leach,	June 25,	1767
Daniel Briant & Sarah Washburn,	July 16,	1767
Timothy Hayward & Hannah Pratt,	July 16,	1767
Luther Keith & Sarah Thompson,	July 23,	1767
Daniel Conant & Joanna Washburn,	Aug. 2,	1767
Samuel Willis, 3d, & Bethiah Lothrop,	Sept. 3,	1767
Jonathan Ames & Keziah Hayward,	Sept. 16,	1767
Stoughton Willis & Mary Monk,	Nov. 16,	1767
Silas Read & Rebecca Russell,	Jan. 28,	1768
Luke Keith & Martha Littlefield,	Feb. 4,	1768
Jonathan Leach, Jr., & Experience Hartwell,	Feb. 23,	1768
ᵛ Josiah Woods & Salome Woods,	March 31,	1768
George Briggs & Molly Keith,	April 4,	1768
Reuben Snow & Hannah Willis,	May 5,	1768
Joseph Newcomb & Mary Aldrich,	July 28,	1768
Jonathan Waterman & Abigail Washburn,	Oct. 24,	1768
Lemuel Keith & Abihail Lothrop,	Nov. 24,	1768
Micah White & Bettie Tolman,	Dec. 22,	1768
Ebenezer Dickerman & Mercy Stone,	Jan. 18,	1769
James Stertevant & Ann Leach,	Jan, 19,	1769
Noah Phinney & Betty Conant,	Jan. 24,	1769
Eleazer Washburn & Huldah Woods,	Feb. 23,	1769
Jonath Caswell & Tabitha Keith,	Feb. 23,	1769
Joseph Allen & Damaris Keith,	Jan. 13,	1769
Samuel Whitman & Susannah Lennard,	Sept. 29,	1761
America Peirce & Ann Freeman (negroes),	June 7,	1764
Shubael Tinkham of Middleboro & Sarah Woods,		
	Aug. 7,	1765
Elijah Edson & Martha Washburn,	March 13,	1766
Nathaniel Orcutt & Mary Lennard,	Aug. 1,	1768
Jonathan Hayward & Mary Johnson,	March 7,	1769
Elijah Ames & Betty Johnson,	May 30,	1769
Issachar Snell & Sarah Hayward,	Nov. 8,	1769
David Keith of Easton & Sarah Copeland,	Nov. 16,	1769

George Keith & Deborah Clift,	Sept. 29,	1768
Eleazer Hill & Hannah Field,	Jan. 30,	1769
Joshua Barrel & Olive Bass,	Nov. 23,	1769
James Loring & Jane Kingman,	Jan. 31,	1770
Isaac Kingman & widow Ruth Loring,	March 15,	1770
Abraham Josselyn, Jr., of Pembroke & Eunice Hill,		
	May 18,	1769
Joseph Foord & Betty Haward,	July 6,	1769
John Hudson & Bethiah Otis,	Oct. 2,	1769
Seth Brett, Jr., & Susanna Latham,	Nov. 15,	1769
Moses Simmons & Lois Hayward,	Nov. 23,	1769
Isaac Kingman, Jr., & Content Packard,	Dec. 4,	1769
Nehemiah Washburne & Ruth Eggarton,	March 29,	1770
Ebenezer Colewell & Sarah Price,	Sept. 27,	1769
Daniel Fobes & Hannah Standish,	Dec. 7,	1769
George Knap, Jr., of Raynham & Tabitha Peters,		
	Dec. 8,	1769
Lemuel Turner of Easton & Mary Fuller	Dec. 14,	1769
Zachariah Standish of Plimton & Olive Pool,	Jan. 9,	1770
Lewis Edson & Hepsibah Washburne,	Jan. 30,	1770
Joseph Ames, Jr., & Martha Williams,	March 15,	1770
John Jones of Middleboro & Olive Leach,	April 3,	1770
Azariah Hayward & Ann Pratt,	Aug. 28,	1768
John Ward of Middleton & Sarah Hudson,	Oct. 27,	1768
Samuel Blake & Abigail Rikard,	Nov. 30,	1768
Jessee Allen & Abigail Willis,	Dec. 1,	1768
Ebenezer Dean of Plimton & Hannah Whitman,		
	May 11,	1769
Thomas Laurance & Sarah Hooper,	Oct. 5,	1769
Josiah Mahurin & Bithia Pratt,	Oct. 26,	1769
Benjamin Crane & Unice Washburn,	June 13,	1770
Nathan Snell & Bettie Haward,	Feb. 22,	1770
Seth Bailey & Deborah Packard,	Oct. 26,	1770
Clifford Belcher of Stoughton & Bettie Copeland,		
	Nov. 22,	1770
Daniel Carr & Martha Edson,	Dec. 27,	1770
Jessee Fuller Sturtevant & Nanne Alger,	March 14,	1771
Robert Dunbar & Bettie Kingman,	June 13,	1771

Thomas Johnson & Molly Lothrop,	June 26,	1771
Ebenezer Collwell & Sarah Price,	Sept. 27,	1769
Daniel Fobes & Hannah Standish,	Dec. 7,	1769
George Knap, Jr., of Raynham & Tabitha Peters,		
	Dec. 8,	1769
Lemuel Turner of Easton & Mary Fuller,	Dec. 14,	1769
Zachariah Standish of Plimton & Olive Pool,	Jan. 9,	1770
Luice Edson & Hepbzibah Washburn,	Jan. 30,	1770
Joseph Ames, Jr., & Martha Williams,	March 15,	1770
John Jones of Middleboro & Olive Leach,	April 3,	1770
William Tory & Molly Perry, both of Plimton,	July 2,	1770
Chiltan Latham & Mary Howard,	Aug. 16,	1770
Benjamin Bennson & Abigail Pratt,	Sept. 27,	1770
Ichabode Leach & Penelope Cobb,	Oct. 11,	1770
Samuel Coney of Easton & Susanna Jonson,	Oct. 15,	1770
Benaiah Niles & Martha Allen,	Oct. 22,	1770
Samuel Warren, Jr., of Middleboro & Bellie Snow,		
	Oct. 30,	1770
Benjamin Mahurin & Mary Wetherel,	Jan. 28,	1771
Abel Edson, Jr., & Bellie Trask,	May 2,	1771
Joshua Williams of Middleboro & Bethia Clerk of Ab-		
ington,	May 30,	1771
Michael Fitchgerald & Margaret Mattison,	July 9,	1771
Barnabas Keith & Hannah Jackson,	Aug. 1,	1771
Samuel Noyes of Abington & Hannah Pratt,	Oct. 30,	1771
Nathan Leach & Deborah Leach,	Nov. 14,	1771
Livi Leach & Hannah Fobes,	Nov. 18,	1771
Pompie Stephens & Sarah Sckips (negroes),	April 28,	1771
Jonathan Whitmarsh & Susanna Shaw of Abington,		
	June 13,	1771
Seth Lennard & Silence Packard,	June 1,	1769
Jonathan Woods & widow Ann Edson,	Feb. 11,	1771
Jonathan Crane & Mary Edson,	Sept. 7,	1771
Daniel Dean of Norton & Lidia Whittman,	Sept. 27,	1771
John Dickerman of Roxbury & Lidia Leach,	Nov. 8,	1771
Samuel Noyes, 3d, of Abington & Millicent Orcut,		
	Dec. 31,	1771
Robert Pegin & Alice James,	Jan. 6,	1771

James Perkins, Jr., & Mary Hooper,   Feb. 14, 1771
Livi Chase of Sandwich & Silence Fobes,   March 20, 1771
James Hooper, Jr., & Susanna Washburn,   Feb. 6, 1772
David Keith & Charity Brett,   March 5, 1772
Samuel Kingsley & Hannah Hayward,   April 22, 1772
Hugh Orr & Agnis Corbit,   Oct. 10, 1771
Christopher Sever & Hannah Hardin,   Oct. 17, 1771
Ephraim Cary, Jr., & Jane Holman,   Dec. 25, 1771
Thomas White of B. & Hannah Green of Abington,
                                                 Jan. 2, 1772
Joseph Cowing & Abigail Fobes,   Feb. 13, 1772
Nathaniel Conant & Silence Fobes,   April 14, 1772
Joab Willis, Jr., & Alice Reccord,   April 14, 1772
Abner Hayward, Jr., of B. & Abigail Hayward of
    Easton,   April 17, 1772
Ebenezer Washburn & Mary Leach,   April 27, 1772
John Doty, Jr., & Zobiah Ward,   May 7, 1772
Nehemiah Leach & Constant Keith,   June 2, 1772
William Hollowell & Molly Trask,   June 23, 1772
Seth Washburn of Middleboro & Elisabeth Dunbar,
                                                July 21, 1772
Jeremiah Keith of B. & Eggatha Briant of Middleboro,
                                               Sept. 10, 1772
Terry Owen & Mary Edey,   Sept. 20, 1772
Icabode Warren of Middleboro & Mary Lennard,
                                               Sept. 22, 1772
Daniel Bolton & Alice Leach,   Oct. 22, 1772
Jeremiah Leach & Alice Hayward,   Dec. 8, 1772
Jireh Swift & Luice Keith,   Dec. 17, 1772
Sylvanus Packard of B. & Elisabeth Marston of Bos-
    ton,   Aug. 19, 1777
Francis Gray of Boston & Sarah Harris,   Nov. 6, 1777
Zachariah Shaw & Hannah Bisbe,   Oct. 7, 1777
Jonathan Allen & Hanah White,   Dec. 4, 1777
Ebenezer Bisbe & Mehitable Shaw,   March 12, 1778
John Thomson & Jennet Allen,   March 12, 1778
Jacob Hardin of Abington & Mehitable Gannett,
                                              March 26, 1778

Pero Jeffry (negro of Dr. Otis) & Creely Williams
   (living with Seth Williams),   May 28, 1778
George Vining & Abigail Alden,   July 27, 1778
Joseph Whiten & Nabby Alden,   Sept. 17, 1778
William Shaw, Jr., & Deliverance Washburn, Oct. 1, 1778
Robert Latham & Jerusha Hooper,   Nov. 18, 1778
James Allen & Polly Whitman,   Nov. 23, 1778
Anthony Peirce & Silu (?) Pratt,   Dec. 17, 1778
John Bisbe & Huldah Shaw,   March 11, 1779
Isaac Lazell & Jane Byram,   June 10, 1779
Solomon Packard & widow Sarah Stetson,   June 23, 1779
John Smith & Ruth Cornish,   July 1, 1779
Josiah Hill, Jr., & Abigail Beal,   Sept. 16, 1779
Edward Hayford & Lehity (?) Kingman,   May 19, 1779
Theophilus Howard, Jr., of B. & Bethsheba Keith of
   Easton,   Oct. 29, 1778
Zadoc Packard & Martha Howard,   Jan. 14, 1779
Nathan Willis, 2d, & Elisabeth Spear,   April 1, 1779
Philip Bryant & Hannah Richards,   May 25, 1779
Prince Ford & Keziah Powers,   Sept. 9, 1779
Daniel Hartwell & Mehitable Copeland,   Nov. 8, 1779
Thaxter Dunber & Phebe Alger,   Dec. 9, 1779
Noah Whitman & Zilpah Washburn,   July 1, 1779
Josiah Mehurin & Martha Conant,   Oct. 14, 1779
John Willis & Sarah Richards,   Dec. 9, 1779
Barnabas Leonard & Phebe Bassett,   Feb. 5, 1780
James Keith, Jr., & Molly Mitchell,   May 4, 1780
William Johnson & Jane Robinson,   Nov. 8, 1779
John Harden, Jr., of Abington & Lydia Hearsey, Dec. 9, 1779
Matthew Ramsdell & Mary Allen,   Dec. 20, 1779
Ichabod Howland of Pembroke & Mary Hatch, Feb. 18, 1780
Ens. Cushing Mitchell & Hannah Newton, March 15, 1780
Ephraim Snell & Anna Keith,   March 23, 1780
George Keith & Elisabeth Ford,   June 14, 1780
Joseph Whitman & Mary Phillips,   Sept. 7, 1780
Elijah Snow & Sarah Shaw,   Sept. 7, 1780
Walter Hatch & Eunice Kingman,   Oct. 5, 1780
Ichabod Packard of Lebanon, N. H., & Rachel Cham-
   berlin,   Oct. 17, 1780

Job Bearce & Sarah Keith,	Nov. 2, 1780
Jonathan Beal & widow Abigail Egerton,	Nov. 7, 1780
William Robinson & Hannah Egerton,	Nov. 9, 1780
Benjamin White, Jr., of Hanover & Mary Chamberlin,	
	Dec. 12, 1780
Joseph Samson & Hannah Gurney,	Dec. 28, 1780
Jonathan Keith & Hannah Snell,	Aug. 28, 1777
Benjamin Ruller (?) & Sarah Ames,	Sept. 8, 1777
Jonas Packard & Mehitable Brett,	Sept. 11, 1777
Noah Pratt & Desire Cole,	Sept. 25, 1777
Oliver Packard & Relief Edson,	Nov. 20, 1777
Ephraim Cole & Silence Webb,	Dec. 18, 1777
Benjamin Hayward & Abigail Perkins,	Dec. 25, 1777
Simeon Brett & Susannah Perkins,	Dec. 25, 1777
Elisha Hayward & Polly Blanchard,	Jan. 13, 1778
Boston Roye & Betty Cordner (blacks),	Feb. 26, 1778
Samuel Brett & Molly Packard,	March 18, 1778
Cesar Eason & Eunice Sewell (blacks),	March 19, 1778
Seth Keith & widow Hannah Keith,	April 2, 1778
Luther Jotham & Mary Mitchell (blacks),	April 8, 1778
Permenas Packard & Martha Reynolds,	April 9, 1778
Charles Snell & Mary Kingman,	April 16, 1778
Daniel Cary & Mehitable Brett,	May 14, 1778
Nathan Edson & Susanna Allen,	May 28, 1778
Cuffee Wright & Anna Cordner (blacks),	Aug. 6, 1778
Nathan Billings & Sarah Warren,	Aug. 19, 1778
James Packard & Jemima Churchill,	Aug. 27, 1779
Noah Ames & Ruhamah French,	Oct. 5, 1779
Archippus Taylor & Hannah Warren,	Oct. 27, 1779
Seth Snow & Mary Snow,	Nov. 17, 1779
Timothy Ames & Abigail Howard,	Nov. 19, 1779
John French & Damaris Howard,	1779
Abijah Thayer & Betty Howard,	March 16, 1779
Cary Hayward & Mary Thomson,	April 29, 1779
Oliver Wentworth & Sarah Leach,	June 15, 1779
Zephaniah Lathrop & Sarah Packard,	Sept. 2, 1779
Ebenezer Thayer & Lydia West,	Sept. 23, 1779
Ephraim Willis & Eunice Egerton,	Sept. 23, 1779

Israel Burr & Hannah Ames,	Oct. 26, 1779
Silas Hayward & Mary Thayer,	Dec. 9, 1779
Thomas Packard & widow Martha Packard,	Jan. 16, 1780
Ephraim Noyes & Sarah Dyke,	Jan. 20, 1780
Simeon Snow & Priscilla Snow,	Feb. 9, 1780
Daniel Ames & Mehitable Perkins,	March 7, 1780
Eleazer Snow & Hannah Dunber,	April 20, 1780
William Curtis & Hannah Linsfield,	June 7, 1780
William Jameson & Eunice Packard,	Sept. 11, 1780
Oliver Howard & Susanna Reynolds,	Nov. 2, 1780
Adam Kingman & widow Anna Hollis,	Nov. 2, 1780
Adin Packard & Keziah Finney,	Nov. 16, 1780
Amasa Tribou & Molly Pratt,	Nov. 16, 1780
Jeremiah Thayer & Katharine Pratt,	Jan. 17, 1781
Josiah Churchill & Sarah Rogers,	Feb. 1, 1781
Edward Johnson & Abigail Bennett (blacks),	March 15, 1781
Matthew Packard & Kezia Perkins,	April 17, 1781
Ebenezer Packard & widow Content Harlow,	April 26, 1781
Nathan Orcutt & Jane Ingley,	May 1, 1781
John Willis & Molly Egerton,	July 5, 1781
Gideon Lincoln & Martha Perkins,	Aug. 13, 1781
Simeon Shurtleff & Submit Kingman,	Aug. 16, 1781
Ezekiel Washburn & Naomi Thayer,	Nov. 1, 1781
Ebenezer Drake & Martha Gurney,	Jan. 17, 1782
Eliphalet Packard & Lydia Barrell,	Jan. 24, 1782
Warren Howell & Mary Kingman,	Feb. 27, 1782
Nathan Witherell & Mary Doty,	July 18, 1780
Solomon Snow & Betty Perkins,	Oct. 5, 1780
Asa Keith & Susanna Hartwell,	Oct. 17, 1780
Robert Wade & Molly Edson,	Nov. 2, 1780
Joseph Fobes of Easton & Olive Hayward,	Nov. 24, 1780
Noah Hill & Hannah Beal,	Nov. 26, 1780
Abraham Harkley of Attleboro & Miriam Thomas,	
	Dec. 6, 1780
David Benson & Charity Besse,	Dec. 21, 1780
Samuel Codding of Taunton & Sarah Hills,	March 27, 1781
Joshua Alden & Mary Alden,	April 16, 1781
Isaac Mehurin & Mary Allen,	Jan. 18, 1781

William Donham of Plymouth & Deborah Hooper,

          Feb. 1, 1781

Isaac Washburn & Huldah Allen,   Feb. 6, 1781

Oliver Washburn & Hannah Gannett, March 1, 1781

Isaac Alden & Mary Russell,   May 14, 1781

Arthur Harris & Celia Mitchell,   June 14, 1781

John Mitchell & Anna Byram,   Sept. 24, 1781

Thomas Whitman & Lydia Sherman, Nov. 22, 1781

Seth Whitman & Eunice Bass,   Nov. 26, 1781

Eliphalet Bailey & Martha Robinson, Jan. 29, 1782

Joshua Bowen of Roxbury & Abigail Smith, March 26, 1782

Reuben Harden of Pembroke & Rebecca Harden,

          July 18, 1782

Seth Hobart & Esther Allen,   Aug. 7, 1782

Josiah Torrey & Olive Pratt,   Aug. 29, 1782

Benjamin Richards & Polly Bartlett, Sept. 25, 1782

Ezra Kingman & Susanna Whitman, Nov. 14, 1782

Robert Packard & Ruth Barrell,   Nov. 28, 1782

William Brett & Molly Allen,   Dec. 5, 1782

William Turner & Joanna Pettingill, June 27, 1782

Edmund Williams of Raynham & Mary Harvey,

          Aug. 20, 1781

Nathan Williams of Raynham & Abthia Harvey,

          Oct. 30, 1781

Luther Hall of Raynham & Abigail Mehurin, Dec. 4, 1781

Eliab Snow & Lydia Snow,   Feb. 5, 1782

William Snell & Eunice Cary,   Aug. 30, 1781

Robert Keith & Hannah Southworth, Jan. 1, 1782

Benjamin Edson & Deborah Perkins, Jan. 3, 1782

Elijah Stores & Susanna Swift,   March 7, 1782

Nathaniel Morton & Mary Cary,   March 17, 1782

Jeremiah Conant & Mary Leonard, March 21, 1782

Abishai Besse & Sally Conant,   April 11, 1782

Solomon Hayward & Zerviah Washburn, April 16, 1782

David Conant & Lucy Besse,   April 18, 1782

Caleb Bassett & Bethiah Keith,   April 18, 1782

Thomas Pope & Huldah Edson,   May 2, 1782

Mr. Eliphalet Cary & Mrs. Hannah Edson, May 9, 1782

Benjamin Snell & Rebecca Conant,	May 23, 1782
William Johnson & Mary Owen,	May 29, 1782
Edmund Harvey & Mary Harvey,	June 4, 1782
Robert Edson & Molly Hayward,	June 6, 1782
Noah Edson & Betty Richards,	June 27, 1782
Levi Latham & Hannah Alden,	July 30, 1782
Ebenezer Perkins & Molly Pratt,	Aug. 1, 1782
Ezra Edson, Jr., & Sena Perkins,	Sept. 19, 1782
Brig. Gen. Nathaniel Goodwin & Mrs. Ruth Shaw,	
	Oct. 3, 1782
Edward Hayward & Jenna Mitchell,	Oct. 16, 1782
Benjamin Price & Mehetabel French,	Oct. 18, 1782
Nathaniel Soper & Betty Price,	Oct. 25, 1782
James Hall & Sarah Orcutt,	Oct. 31, 1782
Asa Richmond & Eunice Washburn,	Nov. 28, 1782
Barnabas Washburn & Keturah Conant,	Dec. 5, 1782
Nathan Shaw & Rosamond Leonard,	Dec. 10, 1782
Thomas Danforth & Nancy Woods,	Feb. 1, 1783
Barnabas Snell & Eunice Conant,	Jan. 1, 1783
Benjamin Conant & Betty Hooper,	March 6, 1783
Marlborough Williams & Susanna Mitchell,	March 20, 1783
Barnabas Lathrop & Sarah Bozworth,	Nov. 27, 1777
Benjamin Samson & Anna Packard,	Jan. 1, 1778
Jonathan Belcher & Abigail Corthell,	Jan. 4, 1778
Jonathan Packard, Jr., & Susanna Alger,	May 11, 1778
Silas Leach & Allice Leach,	Sept. 24, 1778
Elisha Bisbe & Martha Keith,	Sept. 28, 1779
Calvin Keith & Martha Alger,	Nov. 11, 1779
Barnabas Dunbar & Silence Alger,	May 24, 1780
John Foster & Phebe Burr,	May 25, 1780
William Morey & Susanna Fobes,	June 26, 1780
Sylvanus Howard & Sarah Snow,	June 11, 1781
John Fann & Mercy Dunbar,	July 31, 1781
Enoch Perkins & Susanna Perkins,	March 26, 1783
Nehemiah Edson & Olive Perkins,	April 5, 1783
Timothy Mitchell & Hannah Leonard,	Aug. 20, 1783
Andrew Pompy & Hagar Hill (blacks),	April 9, 1780
Asa Wilbore & Sylvia Jackson,	March 27, 1783

Elijah Alden & Rebecca Fuller,   Aug. 31, 1783
Ebenezer Snow, Jr., & Sarah Pool,   Oct. 7, 1783
Nathaniel Ames & Mary Hill,   Nov. 2, 1783
Charles Ramsdel of Pembroke & Betty Terrill, Jan. 23, 1783
Matthew Gannett of Abington & Alice Latham,
  March 20, 1783
Rotheus Mitchell & Hepza Hayward,   April 3, 1783
Solomon Inglee of Hallifax & Bathsheba Orr, April 15, 1783
David Snell & Molly Baker,   July 17, 1783
Joshua Pool of Abington & Lucinda Latham, Aug. 11, 1783
Jacob Mitchell & widow Sally Whitman,   Sept. 4, 1783
Reuben Mitchell & Anna Wade,   Oct. 23, 1783
Joshua Pratt & Mary Pratt,   Oct. 30, 1783
Thomas Phillips & Martha Whitman,   Oct. 30, 1783
Capt. Simeon Whitman & widow Sarah Byram, Nov. 6, 1783
Samuel Faxon & Priscilla Thomas,   Dec. 11, 1783
Edward Howard, Jr., & Molly Howard,   Sept. 25, 1780
Jacob Hill, Jr., & Ann Tribou,   Sept. 25, 1780
John Lathrop & Sarah Cook,   Dec. 7, 1780
Jonathan Ames & Deborah Pratt,   Dec. 10, 1780
Dr. Simeon Dunbar & Abigail Packard,   Jan. 1, 1781
James Alger, 2d, & Olive Snell,   Jan. 2, 1781
John Robbinson & Molly Packard,   Feb. 22, 1781
Alpheus Fobes & Mehetabel Lathrop,   April 5, 1781
Thomas Hayward & Hannah Hayward,   July 19, 1781
David Ames & Rebecca Johnson,   Nov. 15, 1781
Waldow Hayward & Lucy Bartlett,   Dec. 5, 1781
Caleb Packard & Sarah Howard,   June 20, 1782
Daniel Briggs & Jane Lathrop,   July 4, 1782
Joseph Fobes & Susanna Ames,   July 11, 1782
Daniel Manley & Phebe Howard,   Aug. 1, 1782
Ebenezer Bailey & Sylva Howard,   Sept. 26, 1782
Solomon Shaw & Anna Hayward,   Oct. 31, 1782
Caleb Dunbar & Hannah Drake,   Nov. 7, 1782
Seth Howard & Desire Bailey,   Nov. 7, 1782
Sipio Sutton & Mary Cook,   April 22, 1783
Peter White & Rebecca Nero,   April 22, 1783
Daniel Perkins & Bathsheba Williams,   Sept. 8, 1783

Levitt Thayer & Abigail Snell,	Oct. 21,	1783
Elijah Packard & Keziah Ames,	Oct. 21,	1783
Thomas Mitchell & Abigail Howard,	Oct. 27,	1783
Jonathan Ames & Patience Sturtevant,	Dec. 28,	1783
Amasa Howard & Molly Howard,	Jan. 26,	1784
Benjamin Taylor & Sarah Torrey,	March 7,	1784
Rufus Conant & Thankful Leonard,	Sept. 28,	1783
Nathan Lazell & Deborah Conant,	Dec. 22,	1783
Daniel Tolman & Cloe Bozworth,	Feb. 10,	1783
Joseph Knap, Jr., of Easton & Eunice Carver,	Jan. 15,	1784
David Conant & Sylvia Whitman,	April 15,	1784
Solomon Conant & Lois Conant,	April 28,	1784
Theodore Perkins & Patte Conant,	May 2,	1784
John Snow, Jr., & Mary Ames,	May 5,	1784
Israel H. Baker & Barsheba Carver,	June 21,	1784
Joseph French & Hannah Mehurin,	Nov. 18,	1784
Sylvester Conant & Sylvia Conant,	Nov. 25,	1784
Seth Lathrop, Jr., & Abigail Bassett,	Nov. 25,	1784
Isaac Smith of Braintree & Mary Conant,	Jan. 24,	1785
Ebenezer Willis & Joanna Atwood,	Jan. 30,	1785
James Reed of Abington & Ruth Porter,	Jan. 1,	1784
Reed Erskine of Abington & Mary Whitmarsh,		
	March 1,	1784
Jacob Whitmarsh, Jr., & Anna Pool,	April 22,	1784
Isaiah Whitman & Cloe Phillips,	April 29,	1784
Rev. William Reed of Easton & Olive Pool,	May 20,	1784
Isaac Keith & Betty Keith,	May 25,	1784
George Erskine & Huldah Whitmarsh,	June 10,	1784
Spencer Forest of Hallifax & Abigail Wade,	June 17,	1784
John Ramsdel of Pembroke & Hannah Allen,	Sept. 30,	1784
John Phillips & Jennet Young,	Oct. 21,	1784
Daniel Orcutt & Olive Whitman,	Nov. 16,	1784
Josiah Johnson, Jr., & Eunice Allen,	Nov. 23,	1784
Jacob Allen & Susanna Alden,	Nov. 25,	1784
Thomas Osburne & Hannah Wade,	Dec. 16,	1784
Joseph Chamberlain & Sarah Bass,	Dec. 22,	1784
Samuel Hardin of Abington & Relief Spear,	Jan. 13,	1785
Benjamin Darling of Pembroke & Sarah Lowden,		
	Jan. 27,	1785

Thomas Chamberlain & Molly Whitman, Feb. 3, 1785
Peter Salmon of Hanover & widow Eunice Whitman,
           Feb. 17, 1785
Holman Keith & Sylvia Keith, March 8, 1785
Hugh Orr, Jr., & Sylvia Mitchell, March 9, 1785
Samuel Dunbar (a mulatto) & Hannah James, March 10, 1785
John Edson, 3d, & Susanna Orcutt, March 15, 1785
Simeon Allen & Huldah Cary, May 26, 1785
Capt. Isaac Whitman & Bathsheba Allen, June 2, 1785
James Lovell & Jemima Leach, July 14, 1785
James Barrell & Betsey Russell, Sept. 15, 1785
James Ramsdell & Eunice Allen, Nov. 17, 1785
Daniel Rinsley & Molly Keith, Dec. 1, 1785
Daniel Tolman & Cloe Bozworth, Feb. 10, 1783
Rufus Conant & Thankful Leonard, Sept. 28, 1783
Joseph Knap of Easton & Eunice Carver, Jan. 15, 1784
David Conant & Sylvia Whitman, April 15, 1784
Solomon Conant & Lois Conant, April 28, 1784
Theodore Perkins & Patte Conant, May 2, 1784
John Snow, Jr., & Mary Ames, May 5, 1784
Israel Buker & Bathsheba Carver, June 21, 1784
Joseph French & Hannah Mehuren, Nov. 18, 1784
Sylvanus Conant & Sylvia Conant, Nov. 25, 1784
Seth Lathrop, Jr., & Abigail Bassett, Nov. 25, 1784
Nathan Lazell & Deborah Conant, Dec. 22, 1783
Isaac Smith of Braintree & Mary Conant, Jan. 24, 1785
Ebenezer Willis & Joanna Atwood, Jan. 30, 1785
John Shaw of Cummington, Co. of Hampshire, &
  Hannah Dyer of Abington, Sept. 20, 1784
Daniel Lathrop, Jr., & Mary Turner, Sept. 1, 1785
Abial Lapham of B. & Susanna Lathrop of Easton,
           Jan. 12, 1786
Isaac Lathrop & Betty Hacket, Feb. 9, 1786
Daniel Brett & Huldah Snell, March 25, 1784
Ephraim Cary & Mary Kingman, May 21, 1784
Barnabas Dunbar & Mary Howard, May 28, 1784
Benjamin Packard & Mehetabel Fobes, Sept. 8, 1784
Prince Derby & Mary Drake (blacks), Nov. 4, 1784

Thomas Reynolds & Tabitha Thayer,	Feb. 20, 1785
Josiah Williams & Hannah Kingman,	March 10, 1785
Luther Burr & Jane Howard,	April 7, 1785
Azel Kinsley & Patte Howard,	June 16, 1785
Joseph Alger & Olive Ames,	July 7, 1785
Calvin Snell & Polly Packard,	Sept. 8, 1785
Solomon Washburn & Hannah Alcutt,	Sept. 15, 1785
Ebenezer Dunbar & Rebecca Copeland,	Sept. 15, 1785
Luther Hayward & Betty Willis,	Dec. 12, 1785
David Packard & Mary Robinson,	Dec. 15, 1785
Josiah Lathrop & Susanna Howard,	Dec. 15, 1785
Israel Alger & Rachel Howard,	Dec. 26, 1785
Samuel Bartlett & Lucy Jenkins,	Jan. 22, 1786
Thaddeus Howard & Keziah Ames,	March 1, 1786
John Drake & Molly Cole,	April 4, 1782
Enos Thayer & widow Hannah Reynolds,	May 30, 1782
Josiah Dunbar & Abia Goodspeed,	July 8, 1782
Lewis Dailey & Mary Willis,	Aug. 8, 1782
Josiah Packard, Jr., & Rebecca Perkins,	Oct. 10, 1782
Bela Howard & Mehetabel Cary,	Nov. 28, 1782
Job Ames & Mary Dike,	Dec. 12, 1782
Henry Thayer & Philebert Packard,	Jan. 27, 1783
Nathan Warren & Lucy Terril,	June 12, 1783
Benjamin Kingman & Rhoda Packard,	Sept. 28, 1783
James Perkins & Rebecca Packard,	Sept. 25, 1783
Zachariah Gurney & Mehitabel Packard,	Sept. 30, 1783
Thomas Knowlton & Susanna Hollis,	Oct. 6, 1783
George Lathrop & Molly Thayer,	Nov. 6, 1783
John Dyer & Susanna Thayer,	Nov. 6, 1783
Prince Brown & Sarah Talbut (blacks),	Dec. 4, 1783
James Eason & Sarah Dunbar (blacks),	Dec. 11, 1783
Eliab Snow & Dorcas Churchell,	Dec. 23, 1783
Ephraim Churchill & Silence French,	Dec. 25, 1783
Jonathan Cary & Abigail Perkins,	Jan. 19, 1784
Ephraim Jackson & Hannah Delino,	Feb. 5, 1784
William Pettingill & Lydia Cobb,	Feb. 16, 1784
William Packard & Sarah Wales,	Feb. 18, 1784
Jonas Howard & Nabby Packard,	Feb. 26, 1784

Abel Dunbar & Sarah Howard,	March 23, 1784
Enoch Pratt & Saloma Richard,	April 20, 1784
John Pettingill & Elisabeth Thomson,	July 15, 1784
Calvin Snow & Hannah Churchill,	July 20, 1784
Mark Perkins & Tabitha Washburn,	Oct. 17, 1784
Abner Hayward & Grace Turner,	Dec. 4, 1784
John Stock (?) & Phebe Coatheral,	Feb. 24, 1785
Christopher Young & Molly Bonney,	March 21, 1785
Joseph Snell, Jr., & Hannah Cook,	May 10, 1785
Oliver Packard & Mary Dunbar,	May 19, 1785
Samuel Cordiner & Tamer Talbut (blacks),	June 16, 1785
Jonathan Perkins & Abigail Howard,	Oct. 18, 1785
John Fay & Dinah Talbut (blacks),	Sept. 29, 1785
Joel Packard & Harmony Kingman,	Nov. 1, 1785
Howard Cary & Huldah Packard,	Dec. 15, 1785
William Badger & Polly Dickerman,	Jan. 15, 1786
Phillip Packard & Polly (or Patty) Edson,	March 2, 1786
Isaiah Randal & Deborah Leach,	March 30, 1786
Nathan Keith & Lois Howard,	June 13, 1786
Daniel Field & Hannah Snell,	July 13, 1786
Joseph Silvester & Hannah Howard,	Aug. 15, 1786
Alpheus Cary & Ruby Perkins,	Sept. 21, 1786
Timothy Ames & Ruth Carver,	Oct. 1, 1786
Joshua Ames & Hannah Ford,	Oct. 5, 1786
Daniel Alden & Sarah Cary,	Dec. 18, 1786
Rev. Thomas Crafts & Polly Porter,	Dec. 28, 1786
Rev. Zachariah Howard & Polly Crafts,	March 6, 1787
Byram Allen & Elisabeth Child,	Feb. 7, 1787
Thomas Blanchard, Jr., & Susanna Latham,	Feb. 9, 1787
Levi Keith, 2d, & Huldah Keith,	Feb. 9, 1787
Samuel Pool, Jr., & Abigail Porter,	March 2, 1787
Nathaniel Dammon & Molly Allen,	May 25, 1787
Roger Sutman & Phillis Suel (negroes),	May 25, 1787
Henry Jackson & Mehitabel Alden,	Aug. 24, 1787
James Willis & Sarah Jackson,	Sept. 26, 1787
Matthew Allen, 2d, & Jane Keen,	Dec. 21, 1787
Thomas Lindsey, Jr., & Thankful Bailey,	April 20, 1786
Isaac Willis, 3d, & Huldah Ames,	April 27, 1786

Jotham Ames & Sarah Bryant,	June 24,	1786
John Dickerman & Kezia Alger,	July 10,	1786
Richard Thayer & Eunice Edson,	July 14,	1786
Ceasar Smith & Elisabeth Fortune,	Aug. 8,	1786
Edmund Alger & Huldah Lathrop,	Dec. 27,	1786
Joseph Lazell & Abigail Ames,	Jan. 4,	1787
Oliver Washburn & Martha Fobes,	Jan. 19,	1787
Prince Richards & Nancy P—gi—,	March 5,	1787
Eleazer Carver & Nancy Jones,	Sept. 26,	1787
William Torrance & Susanna Stoddard,	Oct. 15,	1787
John Lazell, Jr., & Lucinda Stetson,	Nov. 8,	1787
Nathaniel Tomson of Hallifax & Sarah Thayer,	April 28,	1785
James Thatcher of Plymouth & Susanna Hayward,		
	April 28,	1785
Phineas Conant & Joanna Washburn,	Aug. 25,	1785
Benjamin Sprague & Priscilla Churchill,	Nov. 17,	1785
Ichabod Packard & Rachel Cole,	Jan. 9,	1786
Bezaliel Flagg of Petersham & Abigail Edson,	Jan. 17,	1786
Joshua Washburn & Lucy Rickard,	March 2,	1786
Samuel Reed of Comington & Metilda Doty,	March 7,	1786
Samuel Brattle of Stoughton & Dorothy Dyer,		
	March 29,	1786
Timothy Willis & Lavina Pratt,	May 4,	1786
William Peirce Meed (?) of Braintree & Jane Eddy,		
	June 27,	1786
Azur Eddy & Hannah Fuller,	Dec. 14,	1786
Pompey (negro) & Dina Little,	March 8,	1787
Eliab Latham of Gray & Lucy Latham,	Sept. 2,	1787
Nathan Pratt & Lois Fuller,	Oct. 7,	1787
Solomon Leonard, Jr., & Huldah Orcutt,	Oct. 18,	1787
Peres Snell & Hannah Kinsley,	Oct. 28,	1787
Salmon Rickards & Olive Edson,	Nov. 4,	1787
Sylvanus Leonard & Eunice Kinsley,	Nov. 19,	1787
Joseph Keith, 2d, & Betsey Sherman,	Feb. 15,	1787
Asa Forrest of Hallifax & Susa Mitchell,	Feb. 20,	1787
Ephraim Tinkham of Middleboro & Molly Gurney,		
	March 1,	1787
Samuel Whitman, Jr., & Hannah Egerton,	March 20,	1787

Turner Phillips & Huldah Whitman,	April 3, 1787
Benjamin Tayler & Martha Childs,	April 5, 1787
Oliver Pratt & Susanna Lowden,	May 17, 1787
Dyer Robbinson & Abigail Stetson,	June 21, 1787
Jacob Pool, Jr., of Abington & Zerviah Whitmarsh,	
	Aug. 23, 1787
Jonah Besse & Eunice Washburn,	Sept. 20, 1787
Seth Allen Whitman & Philebert Whitman,	Nov. 1, 1787
Benjamin Pinchin & Molly Stetson,	Nov. 15, 1787
Daniel Cushing & Zerviah Chamberlin,	Nov. 22, 1787
Joseph Edson & Mary Vinal,	Jan. 4, 1786
Phillip Botton & Bethiah Hayward,	April 7, 1787
Amos Fisher & Rebecca Edson,	June 21, 1787
David Snow & Jemima Hayward,	June 26, 1787
Caleb Copeland & Sarah Byram,	Aug. 2, 1787
Ichabod Shurtleff & Betty Pettingill,	Sept. 8, 1787
Lott Pratt & Polly Aldrich,	Oct. 22, 1787
James Ingley & Keziah Richards,	Nov. 25, 1787
Richard Simons & Cloe Squib (blacks),	Jan. 20, 1788
Mr. Timothy Reed & Hannah Kingman,	Jan. 31, 1788
Jonah Willis & Abigail Hayward,	Feb. 11, 1788
Peter Peirce & Metilda Talbut (blacks),	March 31, 1788
Noah Powers & Rhoda Williams,	May 14, 1787
Marlborough Ripley & Ruth Whiting,	July 16, 1787
Jacob Lathrop & Sarah Snow,	Aug. 22, 1787
Joseph Jones & Elizabeth Eames,	Dec. 9, 1787
Mark Howard & Martha Alger,	April 13, 1788
Benjamin Munro & Mary Washburn,	Dec. 6, 1787
Timothy Conant & Nancy Pratt,	Feb. 25, 1788
Enoch Leonard & Abigail Hammond,	April 10, 1788
Jacob Leonard & Mary Swift,	Dec. 4, 1788
Thomas Conant & Lydia Edson,	April 22, 1789
Asa Leach of Killingly, Ct., & Eunice Turner of Bridge-	
water,	March 15, 1787
Seth Gurney & Rebecca Packard,	Jan. 10, 1788
James Lincoln of Cohasset & Nabby Mitchel,	————
Alexander Terril & Lydia Bryant,	March 17, 1788
Nathan Whitman & Mercy Byram,	March 27, 1788

Timothy Allen & Celia Whitman,	April 3, 1788
William Harris & Alice Mitchell,	May 14, 1788
Isaac Allen of B. & Susanna Allen of Brookfield,	
	July 10, 1788
Josiah Parris of Pembroke & Experience Lowdin,	
	July 23, 1788
Ebenezer Whitman, Jr., & Lydia Whitman,	Oct. 7, 1788
George Byram & Phebe Randall,	Oct. 16, 1788
Solomon Johnson & Sally Robinson,	Oct. 22, 1788
Israel Cowing & Rebecca Wade,	Nov. 25, 1788
Charles Lathrop & Rowena Howard,	April 24, 1788
Zenas Lathrop & Sally Tower,	April 27, 1788
Gideon Howard & Molly Willis,	May 4, 1788
Isaac Alger & Susanna Johnson,	Aug. 11, 1788
Perez Williams & Huldah Kingman,	Aug. 22, 1788
Nathan Johnson & Polly Johnson,	Jan. 11, 1789
Benjamin Pratt & Olive Perkins,	Jan. 16, 1789
Thomas Ames, Jr., & Nanny Sturtevant,	Feb. 4, 1789
Solomon Thayer & Sarah Hobart,	April 20, 1789

✓ ABINGTON.

June 10, 1712. "Part of Bridgewater and certain lands adjoining established as ' Abingdon.'" First (Congregational) Church organized 1712.

Samuel Petingill & Martha Jackson,	Dec. 14, 1733
Jacob Reed & Hannah Noyes,	Dec. 21, 1733
Ebenezer Joslin & Esther Hersey,	June 5, 1733
Samuel Pool & Rebecca Shaw,	Nov. 15, 1733
Jacob Ford & Sarah Pool,	Nov. 22, 1733
J. Hezekiah Ford & Deborah Beal,	Nov. 22, 1733
Eleazer Bate & Rachel Ager,	March 17, 1735
Nicholas Shaw & Ruth Beal,	Feb. 6, 1735
Peter Nash & Mary Noyes,	Nov. 13, 1735
Jonathan Tory & Deborah Shaw,	Dec. 18, 1735
Joseph Pool & Ruth Ford,	Nov. 27, 1735

Benjamin (negro) & Sarah Jonas,	March 17, 1737
James Torey & Sarah Nash,	Dec. 25, 1735
John Reed & Abigail Niels,	Dec. 28, 1738
John Shaw & Lydia Shaw,	April 14, 1737
Samuel Reed & Elizabeth Hayward,	April 28, 1737
James Richards & Hannah Shaw,	Nov. 10, 1737
John Cobb & Ruth Chard,	Feb. 1, 1737
John Shaw & Silence Bate,	Dec. 14, 1738
Daniel Bate & Lydia Symmys,	Dec. 14, 1738
Peter Bate & Sarah Randall,	Dec. 14, 1738
William Tirrell & Hannah Whitmarsh,	Jan. 25, 1738-9
John Dyer & Mary Reed,	April 17, 1739
James Reed & Abigail Nash,	May 10, 1739
Benjamin Edson & Anna Thayer,	Oct. 1, 1739
Samuel Noyse & Rebeckah Harden,	March 3, 1736
Samuel Tirrell & Sarah Gurney,	Nov. 1, 1739
Barnabas Tomson & Hannah Porter,	March 13, 1740
James Richards & Susanna Pratt,	May 15, 1740
Ephraim Spooner & Ruth·Whitmarsh,	July 24, 1740
James Reed & Ruth Pool,	Aug. 30, 1741
Alexander Nash & Mary Tirrell,	Oct. 22, 1741
Isaac Tirrell & Mary Whitmarsh,	Oct. 22, 1741
Abraham Joslin & Rebeckah Tirrel,	Oct. 29, 1741
Jacob Reed & Mary Ford,	Nov. 26, 1741
Edward Jackson & Silence Allen,	Feb. 24, 1741
Ezekiel Reed & Hannah Beal,	Nov. 25, 1742
Andrew Ford & Sarah Shaw,	Nov. 25, 1742
Samuel Nash & Abigail Hearsey,	Nov. 10, 1743
Daniel Noyse & Hannah Thayer,	Nov. 24, 1743
Isaac Hearsey & Mary Gurney,	Jan. 5, 1743-4
Samuel Green & Hannah Jackson,	April 25, 1745
Jonathan Shaw & Susanna Hearsey,	Aug. 17, 1744
Elexander Robinson & Abigail White,	—— 26, 1744
Thomas White & Rachel Lincoln,	Oct. 3, 1745
William Hearsey & Lydia Gurney,	Nov. 7, 1745
Ebenezer Bisbe & Bathsheba Whitmarsh,	Jan. 9, 1745-6
James Terril & Rebecca Gurney,	Jan. 9, 1745-6
Joseph Bate & Sarah Pettingal,	Jan. 9, 1745-6

Thomas Moore of Bridgewater & Mary Hamblin,

Sept. 24, 1746

Isaac Hamblin & Sarah Shaw, Jan. 23, 1746-7

Benjamin Shaw & Susannah Vining, June 21, 1750

William Reed, Jr., & Silance Nash, Sept. 13, 1750

Mr. Josiah Torrey & Mrs. Mary Brown, Nov. 1, 1750

Lemuel Gurney & Rebekah Dorby, Dec. 3, 1750

Abel Packard of Bridgewater & Ester Porter, Jan. 9, 1750-1

Josiah Vining & Abigail Dawes, Jan. 31, 1750-1

Isaac Tirrell of A. & Lidia Dawes of Bridgewater,

May 19, 1757

Robert Townsend, Jr., & Hepzebah Jackson, May 26, 1757

Noah Gurney & Ruth Pool, Dec. 15, 1757

William Wethrell of Hanover & Sarah Pilsbury,

Dec. 29, 1757

Joseph Gurney & Sarah Shaw, Sept. 8, 1758

Samuel Porter, Jr., of Bridgewater & Hannah Green,

Sept. 28, 1758

Ezekiel Lincoln & Miriam Tirrel, Nov. 9, 1758

Elijah Bate & Rachel Glyde, Dec. 2, 1758

Caleb Chard & Hannah Burrell, Dec. 21, 1758

Joshua Shaw, Jr., & Mary Pratt, Jan. 25, 1759

Jacob Thayer & Bathsheba Bate, Feb. 22, 1759

Jeremiah Asken (?) & Elisabeth Reed, June 21, 1759

Josiah Thomson & Mary Ha—y, Nov. 8, 1759

David Jones, Jr., of A. & Lidia White of Weymouth,

April 24, 1759

John Glyde & Silence Bate, Nov. 15, 1759

Benjamin Bate, Jr., & Betty Dyer, Nov. 15, 1759

John Shaw, 3d, & Mary Burrett, Nov. 22, 1759

William Reed, Jr., & Ruth Shaw, Dec. 27, 1759

Daniel Shaw & Rebecca Beal, Dec. 27, 1759

Daniel Hovey of Oxford & Content Ramsdell, Dec. 31, 1759

Ezekiel Townsend & Mary Hyde, Jan. 2, 1760

Obedience Reed & Content Lincoln, Jan. 4, 1760

Samuel Pool, 3d, & Ruth Fullerton, Jan. 24, 1760

Samuel Norton & Mary Porter, May 29, 1760

Samuel Brown & Deborah Torrey, Sept. 25, 1760

Barnabas Packard of Bridgewater & Sarah Ford,
Nov. 27, 1760
Gideon Randall of Hanover & Rebecca Pool, Dec. 18, 1760
Peter Nash & Sarah Torrey, May 7, 1761
Samuel Noyes, tertius, & Lois Whitmarsh, May 11, 1761
John Lincoln & Joanna Lincoln, May 21, 1761
Daniel Torrey of Taunton & Keziah Stockbridge,
May 27, 1761
Lemuel Bate & Lucretia Lincoln, May 28, 1761
Ensign Chubbuck & Sarah Tirrell, June 11, 1761
Benjamin Vining & Mehitable Brooks, Oct. 22, 1761
Moses Bate & Hannah Norton, Nov. 28, 1761
James Nash & Tamar Bate, Dec. 31, 1761
John Ramsdell & Eunice Cobb, Dec. 31, 1761
Isaac Stetson & Hannah Bicknell, Jan. 7, 1762
David Reed & Mercy Foord, April 22, 1762
Josiah Baker & Mary Bate, May 18, 1762
Joseph Taylor of Pembroke & Sarah Bate, Dec. 29, 1762
Abner Browne & Eunice Bate, Dec. 17, 1762
Jacob Porter, Jr., & Rachel Reed, Jan. 6, 1763
Ezra Tillson of Plinton & Rebecca Whitten, April 27, 1763
Jonathan Reed & Mary Tirrell, April 28, 1763
William Tirrell, Jr., & Mercy Reed, April 28, 1763
Samuel Reed & Mary Young, May 26, 1763
Solomon Clark & Betty Parkman, May 26, 1763
David Cobb-& Hannah Orcutt, June 11, 1763
Seth Copeland of Brantree & Rebecca Josselyn, June 30, 1763
John Wilks & Remember Gurney, July 21, 1763
Josiah Browne of A. & Molly Goosh of Milton, Oct. 6, 1763
John Tirrell, Jr., & Sarah Gurney, Oct. 27, 1763
John Browne & Lidia Hersey, Nov. 3, 1763
Benoni Gurney & Caroline Wilks, Nov. 24, 1763
Elisha Lincoln, tertius, & Tabitha Whitman, Dec. 24, 1763
Moses Reed & Phebe Tirrell, May 10, 1750
Joseph Richards & Lidia Tower, May 10, 1750
David Torrey & Deborah Briscow of Hanover, Feb. 20, 1751
Jacob Whitmarsh & Hannah Shaw, Nov. 7, 1751
Benjamin Gurney & Elisabeth Harden, Jan. 1, 1752

Joseph Mitchell of Kingston & Hannah Hersey, Jan. 11, 1753
Ephraim Spooner & Mary Jackson,   Nov. 16, 1752
Jacob Tirrell & Susannah Jackson,   Jan. 4, 1753
William Wales & Lidia Sprague,   Jan. 11, 1753
Noah Pratt & Mary Jones,   Jan. 11, 1753
Joseph Porter of Bridgewater & Elizabeth Burrel,
                                               Jan. 25, 1753
John Shaw & Susanna Richards,   Sept. 11, 1753
John Noyes, Jr., & Sarah Hearsey,   Oct. 4, 1753
Jacob White & Mary Hobart,   Oct. 18, 1753
Aaron Hobart & Elizabeth Pilsbury,   Nov. 1, 1753
Jacob Noyes & Anna Whitmarsh,   Jan. 24, 1754
David French, Jr., & Susanna Glyde,   Feb. 27, 1754
Christopher Dyer, Jr., & Betty Reed,   Dec. 19, 1754
Joshua How of Dighton & Hannah Reed,   Dec. 26, 1764
Joseph Hersey, Jr., & Mary Reed,   Feb. 1, 1755
Eliakim Briggs & Sarah Dyer,   Feb. 5, 1756
Nathaniel Cushing & Lidia Stetson of Pembroke,
                                               Feb. 15, 1758
Jacob Glyde & Silence Richards,   Jan. 24, 1755
Daniel Richards & Mary Tirrell,   April 10, 1755
Ebenezer Beal & Sarah Bate,   April 26, 1755
John Fullerton & Molly Noyes,   June 12, 1755
Elijah Reed & Sarah Reed,   July 10, 1755
Alexander Morrison of Bridgewater & Mary Asken (?),
                                               Aug. 21, 1755
Micah Samson & Hannah Pool,   Nov. 3, 1755
Joshua Pool & Mary Burrel,   Jan. 22, 1756
James Hearsey & Betty Noyes,   March 18, 1756
Samuel Noyes, Jr., & Bethiah Beal,   May 20, 1756
Edward Sears of Hallifax & Mary French,   May 28, 1756
Joshua Clap of Scituate & Lidia Short,   July 12, 1756
Jonathan Hearsey & Jane Noyes,   Dec. 9, 1756
John Tirrell & Dorcas Derby,   March 24, 1757
David Jones & Lidia Shaw,   March 21, 1757
Thomas Reed & Mary White,   May 11, 1757
Elisha Vining, Jr., & Deborah Fullington,   May 2, 1764
Thomas Townsend & Mercy Stetson,   March 14, 1764

Joseph Pool & Mary Pilsbury,   April 5, 1764
Andrew Thompson of Hallifax & Judith Noyes, May 3, 1764
Rev. Solomon Reed of Middleboro & Sarah Reed,
                                            July 12, 1764
Jacob Pool & Rachel Beal,   Oct. 26, 1764
Joshua Shaw, Jr., of A. & Naomi Bate of Weymouth,
                                            Nov. 22, 1764
Robert Garnet of Hingham & Mary Stockbridge,
                                            Nov. 26, 1764
Daniel Reed, 3d, & Anna Daws,   Dec. 5, 1764
David Hersey & Elisabeth Jenkins,   Dec. 27, 1764
John Porter & Deborah Shaw,   Jan. 17, 1765
Jonah Vining & Olive Leaverett,   Sept. 4, 1765
Solomon Reed & Mercy Tirrill,   Sept. 28, 1765
John Whitman of Bridgewater & Hannah Mitchel,
                                            Sept. 30, 1765
Capt. Daniel Reed of A. & Sarah Dawes of Bridgewater,
                                            Sept. 30, 1765
Benjamin Clark & Jane Burril,   Dec. 17, 1765
Noah Porter & Mary Norton,   Feb. 2, 1766
Jacob Dyer & Abigail Reed,   Feb. 24, 1766
Benjamin Wood, Jr., of Weymouth & Abigail Sprague,
                                            May 1, 1766
Luke Ford & Hannah Reed,   May 1, 1766
Benjamin White of Weymouth & Anne White,   Aug. 2, 1766
Hezekiah Reed of Bridgewater & Deborah Turril,
                                            Aug. 21, 1766
Gideon Ramsdale & Ruth Palmer,   Sept. 11, 1766
George Asken & Joanna Pratt,   Oct. 20, 1766
William Waters of Hingham & Cloe Jones,   Nov. 2, 1766
Thomas Atwood & Phebe Glyde,   Nov. 2, 1766
William Lord & Elisabeth Vining,   Nov. 4, 1766
Mathew Tower & Lydia Beal,   Nov. 27, 1766
Adam Blancher of Weymouth & Huldah Pain,   Dec. 11, 1766
Samuel Whitman & Rhoda Parkman,   Dec. 23, 1766
Levi Stetson & Elisabeth Pratt,   Dec. 30, 1766
Nathan Noyes of A. & Elisabeth Phillips of Easton,
                                            May 18, 1768

11

Silas Gurney & Ruth Palmer,   Jan. 7, 1767
David Torrey & Lydia Shaw,   Jan. 22, 1767
Jeremiah White & Sarah Thayer,   Feb. 5, 1767
Jonathan Shaw, Jr., & June Bate,   July 30, 1767
Stephen Shaw & Dorothy Southgate,   Nov. 22, 1767
John Bicknell, 3d, & Prudence White,   Nov. 26, 1767
Joseph Pool of Weymouth & Mehitable Jackson, Dec. 3, 1767
John Ford of A. & Lydia Agaur of Weymouth, Dec. 18, 1767
Joseph Joshlyn & Experience Reed,   Dec. 21, 1767
Robert Dawes & Lydia Tirrill,   Jan. 13, 1768
William Daniels of A. & Bethiah Pratt of Bridgewater,
                                               Jan. 14, 1768
Noah Pratt & Mary Whitmarsh,   March 17, 1768
Adam Reed & Silence Reed,   July 14, 1768
Thomas Hunt, of Weymouth & Experience Thayer,
                                               Oct. 27, 1768
Joseph Blancher of North Yarmouth & Mary Andrew,
                                               Aug. 8, 1768
Josiah Baker & Mercy French,   Sept. 20, 1768
Samuel Bate & Hannah Reed,   Nov. 17, 1768
Isaac Peterson of Scituate & Hannah Corthell, Dec. 29, 1768
Nehemiah Pratt of Weymouth & Ruth Torrey, Jan. 7, 1769
Elijah Shaw of Weymouth & Hannah Smith,   Jan. 12, 1769
David Whitmarsh & Peggy Bate,   Feb. 19, 1769
Isaac Tirrill, Jr., & Hannah Porter,   Oct. 25, 1770
Micah Stockbridge of Weymouth & Lydia White,
                                               Sept. 11, 1770
James Dyer & Martha Harden,   Dec. 27, 1770
Isaac Atwood of Plimouth & Hannah Chubbuck, Nov. 2, 1770
John Jeffers & Sarah Whalburn (Indians),   May 16, 1771
John Bicknell, 3d, & Rebecca Nash,   March 22 1771
David Jenkins, Jr., & Sarah Spooner,   Oct. 3, 1771
Winsor Jones & Sarah Cozens,   Oct. 3, 1771
Isaiah Jenkins & Huldah Gurney,   June 6, 1771
Zenas Cushman of Middleboro & Susanna Wild,
                                               May 10, 1772
Ezra Cushman & Susannah Shaw,   Nov. 10, 1772
Silas Reed & Experience Joselyn,   Dec. 6, 1772

Isaac Hersey & Mary Bicknell,   Dec. 29, 1772
Gideon Ramsdale & Sarah Nash,   Feb. 20, 1773
Daniel Lane & Bethiah Cushing,   Aug. 14, 1773
Levi Whitman & Bethiah Chubbuck,   May 4, 1773
Nathaniel Thomas of Pembroke & Betty House,
                                   Feb. 26, 1774
Barnabas Reed & Silence Sprague,   April 20, 1774
Luke Bicknell & Olive Gurney,   Dec. 1, 1774
Daniel Lane, Jr., & Hannah Andrews,   Feb. 20, 1774
Abijah Pool & Sarah Turrill,   Oct. 12, 1774
Joshua Whitman & Hannah Tirril,   Oct. 12, 1774
Jacob Gannet & Ruth Reed,   Aug. 12, 1774
Simeon Gannet of Bridgewater & Mary Reed, Nov. 26, 1775
Nathan Daws & Abigail White,   Nov. 20, 1775
Anthony Dike of Bridgewater & Mary Pool, April 12, 1775
John Norton of A. & Sarah Whitmarsh of Bridgewater,
                                   Dec. 21, 1775
Jacob Bicknell & Anna Harden,   April 15, 1775
Solomon Hersey & Judith Foster,   May 10, 1775
John Hunt & Sarah Cobb,   May 20, 1775
Lemuel Packard of Bridgewater & Sarah Hunt,
                                   Aug. 20, 1775
Thomas Pratt of North Yarmouth & Sarah Blanchard,
                                   May 2, 1775
Luther Lazell of Bridgewater & Sarah Hersey, July 1, 1776
Calvin Shaw & Hannah Shaw,   Nov. 15, 1776
Phillip Shaw & Susannah Lane,   Dec. 15, 1776
Benjamin Wood & Mercy Reed,   Dec. 20, 1776
James Gloyed & Mary Snow,   April 1, 1777
Seth Harris of A. & Mary Phillips of Bridgewater,
                                   May 8, 1777
James Porter & Mary Whitman,   Aug. 1, 1777
David Porter, Jr., & Lydia Hammon,   June 21, 1777
Ephraim Orcutt of Bridgewater & Abiah Thomas,
                                   July 23, 1777
Samuel Bate of Weymouth & Cela White, March 24, 1778
Jacob Thayer & Mary Orcut,   Dec. 21, 1778
Isaac Burrit & Grace Pratt,   June 20, 1778

Simeon Chubbuck & Lydia Pratt,   Jan. 24, 1778
Jonathan Marsh of Braintree & Meriam Reed, April 21, 1778
Samuel Gorham & Hannah Whitman,   March 2, 1778
Thomas Gurney of Bridgwater & Olive Hersey,
                      Dec. 26, 1778
Dr. David Jones & Elizabeth Hobart,   June 17, 1778
Benjamin Townsend & Eunice Stoddard,   Dec. 8, 1778
Eleazer Whitmarsh, Jr., & Mary Brown,   Feb. 20, 1779
Joseph Barn of Pembroke & Molly Hobart, March 3, 1779
Jepthah Pool & Olive Noyes,   April 16, 1779
James Reed & Ruth Nyles,   March 19, 1779
Jonathan Torrey & Abigail Howell,   Jan. 16, 1779
John Totman & Sarah Vining,   Sept. 7, 1779
Barzillai Whitten & Nabby Beals,   Dec. 29, 1779
Laban Stetson & Mary Stoddard,   Dec. 20, 1779
Elisha Lincoln & Tabitha Reed,   Oct. 5, 1779
John King & Hannah How,   May 12, 1779
Ebenezer Kingman Hunt & Mary Beals,   Nov. 5, 1779
Dr. Daniel How of Andover & Susanna Tirril, March 5, 1780
Jacob Bute & Lydia Gurney,   Nov. 9, 1780
Levi Cook & Sarah Pool,   Feb. 10, 1780
Nathaniel Nottage of Boston & Olive Burrit, Oct. 30, 1780
Jacob Nash & Lydia Cushman,   Nov. 3, 1780
Nathan Orcutt of Bridgewater & Eunice Whitmarsh,
                      May 29, 1780
James Rickard & Lydia Shaw,   May 1, 1780
Frederick Reed & Hannah Whitman,   Nov. 12, 1780
Joseph Ai—s of Boston & Sarah Burrit,   Dec. 21, 1780
Noah Pratt & Alce Jenkens,   Nov. 24, 1780
Micah Samson & Deborah Richmond,   Nov. 31, 1780
Daniel Bicknell & Hannah Reed,   Oct. 25, 1780
John Cobb & Anna White,   Oct. 1, 1781
Bela Dyer & Ruth Hunt,   Feb. 21, 1781
Asa Gurney & Mary Hersey,   April 26, 1781
William Hersey of Bridgewater & Naomi Hunt, Feb. 12, 1781
Stephen Hersey & Mary Hunt,   Oct. 9, 1781
Obadiah Stoddard of Scituate & Ceta Vining, Jan. 27, 1781
Thomas Tirrel & Mary Stoddard,   May 10, 1781

Bela Townsend & Hannah Burrel, Oct. 2, 1781
Ephraim Whitman & Mehitable Brown, Dec. 20, 1781
Ishmael Buker of Pembroke & Molly Buker, March 21, 1782
David Byrum of North Yarmouth & Abigail Townsend,
April 20, 1782
John Doty & Bathsheba Buker, March 20, 1782
Clerk Estes of Hanover & Ruth Spooner, Sept. 14, 1782
Asa Fullington & Mary Hunt, Jan. 29, 1782
Joseph Gurney, Jr., & Tamer Jackson, June 10, 1782
Nehemiah Noyes & Abigail Thomson, Jan. 21, 1782
Moses Orcutt of Weymouth & Silence Kingman,
Jan. 26, 1782
Seth Porter & Mary Cobb, March 6, 1782
Samuel Beals & Susannah Cobb, March 6, 1782
Jacob Reed, Jr., & Sarah Noyes, Feb. 21, 1782
Daniel Reed, Jr., & Anna Blanchard, April 4, 1782
Samuel Sprague & Mary Benner, April 4, 1782
Benjamin Vining & Cloe Lane, Nov. 20, 1782
Nathaniel Shaw & Betty House, June 14, 1782
Thomas Whitten & Jane Smith, Aug. 20, 1782
William Wales & Mary Noyes, Jan. 20, 1782
Benjamin Burril & Mary Dammons, Oct. 25, 1782
Samuel Thayer & Abigail Cobb, Aug. 26, 1782
David Edson of Bridgewater & Lydia Shaw, March 18, 1783
Noah Foord & Abigail Whitman, Dec. 11, 1783
Joseph Pool Gurney & Sarah Reed, Dec. 18, 1783
Noah Hersey of North Yarmouth & Ruth Beals,
Nov. 25, 1783
Matthew Noyes & Abi Randal, Feb. 6, 1783
John Nash & Molly Townsend, April 20, 1783
Thomas Reed, Jr., & Joanna Shaw, Jan. 24, 1783
Benjamin Thaxter & Sarah How, Jan. 10, 1783
Josiah Torrey, Jr., & Ruth Reed, March 20, 1783
Christopher Bate of A. & Mary Brown of Bridgewater,
May 12, 1784
Adams Bailey of Bridgewater & Ruth Reed, Oct. 20, 1784
Dr. Richard Briggs & Huldah Reed, Aug. 12, 1784
Ebenezer Whitmarsh & Mary Humphrey, Sept. 22, 1784

Abel Stodard & Susannah Harden,   May 20, 1784
Brackly Shaw & Anna Noyes,   Aug. 29, 1784
Jacob Reed & Anna Harden,   Dec. 2, 1784
Seth Jones Pratt & Hannah Hunt,   Jan. 21, 1784
David Pratt of Bridgewater & Phebe Atwood,   July 5, 1784
Zebulon Pain of A. & Hannah Terril of Braintree,
                                              Dec. 20, 1784
Josiah Shaw & Anna Noyes,   Nov. 16, 1784
David Noyes & Hannah Hunt,   Nov. 25, 1784
James Loud of Weymouth & Anna Dyke,   Dec. 14, 1784
Enoch Hunt of Weymouth & Lydia Wilks,   Dec. 1, 1784
Levi Garnet of Hingham & Mary Vining,   March 24, 1784
Job Beals & Elisabeth Totman,   Nov. 25, 1784
Barnabas French & Mary Foster,   Jan. 20, 1785
Benjamin Gardner & Molly Tirrel,   Sept. 25, 1785
Aaron Hobart, Jr., & Susannah Adams,   Oct. 12, 1785
Caleb Lovel & Ruth Fullington,   Jan. 1, 1785
Jonathan Nash & Rebecca Whitmarsh,   Feb. 15, 1785
James Nash & Sarah Brown,   Oct. 5, 1785
Whitcom Pratt & Ruth Lovel,   Dec. 5, 1785
Josiah Runels of Bridgewater & Mary Phillips
                                              Feb. 5, 1785
Ebid Vining & Abigail Curtis,   Oct. 29, 1785
Peter Benner & Abigail Hunt,   Sept. 20, 1785
Samuel Beals & Sarah Remington,   Oct. 7, 1785
Joshua Birrel of A. & Lydia Bonney of Bridgewater,
                                              Nov. 5, 1785
James Donnahue & Molly Nash,   Oct. 13, 1786
Joshua Hayward of Braintree & Submit Erskins,
                                              Dec. 4, 1786
Phillip Pratt & Rebeckah Shaw,   April 13, 1786
Benjamin Pool & Olive Porter,   May 17, 1786
James Pool of A. & Eunice Lazel of Bridgewater
                                              July 11, 1786
Obadiah Reed, Jr., & Elisabeth Richmon,   Nov. 5, 1786
Ichabod Taylor of Pembroke & Sarah Dyer,   Dec., 1786
Caleb Beal & Sarah Shaw,   March 13, 1786
Woodbridge Brown & Hannah Norton,   April 9, 1786

Benjamin Bate, 3d, & Susannah Reed,   Nov. 27, 1786
Hezekiah Foord of Comington & Huldah Cobb,   Feb., 1787
Silas French & Polly Brown,   April 12, 1787
Samuel Norton, Jr., & Silence Hersey,   Jan. 13, 1787
Luther Packard of Bridgewater & Abigail Thomas,
                                               April 13, 1787
Lot Whitmarsh & Susannah Pool,   May 17, 1787
John Gardner & Hannah Samson,   Aug. 18, 1785
Micah Joy & Mercy Tirril,   Nov. 24, 1785
Christopher Dyer & Deborah Reed,   March 30, 1786
Daniel Smith & Cloe Kingman,   June 13, 1786
Amos (?) Tirril & Lydia Pratt,   Oct. 2, 1786
Benjamin Beal & Mary Noyes,   June 21, 1787
Anthony Dwight & Violet Travellor,   July 25, 1787
Samuel Reed & Mary Pool,   Aug. 23, 1787
Asa Lewis of North Yarmouth & Sarah Hobart,   Oct. 7, 1787
Ezra Reed of Weymouth & Mary Lovell,   Nov. 6, 1787
Joseph Ramsdell of Bridgewater & Lydia Gloyed,
                                               Oct. 10, 1787
Rev. David Gurney of Middleboro & Jane Reed,
                                               Sept. 18, 1787
Nathaniel How & Ruth Colson,   Nov. 24, 1787
Lemuel Tirril, Jr., of A. & Pedy Trask of Braintree,
                                               Dec. 25, 1787
Joshua Reed & Deborah Noyes,   Jan. 7, 1788
Gideon Gurney & Rachel Gardner,   Feb. 21, 1788
Jonathan Reed & Deborah Porter,   May 5, 1788
Oliver Stetson & Abigail Lane,   June 1, 1788
James Chubbuck, Jr., & Sarah Stoddard,   June 22, 1788
Aminadab Hayward of Braintree & Isabel Gloyd,
                                               July 2, 1788
Levi Whitmarsh & Hannah Jackson,   July 7, 1788
Andrew Richmon of Middleboro & Susanna Porter,
                                               Aug. 7, 1788
Charles Lane & Rachel Jenkins,   Aug. 17, 1788
John Hobart & Charlotte Spear,   Oct. 12, 1788
Thomas Gurney & Mary House,   Nov. 27, 1788
Asa Shaw & Hannah Stetson,   Jan. 1, 1789

Benjamin Dyer & Experience Stetson, Jan. 5, 1789
Nathaniel Cushing of Pembroke & Mehitable Dodge,
Feb. 9, 1789
James White of Weymouth & Jerusha Hollas,
March 2, 1789
Nathaniel Eells Bennett & Dolly Bicknell, April 19, 1789

√ HANOVER.

June 14, 1727. "Parts of Abington and Scituate established as Hanover." First (Congregational) Church organized 1728. Baptist, 1806.

William Estes of H. & Elizabeth Stetson of Scituate,
Aug. 23, 1736
Andrew Linsey & Ruth Parrish, both of Pembroke,
Sept. 30, 1736
John Barker of H. & Grace Turner of Scituate, June 1, 1737
Ebenezer Rogers & Sarah Stetson, both of Marshfield,
June 29, 1738
Ebenezer Woodword & Hannah Stetson, July 4, 1739
Shedreck Keen & Elizabeth Turner, July 8, 1740
Caleb Rogers of Scituate & Mary Harlow, July 2, 1741
James Hanks of Pembroke & Abigail Phillips of Bridge-
water, June 30, 1742
Theophilus Cushing & Hannah White, both of Pem-
broke, Jan. 27, 1742
Silas Stetson & Mary Bracket, both of Scituate, Jan. 11, 1743
Joshua Staples of H. & Elizabeth Conaway of Pem-
broke, Jan. 29, 1744
Ebenezer Record & Joanna Bowls, both of Pembroke,
March 7, 1744
Prince Palmer of Scituate & Ruth Bowker, Sept. 19, 1746
Josiah Ripley & Alice Stetson, March 29, 1744
Eleazer Donham of Plymouth & Elizabeth Conner,
April 28, 1744
Jesse Torrey & Mary Baker, Dec. 6, 1744

* Daniel Cothorel of Bridgewater & Hannah Rose,

May 31, 1746

* Daniel Corthrel of Bridgewater & Hannah Rose,

May 13, 1746

Seth Woodward & Mary Cornish, Aug. 13, 1750

Edward Dillingham of H. & Marcy Doty of Scituate,

Aug. 5, 1751

Andrew Alden & Rebecca Stanford, both of Duxborough, Nov. 25, 1751

John Bearse & Abigail Holmes, both of Kingston,

July 12, 1753

Amos Silvester & Desire Rose, Jan. 19, 1757

Samuel Barstow, Jr., & Hulda House, Dec. 27, 1757

Seth Bates & Ann Neal, both of Scituate, Dec. 21, 1757

James Barstow of Pembroke & Rhoda House, Feb. 20, 1757

Joshua Stetson of Scituate & Lillis Stetson, July 8, 1747

William Curtis, Jr., & Martha Man, Nov. 13, 1747

Henchman Silvester & Sarah Stockbridge, Feb. 24, 1747

Jeremiah Hall & Elizabeth Bailey, Jr., Dec. 22, 1748

Eliezer Curtiss & Elizabeth Randal, Feb. 2, 1748

Windsor Jonas (negro) & Mary Ned, March 9, 1748

Oliver Winslow of Scituate & Bethiah Prior, Dec. 5, 1749

John Good of Bridgewater & Rachel Curtiss, Oct. 26, 1749

Benjamin Mann, Jr., & Abigail Gill, Nov. 23, 1749

Joshua Whiton of Hingham & Silence Forres, Dec. 7, 1749

Joshua Briant of Scituate & Elizabeth Perry, Feb. 19, 1749

Joseph Soper of Scituate & Ruth Curtis, May 9, 1750

Thomas Hubbart of Abington & Jane Bailey, July 5, 1750

Caleb Sylvester & Desire Stetson, Nov. 1, 1750

Jack & Bilhas (servants of Mr. Joseph Tilden), Nov. 8, 1750

William Gold, Jr., of Bridgewater & Mary Curtiss, Jr.,

Dec. 25, 1751

Benamin Curtiss & Ruth Man, Jan. 6, 1752

Edmund Sylvester & Elizabeth Bass, Jan. 30, 1752

Bezaleel Palmer of Scituate & Sarah Ells, April 8, 1752

John Shaw, Jr., of Abington & Martha Studley, April 16, 1752

---

* As written.

Joseph Dunbar of Halifax & Zerviah Lambert, June 3, 1752
Jeremiah Stetson & Lucy Bates, Jan. 3, 1753
Joseph Curtiss, Jr., & Abigail Soaper, Jan. 13, 1753
Isaac Hatch & Hannah Randall, May 21, 1753
Richard Baker of Scituate & Phebe Hill, July 12, 1753
Richard Hill & Hannah Torrey, Aug. 30, 1753
Jacob Silvester & Mary Bates, Jr., Nov. 5, 1753
Marlborough Turner of Scituate & Mary Curtiss,
Nov. 26, 1753
Jeremiah Hatch & Abigail DeCrow, Dec. 30, 1753
Reuben Curtiss & Mary Randall, Dec. 27, 1753
Thomas Barstow & Sarah Studly, Jan. 24, 1754
John Robinson of Plymouth & Elizabeth Studley,
Feb. 12, 1754
Seth Harden of Pembroke & Susanna Taylor, Dec. 26, 1754
Joseph House & Sage Randall, Feb. 13, 1755
Daniel Tower of Hingham & Persis Curtiss, Feb. 26, 1755
Thomas Pincheon, Jr., of Scituate & Anna Taylor,
Feb. 27, 1755
John Ruggles, Jr., of Scituate & Susannah Barstow,
March 1, 1775
Elijah (?) Waters of Hingham & Mehitable Curtiss,
March 31, 1755
Charles Barker & Susannah Estes, Aug. 16, 1756
Abner Curtiss & Rebecca Man, Nov. 6, 1756
Joshua Keen (?) of Pembroke & Abigail Eames, Nov. 6, 1756
Lawrence Ekings (?) & Sylvester Howland, Sept. 14, 1758
Michael Jackson of Abington & Thankful Studley,
Feb. 15, 1759
George Bennet of Abington & Hannah North—els,
April 5, 1759
William Norton of Abington & Sarah Sylvester,
Nov. 22, 1759
Thomas Hill of Pembroke & Mary Wardell, Nov. 29, 1759
Elisha Curtis of Scituate & Betty Studley, Jan. 15, 1760
Michael Sylvester & Ruth Turner, Jan. 17, 1760
Elisha House & Orphan (?) Peterson, Jan. 23, 1760
Robert Gardner, Jr., of Hingham & Sarah Mann,
June 5, 1760

Joshua Baker of Rochester & Lidia Clark,   Aug. 3, 1760

David Cudworth of Scituate & Rebecca Stetson,

                             Nov. 27, 1760

Joseph Bates & Elisabeth Curtis,   Jan. 8, 1761

Thomas Rose, Jr., & Rhoda Rogers,   Nov. 12, 1761

Joseph House & Hannah Randall,   May 25, 1761

Nathaniel Turner of Pembroke & Luscinda Turner,

                             Sept. 7, 1761

Abner Sylvester & Susannah Stetson,   Dec. 3, 1761

John Stetson & Thankful Curtis,   Dec. 3, 1761

Stevens Hatch & Ruth Prior,   Dec. 3, 1761

John Wetherell & Content Connenay,   Dec. 17, 1761

Joshua Curtis & Abigail House,   Dec. 17, 1761

Joshua Dwell & Avis Ramsdell,   Dec. 24, 1761

Theophilus Wetherell & Freelove Stetson, Dec. 31, 1761

Gideon Studley & Rosamond Church,   Jan. 14, 1762

Zachariah Curtis of Scituate & Lidia Palmer, Jan. 21, 1762

Seth Bailey & Lidia Barstow,   Feb. 11, 1762

Daniel Alden of Stafford, Ct., & Rebecca Curtis,

                         March 30, 1762

Amos Berry & Sarah Peters,   April 8, 1762

Job Young & Betty Stockbridge,   June 6, 1762

Jonathan Pratt & Lucy Church,   Dec. 30, 1762

Mark Rogers & Mary Bray,   Aug. 11, 1763

Seth Latham of Bridgewater & Rachel House, Nov. 24, 1763

Leonard Hill of Pembroke & Jerusha Bates, Jan. 19, 1764

Daniel Crooker & Abigail Studley, both of Pembroke,

                          Feb. 16, 1764

Adam Curtis & Betty Stetson, Jr.,   March 25, 1758

Nicholas Whitman of Bridgewater & Mary House,

                         Nov. 16, 1758

Joseph Soper & Relief Curtis,   July 30, 1759

Charles Randall & Experience Brooks, both of Scituate,

                         Sept. 4, 1760

Williams Simmons & Hannah Peirce, both of Duxboro,

                         Dec. 4, 1760

Amos Garnett of Abington & Betty Warren, June 29, 1764

Gershom House & Deborah Curtis,   July 26, 1764

Seth Wetherell & Hannah Clark, Jr.,	Nov. 29,	1764
James Still & Sarah Toto (Indians),	Dec. 20,	1764
David Ripley & Priscilla Dunbar,	Jan. 3,	1765
Joseph Studley & Rebecca Stetson, Jr.,	Jan. 10,	1765
John Curtis, Jr., & Anna Curtis,	March 28,	1765

Hezekiah Bunker of Sherborn, in Nantucket, & Margaret Fitz-Gerald, April 7, 1765

Seth Stetson, Jr., & Lucy Studley,	April 11,	1765
Benjamin Stetson & Bradbury Eelles,	April 30,	1765
Job Silvester & Margaret Stetson,	July 18,	1765
Timothy Church & Elisabeth Rose,	Sept. 5,	1765
Othniel Pratt & Deborah Hatch,	Nov. 11,	1765
Joseph Nicholson & Lurana Ned (Indians),	Jan. 19,	1766
Timothy Rose & Lidia Soper,	Jan. 23,	1766

Thomas Collamer of Scituate & Elisabeth Turner,
Jan. 23, 1766

John Chapman, Jr., of Pembroke & Ruth Torrey,
March 13, 1766

Solomon Bryant of Plimton & Elisabeth Curtis, May 1, 1766

Abner Curtis of H. & Sarah Foord of Scituate, July 3, 1766

Jesse Curtis of H. & Hannah Peterson of Scituate,
July 27, 1766

Lemuel Bates & Mercy Wetherell,	Oct. 16,	1766
Samuel Stetson & Alice Rogers,	Dec. 14,	1766
Joseph Ramsdel, 2d, & Mercy Bates,	Jan. 1,	1767
Daniel Parkman of Abington & Hannah House,	Jan. 29,	1767
Thomas Bates & Hannah Torrey,	Jan. 29,	1767
Samuel Harden of Pembroke & Mary Rogers,	April 2,	1767
Elijah Cushing of Pembroke & Mary Turner,	Jan. 18,	1768

Ebenezer Edy of Pembroke & Deborah Palmer,
March 17, 1768

Atherton Wales & Ruth Turner, Jr.,	April 3,	1768
Benjamin Clarke & Tabitha Chubbuck,	April 21,	1768
Abner Bourn & Mary Torrey,	Dec. 29,	1765

Samuel Hill & Lidia Ramsdel, both of Pembroke,
Feb. 4, 1768

Seth Bailey & Alice Neal,	July 28,	1768
Samuel Hayford & Diadama Bishop,	Nov. 28,	1768

Cornelius Turner & Michal Sylvester,   Dec. 8, 1768
Thomas Hatch & Susanna Curtis,   Jan. 12, 1769
Joseph Nicholson & Desire Peten (?) (Indians), Jan. 26, 1769
Josiah Man, Jr., of Scituate & Sage Clark,   March 2, 1769
Samuel Brimhall of Abington & Hannah Ramdell,
                                              May 4, 1769
Thomas Willet of Boston & Hannah Lambert, May 11, 1769
Levi Corthell of Abington & Deborah Curtis,   Oct 12, 1769
Elisha Foster, Jr., of Scituate & Grace Bartow, Oct. 19, 1769
James Orr & Susanna Tilden,   Feb. 8, 1770
Nicholas Bowker & Tamsen Woods,   March 22, 1770
Thomas Curtis, Jr., & Abigail Studley,   June 6, 1770
Bosworth Collier of Hull & Anna House,   Jan. 31, 1771
Jonathan Bates of Rochester & Ruth Stetson, Feb. 11, 1771
Asa Turner & Abigail Man,   June 30, 1771
Daniel Bartow & Betty Tilden,   July 4. 1771
David Torrey & Susanna Rogers,   Sept. 5, 1771
Gamaliel Bates of H. & Mary Carver of Pembroke,
                                              Sept. 5, 1771
James Curtis & Zilpha Stetson,   Oct. 17, 1771
Lot Ramsdell & Rache Torrey,   Nov. 21, 1771
John Barns, Jr., of Hingham & Martha Curtis, 3d,
                                              Feb. 16, 1772
Batcheler Wing & Elisabeth Barker,   Sept. 13, 1770
Caleb Howland of Plymouth & Mary Silvester, Jan. 20, 1785
George Sterling & Ruth Bailey,   March 13, 1785
Morgan Brewster & Martha Stetson,   March 31, 1785
Homar Whiting & Anna Studley,   May 8, 1785
Nathaniel Hill of Pembroke & Mary Ramsdel,   Oct. 4, 1785
John Read Josselyn & Nabby Studley,   Nov. 1. 1785
Clemond Bates, Jr., & Rebecca Stetson,   Dec. 25, 1785
Samuel Baker Perry of Pembroke & Anna Bates, Feb. 2, 1786
Jabez Bates & Elisabeth Barker,   April 11, 1786
Asa Whiting & Debby Dwelly,   April 13, 1786
Caleb Whiting & Susanna Gillman,   April 23, 1786
Nathaniel Barstow of Scituate & Elisabeth Cushing,
                                              Aug. 31, 1786
Paul Webb of Scituate & Deborah Silvester,   Jan. 25, 1787

Dr. Nathaniel Parker of Salem & Mara Mellen,

March 12, 1787

Joseph Ramsdell, Jr., & Elisabeth Ellis, May 17, 1787

Capt. Albert Smith of Pembroke & Anna Lenthel
Eells, Aug. 23, 1787

Robert Salmon & Mary Baldwin, Nov. 1, 1787

Joseph Daws Ramsdale of H. & Eunice Nash of Scituate, Nov. 29, 1787

Oliver Bonney & Cythia Silvester Josselyn, Nov. 29, 1787

Elisha Curtis, Jr., of Scituate & Hannah Curtis, 3d,

Nov. 29, 1787

Shubael Mann, Jr., & Abigail Stetson, Jan. 27, 1788

John Burden Barstow of Scituate & Betsy Eells, Feb. 7, 1788

Abel Whiting & Priscilla Peaks, Feb. 19, 1784

Ezra Briggs & Margaret Curtis, May 13, 1784

Capt. Luther Bailey & Sylvester Little, Oct. 21, 1784

Benjamin Stetson & widow Betty Young, Nov. 8, 1784

Josiah Chamberlain & Lucy Pratt, Nov. 25, 1784

Levi Bates & Lydia Silvester, Dec. 30, 1784

Shubael Munro, Jr., & Abigail Stetson, Jan. 27, 1788

Ezekiel Turner Hatch & Hannah Bailey, May 8, 1788

Benjamin Dwelly of Pembroke & Bradbury Stetson,

Dec. 7, 1788

Elijah Stetson & Susannah Curtis, April 9, 1772

Benjamin Thomas of Marshfield & Betty Robbins,

April 12, 1772

Thomas Stetson & Olive Man, June 18, 1772

Elisha Witherel of Chesterfield & widow Rebecca
Studley, Dec. 30, 1772

Stephen Mott of Scituate & Nabby Staples, Feb. 25, 1773

Isaac Josselyn of Pembroke & Lois Ramsdale, Sept. 12, 1773

Joseph Bates, Jr., & Tamzin Bowker, Dec. 23, 1773

Oliver Pool & Sarah Ramsdel, Jan. 13, 1774

Charles Tolman of Scituate & Mary Sylvester, May 19, 1774

William Stockbridge & Ruth Bailey, Oct. 9, 1774

James Cole, Jr., of Scituate & Lucy House, Nov. 6, 1774

William Curtis, Jr., & Deborah Curtis, Jan. 5, 1775

James Torrey & Lydia Caswell, March 16, 1775

Stephen Damon of Scituate & Rebecca Curtis,   July 6, 1775
Joseph Bicknell, Jr., of Abington & Nabby Turner,
                                              Nov. 8, 1775
Elisha Silvester, Jr., of Scituate & Abigail Palmer,
                                              Nov. 23, 1775
James Clark, Jr., of H. & Deborah Cudworth of Pem-
      broke,   Nov. 23, 1775
Abel Curtis & Ruth Turner, Jr.,   Feb. 12, 1776
Ebenezer Wing, Jr., & Betty Oldham,   April 4, 1776
John Oldham of Pembroke & Lydia Silvester, April 28, 1776
Elijah Gilbert & widow Hannah Randall,   June 13, 1776
Adam Perry of Pembroke & Elisabeth House,   Oct. 20, 1776
Tilson Gould of Pembroke & Mary Hatch,   Dec. 2, 1776
Malbrey Turner & Abigail Curtis,   Jan. 1, 1777
David Torrey of H. & Miriam Manson of Scituate,
                                              Jan. 2, 1777
Robert White & Anna House,   March 20, 1777
Ellis Damon of Scituate & Huldah Curtis,   May 1, 1777
Elisha Curtis of Scituate & Elisabeth Church,   July 20, 1777
Nathaniel House & Lillis Palmer,   Aug. 29, 1777
Amos Perry of Scituate & Sarah Josselyn,   Sept. 7, 1777
Joseph Waterman, Jr., of Hallifax & Lucy Josselyn
      Munro,   Nov. 18, 1777
Joseph Torrey & Mary Torrey,   Jan. 15, 1778
Jacob White of Abington & Hannah Wetherel Eells,
                                              March 12, 1778
Abner House & Abigail Silvester,   April 30, 1778
Dr. Gad Hitchcock of Pembroke & Sage Bailey,
                                              July 9, 1778
William Graham of Spencer & Hannah Hatch,   Sept. 6, 1778
Samuel Whitten & Elisabeth Gardner,   Sept. 6, 1778
Richard Eustis & Mercy Ramsdall,   Nov. 4, 1778
Isaac Turner, Jr., & Mary Whitten,   Dec. 20, 1778
Joseph Curtis & Lydia Oldham,   Dec. 24, 1778
Solomon Shaw, Jr., of Abington & Betty Dillingham,
                                              Jan. 14, 1779
Adams Bailey of Bridgewater & Mary Little,   June 17, 1779
William Morrice of Scituate & Rhoda House, June 27, 1779

Ephraim Palmer of Scituate & Desire Oldham, July 15, 1779
Luther Robbins & Anna Barker,   Sept. 16, 1779
David Stockbridge, Jr., & Ruth Cushing,   Dec. 23, 1779
Caleb Rogers, Jr., & widow Hannah Bates,   Dec. 26, 1779
Ephraim Stetson & Olive Ramsdell,   Feb. 17, 1780
Samuel Gross & Betty Torrey,   Feb. 24, 1780

✓ SCITUATE.

July 1, 1633. "The brooke at Scituate is mentioned." October 4, 1636. "The towne of Scituate (viz., the purchasers and freemen) was authorized to dispose of lands." March 7, 1643. Bounds were established. First Church (Unitarian) organized 1634. Congregational, 1635.

John Dwelley (?) & Rachel Bu——,   Jan. 4, 1692-3
Robert Stetson, son of Joseph, & Mary Callomer,
                                                 Jan. 12, 1692-3
Samuel Stodder & Elisabeth ————,   March 1, 1692-3
John Buck of Scituate & Sarah Dotey of Plymouth,
                                                 April 26, 1693
Elisha Prouty & Martha Silvester,   March 17, 1747
Thomas Bourne of Sandwich & Mary Randal, Nov. 26, 1747
John Briggs & Abigail Neal,   May 11, 1747
Zachary Damon, Jr., & Anna Lenthel Els,   Nov. 30, 1748
George Philips of Middleton & Hannah Phillips, May 5, 1748
James Thomas & Ruth Brooks,   May 12, 1748
Samuel Oakman of Marshfield & Deborah Turner,
                                                 June 9, 1748
Josiah Lothrop of Bridgewater & Sarah Church,
                                                 June 21, 1749
Isaac Stetson & Ruth Prouty,   Nov. 16, 1749
Samuel Cushing, Esq., of Hingham & Mrs. Hannah
     Sparhawk,   Aug. 10, 1749
Thomas Merritt & Jane Nichols,   Nov. 2, 1749
James Barrel & Deborah Barker,   April 5, 1750
Mr. Lemuel Briant of Braintree & Mrs. Abigail Bar-
     stow,   Aug. 23, 1749

Elisha West of Pembroke & Mehitable Northy, Nov. 30, 1749
Mr. Ebenezer Pierpont of Roxbury & Mrs. Sarah Cush-
 ing, Aug. 16, 1750
Mr. Shearjashub Bourn & Mrs. Deborah Barker,
 June 6, 1750
Nathaniel Church, 3d, & Mehitable North, Aug. 16, 1750
Ezra Randal & Margaret Foster, Nov. 14, 1751
Elisha Silvester, Jr., & Grace Ruggles, Dec. 17, 1751
Jonah Stetson, Jr., & Elizabeth Hatch, Dec. 19, 1751
Lemuel Ford of Marshfield & Priscilla Turner, Feb. 20, 1752
Nehemiah Prouty & Lettice Taylor, Aug. 3, 1752
Luke Bowker & Joanna Dunbar, Dec. 14, 1752
Abijah Whitten of Hingham & Mary Lambert, Jan. 22, 1753
William Gray & Abigail Perry, Jan. 30, 1753
William Davis of Freetown & Surviah Hatch, March 1, 1753
Nehemiah Liscom of Stoughton & Rachel Clap,
 March 26, 1753
Nathaniel Brooks, Jr., & Sarah Collamer, April 26, 1753
Cornelius Brigs & Jerusha Church, May 23, 1753
Isaiah Stodder & Mary Bowker, Dec. 5, 1754
Nehemiah Hatch & Keziah Torrey, June 17, 1755
William Corlile, Jr., & Elizabeth Davis, Nov. 17, 1755
Benjamin Curtis, Jr., & Mary Cole, Dec. 3, 1755
Benjamin Stetson of Hingham & Lebiah Elmes, Feb. 5, 1756
Thomas Young & Jael Whitten, Feb. 19, 1756
Elijah Curtis & Abigail Soul, June 28, 1756
Edmond Bowker & Lidia Lambert, Dec. 2, 1756
Anthony Eames of Marshfield & Hannah Els, Jan. 4, 1757
Joseph Clap, Jr., & Elisabeth Turner, Aug. 22, 1757
Gideon Stetson, Jr., & Elisabeth Perry, Nov. 14, 1757
Anthony Collamer & Mercy Barker, Dec. 13, 1757
Galen Clap & Patience Brooks, Jan. 13, 1758
John Elmes & Betty Perry, Jan. 19, 1758
Nicholas Vinal & Desire Cole, July 13, 1758
Benjamin Briant & Ruaby Perry, July 16, 1758
Nathaniel Church & Mary Curtis, Nov. 2, 1758
John Jacob & Hannah Tolman, Nov. 2, 1758
William Baker of Marshfield & Hannah Lincoln, Nov. 2, 1758

Mordecai Lincoln of Taunton & Abiah Els,	Nov. 30,	1758
Simeon Swift & Cateron Turner,	Dec. 26,	1758
Rev. Samuel Baldwin of Hanover & Mrs. Hannah Cushing,	Jan. 4,	1759
Jonathan Brown, Jr., & Mary Cowing,	Nov. 1,	1759
Michael Clap & Sarah Lambart,	Nov. 20,	1759
Joshua Gardner of Hingham & Mary Totman,	Nov. 29,	1759
Joseph Elmes, Jr., & Mary Lincoln,	Nov. 29,	1759
Seth Taylor of Pembroke & Martha Stetson,	Nov. 29,	1759
Josiah Litchfield, Jr., & Abigail Studley,	Dec. 24,	1759
Elisha Jacob & Lucy Randal,	May 1,	1760
Joseph Bowker & Elizabeth Cowing,	May 26,	1760
Israel Vinal, Jr., (?) & Mercy Cushing,	Sept. 25,	1760
Dwelly Clap & Elisabeth Elmes,	June 5,	1760
Lott Silvester of Marshfield & Lidia Ewel (?),	Oct. 5,	1760
Aaron Clark of Wells & Betty Jones,	Oct. 24,	1760
James Turner, Jr., & Deborah Lincoln,	Oct. 24,	1760
Daniel Thomas of Marshfield & Sarah Ewel,	Nov. 13,	1760
Solomon Bates of Hanover & Equila Bates,	Nov. 20,	1760
Jonathan Hatch & Lucy Cole,	Nov. 27,	1760
William Perry & Lidia Turner,	Nov. 27,	1760
Thomas Young & Hannah Barker,	Dec. 11,	1760
Solomon Brigs of Norton & Remember Litchfield,	Dec. 15,	1760
Elijah Crooker of Marshfield & Egathy Hatch,	Dec. 18,	1760
James Stockbridge of S. & Martha Dunbar of Hingham,	Feb. 12,	1761
Samuel Tower (?) of Hingham & Hannah Collamer,	Feb. 12,	1761
Ignatius Vinal & Patience Elmes,	April 2,	1761
Job Cowing, Jr., & Zillah Perry,	May 20,	1761
Colburn Barrel & Desire Bowker,	May 28,	1761
Daniel Damon, Jr., & Hannah Bowker,	May 28,	1761
Thomas Josselyn of Hanover & Patience Barker,	June 10,	1761
John Stetson, Jr., & Bathsheba Dunbar,	Sept. 10,	1761
Elisha Lapham & Elisabeth Cole,	Oct. 15,	1761
Thomas Rogers, Jr., of Marshfield & Submit Hatch,	Nov. 19,	1761

Jonathan Hatch & Rachel Curtis, Nov. 21, 1761
Thomas Southworth of Duxboro & Anna Hatch,
              Nov. 26, 1761
Joshua Richmond of Dartmouth & Elizabeth Cush-
 ing, Nov. 26, 1761
Israel Cowing of Rochester & Elizabeth Cudworth,
              Jan. 5, 1762
David Jones of Hingham & Eunice Davis, May 27, 1762
Joseph Bonney of Pembroke & Elizabeth Delano,
              May 15, 1762
Samuel Boe (negro) & Hannah Richard, July 15, 1762
Seth Byram of Bridgewater & Sarah Vinal, Aug. 12, 1762
Joseph Lambert & Hannah Brooks, Nov. 16, 1762
Stephen Stetson & Experience Palmer, Dec. 19, 1762
Seth Hammond & Mary Buck, Feb. 17, 1763
David Merrit & Sarah Curtis, Feb. 17, 1763
John James, Jr., & Hannah Jacob, March 24, 1763
Benjamin Stetson & Mercy Turner, June 14, 1763
Rev. Ebenezer Gay of Suffield & Mrs. Mary Cushing,
              Nov. 10, 1763
Benjamin Bowker & Hannah Sparhawk, Nov. 10, 1763
Israel Chittenden & Abigail Turner, Nov. 24, 1763
Elisha Turner & Abigail Foster, Dec. 29, 1763
Jehiel Simmons of Duxboro & Rhoda Stetson, April 10, 1764
Seth House of Hanover & Bathsheba Foster, May 31, 1764
John Colman, Jr., & Sarah Hammon, June 7, 1764
Asher Sprague of Hingham & Susanna Buck, July 12, 1764
William Stetson & Mary Lincoln, July 19, 1764
Mr. Abraham Burbank of Suffield & Mrs. Bethiah
 Cushing, Nov. 1, 1764
Anthony Waterman of Hallifax & Sarah Curtis,
              Nov. 15, 1764
William Gardner of Hingham & Thankful Collamer,
              Dec. 5, 1764
John Cushing, Jr., & Mary Jacob, Dec. 6, 1764
Joseph Woodworth & Sarah Jones, Oct. 7, 1743
David Studley, Jr., & Elizabeth Curtis, Oct. 18, 1744
Isaac Lincoln & Mary Neal, Oct. 10, 1749

James Woodworth & Mary Vinal,	Feb. 15, 1749
William Rogers & Lidia Barker,	July 24, 1756
Robert Lenthel Eels of Hanover & Ruth Coplen (?),	
	Dec. 1, 1757
David Studley & Anna Price,	Dec. 26, 1757
Benjamin Briggs & Rebecca Curtis,	Aug. 1, 1758
Ezekiel Merrit & Rachel Vinal,	Aug. 3, 1758
Henry Ewel & Mary Benson Studly,	Nov. 16, 1758
Nathaniel Pitcher & Experience Jones,	Feb. 5, 1761
Jacob Lincoln & Susanna Marble,	March 17, 1762
Timothy Hunt & Sarah Young, both of Boston,	July 26, 1762
Henry Merrit & Ann Studley,	March 17, 1763
Joshua Rogers, Jr., & Sarah Nash,	March 15, 1764
Hezekiah Hatch & Mary Cudworth,	June 23, 1755
Joseph Nash, Jr., & Thankful Hammon,	Dec. 16, 1755
Simeon Turner & Sarah Buck,	Jan. 20, 1756
John Studly & Mary Benson Jones,	Feb. 10, 1756
Robert Peirce & Mercy Hatch,	March 15, 1756
Peleg Simmons & Ruth Bowker,	July 6, 1758
James Cudworth of Freetown & Ann Briant,	Dec. 7, 1758
Constant Church & Hannah Franklin,	May 24, 1759
John Curtis & Sarah Jenkins,	June 3, 1762
Abner Stetson & Deborah Stetson,	Oct. 7, 1762
Benjamin Perry & Mary Stetson,	June 16, 1763
Benjamin Lapham of Marshfield & Content Barker,	
	Sept. 26, 1763
Joseph Vinal & Thankful Vinal,	Nov. 8, 1763
Nathaniel Clark of Hanover & Alice Healy,	Nov. 17, 1763
Timothy White, Jr., & Caterine Elmes,	Dec. 29, 1763
Abiezer Turner & Hannah Thrift (?),	Jan. 5, 1764
James Briggs & Rhoda Nash,	July 17, 1764
William Cole & Rachel Buck,	Aug. 21, 1764
Jacob Vinal, 3d, & Lidia Jenkins,	Oct. 4, 1764
King Lapham of Marshfield & Lucy Barker,	Nov. 8, 1764
Ezra Brigs & Lidia Neal,	Dec. 9, 1764
James Bates of Hingham & Abigail Litchfield,	Jan. 17, 1765
Nehemiah Curtis & Joanna Hammon,	Jan. 23, 1765
Jonathan Vinal & Chloe Pope,	Feb. 11, 1765

James Silvester & Anna Brooks, Dec. 20, 1764
Joseph White of Marshfield & Temperance Clap,
Feb. 28, 1765
Samuel Brooks & Elisabeth Gray, March 14, 1765
John Foster & Sarah Jacob, May 23, 1765
Jabez Standley & Mary Thrift, June 2, 1765
Ezekiel Turner & Leah Simmons, June 6, 1765
Joseph Carrel & Tamer Furrows, Oct. 2, 1765
Moses Dunbar, transient, & Deborah Prouty, Oct. 28, 1765
Benjamin Bass of Hanover & Mercy Tilman, Oct. 28, 1765
John Pincin & Judah Pincin, Jan. 9, 1766
Thomas Jenkins, Jr., & Hannah Clap, Feb. 11, 1766
Lothrop Leichfield & Rhoda Perry, Feb. 11, 1766
Noah Otis & Phebe Cushing, May 1, 1766
John Dorrittrey & Mary Murphrey, Aug. 11, 1766
Elisha Turner & Prudence James, Sept. 18, 1766
Abiel Turner, Jr., & Lurana Silvester, Nov. 13, 1766
Jabez Wilder, Jr., of Hingham & Martha Collamer,
Nov. 13, 1766
Dearing Jones & Hannah Ewell (?), Nov. 20, 1766
Seth Peine & Jemima Turner, Nov. 27, 1766
Thomas Tilden & Abigail Hatch, Dec. 4, 1766
Benjamin Thomas of Duxboro & Abigail Turner,
June 6, 1767
Joshua Lincoln & Anna Bryant, June 8, 1767
Peleg Bryant, Jr., & Lydia Collamer, Nov. 19, 1767
Aaron Magoon of Pembroke & Mary Church, Jan. 21, 1768
Constant Clapp & Rebecca Bailey, March 3, 1768
Nehemiah Randall & Rebecca Collamer, April 21, 1768
Silvanus Clapp & Elisabeth Brooks, June 9, 1768
Benjamin Clap & Sarah Ruggles, June 23, 1768
Gethelar Cowing & Lucy Hatch, July 11, 1768
Nehemiah Palmer & Abigail Barrel, July 14, 1768
Israel Damon & Lydia Rogers, Aug. 8, 1768
David Foster of Pembroke & Christian Farrow, Dec. 29, 1768
Elijah Curtis & Ziporah Randall, Jan. 5, 1769
John Rice & Molly Woodard, Feb. 2, 1769
Josiah Cushing, Jr., of Pembroke & Deborah Cush-
ing, Feb. 16, 1769

Samuel Dunbar of Hingham & Rhoda Cortherel,

    May 29, 1769

Joseph Brooks of Hanover & Lydia Stetson,   July 27, 1769

Shearjashub Bourn & Sarah Woodward,   Oct. 19, 1769

William Gorham of Barnstable & Temperance White,

    Oct. 26, 1769

Benjamin Delano & Mary Brooks,   Nov. 2, 1769

Adam Hunt of Braintrey & Hannah Stetson,

    March 29, 1770

Abner Pinim & Hannah Cowing,   April 22, 1770

Isaiah Wing of Hanover & Elisabeth Rose,   June 12, 1770

Simeon Prouty & Sarah Griffen,   July 19, 1770

Gersham Farrow of Kingston & Jemima Farrow,

    Sept. 13, 1770

Israel Sylvester, Jr., & Margaret Bowker,   Nov. 15, 1770

Joseph Benson & Susanna Clap,   Dec. 5, 1770

Benjamin Simons of Marshfield & Sarah Damon,

    Dec. 20, 1770

Isachar Cato (negro) & Dinah Compset (Indian), Jan. 3, 1771

Knight Brown & Priscella Beals,   Jan. 17, 1771

Hezekiah Stodder, Jr., & Lydia (Stodder ?),   Jan. 21, 1771

Charles Curtis & Lydia James,   Feb. 7, 1771

Amos Sprague of Hingham & Desire Stodder, Feb. 21, 1771

John Damon & Eunice Bowker,   April 11, 1771

Isaac Collier & Tamsen Hayden,   April 11, 1771

Zephaniah Hatch & Mary Vinal,   May 7, 1771

Solomon Lincoln & Deborah Randall,   May 26, 1771

George Cushing & Lydia Cushing,   June 19, 1771

Samuel Damon & Anna Bowker,   Sept. 5, 1771

David Jorden & Lydia Nu——lmon (?),   Sept. 8, 1771

Joseph Tolman & Bethia Turner,   Nov. 4, 1771

Thomas Tolman & Sarah Carman,   Jan. 15, 1772

Lemuel Mayho of Marshfield & Anna Mott,   June 18, 1772

John Beals of Hingham & Rhoda James,   July 1, 1772

Joshua Turner & Eunice James,   July 2, 1772

James Barrel & Martha Farrow,   Dec. 10, 1772

Thomas Sylvester, Jr., & Releife Jordan,   Jan. 18, 1773

David Farrow, Jr., of Hingham & Judeth Stodder,

    Jan. 28, 1773

David Kent & Lydia Damon,   Feb. 1, 1773
Gersham Bowker & Elisabeth Stetson,   Feb. 18, 1773
John Humphries & Mary Palmer,   March 9, 1773
Francis Cushing & Temperance Foster,   April 8, 1773
James Bates of Hingham & Abigail Leichfield, Jan. 17, 1765
Nehemiah Curtis & Joanna Hammond,   Jan. 23, 1765
Jonathan Vinal & Cloe Pope,   Feb. 11, 1765
Joseph Colman & Mercy Studley,   May 13, 1765
James Nash & Hopestill Agrey (?),   May 23, 1765
Timothy Cushing of Hingham & Desire Jenkins, June 4, 1765
Caleb Nichols & Meriam Nash,   July 8, 1765
William Hayden & Margaret Woodworth,   Oct. 10, 1765
Barnabas Leichfield & Lydia Partrick,   Oct. 24, 1765
Elisha Lapham & Sabre Hyland,   Jan. 8, 1766
Daniel Leichfield & Sarah Whitcomb,   Jan. 23, 1766
Gera Jenkins & Lillis Colman,   Feb. 6, 1766
William Gray of Boston & Sarah Hayden,   April 21, 1766
Samuel Stockbridge, Jr., & Sarah Leichfield,   May 29, 1766
Ezra Vinal & Lucy Nash,   June 5, 1776
Ephraim Leichfield & Penelope Leichfield,   June 30, 1766
Nathaniel Chubbuck of Warham & Martha Damon,
                                                        Oct. 20, 1766
Joshua Barker of Boston & Mary Copeland,   Oct. 28, 1766
John Mansail, Jr., & Sarah Price,   Nov. 5, 1766
William Hayden, Jr., & Sarah Wade,   Nov. 27, 1766
Elijah Stodder & Thankful Whitcomb,   Dec. 25, 1766
Joseph Nash, Jr., & Lucy Peaks,   Jan. 13, 1767
Joseph Cudworth of S. & Lydia Tower of Hingham,
                                                        Jan. 22, 1767
Samuel Lapham of Mansfield & Ruth Bryant, Jan. 29, 1767
William Downs of Boston & Ruth Morris,   Feb. 25, 1767
Jonathan Mann of S. & Mary Gilbert of Hingham,
                                                        June 22, 1767
Benjamin Vinal & Sarah Merrit,   Dec. 1, 1768
James Merrit, Jr., & Mary Northey,   Dec. 1, 1768
Abner Dwelley, Jr., & Deborah House,   Jan. 26, 1769
Daniel Carloo & Deborah Price,   Feb. 16, 1769
Thomas Jenkins & Deborah Nash,   Feb. 28, 1769

Edsel Bates of Abington & Desire Haysen,　March 23, 1769
Benjamin Peine, Jr., & Priscella Wade,　March 23, 1769
Ebenezer Foster & Mary Jenkins,　March 30, 1769
John Elmes, Jr., & Molly Whitcomb,　May 22, 1769
Samuel Curtis & Rhoda Vinal,　Aug. 31, 1769
Micka Mott & Ruth Merritt,　Dec. 26, 1769
Elijah Orcutt of Abington & Prudence Hayden, Jan. 4, 1770
James Leichfield & Elisabeth Leichfield,　Jan. 9, 1770
John Rogers & Sarah Lambert,　March 26, 1770
Jacob Lincoln & Hannah Woodworth,　Aug. 2, 1770
Amasa Orcutt of Abington & Ann Mansail,　Aug. 8, 1770
Timothy Robins of Hanover & Mary Tilden,　Oct. 25, 1770
Thomas Whitten of Hanover & Rachel Peaks, Nov. 15, 1770
Samuel Jenkins, Jr., & Abigail Cole,　June 6, 1771
Belcher Clarke of Hanover & Ann Wade,　June 27, 1771
Levi Bates of Cohasset & Hannah Leichfield, Jan. 2, 1772
Thomas Osyer (?) of Marshfield & Martha Orcutt,
　　　　　　　　　　　　　　　　Jan. 30, 1772
Tenex (negro servant of Mrs. Holbrooke of Boston)
　　& Lurana Cato (negro),　July 9, 1772
John Cudworth, Jr., & Elisabeth Clap,　Sept. 7, 1772
Thomas Soper & Luranna Vinal,　Oct. 15, 1772
Barnabas Leichfield & Peinis Peine,　Oct. 15, 1772
Mr. John Turner & Mrs. Mary Vinal,　March 15, 1769
Mr. James Lambert & Mrs. Mary Woodard,　Nov. 28, 1770
Abner Hersey Litchfield & Mary Lyncoln,　March 19, 1780
Zebulon Willcut of Cohasset & Mary Litchfield,
　　　　　　　　　　　　　　　　March 21, 1780
Jared Battles of Cohasset & Elisabeth Litchfield,
　　　　　　　　　　　　　　　　March 30, 1780
William Bailey of Cohasset & Sarah Morris,　April 10, 1780
Reuben Young & Abigail Bates,　July 2, 1780
David Dunbar & Mary Carlile,　Sept. 14, 1780
Zadock Damon & Thankful Wade,　Jan. 4, 1781
Francis Litchfield & Lucy Lincoln of Cohasset,　Feb., 1781
Daniel Dunbar of Hingham & Phillipa Damon,
　　　　　　　　　　　　　　　　April 26, 1781
Stephen Vinal & Christiana Buck,　June 4, 1781

Caleb Bailey & Thankful Nash,   Aug. 23, 1781
Samuel Hyland & Hannah Studley,   Nov. 8, 1781
Joshua Damon & Wealthy Litchfield,   March 2, 1782
Seth Merritt & Susannah Gannett,   Nov. 28, 1782
Isachar Wade & Mary Peirce,   May 25, 1782
Beriah Curtis of Chesterfield & Desire Litchfield,
                    Sept. 14, 1782
Snell Wade & Charlotte Otis,   Oct. 20, 1782
Silvanus Damon & Lydia Rogers,   Jan. 8, 1784
Capt. William Russell of Boston & Eunice Wade,
                    Jan. 28, 1784
Amasa Whitten of Hingham & Lydia Jacob, May 23, 1773
Deacon Elisha James & Sarah Foster,   July 23, 1773
Thomas Cushing of Hingham & Elisabeth Turner,
                    Sept. 30, 1773
Caleb Prouty of S. & Sarah Lincoln of Pembroke,
                    Oct. 29, 1773
William Turner, Esq., & Eunice Clap,   Nov. 18, 1773
Zephaniah Cudworth & Elisabeth Studley, Nov. 25, 1773
Ezekiel Whitton of Hingham & Olive Studley, Dec. 3, 1773
Elisha Barrell & Mary Collamer,   Jan. 6, 1774
Calvin Curtis of Hanover & Martha Bryant, Jan. 6, 1774
Ozios Whitton of Hanover & widow Lucy Vinal,
                    April 4, 1774
Theophilus Corthrell & Jenny Macondy,   June 2, 1774
Israel Levitt, Jr., of Abington & Mary Buck, June 2, 1774
William Brooks & Betty Stoddar,   June 23, 1774
Nathaniel Cushing of Hingham & Alice Cushing,
                    June 30, 1774
Eli Lane of Cohasset & Lucy Gray,   July 31, 1774
Josiah Cushing of Pembroke & Lucy Cushing, Aug. 14, 1774
Seth Turner & Mary Stetson,   Dec. 11, 1774
Benjamin Mann of Hanover & Hannah Sears, Dec. 15, 1774
William Gardner of S. & widow Mary Chubbuck of
   Hingham,   Jan. 17, 1775
Benjamin Bailey & Mercy Bailey,   Jan. 18, 1775
Thomas Farrow, Jr., & Rebecca Stodder,   Feb. 1, 1775
Joshua Bryant, Jr., & Abiel Stockbridge,   Feb. 2, 1775

Micah Foord & Rhoda Copeland,	Feb. 16,	1775
Ensign Otis & Lucy Lapham,	April 30,	1775
Abner Curtis of Hanover & Lydia Bowker,	May 25,	1775
Elijah Turner & Mary Foster,	Aug. 10,	1775
Richard Humphries & widow Lydia Briant,	Aug. 20,	1775
Nathaniel Chittenden & Ruth Foster,	Nov. 2,	1775

Peter Boardman (free negro) of Hingham & Tamer
Cato,   Nov. 19, 1775
Samuel Randal & Desire Curtis,   Nov. 23, 1775
Ebenezer Curtis of Hanover & Mary Randall, Dec. 14, 1775
Jeremiah Gardner of Hingham & Lydia Stodder,
                                                      Dec. 18, 1775
Thomas Studley, Jr., & Olive Gross,   Jan. 1, 1776
Lot Lincoln of Hingham & Joanna Elmes,   Feb. 29, 1776
Stephen Tower of Hingham & Anna Bowker, April 21, 1776
Dwelly Clap & Abigail Gray,   May 3, 1776
John Slade of Boston & Hannah Torrey,   Aug. 1, 1776
Ezekiel Dunbar & Lucy Hammon,   Sept. 29, 1776
Elisha Silvester & Lillice Young,   Nov. 12, 1776
Simeon Wethrell of Hanover & Mary Peirce, Jan. 2, 1777
Jeremiah Haskins of Lancaster & Latice Cothrell,
                                                      Jan. 7, 1777
Peter Sears & Susa Collamore,   March 25, 1777
Gad & Lattice Taylor (negroes),   Feb. 13, 1777
William Tincin (?) of S. & Elisabeth Beals, March 25, 1777
Welcome Beach of Hingham & Susanna Brown,
                                                      May 26, 1777
Samuel Brown of S. & Rany Haskins of Abington,
                                                      July 24, 1777
Stephen Totman & Hannah Damon,   Oct. 16, 1777
George Stetson, Jr., & Bettey Torrey,   Oct. 23, 1777
Edward Damon & Celia Sylvester,   Dec. 20, 1777
Samuel Curtis & Mehitable Young,   April 9, 1778
Elijah Clap & Martha Turner,   Oct. 8, 1778
Jonathan Barrell of George Town & Elizabeth Brooks,
                                                      Nov. 26, 1778
David Jacob of Hanover & Release Jacob,   Nov. 28, 1778
Joshua Whitten of Hanover & Jemima Dagget,
                                                      March 20, 1778

Capt. Joseph Stetson & Martia Gross, March 20, 1778
Nathaniel Jorden & Eunice Nash, Jan. 19, 1779
Matthew Est—s of Hanover & Jenny Palmer, Feb. 23, 1779
David Dunbar, Jr., & Betty Elmes, May 10, 1779
Thomas Church, Jr., & Hannah Woodard, May 27, 1779
Samuel Hatch of Gillmantown & Rachel Farrow,
June 3, 1779
Jonathan Brown & widow Elisabeth Hamon, Aug. 21, 1779
Isaac Lincoln of Bristol & Mary Brooks, Oct. 10, 1779
David Clap & Elisabeth Church, Sept. 26, 1779
Isaiah Damon, a transient person, & Lucy Stetson,
Oct. 28, 1779
Samuel Wooddard of Bristol & Sarah Barstow, Dec. 30, 1779
Nathaniel Jacob & Lucy Jacob, Jan. 6, 1780
Jacob Turner & Rachel Cushing, Feb. 13, 1780
Seth Orcutt & Rhoda Collamore, Feb. 24, 1780
Ebenezer Belcher & Ruth Peterson, March 2, 1780
William James & Mary Randell, April 20, 1780
Jonathan Oldham & widow Patience Clap, May 7, 1780
Caleb Silvester of Hanover & Abigail Jacob, May 18, 1780
James Tower of S. & Lucy Dunbar of Hingham,
May 23, 1780
Simeon Damon & Lucy Bowker, June 8, 1780
Samuel Stetson, Jr., & Deborah Gross, July 16, 1780
Nathaniel Sylvester of Hanover & Lucy Clap, July 20, 1780
George Pitts of Dighton & Lydia Stetson, July 22, 1780
Thomas Chubbuck, Jr., of Hingham & Margaret
Stodder, Aug. 9, 1780
William Vinal & Lucy Mann, Aug. 10, 1780
Thomas James & Sarah Clap, Aug. 17, 1780
Silvanus Hatch of Falmouth & Anna Turner, Nov. 8, 1780
Joseph Jacob & Hannah Eells, Dec. 3, 1780
Snow Stetson & Lydia Tolman, Dec. 7, 1780
Benjamin Bowker & Anna Sylvester, Dec. 25, 1780
Lazarus Bowker of S. & Ruth Daniels of Milton, Jan. 18, 1781
Peleg Curtis & Ruth Bowker, Feb. 10, 1781
Dr. William Whitridge of Tiverton & Mary Cush-
ing, March 10, 1781

William Mayhew & Joanna Farrow, April 2, 1781
Obadiah Stodder of S. & Selah Vining of Abington,
May 13, 1781
James Briggs, 3d, & Deborah Clap, May 17, 1781
Thomas Sheverick of Falmouth & Mary Rundell,
May 24, 1781
James Clap & Elisabeth Jenkins, June 7, 1781
Nathaniel Eells & Sarah Woodward, June 18, 1781
Calvin Jenkins & Elisabeth Litchfield, July 12, 1781
Thomas Colman, Jr., & Molly Bates, Aug. 23, 1781
Asa Copeland of Norton & Rachel Briggs, Jr., Oct. 25, 1781
Caleb Torrey & Hannah Sylvester, Nov. 13, 1781
Job Tilden, Jr., of Hanover & Lydia Jackson, Nov. 15, 1781
Thomas Barstow of S. & Lydia Silvester, Nov. 22, 1781
Esau Cloud of Weymouth & Huldah Palmer, Dec. 3, 1781
Laban Rose & Mable Nash, March 7, 1782
Stephen Wade & Mercy Peirce, March 24, 1782
James Little of Marshfield & Lydia Young, April 4, 1782
Nathaniel Church & Rebecca Barstow, April 4, 1782
Robert Peirce & Zilpha Coleman, April 10, 1782
Gamaliel Merritt & Hannah Mott, June 9, 1782
Melzer Stodder & Lucy Turner, July 25, 1782
Isaac Chittenden & Molly Bryant, Aug. 8, 1782
Rowland Litchfield & Lucy Curtis, Aug. 15, 1782
William Copeland & Polly Church, Aug. 27, 1782
Benjamin Vassel of Charlton & Lucy Stetson, Sept. 8, 1782
Zina Briant & Eunice Wade, Sept. 9, 1782
George Torrey & Thankful Otis, Sept. 22, 1782
Eli Curtis & Bathsheba Nichols, Nov. 14, 1782
John Barns of Hingham & Mary Nichols, Nov. 14, 1782
Hezekiah Bozworth of Boston & Sarah Eells, Nov. 18, 1782
James Torrey & Eunice Turner, Nov. 28, 1782
Joseph Turner & Patience Oldham, Dec. 25, 1782
Elisha Magoun of Pembroke & Abigail Neal, Dec. 29, 1782
Capt. George Pillsbury of Boston & Polly Otis, Jan. 6, 1783
Isaac Perry of Hanover & Jemima Farrow, March 9, 1783
Joseph Neal Bates & Eunice Oldham, March 20, 1783
Micah Stetson & Sarah Copeland, March 23, 1783

Calvin Damon & Desire Eells, April 10, 1783
Snow Curtis & Bathsheba Hatch, April 17, 1783
Abner House & Rebecca Morton, June 2, 1783
Paul Merritt & Deborah Nash, Oct. 12, 1783
Ward Litchfield & Betty Merritt, Oct. 12, 1783
Samuel Jackson & Mary Southward, Oct. 12, 1783
Gershom Collier & Abigail Nash, Nov. 2, 1783
William Hoskins & widow Lydia Nickolson, Nov. 13, 1783
Noah Barrell & Martha Palmer, Nov. 18, 1783
Daniel Hayden & Nancy Doane, Nov. 24, 1783
Nathaniel Brooks, Jr., & Deborah Brooks, Nov. 27, 1783
Nathaniel Vinal & Priscilla Mott, Nov. 30, 1783
Ichabod Briggs & Sarah Collier, Nov. 30, 1783
Laben Souter & Betty Randall, Dec. 15, 1783
John Sylvester & Bathsheba Hiskins, Feb. 1, 1784
Bryant Stephenson & Deborah Turner, Feb. 1, 1784
John Keith of Easton & Abigail House, Feb. 26, 1784
Thomas Hatch of Hanover & Sarah White, March 4, 1784
Consider Turner & Mary Brown, March 11, 1784
Job Cushing, Esq. of Cohasset & widow Abigail Peirce,
April 27, 1784
Joseph Nicolson & Mary Samson, May 20, 1784
Samuel Nash & Jerusha Briggs, June 13, 1784
Elijah Whitman of Bridgewater & Mary Randall,
July 1, 1784
Thomas Barker Briggs & Lucy Otis, Oct. 10, 1784
Zeba Harris & Jenny Willis, Oct. 28, 1784
Hezekiah Stodderd & Elisabeth Garnett, Dec. 12, 1784
Israel Cudworth & Mercy Cudworth, Dec. 25, 1784
Thomas Lapham, Jr., & Abigail Lincoln, Nov. 25, 1784
Nathaniel Wade, Jr., & Deborah Turner, Nov. 25, 1784
Samuel Tolman & Rebecca Copeland, Nov. 25, 1784
Elijah Randall & Hannah Stetson, Dec. 22, 1784
John Doane & Lucy Litchfield, Dec. 22, 1784
Hezekiah Ripley of Kingston & Hannah Tilden, Jan. 20, 1785
Lemuel Jacob & Sarah Randall, March 31, 1785
Benjamin Elmes & Elisabeth Litchfield, May 16, 1785
Peleg Simmons & widow Sarah Clap, May 22, 1785

Charles Jenkins of Bridgewater & Jennie Collier,
June 14, 1785
Robert Northey & Alice Thomas, June 16, 1785
Thomas Josselyn, Jr., of Hanover & Polly Loring,
Sept. 11, 1785
John Morton & Anna Stetson, Nov. 13, 1785
James Gray & Bethiah Curtis, Nov. 16, 1785
Joseph Northey & Betty Brown, Dec. 12, 1785
John Studley & Sarah Gannett, Dec. 12, 1785
Elijah Curtis, Jr., & Rachel Clap, Jan. 16, 1786
Eliphalet Northey of Landiff, in Hampshire State, & ·
Abigail Stodder, Jan. 16, 1786
Isaac Porter of Marshfield & Sally Hull, Jan. 24, 1786
Peleg Hayden & Rhoda Jenkins, Feb. 12, 1786
Abiel Farrow & Bethiah Cushing, May 30, 1786
Daniel Williams of Carlton & Mercy Stetson, June 4, 1786
Israel Vinal, 3d, & Rebecca Bailey, June 22, 1786
Charles Cole & Esther Clap, July 30, 1786
Joel Sylvester of Hanover & Sarah Damon, Aug. 31, 1786
Eli Curtis, Jr., & Deborah Merritt, Aug. 31, 1786
John Russell & Lydia Gray, Sept. 3, 1786
Job Vinal & Sarah Elmes, Oct. 15, 1786
Elkanah Gannett & Mercy Studley, Nov. 12, 1786
Hosea Dunbar & Lucy Simons, Nov. 15, 1786
Seth Webb & Desire Cudworth, Nov. 16, 1786
Samuel Simmons, Jr., & Thankful Curtis, Nov. 28, 1786
Elisha Foord, Jr., of Marshfield & Lydia Turner, Jan. 4, 1787
Noah Merritt & Betty Bryant, Jan. 11, 1787
Charles Otis & Sarah Tilden, Feb. 8, 1787
Melzar Vinal & Rhoda Beals, Feb. 18, 1787
Prince Gannett of S. & Molly Joy of Cohasset, April 2, 1782
Elisha Dunbar & Fanny Hayden, May 2, 1784
Silas Hamilton & Sarah Studley, Sept. 23, 1784
John Fowler of Winslow, County of Lincoln, & Sarah
James, Aug. 25, 1785
Daniel Merritt & Molly Simmons, March 23, 1786
John Lincoln & Ruth Stetson, 1779
Isaac Chittenden of Malden & Mary Turner, 1780

John Gibbs & Betty Woodworth,   1780
Asher Freeman & Dinah Cato,   1780
John Merritt & Lucy Gross,   1780
Joshua Merritt & Priscilla Litchfield,   1780
James Chubbuck of Abington & Martha Studley,   1782
Joseph House & Huldah Coleman,   1782
David House, Jr., of Hanover & Rachel Merritt,   1783
Israel Turner of S. & Mary Oakman of Marshfield,   1784
Elisha Stetson & Rebecca Curtis,   1784
Gamaliel Curtis & Patience Wade,   1784
Capt. Joseph Northey of Marblehead & Elisabeth
    Northey,   1785
Thomas Stodder of Cohasset & Sally Stodder,   1786
James Stetson & Nancy Elmes,   1786
Samuel Silvester & Desire Cole,   1786

ROCHESTER.

June 4, 1686. "Sippican alias Rochester made a township with the privileges of a town."
First Church (Congregational) organized 1703.   Second at North Rochester, 1753.

Samuel Ruggles & Allis Sherman,   June 25, 1738
Josiah Jenkins of Barnstable & Mary Ellis,   July 6, 1738
Joseph Edwards, Jr., & Sarah Burge,   July 13, 1738
David Bessey, Jr., & Dinah Muxum,   July 20, 1738
Nathaniel Whitcomb & Phebe Blackmer,   July 27, 1738
Uriah Savoy & Deborah Bumpass,   Sept. 3, 1738
Nathan Bumpas & Lydia Bumpas,   Oct. 19, 1738
Zacheus Bumpas & Reliance Morey,   Oct. 19, 1738
Samuel Hix of Dartmouth & Ruth Hoskens,   Jan. 9, 1738-9
Samuel Doty & Zerviah Lovel,   Jan. 18, 1738-9
Elisha Tupper & Mary Hammond,   April 10, 1740
Daniel Wing & Mary Clifton,   Nov. 26, 1740
Marke Haskell, 3d, & Elisabeth Witredge,   Aug. 6, 1741
John Penny of Harwick & Elizabeth Dellano,   Oct. 15, 1741
Simon Burge & Deborah Edwards,   Dec. 20, 1741

Samuel Rider, Jr., & Mary Chapman,	April 13, 1742
William Tereth & Dinah Dexter,	Nov. 16, 1742
Lemuel Claghorne & Deborah Wing,	March 15, 1742
Elijah Caswell & Hannah Freeman,	May 2, 1743
Job King & Uniss Hammond,	July 12, 1743
Joshua Lawrence & Jane Haskell,	July 13, 1743
Amos Mendal & Susanna Church,	Oct. 20, 1743
Haneniah Gifford & Joanna Mendal,	Jan. 4, 1743
John Mattkeless & Rebecca Crapoo,	Jan. 4, 1743
Peleg Dexter & Catharine Cosby,	1743
Thomas Southworth of Dartmouth & Abigail Bools,	
	March 20, 1745-6
Isaac Stephens & Elisabeth Dextor,	Nov. 26, 1747
Samuel Randall of R. & Patience Fish of Sandwich,	
	March 20, 1747-8
Nehemiah Randall & Hope Peterson,	June 17, 1748
Josiah Hammond, Jr., & Rebecca Hammond,	Jan. 10, 1750
Joseph Cook & Sarah Randall,	Jan. 29, 1750
Mideon Cowing & Sarah Howard,	Feb. 21, 1750
Pollycarpus Hammond & Barthsheba Randall,	
	March 21, 1751
Thomas Bools & Ann Cowing,	Oct. 17, 1751
Jabez Dexter & Patience Hammond,	Nov. 7, 1751
Josha Shaw & Ruth Bools,	Jan. 2, 1752
Caleb Coombs of Brunswick & Eunice (?) Combs,	
	July 11, 1751
Charles Stertevant & Elisabeth Bourn,	Aug. 1, 1751
Joseph Pain & Elenor Stewart,	Dec. 11, 1751
John Williams & Rhoda Crowle,	March 5, 1752
Nathaniel Jenkins & Meriah Ellis,	March 31, 1752
Reuben Ellis & Deborah Chubbock,	June 21, 1752
John Clarke of Hanover & Thankful Wing,	July 28, 1752
Zacheus Burge & Joanna Barrow,	July 30, 1752
Jonathan Wing & Phebe Handy,	Oct. 29, 1752
Nathaniel Ruggles & Deliverance Barrow,	Nov. 5, 1752
Silvanus White & Ann Williams,	Nov. 16, 1752
James Hammond & Hannah Barlow,	April 3, 1753
John Clarke, Jr., & Elisabeth Hammond,	April 5, 1753

James Hammond & Hannah Barlow,	April 3, 1763
John Clark & Elisabeth Hamond,	April 5, 1763
Jonathan Bolles, Jr., & Deliverance Randal,	Oct. 4, 1754
William Ratch & Anne Barlow,	Nov. 17, 1754
David Bolles & Lydia Carby,	Dec. 12, 1754
John Danford & Jane Henderson,	Dec. 13, 1754
Abiel Tri— (?) of Freeton & Sarah Haskel,	Feb. 6, 1750
Samuel Swift of Plymouth & Thankful Ashley,	Nov. 7, 1757
Amos Crepo & Mary Andrews,	Aug. 5, 1753
Seth Blackwell & Ruth Sturtevant,	Dec. 25, 1753
Joseph Williams of Hebron & Sarah Holmes,	Dec. 13, 1754
David Wood & Rebacka Preet (?),	Nov. 13, 1746
James Barrow & Mary Cofin,	March 23, 1746
Francis Attwood & Elisabeth Lucas,	Aug. 27, 1747
Lt. Nathaniel Attwood & Abigail Lucas,	Oct. 7, 1747
Jonathan Tillson & Luce Cobb,	May 4, 1748
Elizer Crocker & Hannah Cobb,	May 10, 1748
Isaac Weston & Inoley (?) Ripley,	June 30, 1748
James Cole & Bennett Barrows,	Aug. 16, 1748
Archibus Fuller & Mary Pratt,	Aug. 23, 1748
James Lucas & Ruth Murdock,	Sept. 15, 1748
Elkanah Shaw & Elisabeth Attwood,	Oct. 13, 1748
Nathaniel Attwood & Susanna Shurtleff,	Dec. 5, 1748
Bartlett Murdock & Sarah Lucas,	March 9, 1748
Samuel Lucas & Abigail Shaw,	Nov. 9, 1749
Samuel Noyes (?) & Hannah Doten,	Sept. 28, 1750
James —ove— (?) & Patience Barrow,	Dec., 1750
John Bush— (?) & Zilpha Sampson,	May 6, 1754
Joshua Fobes & Mercy Churchill,	June 5, 1754
John Eaverson, Jr., & Elisabeth Richard,	Oct. 24, 1754
Ebenezer Porter & Lydia Loring,	Oct. 24, 1754
John Mackarlin & Martha Glover (?),	Nov. 26, 1754
Benjamin Ranson & Abigail Whiton,	March 27, 1755
Solomon Doten & Joannah Bryant,	Sept. 13, 1755
George Little & Abigail Soul,	Nov. 13, 1755
Dr. Thomas Ruggles & Mary Loring,	Dec. 4, 1755
Josiah Bryant & Mary Griffeth,	Jan. 1, 1756
Joseph Joseling & Mary Waterman,	April 1, 1756

13

Joseph Bryant & Zilpha Sampson,	Nov. 23, 1756
Enoch Dexter & Jedediah (?) Morse,	Sept. 7, 1755
Gershom Dexter & Mehitable Bolls,	Oct. 1, 1755
Daniel Randal & Mary Steward,	Nov. 2, 1755
Samuel Sherman & Rachel Hatch,	Nov. 6, 1755
Nathaniel Clerk & Mary Clap,	Nov. 17, 1755
Stephen Perrey & Sarah Dexter,	Nov. 20, 1755
Isaiah Hatch & Joanna Whitcomb,	Feb. 26, 1756
Ebenezer Wright & Anna Trip,	July 1, 1756
Benjamin Dexter & Priscilla Benson,	Oct. 19, 1756
Noah Sprague, Jr., & Mary Dexter,	Nov. 28, 1756
Seth Mendal & Mary Ellis,	Dec. 16, 1756
Nathaniel Parlow & Sarah Wing,	June 16, 1756
Abiel Trip of Freetown & Sarah Haskell,	Feb. 6, 1750
Samuel Swifte of Plimouth & Thankful Ashly,	Nov. 7, 1751
Amos Crepo & Mary Andrews,	Aug. 5, 1753
Seth Blackwell & Ruth Stertevant,	Dec. 25, 1753
Joseph Williams of Hebron & Sarah Holmes,	Dec. 30, 1754
Peter Crapo of R. & Hannah Axdil of Middleboro,	
	Feb. 23, 1755
Thomas Handy of Dartmouth & Priscilla Hammond,	
	Nov. 1, 1753
Joseph Lovell & Mary Lewis,	March 5, 1754
Benjamin Hamond, Jr., & Sarah Hamond,	Feb. 27, 1754
Joseph Jedson & Rebecca Rider,	March 27, 1755
Ebenezer Dexter & Lydiah Rider,	March 27, 1755
Zacheus Mead & Sarah Balow,	Nov. 27, 1755
Simeon Clerk & Mercy Bump,	Dec. 9, 1755
Peter Tomson of Hallifax & Lydia Cowing,	Jan. 6, 1756
John Bolles & Susannah Eldridge,	Feb. 19, 1756
Samuel Tanne, Jr., of Dartmouth & Bethiah Rider,	
	Dec. 11, 1755
Mose Hamond & Marcy House,	April 11, 1756
Ichabod Peterson of Richmond, Kings County, &	
Sarah Clark,	April 13, 1758
Barzella Hammond & Sarah Dotey,	July 4, 1758
Isaac Stevens & Mary Clark,	Dec. 27, 1759
Dr. (?) John Pitcher & Elizabeth Sprague,	May 18, 1760

Jabez Griffith & Mary Hiller,   Jan. 22, 1761
Samuel Sherman & Lidia Pope,   Feb. 22, 1758
Elnathan Dexter & Mary Snow,   Feb. 26, 1758
Joseph Child of Barnstable & Meribah Dexter,
                       March 16, 1758
Benjamin Hammond, Jr., & Susannah Meggs,   July 4, 1758
Stafford Hammond & Hannah Dotey,   Aug. 2, 1761
Peaceful Ashley of Freetown & Anne Bishop, Aug. 27, 1761
Nathaniel Snow, Jr., & Azubah Nickerson,   Oct. 13, 1761
Samuel Briggs, Jr., & Susannah Nye,   Dec. 10, 1761
David Eving & Sarah Parker,   Dec. 14. 1758
Thomas Atkins of Sandwich & Ruth Snow,   Jan. 4, 1759
Nehemiah Bozworth & Sarah Goodspeed,   Jan. 23, 1759
Samuel Wing, Jr., & Joanna Haskel,   April 8, 1759
Elijah Williams & Ruth Nye,   June 24, 1759
Perez Clark & Unice Bourn,   Sept. 20, 1759
John Stevens & Thankful Hammond,   Jan. 21, 1760
Elisha Barrow & Nelle Lambert,   April 24, 1760
Jabez Delano & Ruth Goodspeed,   Aug. 24, 1760
Benjamin Benson of Middleboro & Hannah Stewart,
                       Aug. 28, 1760
Joseph Wing & Rebecca Hathaway,   Jan. 8, 1761
Stephen Bennet of Dartmouth & Zerviah Hammond,
                       Jan. 15, 1761
James Stewart & Lidia Crandal,   March 12, 1761
Benjamin Bailey of Scituate & Patience Bates, April 21, 1761
Joseph Morse & Thankful Packard,   May 18, 1761
Theophilus Peas, Jr., & Ruth Brigs,   July 2, 1761
Simon Sherman & Deliverance Griffith,   Aug. 6, 1761
————Clap & Sarah House,   Sept. 3, 1751
Timothy White of Scituate & Sarah Haskel, Oct. 27, 1761
Ebenezer Clap & Lucy Sprague,   May 27, 1762
George Nye & Rebecca Marshall,   Oct. 7, 1762
Nathaniel Briggs & Mary Parker,   Nov. 7, 1762
Joseph Strane (?), resident of Dartmouth, & Sarah
    Crapeo,   Dec. 30, 1762
Timothy Haskell & Deliverance Hatch,   Nov. 19, 1761
Nathaniel Sears & Elisabeth Winslow,   Nov. 26, 1761

Philip Simond & Rachel Randal,   April 8, 1762
Edward Hamond & Mary Lumbert,   June 17, 1762
David Lewis & Abigail Perry,   Aug. 26, 1762
Thomas Hix of Sandwich & Sarah Smith,   Dec. 8, 1762
Beraliel Washburne of Dartmouth & Barsheba Ham-
    mond,   Dec. 23, 1762
Ebenezer Clarke, Jr., & Elisabeth Dexter,   Jan. 5, 1764
Jonathan Wing & Hannah Hammond,   Jan. 15, 1764
John Rider & Sarah Ruggles,   June 26, 1764
Rev. Thomas West of Dartmouth & Mrs. Priscilla
    Hammond,   Nov. 30, 1763
George Barlow & Abigail Allen,   Dec. 8, 1763
Stephen Wing & Ollive Hamond,   Jan. 5, 1764
Ichabod Norton of R. & Hannah Pattin of Bridgewater,
                                           Feb. 26, 1764
Nathaniel Myrick of Hartwick & Louis Hamond,
                                           May 29, 1764
Robert Clark & Rebecca Meggs,   Aug. 22, 1764
William Barlow & Content Barstow,   Oct. 4, 1764
Charles Hammond & Eliphal (?) Hamond,   Oct. 4, 1764
David Hammond & Elisabeth Annable,   Dec. 5, 1764
William Reed & Mary Peirce,   March 27, 1755
Joshua Whitcomb & Mariah Ashley,   Dec. 4, 1755
Benjamin Bump of Wareham & Ruth Sprague,
                                           Jan. 15, 1756
Melatiah White & Mary Sprague,   Feb. 12, 1756
Lemuel Swift of Plimouth & Rebecca Whithead, Dec. 8, 1756
John Bly of Middleboro & Mercy Holmes,   Feb. 17, 1757
Levi Hiller & Rebecca Palmer,   May 19, 1757
John Doty & Elisabeth Clark,   Dec. 28, 1758
Asa Whitcomb of Hardwich & Joanna Raymond,
                                           March 15, 1759
Malachi Ellis of Sandwich & Susanna Denis,   Nov. 7, 1759
Elnathan Comes of R. & Mary Taylor of Dartmouth,
                                           Nov. 29, 1759
Zacheus Handy, Jr., & Joanna Whitridge,   April 9, 1761
Barnabas Freeman of Liverpool & Thankful Denis,
                                           Dec. 16, 1761

John Lowden of Dartmouth & Mary Whitridge,
Dec. 17, 1761
Joseph Basset & Martha Lewis,   Jan. 7, 1762
Scipio & Deborah Cato (negroes),   Aug. 2, 1762
Ichabod Johnson & Mary Ashley,   Jan. 26, 1763
Hezekiah Purrington of Middleboro & Susanna Holmes,
Feb. 10, 1763
John Nye & Sarah Denis,   Nov. 13, 1763
Thomas Washburn of Dartmouth & Mary Crapoo,
Dec. 8, 1763
James Cowing & Mary Cottle,   Dec. 29, 1763
James Hoskins of R. & Abigail Man of Middleboro,
Feb. 22, 1764
Job King & Mary Ashley,   Oct. 18, 1764
Abram Niles & Mary Caswel,   March 7, 1765
Joshua Morse & Mary Goodnuff,   Sept. 8, 1763
Robert Durfey of Freetown & Eleanor Griffith. Sept. 22, 1763
Prince Stevens & Reliance Hinkley,   Jan. 19, 1764
Benjamin Bessee of Wareham & Elisabeth Dotey,
Jan. 31, 1764-5
Samuel Balkman, Jr., of Douglas & Thankful Griffith,
June 12, 1766
John Clark, 4th, of R. & Susannah Harris of Middle-
boro,   Sept. 11, 1766
Lewis Randal & Patience Briggs,   Sept. 14, 1766
Joseph Oliver, Jr., & Dorothy Pettes,   Nov. 14, 1766
John Briggs of Wareham & Desire Griffith,   Nov. 27, 1766
Henry Bishop & Lidia Peirce,   Jan. 15, 1767
Seth Ames & Sarah Shreave,   May 10, 1767
Joshua Morse & Mary Goodnuff, late residents of R.,
Sept. 8, 1763
Robert Durfee of Freetown & Eleanor Griffeth, Sept. 22, 1763
John Morse & Elisabeth Clark,   Dec. 22, 1763
Samuel Boulkcum, Jr., of Douglas & Thankful Griffeth,
June 12, 1766
Cyrus West of Cornwallis & Mary Freeman,   Dec. 3, 1767
Seth Ames & Sarah Shreave,   May 10, 1767
Silas Hathaway of Dartmouth & Mary Griffeth, Aug. 9, 1767

Noah Bumpas of Wareham & Mary Haskens, March 10, 1768
Timothy West & Lois Dexter, Aug. 28, 1768
Charles Hammond & Anna Stewart, Nov. 23, 1768
Joseph Cannon & Abigail Dexter, Nov. 24, 1768
Isaac Tinkham of Plymouth & Lidia Rider, Dec. 4, 1768
Benjamin Ingram of Freetown & Jane Crapo, Dec. 24, 1768
Nathaniel Bessee of Wareham & Susannah Hammond, March 14, 1764
Amos Bates & Mercy Morse, Oct. 24, 1765
Asaph Price & Thankful Hammond, Dec. 19, 1765
John Clap & Ruth Haskell, Jan. 9, 1766
Eleazer Allen & Mary Sherman, Jan. 23, 1766
Thomas Mitchell & Dinah Norton, Jan. 29, 1766
Samuel Eldrege & Mary Barlow, Jan. 30, 1766
Savory Hathaway & Dorithy Clifton, Feb. 13, 1766
Jeremiah Jackson of Abington & Eleanor Doty, Oct. 10, 1766
Jonathan Hatch of Falmouth & Mary Sears, Nov. 13, 1766
Cephas Cushman of Dartmouth & Judith Clark, Dec. 27, 1766
Toby & Judith (negroes), March 7, 1767
John Sherman, 4th, & Ann Nickerson, June 27, 1767
Seth Barlow & Mary Hammond, Oct. 26, 1767
Silas Cross & Deborah Howland, March 13, 1768
James Clark of Norton & Mary Randal, April 15, 1768
Timothy Hammond & Deborah Hammond, Oct. 26, 1767
Barnabas Dotey & Catharine Freeman, Dec. 24, 1767
Gideon Hammond & Abigail Barlow, April 21, 1768
Samuel Jenkins of Falmouth & Rest Snow, Dec. 21, 1768
Amos Cross & Hannah Austin, Jan. 22, 1769
David Sears & Susannah Handy, Feb. 13, 1766
Alexander Kennedy of Middleboro & Mary Smith, Dec. 1, 1768
Nicholas Snow & Hannah Dexter, Dec. 8, 1768
Ephraim Haskel, Jr., & Eunice Nye, Jan. 22, 1769
Joseph Hammond & Rachel Winslow, Feb. 23, 1769
Daniel Mendall & Hannah Mendall, March 23, 1769
Charles Church & Alice Sears, March 29, 1769
John Bennet, 3d, of Dartmouth & Lois Church, March 30, 1769

Job Randal & Mercy Randall, April 13, 1769

Abisha Sherman of Dartmouth & Aurelia Bassett,

Aug. 31, 1769

David Bessee of Wareham & Experience Snow, Aug. 31, 1769

Rev. Bezaliel Shaw of Nantucket & Miss Elisabeth
Hammond, Sept. 17, 1769

Nathaniel Meggs & Hannah Holmes, Nov. 12, 1769

Josiah Peirce & Mary Kennedy, Nov. 16, 1769

Edminster Hammond & Mary Meggs, Nov. 23, 1769

Stephen Bassett & Thankful Handy, Nov. 30, 1769

John Wing & Margaret Look, Nov. 30, 1769

Kenelm Clap & Deliverance Haskell, Dec. 28, 1769

Thomas Ayres of Nantucket & Lidia Henderson,

Nov. 20, 1769

Luther Burge of Dartmouth & Allice Southworth,

Feb. 8, 1770

Amaziah Bowles of Dartmouth & Mary Stewart,

May 14, 1770

John Elles, Jr., & Ellenor Randel, Aug. 16, 1770

David Edwards & Deborah Clark, Nov. 22, 1770

Benjamin Hammond of Dartmouth & Anna Williams,

Feb. 21, 1771

Jonah Hammond & Mary Barlow, July 7, 1771

Ebenezer Parker, Jr., & Lydia Haskell, Sept. 19, 1771

Joseph Dotey of Middleboro & Susannah Smith,

Oct. 17, 1771

Daniel Eggery of Dartmouth & Mary Perry, Nov. 21, 1771

Joseph Haskell, 2d, & Mercy Parker, Dec. 1, 1771

Resolved White & Charity Clap, Dec. 19, 1771

Ebenezer Morse & Anna Stetson, Dec. 26, 1771

William Bassett, Jr., & Bethiah Goodspeed, Dec. 26, 1771

Joseph Brown of R. & Sarah Snow of Abington,

Dec. 26, 1771

Ephraim Dexter, Jr., & Kezia Sober, Dec. 29, 1771

David Hathaway & Priscilla Hiller, Dec. 2, 1770

Ebenezer Baker & Phebe Randall, Jan. 9, 1771

Samuel Hackett of Middleboro & Mary Randall,

Jan. 10, 1771

Aaron Jenkins & Tabitha Raymont, both of Plimouth,

	May 29, 1771
Edmond Freeman & Sarah Jorden,	June 10, 1771
Ebenezer Holmes & Lydia Cliffton,	Sept. 29, 1771
William Wiltshire & Mabel Southworth,	Jan. 12, 1772
George Bonum Nye & Sarah Handy,	March 11, 1772
Elijah Dexter & Keziah Winslow,	March 27, 1772
Thomas Francis & Mary Horsnot (Indians),	April 2, 1772
William Nye & Eunice Handy,	Nov. 15, 1772
Anthony Haskins of Middleboro & Rest Crapo,	Dec. 3, 1772
Seth Hammond of Dartmouth & Mary Bolls,	March 1, 1773
Charles Sturtevant & Martha Sturtevant,	April 29, 1773
Tisdale Winslow & Jane Blackwell,	Aug. 15, 1773
Caleb Randal & Elisabeth Haskins,	Sept. 23, 1773
Shubael Hammond & Ann Barden,	Oct. 7, 1773

Ephraim Leonard, Esq., of Mansfield & Anna Ruggles,

	Oct. 27, 1773
Job Haskell & Elisabeth Hammond,	Dec. 8, 1773
Nathaniel King & Hannah Doty,	Jan. 13, 1774
Amos Bolles & Mary Southworth,	March 17, 1774
Benajah Davis & Phebe Randall,	Aug. 18, 1774
Timothy Hewet & Elisabeth Hallowell,	Aug. 18, 1774
Nathaniel Snow & Abigail Dexter,	Sept. 8, 1774
Robert Clark & Dorcas Bishop,	Oct. 30, 1774
Belcher Manter & Rebecca Hiller,	Oct. 31, 1774
Silas Handy & Lois Hiller,	Oct. 31, 1774
Josea Bolls & Sarah Dexter,	Oct. 31, 1774
David Winslow & Sarah Hollowell,	Dec. 14, 1774
Micah Haskell & Lucy Clap,	Dec. 15, 1774
Timothy Ruggles & Judith King,	Dec. 15, 1774
Church Mendal & Patience Mendal,	Jan. 1, 1775
Nathaniel Haskins & Hopstill Randall,	Jan. 26, 1755
Ebenezer Bolles & Anna Clifton,	March 2, 1775
Daniel Mendal & Thankful Hammond,	March 9, 1775
Joseph Edwards & Mary Randall,	March 30, 1775
Thomas Haskell & Deborah Allen,	April 27, 1775

Nathaniel Mirick of Hardwick & Elisabeth Haskell,

	June 26, 1775

John Barker of Dartmouth & Hosa Francis (Indians),

	July 13, 1775
John Smith & Patience Bailey,	Sept. 3, 1775
Stephen Delano & Lydia Clap,	Oct. 3, 1775
Isaiah Dexter & Mary Davis,	Oct. 29, 1775

Rowland Blackwell of Sandwich & Mary Hammond,

	Nov. 9, 1775
Lemuel Randall, Jr., & Mary Hammond, Jr.,	Nov. 12, 1775
Isaac Briggs & Lois Mendall,	Nov. 30, 1775
Jeremiah Crapo & Waitstill West,	Dec. 27, 1775
David Snow & Phebe Stetson,	Jan. 18, 1776
Cornelius Clark, Jr., & Bethiah Sherman,	Jan. 31, 1776
Seth Pope & Sarah Freeman,	May 21, 1776
Jabez Sherman & Thankful Winslow,	June 23, 1776
Rufus Bassett & Jedida Handy,	June 23, 1776
John Hiller & Lucy Burge,	Aug. 21, 1776
Edmond Snow & Abigail Sherman,	Oct. 31, 1776
Thomas Ellis & Eunice Reed,	Nov. 21, 1776
John Phillips of Dartmouth & Dorothy Nye,	Dec. 8, 1776
Abraham Holmes & Bethiah Nye,	Dec. 26, 1776
John Beard & Hanah Courby,	Jan. 27, 1777
James Blankenslip, Jr., & Alice Hammond,	Feb. 6, 1777
Timothy Snow & Anna Jenne, Jr.,	Feb. 20, 1777
Weston Allen & Thankful Clark,	Feb. 27, 1777

Lenen (?) Dexter of Dartmouth & Vashti Sturtevant,

	Feb. 27, 1777
John Dexter, Jr., & Rebecca Hiller,	March 9, 1777

Abisha Sherman of Dartmouth & Mary Goodspeed,

	March 27, 1777
Josiah Clark & Mercy Caswell,	April 17, 1777
Lot Cowing & Mary Courby,	June 18, 1777
Samuel Sherman of Dartmouth & Olive Clark,	July 13, 1777
John Faunce of Plymouth & Susanna Clark,	Sept. 18, 1777

John Gibbs, Jr., of Wareham & Joanna Dexter,

	Nov. 13, 1777
Jonathan King & Mary Clark,	Nov. 20, 1777
George Vaughan of Middleboro & Mary Rider,	Dec. 18, 1777
Nathaniel Sherman & Abigail Haskell,	Dec. 28, 1777

Sylvester Bates & Sarah Sears,   Jan. 1, 1778
Nicholas Davis, Jr., of Dartmouth & Hannah Pope,
                                                March 1, 1778
David Randall & Priscilla Symonds,   March 12, 1778
John Omey & Hannah Clark,   March 17, 1778
Joshua Lawrence of Fretown & Thankful Snow, May 7, 1778
Noah Hammond & Eunice Hammond,   May 31, 1778
Silas Dexter & Eleanor Bumpus,   Oct. 25, 1778
Hunnowell Hammond & Mary Andrews,   Nov. 26, 1778
Rowland Lun & Elizabeth Clark,   Nov. 27, 1778
Seth Bumpus & Experience Dexter,   Dec. 24, 1778
Malatiah White & Mercy Sprague,   Jan. 10, 1779
Nathaniel Hammond of Dartmouth & Deborah Bolls,
                                                Jan. 31, 1779
Elijah Dexter & Martha Clark,   April 4, 1779
Jethro Randall & Huldah Oliver,   April 15, 1779
John Crapo & Abigail Yeomans,   Aug. 12, 1779
Nathan Hatheway of Wareham & Tamer Gurney,
                                                Aug. 19, 1779
John Collins & Hannah Haskins,   Aug. 19, 1779
Nathan Sears & Thankful Bassett,   Sept. 18, 1779
Jesse Lombard & Ruth Clark,   Oct. 7, 1779
Prince Parker of Yarmouth & Mercy Handy,   Oct. 7, 1779
Ebenezer Sears & Jane White,   Oct. 21, 1779
John Macomber of Middleboro & Eleanor Pierce,
                                                Oct. 21, 1779
Elnathan Foster of Dartmouth & Thankful Hammond,
                                                Feb. 27, 1780
John Symonds & Huldah Randall,   March 7, 1780
Timothy Hiller & Bathsheba Luce,   March 17, 1780
James Haskell & Abigail Doty,   April 5, 1780
Thomas Dotey & Asenath Bassett,   April 5, 1780
Joshua Vincent of Dartmouth & Hannah Church,
                                                April 16, 1780
Jashub Wing of Dartmouth & Eleanor Handy, June 8, 1780
Lot Conant of Bridgewater & Rhoda Perry,   Oct. 12, 1780
Benjamin Hammond & Lydia Haskell,   Oct. 22, 1780
John Clark & Bethiah Haskell,   Oct. 29, 1780

Seth Mendall & Meribah Clifton,	Nov. 16, 1780
William Randall & Deborah White,	Dec. 7, 1780
Arthur Hathaway of Wareham & Sarah Gurney,	
	Dec. 14, 1780
James Cowing & Sarah Randall,	Dec. 31, 1780
Thomas Bassett & Lydia Mendall,	Jan. 7, 1781
Joseph Hayward of Easton & Lydia Barrow,	Jan. 24, 1781
Samuel Lombard & Mercy White,	Feb. 8, 1781
Jethro Bennet of Dartmouth & Mary Devol,	Oct. 10, 1781
Jonathan Delano of Dartmouth & Lydia Briggs,	Oct. 21, 1781
Seth Hall of Middleboro & Rebecca Rider,	Nov. 4, 1781
Melatiah Bassett & Susanna Briggs,	Dec. 14, 1781
Jabez Delano & Rhoda Blankenship,	Jan. 13, 1782
Silas Briggs, Jr., & Elisabeth Leach,	Feb. 3, 1782
Zebulon Haskell & Thankful Dexter,	Feb. 3, 1782
Melatiah Clark & Hannah Snow,	Feb. 14, 1782
William Briggs & Mary Cowing,	March 10, 1782
Joshua Randall & Hannah Randall,	March 28, 1782
David Dexter & Mary Butler,	April 11, 1782
Ezra Perry of Woodstock, Vt., & Rachel Allen,	Oct. 6, 1782
Barnabas Clark & Hope White,	Oct. 11, 1782
Timothy Clifton & Bethiah Delano,	Nov. 28, 1782
Jesse Briggs of Wareham & Bette Jenne,	Dec. 12, 1782
Lemuel Clark & Elizabeth Perry,	Dec. 19, 1782
Zadock Cowing & Deborah Stuart,	March 29, 1772
Wiatt Barlow & Susanna Hammond,	April 6, 1772
Davis Collamore & Lydia Sturtevant,	Sept. 20, 1772
Richard ——— & Lucy Bumpus,	Oct. 16, 1772
Elijah Allen of Dartmouth & Villary (?) Church,	
	July 23, 1773
Malachi Ellis & Mercy Trip,	Nov. 25, 1773
Nathan Briggs & Mary Hammond,	Dec. 2, 1773
Joshua Austin & Esther Grinnall,	March 23, 1774
Jonathan Snow & Hannah Burge,	Feb. 6, 1783
Simon Hatheway & Eunice Wing,	Feb. 13, 1783
William Bassett & Thankful Haskell,	April 27, 1783
William Clark & Catey Luce,	May 22, 1783
Freeman Handy & Phebe Wing,	June 8, 1783

Shubael Nye of Falmouth & Mary White,	Aug. 10, 1783
Nathaniel Clarke of Pembroke & Mercy Sturtevant,	
	Oct. 5, 1783
William Smith & Desire Lombard,	Dec. 11, 1783
Jonathan Church & Sarah Nye,	Dec. 11, 1783
Elisha Briggs & Deborah Delano,	Jan. 15, 1784
Robert Foot & Thankful Ruggles,	Feb. 19, 1784
Timothy Ruggles & Clarinda Morse,	Feb. 19, 1784
Seth Clap & Charlotte Barden,	March 28, 1784
Joel Ellis & Deborah Briggs,	April 1, 1784
Peleg Tripp of Dartmouth & Sarah Haskell,	April 25, 1784
Robert Rider & Abia Parker,	April 25, 1784
Nathaniel Peirce of Middleboro & Mercy Rider,	
	May 13, 1784
Moses Mendal & Huldah Barrow,	Aug. 19, 1784
Nathaniel Ruggles & Drusilla Briggs,	Sept. 2, 1784
Stephen Barden & Lydia Clark,	Sept. 5, 1784
Paul Blankenship & Joanna Pease,	Nov. 7, 1784
Elnathan Hammond & Temperance Clark,	Oct. 3, 1776
Thomas Tobey & Betty Norton,	Oct. 17, 1776
Rev. Jonathan Moore & Nancy Hammond,	April 3, 1776
Nathan Brooks & Margaret Allen,	Sept. 28, 1776
Reuben Trip of R. & Susanna Delano of Dartmouth,	
	Nov., 1776
Haman Higgins & Hannah Randal,	Jan., 1778
Silas Jenny & Austris (?) Hammond,	April, 1778
Solomon Cutter of Brookfield & Sally Southward,	
	Dec. 8, 1778
Edward Phelps & Sarah Black,	Dec. 8, 1778
Nathaniel Cushing & Phebe Snow,	Feb. 4, 1779
Ichabod Samson of Wareham & Martha Dexter,	June 6, 1779
David Dexter & Sarah Allen,	Nov. 5, 1779
Ichabod Hatheway & Mary Ellis,	Nov. 14, 1775
Benjamin Hoskins, Jr., & Mary Hoskins,	Nov. 27, 1780
Joseph Parker & Hannah King,	Jan. 7, 1787
Barnabas Hammond & Huldah Holmes,	May 1, 1780
Dr. Samuel Cheever of Eastham & Thankful Hammond,	
	July 12, 1781

John Wallace & Eunice Clark, July 22, 1781
Edward Wanton Westgate & Lydia Randall, Nov. 13, 1781
Gideon Barstow & Anna Mead, Oct. 10, 1782
Joshua Dexter & Thankful Dexter, Dec. 30, 1782
Ebenezer Chace of Dartmouth & Sarah Snow, Jan. 21, 1783
Ebenezer Snow & Eleanor Young, Jan. 29, 1783
Isaac Benson of Middleboro & Zerviah Nye, July 15, 1783
Phillip Spooner of Dartmouth & Lydia Parker, Dec. 10, 1783
Humphrey Eldredge & Martha Austin, Jan. 1, 1784
Justus White & Content Clark, March 8, 1784
Benjamin Hammond & Anna Jenny, Sept. 1, 1784
Freeman Tabor of Dartmouth & Mary Stevens,
Nov. 10, 1784
Job Niel & Mary Hammond, Jan. 24, 1785
Richard Green & Abigail Barlow, July 28, 1785
William Nye & Ruth Snow, Aug. 19, 1785
Jerathmeel Doty & Sarah Look, Nov. 10, 1785
Richard Sherman & Hannah Eldridge, Dec. 8, 1785
James Hammond & Debby Snow, May 10, 1786
Ebenezer Mead & Priscilla Norton, June 10, 1786
Noah Hammond & Lydia Barlow, Nov. 19, 1786
Phillip Dexter & Patience Randall, Dec. 28, 1786
John Look & Hannah Holmes, Jan. 20, 1787
Jeremiah Clap & Polly Briggs, Feb. 21, 1787
Joseph Davis & Mercy Hammond, March 15, 1787
Noah Stevens & Mary Snow, April 15, 1787
Benjamin Wing & Lydia Ellis, Feb. 14, 1785
Jonathan Parlow & Katherine Wing, March 8, 1785
Gideon Jenne of R. & Hannah Briggs of Wareham,
April 14, 1785
William Packer of Dartmouth & Rebecca Randall,
May 1, 1785
Daniel Butler of Falmouth & Sarah Church, Sept. 22, 1785
Arnold Briggs of R. & Rhoda Benson of Wareham,
Oct. 6, 1785
Samuel Briggs, 3d, & Elisabeth Randall, Oct. 13, 1785
Theophilus Pitcher & Sarah Foster, March 17, 1786
Elisha Bassett of Tisbury & Mercy Sherman, March 23, 1786

Joel Ellis, Jr., & Tabitha White,   March 27, 1786
Richard Tabor of Dartmouth & Lydia Foster, April 27, 1786
Joseph Clagham of Tisbury & Anna Mendell, April 30, 1786
John Delano of Dartmouth & Polly Caswell,   May 14, 1786
Abraham Tabor of Dartmouth & Sarah Sherman,
                                             Sept. 5, 1786
Lewis Tobey of Sandwich & Abigail Bassett,   Sept. 7, 1786
Andrew Stephens & Sarah Clark,   Dec. 27, 1786
Benjamin Rowley of Falmouth & Susanna Clark,
                                             April 17, 1787
Levi LeBaron of Middleboro & Temperance Morse,
                                             July 5, 1787
Reuben Hamlin & Phebe Parlow,   Aug. 5, 1787
Seth Spooner, 3d, of New Bedford & Mary Reed,
                                             Dec. 17, 1787
John Smith & Mercy King,   Dec. 20, 1787
Butler Wing & Thankful Ellis,   March 2, 1788
Francis Le Baron of Middleboro & Jane Haskell,
                                             April 3, 1788
Abner Vincent of New Bedford & Phebe Stevens,
                                             June 15, 1788
William Claghorn, Jr., of New Bedford & Dolly Has-
    kell, Jr.,   Nov. 9, 1788
Joshua Sherman & Sally Pope,   Nov. 27, 1788
Stephen West of New Bedford & Asebra Mackfarling,
                                             Aug. 26, 1787
Seth Hiller, Jr., & Mary Hatheway,   Dec. 16, 1787
Simeon Bowerman of New Bedford & Susanna Cham-
    berlain,   Jan. 22, 1788
Major Elisha Ruggles & Mary Clap,   July 20, 1788
Thomas Freeman of Barnard, Vt., & Rebecca Swift,
                                             Sept. 25, 1788
Jabez Goram & Abigail Tobey,   Nov. 26, 1788
Noah Dexter & Mary Delano,   Nov. 27, 1788
Silvanus Wistgate of Tiverton, R. I., & Deborah
    Hammond,   Jan. 11, 1789
Job Randall & Mary Reynolds,   Feb. 10, 1789
Manassah Washburn of Middleboro & Sylva Caswell,
                                             April 23, 1789

MARRIAGES BY TIMOTHY RUGGLES, AT ———

Thomas Weeks of Hardwick & Katherine Clarke of R.,
April 3, 1743
George King & Lydia Snow, Aug. 4, 1743
James Francis & Hosea Nummuch (Indians), Sept. 28, 1743
David Pecker of Newport & Dorothy Robinson, Oct. 27, 1743
Joseph Tharp & Charity Andrews, Jan. 1, 1743
John Goodspeed & Mercy Hammond, Feb. 5, 1743
Samuel Savory & Elisabeth Bumpas of Wareham,
Dec. 25, 1739

INDEX.

EARLY MASSACHUSETTS MARRIAGES, BOOK II.

PLYMOUTH COUNTY.

Early Massachusetts Marriages

PRIOR TO 1800

AS FOUND ON

ANCIENT COURT RECORDS

of the Counties of

MIDDLESEX, HAMPSHIRE, BERKSHIRE AND BRISTOL

THIRD BOOK

EDITED BY THE

REV. FREDERIC W. BAILEY, B.D.

EDITOR "EARLY CONNECTICUT MARRIAGES," DESIGNER OF BAILEY'S PHOTO-ANCESTRAL RECORD—"THE RECORD OF MY ANCESTRY": MEMBER NEW ENGLAND HISTORIC GENEALOGICAL SOCIETY, CONNECTICUT HISTORICAL SOCIETY, WORCESTER SOCIETY OF ANTIQUITY, SONS OF THE AMERICAN REVOLUTION. (MASS.)

Published by
FREDERIC W. BAILEY
Worcester, Massachusetts

PREFACE

The following Middlesex County marriages were furnished us years ago by Mr. Frederic W. Parke now deceased, long a member of the New England Historic Genealogical Society, who copied from A. H. Ward's transcript of the old B. & M. records on file in the County Clerk's office at East Cambridge. For this reason they are believed to be both accurate and complete.

The Hampshire County marriages came from the County Clerk's office at Northampton covering all to be found on the old court records there.

The Berkshire County marriages are taken from the old court records at Pittsfield and include them all.

Of Bristol County we are able to print here the marriages of but one of the several towns recorded at the County Clerk's office, reserving for another issue the many other marriages of this county.

By including herein a number of early marriages of Plymouth County overlooked in the preparation of Book II, and thus completing in these issues the records from the courts of that county, the limits of this number have been reached.

Incidentally, there have been added herein some Springfield marriages pertaining to Connecticut people only as found on the town records there, being especially valuable to such as are tracing Connecticut family lines.

It is now some fourteen years since Book II was issued. That book has well served its intended purpose without, however, much profit to the editor. With this Book III we can see the accomplishment of another step in our endeavor of bringing to light and to service these old court records of marriages that few have access to or even suspect of existence.

Of course, there will be some errors, even though special care be taken to avoid them, and there will be those carping individuals, especially among genealogists, who will enjoy dwelling upon them often.

There are many reasons why in such a work mistakes are liable to occur even among the most efficient. But freely confessing to our own fallibility it will not deter us from offering this issue to all original seekers after family data to whom any fresh clue has precious meaning. To further, then, this intensely fascinating cause, we offer Book III as our humble contribution.

FREDERIC W. BAILEY.

Worcester, Mass., Nov. 1, 1914.

CONTENTS

MIDDLESEX COUNTY

Middlesex Co. was established May 10, 1643, being the same date with the establishment of both Suffolk and Essex.

The following marriages though in the county are not classified by their towns.

Tho. Elyott & Hannah Goold,	April 10, 1675
Wm. Sair & Martha Barber,	May 8, 1675
John Burrage & Susannah Cutler,	April 15, 1675
Edw. Johnson & Mirriam Holebrook,	March 24, 1675
Wm. Crouch & Elizab. Bredsha,	April 20, 1675
Jacob Hurd & Hannah Wilton,	Oct. 21, 1675
James Popley & Barbare Legorwell,	Oct. 23, 1675
Zach. Fowle & Mary Payne,	Oct. 24, 1675
Jonath. Carey & Hannah Windsor,	July 30, 1675
Jonath. Kettle & Abigail Convars,	Jan. 30, 1676
Tho. Chapman & Sarah Mirrick,	July 8, 1675
Wm. Ellis & Mary Mitchel,	5-5, 1675
James Smith & Mary Foster,	June 8, 1676
Samll. Carter, Jr. & Abigail Daman,	July 9, 1676
Capt. Wm. Hudson & Mary Fownell,	Nov. 23, 1676
Henry Sandeford & Mary Long,	Nov. 23, 1676
Hen. Kerly & Elizab. How,	Feb. 18, 1676
Samuel Phips & Mary Philips,	June 8, 1676
John Allin & Mercy Lee,	Aug. 25, 1677
Wm. Jamison & Sarah Price,	Aug. 18, 1677
John Smith & Mary Horne,	Aug. 22, 1677
Samuel Dowss & Faith Jewitt,	Jan. 7, 1677
Thomas Tarboll & Susannah Lawrence,	June 15, 1677
John Whittamore & Mary Miller,	Sept. 8, 1677
William Marshall & Lydia Hale,	June 14, 1681
John Reyner & Katharine Adams,	Sept. 7, 1681
John Brackenbury & Dorcas Greene,	Aug. 10, 1681
Thomas Barlow & Elizabeth Mellins,	Oct. 29, 1681
John Gill & Mary Carwithy, both of Dedham,	Dec. 31, 1686
Thomas Lewis & Mary Bread of Lynn,	Oct. 25, 1686
Thomas Robinson of Salem & Rebecca Lawrence of Dorchester,	Feb. 23, 1686/7

Matthew Castle & Mary Stowers,	Aug. 4, 1687
Richard Wild & Margaret Dollin,	Aug. 22, 1687
Ebenezer Orton & Abigail Furbur,	Oct. 28, 1687
John Searl & Margaret Hinksman,	Nov. 14, 1687
Robert Price & Hannah Chanler, both of Boston,	Apr. 16, 1688
Joseph Palmer of Stonington & Frances Prentice of Cambridge Village,	Nov. 13, 1687
William Hide & Elizabeth Hide of Cambridge Village,	Jan. 3, 1687
Nathaniel Hawes of Dedham & Sarah Newell of Roxbury,	Mch. 29, 1688
John Parker & Elizabeth Woodward, both of Boston,	Apr. 15, 1687
Ephraim Wheeler & Sarah Spring both of Cambridge Village,	Jan. 1, 1688
George Roseborough & Mary Lovell,	Aug. 6, 1686
James Bishop & Elizabeth Morsly,	Nov. 16, 1692
Nathaniel Call & Temperance Hurry,	May 15, 1690
Jonathan Richardson & Elizabeth Bates,	May 3, 1693
Edmund Rice & Ruth Parker of Roxbury,	Nov. 15, 1692
Nathaniel Harrad & Hannah Taylor,	Feb. 5, 1727-8
Barnad McNitt & Jane Clark,	Feb. 19, 1727-8
John Smith & Rebecca Bettyes,	Apr. 23, 1727
William Temple & Sarah Miller,	May 16, 1729
John McAlister & Margaret Johnson,	Oct. 6, 1729
Thomas Stearns & Mary Jennison,	Dec. 29, 1729

MENDON

May 15, 1667. "Ordered that the name of Mendon be given to "the Court's grant to Qunstipauge, being the township of Qunshapage as it was laid out according to the grant of the General Court" and that Mendon be settled as a town."

James Lovett & Hannah Tiler,	Jan. 20, 1668
Hopestill Tiler & Mary Lovett,	Jan. 20, 1668
John Aldridge & Sarah Thompson,	June 9, 1670
Joseph Steevens & Sarah Tayer,	July 2, 1671

BILLERICA

May 29, 1655. Certain proprietors and inhabitants of Shawshine granted a tract of land on Concord River, the name of the plantation to be "Billirikeyea."

John Baldwin & Mary Richardson,	15-3-1655
Jonathan Danforth & Elizab. Powlter,	Sept. 22, 1655
Jno. Stone & Mary Lathrop,	Oct. —, 1656
Samuel Champney & Sarah Hubbard,	Aug. 13, 1657
John Trull & Sarah French,	Oct. 11, 1657
John Sheldon & Mary Thompson,	Dec. 1, 1658
John French & Abigail Coggin,	April 21, 1659
Ralph Hill, Jr., & Martha Toothaccre,	Sept. 15, 1660
Benjamin Parker & Sarah Hartwell,	Feb. 18, 1661
John Brackett & Hannah French,	July 6, 1661
Jacob Browne & Mary Taplease,	Aug. 16, 1661
Ensign Oliver Whiting & Anna Danforth,	22-1-1689/0
George Brown & Sarah Kidder of Chelmsford,	Jan. 30, 1689/0
John Baldwin & Sarah Haywood,	Feb. 12, 1689/0
Jonathan Danforth & Easter Converse of Woburn,	
	Nov. 17, 1690
John Sheldon & Deborah Hill,	Nov. 29, 1690
Sergt. Thomas Richardson & Sarah Pattin,	Dec. 29, 1690
Joseph Crossbey & Sarah French,	May 6, 1691
Joseph Davis of Redding & Elizabeth Pattin,	June 18, 1691
Benjamin Dutton & Joanna Dunkin,	July 1, 1690
Edmund Chamberlain & Mercy Abbott,	26-6-1691
Zechariah Shedd & Lydea Farley,	March 9, 1692/3
James Frost, Jr. & Hannah Trull,	Nov. 22, 1693
Justinian Holden & Susanna Durant,	Dec. 6, 1693
Nathan Shed & Mary French,	Feb. 21, 1693/4
Nathaniel Duntlin of Woburn & Mary Sharp,	
	March 23, 1693/4
John Biglow & Sarah Bernus (?) both of Water- town,	Oct. 2, 1694

John Wilson, Jr. & Elizabeth Foster,	Nov. 27, 1694
Daniel Kitteridge & Elizab. Foster,	Dec. 19, 1694
Thomas Pattin & Rebecca Payne,	April 1, 1662
Samuel Kemp & Sarah Foster,	May 23, 1662
James Pattershin & Rebeccah Steevenson,	May 29, 1662
Joseph Thompson & Mary Brackett,	July 2, 1662
Thomas Hubbards & Elizabeth Hewett,	Oct. 15, 1662
John Marshall & Hannah Adkinson,	Nov. 19, 1662
John Poulter & Rachel Eliot,	Dec. 29, 1662
John French & Hannah Burrage,	July 3, 1663
Joseph French & Experience Foster,	Nov. 4, 1663
Lewis Allin & Sarah Ives,	April 6, 1665
John Kitterige & Mary Littlefield,	Nov. 2, 1665
James Frost & Rebeccah Hamlet,	Dec. 17, 1665
Roger Toothacre & Mary Allin,	June 9, 1665
Jacob French & Mary Champney,	Sept. 20, 1665
John Marshall & Mary Burrage,	Nov. 27, 1665
Caleb Farly & Rebeccah Hill,	5-5-1667
Henry Jeffs & Mary Bird,	Aug. 3, 1667
Jonathan Hill & Mary Hartwell,	Oct. 11, 1667
James Frost & Elizabeth Foster,	Nov. 22, 1667
Nathaniel Hills & Elizab. Holmes,	April 21, 1667
John Rogers, Jr. & Mary Shed,	Aug. 10, 1667
John French & Mary Rogers,	Nov. 14, 1667
Samuel Trull & Ann Hayle, widow,	April 15, 1668
Jacob Hamlett & Hannah Parker of Chelmsford,	22-7-1668
Lt. Willm. French & Mary Sternes, widow,	6-3-1669
John Rogers, Sen. & Elizabeth Browne, widow of Boston,	May 6, 1669
Caleb Farly & Lidea Moore,	Sept. 3, 1669
Joseph Walker & Sarah Wyman,	Oct. 15, 1669
Jacob Hamlett & Mary Dutton,	Oct. 21, 1669
Thomas Richardson & Mary Steevenson,	Nov. 5, 1669
Daniel Shed & Ruth Moore,	May 5, 1669
Willm. Deane & Martha Bateman,	July 1, 1669
John Durant & Susan Dutton,	Sept. 16, 1669
John Sanders & Mary Farly,	16-10-1671
Thomas Rogers & Hannah Shed,	Sept. 30, 1672

Joseph Foster & Aliz Gorton of Roxbury,	Dec. 11, 1672
Jonathan Hides, Jr. & Dorothy Kidder,	6-3-1673
Tho. Carrier Als Morgan & Martha Allin,	7-3-1674
Steeven Richardson & Abigail Wyman,	31-10-1674
John Dunkin & Johannah Jeffs,	23-12-1674
John Brackett & Ruth Ellis,	31-1-1675
Saml. Farley & Elisabeth Shed,	11-2-1677
Benj. Bullard & Elizabeth Ellice,	1-3-1677
Nathl. Toy (Tay)? & Bathshaba Wiman,	30-3-1677
John French & Mary Kitterige,	16-11-1677
Zach. Shed & Ann Dray,	16-11-1677
John Parker of Chelmsford & Mary Danforth,	4-4-1678
Isaac Fox & Abigail Osborn,	18-5-1678
James Kidder & Elisabeth Brown,	23-7-1678
Tho. Dutton, Jr. & Rebecca Draper,	1-11-1678
Tho. Rogers & Mary Browne,	16-1-1681
Ens. Joseph Tomson & Mary Denison,	17-1-1681
Hen. Jeffs, Jr. & May Baldwin,	13-2-1681
Hen. Jeffs Sen. & Mary Baker, widow, of Concord,	5-3-1681
Jno. Lavistone & Margaret Ross,	12-7-1681
Jno. Dutton & Sarah Shed,	20-7-1681
Sergt. Jno. Marshall & Damaris Wayte, widow,	30-9-1681
Jno. Chamblaine & Deborah Jaco,	6-10-1681
Jno. Lane & Susan Swipple,	20-1-1682
Jonathan Danforth & Rebecca Parker,	27-4-1682
Jno. Hinds & Mary Buttlar, widow,	9-12-1682
Samuel Lewis & Sarah Dutton,	3-2-1683
Benjamin Parker & Mary Trull,	11-8-1684
Tho. Dutton, Sr., & Ruth Hooper,	10-9-1684
Jacob French & Mary Converse,	30-4-1685
John Kitteridge & Hannah French,	3-6-1685
Ephraim Kidder & Rachel Crosbee,	1-6-1685
Nathl. Rogers & Martha Cloyce,	25-9-1685
Peter Bracket of B. & Sarah Foster of Cambridge,	Mch. 16, 1686/7
Timothy Baldwin of Wooburn & Elizabeth Hill,	June 2, 1687
Isaac Mixar of Watertown & Mary French,	June 29, 1687
David Carey of Bristol & Elizabeth Bracket,	Dec. 10, 1687

Caleb Farley, Jr. & Sarah Godfrey of Haverhill,   Apr. 8, 1686
Thomas Pattin, Sr. & Sarah Ditson of Redding, May 20, 1686
Anthony Goff of B. & Sarah Polley of Wooburn, Sept. 29, 1686
Josiah Wood of Wooburn & Abigail Bacon,   Dec. 13, 1686
Daniel Rogers of B. & May Russell of Concord, Dec. 28, 1686
Thomas Hayward of Concord & Elizabeth Danforth,
                                        Mch. 7, 1686/7
Geo. Walcup & Naomi Stevenson, both of Redding,
                                        Nov. 4, 1688
Peter Procter of Chemsford & May Paterson of B.
                                        Jan. 30, 1688
John Rogers of B. & Abigail Rogers of Charlestown,
                                        Feb. 7, 1688
Nathl. John Gefts of B. & Lydia Fisk of Sandwich,
                                        Ap. 6, 1688
John Smith & Sarah Blanchard, both of Charlestown,
                                        Feb. 18, 1691

CAMBRIDGE

Sept. 8, 1636 "Newe Towne" now called Cambridge.

Edward Jacson & Elizabeth Oliver,	14-1-1648–49
George Bowers & Eliz. Worthington,	Feb. 15, 1649
Robert Browne & Barbara Eden,	March 8, 1649
John Shepard & Rebecca Grenhill,	Aug. 4, 1649
Abraham Errington & Rebecca Cutler,	——, ——
Jonas Clearke & Eliz. Clearke,	May 30, 1650
John Swan & Rebecca Palfory,	Nov. 1, 1650
William Wilcocke & Mary Powell,	Nov. 22, 1650
Frances Moore & Albee Eaton,	July 7, 1650
Jonathan Michell & Margeret Shepard,	Sept. 19, 1650
Nath. Sparhauke & Patience Newman,	Aug. 3, 1649
Samuel Andrews & Elizabeth White,	July 22, 1652
Zach. Hickes & Elizab. Scill,	Aug. 28, 1652
Jonath. Padlfoot & Mary Blanford,	Aug. 5, 1652

Benj. Bowers & Elizabt. Dunster,	Oct. 9, 1653
Thomas Moore & Sarah Hodges,	Sept. 9, 1653
Robert Daniel & Reana Andrew,	March 2, 1654
Isacke Amsden & Franc. Perriman,	April 8, 1654
Jno. Marritt & Abigail Richardson,	April 20, 1654
Jno. Swan & Mary Prat,	Jan. 2, 1655
Walter Hastings & Sarah Meen,	Feb. 10, 1655
Thomas Fanning & Elizabt. Daniel,	March 17, 1655
Francis Moore & Elizabeth Periman,	Oct. 6, 1653
David Fiske & Seaborne Wilson,	July 6, 1655
Samuel Stone & Sarah Sternes,	April 7, 1655
Samuel Goffe & Hannah Barnard,	April 25, 1656
Thomas Browne & Martha Oldam,	Aug. 7, 1656
Hen. Bowtell & Elizth. Bowers,	April 25, 1657
Willm. Heale & Grace Butterice,	Aug. 14, 1653
Willm. Michelson & Mary Bradshaw,	Feb. 26, 1654
Jno. Green & Ruth Michelson,	Aug. 20, 1656
Willm. Barrat & Sarah Champneys,	June 19, 1656
Charles Sternes & Rebecca Gibson,	April 22, 1656
Edmund Angier & Anna Batt,	April 12, 1657
Gilbert Crackbone & Elizabeth Coolidge,	April 17, 1656
Thomas Danforth & Mary Withington,	23-2-1643
William Ward & Abigail ———,	Dec. 31, 1689
John Staples & Mary ———,	July 24, 1690
Richard Ward & Thankful ———,	Dec. 15, 1690
John Bunker & Rebecka Eaton,	28-2-1690
William Johnson & Mary Cook, Jr.,	Dec. 18, 1690
John Stedman & Sarah Gibson,	Feb. 9, 1691
Richard Fergison & Sarah Hurly,	May 31, 1690
John Hastings & Rebecka Eaton,	July 28, 1691
Joseph Pierce & Hannah Munroe,	21-12-1692
James Hews of Boston & Bethiah Swetman,	Dec. 12, 1692
David Stowell & Mary Stedman,	April 7, 1693
Jno. Eveleth of Chebacco & Mary Bowman,	Dec. 2, 1693
John Cutler & Mary Sternes,	July 19, 1693
William Man & Alice Tid,	June 11, 1657
William Clemance & Ann Taylor,	April 3, 1660
John Goave & Mary Aspinwall,	Oct. 6, 1658

Benjamin Crackbone & Elizabeth Dutton,	Nov. 6, 1657
Samuel Wood & Alice Rushton,	Sept. 28, 1659
Thomas Woolson & Sarah Hide,	Nov. 20, 1660
John Swan & Mary Pratt,	March 1, 1655
Willm. Healy & Phebe Greene,	Aug. 15, 1661
Seth Switzer & Elizab. Oakes	April —, 1661
John Lowden & Sarah Steevenson,	May 29, 1662
James Patteson & Rebecca Steevenson,	May 29, 1662
Thomas Hamond & Elizabeth Stedman,	Dec. 17, 1662
Joseph Scil & Jemima Belcher,	Dec. 5, 1662
William Barratt & Mary Barnard,	June 16, 1662
Samuel Greene & Sarah Clarke,	Feb. 23, 1662
John Gibson & Joanna Prentice,	July 24, 1662
Richard Cutter & Francis Emsden,	Feb. 14, 1662
Thomas Parkes & Abigail Deekes,	Dec. 1, 1653
Thomas Ross & Seth Holman,	Jan. 16, 1661
Joseph Russell & Mary Belcher,	June 23, 1662
Samuel Hastings & Mary Meene,	Nov. 12, 1661
James Hubbard & Sarah Winship,	Sept. 29, 1659
John Pitchfeild & Margarett Goffe,	Dec. —, 1662
Samuel Sternes & Hannah Manning,	Feb. 1, 1662
Nathaniel Upham & Elizabeth Stedman,	March 5, 1661/2
Richard Jackson & Elizabeth Browne,	May 12, 1662
Daniel Farrabas & Rebecca Perriman,	March 27, 1660
Jonathan Remington & Martha Belcher,	July 13, 1664
John Palfrey & Rebeccah Bordman,	Aug. 4, 1664
Isaac Sternes & Sarah Beers,	June 28, 1660
Nathaniel Hancocke & Mary Prentice,	March 8, 1663/4
John Hastings & Hannah Moore,	March 1, 1665/6
Joseph Cooke & Martha Stedman,	Dec. 4, 1665
John Stedman & Elizabeth Remington,	May 14, 1666
John Brackett & Sarah Stedman,	Aug. 23, 1662
John Mirriam & Mary Cooper,	Oct. 21, 1663
Edmund Pinson & Anna Cooper,	Aug. 2, 1664
Daniel Champney & Dorcas Bridge,	Jan. 3, 1665
John Frost & Rebeccah Andrews,	26-4-1666
Humphrey Osland & Elizabeth Hide,	Jan. 7, 1666–67
Joseph Hassull & Mary Perry,	June 21, 1667

James Hubbard & Hannah Ive,	Nov. 8, 1667
Samuel Alcock & Sarah Brackett,	Jan. 24, 1668
Piam Blower & Elizabeth Belcher,	Jan. 31, 1668
Robert Houghton & Sarah Phipeny,	July 8, 1668
Samuel Frost & Mary Coale,	Aug. 12, 1663
Samuel Gibson & Sarah Pemberton,	Aug. 30, 1668
Thomas Oliver & Grace Prentice,	Sept. 27, 1667
John Macoone & Deborah Bush,	Sept. 8, 1656
John Macoone & Sarah Wood,	April 14, 1665
Francis Whitmore & Margerett Harty,	Sept. 10, 1666
John Elyott & Elizabeth Gookin,	March 23, 1666
John Gibson & Rebecca Errington,	Oct. 9, 1668
Henry Thompson & Elizabeth Upham,	27-4-1669
Daniel Markham & Elizab. Whitmore,	Nov. 3, 1669
John Hastings & Lidea Champney,	May 20, 1668
Thomas Richardson & Mary Steevenson,	Jan. 5, 1669
Samuel Bucke & Rachel Leven,	March 16, 1669/70
Humphrey Bredsha & Martha Russell,	March 24, 1665
Israel Mede & Mary Hall,	Feb. 26, 1669
Nathaniel Patten & Rebeccah Adams,	Nov. 24, 1669
Nicholas Parlen & Sarah Hanmore,	Nov. 30, 1665
Nathaniel Robbins & Mary Brasier,	Aug. 4, 1669
Marmaduke Johnson & Ruth Cane,	April 28, 1670
Ephraim Winship & Hannah Reyner,	April 7, 1670
Jonathan Stevenson & Elizabeth Stubs,	July 8, 1669
Steeven Francis & Hannah Hall,	————, 1670
Benjamin Willington & Elizabeth Swatman,	Dec. 7, 1671
John Woodmancy & Elizabeth Clarke,	July 23, 1672
John Richardson & Mary Peirson,	Oct. 28, 1673
Henry Smith & Lidea Bucke,	March 3, 1672/3
Richard Robbins & Elizabeth Crackbone,	March 26, 1673
Samuel Manning & Abiah Weight,	May 6, 1673
Willm. Steevens & Abigail Greene,	July 1, 1673
Walter Davis & Mary Davis,	19-8-1674
John Sewall & Hannah Fisenden,	Aug. 28, 1674
John Wyatt & Elizab. Long,	Aug. 8, 1674
John Dolittle & Sibilla Nutt,	Aug. 30, 1674
Jno. Chadwick & Mary Barlow,	Aug. 30, 1674

David Stone & Sarah Hildreth,	Oct. 31, 1674
Edm. Bloyce & Ruth Parsons,	27-7-1675
Elisha Bull & Deborah Wilson,	June 7, 1689
Barnabas Cook & Mary Goodwin,	Dec. 4, 1689
Benjamin Goddard & Martha Palfry,	May 30, 1689
Nicholas Bow & Dorcas Champney,	May 6, 1690
Israil Chevers & Bridget Woodhead,	June 10, 1690
Samuel Kidder & Sarah Griggs,	Oct. 23, 1689
Benjamin Dana & Mary Buckmaster of Muddy River,	May 24, 1688
Thomas Phillibrowne of Charlestown & Rebekah Cutter of Cambridge,	Dec. 19, 1688
Saml. Parker of Redding & Mary Browne,	Jan. 3, 1688/9
Saml. Newman of Rehoboth & Hannah Bunker,	May 2, 1689
Daniel Lawrence & Sarah Counts, both of Charlestown,	June 19, 1689
Joseph Pike & Prudence Edminster, both of Charlestown, at Boston,	July 1, 1689
William Barrett & Mary Sparhawk,	8-8-1673
Seabas Jackson & Sarah Baker,	19-2-1671
Jonathan Sanders & Abiah Bartlett,	24-8-1669
Hen. Seogr ? & Sarah Bishop,	21-11-1673
Andrew Grover & Hannah Hill,	7-12-1673
Jonath. Hide & Mary Rediat,	8-11-1673
Saml. Hide, & Hannah Stedman,	20-11-1673
Tho. Andrew & Martha Eccles,	30-8-1673
James Minott & Hephziba Corlett,	21-3-1673
Arthur Coale & Lidea Barrett,	27-9-1673
Daniel Thurston & Mary Stedman,	1-2-1674
Jonath. Cane & Rebecca Welsh,	14-3-1674
Saml. Scripture & Elizab. Knap,	11-7-1674
Jno. Oldam & Abigail Wood,	22-5-1675
Fra. Everitt & Mary Edwards,	7-10-1675
Walter Hastings & Elizab. Bright,	23-5-1674
Jno. Smith & Sarah Prentice,	8-4-1676
Ephr. Winship & Elizab. Kendall,	9-9-1675
Jno. Oldam & Abigail Wood,	22-5-1675
Fran. Everitt & Mary Edwards,	7-10-1675

Walter Hastings & Elizab. Bright,	23-5-1674
Jno. Smith & Sarah Prentice,	8-4-1676
Jno. Warner & Sarah Wood,	12-4-1677
Edw. Hall & Mary Reyner,	18-4-1677
Humph. Miller & Elizab. Smith,	12-7-1677
Ri. Eccles & Susannah Carter,	4-4-1677
Samuel Oldam & Hannah Dana,	5-11-1670
Jonas Clark & Elizab. Cook,	19-6-1673
Jonath. Lawrence & Rebecca Rutter,	5-9-1677
Wm. Healy & Sarah Brown,	29-9-1677
Timothy Willy & Elizab. Danes,	4-10-1677
Tho. Lun & Elizab. Bowker,	28-1-1679
Owen Warland & Hannah Guy,	3-2-1679
Daniel Farrabas & Deborah Rideatt,	22-3-1679
Jonathan Rice & Rebecca Watson,	1-9-1677
Samuel Gibson & Elizab. Stedman,	14-4-1679
Jno. Needham & Elizab. Hicks,	10-8-1679
Jno. Gove, & Mary Woodhead,	15-1-1677
Andrew Bordman & Ruth Bull,	15-8-1669
Isaac Hill & Sarah Bicknall	12-11-1679
Ephraim Cutter & Bethya Wood,	11-12-1678
Joshua Fuller & Elizab. Ward,	7-3-1679
Nathl. Pattin & Sarah Cooper,	8-8-1678
Isaac Aemsden & Janet Rutter,	17-3-1677
Tho. Greenwood & Hannah Ward,	8-4-1670
Joseph Bartlett & Mary Wayte,	27-8-1668
David Mede & Hannah Warren,	26-7-1675
Tho. Prentice & Elizab. Jackson,	28-4-1677
Gershan Cutter & Lidea Hall,	6-1-1677/8
Noah Wiswall & Theodosiah Jackson,	14-10-1664
Gershom Swann & Sarah Holden,	20-10-1677
Nehemiah Hubbart (Hobart) & M—? Sarah Jackson,	
	21-1-1676/7
Renold Bush & Susannah Lovett,	2-7-1678
Joshua Woods & Elizab. Buck,	28-6-1678
Sam'l Ballard & Hannah Belcher,	2-7-1678
Joseph Fuller & Lidea Jackson,	13-12-1678-9
Jonath. Dunster & Abigail Elyott,	5-10-1678

Sam'l Stone & Dorcas Jones,	12-4-1679
Wm. Aegur? & Hester (Lidea)? Cole,	13-2-1680
Jno. Hinckson & Mary Harrington,	13-2-1680
Philip Russell & Joannah Cutter,	19-4-1680
Joseph Simons & Mary Teed,	7-1-1680/1
Thomas Brown & Mary Hall,	23-3-1681
Jno. Willington & Susannah Strayts ?,	9-4-1681
Nicholas Withe & Lidea Fisk,	6-7-1681
Amos Marritt & Bethya Longhorn,	2-9-1681
Jno. Ward & Mary Spring,	30-9-1681
Jno. Mirrick & Elizab. Trowbridge,	9-12-1681/2
Henry Prentice & Mary Gove,	7-2-1682
Isaac Laurance & Abigail Bellows,	19-2-1682
Stephen Sewall & Margaret Mitchell,	13-4-1682
Thomas Oliver & Mary Wilson,	19-2-1682
Jno. Fuller & Abigail Balstone,	30-4-1682
Sam'l Cooke & Abigail Griggs,	14-9-1681
Tho. Chamberlain & Elizab. Hammond,	18-2-1681
Francis Foxcroft & Elizabeth Danforth,	3-8-1682
James Nicolls & Mary Poole,	9-9-1682
Sam'l Goffe & Mary Saxton,	9-9-1682
Jno. Hide & Mary Kinnericke,	20-11-1682
Sam'l Cooper & Hannah Hastings,	4-10-1682
John Wythe & Deborah Ward,	2-11-1682
Thomas Johnson & Elizab. Green,	8-11-1682/3
Edward Winship & Rebecca Barsham,	14-3-1683
Will. Russell & Abigail Winship,	18-1-1682/3
Tho. Stacie & Hannah Hicks,	20-4-1683
Tho. Hall & Martha Bradshaw,	24-3-1683
Will. Wythe & Ruth Shepard,	16-8-1683
Will. Taylor & Mary Cheevers,	28-9-1683
Stephen Francis & Hannah Dickson,	16-7-1683
Geo. Addams & Martha Fisk,	28-11-1683
Will. Burgess & Hannah Stewinson ? (Stevenson),	20-3-1684
Jaason Russell & Mary Hubbard,	27-3-1684
Daniel Champney & Hephsibah Minott,	9-4-1684
Jonathan Fuller & Mindwell Trowbridge,	2-3-1684
John Green & Mary Broadish,	22-9-1684

Edwd. Wyer, Jr. & Abigail Lawrence, 1-7-1684
James Clarke & Sarah Champney, 24-7-1685
Thomas Fox & Rebek. Wythe, Dec. 16, 1685
Zech. Hicks & Ruth Greene Nov. 18, 1685
Sam. Greene & Elisabeth Sill, Nov. 18, 1685
Sam. Whitmore & Rebekah Gardner, Mch. 31, 1686
John Cooper & Elisabeth Bordman, Ap. 28, 1686
Thomas Foster & Experience Parker, Nov. 30, 1686
Isaac Wilson & Susannah Andrew, July 19, 1685
Ebenezer Stone & Margaret Trowbridge, Mch. 1, 1686
Nicholas Bow & Sarah Hubbard, June 26, 1684
Samuel Winship of C. & Mary Powter of Meadford,
Ap. 12, 1687
John Stone of C. & Rachel Shepard of Concord, Ap. 27, 1687
John Dixon & Margery Winship, May 12, 1687
Isaac Parker & Mary Parker, May 4, 1687
John Ruggles, Sr. & Ruth Swan, both of Roxbury,
Oct. 12, 1687
John Francis & Lydia Cooper, Jan. 5, 1687/8
Joseph Addams & Margaret Eames, Feb. 21, 1687/8
Matthew Abdey ? & Debrah Wilson, Ap. 10, 1688
William Shattuck, Jr. of Groton & Hannah Under-
wood, Mch. 19, 1687/8
Thomas Dean of Concord & Sarah Blanchard of
Charlestown, Aug. 22, 1687
Jacob Taylor & Deborah Hutting, both of Concord,
Nov. 29, 1687
Josiah Blood & Mary Barret, both of Concord, Mch. 21, 1687/8
Nath'l Ball & Mary Brooks, both of Concord, Ap. 19, 1688
Nath'l Cutter of C. & Mary Phillibrowne of
Charlestown, Oct. 8, 1688

CHARLESTOWN

Aug. 23, 1630. The first court of Assistants was held at "Charlton."

William Roswell & Katherin Russell,	29-2-1654
John Anderson of Boston & Mrs. (?) — Hodges,	Jan. 3, 1654
Mathew Griffin & Hannah Cutler,	Aug. 29, 1654
Saml. Blanchard & Mary Switcher,	3-11-1654
Saml. Ruggles & Hannah Fowle,	10-11-1654
John Knight & Ruhama Johnson,	April 25, 1654
Thomas Gennar & Rebecca Terrice,	22-3-1655
John Brackenbury & Amye Anderson,	17-5-1655
Joseph Noise & Mary Norton,	Oct. 30, 1656
Joseph Noyse & Sarah Line,	Feb. 18, 1656
John Johnson & Elizabeth Mavericke,	Oct. 15, 1656
Thomas Adams & Alice Roper,	Dec. 2, 1656
Thomas Shepard & Hannah Tingentred,	Nov. 3, 1656
Jno. Cole & Hannah Kettle,	Jan. 22, 1656
Thomas Rann & Sarah Idends,	March 12, 1655/56
Edward Wilson & Mary Hale,	Nov. 6, 1656
Elias Roe & Rebecca Long,	July 17, 1656
Samuel Whiteing & Dorcas Chester,	Nov. 12, 1656
Henry Kemball & Sarah Founell,	Nov. 13, 1656
Zach. Long & Sarah Tid,	Sept. 24, 1656
Jno. Philips & Katherine Anderson,	July 19, 1655
Henry Cookery & Hannah Long,	Oct. 22, 1657
Josiah Wood & Lidia Bacon,	Oct. 28, 1657
Walter Adams & Hannah Moulton,	Dec. 15, 1657
Samuel Hossier & Urslin Streeter,	Oct. 13, 1657
Edward Weyer & Elizab. Johnson,	5-11-1658
John Mathews & Margarett Hunt,	Nov. 7, 1658
Willm. Evered & Sarah Fillibrown,	Nov. 30, 1658
John Fowles & Annah Carter,	Nov. 25, 1658
John Mason & Annoer Colliham,	Nov. 30, 1658
Jno. Baxter & Hannah Thrumble,	Jan. 2, 1659

Nathall. Hutchinson & Sarah Baker,	Jan. 16, 1659
Nath. Blancherd & Mahettable Nowett,	Oct. 16, 1659
Willm. Hilton & Mahettable Nowett,	July 16, 1659
Richard Astin & Abigail Bachelder,	Sept. 11, 1659
Thomas Haile & Mary Nash,	Oct. 14, 1659
Henry Cookery & Mary Beman,	23-1-1689
Thomas Gilberd & Lydia Ballatt,	26-9-1690
Thomas Bly & Sarah Everton,	July 10, 1691
Samll. Ballatt & Lydia Hale,	April 4, 1691
William Rouse & Mary Peache,	19-1-1691/2
John Kent & Sarah Smith,	Dec. 22, 1692
Joseph Austin & Elizab. Pitts,	Nov. 10, 1692
Jno. Crawford of Liverpool, England & Mary Alford,	22-9-1692
Robert Ward of Yohall & Margaret Peache,	Dec. 22, 1692
Thomas Swan of Roxbury & Prudence Wade of Medford,	27-10-1692
Thomas Barber & Hannah Stedman,	Jan. 12, 1692
Jonathan Dunster & Deborah Wade,	April 5, 1692
Joses Bucknam of C. & Hannah Peabody of Boxford at Topsfield,	Feb. 24, 1690/1
Benjamin Gary & Abigail Goold,	May 15, 1693
Eleazer Dowse & Mary Edmonds,	Sept. 21, 1693
Joseph Richardson & Mary Bloghead, both of Woburn,	Oct. 24, 1693
John Edmunds & Sarah Blany,	Nov. 1, 1693
Archibald Macquarring of Lofin in Scotland & Sarah Lawden,	Jan. 2, 1693/4
Nathanll. Frothingham & Hannah Rand,	April 12, 1694
Samuel Kettle & Mary Frothingham,	May 3, 1694
Capt. Thomas Fisk of Wenham & Martha Fitch of Boston,	May 14, 1695
William Welsted & Katherine Long,	May 24, 1694
Samuel Brackenbury & Ann Chickering,	Oct. 22, 1694
Jonathan Dowse & Elizabeth Ballatt,	Nov. 18, 1694
Edward Park of New Town & Martha Fisk of Watertown,	March 13, 1694/5
Capt. Thomas Fiske of Wenham and Martha Fitch of Boston,	May 14, 1695

Thomas Fosdick & Mary Martin,	May 16, 1695
Jonathan Wardwell of Ipswich & Katherine Chickering,	Dec. 12, 1696
Michael Gill & Releife Dowse,	May 26, 1696
Thomas Hodges & Exercise Razor,	March 23, 1663
John Wheeler & Sarah Larkin,	March 25, 1663
Luke Perkins & Hannah Coockery,	March 9, 1663
Thomas Tucke & Elizabeth Nichols,	May 21, 1663
Robert Parris & Seaborne Cromwell,	May 22, 1663
John Badger & Elizabeth Hayden,	June 16, 1663
Nathaniel Dade & Hannah Miller,	June 17, 1663
Jno. Chester & Elizabeth Pittman,	June 30, 1663
Jacob Moulton & Ruhama Haydon,	July 3, 1663
Jno. Whiple & Mary Steevens,	July 21, 1663
Robert Smith & Elizabeth Kelly,	Aug. 4, 1663
Jno. Avery & Sarah Browne,	Aug. 21, 1663
Henry Blackmore & Mary Thrumball,	Aug. 25, 1663
John Trerice & Hannah Lines,	Sept. 3, 1663
James Tally & Martha Baistow,	Oct. 14, 1663
Richard Shepard & Jane Talby,	Oct. 14, 1663
Daniel Whittemore & Mary Mellins,	March 7, 1662
Inego Potter & Mary Laurance,	Aug. 25, 1665
Richard Holly & Joanna Downing,	Oct. 29, 1663
Thomas White & Mary Frothingham,	Nov. 17, 1663
Philip Bullis & Judith Keep,	Dec. 3, 1663
Samuel Dingles & Elizabeth Call,	Sept. 20, 1663
John Hamon & Sarah Nicholls,	March 2, 1663
Stephen Smith & Decline Lamb,	Dec. 7, 1663
Joseph Johnson & Mary Soatly,	April 19, 1664
John Barratt & Elizabeth Cousons,	June 6, 1664
Willm. Pitts & Ann Patridge,	July 29, 1664
Nathaniel Graves & Elizabeth Russell,	Aug. 24, 1664
Nathaniel Rand & Mary Carter,	Sept. 2, 1664
Richard Rosemorgan & Hopestill Mirrick,	Oct. 7, ——
Willm. Ginningham & Agnes Walden,	Oct. 13, 1664
John Laurance & Susanna Bachelder,	Nov. 2, 1664
Joseph Shaw & Sarah Potter,	Dec. 16, 1664
Joseph Widney & Mary Buckmaster,	Nov. 20, 1664

John Larkin & Joanna Hale,	Nov. 9, 1664
Timothy Prout & Deborah Simes,	Dec. 13, ——
John Coggin & Mary Long,	Dec. 22, 1664
William Browne & Elizabeth Downe,	
William Brigs & Mary Yelling,	Jan. 10, 1664
Mark Wood & Elizabeth Hancock,	Feb. 2, 1664
Theophilus Marsh & Elizabeth Hunt,	Feb. 3, 1664
John Newell & Hannah Lurkin,	Feb. 15, 1664
Joseph Lindes & Sarah Davison,	March 29, 1665
Peter Frothingham & Mary Lowden,	March 14, 1665
Elihue Wardle & Elizabeth Wade,	May 27, 1665
Laurence Hamond & Abigail Willett,	May 12, 1665
Joseph Shapley & Abiell Howard,	June 8, 1665
Thomas Peachy & Mary Robinson,	May 3, 1665
Joseph Kettle & Hannah Frothingham,	July 5, 1665
Samuel Kettle & Mercy Haydon,	July 11, 1665
Mathew Smith & Ales Leader,	July 14, 1665
John Thrumble & Mary Jones,	Sept. 26, 1665
Randall Foster & Sarah Martin,	Oct. 19, 1665
John Winsor & Mary Neybours,	Sept. 22, 1665
George Read & Hannah Rockwell,	Nov. 9, 1665
William Welsted & Mehettabell Cary,	Nov. 24, 1665
Thomas Boylson & Mary Gardner,	Dec. 13, 1665
Nathan Ransford & Mary Allen,	Nov. 28, 1665
Samuel Sevornes & Sarah Grant,	Feb. 23, 1665
John Simson & Abigail Smith,	Dec. 1, 1665
Thomas Lindes & Rebeccah Trerice,	Dec. 6, 1665
John Newton & Elizabeth Larkin,	June 5, 1666
Roger Prosser & Mary Collins,	July 5, 1666
Willm. Teirce & Sarah Kein,	July 3, 1666
Nathaniel Howard & Sarah Willard,	July 2, 1666
Willm. Guard & Martha Gimson,	July 30, 1666
Samuel Leamon & Mary Longley,	July 30, 1666
Samuel Goolethirt & Elizabeth Cheaver,	Sept. 6, 1666
John Goose & Sarah Trerise,	Aug. 10, 1666
John Jones & Rebecca Sallie,	Sept. 10, 1666
Isaac Winslow & Mary Nowell,	Aug. 14, 1666
Philip Kneale & Ruth Allin, widow,	Oct. 5, 1666

Willm. Marshall & Mary Hilton,	Aug. 2, 1666
Willm. Barber & Elisab. Brickford,	Dec. 2, 1666
Benjamin Chadwell & Elizab. Hawes,	Dec. 20, 1666
Thomas Hett & Dorothy Edmunds,	Jan. 8, 1666
Samuel Pettefer & Mary Baker,	Feb. 7, 1666
Henry Balcome & Elizabeth Haynes,	Aug. 12, 1666
Richard Pritchard & Margery Benham,	Feb. 20, 1666
Thomas Larkin & Hannah Remington,	Sept. 13, 1666
Daniel Sutton & Mary Cole,	April 15, 1667
John Powell & Sarah Sallie,	May 20, 1667
David Anderson & Hannah Nicholls,	June, 1667
Thomas Barber & Hannah Roper,	June 25, 1667
James Johnson & Ann Furnell,	June 28, 1667
George Welby & Ann Carpenter,	July 16, 1667
Thomas Greene & Elizab. Web,	Aug. 19, 1667
Manasses Marston & Mercy Peirce,	Aug. 22, 1667
Samuel Carter, Jr. & Bethia Cowdry,	Sept. 18, 1667
John Edmunds & Hannah Dady,	Oct. 4, 1667
Samuel Lords & Elizab. Ted,	Oct. 15, 1667
Henry Edwards & Ursula Huson,	Nov. 7, 1667
Thomas Verny & Ann Browne,	Dec. 23, 1667
Thomas Lovell & Elizabeth Watson,	Dec. 28, 1667
Joseph Frost & Hannah Miller,	May 22, 1666
Solomon Phips, Jr. & Hannah Pickard,	Nov. 13, 1667
Samuel Hale & Lidea Maynard,	March 19, 1668
Edward Willis & Ruth Simes,	June 15, 1668
John Knight & Mary Bridge,	June 22, 1668
Henry Herbert & Elizabeth George,	June 9, 1668
Thomas Deane & Elizabeth Burrige,	Sept. 15, 1668
James Elson & Sarah Hayman,	Oct. 13, 1668
John Beacon & Susanna Draper,	Sept. 2, 1668
Moses Newton & Joannah Larkin,	Oct. 28, 1668
Thomas Knowlton & Hannah Greene,	Nov. 24, 1668
Nathaniel Johnson & Joanna Long,	Nov. 24, 1668
Samuel Frothingham & Ruth George,	Dec. 4, 1668
Timothy Simes & Mary Nicholls,	Dec. 10, 1668
Jonathan Shoare & Priscilla Hawthorne,	Jan. 15, 1668
Samuel Long & Elizab. Pinkham,	Jan. 20, 1668

Nathaniel Cutler & Elizabeth Carter, Sept. 2, 1668
Zachariah Soaftly & Elizabeth Harris, 13-2-1669
Willm. Rogers & Abigail Goold, April 1, 1669
John Strapen & Sarah Palefield, May 7, 1669
John Swayne & Mary Moore, June 4, 1669
Jacob Cole & Sarah Trayne, Aug. 12, 1669
Zachary Simmes, Jr. & Susanna Graves, Sept. 18, 1669
Christopher Hayes & Sarah King, Oct. 2, 1669
John Goodwin & Martha Lathrop, Oct. 2, 1669
Samuel Bignell & Mary Bell, Oct. 2, 1669
Elijas Maverick & Margarett Sheerwood, Oct. 8, 1669
Thomas Skinner & Mary Goold, Oct. 22, 1669
Thomas Russell & Prudence Chester, Oct. 30, 1669
Nathaniel Kettle & Hannah Eville, Nov. 13, 1669
James Browne & Hannah House, Jan. 16, 1670
John Betts & Mary Haws, March 17, 1669/70
John Munnell & Sarah Thamar, Aug. 7, 1669
John Heyden & Hannah Mayner, Aug. 14, 1669
John Hallyday & Ann Sady, March 21, 1670
Solomon Phelps, Jr. & Mary Danforth, July —, 1669
Francis Shepard & Sarah Osburne, April 28, 1670
Thomas Bonfeild & Elizab. Long, June 2, 1670
Robert Manser & Elizabeth Brookes, June 6, 1670
John Greenland & Lidea Sprague, July 5, 1670
Willm. Dady & Elizabeth March, June 29, 1670
Samuel Hayman & Hannah Trumbell, Aug. 18, 1670
Samuel Douss & Hannah Ludkin, Aug. 8, 1670
Deacon Willm. Stitson & Mrs. Mary Norton, widow,
                                                    Aug. 22, 1670
Owen Headen & Martha Clarke, Aug. 25, 1670
Peter Tufts & Elizabeth Linde, Aug. 26, 1670
John Mallesie & Izabell Wells, Oct. 4, 1670
Henry Swayne & Mary Smith, Nov. 16, 1670
John Bachelder & Agnes Gillingham, widow, Dec. 22, 1670
Samuel Hayward & Susannah Wilkinson, March 10, 1670
John Baker & Ruth Wally, widow, March 7, 1670
John Pike & Elizabeth Engleby, March 28, 1671
George Cannoway & Anna Wilson, widow, April 23, 1671

David Macomy & Hester Hardy,	Sept. 6, 1671
Timothy Simmes & Elizabeth Norton,	Sept. 21, 1671
Abell Benjamin & Amalthya Mirriacke,	Nov. 6, 1671
Seabred Taylor & Mary Arrington,	Nov. 21, 1671
Isaac Johnson & Mary Stone,	Nov. 22, 1671
Mathew Soby (?) & Sarah Strapen,	Dec. 7, 1671
Caleb Savon & Sarah Inglesby,	Dec. 15, 1671
Isaac Fowle & Berriah Bright,	Nov. 30, 1671
John Hunt & Ann Carter,	Jan. 2, 1671
Daniel Smith & Elizabeth Walden,	Jan. 2, 1671
Nehemiah Willoughby & Abigaill Bartholomew,	Jan. 2, 1671
George Bullard & Jane Elce,	May 2, 1672
Giles Fifeild & Judeth Convers,	May 2, 1672
William Browne, Jr. & Mary Goodin,	Feb. 29, 1672
John Blany & Sarah Powell,	June 26, 1672
John Walker & Hannah Mirricke,	Aug. 1, 1672
David Anderson & Katherine Richeson,	Sept. 12, 1672
John Douse & Releife Holland,	Oct. 31, 1672
Nathaniel Kettle & Hannah Kidder,	Oct. 30, 1672
Jeremiah Gatchell & Hannah Saith,	Feb. 2, 1672
Richard Sprague & Eunice Chester,	Feb. 25, 1672
Christopher Goodwin, Jr. & Mercy Crouch,	May 11, 1671
John Marable & Mary Whettemore,	May 3, 1673
Thomas Bathricke & Elizabeth Wells,	April 5, 1673
Thomas Wheeler & Elizabeth Chamberlin,	May 5, 1673
George Mudge & Elizabeth Shippie,	May 27, 1673
Samuel Linde & Rebeccah Jenners,	June 3, 1673
Samuel Blancher & Hannah Dagget,	June 23, 1673
Willm. Sheafe & Ruth Wood,	Aug. 15, 1673
John Parrack, & Sarah Smith	July 17, 1673
Nehemiah Goodall & Havens,	July 30, 1673
Steeven Geary & Mary Manuell,	Aug. 14, 1673
Increase Turner & Mehettabell Hett,	Oct. 3, 1673
James Miller & Hannah George,	Nov. 25, 1673
Zacheriah Ferris & Sarah Blouds,	Nov. 12, 1673
Thomas Ricks & Sarah Blithe,	Dec. 31, 1673
Thomas Haul & Elizabeth Miles,	Dec. 24, 1673
Nicholas Hookie & Mary Bredshaw,	Dec. 17, 1673

Timotny Cutler & Elizabeth Hilton,	Dec. 22, 1673
Jonathan Simpson & Wayte Clap,	April 3, 1673
Daniel Davison & Abigail Coffin,	Dec. 16, 1673
Benjamin Redknop & Sarah Tompson,	March 19, 1673/4
Nathan Hayman & Elizabeth Allin,	March 11, 1673/4
George Stedman & Hannah Osburn,	4-2-1674
Steeven Waters & Sarah Carter,	April 12, 1674
Jno. Long & Mary Winslow,	July 10, 1674
Ande. Robinson & Elizab. Whafe,	July 23, 1674
Saml. Burnell & Anny Moore,	Aug. 9, 1674
Jno. Nutter & Mehett. Edengton,	Aug. 7, 1674
Alex. Forbas & Kal. (?) Robinson,	Aug. 29, 1674
Wm. Vine & Elizab. Arrington,	Aug. 15, 1674
Steeven Codman & Elizab. Randall,	Sept. 19, 1674
Tho. Larkin & Elizab. Dowse,	April 18, 1674
Jno. Edes & Mary Tufts,	Aug. 15, 1674
Capt. Laur. Hamond & Margt. Willoughby,	Dec. 8, 1674
George Grines & Elizab. Blancher,	Feb. 15, 1675
David Wyman & Izabell Farmour,	Feb. 27, 1675
Math. Farrinden & Sarah Potter,	Feb. 28, 1675
Jno. Cutler & Martha Wiswall,	Feb. 23, 1675
Joseph Dowss & Mary George,	11-5-1678
Nathl. Havard & Sarah Parker,	1-5-1678
Jacob Green & Mary Robinson,	8-11-1676
Caleb Carter & Mary Tuttle,	4-10-1678
Walter Allen & Abigail Rogers,	29-9-1678
John Knight & Mary Clements, widow,	19-10-1678
Andrew Stevenson & Abigail Switzer,	1-9-1678
Sam'l Ballatt & Hannah Belcher,	1-7-1678
Christopher Goodwin & Joanna Johnson, widow,	10-10-1679
James Lowden & Mary Bunker, widow,	12-10-1679
William Wilson & Remember Ward,	May 1, 1679
Capt. Ri. Sprague & Mrs. Katharine Anderson,	May 7, 1679
John Betts & Elizabeth Lisley,	June 17, 1679
Samuel Read & Elisabeth Mousall,	June 19, 1679
Tho. Rand & Sarah Langley,	June 17, 1679
William Brown & Mary Lathrop,	May 21, 1679
Abram Fowl & Hannah Harris,	July 14, 1679

Tho. Monsall & Mary Moore,	Ap. 31, 1679
Hen. Swayne & Hannah Lathrop,	Aug. 21, 1679
John Edminster & Sarah Tomson,	June 17, 1679
Samuel Johnson & Elisabeth Martin,	Sept. 2, 1679
Tho. Carter, Sr. & Elisabeth Johnson,	Oct. 24, 1679
James Kelling & Hannah Frerice ?,	Dec. 22, 1679
Timothy Pratt & Grace Sheepie,	Nov. 19, 1679
Joseph Lampson & Elisabeth Mitchell,	Dec. 12, 1679
Alexander Logan & Susannah Burrige,	Jan. 15, 1679
Tho. Welsh & Hannah Monsall,	Jan. 21, 1679
Isaac Lewis & Mary Davis,	Mch. 25, 1680
Solomon Green & May Goose? (Grose)?,	Dec. 19, 1679
Joseph Lind & widow Brackenbury,	Dec. 24, 1679
John Carter & Sarah Stowers,	Ap. 21, 1680
Steeven Barratt & Elizabeth Mellins,	May 14, 1680
Tho. Addams & May Blackmore,	Ap. 28, 1680
James Kebbe & Sarah Lowden,	Oct. 23, 1679
Sam'l Blunt & Hannah Fosdick,	June 9, 1680
John Poore & Elisabeth Deane,	Aug. 12, 1680
Geo. Mannings & Mary Mixtur,	Nov. 1, 1680
Joseph Newall & Sarah Tuttle,	Nov. 11, 1680
Joseph Pike & Susannah Smith,	Nov. 10, 1680
John Ireland & Grace Healy,	July 15, 1680
John Rupling & Sarah Healy,	Dec. 14, 1680
James Bennett & Elizabeth Tarbole,	Feb. 4, 1680
Sam'l Phips & Katharine·Brackenbury,	Feb. 16, 1680
Jonath. Tufts & Rebecca Wayte,	Mch. 31, 1681
Sam'l Griffin & Priscilla Croswell,	June 19, 1680
Timothy Philip & Mary Smith,	Ap. 18, 1681
William Johnson & Sarah Burrage,	5-2-1682
Robert Lewis & Rebecca Linde,	6-2-1682
Thos. Graves & Mrs. Sarah Alcock,	15-3-1682
Joseph Stacy & Elizabeth Addams,	29-4-1682
Jno. Perry ? & Elizabeth Rand,	4-5-1682
Zach. Long & Sarah Moore,	9-6-1682
Tho. Shepard & Mrs. Mary Linde,	27-5-1682
Joshua Benjamin & Thankful Stone,	24-6-1682
James Capen & Hannah Laurance,	21-7-1682

Sam'l Lawrance & Rebecca Luen,	14-7-1682
Hopewell Davis & Sarah Boynton,	14-9-1682
William Johnson & Hester Taylor,	21-10-1682
Jeremiah Wherry & Jane Wayt,	21-2-1683
Ignatius White & Ruth Burrage,	4-4-1683
John Knight & Sarah Holsworth,	24-3-1683
Joseph Hunscot & Mary Maccarty,	17-7-1683
Thomas Call & Elisabeth Chesswell,	23-3-1683
Nathaniel Wilson & Thankful Beamont,	27-7-1683
Tho. Shepard, Jr. & Hannah Blanchar,	7-10-1682
William Morrice & Lettice Carter,	15-7-1683
Matthew Smith & Mary Cutler,	2-1-1682/1
Jno. Ross & Susannah Goose,	28-9-1681
Andrew Phillip & Sarah Smith,	11-19-1683
Daniel Willard & Hannah Cutler,	6-10-1683
Thomas Foskett & Miriam Cleveland,	13-10-1683
John Bennet & Ruth Bradshaw,	3-11-1683
John Burnett & Mary Rice of Redding,	7-2-1684
Deacon Aron Ludkin & Hannah Edmond,	22-3-1684
Allen Bread & Elizab. Ballard,	22-3-1684
Jonathan Pierce & May Lobden,	4-10-1683
John Whittamore & Elizab. Anniball,	26-3-1684
David Robertson & Eliza Bird,	23-4-1684
John Lowden & Elizab. Spencer,	5-4-1684
John Brigden & Sarah Barrett,	15-8-1684
John Herbert & Elizab. Graves,	15-8-1684
Deacon John Cutlar & Mehittabel Hilton,	29-8-1684
Thomas Lord & Rebeckah Edington,	16-10-1684
Thomas Clarke & Sarah Lynde,	15-8-1684
Capt. Lawr. Hammond & Mrs. Ann Gearish,	14-11-1684
William Everton, Jr. & Ruth Wally,	19-9-1684
John Salter & Mary Adams,	27-12-1684
Thomas White, Jr. & Sarah Rand,	4-1-1684/5
Jonathan Crouch & Elizab. Foskett,	16-10-1684
George Luke & Hannah Bagster,	30-2-1685
William Dodge & Joanna Larkin,	26-3-1685
Francis Shoorin & Sarah Kettle,	12-4-1685
Thomas Jenner & Marah March,	9-5-1685

John Reyner & Abigail Hathorne,	31-5-1685
Mark Athy & Martha Smith,	13-6-1685
Nathaniel Dows & Dorothy Edmonds,	7-7-1685
Sam'l Wilson & Sarah Bagster,	10-7-1685
William Wilson & Mary Pearce,	1-8-1685
Ebenezer Austin & Thankful Benjamen,	8-5-1685
Jno. Rand & Mehetabel Call,	Dec. 2, 1685
Richd. Merrit & Mary Simmons,	Jan. 12, 1685
Jno. Tayler & Kather. Johnson,	Dec. 24, 1685
Wm. Williams & Sarah Hurd,	Jan. 21, 1685
Wm. Case & Mary Starky,	Jan. 28, 1685
Henry Cookery & Mary Masson,	Jan. 21, 1685
Wm. Wally & Sarah Marshal,	Feb. 18, 1685
Thomas Harris & Hephsiba Creswel,	Feb. 25, 1685
Isaac Fensem of Malden & Hannah Dickerman,	Mch. 15, 1685
John Monsal & Elenor How of Cambridge,	Mch. 26, 1686
Richd. Foster & Parnel Winslow,	May 4, 1686
Tho. Adams & Margaret Watts,	May 24, 1686
Elias Stone & Abigail Long,	May 10, 1686
Mingo, negro servant to Mr. Daniel Smith & Moll,	
negro servant to Mrs. Sarah Soley, widow,	Dec. 10, 1686
John Everton & Sarah Taylor,	Dec. 15, 1686
Sam'l Hayman & Mrs. Mary Shepard, widow,	June 16, 1686
Andrew Mitchel & Abigail Atwood,	Nov. 12, 1686
Thomas Bennet & Elizabeth Giningham,	Dec. 9, 1686
Richard Waite & Lydia Hale,	Dec. 9, 1686
Nathan Dunkin & Hannah Wyer,	Dec. 15, 1686
Joseph Whittemore & Joanna Monsal,	Mch. 30, 1687
Samuel Mould, seaman & Mary Swaine,	Feb. 3, 1686/7
John Wait & Ruth Edmonds,	Ap. 28, 1687
Joseph Phipps & Mary Kettle,	May 12, 1687
Nicholas Lobdill & Elisabeth ————,	Aug. 18, 1687
Thomas Atkins of Boston & Abigail Jones of C.	
widow,	Aug. 11, 1687
Thomas Walter & Abigail East, both of Boston,	Sept. 19, 1687
Thomas Pope, mariner & Elizabeth Manser,	Dec. 3, 1687
Sampson Moor & Elisabeth Matson, both of Boston,	
	Dec. 15, 1687

Michael Brigden & Joanna Wilson,   Jan. 11, 1687/8
Charles Chambers & Rebekah Patefield,   Jan. 30, 1687/8
John Hall of Meadford & Jeremiah Sill of Cam-
     bridge,   Dec. 21, 1687
John Tenney & Sarah Atkins, both of Boston,   May 9, 1688
Benjamin Pierce & Mary Reid, both of Woburn,   Oct. 10, 1688
Joseph Wait of Malden & Mercy Tufts of C.,   Oct. 24, 1688
William Eustis of Boston & Sarah Curtis of C.,   Oct. 29, 1688
Joseph Maylern ? of Boston & Hannah, da. of
     widow King of C.,   Oct. 31, 1688
Edward Larkin & Mary, da. of John Walker
     of C.,   Nov. 1, 1688
Joshua Lee & Mary Engs, widow, both of Boston, Dec. 14, 1688
Luke Greenough of Boston, & Abigail Hammond
     of Charlestown,   Jan. 30, 1689/90
Thos. Lemon & Margaret Hutchinson,   Feb. 20, 1689/90
John Shepard & Purces Peirce,   Mch. 26, 1690
Joseph Blanchard & Hannah Shepard,   Ap. 13, 1681
John Stride & Elisabeth Oker,   Ap. 26, 1681
Sam'l Cutler & Dorothy Bell,   June 30, 1681
John Call & Martha Lowden,   July 29, 1681
John Watkins of Charlestown & Mary Russell, at
     Boston,   July 22, 1691
John Miriam of Cambridge & Mary Wheeler of
     Concord,   Nov. 14, 1688
John Newell, Jr. and Hannah Hurry,   Dec. 22, 1687
Geo. Blanchard and Sarah Basset,   Dec. 15, 1687
Nathaniel Coolidge & Lydia Jones,   Jan. 2, 1687/8
Samuel Mattock of Boston & Anne March, da. of
     the widow Dadey of C.,   Ap. 12, 1688
Capt. Ephraim Savage of Boston & Mrs. Elizabeth
     Symmes of Charlestown, widow of Mr. Timo.
     Syms,   Ap. 12, 1688
John Row & Ruth Knil,   Sep. 15, 1687
Joseph Hobkins of Boston & Ruth Long,   Dec. 1, 1686
Abraham Bryant of Redding & Ruth Frothingham, June 7, 1688
John George & Mary, da. of John Lowden, dec., Sept. 11, 1688
John Kettle, Jr. & Abigail, da. of Richard Austin, Sept. 13, 1688

David Jenner & Mabel Russell,   ———, 1688
Ralph Monsel & Anne Fowle,   Aug. 6, 1689
Thos. Marable & Sarah Bell,   Aug. 30, 1689
John Fowl, Jr. of C. & Katharine Gutridge of Bos-
    ton,   Feb. 18, 1689
Richard Martin & Elizabeth Edmunds, widow,   Nov. 28, 1689
William Hurry & Hannah Call,   Mch. 13, 1689/90
Robert Smith of C. & Margaret Swilloway? of
    Malden,   Aug. 15, 1687
James Tompson of Woburn & Abigail Gardner of C.,
                                               Ap. 13, 1687
Thomas Shepey & Mabel Mitchel,   April 17, 1690
Capt. Caleb Stanley of Hartford in Connecticut,
    & Sarah Long widow of Zech. Long,   Sept. 24, 1690
John Curtice & Elizabeth Pierce,   Jan. 3, 1689
Thomas Pierson of Boston & Elizabeth Hammond
    of Charlestown,   Oct. 19, 1691
John Price & Hannah Luke,   June 3, 1691
Abraham Miller & Deborah Chamberlin,   Aug. 13, 1691
Richard Austin & Mehitable Welsted,   Nov. 27, 1691
Jonathan Edmonds, son of Daniel Edmds. & Ruth
    Frothingham, daughtr. of Samuel Frothing-
    ham,   Nov. 26, 1691
Thomas Bligh of Boston & Sarah Everton, widow
    of William Everton, Sen., of Charlestown, Sept. 10, 1691
Ebenezer Austin of Charlestown & Rebekah
    Sprague, daughter of Sam. Sprague, of Mal-
    den,   Jan. 27, 1691
Seth Sweetsir & Sarah Clark, widow of Thos. Clark
    late of ye Island of Barbados,   Jan. 12, 1691
William Paine of Charlestown & Ruth Grover of
    Malden,   March 9, 1691/2
Joseph Leman & Mary Bradley,   June 12, 1690
William Rows & Mary Peachee,   Dec. 31, 1692
Nicholas Laurence & Abigail Wyer   Dec. 25, 1689
John Foster of Charlestown & Sarah Richardson
    of Newberry,   May 31, 1692
Norton Long & Sarah Fowl,   May 31, 1692

James Gouge of Wells & Hannah Emmans of
    Charlestown,   Feb. 10, 1691/2
Nathaniel Davis & Mary Edmunds,   July 15, 1692
Deacon Joseph Kettle & Widow Dorothy Hitt, Dec. 20, 1693
Thomas Cammon & Sarah Davis.   Nov. 20, 1716
Benjamin Lawrance & Anna Adams,   Nov. 8, 1716
William Gowen & Naomi Harris,   Nov. 8, 1716
Edmund Angier & Abiel Hovey,   April 9, 1717

CHELMSFORD

May 29, 1655. A new plantation "the name of thereof to be called Chelmsford" is mentioned.

Daniel Blogget & Mary Butterfield,	Sept. 15, 1653
Joseph Parker & Rebecca Read,	June 24, 1656
Josiah Richeson & Remembrance Underwood,	June 6, 1659
James Hildreth & Margaret Ward,	June 1, 1659
Samuel Fletcher & Margarett Hailstone,	Oct. 14, 1659
James Richeson & Bridgett Hinksman,	Nov. 28, 1660
John Wright & Abigail Warren,	May 10, 1661
John Gilson & Mary Cooper,	Nov. 18, ——
Joseph Keyes & Joanna Cleveland,	May 28, 1690
Benjamin Parker & Sarah Howard,	Jan. 14, 1690
Thomas Chamberlain & Elizabeth Hall,	Jan. 9, 1690
Gershom Proctor & Sarah Whittacres,	——, 1690
John Perram & Lydia Flecher,	Dec. 27, 1692
John Swallow & Anna Barratt,	Jan. 3, 1692/3
John Stevens & Sarah Snow of Woburn,	Jan. 17, 1692/3
John Miriam of Concord & Sarah Spalden,	Feb. 16, 1692/3
Moses Keyse & Mehetabell Kemp,	June 27, 1693
Nathanll. Collar of Sudbury & Mary Barrett,	Oct. 10, 1693
Robert Usher & Sarah Blanchard,	Jan. 23, 1693/4
John Richardson & Elizabeth Farewell,	Jan. 31, 1693/4
John Snow of Woburn & Sarah Stevens,	Feb. 13, 1693/4
Moses Parker & Abigail, da. of Rich. Hildrick,	June 19, 1684

Sam'l Fletcher & Mary Cotton of Concord,	Sept. 3, 1684
Moses Barret & Anna Smith of Dorchester,	Sept. 10, 1684
John Kidder & Lidia Parker,	Sept. 3, 1684
William Underwood & Anna Kidder of Bellerica,	Mch. 17, 1685
Daniel Coburn & Sarah, da. of Robt. Blood,	June 18, 1685
Isaac Hildrick & Elisabeth Wilson of Wooburn,	July 24, 1685
James Borne & Mary Proctor,	Ap. 3, 1685
Capt. William Greenough of Boston & Mrs. Sarah	
Shove of C.,	Nov. 29, 1688
Noah Fisk & May Goold,	June 16, 1686
John Graves of Hatfield & Sarah Bawke,	Oct. 25, 1686
Joseph Perkis & Eunice Spalden,	Nov. 4, 1686
Sam'l Webb of Braintree & Mary Adams,	Dec. 16, 1686
Richard Stratton of C. & Naomi Lovejoy of An-	
dover,	Jan. 6, 1686
George Robbins & Mary Barret,	Jan. 21, 1686
Benjamin Butterfield & Hannah Whittamore,	June 3, 1663
Edward Spalden & Priscilla Underwood,	July 6, 1663
Thomas Corey & Abigail Goole, Ware,	Sept. 19, 1665
John Batts & Mary Farwell,	Dec. 22, 1665
John Fiske & Lidea Fletcher,	March 27, 1666
John Stevens & Elizabeth Hildreth,	Dec. 15, 1664
Jno. Perum & Lidea Shiple,	Dec. 15, 1664
Thomas Chamberline & Sarah Proctor,	Aug. 10, 1666
John Waddell & Mary Goole,	Dec. 25, ——
Joseph Farwell & Hannah Learned,	Dec. 25, 1666
Joshua Fletcher & Grisoll Jewell,	May 4, 1668
Samuel Adams & Hester Sparhawke,	May 7, 1668
Benjamin Spalding & Olive Farwell,	Oct. 30, 1668
Ambrose Fearlon & Mary Martin,	Dec. 2, 1668
Nathaniel Butterfield & Deborah Underwood,	Dec. 31, 1668
Daniel Blogget & Sarah Underwood,	March 10, 1669
Willm. Woodhead & Mary Browne,	June 21, 1669
Edmund Chamberline & Hannah Burden,	June 22, 1670
Cornelius Church & Sarah ————,	June 4, 1670
Nathaniel Bloud & Hannah -————,	June 13, 1670
Joseph Laurance & Lidia,	1670/71
Josiah Brackett & Elizabeth Waldo,	Feb. 4, 1672

✓CONCORD

Sept. 3, 1635—"Ordered, that there shall be a plantation at Musketequid and the name of the place is changed and hereafter to be called Concord."

Thomas Fox & Hanah Brookes,	Oct. 13, 1647	
James Tailor & Isabel Tompkins,	Aug. 19, 1641	
Luke Potter & Mary Edmunds,	Aug. 19, 1644	
Christopher Woolly & Ursilla Wodell,	Dec. 26, 1646	
William Fletcher & Lidia Bates,	Sept. 7, 1645	
Robert Proctor & Jane Hildreth,	Oct. 31, 1645	
Babtist Smedley & Kathrine Shorthose,	Jan. 27, 1645	
Joseph Mirriam & Sarah Stone,	May 12, 1653	
Francis Fletcher & Elizabeth Wheeler,	Aug. 1, 1656	
Jno. Howard & Rebecca Adkinson,	June 17, 1656	
Josiah Willard & Hannah Hosme,	Jan. 20, 1656	
James Bloud & Hannah Purchis,	Aug. 26, 1657	
John Bellowes & Mary Wood,	March 9, 1655	
Robert Bloud & Elizabeth Willard,	Feb. 8, 1653	
Willm. Hall & Sarah Mirriam,	Aug. 14, 1658	
Jno. Hall & Elizath Greene,	Feb. 4, 1656	
James Hosmer & Sarah White,	Aug. 13, 1658	
Thomas Wheeler & Hannah Harrad,	Aug. 10, 1657	
John Farwell & Sarah Wheeler,	Sept. 4, 1658	
Gershom Bulkly & Sarah Chauncy,	Aug. 26, 1659	
Thomas Pellale & Mary Dane,	Jan. 5, 1659/60	
Jno. Law & Lidea Draper,	Jan. 5, 1659/60	
Caleb Brooke & Susan Adkinson,	Feb. 10, 1660	
William Wheeler & Hannah Russe,	Oct. 30, 1659	
Simon Davis & Mary Bloud,	Dec. 12, 1660	
Thomas Daken & Susan Strotne, widow,	June 11, 1660	
Richard Griffin & Mary Harrad, widow,	Dec. 10, 1660	
John Held & Sarah Dane,	June 10, 1661	
John Billings & Elizab. Hastings,	Nov. 11, 1661	
Lt. Jonathan Prescott & Mrs.(?) Rebecka Bulkly,	Dec. 18, 1689	

Joseph Estabrook & Millesent Woodis,	Dec. 31, 1689
Samll. Wheeler & Mary Hoseman,	Jan. 27, 1690
Samll. Palk & Sarah Bralrok,	Feb. 13, 1690
Gershom Heald & Hannah Parling,	Feb. 19, 1690
John Fletcher & Hannah Hunt,	Feb. 18, 1690
Ebenezer Hartwell & Sarah Smedly,	March 27, 1690
John Shepard & Elizabeth Craggin,	March 19, 1690
Robert Blood & Dorcas Wheeler,	May 12, 1690
Richard Parks & Elizabeth Billings,	July 14, 1690
Abraham Tayler & Mary Whitaker,	Dec. 16, 1681
John Ball & Hannah Rugg,	Oct. 16, 1690
John Heald & Mary Chandler,	Dec. 18, 1690
Nathanll. Stow & Ruth Miriam,	Dec. 3, 1690
John Goble & Abigail Rogers of Charlestowne,	May 23, 1693
Samll. Fox & Ruth Knight,	June 13, 1693
Joseph Dane & Elizabeth Fuller,	Nov. 26, 1662
Humphrey Barret & Elizab. Payne,	July 17, 1661
John Wheeler & Sarah Lorkin,	March 25, 1663
Nathaniel Stow & Martha Bigrell,	Aug. 20, 1662
John Mirriam & Mary Cooper,	Oct. 21, 1665
John Mason & Hannah Ramsden,	Dec. 11, 1662
James Addams & Priscilla Ramsden,	May 7, 1662
Jno. Barron—Barns ? & Elizab. Hunt,	April 1, 1664
John Hartwell & Priscilla Wright,	June 1, 1664
Joseph Heyward & Hannah Osmer,	Oct. 26, 1665
Boaz Browne & Mary Winship,	Nov. 8, 1664
Thomas Smith & Mary Hosmer,	June or Jan. 19, 1663
Samuel Hartwell & Ruth Wheeler,	Oct. 26, 1665
Eliphalet Fox & Mary Wheeler,	Oct. 26, 1665
Francis Dudley & Sarah Wheeler,	Oct. 26, 1665
Joseph Emerson & Elizab. Bulkly,	Dec. 7, 1665
John Heywood & Sarah Simons,	Nov. 30, 1665
Stephen Hall & Ruth Davis,	Dec. 3, 1663
Samuel Davis & Mary Meadoes,	Jan. 11, 1665
Peter Bulkly & Mrs. (?) Rebeccah Wheeler,	April 16, 1667
Steeven Hosmer & Abigail Wood,	May 24, 1667
Addam Draper & Rebeccah Brabrooke,	Sept. 15, 1666
Isaac Hunt & Mary Stone,	May 14, 1667

Samuel Smedley & Hannah Wheeler,	July 11, 1667
Nehemiah Hunt & Mary Tooll,	June 1, 1663
John Flint & Mary Oakes,	Nov. 12, 1667
Willm. Frizell & Hannah Clarke,	Nov. 28, 1667
Isaac Shepard & Mary Smedley,	Dec. 10, 1667
Willm. Buttrick & Jane Goodenow,	Feb. 21, 1667
John Barker & Judah Simonds,	Dec. 9, 1668
Nathaniel Buss & Mary Haes,	Dec. 16, 1668
Thomas Bateman & Mary Knight,	Jan. 17, 1668
Benjamin Graves & Mary Hoare,	Oct. 21, 1668
Thomas Baybrooke & Abigail Temple,	March 3, 1668
John Smedley & Sarah Wheeler,	May 5, 1669
Samuel Stow & Elizabeth Stone,	Nov. 16, 1669
Samuel Merriam & Elizabeth Townsen,	Nov. 21, 1669
Timothy Wheeler & Ruth Fuller,	June 29, 1670
Gershom Brooks & Hannah Eccles,	March 12, 1668/69
Nathaniel Baal & Margery Bateman,	Feb. 7, 1670
Willm. Hayward & Anna Stratton,	April 14, 1671
Roger Chandler & Mary Simons,	April 25, 1671
George Harris & Lidea Gross,	Nov. 21, 1671
James Smedly & Mary Barrett,	Dec. 4, 1671
Joseph Buss & Elizabeth Jones,	Dec. 21, 1671
Joseph Brabrooke & Sarah Lewis,	April 23, 1672
Thomas Bateman & Abigail Mirriam,	April 25, 1672
John Hawood & Ann White,	June 2, 1671
Obadiah Wheeler & Elizab. White,	July 17, 1672
Joseph French & Elizab Knight,	Jan. 2, 1672
Abram Shepard & Judeth Philbrook,	Jan. 2, 1672
Samuel How & Mary Woolly,	March 27, 1673
Jno. Graves & Mary Chamberlin,	Dec. 1, 1671
Saml. Jones & Elizab. Potter,	Jan. 16, 1672
Gershom Held & Ann Vinton,	May 6, 1673
Ephr. Jones & Ruth Vinton,	May 7, 1673
John Hadlock & Elizab. Stow,	May 13, 1673
Samuel Wheeler & Mary Perry,	Nov. 10, 1673
Abram Temple & Deborah Hadlock,	Dec. 4, 1673
Samuel Potter & Sarah Wright,	Jan. 8, 1673
Steeven Farr & Mary Tayler,	May 15, 1674

John Barns & Deborah Wright,	Dec. 10, 1674
Ens. Wm. Buff (?) & Dorcas Jones,	Dec. 24, 1674
Humph. Barratt & Mary Potter,	March 23, 1674/75
John Biggalow & Sarah Wheate,	May 27, 1675
Eleaze. Baall & Priscilla Woodward,	Sept. 25, 1675
Saml. Stratton & Hannah Wheat,	Oct. 20, 1675
Eleaz. Flack & Deborah Barnes,	Oct. 10, 1676
Saml. Parry & Hannah Smedly,	Nov. 8, 1676
Saml. Rise & Sarah Hosmer,	Dec. 13, 1676
Nathl Juel & Mary ———,	June 9, 1676
Samuel Buttrick & Elizab. Bloud,	June 21, 1677
Abram Graves & Ann Hayward,	June 28, 1677
Daniel Hoare & Mary Stratton,	July 19, 1677
Tho. Wheeler & Sarah Sternes,	July 23, 1677
Jonath. Prescott & Elizab. Hoare,	Dec. 23, 1675
Tho. Brown & Ruth Jones,	Nov. 12, 1677
Jno. Wood & Elizab. Vinton,	Nov. 13, 1677
Ephr. Roper & Hannah Goble,	Nov. 20, 1677
Joshua Sawyer & Sarah Potter,	Jan. 2, 1677
James Sawyer & Mary Marble,	Feb. 4, 1677
Samuel How & Mary ———,	March 25, 1678
Jno. Taylor & Unice Woody,	March 26, 1678
Ebenezer Prout & Elizab. Wheeler,	May 28, 1678
Jno. Wheeler & Sarah Sternes,	Oct. 27, 1678
Nathll. Billins & Jane Banister,	March 19, 1679
George Hues & Lidea Bennet,	May 3, 1679
James Bloud & Isabel Wyman,	Sept. 9, 1679
John Miles & Susannah Rediat,	Feb. 10, 1679
Adam Hollaway & Hannah Farrar,	Jan. 5, 1681
Wm. Baker & Elizab. Dutton,	March 5, 1681
Joseph Wheeler & Mary Powers,	Jan. 1, 1681
Jonath. Hubbard & Hannah Rice,	Jan. 15, 1681
Eliphalt. & Mary Hunt,	Sept. 30, 1681
Saml. Fletcher & Elizab. Wheeler,	April 15, 1682
Abram Taylor & Mary Whittacer,	Oct. 16, 1681
John Hartwell & Elizab. Wright,	Aug. 23, 1682
Samuel Parry & Ester Comy,	Sept. 7, 1682
Jno. Ball & Martha Bignall,	Sept. 29, 1682

Joseph Daney & Mary Goble,	Nov. 17, 1682
Tho. Estabrook & Sarah Temple,	March 11, 1683
Sam. Stratton & Elizabeth Fletcher,	Sept. 28, 1683
John Wilcockson & Elizab. Buss,	Jan. 14, 1682/3
Peter Wright & Elizab. Lamson,	March 5, 1684
John Wheeler & Elizab. Wells,	April 25, 1684
Peter Rice & Mary Forrd (?),	Aug. 29, 1683
Ephraim Flint & Jane Bulkley,	Jan. 20, 1683/4
John Jones & Sarah Farwell,	March 5, 1681
Timothy Rice & Abigail Marret of Cambridge,	April 27, 1687
Samuel Tayler & Mary Robbins,	Dec. 9, 1685
John Billings & Elizabeth Lamson,	Dec. 31, 1685
Robert Chaffin & Abigail Davis,	April 15, 1719
Jonathan Butterick & Elizabeth Woolley,	Dec. 19, 1717
Joseph Wooly of C & Rachel Bracket of Chelmsford,	Dec. 3, 1688
Eliazar Ball of C. & Sarah Miriam of Cambridge,	June 14, 1688
Isaac Taylor of C. & Elizabeth Knight of Cambridge,	Dec. 19, 1688
William Russell & Hannah Adams,	Ap. 24, 1688
Richard Temple & Sarah Parling,	Ap. 24, 1688
Joseph Fletcher & Mary Dudley,	June 7, 1688
James Hosmer of Marlboro & Elisabeth Sawyer of Lancaster,	Feb. 6, 1687/8
James Minot & Rebekah Jones,	Feb. 9, 1687/8
Robert Wier & Elisabeth, da. of John Fowle, both of Charlestown,	June 26, 1688
Edmund Goodenow & Dorothy Man, both of Sudbury,	June 6, 1686
John How of Sudbury & Elisabeth Woolson of Watertown,	Nov. 3, 1686
Benj. Moore & Dorothy Wright, both of Sudbury,	Nov. 11, 1686
Obadiah Coolidge of Sudbury & Elisabeth Roose of Hartford,	Feb. 28, 1686
David Rice & Hannah Walker, both of Sudbury,	Ap. 7, 1687
Sam'l Gaskel of Charlestown & Elisabeth Sherman of Watertown,	July 20, 1687
Thomas Walker & Marth. How, both of Sudbury,	Dec. 7, 1687

John Peckham & Dorothy Goodenow, both of
    Sudbury,   Dec. 9, 1687

Thomas Drury & Rachel Rice, both of Sudbury, Dec. 15, 1687

Edmund Bouker & Sarah Parmenter, both of
    Sudbury,   Mch. 29, 1688

John Sheares of Sudbury & Alice Mitchelson of
    Cambridge,   Ap. 9, 1688

John Gibbs of Sudbury & Anne Gleason of Sher-
    burn,   Ap. 27, 1688

Alexander Stuart & Deborah Farrowbush, both of
    Marlboro,   May 23, 1688

Ebenezer Brooks & Martha Wilder, both of Wo-
    burn,   June 14, 1687

Robert Sharp & Mary French, both of Billerica, June 20, 1687

Ezek. Richardson of Woburn & Elisabeth Swan of
    Cambridge,   July 27, 1687

Adam Goold of Groton & Hannah Knight of Wo-
    burn,   Sept. 28, 1687

Peter Talbot of Chelmsford & Hannah Frissell of C.
                            Dec. 29, 1687

John Comy of C. & Martha Roe of Cambridge, June 21, 1688

William Frost & Esther Lee, now in Charlestown, Aug. 6, 1688

Thomas Sternes & Rebeckah Chamberlain, both
    of Billerica,   June 20, 1688

Henry Baitman & Abial Shaply,   Aug. 15, 1688

John Randal & Mary Wait, both of Watertown, July 13, 1688

Jonathan Fairbanks of Lancaster & Mary Haward,
    of C.,   Aug. 24, 1688

Thos. Burnap & Sarah Walton, both of Redding, May 28, 1688

John Hayward of Concord & Sarah Blogget of Wo-
    burn,   Jan. 7, 1686/7

William Wilson & Sarah Blood,   July 1, 1686

Joseph Lamson & Elizabeth Adams,   Aug. 18, 1686

Thomas Goble & Sarah Shepard,   Jan. 4, 1686

Thomas Harris & Mary Shepard,   Sept. 17, 1688

John Parlim & Mary Hartwell,   Nov. 1, 1688

Geo. Harris & Sarah Vinton,   Dec. 5, 1688

Simon Davis & Elizabeth Woodis,   Feb. 14, 1688/9

John Greene of Charlestown & Patience, da. of
    Samuel Davis of Groton,
John Mousel, Jr. & Dorothy Hett, both of Charles-
    town,   July 1, 1691
Jonathan Kemp of Chelmsford & Sarah Gilson of
    Groton,   Nov. 19, 1718
Ebenezer Olds of Suffield & Rebecca Temple,   Nov. 6, 1718
Elias Barron & Priscilla Wilson,   Sept. 16, 1718
Abraham Estabrook & Martha Brabrook,   Sept. 30, 1718
Thomas Bodgett & Tabitha Blanchard,   April 21, 1719
James Lane of Billerica & Martha Minott,   April 30, 1719
Benjamin Pool & Sarah Barney, both of Boston, June 15, 1719
Joseph Blodgett & Sarah Stone, both of Lexington, Nov. 5, 1719
Ebenezer Stone & Prudence Pratt, both of Fram-
    ingham,   May 10, 1721
Elnathan Jones & Hanna Pierce,   Sept. 22, 1721
John Bellows of Marlboro & Mary Wheeler,   Dec. 5, 1721
Samll. Fletcher & Abigail Hubbard,   Jan. 18, 1721/2
John Andros of Killingsly & Mary Bigals of Weston,
                              Jan. 28, 1721/2
John Wallis & Sarah Wheeleer, both of Stow, Feb. 15, 1721/2
Isaac Wood & Susana Riscon,   April 26, 1722
Benjamin Stone & Esther Kibbey, both of Lexing-
    ton,   June 28, 1722
James Russel & Susana Farrar,   Aug. 16, 1722
Jonathan Olds & Susana Temple,   Oct. 3, 1722
Joseph Harris & Abigail Goble,   Nov. 8, 1722
Palmer Golding & Abigail Rice, both of Sudbury, Dec. 4, 1722
Samll. Wilson & Elizabeth Hartwell,   Dec. 3, 1722
Thomas Houghton & Joanna Joselin, both of Lan-
    caster,   Dec. 22, 1722
John Sawyer & Sarah Joslin, both of Lancaster, Nov. 22, 1722
John Adams & Love Minott,   Dec. 13, 1722
Samuel Dakin & Mercy Minott,   Dec. 13, 1722
Obadiah Perry of Boston & Elisabeth Chambers
    of Watertown,   Jan. 23, 1723/4
Samll. Hartwell & Elisabeth Fletcher of Chelms-
    ford,   Feb. 6, 1723/4

Bartholew Jones & Ruth Stow,	July 9, 1723
John Varnum & Elisabeth Colburn,	May 26, 1724
David Gowers & Martha Glazier,	May 26, 1724
Joseph Baker of Marlborough & Esther Harwood of Dunstable,	Aug. 20, 1724
John Hosmer & Mehetabel Parker,	Aug. 26, 1724
John Martyn & Mary Marret, both of Cambridge,	Aug. 18, 1724
James Hildreth & Elizebeth Cumings, both of Chelmsford,	Nov. 26, 1724
Thomas Brooks & Hannah Dakin,	June 24, 1725
James Houghton of Lancaster & Mary Jones,	Oct. 8, 1725
➤ John Holding & Mary Wheeler,	Dec. 29, 1725
Daniel Holding & Anne Jones,	Feb. 15, 1725/6
Jonathan Stockwell of Sutton & Rachel Underwood of Lexington,	Dec. 16, 1726
Benjamin Osgood & Hannah Divel, both of Lancaster,	Oct. 9, 1726
David Parlin & Sarah Farrar,	April 9, 1726
Francis Eveleth of Stow & Mary Hunt,	Feb. 7, 1726/7
Saml. Wheat, Jr. & Hannah Hovey, both of Cambridge,	Aug. 2, 1726
Joseph Farnsworth of Groton & Rebecca Gibson,	May 4, 1727
Nathl. Holman & Elizabeth Knight,	April 12, 1726
Thomas Hosmer & Prudence Hosmer,	April 29, 1731
Joseph Harwood & Lydia Brooks,	April 14, 1731
Eleazer Davis of Bedford & Rebecca Chandler,	June 17, 1731
William Conant & Mary Lamson,	June 15, 1731
Eleazer Flegg & Huldah Chandler,	Sept. 28, 1731
' John Page of Bedford & Rebecca Wheeler,	Dec. 23, 1731
Elnathan Jones & Rebecca Barret,	Jan. 13, 1731/2
Samuel Buttrick, Jr. & Mary Parker,	Feb. 3, 1731/2
Samuel Farrer & Lydia Barret,	Jan. 13, 1731/2
Samuel Minot & Sarah Prescot of Westford,	March 7, 1731/2
' John Bateman & Anna Wheeler,	Feb. 10, 1731/2
John Amy & Mary Mathews, both of Hopkinton,	April 4, 1732
Thomas Stratton & Sarah Ball,	May 30, 1732
ᵿ Ephraim Brown & Abigail Wheeler,	June 30, 1732
Israel Conant & Martha Lampson,	July 11, 1732

Stephen Hosmer & Mellessent Wood, Aug. 9, 1732
William Barker & Abigail Rex, Oct. 5, 1732
Ephraim Hartwel & Elizebeth Heywood, Nov. 7, 1732
Amos Gates of Stow & Mary Hubbard, Nov. 7, 1732
David Eaton of Ashford & Dinah Davis, Oct. 19, 1732
Benjamin Brabrook & Dorcas Adams, Nov. 16, 1732
Edward Thompson of Haverhil & Hannah Cocksage, Dec. 13, 1732
James Barret & Rebecca Hubbard, Dec. 21, 1732
Saml. Jones & Sarah Hubbard, Dec. 21, 1732
Hezekiah Wheeler & Sarah Russ, April 12, 1732
Samuel Fellows & Eunice Heald, July 16, 1735
Abishai Brown & Mary Farrar, Sept. 9, 1735
Zechariah Fletcher & Susannah Fassett, Sept. 23, 1735
Phineas Blood & Elisabeth Allen, Oct. 16, 1735
Henry Jefts of Billerica & Dinah Brown, Nov. 13, 1735
Edward Gearfield of Weston & Sarah Brooks, Nov. 13, 1735
Jonathan Billings of Acton & Dorothy Brooks, Feb. 12, 1735/6
Joseph Barnes & Sarah Melvin, March 18, 1735
Benjamin Wheeler & Rebecca Lee, April 6, 1736
Joseph Moffat & Mary Moffat, Jan. 17, 1736
Jonathan Cleveland & Lydia Lampson, Sept. 29, 1736
Abraham Wheeler & Martha Blood, Dec. 15, 1736
Joseph Read & Ruth Underwood, both of Westford,
May 30, 1737
Rev. Thomas Thompson of Londonderry & Frances
Cuming, July 14, 1737
Nathaniel Ball & Mary Wesson, Aug. 25, 1737
Oliver Barret & Hannah Hunt, Dec. 8, 1737
Ebenezer Russell & Abigail Baker, Dec. 20, 1737
Jonathan Miles & Katherine Barron, Feb. 23, 1737/8
Ezekiel Wallingsford of Lancaster & Lydia Brown,
Feb. 2, 1737/8
Zachariah Blood & Elisabeth Whitaker, Feb. 9, 1737/8
Josiah Horsmer & Hannah Wesson, April 11, 1738
James Robbins of Chelmsford & Mary Heald of
Acton, May 24, 1738
John Barrett of Chelmsford & Martha Heald of
Acton, May 24, 1738

Jonathan Hildreth & Mary Spaulding, both of
    Chelmsford, June 13, 1738
David Whitaker & Hannah Hopkinson, June 27, 1738
Josiah Fuller of Stow & Mary Whitaker, Sept. 6, 1738
Joseph Hartwell & Hannah Reed, both of Woburn,
    Sept. 21, 1738
Joseph Haywood & Abigail Horsmer, Oct. 4, 1738
Samuel Estabrook & Huldah Temple, Nov. 16, 1738
Ebenezer Peirce & Joanna Townsend, Nov. 21, 1738
Thomas Mead & Ruth Parlin, Dec. 12, 1738
Joseph Brooks & Esther Durant of Billerica, Feb. 22, 1738/9
Joseph Hapgood of Marlborough & Mary Brooks,
    April 26, 1739
Joseph Nowell of Lynn & Elisabeth Hodgman, May 30, 1739
Daniel Horsmer & Bethia Conant, April 12, 1739
John Baker & Lydia Bradfield, May 16, 1739
Benjamin Willard of Grafton & Sarah Brooks, May 17, 1739
Simon Wheeler & Dorothy Worster, Sept. 18, 1739
John Wheeler & Dorothy Darby, July 24, 1739
Thomas Barron & Anna Blood, Sept. 5, 1739
Ephraim Wheeler & Rebekah Shevally, Oct. 31, 1739
Hugh Riddle of Londonderry & Ann Aikin, Oct. 24, 1739
Isaac Patch & Joanna Butterfield, both of Westford,
    Oct. 29, 1739
Joseph Temple of Worcester & Mary Laughton, Dec. 3, 1739
Benjamin Fay of Westborough & Martha Miles, Dec. 27, 1739
Thomas Parrott & Sarah Robbins, both of Westford,
    Dec. 6, 1739
William Reed of Marlborough & Sarah Wood of Acton,
    May 28, 1740
John Davis & Sarah Flint, July 3, 1740
William Barker & Martha Shepard, Aug. 25, 1740
Joseph Williams & Lydia Monroe of Lexington, Oct. 9, 1740
John Laughton & Esther Davis, Oct. 21, 1740
Nathan Stone & Mary Robbins, both of Sudbury,
    May 5, 1740
Israel How of Rutland & Elisabeth Hubbard, March 24, 1740
Jeremiah Wheeler & Mary Wheeler, Nov. 6, 1740

John Wheate & Grace Brown,   Nov. 10, 1740
David Brooks of Acton & Betty Bass,   Nov. 13, 1740
Jonas Prescott of Westford & Rebekah Barrett, Nov. 25, 1740
Joseph Dudley & Mary Brown,   Jan. 16, 1740/1
Francis Wheeler & Sarah Blood,   Jan. 23, 1740/1
Simon Blood & Abigail Flint,   Feb. 15, 1740/1
Jason Russell & Mary Robbins, both of Chelmsford,
                                                                            Nov. 6, 1740
Thomas Hodgman & Elisabeth Blood,   Dec. 25, 1740
Ebenezer Allen & Dorothy Barron,   Jan. 22, 1740
Joseph Stratton & Elizabeth Dudley,   March 3, 1740/1
Ezekiel Miles & Joanna Wesson,   Feb. 12, 1740/1
Thomas Powers & Hepzibah Hastings, both of Littleton,
                                                                           April 15, 1741
Elisha Smith of Worcester & Sarah Melvin,   Aug. 12, 1741
Walter Powers & Mary Hartwell, both of Medford,
                                                                            June 11, 1741
John Clark & Susanna Maynard, both of Sudbury,
                                                                            June 29, 1741
Benjamin Prescott of Salem & Rebekah Minott, Aug. 12, 1741
William Baldwin & Mary Farmer, both of Billerica,
                                                                            Sept. 23, 1741
John White & Mehitable French, both of Billerica,
                                                                            Sept. 23, 1741
Thomas McGee of Chester & Anne Stewart,   Nov. 26, 1741
Ezekiel Brown & Abigail Davis,   May 14, 1741
Benjamin Brown & Submit Ward,   June 22, 1741
James Haynes of Sudbury & Eleanor Lee,   Aug. 13, 1741
John How of Sudbury & Mary Holdin,   Aug. 26, 1741
Andrew Adams of Grafton & Elizabeth Hunt,   Oct. 15, 1741
Josiah Wheeler & Mary Lee,   Feb. 1, 1741
Samuel Meriam & Jerusha Brooks,   March 17, 1741
Thomas Whiting & Lydia Parker of Dracutt,   March 25, 1742
Moses How of Rutland & Hannah Heald,   Sept. 9, 1741
Hezikiah Smith of Lexington & Elisabeth Billing,
                                                                            Feb. 23, 1742
Samuel Heald & Rebekah Fletcher,   June 9, 1742
John Jones & Abigail Wesson,   July 6, 1742

Humphrey Barrett & Elisabeth Adams,	Dec. 9, 1742
Simon Hunt & Anna Brown,	Jan. 20, 1742
Joseph Flegg & Sarah Harris,	Oct. 21, 1742
Josiah Holdin & Hannah Parker,	Jan. 27, 1742
Timothy Wheeler & Sarah Hunt,	March 3, 1742
David How of Sudbury & Abigail Hubbard,	March 15, 1742
John Knight of Worcester & Experience Ball,	March 29, 1743
Zechariah Davis & Lydia Hubbard,	March 28, 1743
Benjamin Clark & Rebekah Flagg,	April 14, 1743
William Baker & Rebekah Conant,	April 14, 1743
Ephraim Flint & Ruth Wheeler,	March 31, 1743
Amos Haywood of Holden & Mary Buttrick,	Aug. 30, 1743
Joseph Harburd & Abigail Brown,	Aug. 18, 1743
John Gill & Abigail Barker,	Sept. 1, 1743
Jonathan Cleveland & Dorothy Shepard,	June 16, 1743
Jonathan Harris & Mary Moores,	Nov. 17, 1743
Daniel Hoar of Narraganset Township, No. 2 &	
Rebekah Brooks,	Nov. 24, 1743
Peter Buss & Abigail Hodgman,	Feb. 10, 1743
James Miles & Hannah Ball,	Aug. 24, 1743
Jonas Wheeler & Persis Brooks,	Oct. 13, 1743
Peter Holdin & Abigail Jones,	July 4, 1743
John Young of Watertown & Susan Daverson,	Sept. 19, 1743
Robert Estabrook & Olive Townsend,	May 24, 1743
Samuel Edwards of Littleton & Ruth Lee,	May 9, 1743
Henry Yours & Tabitha Fox,	Nov. 24, 1743
Joseph Davis & Hanh. Brown,	Jan. 10, 1743
Joseph Wright & Rebekah Haywood,	Dec. 15, 1743
Joseph Temple & Sarah Mackiney,	June 6, 1744
John Parrot & Margaret Mathis, both of Chelmsford,	
	June 14, 1744
Aaron Brown & Abigail Burk,	July 3, 1744
Ebenezer Lampson & Mary Hopkinson,	July 31, 1744
Samuel Kinney & Lydia Whitney, both of Dunstable,	
	Aug. 17, 1744
Samuel Buttrick & Lucy Wheeler,	Sept. 18, 1744
John Barret & Lois Brooks,	Nov. 15, 1744
John Minott & Sarah Stow of Marlborough,	June 26, 1744

Timothy Rogers & Rebekah French, both of Billerica,
March 12, 1744
Josiah Wheat & Ruth Coolidge, Feb. 12, 1744
Elisha Brown of Cambridge & Eliza. Davis, May 17, 1744
Timothy Wheeler & Mehitable Whittemore, May 31, 1744
Ephraim Hubbard of Rutland & Sarah Billing, June 6, 1744
Jonathan Palmer & Esther Laughton, July 10, 1744
Jonathan Haywood & Sarah Stone, Aug. 28, 1744
Timothy Larrabee & Mary Fletcher, Nov. 22, 1744
Hezekiah Taylor of Grafton & Abigail Hunt, Dec. 13, 1744
Daniel Raymond & Lucy Wooley, Jan. 15, 1744
Jonathan Fisk & Sarah Wheeler, March 5, 1744
Josiah Piper of Stratham & Mehitabel Conant, March 14, 1744
John Parlin & Margaret McColls of Rutland, April 2, 1745
Daniel Taylor of Townsend & Sarah Stow, April 10, 1745
Josiah Hodgman & Rebekah Buss, April 16, 1745
John Perry of Bedford & Lucy Dudley, Dec. 6, 1744
John Flint & Hepzibah Brown, Jan. 12, 1744
John Hedly & Deborah Temple, Jan. 24, 1744
Simeon Hayward & Sarah Hosmer, March 13, 1744
John Adams of Ipswich & Mary Hunt, Oct. 31, 1745
William Hunt & Elisabeth Hildreth of Westford, April 3, 1746
Jonas Reed of Holden & Elisabeth Wright, April 17, 1746
Richard Temple & Sarah Hambleton of Charlestown,
April 24, 1746
David Tyler of Upton & Rachel Brabrook, May 26, 1746
Nathan Meriam & Abigail Wheeler, Jan. 11, 1742
John Brooks & Lucy Hoar, Oct. 23, 1745
Jonathan Lamson & Mary Dudley, Dec. 5, 1745
Thomas Wheate & Mary Ball, Dec. 10, 1745
Ephraim Stow & Grace Wood, Jan. 14, 1745
Samuel Kibbey & Elisabeth Parlin, Jan. 14, 1745
Joseph Darby & Silence Hubbard, Jan. 14, 1745
David Taylor of Bedford & Ruth Jones, Feb. 5, 1745
Jacob Farrar & Mary Meriam, May 8, 1746
Jeremiah Whittemore of Weston & Abigail Wooley, June 5, 1746
Josiah Meriam & Lydia Wheeler, June 17, 1746
Joseph Gould of Nottingham & Mary Piper, June 19, 1746

Nathaniel Ball & Sarrah Meriam of Lexington,   Sept. 10, 1746
Ebenezer Ball & Sarah Gookin,   Oct. 16, 1746
Nathan Winchester of Brookline & Beulah Parks, Oct. 17, 1746
Jacob Whittemore of Lexington & Esther Whitte-
    more,   Oct. 26, 1746
James Flegg & Anna Morse of Cambridge,   Nov. 6, 1746
John Ball of Boston & Sarah Brooks,   Nov. 20, 1746
Stephen Wesson & Lydia Billing,   Nov. 27, 1746
Aaron Estabrook & Bethia Ball,   Feb. 17, 1746
William Brown of Framingham & Elisabeth Conant,
    March 6, 1746
Hezekiah Sleeper & Martha Wood,   May 7, 1747
Joseph Estabrook & Lydia Wheat,   Dec. 24, 1747
James Allen & Ruth Wesson,   Jan. 15, 1747
James Chandler & Mary Flegg,   July 2, 1747
James Cropfield & Rebekah Adams of Acton,   July 15, 1747
James Brooks & Mary Bathrick of Charlestown, July 26, 1747
Samuel Allen of Westborough & Abigail Billing, Aug. 6, 1747
Jonathan Brooks & Lucy Perry,   Nov. 12, 1747
Jeremiah Hunt of Billerica & Hannah Flint,   Nov. 26, 1747
Nathan Brown & Rebekah Adams,   March 10, 1747
Henry Gold & Lydia Blazdill of Billerica,   May 12, 1748
Thomas Brown & Mary Flint,   May 26, 1748
Samuel Dwight of Sutton & Jane Buckley,   Dec. 23, 1731
David Burnet & Hannah Thompson, both of Boston,
    Aug. 15, 1741
John Adams & Elisabeth Shan,   Sept. 3, 1748
Elisha Child & Mary Wheeler,   Jan. 11, 1748
Samuel Buttrick, Jr. & Dorothy Flint,   Aug. 25, 1748
Nathan Stratton & Hannah Brooks,   Oct. 27, 1748
Andrew Cornet & Ruth Brooks,   Nov. 30, 1748
Oliver Brown & Mary Williams,   Feb. 7, 1748
Ebenezer Fletcher & Elisabeth Fletcher,   Feb. 28, 1748
Willard Meriam of Littleton & Sarah Hartwell, April 11, 1749
Ephraim Smith & Abigail Monroe,   April 25, 1749
John Edwards of Acton & Mary Melven,   April 26, 1749
Nathan Wheeler & Mary Hunt,   May 25, 1749
Josiah Hodgman & Dorothy Wheeler,   May 31, 1749

David Fletcher & Jerusha Wheeler,	July 6, 1749
John Beaton & Mary Collins,	Oct. —, 1733
Samuel Ball & Persis Flagg,	March 8, 1749
Noah Brooks & Huldah Horsmer,	March 13, 1749
Joseph Hodgman & Abigail Piper,	July 20, 1749
Jacob Whittemore & Deborah Flagg,	Oct. 19, 1749
Samuel Meriam & Esther Wheeler,	Dec. 21, 1749
Ezra Wheeler & Rebekah Davis,	Feb. 3, 1749
Zachariah Wheeler & Mary Peirce of Weston,	March 29, 1750
Zachariah Wesson & Mary Hoar,	May 10, 1750
Jonathan Putnam of Bedford & Hannah Melven,	Aug. 21, 1750
Nathaniel Williams of Weston & Dorothy Stratton,	
	Sept. 20, 1750
Joseph Emerson & Betty Mason,	April 13, 1780
Ephraim Willson & Esther Hodgman,	April 13, 1780
George Minot & Elizabeth Barret,	Dec. 12, 1776
Farwell Jones & Hanh. Hosmer,	Jan. 1, 1777
Thomas Bond & Esther Meriam,	March 5, 1770
Rev. Ezra Ripley to Phebe Emerson,	Nov. 16, 1780
John White & Esther Kettell,	Nov. 11, 1778
John Prescott Heywood & Elizabeth Wheeler,	Dec. 30, 1778
Roger Brown & Polly Hartwell of Lincoln,	—— ——
Amos Barrett & Polly Hubbard,	March 31, 1779
Ezekiel Miles & Lucy Wood,	April 22, 1779
Amos Flint & Lucy Ball,	May 11, 1779
Peter Ball & Mary Prescott,	July 8, 1779
James Colburn & Rebecca Wheeler,	July 17, 1779
Samuel Spring & Lydia Robertson,	Aug. 22, 1779
William Barron & Sally Benjamin,	Aug. 22, 1779
Nathan Stow & Abigail Meriam,	Jan. 27, 1780
Joshua Brooks of Lincoln & Martha Barrett,	Feb. 27, 1780
Jonas Lee & Elizabeth Cordis,	March 16, 1780
Humphry Barret & Rebecca Heywood,	July 6, 1780
Simon Wheeler & Lydia Hall,	July 13, 1780
Edward Flint & Mary Buttrick,	July 29, 1780
Thomas Thurstain & Lydia Davis,	Aug. 16, 1780
Jonathan Ball & Abigail Child,	Sept. 12, 1780
Jonathan Estabrook & Mary Flagg,	June 22, 1781

Samuel Lewis of Townsend & Sarah Potter,	July 17, 1781
Jacob Farrar & Elizabeth Heywood of Acton,	Aug. 26, 1781
Isaac Hoar & Anna Meriam,	Nov. 1, 1781
Reuben Ball & Rebecca Winship,	Jan. 21, 1782
Silas Man & Lydia Barret,	April 11, 1782
John Curtis & Hannah Tural,	Sept. 19, 1782
Abel Davis & Levinah Hosmer,	Oct. 24, 1782
Jonas Potter & Sarah Jones,	Oct. 24, 1782
Nathaniel Davis & Mellicent Hubbard,	Feb. 10, 1783
Abraham Hapgood of Acton & Mary Wright,	March 13, 1783
Abijah Warren & Rebecca Hubbard,	March 27, 1783
Noah Ripley of Barre & Lucy Barret,	April 8, 1783
Abijah Bond & Sarah Hubbard,	May 22, 1783
Nathaniel French & Susanna Brown of Lunenburg,	
	Sept. 11, 1783
Ephraim Brooks & Susannah Estabrooks,	March 31, 1784
Thomas Whitney & Lydia Jones,	July 22, 1784
Thomas White & Mrs. Mary Buttrick,	Jan. 13, 1785
Deacn. Andrew Parker of Barre & Mary Stearns,	March 3, 1785
Jonas Heywood, Jr. & Ruth Barret,	Feb. 23, 1786
Isaac Hoar & Martha Bliss,	June 22, 1786
William Muzzy of Hubbardston & Mary Chandler,	
	Sept. 8, 1786
Charles Brown & Abigail Buttrick,	Oct. 26, 1786
Charles Miles & Lucy Miles,	Nov. 8, 1786
Jonathan Wright & Mary Brown,	June 9, 1785
John Hayward & Elizabeth Brown of Sudbury,	Sept. 15, 1785
James Hayward & Betty Lee,	Sept. 15, 1785
Nathan Wheeler of Carlisle & Ruth Hunt of West-	
ford,	Nov. 16, 1785
Thomas Hunt & Lydia Ball,	Aug. 16, 1786
Abel Adams of Mason & Rebecca Jones,	Nov. 24, 1786
Robert Marshall & Olive Nutting,	Nov. 7, 1786
John Cuming of Mason & Hannah Parker of Carlisle,	
	May 29, 1787
Timothy Jones of Bedford & Lucy Ball,	July 3, 1787
Nathaniel Hilton & Jane Tullock,	Sept. 20, 1787
James Ledget & Rebecca Brooks,	May 23, 1787

Daniel Dudley of East Sudbury & Lucy Vose, June 23, 1787
John Flint & Submit Hunt, Nov. 7, 1787
Rev. Laban Ainsworth of Jaffrey & Mary Minot, Dec. 5, 1787
Samuel Potter, Jr. & Lucy Hosmer, March 11, 1788
Lewis Richards & Polly Robertson, March 8, 1788
John Caldwell & Susanna Robertson, April 8, 1788
Lt. Emerson Cogswell & Anna Larnard, May 3, 1789
Joseph Dudley & Eunice Darby, July 28, 1789
Amos Whitney & Anna Brown, Aug. 16, 1789
Samuel Buttrick & Elisabeth Blood, Oct. 2, 1750
Peter Hubbard & Mary Adams, Dec. 20, 1750
Joseph Wheeler & Mary Hosmer, Jan. 7, 1750
Ebenezer Jones & Mary Wheeler, Jan. 22, 1750
Abraham Smith of Sudbury & Rhoda Wheeler, Jan. 22, 1750
Henry Flint & Sarah Wheeler, Feb. 19, 1750
Benjamin Adams & Priscilla Adams, April 18, 1751
Benjamin Miles & Mary Hubbard, May 16, 1751
Sampson Wheeler of Acton & Sarah Parlin, May 23, 1751
John Brown & Elisabeth Bateman, June 26, 1751
Joseph Buttrick & Sarah Brown, July 23, 1751
John Fletcher & Sarah Kidder of Chelmsford, Sept. 12, 1751
Hugh Kennedy of Volentown & Elisabeth Werling, Oct. 8, 1751
Jonathan Bradstreet of Lunenberg & Abigail Fletcher,
Oct. 15, 1751
Samuel Parmenter of Sudbury & Mary Tower, Nov. 14, 1751
Oliver Wood & Lucy Hosmer, June 13, 1750
William Flagg of Holden & Abigail Buttrick, July 2, 1751
Samuel Kendall of Woburn & Mehitabel Hosmer,
July 23, 1751
David Melven & Abigail Davis, Dec. 24, 1751
Nathan Meriam of Narraganset, No. 2 & Mary Hosmer,
March 26, 1755
Obadiah Gill & Hannah Holdin, both of Stow, May 28, 1755
David Hartwell & Rachel Wooley, both of Carlisle,
Oct. 23, 1755
Samuel Davis of Acton & Ann Cole, Dec. 5, 1755
Josiah Heywood, Jr. & Thankful Balcom of Sudbury,
April 7, 1755

Simon Hunt, 3d & Lucy Raymond, April 15, 1755
Samuel Hosmer & Ann Parlin of Carlisle, June 5, 1755
Amos Dakin of Lincoln & Thankful Sarah Minot, June 12, 1755
Joseph Sargent of Stow & Elisabeth Wheeler, June 17, 1755
John Meriam & Sarah Jones, Sept. 11, 1755
James Adams of Lincoln & Keziah Conant, Jan. 15, 1756
William Blasdell & Sarah Holmes, Sept. 11, 1755
James Chandler & Mary Whitaker of Carlisle, April 14, 1756
Thomas Baker of Littleton & Bulah Dakin of Sudbury,
March 6, 1755
Samuel Brooks of Worcester & Hannah Brown of
Carlisle, March 14, 1755
William Cory & Dorothy Wood, both of Bedford, May 24, 1755
Joshua Wheeler & Elisabeth Raymond, Sept. 4, 1755
Abraham Tayler & Thankfull Stow, May 20, 1760
John Goddard of Marlborough & Lucy Walker of
Bolton, June 20, 1760
Enos Fox & Lydia Mercer, July 2, 1760
John Buttrick & Abigail Jones, June 24, 1760
Oliver Heald of Steptown (?) & Lydia Spaulding
of Townsend, Dec. 2, 1760
Silas Walker of Brookfield & Mary Wheeler, Nov. 28, 1760
Joseph Stow & Olive Jones, June 14, 1759
Charles Miles & Ruth Barret, May 3, 1759
Ephraim Stow & Elisabeth Wooley, May 29, 1759
Samuel Cheney & Mary Ozlen, Aug. 3, 1759
John Peirce of Lexington & Abigail Knolton, Sept. 3, 1759
Isaac Appleton of New Ipswich & Mary Adams, April 24, 1760
Nathan Barret & Miriam Hunt, May 22, 1760
Nathaniel Stearns & Mary Farrar, Oct. 9, 1760
Edward Brown & Mary Brown, Jan. 15, 1761
Thomas Barret, Jr. & Dorcas Minot, Jan. 15, 1761
Samuel Rice & Hepzibath Flint, Dec. 6, 1765
Samuel Farwell & Mary Parker, Dec. 9, 1765
John Laughton & Hannah Brown, Jan. 23, 1766
Joseph Soper & Rhoda Brown, April 29, 1766
Samuel Fitch of Acton & Mary Blood, May 28, 1760
Ezra Corey & Mary Ramsdell, May 27, 1766

Samuel Darby & Mary Soper,	March 18, 1766
Israel Conant & Mary Heywood,	April 15, 1767
Nathan Davis & Mary Blood,	May 28, 1767
Hezekiah Stratten & Martha Barker,	Aug. 25, 1767
Ebenezer Jones, Jr. and Hannah Fay of Lincoln,	Oct. 22, 1767
Eli Conant & Elisabeth Gardner,	Dec. 23, 1767
Capt. Aaron Jones of Weston & Eliza. Prescott,	Dec. 31, 1767
John Cole & Mary Dudley,	May 28, 1768
Joseph Goodenow of Sudbury & Dorothy Stratton,	July 18, 1768
Solomon Rice & Abigail Cleveland,	Aug. 3, 1768
Samuel Dutton & Ruth Edwards,	Aug. 23, 1768
Redit Jones & Hannah Wheeler,	April 15, 1768
Timothy Jones & Rebekah Bateman, both of Bedford,	Nov. 1, 1768
Daniel Hosmer & Hannah Baker of Lincoln,	Nov. 24, 1768
Samuel Keyen of Westford & Molly Davis of Acton,	March 21, 1769
Ebenezer Jones, Jr. & Sarah Fay,	May 27, 1769
Moses Heynes of Sudbury & Dorcas Jones,	March 9, 1769
Joseph Shed of Temple & Sybill Procter of Chelmsford,	Nov. 16, 1769
Willard Buttrick & Esther Blood,	Nov. 22, 1769
Isaac Ramsdell & Abigail Temple,	Dec. 21, 1769
Benjamin Williams & Hepzibah Brown,	March 8, 1770
Ebenezer Farrar & Elisabeth Mercer,	March 14, 1770
Eliot Powers & Mary Barker, both of Acton,	March 20, 1770
Philip Piper & Ann Gill, both of Acton,	Aug. 7, 1770
Samuel Gilbert of Littleton & Elisabeth Robbins of Westford,	Oct. 9, 1770
Joshua Longley & Elisabeth Melven,	Oct. 16, 1770
John Pushe of Acton & Lucy Blodgett of Westford,	Nov. 22, 1770
John Wood & Lydia Hosmer,	Dec. 6, 1770
William Horsley of Westminster & Abigail Haywood,	July 10, 1771
John Hill of Acton & Sarah Harris of Westford,	
Paul Lamson & Azubah Parlin,	May 2, 1771
Peter Perham & Rebekah Buttrick,	Jan. 7, 1771

Stephen Barker & Rebekah Gibson, both of Stow,

June 8, 1772

Joseph Shed & Rebekah Needham, both of Billerica,

Jan. 7, 1773

Joseph Meriam & Mary Brooks,	Jan. 14, 1768
Ephraim Brown & Sybill Paterson,	March 13, 1768
Benjamin Pollard of Lincoln & Mercy Adams,	April 12, 1768
Thomas Wheat of Hollis & Sarah Temple,	Aug. 23, 1768
James Perrey & Mary Cowdry,	Sept. 1, 1768
David Johnson & Mary Soper,	Sept. 1, 1768
John Stratton & Ruth Wright,	Dec. 1, 1768
Isaac Meriam & Rebekah Davis of Acton,	Dec. 2, 1768
Daniel Brooks of Acton & Lydia Burridge,	Dec. 2, 1768
David Brown of Hollis & Rebekah Foster,	Jan. 13, 1768
David Beard & Hannah Haywood,	Jan. 19, 1769
Samuel Gardner of Woburn & Dorothy Miles,	Aug. 9, 1769
William Barker of Acton & Anna Holdin,	Aug. 31, 1769
Timothy Dix of Littleton & Rachel Burbanks,	Aug. 31, 1769
John Blood & Ruth Brown,	Sept. 7, 1769

John Remington Esqr. of Watertown & Elisabeth

Hartshorn, Nov. 9, 1769

Daniel Holdin & Mellicent Hosmer,	Dec. 14, 1769
David Lock of Ipswich & Betty Kibbey,	Jan. 4, 1770
Reuben Hunt & Rebekah Barret,	Jan. 18, 1770
Nathan Parlin of Acton & Abigail Hodgman,	Jan. 31, 1770
Elisha Jones & Elisabeth Farrar,	Feb. 22, 1770
Jacob Baker of Lincoln & Hannah Ball,	Feb. 28, 1770
Samuel Johnson of Woburn & Lydia Jones,	May 10, 1770
William Meriam of Lexington & Sarah Puffer,	June 21, 1770
Reuben Hodgman & Sarah Stratton,	Aug. 9, 1770
Israel Cook & Submit Stratton,	July 12, 1770
William Bond of Royalston & Mary Fletcher,	Aug. 16, 1770
Samuel Walker of Weston & Janna Peirce,	Aug. 16, 1770
Samuel Jones & Hepzibah Jones,	April 25, 1771
Thomas Davis, Jr. & Ruhamah Andrews,	April 30, 1771
Abel Conant & Katy Johnson,	May 7, 1771
David Blood & Elisabeth Procter,	Sept. 26, 1771
Daniel Billing, Jr. of Lincoln & Ann Hunt,	Oct. 31, 1771

Daniel Jones & Mary Jones,	Nov. 16, 1769
Abijah Wheeler & Mary Hayward,	Dec. 7, 1773
Paul Brown & Mary Wheeler,	Dec. 13, 1773
Samuel Green, Jr. & Sarah Marble, both of Stow,	
	Feb. 28, 1774
Kendall Bancroft & Susanna Evers,	March 9, 1775
Abijah Hodgman & Beulah Kibbey,	March 9, 1775
Stephen Jones & Anna Brooks,	April 27, 1775
Samuel White of Westford & Hepzibah Barret,	May 23, 1775
Jonathan Chandler & Hannah Brooks of Lincoln,	June 8, 1775
Stephen Barret & Sarah Barret,	June 22, 1775
Thomas Fessenden of Lexington & Lucy Lee,	Dec. 7, 1775
Jacob Ames & Ginney Fay,	Dec. 15, 1775
Isaiah Brown of Holdin & Nabby Brown,	Dec. 27, 1775
Ebenezer Stow & Mary Hartwell,	Dec. 28, 1775
Abraham Whitney of Bolton & Rebecca Dudley	
of Acton,	Feb. 28, 1776
Isaiah Whitney of Harvard & Mary Wheeler,	Feb. 28, 1776
Timothy Wheeler of Mason & Sarah Hubbard,	April 11, 1776
Elijah Hosmer & Sarah Gardner,	June 26, 1776
Noah Wheeler & Sarah Meriam,	July 30, 1776
Joseph Wright & Mary Meriam,	Nov. 22, 1776
Amos Hosmer & Lucy Meriam,	Nov. 22, 1776
Amos Lowell of Holdin & Mary Ball,	Nov. 20, 1776
Ralph Hill & Mary Jones, both of Ashby,	April 15, 1777
William Shaw & Lucy Handley,	April 7 1777
Doctr. Abel Prescott & Mrs (?) Mary Beaton,	June 12, 1777
John Hosmer, 2d. & Dorothy Wheeler,	Aug. 10, 1777
John Blood & Mary Davis,	Nov. 7, 1777
Ephraim Robbins of Groton & Thankful Ball,	Dec. 19, 1777
Ebenezer Phillips of Littleton & Experiance Shepard,	
	March 5, 1778
David Hubbard & Mary Barrett,	April 15, 1778
Josiah Meriam, Jr. & Mary Brown,	Aug. 6, 1778
Thomas Meads of Westford & Sarah Foster,	Nov. 7, 1778
John Parlin & Rachel Harris,	Sept. 20, 1779
Jeremiah Hunt & Nancy Blodgett,	Dec. 10, 1780
Daniel Brown & Elizabeth Briant,	Dec. 14, 1780

Joel Hosmer & Abigail Whittemore,	Jan. 11, 1781
William Bass of Bolton & Abigail Dudley,	Jan. 19, 1781
Francis Legross & Dolly Barker,	Feb. 11, 1787
John Hodgman & Mary Willson,	Feb. 26, 1778
Jacob Kemp & Susannah Lock,	Feb. 26, 1778
Thaddeus Munro of Hillsborough & Hannah Richardson of Chelmsford,	Feb. 17, 1780
William Spaulding & Lucy Spaulding, both of Chelmsford,	April 6, 1780
Abraham Conant of Stow & —— Merrill,	Aug. 27, 1789
Thomas Fox & Hannah Brooks,	(no date)
William Wheeler & Hannah Russe,	(no date)

√ DUNSTABLE

Oct. 13, 1680 Dunstable is mentioned in a military list.

John Goole & Elixabeth Cummings,	July 2, 1686
Thomas Welds & Elizabeth Wilson,	Nov. 9, 1681
Samuel Warner & Marah Swallow,	May 4, 1684
John Cummings & Elizabeth Kinsley,	Sept. 13, 1681
Samuel French & Sarah Cummings,	Feb. 7, 1683
John Salindon & Elisabeth Usher,	Ap. 2, 1679
John Lovewell & Anna Hassell,	Dec. 7, 1686
Samuel Whiting, Jr. of Billerica & Mrs. Elizabeth Read at D.,	Jan. 27, 1686/7
James Richardson of Chelmsford & May Parris,	Dec. 14, 1687
Thomas Blancher of D. & Tabitha Lipperwell of Woburn,	Feb. 13, 1688/9

GROTON

May 29, 1655. A plantation formerly called Petapawag established as "Groton."

Joshua Parker & Abigail Morss,	Sept. 22, 1690
James Dutten & Mary Robin,	Dec. 9, 1690
Jno. Page & Faith Dunster,	May 12, 1664
Samuel Willard & Abigail Shearman,	Aug. 8, 1664
Jonathan Sawtle & Mary ———,	July 3, 1665
Thomas Williams & Mary ———,	Aug. 11, 1666
Thomas Tarbole & Hannah ———,	June 30, 1666
James Robertson & Elizab. ———,	Jan. 16, 1667
Timothy Cooper & Sarah Morss,	June 2, 1669
James Bloud & Elizabeth Longly,	Sept. 7, 1669
Cornelius Church & Mary ———,	June 4, 1670
Nathaniel Bloud & Hannah ———,	June 13, 1670
Willm. Longley & Lidea ———,	May 15, 1672
Alexande. Rouse & Judah ———,	May 15, 1672
Hen. Willard & Mary (Lakin)?	18, 5, 1674
John Nuttin & Mary,	11, 10, 1674
Thomas Tarball & Elisabeth Wood,	Dec. 1, 1686
John Fanworth of G. & Hannah Aldis of Dedham,	Dec. 8, 1686
James Blood & Abigail Kemp,	Dec. 20, 1686
James Fish & Tabitha Butterick,	Feb. 2, 1686/7
John Lawrence & Hannah Tarbol,	Nov. 9, 1687
John Green of Groton & Mary Pierce of Watertown,	Dec. 25, 1688
Christopher Hall of G. & Ruth Garfield of Watertown,	Feb. 2, 1687/8
Samll Winter of Killingsley & Elizabeth Philbrook,	Feb. 16, 1713
Gershom Hobart & Lydia Nutting,	Feb. 26, 1713
Wm. Powers of Concord & Lydia Parham,	March 16, 1713/4
Thomas Farr & Elisabeth Powers, both of Nashoah,	March 16, 1713/4

Joseph Powers & Hannah Whetcom,	March 16, 1713/14
Joseph Sanderson & Sarah Page,	July 30, 1714
John Parker & Mary Bradstreet,	Nov. 29, 1715
Joseph Parker, Jr. & Abigail Sawtell,	Jan. 24, 1715/16
Jonathan Whetcomb & Deliverance Nutting,	May 15, 1716
John Holden & Sarah Davis,	Nov. 22, 1716
William Lun of Dunstable & Rachel Holdin,	Dec. 20, 1716
Thomas Tarbell & Abigail ———,	Jan. 1, 1716/17
Benjamin Parker & Mary Sawtel,	Oct. 23, 1718
Nathanll. Holdin & Abigail Stone,	Dec. 11, 1718
William Shattuck & Deliverance Pease,	March 24, 1718
Eleazer Gilson & Hannah Farwell,	May 6, 1719
John Parker & Joanna Am's,	May 22, 1719
Eleazer Nutting & Abigail Davis,	June 23, 1719
Moses Bennit & Anna Blanchard,	Aug. 11, 1719
Stephen Holdin & Hannah Sawtell,	Sept. 2, 1719
John Spencer & Bethiah Kemp,	Nov. 12, 1719
Daniel Pierce & Elenor Boynton,	Dec. 9, 1719
Joseph Farwell & Mary Gilson,	Dec. 24, 1719
Jonathan Parker & Sarah Pierce,	Oct. 27, 1720
Samll. Woods & Patience Biggelow,	Nov. 29, 1720
Robert Robins of Littleton & widow Elizabeth Cummins,	Jan. 23, 1721
Zechr. Maynard & Widow Waters,	May 22, 1721
Ebenezer Prescott & Hannah Farnsworth,	May 24, 1721
Daniel Boynton & Jemima Brown,	June 1, 1721
Nathnll Woods & Sarah Brown of Stow,	July 3, 1721
Ephraim Pierce & Esther ———,	Oct. 30, 1721
Obadiah Sawtle & Rachel Parker,	Nov. 16, 1721
Richard Rice & Sarah Caree,	Feb. 1, 1721
Robert Dickson & Abigail Parker, widow,	Feb. 7, 1721
Eleazer Green & Annah Tarbell,	March 8, 1721
Jonathan Shead & Sarah Farnsworth,	April 3, 1722
Collins Mores of Oxford & Bathsheba Woods,	May 2, 1722
John Blanchard of Dunstable & Mary Sawtell,	May 30, 1722
William Lawrence & Susanna Prescott,	June 27, 1722
Joshua Hutchins & Sarah Shead,	July 12, 1722
John Gilson & Mary Shattuck,	July 12, 1722

John Stone, Jr. & Elisabeth Farwell,   Dec. 26, 1722
William Banks & Hannah Wansamug of Lancas-
    ter,   Dec. 21, 1719
Benjamin Bennit & Mary Larkin,   March 27, 1723
Thomas Wood & Abigail Chamberlin,   April 30, 1723
Isaac Williams & Lydia Shattuck,   May 22, 1723
John Davis & Rebeckah Burt,   June 13, 1723
Thomas Farwell & Elizabeth Pierce,   Dec. 24, 1723
Jeremiah Shattuck & Sarah Parker,   July 7, 1724
Jonathan Green & Sarah Lakin,   Feb. 25, 1724
John Farmer of Billerica & Hanah Woods,   April 27, 1725
John Woods & Sarah Longley,   June 3, 1725
David Peace & Elizabeth Bowers,   June 15, 1725

HOLLISTON

Dec. 3, 1724. Part of Sherborn established as Holliston.

John Death & Hannah More,   May 15, 1729
Eli Jones & Mercy Underwood,   May 15, 1729
Moses Hill & Hannah Hill,   June 27, 1729
Edward Kebly of Medway & Abia Morse,   July 3, 1729
Ephraim Bigloe & Lydia Johnson,   July 24, 1729
Aaron Morse & Abigail Dunton,   Jan. 15, 1729/30
Ebenezer Marshall & Elisabeth Jones,   Jan. 15, 1729/30
Sam'l Daniels & Lydia Hill,   Jan. 15, 1729/30
John Fisk & Abigail Babcock, both of Sherborn,
                                                        Sept. 21, 1731
Francis Dudley of Sutton & Sabilla Laland of Sher-
    born,   May 23, 1732
John Haven of Framingham & Mary Bullard,   Mch. 9, 1731/2
Moses Johnson of H. & Sabilla Plymton of Sher-
    born,   May 18, 1732
John Leland & Ruth Morse, both of Sherborn,   June 21, 1732
Eleazar Perry & Mary Johnson,   June 14, 1732

LANCASTER

May 18, 1653. "Nashaway" to be a township to be called Lancaster.

James Fairbanks & Lidea Prescott,	March 28, 1658
George Bennitt & Lidea Kibby,	April 13, 1658
Richard Wheeler & Sarah Prescott,	June 2, 1658
Willm. Kerly & Brichett Rowlandson	March 31, 1659
William Kerly & Rebeccah Joselin,	March 16, 1664
John Deuall & Hannah White,	Oct. 23, 1663
Josiah Whetcombe & Rebeccah Waters,	Nov. 4, 1664
Jonathan Whetcome & Hannah ———,	Nov. 25, 1667
John Farrer & Mary ———,	June 30, 1667
John Rug & Hannah ———,	May 4, 1660
John Prescott & Sarah ———,	Nov. 11, 1668
Thomas Wilder & Mary ———,	June 25, 1668
Jacob. Farrer & Hannah ———,	Nov. 11, 1668
John Rigby & Elizabeth ———,	Aug. 30, 1662
Reuben Luxford & Margarett ———,	June 22, 1669
Henry Maze & Ales ———,	Sept. 14, 1669
John Whetcombe & Mary ———,	May 19, 1669
Jonathan Prescott & Dorothy ———,	3-6-1670
Thomas Sawyer & Sarah ———,	11-8-1670
Jno. Whitcomb & Mary ———,	16-1-1670/1
Benj. Bosworth & Beatris,	16-9-1671
Mordecay Muckload & Lidea,	31-11-1670
Cipryan Steevens & Mary (Willard)?,	22-11-1671
John Wilder & Hannah,	17-5-1672
John Houghton & Mary,	22-11-1671
Tho. Sawyer & Hannah,	21-9-1672
Jerimiah Rogers & Dorcas,	11-10-1672
Abram Jocelyn & Ann,	29-9-1672
Samuel & Mary Waters,	21-1-1672
Nathl. Wilder & Mary,	24-11-1673
Jonas Prescott & Mary (Loker)?	14-9-1672
John Sawyer & Mary Bull of Worcester,	June 16, 1686

John Moor & Mary Whitcomb,	Aug. 23, 1683
John Pope & Beatrix Haughton,	Sept. 20, 1683
Jonah Haughton of L. & May Berbeane of Woburn,	
	Feb. 15, 1681
James Atherton & Abigail Hudson,	June 6, 1684
Caleb Sawyer & Sarah Houghton, both of L. at	
Marlboro,	Jan. 21, 1687
Joseph Fairbank & Mary Brown,	April, 1718
John Bennet & Bathsheba Phelps,	July 23, 1718
Jethro Emes & Abigail Wheelock,	Sept. 10, 1718
Joseph Sawyer & Abigail Wilder,	Nov. 12, 1718
Edward Phelps & Mary Bennet,	Nov. 24, 1718
Deliverance Brown & Elisabeth Fairbank,	Dec. 24, 1718
Jabez Fairbank, Jr. & Hephzibah Sawyer,	Jan. 28, 1718/19
Ephraim Brown & Mary Fairbank,	Feb. 9, 1718/19
Jabez Fairbank, Sen. & Elisabeth Whetcomb,	March 25, 1719
Thomas Sawyer & Mary White,	July 15, 1718
John Houghton & Mehetable Wilson,	Nov. 18, 1718
John Goodman & Mary Atherton,	Jan. 20, 1718/19
Jonathan Whitney & Alice Willard,	Feb. 25, 1718/19
Eliezer Houghton & Elisabeth Divall,	March 11, 1718/19
Joshua Houghton & Elisabeth Bennit,	April 8, 1719
Amos Sawyer & Abigail Houghton,	May 14, 1719
Nathanll. Whitney & Mary Holeman,	Nov. 18, 1719
Jonathan Willard & Keziah White,	Aug. 17, 1719
Jno. Smith & Martha Butler,	Dec. 14, 1719
Jno. Houghton & Sarah Gulliver,	Jan. 7, 1719/20
Joseph Atherton & Hannah Rogers,	June 9, 1720
Benjamin Houghton, Jr. & Ruth Wheelock,	July 20, 1720
Benjamin Houghton, Sen. & Zeriah Moore,	July 28, 1720
Ephraim Wheeler & Meriah Glazier,	Nov. 1, 1720
John Longley & Deborah Houghton,	Nov. 30, 1720
John Nicholls & Mary Priest, Jr.,	March 20, 1720/1
Jeremiah Holman & Anna Priest,	March 23, 1720/1
Ebenezer Houghton & Mary Priest, *Jr.,	March 23, 1720/1
Thomas Tucker & Mary Divell,	*May 25, 1720/1*
James Fairbanks & Lidea Prescott,	(no date)
Jonathan Whitcome & Hannah ———,	(no date)

MARLBOROUGH

May 31, 1660. The grant to the Whip-sufferage planters confirmed the name of the plantation to be "Marlborow."

Thomas Barence & Abigail Goodenow,	July 2, 1662
Thomas Goodenow, Jr. & Johanah,	Dec. 18, 1662
John Howe, Jr. & Elizabeth ————,	Jan. 22, 1662
Jonathan Johnson & Mary ————,	Aug. 14, 1663
John Barrence & Joanna ————,	————, 1664
Thomas Brigham & Mary ————,	Dec. 27, 1665
Henry Axdell & Hannah ————,	June 14, 1665
John Nuton & Elizabeth ————,	Jan. 5, 1666
Joseph Johnson & Susanna ————,	Nov. 19, 1667
Samuel Ward & Sarah ————,	June 6, 1667
Obadiah Ward & Mary ————,	Nov. 28, 1667
William Hunt & Mercy ————, Oct. or Nov. ——, 1664	
Moses Nuton & Joannah Larkin,	Oct. 27, 1668
Richard Barrence & Deborah Dicks,	Oct. 16, 1667
William Taylor & Mary Johnson,	Nov. 15, 1671
Nathaniel Johnson & Mary Phimpton,	Nov. 16, 1671
Isaac How & Francis Woods,	Jan. 17, 1671
John Wetherby & Mary How,	Sept. 18, 1672
Jonathan Johnson & Mary,	(no date)
Jeremiah Wilson & Hannah Beman, both of Lancaster,	
	Dec. 27, 1687
Joseph How & Dorothy Martin,	Dec. 29, 1687
John Warner & Elisabeth Newby,	Feb. 9, 1687/8
Abiel Bush & Grace Barret,	June 27, 1688
John Barret, Jr. & Deborah How,	Sept. 27, 1688
Eleazar Bellows & Easter Barrett,	Oct. 11, 1692
John Witherby & Mary How,	13-6-1672
James Wood & Hopestill Ward,	22-2-1678
Josiah White & Mary Rice,	28-9-1678
John Bowker & Mary How,	8-11-1678
Tho. Remond (Beaman)? & Eliz. Williams,	26-5-1678

Will. Ward & Hannah Ward,	4-6-1679
Nath. of John & Eliz. Newton,	28-11-1680
Dan. Newton & Susannah Moss,	30-10-1679
Tho. How & Sarah Osmer,	21-4-1681
Daniel Rice & Bethiah Ward,	10-11-1681
Thomas & Ann Rice,	10-11-1681
Nathl. Joslin & Hesther Moss,	8-12-1682
Eliazar Ward & Hannah Rice,	10-5-1675
Will. Taylor & Hannah Axtell (widow),	16-5-1677
Nathaniel Oke & Mehetabel Rediat,	Dec. 14, 1686
Lieut. John Rudduck & Jane Brimsmead,	Dec. 30, 1686
Charles Williams & Elizabeth Weekes, both of Worcester,	Jan. 11, 1686
Henry Jefts & Elisabeth Hayward,	July 10, 1716
Joseph Mors & Abigail Barn,	Nov. 1, 1716
James Holmes & Jane Stephens, both of Worcester,	Jan. 26, 1687/8
Benjamin Rice & Mary Rice,	Nov. 15, 1692
Abraham Eager & Lydia Woods,	Nov. 15, 1692
Jacob Hues (Hinds) & Grace Morse,	Dec. 6, 1716
Daniel Bartlet & Martha How,	Feb. 12, 1716
Nathl. Wells & Mary Hall,	Ap. 11, 1717
Nathan Brigham & Dina Rice,	Dec. 24, 1717
Benjamin Woods & Elisabeth Morse,	Aug. 8, 1717
John Wheeler & Mary Hapgood,	Oct. 8, 1717
William Taylor & Elisabeth Hapgood,	Nov. 28, 1717
Joseph Wheeler & Elisabeth Holloway,	Jan. 16, 1717
Asa Bowker & Martha Eager,	Feb. 28, 1717
Peter How & Grace Bush,	Dec. 24, 1718
Isaac Amsden & Mary Martin,	May 23, 1718
Benjamin Mills of Needham & Sarah Taylor,	Nov. 10, 1718
Thomas Green & Mary Johnson,	Nov. 12, 1718
Simon Mainard & Sarah Church,	Nov. 18, 1718
Isaac How & Susan Sible of Sutton,	Dec. 2, 1718
John Mathes & Jerusha Biglo,	Dec. 11, 1718
Benjamin Bayle of Lancaster & Elisabeth How,	Dec. 18, 1718
Peter Smith & Mercy Wright,	Dec. 18, 1718
Elias Keyes & Kezia Brigham,	Dec. 19, 1718

Thomas Forbush & Hannah Bellows,	Jan. 6, 1718
James Mainard & Mary Morse,	Jan. 6, 1718
Aaron Forbush & Susanna Morse,	Jan. 13, 1718
Abijah Bruce & Mary Morse (Woods)?	Jan. 14, 1718
John Mathewes & Mary Johnson,	Sept. 20, 1686
Daniel How & Elisabeth Kerley,	Oct. 12, 1686
Henry Bartlet & Mary Bush,	Dec. 6, 1682
Sam'l Bridgam & Elisabeth How,	——, 1683
Eliazer How & Hannah How,	Nov., 1684
William Johnson & Mary Larkin,	Jan. 27, 1684
Thomas Barnes & Mary How,	Ap. 14, 1685
Joseph Morse & Abigail Barnes,	Nov. 1, 1716
Jacob Hines & Grace Morse,	Dec. 6, 1716
Daniel Bartlet & Martha How,	Feb. 12, 1716/7
Nathan Wells & Mary Hall,	Ap. 15, 1717
Nathan Brigham & Dina Ruskin?,	Dec. 24, 1717
Benjamin Woods & Elisabeth Morss,	Aug. 8, 1717
John Wheeler & Mary Hapgood,	Oct. 8, 1717
William Taylor & Elisabeth Hapgood,	Nov. 28, 1717
Joseph Wheeler & Elisabeth Holloway, Jr.,	Jan. 16, 1718
Asa Bowker & Martha Eager,	Feb. 28, 1718
Hezekiah Bush & Abigail Joslin,	Oct. 31, 1721
Cyprian Rice & Lydia Rice,	Dec. 23, 1721
Joseph Wright & Mary Holland,	Jan. 1, 1721
John Crosby & Bathsheba Newton,	Jan. 23, 1721
Thomas Rich & Ruth Banister,	Feb. 1, 1721
Josiah Holden & Sarah Axtill,	Feb. 7, 1721
John Stow & Elisabeth Brigham,	Ap. 25, 1722
Nathaniel Joslin & Elisabeth Taylor,	Sept. 6, 1722
Thomas Rice & Mary Oakes,	Nov., July 2, 1722
Henry Emmes & Ruth Newton,	Nov. 7, 1722
David Goodenough & Dina Fay of Westborough,	Nov 8, 1722
Abraham Amsden & Hannah Newton,	Dec. 29, 1722
Amos Pratt & Ann Allen of Shrewsbury,	Dec. 12, 1722
Ephraim How (Stow?) & Elisabeth Rice,	Jan. 8, 1722
Joseph How & Surviah How,	Feb. 20, 1722
Isaac Temple & Elisabeth Holland,	June 4, 1725
Othniel Taylor & Mary Newton,	Sept. 1, 1725

Abraham Williams & Elisabeth Breeck,	Dec. 22, 1726
Nathaniel Hudson & Jane Banester,	Dec. 20, 1725
Jesaniah Newton & Deliverance Newton,	Jan. 5, 1725
John Eddy & Mary Bellows,	Jan. 20, 1725
David Woods & Ruth Johnson,	Jan. 26, 1725
Moses Newton & Sarah How,	Feb. 22, 1725
Joseph Biglow & Martha Brigham,	Feb. 22, 1725
Eleazer Bemont & Hannah How,	Mch. 2, 1726
Jonathan Keys & Patience Morse,	Nov. 11, 1726
Caleb Wheeler & Joanna Wheeler,	Jan. 12, 1727
Jacob Wheeler & Amity Amsden,	Jan. 12, 1727
William McAllister & Jane Campbell,	Jan. 21, 1727
James Bellows & Thankful Willis,	Jan. 18, 1727
Simon Rice & Grace Newton,	Jan. 23, 1727
Joseph How & Ruth Brigham,	Feb. 20, 1727
David Bruce & Mary Brigham,	Feb. 20, 1727
Jonathan Goodenough & Lydia Rice,	Feb. 20, 1727
Nath'l Oak & Tabitha Rice,	Feb. 20, 1727
Uriah Eager & Sarah Brigham,	Mch. 14, 1727
Moses Johnson & Sarah Rush (Bush)?,	Mch. 13, 1727
James Brown & Mary Claice?	Dec. 7, 1727
Jonathan Jennings of Brookfield & Esther Rice,	July 17, 1727
Ebenezer Snow & Experience Joslin,	Oct. 11, 1727
Robert Sennet of Hopkinton & Elisabeth Witherby,	
	Nov. 16, 1727
Joseph Johnson & Susanna Joslin,	Nov. 30, 1727
Daniel Ward & Mary Biglow,	Dec. 10, 1727
Pelatiah Rice of Westborough & Sarah Newton,	Jan. 11, 1727
Sam'l Eddy of Oxford & Elisabeth Bellows,	Jan. 30, 1727
Nath'l Harthorn & Sarah Stevens,	Mch. 7, 1727/8
Hezekiah Wetherby & Huldah Martyn,	Ap. 23, 1728
John Biglow & Rebecca How,	July 4, 1728
Joseph Brigham & Comfort Biglow,	Aug. 26, 1728
Joseph Rice, & Elisabeth Robinson,	Dec. 4, 1728
Benjamin Gott & Sarah Breck,	Jan. 20, 1728
Zerubbabel Rice, & Elisabeth Barrett,	Feb. 4, 1728
John Snow & Abigail Brigham,	Mch. 25, 1729
Jonathan Morse & Mary Church,	May 1, 1729

√ MALDEN

May 2, 1649.   "Misticke side men" granted to be a town to be called "Maulden."

John Lewis & Mary Brown,	10-2-1650
John Sprague & Lidea Goffe,	March 2, 1651
John Winslow & Sarah Moulton,	March 5, 1652
Robert Burdit & ———— Winter,	Sept. —, 1653
Joseph Hills, Jr. & Hannah Smith,	Sept. —, 1653
George Bunker & Hannah Miller,	July —, 1655
Joseph Hills, Sen., & Helen Adkinson,	Nov. —, 1655
Samuel Sprague & Rebecca ————,	————, ————
Thomas Michell & Mary Molton,	Sept. —, 1655
Willm. Leraby & Eliz. Felt,	Sept. —, 1655
Jno. Paul & Lidea Jenkins,	March 3, 1657
Thomas Call, Jr. & Lidea Shepdson,	May 22, 1657
Phineas Upham & Ruth Wood,	Feb. 14, 1658
Thomas Shepard & Hannah Ensigne,	Sept. 9, 1658
Thomas Greene, Sen. & Francis Cooke,	July 5, 1659
Willm. Green & Elizabeth Wheeler,	July 13, 1659
Willm. Augur & Ruth Hill,	Oct. 7, 1659
Job Lane & Anna Reyner,	July —, 1660
James Nicholls & Mary Felt,	Feb. —, 1660
John Greene & Sarah Wheeler,	Oct. 18, 1660
Walter Power & Triall Shepard,	Jan. 11, 1660
Phineas Sprague & Mary Carrington,	Oct. 11, 1661
Joseph Wayt & Mercy Tufft,	24-10-1688
John Upham & Abigail Haward,	Oct. 31, 1688
Phillip Coriell (?) & Elisabeth Atwood,	Sept. 26, 1688
Thomas Oaks & Sarah Tufft,	May 22, 1689
Thomas Kimball of Bradford & Deborah Pemerton of M.	Dec. 22, 1686
Samuel Green & Mary Wheeler,	May 4, 1694
Lemuel Jenkins & Marcy Waite,	June 11, 1694
Jonathan Haward & Elisabeth Lee,	May 24, 1690

Jacob Winslow & Elisabeth Whittemore,	May 26, 1690
Joseph Baldwin & Elisabeth Grover,	June 26, 1691
Samll. ——— & Elisabeth Upham,	Oct. 28, 1691
John Lynde & Elisabeth Green,	Aug. 25, 1691
Roger Kenicott & Joanna Sheperson,	Nov. —, 1661
Samuel Haward & Elizabeth Switcher,	———, ———
Samuel Lee & Mercy Call,	Nov. 4, 1662
Edward Conats & Sarah Addams,	Feb. 25, 1662
Isaac Hill & Hannah Haward,	4 Mo., 1666
Abram Hill & Hannah Stower,	Aug. —, 1666
Samuel Greene & Mary Cooke,	———, ———
Jno. Winbourne & Elizab. Hart,	Feb. 2, 1667
Gershom Hill & Elizab. Chadwicke,	11-11-1667
Thomas Greene & Elizab. Web,	———, ———
Benjamin Web & Mercy Bucknam,	Dec. 7, 1669
Thomas Grover & Sarah Chadwick,	May 23, 1668
Zachariah Sautle & Elizab. Harris,	April —, 1668
Daniel Shepardson & Elizab. Tingle,	April —, 1667
John Sergent & Mary Bense,	Sept. 3, 1669
Phineas Sprague & Sarah Hasse,	Jan. 5, 1669
Lemuel Jenkins & Elizab. Oakes,	12-5-1670
Samuel Haward & Susanna Wilkinson,	Jan. —, 1671
John Martinn & Mary Mudge,	Feb. 14, 1671
Henry Greene & Hester Hasse,	Nov. 11, 1671
James Barrett & Dorcas Greene,	Nov. 11, 1671
John Uppam & ——— Hollie,	June —, 1671
Joseph Wayte & Hannah Oakes,	6-7-1672
Andrew Grover & Hanna Hills,	Dec. 7, 1673
Jno. Wayte & Sarah Muzzy,	April 12, 1674
Jno. Shaw & Eliz. Ramsdel,	June 12, 1674
Benj. Blackman & Sarah Scottow,	Feb. 1, 1675
Phillip Attwood & Eliz. Grover,	Feb. 7, 1675
Jno. Wayte & Sarah Parker,	June 4, 1675
Tho. Green & Mary Weeks,	Jan. 22, 1675/6
Wm. Bucknam & Hannah Wayte,	Aug. 11, 1676
Obadiah Jenkins & Mary Lewis,	Nov. 11, 1676
James Chadwick & Hannah Butler,	Dec. —, 1676
Richard Weeks & Mary Lee,	Dec. 2, 1686

James Nickols & Hannah Whittemore of Wooburne, Nov. 15, 1686

John Prat & Martha ——,	——, ——
Josiah Blanchard & Elisabeth Merriam,	Dec. 6, 1721
Richard Pratt & Joana Ong,	Dec. 29, 1721
John Burditt & Hannah Coal,	July 5, 1722
John Sweetser & Martha Green,	Oct. 2, 1722
Thomas Wayte & Abigail Hessey,	Jan. 10, 1723
James Holden & Mary Storer,	Feb. 7, 1723
John Coleman & Dorothy Upham,	April 23, 1723
Abiather Vinten & Lydia Green,	April 30, 1723
Jacob Freese & Dorothy Moulton,	March 31, 1725
Thomas Douglas & Mary Sergeant,	June 10, 1725
Thomas Pratt & Lydia Lynds,	June 24, 1725
Benjamin Blaney & Abigail Buckman,	Oct. 13, 1725
John Thomas & Elizth Nichols,	Nov. 30, 1725
Phillips Sweetser & Mary Green,	Dec. 30, 1725
Thomas Green & Martha Lynds,	Jan. 13, 1725/6
Joseph Green & Ruth Dexter,	Jan. 25, 1725/6
Thomas Blanchard & Judith Hill,	Feb. 21, 1725/6
Timothy Wait & Mary Oaks,	April 28, 1726
Jonathan Howard & Mary Harndel,	June 1, 1726
Robert Snelling & Lydia Dexter,	June 30, 1726
Joseph Woolson & Elizabeth Upham,	Oct. 26, 1726
Amos Puttnam & Hannah Lynds,	Dec. 27, 1726
Daniel Floyd & Margaret Jenkins,	Feb. 7, 1726/7
Jotham Tutle & Martha Hallwere,	March 1, 1727
Jacob Freese & Dorothy Moulton,	March 31, 1725
Thomas Douglas & Mary Sergeant,	June 10, 1725

Edward Hullwell & Huldah Furrington of Lynn, Dec. 25, 1730
Phineas Upham & Hannah Waite, Dec. 30, 1730
Benja. Tufts of Medford & Mary Hutchinson, Jan. 7, 1730/1

Samuel Waite & Elisabeth Pratt,	March 16, 1730/1
Jacob Burditt & Rebekah Brown,	March 30, 1731
Thomas Parker, Jr. & Mary Upham,	April 5, 1731
James Barnet of Killingsly & Tabitha Hill,	May 6, 1731
Michael Sweetser & Mary Smith,	Nov. 18, 1731
Ezekiel Jenkins & Phebe Sprague,	Aug. 3, 1732

Joseph Chadwick of Falmouth & Mary Jenkins, Nov. 2, 1732
John Goddard of Roxbury & Mary Sprague, Nov. 15, 1732
David Green of Reading & Hannah Marble, March 15, 1732/3
Patrick Cowen & Jane Crawford of Lynn, Feb. 22, 1732/3
Thomas Richardson & Ruth Bucknam, June 26, 1733
Thomas Mighills of Pomfret & Mary Haward, Sept. 6, 1733
Benjamin Faulkner & Anna Green, Oct. 25, 1733
Nathaniel Pain & Abigail Hasey, Feb. 5, 1733/4
Ebenezer Harnden & Lydia Wade of Medford, Feb. 25, 1733/4
John Sprague & Judith Green of Stoneham, April 11, 1734
David Pratt & Mercy Upham, April 18, 1734
Joshua Whittemore & Elisabeth Whittemore, April 25, 1734
Asa Hill of Sherborn & Sarah Hill, May 29, 1734
Ebenezer Barrett & Elisabeth Sergant, Nov. 7, 1734
Isaac Waite & Deborah Waite, Nov. 28, 1734
Thomas Lynds & Joanna Parker, Dec. 27, 1735
Richard Whittemore of Killingsley & Elizabeth
  Baldwin, Dec. 26, 1735
Samuel Evans of Reading & Sarah Marble, Nov. 3 1735
Benjamin Farnsworth of Groton & Rebekah Pratt,
  May 19, 1736
William Dana of Cambridge & Mary Green May 20, 1736
Phinehas Walker of Brookfield & Ruth Chadwick,
  July 3, 1736
Theophilus Burrill of Lynn & Mary Hills, Sept. 24, 1736
Samuel Grover & Abigail Oakes, Nov. 8, 1736
Samuel Sprague & Martha Hills, Jan. 11, 1736/7
Samuel Bleigh of Boston & Mary Tufts, Nov. 12, 1736
Nathaniel Townsend of Lynn & Margaret Chamberlain,
  Dec. 9, 1736
Daniel Mansfield of Lynn & Elisabeth Tufts, Jan. 6, 1736/7
David Howard & Sarah Degrusha, Jan. 20, 1736/7
Samuel Newhall & Martha Upham, March 18, 1737
Timothy Sprague & Mary Legg, April 14, 1737
Thomas Jenkins of Boston & Anna Sergeant, June 15, 1736
Samuel Sweetser & Mary Burditt, July 8, 1736
Samuel Hasey of Boston & Sarah Upham, May 9, 1737
Charles Lemoyne & Mary Marble, May 19, 1737

Moses Gleason of Oxford & Deborah Whittemore,
Feb. 2, 1737/8
Stephen Sweetser & Mary Mudge,   Feb. 8, 1737/8
Reuben Derbe of Pomfret & Zibilla Howard,   Dec. 27, 1738
William Waite & Deborah Bucknam,   Dec. 28, 1738
Abraham Skinner & Anna Emmes,   March 13, 1739
Robert Willson & Anna Jackson,   July 12, 1738
Joseph Barrett & Phebe Waite,   April 27, 1739
John Sweetser of North Yarmouth & Elisabeth
Stevens,   Nov. 16, 1738
Jonathan Oakes & Martha Bucknam,   Feb. 1, 1738/9
Timothy Dexter & Sarah Bucknam,   March 22, 1738/9
Timothy Green & Dorothy Waite,   Nov. 8, 1737
Joseph Burditt & Tabitha Paine,   Dec. 16, 1737
Benjamin Faulkner & Anna Sprague,   March 22, 1738
John Mudge & Mary Waite,   May 4, 1738
Jonathan Lynds & Elisabeth Mower,   Dec. 21, 1739
David Parker & Mary Upham,   Sept. 5, 1740
Joseph Lynds & Mary Lynds,   July 4, 1740
John Seargeant & Hannah Wadkins,   July 24, 1740
John Nichols & Agnes Leveston,   Dec. 11, 1740
Ezra Green & Sarah Hutchinson,   Feb. 12, 1740/41
Jabez Clark of Stoughton & Sarah Whittemore, March 30, 1741
Capt. Daniel Goffe of Boston & Mary Upham, March —, 1740
Daniel Merrit of Boston & Lydia Sweetser,   Dec. 11, 1739
Jabez Burdett & Hannah Seargent,   Feb. 7, 1739/40
Nathan Richardson of Woburn & Lydia Whittemore,
April 3, 1740
Samuel Wade of Medford & Martha Newhall,   Dec. 2, 1741
Joshua Tucker of Woodstock & Mary Wright, Feb. 11, 1741/2
Nathan Sergeant of Leicester & Mary Sergeant, June 24, 1742
James Dumbar & Mary Woods of Boston,   Jan. 11, 1742/3
Joseph Mudge & Phebe Green,   Jan. 19, 1742/3
William Barnes of Boston & Mary Mansar,   Jan. 26, 1742/3
John Hoyle of Providence & Anna Waite,   Aug. 11, 1743
Samuel Sargeant & Louis Waite,   Oct. 25, 1743
Nathan Newhall & Tabitha Waite,   Oct. 26, 1743
Benjamin Bucknam & Rebekah Parker,   Nov. 12, 1743

John Waite of Chelsea & Sarah Faulkner,   Nov. 25, 1743
Benjamin Sprague & Phebe Lynde,   March 20, 1743/4
Samuel Shute & Elisabeth Pratt,   May 23, 1744
James Milliner of Mansfield & Ruth Peirce,   June 12, 1744
Benjamin Rice of Brookfield & Sarah Upham,   June 30, 1744
Edward Sprague & Lydia Howard,   July 4, 1744
Israel Cook of Boston & Hannah Upham,   Jan. 11, 1744/5
Bartholomew Flagg & Susanna Marble,   March 27, 1745
John Goddard & Sarah Sargeant,   Aug. 3, 1745
John Martin lately of Boston & Sarah Manser,   Sept. 18, 1745
Charles Crouly of Charlestown & Mary Marks,   Oct. 1, 1745
Thomas Parlen & Jemima Brintnal,   Dec. 4, 1745
Thomas Boston & Anna Taylor late of Maldon, Jan. 7, 1745/6
John Burdett & Jemima Green,   Feb. 6, 1745/6
Silas Sergant & Mary Winslow,   Feb. 14, 1745/6
Joses Bucknam & Mary Sprague,   June 8, 1743
James Whittemore & Mary Shearman,   June 4, 1744
Nathan Dexter & Esther Brintnal of Chelsea,   June 26, 1744
John Dunten & Mercy Johnson,   Aug. 17, 1744
David Bucknam of Salem & Esther Sprague,   March 4, 1745/6
John Dexter & Abigail Hill,   April 18, 1746
Nathaniel Jenkins & Abigail Baldwin,   May 1, 1746
Abraham Hill & Abigail Upham,   May 8, 1746
Moses Collins of Roxbury & Lydia Whittemore, May 20, 1746
Thomas Waite & Mary Sprague,   June 13, 1746
John Knower & Phebe Sprague,   June 17, 1746
Jabez Sargeant & Rachel Waite,   Oct. 9, 1746
Benjamin Waite & Barbara Unthank of Chelsea,
   March 20, 1746/7
Ebenezer Pratt & Elisabeth Knower,   May 7, 1747
Nathaniel Jenkins & Katherine Grant of Malden, June 19, 1747
Joseph Sprague of Dudley & Phebe Hutchinson, Jan. 7, 1747/8
Jacob Upham & Rebekah Burnitt of Reading, Jan. 19, 1747/8
Thomas Shute & Sarah Baldwin, of Malden,   Jan. 21, 1747/8
John Dexter & Joanna Lynds,   March 15, 1747/8
Edward Oliver & Sarah Wayte of Chelsea,   March 23, 1747/8
Joseph Sargeant & Hannah Whittemore,   Jan. 20, 1746/7

William Thomas & Mary Hill,	March 28, 1747
John Sargeant & Hannah Knower,	Oct. 1, 1747
John Bucknam & Hannah Lynds,	Nov. 12, 1747
John Nicholls & Elisabeth Burditt,	April 21, 1748
James Bayley of Boston & Mary Wayte,	May 16, 1748
Ebenezer Upham of Leicester & Lois Wayte,	Oct. 28, 1748
Jacob Breeden of Chelsea & Hannah Floyd,	March 2, 1749/50
Samuel Sprague & Elisabeth Wade,	Jan. 24, 1749/50
Thomas Burrige of Lynn & Anna Wayte,	Nov. 15, 1750
Jacob Shute & Mary Pratt,	Dec. 27, 1750
Nathaniel Sprague & Mary Hovey,	April 17, 1750
Thomas Hill & Mary Shute,	April 26, 1750
Richard Shute & Mary Green,	Jan. 4, 1750/51
Richard Stower & Judith Wayte,	Feb. 6, 1750/51
Jonathan Oakes & Esther Bucknam,	Sept. 13, 1750
Thomas Sargeant & Mary Wayte,	Jan. 17, 1748/49
William Gill & Martha Flynn,	March 9, 1748/9
James Sargeant & Elisabeth Upham,	April 25, 1749
Jabez Burditt & Deborah Richardson,	Jan. 16, 1749/50
Ezra Sargeant & Deborah Sargeant,	May 23, 1751
David Sargeant & Mehitabel Green,	June 27, 1751
Deacon James Hovey & Susanna Dexter,	May 17, 1751
Thomas Pratt & Sarah Simms,	Aug. 29, 1751
Daniel Floyd & Elisabeth Jenkins of Chelsea,	Oct. 4, 1751
John Green & Elisabeth Sprague,	Nov. 1, 1751
Joseph Howard & Rebekah Sprague,	Nov. 27, 1751
Rev. Daniel Little of Wells & Mary Emerson,	Dec. 5, 1751
Samuel Pratt of Chelsea & Elizabeth Wayte,	Jan. 1, 1752
John Paine & Abigail Collins of Boston,	Feb. 6, 1752
John Haskins of Boston & Hannah Upham,	March 12, 1752
Hugh Floyd & Abigail Hasey of Chelsea,	April 15, 1752
Peter Edes & Mary Morfin,	June 9, 1752
Ebenezer Cutter of Medford & Eleaner Floyd,	Sept. 2, 1752
Nathan Wayte & Dorothy Pratt,	March 28, 1753
John Manser & Sarah Bradish,	July 26, 1753
James Phillips & Elisabeth Clepson,	Nov. 20, 1754
Nathan Dexter & Tabitha Burditt,	Feb. 20, 1753
Jabez Burditt & Elizabeth Winslow,	May 3, 1753

John Hopkinson of Bradford & Sarah Dexter,   June 28, 1753
Joseph Willson of Boston & Huldah Blaney,   Sept. 20, 1753
Isaac Wheeler & Sarah Stone of Charlestown,   April 18, 1754
Ebenezer Willey of Reading & Elisabeth Sprague, Jan. 2, 1754
Hezekiah Blanchard of Charlestown & Susanna
    Dexter,   Feb. 22, 1754
Isaac Walton of Reading & Mary Cowen,   Nov. 29, 1754
Isaac Cluly & Sarah Burditt,   Jan. 10, 1755

MEDFORD

Sept. 28, 1630. "Meadford" is mentioned in a Tax Act.

Peter Tufts & Mary Cotton,   16-10-1684
John Bradshaw & Mary Hall,   June 29, 1686
Thomas Swan of Roxbury & Prudence Wade,   Oct. 27, 1692
Nathaniel Hall & Elizabeth Cutter,   April 16, 1690
Francis Lock & Elizabeth Winship,   Feb. 25, 1713
Jonathan Tuffs & Sarah Wait of Malden,   Jan. 27, 1713
Benjamin Willis & Ruth Bradshoe,   Feb. 10, 1713/14
Benjamin Parker & Mary Willis,   April 22, 1714
John Willis & Rebekah Tuffts,   April 17, 1717

NEWTON

Dec. 15, 1691. Petition of inhabitants of "Cambridge Village sometimes called "Little Cambridge" for a name for their town was granted, the name to be Newton and the town's brandmark to be N.

Joseph Bush & Hannah ———,   Dec. 22, 1691
Abraham Chamberlain & Elizabeth ———,   March 9, 1691/2
Nathanll. Wilson & Elizabeth Osland,   March 11, 1692/3
Thomas Greenwood & Elisabeth Wiswell,   Dec. 28, 1693

William Whitney, & Margaret Mirick,	Ap. 25, 1717
Isaac Ham——? & Mary Chamberlain,	Feb. 11, 1716/7
Richard Parks & Sarah Fuller,	July 17, 1717
Geo. Allen & Elisabeth Chamberlain,	Aug. 8, 1717
Jonathan Fuller & Sarah Mirick,	Oct. 3, 1717
John Cheany & Elizabeth Burrig, Jr.,	Oct. 22, 1717
Joseph Jackson & Patience Hides,	Nov. 28, 1717
Thomas Ward & Sarah Mattocks,	Dec. 5, 1717
John Stone & Lydia Hides,	Dec. 17, 1717
John Mash of Hadly & Sarah Williams,	Oct. 9, 1718
John Burrig & Lydia Ward,	Oct. 9, 1718
James Livermore of Weston & Rebecca Mirick,	Oct. 28, 1718
John Tozer & Experience Jackson,	Oct. 15, 1718
John Harris, late of Brookline & Hannah Wilson,	Dec. 8, 1718
Joseph Garfield & Abigail Fuller of Cambridge,	Dec. 31, 1718
Eliezer Stoddar & Susanna Hull,	Jan. 1, 1718/9
John Hamond & Margaret Wilson,	Dec. 8, 1718
John Wedge of Brookline & Hannah Mackey,	Dec. 18, 1718
David Newman of Rehoboth & Hannah Wiswell,	June 18, 1719
Josiah Bond & Elizabeth Fuller,	Jan. 13, 1719/20
Jonathan Woodward & Thankful Myrick,	June 8, 1720
Joseph Brown & Hannah Fuller,	June 9, 1720
John Park & Abigail Lawrence,	July 14, 1720
William Stanton & Mary Langwell of Boston,	Sept. 15, 1720
Joseph Moss & Elizabeth Park,	Nov. 20, 1720
Noah Wiswell & Thankful Fuller,	March 15, 1720/21
Nathan Ramsdel & Mary Phipps,	Sept. 30, 1725
James Bennet & Mary Dill,	Sept. 30, 1725
David Stowel & Mary Deleway,	Dec. 1, 1725
Judah Warden & Rebecca Prentice,	Dec. 2, 1725
Benjamin Murdock & Mary Hide,	Dec. 9, 1725
John Hastings & Mercy Ward,	April 6, 1726
John Ellis & Hannah Cheeny,	June 16, 1726
David Robinson & Mercy Segur,	July 13, 1726

Edward Fuller & Esther Brown,	Sept. 21, 1726
David Richardson & Remember Ward,	Oct. 19, 1726
Joseph Cooke & Mindwell Hide,	Nov. 10, 1726
Saml. Chamberlin & Esther Hammond,	March 23, 1727
John Knap & Deliverance Prentice,	
Ebenezer Warren & Elizth. Hide,	
James Ward & Mary Bacon,	Marriages
Nathaniel Stratton & Ester Parker,	from
Isaac Sanger & Mary Knap,	March
Timothy Hide & Mary Whitmore,	25,
Ebenezer Ward & Mary Fisher,	1727
Robert Brown & Mercy Fowle,	
Thomas Clark & Mary Brown,	
Isaac Jackson & Ruth Greenwood,	July 10, 1729
George Bacon & Susanna Greenwood,	July 30, 1729
Nehemiah Hide & Hannah Murdock,	Nov. 10, 1729
Moses Craft & Esther Woodard,	Nov. 15, 1729
Edward Prentice & Abigail Burridge,	Jan. 8, 1730
John Cheeny & Lydia Burridge,	April 24, 1730
Richard Coolidge & Mary Trowbridge,	Aug. 6, 1729
Isaac Clark & Experience Willson,	Aug. 7, 1729
Ebenezer Dorr & Hannah Loreing,	Aug. 28, 1729
Isaac Shephard & Sarah Cheeney,	Sept. 3, 1729
Israel Stowel & Sarah Cheeny,	Oct. 8, 1729
Benjamin Whitmore & Elizth Cheny,	Oct. 23, 1729
Josiah Reed, & Elizabeth Williams,	Dec. 31, 1729
Edward Park & Eunice Barnes,	Jan. 1, 1730
Joseph Norcross & Hannah Shephard,	Jan. 8, 1730
Oaks Angier & Abigail Coolidge,	Feb. 12, 1730
William Spring & Abigail Squire,	Feb. 19, 1730
John Newman & Sarah Wiswall,	March 3, 1730
John Taylor & Jenisha Littlefield,	March 11, 1730
Saml. Trusedall & Elizabeth Ward,	May 7, 1730
Edward Hall & Mary Miller,	May 21, 1730
Michael Jackson & Phebe Patten,	Oct. 17, 1733
Benjamin Edy & Elizabeth Trusdale,	Nov. 13, 1733
Nathaniel Biggelo & Hannah Robbinson,	Nov. 22, 1733
Ebenezer Chamberlin & Mary Trowbridge,	Nov. 28, 1733

Jonathan Trowbridge & Jemima Bright,	Jan. 3, 1734
Josiah Peas & Abigail Stowel,	Feb. 7, 1734
Thomas Hammond & Anna Farley,	April 10, 1734
Thomas (?) Hammond & Anna Longley,	May 21, 1734
Samuel Willson & Abigail Prentice,	July 25, 1734
Henry Prat & Sarah Fuller,	Sept. 30, 1741
Timothy Ward & Margaret Woodward,	Nov. 4, 1741
Nathaniel Spring & Martha Williams,	Dec. 10, 1741
Ephraim Hammond & Martha Steel,	Dec. 10, 1741
William Baldwin & Elisabeth Wiswall,	Dec. 17, 1741
Jeremiah Woodcock & Hannah Ward,	May 25, 1742
Rev. Samuel Cook & Anna Cotton,	Sept. 23, 1742
Jonathan Dike & Hannah Hide,	Oct. 28, 1742
William Chubb & Mary Prentice,	Nov. 11, 1742
Samuel Miller & Elisabeth Hammond,	Feb. 3, 1742/3
Timothy Parker & Kezia Hammond,	Feb. 17, 1742/3
John Ball & Mary Clark,,	Nov. 12, 1730
Abraham Brown & Abigail Dike,	Dec. 1, 1730
Eleazer & Sarah Chamberlin,	Dec. 17, 1730
Joseph Lovering & Hannah Bacon,	Jan. 22, 1731
Joseph Bartlit & Zabillah Collar,	Feb. 11, 1731
Josiah Greenwood & Phebe Sterns,	April 1, 1731
Joshua Herrington & Elizabeth Truesdale,	June 17, 1731
Nathaniel Hill & Patience Quassen,	July 7, 1731
Ebenezer Segur & Ruth Burridge,	Oct. 20, 1731
Josiah Hide & Elizabeth Ossland,	Oct. 21, 1731
Nathaniel Stowel & Margaret Trowbridge,	Oct. 22, 1731
Richard Herrington & Abigail Hammond,	Oct. 28, 1731
Seabus Jackson & Abigail Patten,	Dec. 2, 1731
Daniel Robbins & Hannah Trowbridge,	Dec. 16, 1731
Ephraim Ward & Mary Stone,	Jan. 6, 1732
Henry Tucker & Judeth Cheny,	Jan. 13, 1732
William Robinson & Hannah Ball,	Feb. 17, 1732
Isaac Stowel & Abigail Hide,	Feb. 17, 1732
Joshua Gay & Hannah Ward,	March 15, 1732
Thomas Bishop & Mary Blackman,	March 16, 1732
Eliphalet Gay & Dorothy Hall,	April 20, 1732
John Woodward & Abigail Ward,	May 17, 1732

Joseph Bartlet & Mercy Hide,	June 14, 1732
Joseph Park & Abigail Green,	June 15, 1732
Simon Howard & Deborah Pattin,	June 22, 1732
Simon Stone & Priscilla Dike,	Aug. 16, 1732
James Cheny & Lydia Myrick,	Aug. 31, 1732
Moses Allen & Hannah Knap,	Oct. 25, 1732
Nicholas Bartlet & Mary Cook,	April 17, 1733
Isaac Brown & Jerusha Prentice,	June 20, 1733
Joseph Ward & Experience Stone,	July 5, 1733

√READING

May 29, 1644. "Linn Village shall be called Redding."

John Wesson & Sarah Fitch,	Feb. 18, 1653
Nathaniel Cowdrey & Elizabeth, ———,	Nov. 21, 1654
Mathew Edward & Mary ———,	2-10-1657
Thomas Clarke & Mary ———,	June 31, 1658
Tho. Wiggins & Sarah ———,	27-6-1649
Benjamin Belflower & Abigaill ———,	Dec. 3, 1658
John Eaton & Elizabeth ———,	Jan. 8, 1658/9
John Browne & Elizab. ———,	Aug. 18, 1659
George ——— & Hannah ———,	Sept. 15, 1659
Nathaniel Cowdry & Mary ———,	22-11-1660
Thomas Cutler & Mary ———,	March 19, 1659/60
Benjamin Smith & Jehodan,	March 27, 1661
Thomas Hartshorn & Sarah ———,	April 10, 1661
James Steevenson & Naomy, ———	April 18, 1661
Joseph Fitts & Hannah ———,	July 2, 1661
Robert Burnap, Jr. & Sarah ———,	May 28, 1662
Thomas Tower & Hannah ———,	Oct. 30, 1662
John Brocke & Sarah Haugh widow,	Nov. 13, 1662
John Parker & Thankful ?———,	Jan. 28, 1689/0
Samll Pool & Mary ———,	Nov. 19, 1690
Joshua Eaton & Ruth ———,	Dec. 18, 1690

James Bowtwell & Elizabeth ———,	Jan. 20, 1690/1
Joseph Barnap & Tabitha ———,	Jan. 31, 1690/1
Benjamin Hardell & Mary ———,	Feb. 10, 1690/1
Samll. Lilley & Hannah Boutell,	Dec. 22, 1692
John Parker son of Nathan Parker of Andover &	
Hannah, da. of John Brown of Redding,	May 24, 1687
Joseph Fitch & Anne Kilby,	June 29, 1688
Samuel Wesson of R. & Abigail Eames of Woburn,	Aug. 29, 1688
William Eaton of Linn & Mary Barnap,	Jan. 11, 1692/3
John Smith & Ruth Cutler of Charlestowne,	May 18, 1693
Samuel Dix & Hannah Smith of Charlestown,	July 10, 1693
Thomas Smith & Mary Cook of Linn,	Aug. 30, 1693
Abraham Bryant, Jr. & Sarah Bancroft,	Nov. 29, 1693
Joseph Dutton & Mary Smith of Charlestowne,	Dec. 7, 1693
Robert Knowls & Katherine Graves of Charlestowne,	
	Dec. 27, 1693
Abraham Bryant, Sen. & Dorcas Eaton,	Dec. 28, 1693
Ezekiel Upton & Rebecka Preston of Salem village,	
	Dec. 28, 1693
John Boutell & Sarah Burnap,	Feb. 9, 1692/3
Stephen Wessen & Sarah Townsend of Lynn,	March 22, 1694
John Brown, Jr. & Elizabeth Fitch,	May 29, 1694
James Barrett & Anna Bryant,	May 30, 1694
John Gibbs of Sudbury & Sarah Cutler,	May 31, 1694
Samuel Bachelder & Mary Procter,	June 25, 1694
Thomas Bancroft, Jr. & Mary Webster,	Aug. 1, 1694
Isaac Greenwood of Boston & Anna Lynde of	
Charlestowne,	Sept. 6, 1694
Thomas Wesson & Elizabeth Brown,	Nov. 13, 1694
John Smith & Mary ———,	Jan. 6, 1662
John Bachelder & Sarah ———,	Jan. 6, 1662
Thomas Hodgman & Mary ———,	Aug. 12, 1663
Hannaniah Parker & Elizabeth ———,	Sept. 30, 1663
Thomas Barnap & Mary ———,	Dec. 3, 1663
Jeremiah Swaine & Mary ———,	Nov. 5, 1664
Abram Briant & Mary ———,	Feb. 2, 1664
Cornelius Browne & Sarah ———,	March 6, 1664/65
Edward Marshall & Mary ———,	June 9, 1665

Nathaniel Goodwin & Mary ———,	Oct. 18, 1665
James Bowball & Rebeccah ———,	July 15, 1665
Benjamin Fitts & Elizabeth ———,	Feb. 27, 1665
Philip Makentier & Mary ———,	6-7-1666
Richard Hordell & Mary ———,	Aug. 24, 1666
William Cowdrey & Ales ———,	Oct. 5, 1666
Josias Browne & Mary ———,	Nov. 23, 1666
George Lilly & Jane ———,	6-5-1667
John Parker & Hannah ———,	Nov. 13, 1667
Thomas Parker & Deborah ———,	Nov. 13, 1667
Adam Calston & Mary ———,	Sept. 7, 1668
John Boutall & Hannah ———,	May 10, 1669
Thomas Hartshorne & Hannah ———,	May 10, 1671
Thomas Taylor & Mary ———,	Oct. 1, 1671
Jeremiah Pike & Rachell ———,	Nov. 15, 1671
Seabred Tayler & Mary ———,	Nov. 21, 1671
Joseph Dodge & Sarah ———,	Feb. 28, 1671
Tho. Bancroft & Sarah ———,	10-2-1673
Saml. Fits & Sarah ———,	23-2-1673
Sam'l Dunton & Sarah ———,	17-4-1673
Edw. Taylor & Elizabeth Bridge, widow,	29-5-1673
Joseph Brown & Elisabeth, ———	26-3-1674
Jno. Eaton & Dorcas ———,	26-9-1674
Francis Everet & Mary ———,	8-10-1675
Sam'l Lamson & Mary ———,	18-3-1676
Jno. Niccols & Abigail,	18-3-1676
Nathl. Goodin & Susannah,	25-8-1676
John Brown & Hannah,	30-2-1677
Jonas Eaton & Hannah,	25-7-1677
Nathl. Parker & Bethia,	24-7-1677
Jno. Cuttlar & Hanna ———,	25-1-1678
Joshua Eaton & Rebecca,	25-2-1678
Jno. Damon & Susan,	15-3-1678
Timothy Weyly & Elisabeth,	4-11-1678
David Bachelder & Hannah,	30-10-1679
Fr. Smith & Ruth ———,	1-1-1680
William Robins & Priscilla ———,	2-5-1680
Tho. Nicholes & Rebecca,	1-10-1680

Jno. Upto & Sarah,	19-10-1680
Wm. Halsey & Judah,	16-3-1681
Jno. Polley & Mary,	16-3-1681
Sam'l Fitts & Rebecca,	26-5-1681
Jno. Brown & Sarah,	14-9-1681
James Pike & Hannah,	25-9-1681
Benj. Hartshorn & Mary	28-12-1681
Jno. Brown & Elisabeth,	29-1-1682
David Hartshorn & Rebecca,	Mch. 15, 1683
Tho. Damond & Lusian ———	May 15, 1683
Jonathan Eaton & Elizabeth ———,	15-6-1683
Nathaniel Stow & Mehetabel Bryant,	May 24, 1721
Enoch Sawyer of Newbury & Sarah Parpoint,	Sept. 29, 1721
Stephen Wesson & Elisabeth Parker,	Dec. 6, 1721
Joseph Bancroft & Ruth Parker,	Jan. 3, 1721
Crispen Bedford & Poegis Cummings, negros,	Jan. 23, 1721
John Hartshorn of R. & Abigail Bancroft of Lynn,	
	July 26, 1721
James Parsons of Lynn & Hepsebah Hartshorn,	Nov. 3, 1721
John Eaton & Abigail Roberts,	Dec. 28, 1721
Stephen Payn of Charlestown & Rebecca Bachelor,	
	Nov. 23, 1721
John Emerson of Mendham & Mary Rice?	Nov. 16, 1721
John Woodard & Sarah Bancroft,	July 7, 1686
Nathl. Gowing & Martha Proctor,	July 22, 1686
John Poole & Mary Gooding,	Nov. 17, 1686
Thomas Cutler & Elisabeth Feltch,	Dec. 30, 1686
Sam'l Lamson & Abigail Bryant,	July 3, 1722
Abram Knowlton & Mary Smith	Sept. 20, 1722
Ebenezer Parker of R. & Hannah Green of Malden,	
	Dec. 13, 1722
Joseph Burnap & Sarah Nichols,	Dec. 20, 1722
Thomas Taylor & Mary Goodwin,	Dec. 20, 1722
John Towned & Tabitha Damon,	Jan. 1, 1722/3
John Damon & Rebecca Pratt,	May 7, 1722
Barachias Farnum of Andover & Hepsibah Harden,	
	Jan. 1, 1722/3
Ebenezer Burt & Ruth Fisk,	Nov. 5, 1722

Stephen Fisk of R. & Abigail Parks of Sudbury, Jan. 7, 1722/3
Jonathan Fisk & Mary Hart, Feb. 18, 1722
John Parker & Sarah Lilly, Feb. 23, 1722
John Lilly & Abigail Burnap, Mch. 7, 1722
Thomas Rich & Rachel Sawer, Mch. 12, 1722/3
Joseph Burrill of Boston & Susan Cowdry, Nov. 7, 1723
Israel Eaton of R. & D——— Howard of Salem, June 21, 1726
Nath'l Sherman of Lynn & Dorcas Sawyer, June 30, 1726
Oliver Attwood of Medford & Elizabeth Phelps, July 12, 1726
Thos. Stimpson & Elisabeth Bryant, Sept. 15, 1726
Hezekiah Williams of Boxford & Mehetable Upton, Aug. 4, 1726
Dan'l Townsend of Lynn & Lydia Sawyer, Oct. 18, 1726
Benj. Wesson & Eunice Upham, Ap. 18, 1726
Ebenezer Cutler of Shrewsbury & Abigail Felch, Ap. 26, 1726
Abraham Roberts & Elisabeth Peirce, June 8, 1726
John Ordoway of Newbury & Margaret Allen, Aug. 18, 1726
Ephraim Wesson & Rebecca Burnap, Sept. 20, 1726
Joseph Bryant of R. & Sarah Goold of Stoneham, Nov. 8, 1726
Ebenezer Wesson & Mehetable Sodorich, Nov. 29, 1726
William Upton of Salem & Lydia Burnap, Jan. 4, 1726/7
Jonathan Lawrence of Lexington & Elisabeth Swain,
Feb. 23, 1726

SHERBORN

Oct. 7, 1674. More land granted to the inhabitants and proprietors of the land at or near Boggestow, the place to be called Sherborne.

William Goddard & Leah Fisher, Dec. 10, 1685
John Pond of Wrentham, Son of Lieut. Daniel Pond
& Hannah, da. of Goodman Hill of S. Sept. 30, 1686
Jonathan Morss & Jane Whitney, Jan. 4, 1692/3
Wm. Mackentosh & Experience Holebrook, both
of Dedham, Feb. 28, 1692/3
John Holebrook & Silence Wood, March 6, 1692/3
Thomas Thurstane of Rentham & Esther Clark of
Medfield, June 15, 1693

Thomas Holebrook & Mary Rogers of Weymouth, Oct. 31, 1693
William Patrige & Hannah Fisher, both of Med-
    field, Nov. 15, 1693
Samuel Hinsdell & Susannah Rocket of Medfield, Dec. 20, 1693
Samuel Ellis & Deborah Lovell, both of Medfield, Dec. 20, 1693
Samuel Williams & Abigail Goddard, May 14, 1716
Samuel Biglow of Marlborough & Mary Gleason, Dec. 4, 1716
Ellcanah Haven of Framingham & Patience Lea-
    land, Feb. 5, 1716/7
Eleazer Morse of S. & Abigail Clap of Dedham, Feb. 7, 1716/7
Richard Gookin & Margaret Morse, ————
Ebenezer Twitchell & Sarah Pratt, Dec. 3, 1717
Joseph Twitchell & Elisabeth Holebrook, Mch. 27, 1718
Samuel Fairbank & Susana Watson, June 30, 1718
Samuel Holebrook & Keziah Morse, Sept. 4, 1718
John Holebrook & Ruth Hill, Mch. 13, 1718
David Morse & Sarah Dyer, Ap. 14, 1719
William Adams of Uxbridge & Mary Cozzens, Aug. 19, 1730
John Carpenter of Holliston & Margaret Lealand, Oct. 29, 1730
Jonathan Holbrook & Abigail Breek, Nov. 5, 1730

STOW

May 16, 1683. The plantation between Concord and Lancaster called Pomositticut established as Stow.

Stephen Gates of S. & Jemima Benjamin of Pli-
    mouth Colony, Nov. 8, 1686
Jonathan Heald & Martha Taylor, Oct. 27, 1719
Moses Whiting (Whitney) of S. & Sarah Knight of
    Cambridge, Sept. 30, 1686
Ephraim Hildreth & Anna Moor of Sudbury, Oct. 8, 1686
John Butterick & Mary Blood, Ap. 8, 1679
Henry Rand & Mary Crane, Sept. 29, 1682
James Wheeler & Sarah Randall, June 24, 1682
John Whitherby & Lidia Moore, Sept. 16, 1684

Ephraim Hildreth & Dorothy Barnes,	June 11, 1685
Thomas Williams & Sarah Foster,	Sept. 22, 1686
Moses Whitney & Sarah Knight,	Sept. 30, 1686
John Wedge & Sarah Hall,	Sept. 30, 1693
Simon Gates & Hannah Benjamin,	May 4, 1688
Robert Hues & Mary Crane,	Sept. 21, 1688

√ SUDBURY

Sept. 4, 1639.   The new plantation by Concord to be called Sudbury.

Philemon Whale & Sarah Cakebread,	Nov. 7, 1649
Josiath Haine & Elizabeth Freeman,	Nov. 13, 1649
Mathew Rice & Martha Lamson,	July 7, 1654
Henry Kerly & Elizabeth White,	Nov. 2, 1654
John Morse & An Smith,	Nov. 16, 1654
Peter Noice & Elizabeth Darrell,	Nov. 30, 1654
Edward Rice & Mary Brigham,	March 1, 1655
Samuel Rice & Elizabeth King,	Nov. 8, 1655
Thomas King & Bridget Davis,	Dec. 26, 1655
James Pendlton & Hannah Goodenow,	April 29, 1656
Jonathan Stanap & Susanna Aye,	April 16, 1656
John Barrat & Mary Pond,	Sept. 19, 1656
John Goodenow & Mary Axdell,	Sept. 19, 1656
Philemon Whale & Elizabeth Griffine,	Nov. 9, 1657
John Johnson & Deborah Ward,	
Thomas Knapp & Mary Grout,	Sept. 19, 1688
Thomas Rutter & Jeremiah Stanhop,	Oct. 15, 1689
Thomas Read & Arabella Thong,	Dec. 29, 1689
James Haines & Sarah Noise,	Dec. 21, 1689
John Goodenow Jr. & Ruth Willis,	Feb. 28, 1689/90
John Rutter & Hannah Bush,	March 12, 1690
Jonathan Willard & Mary Brown,	Jan. 8, 1690/1
Noah Clap & Mary Wright,	July 28, 1690
Benjamin Wright & Elizabeth Newell of Boston,	April 10, 1690

Ephraim Rice of S. & Hannah Livermore of Water-	
town,	Feb. 21, 1688/9
Benjamin Rice & Graves ———,	Ap. 1, 1691
Thomas Frost & Hannah Johnson,	July 9, 1691
Josiah Haiden of Braintree & Elizabeth Goodenow,	
	Mch. 22, 1691/2
Jonathan Rice & Elizabeth Wheeler,	Feb. 12, 1690/1
Samll. How & Abigail Mixter of Watertown,	Oct. 1690/1
James Smith & Hannah Rutter,	May 5, 1693
Thomas Brentnel & Hannah Willard,	May 23, 1693
John Brewer & Hannah Jones of Watertowne,	July 5, 1693
Obidiah Ward & Johannah Harrington of Water-	
towne,	Dec. 20, 1693
Joseph Noyse & Ruth Haynes,	Dec. 20, 1693
John Maynard & Mary Gates,	April 5, 1658
Joseph Rice & Mercy King,	May 4, 1658
John Bent & Hannah Stone,	July 1, 1658
James Ross & Mary Goodenow,	Dec. 5, 1658
Edward Wright & Hannah Epson,	June 18, 1659
Nathaniell Laurance & Sarah Moss,	March 13, 1660
Richard Ward & Mary Moores,	Sept. 8, 1661
Joseph Noyes & Mary Darrell,	Nov. 12, 1662
Samuel How & Martha Bent,	June 5, 1663
Daniel Goble & Hannah Brewer,	Feb. 25, 1663
Samuel Wright & Lidea Moores,	May 3, 1664
Joseph Frost & Mary Bradish,	April 10, 1664
Robert Man & Deborah Draper,	April 1, 1664
Shedrack Habgood & Elizabeth Tredaway,	Oct. 21, 1664
Samuel Moss & Elizabeth Wood,	Feb. 10, 1664
John Perry & Bethia Moss,	May 23, 1665
James Cutler & Lidea Wright,	June 15, 1665
Elias Keies & Sarah Blandford,	Sept. 11, 1665
John Fisher & Mary Tredaway,	Sept. 12, 1665
Joseph Graves & Elizabeth Maynard,	Jan. 15, 1665
John Grout & Rebeccah Toll,	April 15, 1667
Jacob Moore & Elizath. Looker,	May 29, 1667
Thomas Browne & Patience Foster,	Sept. 29, 1667
Daniel Stone & Mary Ward,	Nov. 22, 1667

Jabez Browne & Hanna Blanford,	Dec. 23, 1667
Richard Burke & Mary Parmenter,	June 24, 1670
Thomas Gates & Eliz. Freeman,	July 6, 1670
Josiah How & Mary Haynes,	May 18, 1671
Ri. Chamberlyn & Elizb. Jaques,	March 30, 1672
Saml. Winch & Hannah Gibs,	Feb. 11, 1672
Jonath. Stanhop. & Sarah Griffin,	May 11, 1674
Daniel Hudson & Mary Maynard,	July 21, 1674
Jno. Rice & Tabitha Stone,	Nov. 2, 1674
Jno. Goodridge & Mary Gibbs,	March 23, 1674
Wm. Brown & Margaret Stone,	Jan. 11, 1675
Jonath. Rice & Martha Eames,	March 23, 1675/6
Lewis Dowss & Elizab. White,	Jan. 9, 1676
Jonath. Griffin & Mary Long,	Oct. 25, 1676
Benj. Chamberlin & Sarah Baul,	June 5, 1677
Ri. Taylor & Hannah Ward,	Oct. 17, 1677
Jonath. Rice & Rebeccah Watson,	Nov. 1, 1677
Peter Haynes & Elizab. Rice,	Jan. 2, 1677
Tho. Read & Mary Goodridge,	May 30, 1677
Joseph Dawby & Jane Plimpton,	Jan. 14, 1676
Joseph Curtice & Abigail Grout,	Feb. 5, 1677
Thos. Read, sen. & Mary Wood,	March 7, 16
Zach. Maynard & Hannah Goodridge,	July 15, 1678
Math. Gibs & Mary Moore,	Nov. 12, 1678
Thos. ffrost & Mary Goodridge,	Nov. 12, 1678
Jno. Gleison & May Ross,	Jan. 15, 1678
George Parminte & Hannah Johnson,	Jan. 20, 1678
Jno. Bush & Hannah Pendlton,	Jan. 13, 1679
Richard Adams & Rebeccah Davis,	June 24, 1679
James Shearman & Mary Walker,	May 13, 1680
James Smith & Hannah Goodenow,	March 25, 1680
Joseph Noyes & Mary Willard,	July 14, 1680
Joseph Freeman & Dorothy Hayes,	May 6, 1680
Benj. Parmintr & Tamisen Rice,	Sept. 22, 1680
Edmund Rice & Joyce Russel,	Oct. 13, 1680
Jno. Adams & Hannah Bent,	Feb. 26, 1680
Stephen Blanford & Susannah Long,	April 9, 1682
Tho. Carter & Elizab. White,	April 7, 1682

Joseph Chamberlain & Hannah Gilbert,	Aug. 28, 1682
John Brooks & Hannah Garfield,	Sept. 8, 1682
John Haines, sen. & Ruth Roper,	April 19, 1683
Joseph Gleison & Abigail Garfield of Watertowne,	Dec. 22, 1686
Thomas Williams & Sarah Foster of Cambridge,	Sept. 23, 1686
Samuel Allen of Watertowne & Elizab. Grout,	Dec. 22, 1683
Samuel Allen & Jane Rosse,	Jan. 4, 1683
Thomas Lawine of Sherburn & Deborah Rice,	Jan. 23, 1683
Nathaniel Stone & Sarah Wayt of Malden,	April 25, 1684
Caleb Johnson & Agnes Bent,	July 9, 1684
Joseph Stanhope & Hannah Braddish,	Jan. 1, 1684/5
Samuel How & Sarah Clapp,	Sept. 18, 1685
Hopestill Brown & Abigail Haines,	Nov. 26, 1685
Stephen Jennings & Hannah Stanhop,	April 1, 1686
William Walker & Sarah Goodenow,	May 6, 1686
Henry Rice & Elizabeth Moore,	Dec. 27, 1716
William Moore & Tamar Rice,	Jan. 21, 1716
James Haynes & Susannah Woodward,	March 14, 1716/17
Henry Loker & Mary Rice,	Feb. 20, 1716/17
Jonathan Jackson & Martha Frisell, both of Framingham,	March 7, 1716/17
John Brigham & Sarah Bouker,	May 22, 1717
John Walker & Jemima Stanhope,	May 27, 1717
John Wallis of Billerica & Mary Twichel of Sherburn,	July 19, 1717
Joseph Parmenter & Lydia Rice,	April 23, 1717
Edward Grout & Martha Flegg,	April 23, 1717
Adam Stone & Sarah Wight,	May 22, 1717
Thomas Walker & Elizabeth Mayner,	May 22, 1717
Hopestill Brown & Dorothy Parris,	Nov. 25, 1718
Gershom Wheelock & Abigail Flegg, both of or joining near to Worcester,	Jan. 1, 1718/19
Richard Ward & Lydia Wheelock, both of or near joining to Worcester,	Jan. 1, 1718/19
Thomas Buck & Mary Parmenter,	May 1, 1718
Josiah Brown & Elizabeth Tompson,	Dec. 30, 1718
Hezekiah Rice of Marlborough & Mary Haynes,	April 30, 1719
James Brewer & Abigail Smith of Needham,	March 12, 1719

Peter Moores & Mary Goodenow,	June 10, 1719
Edward Rice & Rachel Estgit,	June 18, 1719
Thomas Frink & Mercy Whitney of Sherborn,	July 16, 1719
William Rice & Martha Rice,	Oct. 7, 1719
Moses Rice & Sarah King,	Nov. 16, 1719
John Graham & Lydia Blanford,	Dec. 9, 1719
John Potter & Martha Jewell,	March 4, 1718/19
James Moore & Comfort Rice,	March 4, 1718/19
John Phips & Hannah Walker,	Jan. 15, 1718/19
Josiah Brown & Bulah Stone,	Jan. 14, 1719/20
James Haynes & Mary Rugg,	Sept. 6, 1720
Edward Goodenow & Hannah Allen of Weston,	June 3, 1720
Edmund Rice of Westboro & Hannah Brown,	June 23, 1720
Joseph Haynes & Mary Gates of Stow,	Dec. 20, 1720
Peter Plimpton & Abigail Thompson,	Nov. 8, 1720
John Hadley & Mary Wait of Weston,	Feb. 2, 1720/1
Edmund Goodenow & Dorothy Man,	June 6, 1686
John How & Elizabeth Woolson of Watertown,	Nov. 3, 1686
Benjamin Moore & Dorothy Wright,	Nov. 11, 1686
Obadiah Coolidge & Elizabeth Roose of Hartford,	
	Feb. 28, 1686
David Rice & Hannah Walker,	April 7, 1687
Samuel Gaskal of Charlestown & Elizabeth Sherman	
of Watertown,	July 20, 1687
Thomas Walker & Marth. How,	Dec. 7, 1687
John Peckham & Dorothy Goodenow,	Dec. 9, 1687
Thomas Drury & Rachel Rice,	Dec. 15, 1687
Edmund Bouker & Sarah Parmenter,	March 29, 1688
John Sheares & Alice Mitchelson of Cambridge,	April 9, 1688
John Gibbs & Anne Gleason of Sherburn,	April 27, 1688
Alexander Stuart & Deborah Farrowbush, both of	
Marlborow,	May 23, 1688
John Bowker & Sarah Clap,	Feb. 21, 1720/1
Isaac Hunt & Martha Goodenow,	Dec. 28, 1721
Joseph Muzzy & Patience Rice,	March 24, 1721
William Wesson & Mary Stanhope,	March 30, 1721
Abraham Bryant & Sarah Frinkes,	May 3, 1721
George Reed & Sibla Rice,	May 24, 1721

Daniel Snow of Woburn & Mary Barney,	July 20, 1721
John Woodward & Sopphira Moore,	Aug. 1, 1721
Josiah Haynes & Persis Knight,	Aug. 9, 1721
John Griffin & Martha Long,	Aug. 8, 1721
Uriah Moore & Abigail Haynes,	Oct. 5, 1721
Daniel Noyes & Sarah Haynes,	Oct. 19, 1721
Thomas Dunton & Sarah Beal,	Jan. 2, 1721/2
Phillip Kitely & Hannah Barney,	Feb. 28, 1721/2
Mathew Poole of Boston & Mary Knight,	March 21, 1721/2
Uriah Parmenter & Sarah Duncan,	July 26, 1722
James Creage of Lexington & Rachel Wallis,	Aug. 6, 1722
John Eveleth of Stow & Hannah Haynes,	Oct. 9, 1722
Joseph Maynerd & Miriam Willard,	Jan. 29, 1722/3
John Clap & Abigail Estabrooks,	March 17, 1723/4
Nicho Stone of Framingham & Abigail Stone,	April 2, 1724
Elias Moore & Susannah Tomson,	July 9, 1724
John Coggin & Elizabeth Jennison,	Oct. 21, 1724
Edward Moor & Keziah Goodenow,	Feb. 19, 1722/3
Samuel Munckley & Rachel Knight,	June 28, 1723
Thomas Bryant of Reading & Abigail Frinks,	July 25, 1723
Peter King of Worcester & Elizabeth Graves,	March 25, 1723
Peter How of Hopkinton & Thankfull How,	April 9, 1723
Thomas Brown & Mary Darbe,	June 27, 1723
Joseph Reed & Sarah Rice,	Nov. 17, 1723
Moses Maynard & Lois Stone of Framingham,	March 18, 1723
David Parmenter & Abigail Brewer,	Feb. 12, 1712/13
Paul Brintnal & Mary Rice,	Nov. 10, 1724
Thomas Brigham & Elizabeth Bowker,	Dec. 24, 1724
Amos Smith & Susannah Holman,	Jan. 31, 1724/5
George Walkup of Framingham & Sarah Greaves,	April 29, 1725
Ephraim Rice & Mary Noyes,	March 24, 1725
Zebediah Allen & Mary Hoar,	Jan. 21, 1724/5
Joseph Brooks of Weston & Jane Jennison,	July 29, 1725
John Haynes & Tabitha Cutler,	July 21, 1725
Isaac Gibbs & Thankfull Wheeler,	Oct. 1, 1725
Timothy Gibbson & Persis Rice,	Dec. 29, 1725
Nathanl. Gibbs & Bathsheba Parmenter,	May 29, 1726
Benjamin Dudley & Elizabeth Rice,	Nov. 7, 1726

Jonathan Snow of Woburn & Esther Barrey "Bar-
    ney,"   May 11, 1727
Peter Bent & Mary Parris,   April 18, 1727
John Hayden of Hopkinton & Lucy Maynard,   Sept. 16, 1726
Abijah Haynes & Elizebeth Smith,   Jan. 18, 1726/7
Peter Noyes & Elizebeth Clap,   Feb. 14, 1726/7
Benjamin Gates of Worcester & Bethula Rice,   April 5, 1727
Thomas Bryant & Sarah Noyes,   May 3, 1727
Ebenezer Hayden & Thankfull Parmenter,   May 11, 1727
Willm. Simpson & Susannah Stanhope,   Sept. 27, 1727
Eliab. Moor & Keziah Stone,   March 5, 1727/8
Daniel Haynes & Lydia Russel,   April 25, 1728
Gershom Rice & Elizth. Battle of Dedham,   May 27, 1728
Benjamin How & Zebiah Moor,   June 4, 1728
Hezekiah Moor & Mary Haynes,   June 27, 1728
Charles Adams & Priscilla Wait,   May 27, 1729
John Curtis & Rebecca Wait,   June 4, 1729
Jeremiah Wesson & Sarah Bent,   July 10, 1729
Isaac Allen & Elizth. Gleason,   June 24, 1729
Daniel Drury of Framingham & Sarah Flegg,   July 14, 1729
Shemuel Griffin & Elizabeth Robbins,   Oct. 31, 1729
Ebenr. Goodenough & Elizth. Allen of Weston, Feb. 5, 1729/30
Daniel Noyes & Sarah Gott,   Feb. 25, 1729/30
Cyprian Keyes of Shrewsbury & Hepsibah How, Dec. 15, 1729
William Brintnal & Zerviah Buckminster of Fram-
    ingham,   Dec. 19, 1729
Nathan Goodenough & Lois Cutler,   Jan. 22, 1729/30
Joseph Axtel of Marlborough & Abigail Hayden,
                               Feb. 4, 1729/30
Isaac Reed & Experience Willis,   Feb. 11, 1729/30
Jacob Moor & Rebecca Robins,   Nov. 4, 1729
Saml. Burbank & Mary Reed,   March 10, 1729/30
John Cheney of Framingham & Mary Clap,   Dec. 25, 1730
Joseph Goodenow & Anna Allen,   July 7, 1730
Samuel Knight & Mary Rice,   Aug. 31, 1730
Sebeas Greaves & Amity Whitney,   Oct. 14, 1730
Samuel Goodenow & Mary Griffin,   April 30, 1730
Cornelius Goodenow & Abigail Griffin,   April 30, 1730

Henry Coggin & Mary Stone of Framingham,	May 25, 1730
Israel Rice & Sarah Rose,	June 5, 1730
John Rose & Submit Hoar,	July 8, 1730
Jonathan Gaffield & Submit Parmenter,	Sept. 15, 1730
James Patterson & Lydia Fisk,	Oct. 14, 1730
James Jackson & Martha Hunt,	Dec. 4, 1730
Isaac Gleason & Jerusha Noyes,	Feb. 23, 1730/1
Benjamin Barney & Abigail Cutting,	March 15, 1730/1
Nathaniel Hayden & Abigail Temple of Bedford,	Sept. 29, 1731
Deliverance Parmenter & Ruth Hayden,	May 12, 1731
Philip Rally & Joanna (Susanna)? Joyner,	Oct. 8, 1731
Ephraim Curtis of Worcester & Mary Rice,	Dec. 23, 1729
Jason Glasson & Mary Curtis,	Dec. 20, 1732
Bezaliel Smith & Sarah Miles of Concord,	Dec. 8, 1731
James Brewer & Mary Smith,	Dec. 8, 1731
Robet Henry of Leicester & Charity Thompson,	April 24, 1731
Hopestil Bent & Bulal Rice,	Oct. 22, 1733
Samuel Osburn & Lydia Griffin,	Nov. 1, 1732
Josiah Coggin & Mary Heard,	April 2, 1733
Phineas Gleason & Rebecca Allen,	April 6, 1732
John Stone of Rutland & Elizebeth Stone,	Jan. 18, 1731
Thomas Bent & Mary Stone,	May 28, 1733
Jonathan Stanhope & Bathsheba Walker,	Oct. 2, 1733
William Rice & Hannah Greaves,	May 10, 1733
Amos Sanderson & Ruth Hoar,	April 20, 1732
Joseph Goodell & Elizebeth Goodell, both of Marl-	
borough,	Sept. 26, 1733
Jonathan Puffer & Mary Maynard,	Jan. 14, 1733/4
Samuel Wood & Lydia Goodenough,	Feb. 5, 1733/4
Joseph Balcome & Deborah Boice,	Feb. 21, 1733
Aaron Goodenow & Elizebeth Goodenow,	Aug. 12, 1733
Zedekiah Maynard & Sarah Morsman,	Oct. 21, 1734
Jonathan Robbins & Mary Parmenter,	Nov. 12, 1734
Joseph Noyes & Elizebeth Gilberd,	Nov. 18, 1734
Timothy Morsman & Martha Whitney of Weston,	
	Feb. 26, 1734/5
William Whitney of Weston & Hannah Harrington,	
of Watertown,	Sept. 10, 1735

Ebenezer Puffer & Thankfull Cutler, June 12, 1735
Jeremiah Knowlton of Concord & Sarah Allen, July 24, 1735
John Barber of Medfield & Hannah Rice, Oct. 23, 1735
Henry Hunt & Elizabeth Rice, Nov. 3, 1735
Joseph Johnson & Thankfull Moore, (Morse?), both of
    Marlborough, Nov. 11, 1735
Abner Cutler of Rutland & Anna Haynes, Dec. 4, 1735
John Johnson & Sarah Hogs, both of Concord, Dec. 25, 1735
John Tompson & Abigail Farnsworth, Feb. 26, 1735/6
John Noyes & Tabitha Stone, July 12, 1736
Hugh Riddel of Londonderry & Agnes Bolton, Oct. 9, 1735
Jonas Livermore of Weston & Elizabeth Rice, Nov. 28, 1735
Rev. Phineas Heminway of Townshend & Mary
    Stevens of Marlborough, May 8, 1735
Ephraim Moore of Rutland & Dorothy Brintnal,
                                        May 11, 1736
Thomas Axtel of Grafton & Elizabeth Shearman of
    Marlborough, May 13, 1736
Henry Pudney & Martha Stevens, both of Marl-
    borough, June 3, 1736
Enos Goodell & Mary Angier both of Marlborough,
                                          Nov. 16, 1736
David Brown of Rutland & Abigail Goodenow, Dec. 28, 1736
William Rice & Mary Eastabrook, March 29, 1737
Ephraim Goodenow & Elizabeth Green, April 5, 1737
Daniel Reed & Rebecca Mead, April 13, 1737
John Putman of Framingham & Sarah Maverick, April 25, 1737
John Balcom & Susannah Haynes, Aug. 23, 1737
Nathaniel Rice & Sarah Smith, Nov. 24, 1737
William Pope & Sarah Walker, Dec. 1, 1737
John Russ? of Lancaster & Eunice Wood of Concord,
                                          Dec. 29, 1737
Daniel Goodenow & Ruth Woods, Dec. 22, 1737
Samuel Robbins & Elizabeth Brown, Jan. 5, 1737
Thomas Parker & Barthsheba Smith, Feb. 20, 1737/8
Nathaniel Sever & Rebecca Willis, Feb. 23, 1737/8
Samuel Gould & Hannah Brintnal, Aug. 16, 1737
Ichabod Druce & Abigail Stow, both of Concord, April 6, 1738

Robert Jennison & Sibilla Brintnal,   Jan. 18, 1738/9
Samuel How & Elizabeth Sever, both of Framingham
Josiah Foster & Anna Dunton,   May 22, 1739
Hezekiah Coller & Elizabeth Rice,   March 17, 1742/3
David Stone & Mary Moore,   May 24, 1743
Jonathan Grout & Hannah Heard,   June 6, 1743
Hezekiah Walker & Hannah Putnam of Framing-
    ham,   April 4, 1738
Paul Brintnal & Dorothy Rice,   April 20, 1738
Joseph Stone of Lancaster & Elizabeth Taylor, April 29, 1738
Cornelius Wood & Mary Eaton,   May 18, 1738
Elijah Willis & Abigail Smith,   June 15, 1738
Benjamin Estabrook & Dinah Moore,   July 13, 1738
Matthias Woodis & Sarah Parry,   Nov. 27, 1738
John Barns & Elizabeth Cranson, both of Marl-
    borough,   Dec. 6, 1738
Thomas How & Dorothy Brigham, both of Marl-
    borough,   Jan. 25, 1738/9
Jonathan Graves & Susannah Graham,   Feb. 13, 1738/9
Joseph Wooley & Mercy Whitney,   March 1, 1738/9
Jonathan Robbins & Elizabeth Putnam,   April 3, 1739
John Tainter & Hannah Goodel, both of Marl-
    borough,   Jan. 1, 1739/40
Joseph Travice of Sherburn & Sarah Dean,   March 29, 1740
Elijah Smith & Abigail Plympton,   March 25, 1740
Ezekiel How & Elizabeth Rice, both of Marlborough,
                                               May 20, 1740
Jabez Mead & Abigail Evelith,   June 1, 1740
Rev. Mr. Stone of Holliston & Mrs. (?) Sarah
    Brown,   Dec. 19, 1740
Nathan Maynard & Betty Jewell,   June 1, 1741
James Mossman & Elizabeth Balcom,   July 10, 1741
Richard Tayler & Submit Brintal of Framingham,
                                               July 23, 1741
David Goodenow of Rutland & Mary Bent,   Sept. 24, 1741
Thomas Car & Grace Sherman of Marlborough, Nov. 2, 1741
Nathaniel Rice & Elizabeth Stone,   Feb. 23, 1742
Daniel Winch of Framingham & Abigail Read, March 11, 1742

James Marverick & Lydia Sanderson,	April 28, 1742
Bezaleel Fisk & Beulah Frost of Framingham,	Nov. 11, 1742
Isaac Lincoln of Boston & Hannah Eveleth,	Sept. 26, 1743
David Moor & Hannah Parker,	Dec. 22, 1743
Ezekiel How & Bathsheba Stone,	Jan. 19, 1743/4
Nathaniel Hayden & Zeruiah Parmenter,	
Obadiah Moor & Eunice Hayden,	May 22, 1744
Nathan Moor & Agnes Bolten,	July 3, 1744
Randal Davis & Susanna Griffin,	July 11, 1744
Joseph Curtis & Jane Plympton,	Sept. 11, 1744
Amos Gates & Mary Trobridge, both of Framingham,	Nov. 28, 1744
Phineas Walker & Beulah Clap,	Dec. 12, 1744
David Stone & Sarah Rice, both of Framingham,	March 26, 1745
Ephraim Stone & Joanna Emmes, both of Framingham,	July 24, 1745
Trustram Cheney & Margaret Joyner,	Nov. 28, 1745
Jonathan Sherman & Elizabeth Bruce of Marlborough,	Dec. 19, 1745
Augustus Moor & Elizabeth Haynes,	Feb. 13, 1745/6
Amos Stow of Concord & Mary Muzzy,	April 29, 1746
Richard Munson & Elizabeth Loring,	June 6, 1746
Richard Bayley of Stoughton & Anna Mossman,	Oct. 9, 1746
Reuben Gibson of Lunenburg & Lois Smith,	Nov. 13, 1746
Hopestill Brown & Sarah Loring,	Dec. 30, 1746
James Boutell & Rachel Walcup, both of Framingham,	March 9, 1743/4
Josiah Farrar & Hannah Taylor,	May 24, 1744
Josiah Richardson of Chelmsford & Experience Wright,	Oct. 23, 1738
Nathaniel Smith of Hopkinston & Mrs. (?) Mary Frink,	(no date)
William Upham & Elisabeth Gregory, both of Weston,	April 10, 1745
John Davis & Mrs. (?) Rebekah Allen, both of Newton,	Nov. 27, 1746
Joseph Ruggles of Billerica & Sarah Roby,	Nov. 2, 1749

Jonathan Wood of Littleton & Abigail Daby, March 8, 1748/9

Elisha Harrington of Holden & Tabitha Haynes,

March 4, 1748/9

Daniel Parks of Concord & Sarah Walker,   June 13, 1749

Joel Clap & Elizabeth Burk,   Oct. 17, 1749

William Hunt & Mary Wheeler,   Jan. 1, 1749/50

Moses Hayden & Priscilla Goodenow,   Jan. 2, 1749/50

Nathaniel Coolidge of Weston & Sarah Parker, Feb. 1, 1749/50

Samuel Maynard & Sarah Noyes,   Feb. 22, 1749/50

Nathan Wood & Rebekah Haynes,   May 2, 1750

Josiah Noyes & Abigail Gilbert,   June 28, 1750

Cyrus Whitcomb & Susanna Wood,   July 25, 1750

Jonathan Graves & Esther Perry,   Oct. 17, 1750

Aaron Haynes & Rebekah Willis,   Oct. 30, 1750

James Parmenter & Mary Carter,   Nov. 4, 1750

David Fisk & Ruth Noyes,   Dec. 5, 1750

Ebenezer Goodenow & Kezia Frost of Framingham,

Dec. 11, 1750

Samuel Fisk & Abigail Rice,   June 14, 1753

Josiah Curtis & Abigail Baldwin,   May 7, 1752

Israel Gates & Elizabeth Brewer,   April 30, 1753

Nehemiah Allen of Rutland & Anna Billing of Con-

cord,   Nov. 28, 1752

Thomas Partridge & Abigail Harrington,   Sept. 14, 1753

John Robinson of Newton & Lydia Warren of Wal-

tham,   Sept. 20, 1753

Samuel Satter & Sarah Knight, both of Stow,   Oct. 15, 1753

Joseph Muzzy & Mrs. (?) Sarah Pope,   Dec. 27, 1753

Peter Mossmee & Patience Pequickss, resident in

Weston,   Jan. 31, 1754

Nathaniel Cutter & Submit Whitcomb of Stow, Nov. 23, 1753

Bezaleel Moor & Ruth Esty,   March 19, 1755

Joseph Hager & Jerusha Forgenson, both of Wes-

ton,   July 10, 1755

Cornelius Melonia & Elizabeth Parks, both of

Lincoln,   March 11, 1756

Edward Shearman, jr. & Mrs. (?) Lydia Moore, Oct. 14, 1756

Josiah Baldwin & Susannah Gould,   March 29, 1763

Moses Hayden & Abigail Barret of Framingham, April 1, 1763
Samuel Graves & Mary Farrar,   May 19, 1763
Samuel Cutting & Lois Willis,   Aug. 9, 1763
Joseph Haynes & Hannah Stratton,   Aug. 11, 1763
Samuel Haynes of Needham & Mary Hammon, Sept. 1, 1763
Timothy Eames & Hannah Hill,   Sept. 26, 1763
Isaac Stone of Framingham & Parris How,   Sept. 28, 1763
Jonathan Hemingway of Framingham & Thankful
   Haywood,   Nov. 3, 1763
Timothy Minott of Concord & Beulah Brown, Nov. 24, 1763
Joseph Livermore & Abigail Parmenter,   Dec. 22, 1763
John Underwood & Barthsheba Rice,   Dec. 29, 1763
Josiah Bennet & Ruth Wood of Southborough, Jan. 10, 1764
John Fassett of Rutland & Isabel Boagle,   Feb. 16, 1764
Ephraim Goodenough & Elizabeth Ball of Framing-
   ham,   Feb. 16, 1764
Jonathan Walker of Weston & Mary Rice,   July 27, 1763
Oliver Curtis & Mary Damon,   April 7, 1763
John Houghton of Bolton & Keziah Ross,   June 14, 1763
Ebenezer Roby, jr. & Abigail Moffat,   Sept. 5, 1763
Nathaniel Carriel of Marlborough & Deborah San-
   derson,   Sept. 16, 1763
Robert Sever of Marlborough & Joanna Parmenter,
                               Sept. 20, 1763
Elijah Goodenow of Needham & Hannah Curtis, Oct. 12, 1763
Joseph Livermore of Spencer & Ann Rice,   Nov. 10, 1763
Daniel Grout & Abigail Learned,   Dec. 28, 1763
Samuel Jackson of Newton & Mary Baldwin, Feb. 7, 1764
Timothy Billing of Concord & Mary Morse, Jan. 27, 1740
Joshua Hemingway of Framingham & Jemima Rut-
   ter,   March 12, 1740
William Fisk & Sarah Cutting,   Nov. 13, 1740
Peter Noyes & Keziah Fisk,   Nov. 12, 1741
Samuel Cutting & Eunice Moore,   April 22, 1742
Ephraim Jennings of Framingham & Sybilla Rice,
                            March 31, 1742/3
Joseph Rutter & Mary Willard,   April 28, 1743
Shrimpton Hunt of Boston & Margaret Cook, Oct. —, 1743

Jonathan Underwood & Lydia Muzzy,	June 4, 1744
John Wait & Eunice Morse,	March 7, 1743/4
Josiah Hoar & Mary Walker,	Feb. 6, 1745
Isaac Livermore & Dorothy Walker,	Feb. 17, 1745/6
Samuel Curtis & Jerusha Cutting,	Feb. 20, 1745/6
James Walker & Abigail Wood,	Nov. 17, 1746
Richard Heard & Sarah Fisk,	April 9, 1746
William Joyner & Hannah Bowker,	March 18, 1745
Henry Smith & Anna Fisk,	June 9, 1747
Daniel Wyman & Dorothy Johnson,	Nov. 28, 1747
Moses Goodenow & Thankfull Griffin,	Dec. 29, 1747
Joseph Green & Patience Winship,	Oct. 26, 1748
Benjamin Garfell of Westborough & Beulah Parmenter,	Sept. 28, 1748
Edmund Allen & Elizabeth Woodward,	March 10, 1747/8
Eleazer Kendall & Mary Brown,	April 13, 1749
Daniel Farrar, jr. & Mary Allen,	Dec. 1, 1748
Aaron Jones of Weston & Silence Cutting,	Jan. 3, 1749
Zebulon Rice & Susannah Allen,	Dec. 7, 1749
Daniel Billing & Elizabeth Farrar, both of Concord,	Jan. 31, 1749
Edmund Rice & Margaret Smith,	Feb. 22, 1749/50
Edward How & Lois Maynard,	Nov. 2, 1750
Elijah Kendall of Framingham & Jemima Smith,	May 24, 1750
Samuel How & Abigail Dudley,	April 12, 1750
Jonathan Kendall of Framingham & Frances Crumpton,	March 14, 1750
Abraham Gould & Hepzibah Maynard,	Feb. 28, 1750
Samuel Frost of Framingham & Rebecca How,	June 19, 1750
Thomas Damon & Elisabeth Stone,	Jan. 10, 1751
Josiah Bennet, of Shrewsbury & Abiel Graves,	Aug. 13, 1751
Jonas Holden & Abigail Kendall,	Jan. 28, 1752
Jonathan Parmenter & Susannah Bryant,	Feb. 14, 1752
William Baldwin & Jane Cook,	Feb. 15, 1753
Thomas Nickolls & Eunice Parmenter,	Nov. 18, 1752
Joseph Goodenow & Hannah Elliot,	Nov. 30, 1752
Samuel Garfield of Waltham & Lydia Livermore,	Nov. 2, 1752

Jonathan Sawyer of Woburn & Elisabeth Tenny, March 5, 1752

William Revies & Mary Nickol, May 5, 1752

John Billing of Concord & Hannah Farrar, April 19, 1753

Timothy Underwood & Susannah Bond, Jan. 24, 1753

Daniel Daby of Stow & Lydia Farrar, Jan. 10, 1754

Israel Haynes & Sarah Daby of Stow, Jan. 10, 1754

Jason Parmenter & Sarah Grout, Jan. 17, 1754

Daniel Rice & Sarah Rice, Nov. 28, 1754

William Grout & Eunice Cutting, Jan. 8, 1754

Jonas Loker & Abigail Barber, March 27, 1754

Joseph Church & Ruth Gould, Jan. 1, 1755

Ebenezer Staples & Abigail Curtis, Feb. 20, 1755

John Moffat & Abigail Johnson, April 17, 1755

Benjamin Cory & Silence Graves, Oct. 24, 1755

Ebenezer King & Mary Livermore of Weston, May 28, 1755

Nathan Livermore of Weston & Lucy Bennet, July 19, 1755

Joel Winship of Lexington & Elisabeth Grout, Jan. 15, 1755

Henry Loker & Hannah Barber, May 22, 1755

Jonathan Carter & Eunice Kendall, Nov. 2, 1756

Longly Bartlett of Newton & Elisabeth Rice, Oct. 14, 1756

Jason Glezen & Catherine Cook, May 11, 1756

Nehemiah Abbot, of Lincoln & Joyes Abbot, July 1, 1756

Timothy Bemis of Weston & Martha Wesson, Jan. 30, 1756

Ephraim Rice & Mary Battle of Dedham, April 14, 1757

Isaac Stone & Sarah Moulton, March 1, 1757

Thomas Grout & Abigail Parmenter, Jan. 19, 1756

Jason Whitney of Natick & Elizabeth Beal, March 3, 1757

Addington Gardner of Sherburn & Mary Bryant, Feb. 21, 1758

Hezekiah Whitcomb of Lancaster & Submit Ross, Nov. 23, 1758

John Walker & Elisabeth Goodenow, June 24, 1758

Josiah Maynard & Mary Noyes, Dec. —, 1758

William Russell & Katherine Bent, Jan. 4, 1758

William Revies & Abigail Wright of Lincoln, Feb. 13, 1760

Jason Glezen & Lydia Graves, Feb. 7, 1760

Francis Benson & Hannah Harry, Sept. 10, 1761

Jacob Johnson & Sarah Moore, Oct. 15, 1761

John Brigham & Abigail Johnson, March 12, 1750

Elijah Rice & Elizabeth Rice, March 26, 1751

Samuel Woods of Rutland & Tabitha Eveleth, Sept. 14, 1751
Ambrose Tower & Jerusha Clap, Oct. 10, 1751
Timothy Mossman & Elisabeth Buttrick, Nov. 6, 1751
Stephen Morse of Leicester & Mary Hayden, Nov. 13, 1751
Caleb Harrington of Marlborough & Hepzibah
    Hayden, Nov. 14, 1751
Micajah Dorman of Norton & Mary Smith, July 9, 1752
Ebenezer Burbank & Sarah Homans, Dec. 22, 1752
William Skinner & Martha Shevally, Jan. 11, 1753
Jonathan Bellows of Southborough & Abigail Knight,
    Feb. 10, 1753
William Rice of Natick & Abigail Willis, Aug. 16, 1753
Josiah Child of Rutland & Experience Read, Oct. 10, 1753
Aaron Johnson & Kezia Bennet, Dec. 6, 1753
Jonas Davis of Harvard & Elisabeth Cheny, Jan. 1, 1754
Micah Goodenow & Abigail Gibbs, Jan. 8, 1754
Bezaleel Fisk of Holden & Rebecca Rand, April 11, 1754
Isaac Hunt, Jr. & Abigail Hayden, June 28, 1754
Benjamin Parks of Lincoln & Lois Gibbs, Aug. 29, 1754
James Thompson & Mary Vorce, Nov. 14, 1754
James Carter & Priscilla Whitney, Nov. 28, 1754
Isaac Read Jr. & Lydia Goodenow, Jan. 16, 1755
Norman Sever & Sarah Read, March 14, 1753
Gideon Rugg of South Hadley & Judith Maynard,
    March 24, 1755
Samuel How & Elisabeth Haynes, May 22, 1755
Thomas Hayden & Mary Ball of Southborough, Nov. 27, 1755
Samuel Knight & Ann Clap, July 1, 1756
Elias Hayden of Hopkinston & Hannah Hayden, Aug. 4, 1756
Aaron Amsden of Southbridge & Mary Win, Sept. 9, 1756
Asa Brown & Silence Noyes, Dec. 1, 1756
Isaac Goodenow & Mary Hunt, Jan. 27, 1757
Jacob Read & Patience Goodenow, Feb. 28, 1757
Eleazer Lawrence of Littleton & Rebecca Haynes, Dec. 15, 1757
Jonas Balcom & Grace Holden, Dec. 20, 1757
Andrew White & Sarah Railey, Jan. 19, 1758
William Hayden & Betty Potter of Marlborough,
    March 16, 1758

Josiah Rice & Sybill Battle,	April 11, 1758
Timothy Goodenow & Sarah Willis,	April 13, 1758
William Dun of Framingham & Eunice Goodenow,	
	May 4, 1758
Isaac Read Jr. & Mary Haynes,	Dec. 12, 1758
Oliver Morse & Elizabeth Osburn,	Feb. 8, 1759
Samuel Dakin & Ann Wheeler,	Feb. 21, 1759
Asael Smith & Mary Puffer,	March 21, 1759
Abijah Brigham & Eunice Willis,	June 5, 1759
Daniel Woodward & Prudence Vorce,	Oct. 18, 1759
Josiah Puffer & Mary Read,	Nov. 29, 1759
James Haynes & Abigail Noyes,	Jan. 24, 1760
Josiah Richardson & Elisabeth Eveleth of Stow,	Jan. 30, 1760
Benjamin Berry & Anna Knight,	Feb. 1, 1760
Asahel Knight & Lucy Goodenow,	Feb. 20, 1760
Nahum Baldwin & Martha Low,	April 22, 1760
John Carruth, Jr. of Westborough & Miriam May-	
nard,	May 20, 1760
Samuel Puffer Jr. & Olive Rice,	June 12, 1760
Rowen Bogle & Elisabeth Goodenow,	Oct. 16, 1760
Samuel Parris & Abigail Fisk,	Nov. 28, 1760
John Brewer & Lydia Daby,	Dec. 1, 1760
Benjamin Tower & Ann Vorce,	Jan. 7, 1761
Samuel Balcom & Mary Brigham,	Jan. 14, 1761
Timothy Baker of Littleton & Mary Dakin,	Jan. 15, 1761
Michael Corlin & Lois Raily,	Feb. 9, 1761
John Goodenow & Mary Read,	March 19, 1761
Silas Goodenow & Mary Bogle,	April 1, 1761
James Thompson of New Braintree District &	
Hannah Walker,	April 23, 1761
James Eaton of Framingham & Lois Goodenow,	May 7, 1761
John Rice & Sarah Smith,	May 7, 1761
Benjamin Muzzy & Elisabeth Wetherbee of Stow,	July 30, 1761
Nathan Russell & Anna Rice,	Aug. 20, 1761
Andrew Paterson & Elisabeth Bond,	Oct. 22, 1761
Zebadiah Allen of Rutland & Hannah Grout,	Oct. 1, 1761
Benjamin Smith & Lucy Maynard,	Nov. 11, 1761
Gilbert Dench of Hopkinston & Anne Gibbs.	Dec. 10, 1761

Capt. Reynolds Seager & Mrs. (?) Hannah Bennet,
Dec. 25, 1761
Nathaniel Brown of Framingham & Eleanor Hay-
den,   Dec. 29, 1761
Isaiah Parmenter & Lydia Hayden,   Jan. 28, 1762
Benjamin Goodenow of Hardwick & Ruth Sander-
son,   March 23, 1762
Joseph Potter Jr. of Marlborough & Zebudah Hay-
den,   March 23, 1762
Micah Parmenter & Rebecca Clark,   July 6, 1762
John Eveleth of Stow & Abigail Knowles,   July 12, 1762
Benjamin Hemingway of Framingham & Luce Stone,
Sept. 2, 1762
Asahel Wheeler & Thankful Goodenow,   Sept. 20, 1762
Jonathan Stearns of Rutland & Abigail Moore, Dec. 9, 1762
Darius Hudson & Dinah Goodenow,   Dec. 30, 1762
Isaac Lincoln & Experience Willis,   Feb. 15, 1763
John Allen & Eunice Glezen,   Nov. 17, 1761
Isaac Baldwin & Eunice Jenison of Natick,   Dec. 31, 1761
Adams Stone & Hannah Barber,   Jan. 26, 1762
James Glover of Framingham & Lois Bent,   Feb. 3 1762
Micah Rice & Elisabeth Bent,   Feb. 11, 1762
Deliverance Parmenter & Mary Osburn,   April 20, 1762
Isaac Atler & Thankful Brewer,   April 26, 1762
Ebenezer Woods & Dorothy Moor,   Sept. 16, 1762
Cuff & Hager, negro servts. of Col. Noyes,   Oct. 14, 1762
Richard Mills of Rutland & Dorothy Bent,   Nov. 9, 1762
Samuel Eaton of Worcester & Millicent Wheeler, April 18, 1748
Solomon Parmenter & Elisabeth Craige,   May 10, 1748
Joseph Tower & Hepzibah Gibbs,   July 21, 1748
Joseph Eveleth & Patience Hunt,   Aug 25, 1748
Samuel Willis Jr. & Sybill Balcom,   Oct. 6, 1748
Micah Stone of Framingham & Rachel Haynes,   Oct. 11, 1748
Theophilus Potter of Marlborough & Lois Walker, Dec. 13, 1748
Joseph Read & Sarah Goodenow,   Jan. 16, 1748/9
George Mossman & Sybill Walker,   Jan. 19, 1748/9
Daniel Parmenter & Mary Knight,   Sept. 20, 1764
Jared Smith & Rebecca Wood, both of Concord, Oct. 3, 1764

Daniel Noyes Jr. & Ruth Read,   Nov. 1, 1764
David Andrews of Shrewsbury & Abigail Nixon, Nov. 29, 1764
Reuben Willis & Sarah Brigham,   March 13, 1765
Aaron Wheaton & Abigail Goodenow,   March 28, 1765
Josiah Brown & Ann How,   April 4, 1765
John Hedley of Lancaster & Eunice Maynard, Jan. 22, 1765
Jesse Gibbs & Ruth How,   March 7, 1765
Abraham Jenkinson & Martha Shearman,   June 13, 1765
Daniel Goodenow Jr. & Katherine Moore,   Sept. 12, 1765
Francis Blanchard of Brookline & Mary Maynard,

                                Sept. 26, 1765
John Rayley & Sarah Peirce,   Oct. 30, 1765
Benjamin Muzzy & Hannah Bennet,   Dec. 25, 1765
Jonathan Smith Jr. & Ann Willis,   Jan. 30, 1766
Daniel Felch of Natick & Ann Bent,   May 12, 1763
Amos Wheeler & Mary Garfield, both of Lincoln, Oct. 22, 1765
Israel Joslin & Ann Newton, both of Marlborough,

                                Oct. 30, 1765
John Abbot & Mary Allen of Weston,   Sept. 25, 1760
Jonas Harrington of Weston & Jane Bent,   Feb. 13, 1766
Nathaniel Bemis & Esther Cox,   July 29, 1766
Eliab Moore & Kezia Parmenter,   April 9, 1766
Stephen Gibson, Jr. of Stow & Rebekah Puffer, April 15, 1766
Hopestill Willis & Olive Smith,   May 1, 1766
Reuben Vorce & Mary Rice,   May 15, 1766
Hopestill Brown & Elisabeth How,   Nov. 27, 1766
Joseph Goodenow & Dinah Moor,   Jan. 8, 1767
Uriah Hayden & Lydia Eaton of Worcester,   Jan. 15, 1767
Asher Cutler & Eunice Goodenow,   Jan. 15, 1767
Joseph Moor & Martha Grout,   Jan. 22, 1767
Samuel Hunt & Submit Graves,   May 15, 1766
Uriah Wheeler & Ann Smith,   March 15, 1768
Moses Noyes & Ellisabeth Eaton,   April 14, 1768
Israel Wheeler & Lucy Ingersoll,   April 14, 1768
Oliver Noyes & Mercy Johnson,   April 27, 1768
Jonathan Heywood of Concord & Rebecca Rice, Aug. 23, 1769
Moses Banter of Prince Town & Mary Moore, Sept. 1, 1768
Benjamin Clark & Abigail Hunt,   Oct. 19, 1768

John Wrighten & Elizabeth Bogle,	Oct. 26, 1768
Eli Leominster & Eleaner Haynes,	Nov. 28, 1768
Nathan Winch of Framingham & Abigail Brown,	Feb. 8, 1769
Isaac Moore & Elizabeth Bryant,	April 21, 1768
John Noyes Jr. & Jane Wyman,	June 15, 1768
Peter Johnson & Mary Rice	Sept. 1, 1768
Ezekiel Rice & Eunice Cutting,	Oct. 27, 1768
Isaac Rice & Mary Johnson,	Nov. 3, 1768
Asa How & Mary Betty,	Nov. 4, 1768
Bulkley How of Prince Town & Elizabeth Moore,	Feb. 21, 1769
Nathl. Maynard & Martha Smith,	June 19, 1764
Samuel Poole & Hannah Choate,	Nov. 27, 1764
Isaac Damon & Lucy Cutting,	March 12, 1765
Peter Haynes & Anna Russell,	April 30, 1765
Jason Gleason, Jr. & Abigail Bent,	June 18, 1765
Silas Bent & Mary Carter,	June 24, 1765
Isaac Whittemore of Weston & Elisabeth Graves,	Aug. 15, 1765
Joseph Grout & Lydia Rice,	Oct. 18, 1765
James Adams of Lincoln & Deliverance Adams,	Aug. 28, 1766
Jona. Haynes & Millicent Russell,	Sept. 21, 1766
Isaac Lock & Ann Brintnal,	Oct. 2, 1766
David Rice & Abigail Rice,	Nov. 20, 1766
James Brewster, Jr. & Mary Hoar,	Dec. 11, 1766
Ebenezer Johnson & Elisabeth Rice,	Dec. 16, 1766
Roland Bennit & Lydia Trask,	Feb. 9, 1767
William Williams & Elisabeth Jennison of Natick,	April 30, 1767
Robert Cutting Jr. & Jerusha Curtis,	Aug. 6, 1767
John Tilton & Mary Williams,	Oct. 15, 1767
Josiah Allen & Deborah Day,	Dec. 1, 1767
David Jackson & Rebekah Wyman,	Jan. 28, 1768
Joseph Eaton & Sarah Hayden,	March 5, 1767
Asa Balcom & Jerusha Willis,	March 5, 1767
Caleb Molton Jr. & Mary Goodenow,	Sept. 10, 1767
Edward Boynton & Abigail Walker,	Nov. 11, 1767
Joshua Fairbanks of Framingham & Mary Parmenter,	Dec. 3, 1767
James Balcom & Ruth Balcom,	Dec. 30, 1767

Capt. Amos Coolidge of Sherburn & Zeruiah Brown,

	Feb. 25, 1768
Elisha Goodenow & Sarah Vickery,	April 26, 1769
Ithamar Rice & Susanna Balcom,	May 10, 1769
Moses Maynard & Sybilla Willis,	Sept. 7, 1769
William Moore & Abigail Wheeler,	Oct. 12, 1769
Samuel Knight & Lois Goodenow,	Nov. 9, 1769
Augustus Moore & Ruth Plympton,	Nov 16, 1769
Daniel Osborn & Sarah Perry,	Nov. 16, 1769

Dr. Joseph Josslin of Marlborough & Hannah Seager,

	Jan. 2, 1770
Isaac Puffer & Sarah Wheeler,	Sept. 14, 1769
Thaddeus Russell & Sarah Poland,	May 4, 1769
Solomon Gearfield of Lincoln & Sarah Stimpson,	Aug. 22, 1769

Thomas Bryant of Sherburn & Mehitabel Bryant,

	Sept. 7, 1769
Ephraim Abbott & Sara Curtis,	Oct. 12, 1769
James Sanderson & Rebekah Abbot,	Nov. 9, 1769
William Damon & Sarah Cutting,	Jan. 7, 1770
Daniel Wait & Abigail Read,	March 18, 1770
Philemon Brown & Anne Rice,	March 8, 1770
William Moulton & Susannah Loring,	April 24, 1770
Daniel Puffer & Mary Balcom,	July 5, 1770
Daniel Loring & Bathsheba How,	Sept. 20, 1770
Nathaniel Puffer & Cate Clap,	Oct. 29, 1770
Daniel Balcom & Mercy Maynard,	Feb. 20, 1771
Ephraim Curtis & Relief Putman,	May 23, 1770
Simeon Smith of Weston & Dorothy Wyman,	July 12, 1770
Nathaniel Reeves & Dorothy Hoar,	Sept. 13, 1770

Moses Kenny of Northborough & Azubah Parmenter,

	Dec. 5, 1770
Joshua Kendall & Mary Rutter,	Dec. 6, 1770
Noah Eaton of Framingham & Mary Tilton,	Feb. 14, 1771
Timothy Shearman & Mary Maynard,	Feb. 20, 1771

Jacob Cranel (?) of Roxbury & Anna Patterson of Cambridge,

	May 30, 1769
Jonathan Edes of Natick & Hannah Stroud,	Dec. 17, 1770
Ephraim Goodenow & Mary Holmes,	Feb. 4, 1771

Ephraim Allen & Thankfull Goodenow,	April 30, 1772
Abraham Whitney & Sarah Adams of Weston,	Nov. 12, 1771
Abishai Crossman & Experience Richardson,	March 31, 1772
Josiah Wellington & Mary Smith,	May 7, 1771
Zebediah Farrar of Lincoln & Katherine Moor,	July 11, 1771
Benjamin Bennet & Susannah Trask,	Sept. 30, 1771
David Stone, Jr. & Elizabeth Bent,	Oct. 17, 1771
Lemuel Veazey of Roxbury & Sarah Abbot,	Dec. 26, 1771
Jonathan Cutting & Persis Hoar,	March 12, 1772
Nathan Stearns of Newton & Lucy Rice,	March 23, 1772
Jonathan Rice & Eunice Willis,	May 26, 1772
Micah Balcom of Stow & Katharine Harrington,	July 2, 1772
Aaron Goodenow, Jr. & Esther Maynard,	July 9, 1772
William Rice, Jr. & Sarah Noyes,	July 23, 1772
Moses Willson of Westminster & Unity Allen,	July 23, 1772
William Maynard & Lucy Balcom,	Aug. 20, 1772
Abel Holden & Lois Cutler,	Aug. 27, 1772
John Brigham & Caty Willis,	Oct. 15, 1772
Abraham Goodenow & Lucy Perry,	Oct. 29, 1772
Silas Parmenter & Molly Hayden,	Nov. 5, 1772
Andrew Paterson & Molly Russell,	Jan. 26, 1773
Samuel Rice & Abigail Underwood,	Feb. 4, 1773
Isaac Gould & Sarah Hoar,	Feb. 11, 1773
Elisha Wheeler, Jr. & Sarah Goodenow,	March 4, 1774
Ephraim Carter & Anne Reeves,	March 4, 1774
Jonathan Hoar & Sarah Heard,	April 1, 1773
Amos Davis & Ruth Warren of Weston,	April 8, 1773
Nathan Drury of Framingham & Abigail Rice,	May 6, 1773
Penuel Park of Watertown & Dorothy Walker,	May 20, 1773
Ariel Nims of Deerfield & Anne Brewer,	June 14, 1773
Thomas Rutter & Abigail Heard,	June 24, 1773
Jonathan Lawrence of Weston & Lucy Moore,	Aug. 11, 1773
Thomas Heard & Elizabeth Reeves,	Nov. 25, 1773
Jonas Shearman & Hepzibath Gallop,	Nov. 25, 1773
Elisha Robinson of Framingham & Eunice Rice,	Nov. 25, 1773
Mark Moore & Mary Stone of Framingham,	Feb. 9, 1774
Joseph Bacon of Needham & Elizabeth Dudley,	March 3, 1774
John Perry & Jerusha Parmenter,	Feb. 4, 1773

Reuben Brown of Concord & Mary How,	May 12, 1773
Matthias Rice & Mary Brown of Stow,	Aug. 25, 1773
Jesse Moore & Lucy Eaton,	Nov. 7, 1773
Joseph Lovering of Westminster & Kezia Carr,	Nov. 24, 1773
Simeon Ingersol & Silence Tower,	Jan. 20, 1774
Israel Moore, Jr. & Mary Dejersey,	Feb. 10, 1774
Ephraim Allen & Thankful Goodenow,	April 30, 1772
Benjamin Rice of Boston & Martha Bent,	Jan. 31, 1775
Capt. Josiah Hoar & Hepzibah Allen,	Feb. 10, 1774
Israel Rice, Jr. & Sarah Goodenow,	April 7, 1774
James Smith, Jr. of Weston & Rebecca Shearman,	Aug. 25, 1774
Rev. Jonathan Barns of Hillsborough & Abigail Curtis,	Dec. 14, 1774
Jonathan Priest of Bolton & Ann Sanderson,	Dec. 16, 1774
Joseph Robbins of Acton & Elizabeth Moore,	Jan. 10, 1775
Alpheus Morse & Lydia Rice, both of Marlborough,	Jan. 17, 1775
John Moore & Mary Bruce,	Jan. 26, 1775
Samuel Glezen & Hannah Brigham,	Feb. 22, 1775
Jonathan Fairbank of Northborough & Hannah Morse,	Feb. 28, 1781
Elijah Dedman of Framingham & Bathsheba Parmenter,	Feb. 28, 1781
Nathaniel Linfield, Jr. & Sarah Balcom,	April 28, 1781
Willm. Hemengway of Framingham & Eunice Parmenter,	Oct. 21, 1781
Aaron How & Mary Foster, both of Marlborough,	Dec. 13, 1781
Danl. Woodward More & Azubah Knight,	Jan. 4, 1782
Thos. Walker & Elizabeth Foskett of Bolton,	Jan. 15, 1782
Ebenezer Plympton & Hannah Ruggles,	Jan. 31, 1782
Jacob Parmenter & Lois Goodenow,	Jan. 31, 1782
Henry Gates of Farmington & Anna Emes,	Feb. 12, 1782
Asahel Goodenow & Frances Baldwin,	April 27, 1780
Abel Billing of Lincoln & Elizabeth Farrar,	May 30, 1780
Saml. Curtis & Mary Mann,	July 25, 1780
Chevey Kendall of Framingham & Dorothy Parns,	Aug. 24, 1780

Zebediah Farrar of Lincoln & Eunice Sharman, Aug. 31, 1780
Benja. Carter & Lois Whittemore,   Sept. 4, 1780
Joseph Bachelor of Grafton & Sarah Tilton,   Sept. 21, 1780
William Wyman & Anna Noyes,   Sept. 26, 1780
John Adams & Elizabeth Billings of Lincoln,
Stephen Merrick of Princeton & Abigail Griffin, Dec. 7, 1780
Joseph Tilton of Ipswich & Elizabeth Russell,   Jan. 9, 1781
Joseph Goodenow of Sudbury & Polly Bond of
    Lincoln,   Jan. 28, 1781
Cuff Kneeland of Lincoln & Dinah Young,   Feb. 8, 1781
Trowbridge Taylor of Sudbury & Jane Curtis, April 19, 1781
Peter Smink of Boston & Abigail Abbot,   May 24, 1781
Rev. David Kellogg & Sarah Bridge, both of Fram-
    ingham,   May 27, 1781
Lieut. Ephraim Barber & Elizabeth Crosby, both
    of Marlborough,   Oct. 11, 1781
Asa Russell of Fitchburg & Lucy Brown,   Jan. 7, 1782

WATERTOWN

Sept. 7, 1630 "The town upon the Charles River to be called Watertown."

Richard Norcas & Mary Brookes,   24-4-1650
Richard Whitney & Mary Coldam,   Jan. 19, 1650
Richard Norcross & Mary Brookes,   April 24, 1650
William Bond & Sarah Bliss,   Dec. 12, 1649
Jno. Bisco & Elizabeth Bittlstone,   Dec. 13, 1650
Samuel Stratton & Mary Fry,   March 25, 1651
Richard Bloiss & Michael Gennison,   10-12-1657
Willm. Price & Mary Mapelhead,   Feb. 9, 1657
Henry Spring & Mehetabel Bartlett,   Nov. 7, 1657
Abram How & Hannah Ward,   — 26, 1657
Nath. Coolidge & Mary Bright,   Aug. 15, 1657
George Laurance & Eliz. Crispe,   July 29, 1657
John Stratton & Elizab. Trayne,   Jan. 1, 1658

Simon Coolidge & Hannah Barron, Sept. 17, 1658
Isack (Jack)? Mixer & Rebeccah Garfield, 10-1-1660
George Woodward & Elizabeth Hamon, Aug. 17, 1659
John Whitney & Judah Clement, Sept. 29, 1659
Francis Boman & Martha Sherman, Sept. 26, 1661
Edward Garfield & Joanna Buckmaster, Sept. 1, 1661
Joseph Morss & Susanna Shattuck, April 12, 1661
Jonathan Browne & Mary Shattuck, Feb. 11, 1661
Richard Child & Mehetabell Dimick, April 17, 1662
Abram Browne & Mary Dix, Feb. 5, 1662
Thomas Traine & Rebecka Sterns, Jan. 25, 1692/3
John Barnard & Elizabeth Shern, Nov. 17, 1692
Jno. Kimball & Sarah Goodhue, both of Ipswich, Dec. 2, 1692
Jonas Bond & Grace Coolidge, Jan. 29, 1688/9
Thomas Knolton & Margery Goodhue, Dec. 2, 1692
James Barnard & Judith Jennison, Dec. 16, 1692
Nathanll Bowman of Cambridge & Ann Barnard, Dec. 16, 1692
Richard Cooledge & Mary Bond, June 21, 1693
John Edy & Sarah Woodard, July 6, 1693
James Hastings & Sarah Tarball of New Towne, Aug. 31, 1693
Wm. Bull & Elizabeth Underwood, Sept. 13, 1693
William Fisk & Hannah Smith of Cambridge, Oct. 25, 1693
Daniel Smith & Hannah Coolidge, Nov. 3, 1693
Samll. Edy & Elizabeth Woodard, Dec. 7, 1693
John Perry & Sarah Price, July 19, 1693
Daniel Maggrige & Elisabeth Robinson, Dec. 20, 1693
James Bigalow & Elizabeth Child, ————, ————
James Ball & Elizabeth Fisk, Jan. 16, 1694
John Park & Elizabeth Miller, April 5, 1694
John Squire & Rebeckah Tappin, both of Cam-
    bridge, April 16, 1694
Samuel Hastings & Elizabeth Nevenson, April 24, 1694
Daniel White of Concord & Mary Winter, May 25, 1694
Adam Eve & Elizabeth Barsham, July 5, 1694
Daniel Netup & Bethiah Breck, March 25, 1664
Samuel Manning & Elizabeth Sternes, April 13, 1664
John Ball, Jr. & Sarah Bullard, Oct. 17, 1665
John Smith & Mary Beck, April 19, 1665

John Morss & Abigail Edwards,	April 27, 1666
Timothy Hawkins & Mary Shearman,	Jan. 18, 1666
John Lawine & Judeth Peirce,	Feb. 16, 1666
Willm. Sanders & Sarah ————,	Dec. 18, 1666
Obadiah Perry & Hester Hassull,	21-6-1667
Joseph Allin & Ann Brazeer,	Aug. 11, 1667
Serjt. John Warren & Michael Bloyce,	May 11, 1667
Josiah Jones & Lidea Tredaway,	Aug. 2, 1667
John Stratton & Mary Smith,	Sept. 20, 1667
John Kemball & Hannah Bartlet,	Nov. 19, 1667
Daniel Smith & Mary Grant,	Dec. 22, 1667
Samuel Livermore & Hannah Bridge,	June 4, 1668
John Child & Mary Warren,	May 29, 1668
Joseph Esterbrookes & Mary Mason,	20-5-1668
Andrew Gardiner & Sarah Mason,	May 20, 1668
Martin Townson & Abigail Trayne,	April 10, 1668
Philip Shattuck & Deborah Bairstow,	Nov. 9, 1670
John Flegg & Mary Gale,	March 30, 1670
John Harris & Mary Sangar,	Sept. 2, 1670
Isaac Ong & Mary Underwood,	May 18, 1670
John Applin & Bathsheba Bartlett,	Nov. 23, 1671
John Cutter & Susan Arrington,	Feb. 9, 1671
Abram Gale & Sarah Fiske,	Sept. 3, 1673
Joseph Shearman & Elisabeth Winship,	Nov. 10, 1673
Nath'l Whitney & Sarah Hagar,	Mch. 12, 1673
Thomas Blanford & Elizabeth Eames,	Dec. 18, 1673
Ri. Norcross & Susannah Shattuck,	Nov. 18, 1673
Sam'l Bigulah & Mary Fleg,	June 3, 1674
Joseph Whitney & Martha Beech,	Jan. 24, 1674
Wm. Rider & Hannah Lovett,	Aug. 11, 1674
Josiah Tredaway & Sarah Swoetman,	June 9, 1674
John Trayne & Sarah Stubs,	Mch. 24, 1674
Joseph Smith & Hannah Teed,	Dec. 1, 1674
David Mead & Hannah Warren,	Sept. 24, 1675
Jno. Trayn & Abigail Bent,	Oct. 12, 1675
Timothy Hawkins & Mary Fisher,	July 21, 1675
John Bright & Mary Barsham,	May 7, 1675
Enoch Laurance & Ruth Shattuck,	Mch. 6, 1676

Josh. Bigulah & Eliz. Fleg,	Oct. 20, 1676
John Hues & Ruth Sawtell,	Mch. 9, 1676
Michael Baistow & Rebecca Trayne,	Dec. 12, 1676
Nath'l Fisk & Mary Child,	Ap. 13, 1677
Jacob Willard & Mary White,	Oct. 23, 1677
Benj. Garfield & Elisabeth Budge,	Jan. 17, 1677
John Gale & Elizabeth Spring,	Sept. 27, 1677
Tho. Hamond & Elisabeth Noyes,	Aug. 21, 1678
R. Child & Hannah Trayne,	Jan. 16, 1678
Dan'l Warren & Elisabeth Whitney,	Dec. 19, 1678
Jno. Fay & Susannah Moss,	July 5, 1678
Benj. Peirce & Hannah Brooks,	Jan. 15, 1678
James Cady & Hannah Barron,	Jan. 14, 1678
Nath'l Barsham & Elisabeth Bond,	Mch. 13, 1678
Tho. Whitney & Elisabeth Laurence,	Jan. 29, 1678
Elliz. ? Baron & Mary Shearman,	May 27, 1679
John Bard & Mary Coolidge,	Aug. 6, 1679
John Coolidge, Jr. & Mary Mattock,	Sept. 16, 1679
Tho. Underwood & Mary Palmer,	Nov. 19, 1679
Steeven Cook & Rebeccah Fleg,	Nov. 19, 1679
Jno. Fisk & Abigail Park,	Dec. 9, 1679
Abram Jackson & Elisabeth Bisco,	Nov. 20, 1679
Philip Shattuck & Rebecca Chamberline,	Feb. 11, 1679
John Hastings & Abigail Hammond,	June 18, 1679
James Cutten & Hannah Coller,	June 16, 1679
Joseph Goddard & Deborah Tredaway,	Mch. 25, 1680
Wm. Bond & Hepzibah Hastings,	June 2, 1680
Timothy Hawkins & Ruhamah Johnson,	June 13, 1680
Joseph Child & Sarah Norcross,	Sept. 23, 1680
Tho. Bond & Sarah Woolson,	Sept. 30, 1680
John Gibson & Hannah Underwood,	Oct. 14, 1680
Dennis Hedley & Johannah Bullard,	Mch. 22, 1680
Nath'l Bright & Mary Coolidge,	July 21, 1681
Daniel Harrington & Sarah Whitney,	Oct. 18, 1681
Jno. Harrington & Hannah Winter,	Nov. 17, 1681
Gregory Cook & Susannah Goodwin,	Nov. —— 1681
Manning Sawing & Sarah Stone,	Dec. 15, 1681
Simon Coolidge & Priscilla Rogers,	Jan. 19, 1681

Nath'l Healy & Rebecca Hagar,	July 14, 1681
Thomas Fox & Elizabeth Chadwick,	Ap. 24, 1683
Jonathan Hastings & Ruth Rice,	31-9, 1682
Jeremiah Moss & Abigail Woodward,	13-11, 1681
Francis Bowman & Lydia Stone,	26-5-1684
John White & Rebecca Bemish,	1-2-1684
Joseph Willington & Elizab. Straight,	6-5-1684
Isaac Mixer & Elizab. Pierse,	17-8-1684
Nathaniel Bond & Bethiah Fuller,	27-12-1684
Joseph Hastings & Martha Shepard,	8-11-1684
Alen Fleg & Sarah Ball,	12-1-1684
Benj. Herrington & Abigail Bigaloh,	10-10-1684
Samuel Hastings & Lydia Church,	Jan. 4, 1686/7
Solomon Johnson & Hannah Grose of Menotaney in Cambridge,	Feb. 1, 1686/7
Abraham Peirce & Isabel Whitherspoone, both of Boston,	Mch. 11, 1686/7
Daniel Benjamin & Elizabeth Browne,	Mch. 25, 1687
James Bigalow & Patience Browne,	Mch. 25, 1687
William Hagar & Sarah Benjamin,	Mch. 31, 1687
Benjamin Whitney & Abigail Hagar,	Mch. 31, 1687
Joseph Allen of Sudbury & Abigail Mirriack,	May 5, 1687
Edward Tayler, Jr. & Rebekah Humphryes, both of Boston,	May 24, 1687
William Clampet & Mary Napper, both of Boston,	May 25, 1687
James Cornish, Jr. & Mary Kay, both of Boston,	May 25, 1687
Nathaniel Norcross & Mehetabel Hagar,	June 20, 1687
Benjamin Laurence & Mary Clough,	July 4, 1689
Palsgrave Willmington & Sarah Bond,	Jan. 29, 1688/9
Richard Lecky & Anne Greenfield, both of Boston,	July 4, 1687
Ebenezer Messenger & Rose Collins, Boston,	July 4, 1687
Eliezer Whitney & Dorothy Rosse, Sudbury,	Aug. 11, 1687
Thomas Fenton & Elisabeth Basset of Boston,	Aug. 17, 1687
William Jones of W. & Abigail Avered of Dedham,	Oct. 18, 1687
Robert Garfield of W. & Deborah Holman of Cambridge,	Nov. 3, 1687
Peter Barber & Sarah Willy, both of Boston,	Nov. 22, 1687

Joseph Winship of Notony & Sarah Harrington, Nov. 24, 1687
Shubal Child & Abigail Saunders, Oct. 27, 1687
John Knap, Jr. & Sarah Park of Cambridge Village, Aug. 4, 1686
Richard Norcross & Rose Woodward, Aug. 10, 1686
George Woodward & Lydia Browne, Dec. 30, 1686
Richard Child & Mary Flegg, Dec. 30, 1686
Thomas Herrington & Rebecca White, Ap. 1, 1686
James Knap & Mary Fiske, Oct. 30, 1716
Daniel Simonds of Lexington & Abigail Smith, Nov. 29, 1716
John Bemis & Sarah Phillip, Jan. 1, 1716/7
Joseph Grout & Mary Rogers (widow of Dan'l), Jan. 3, 1716/7
John Newton of Marlboro & Hannah Parkhurst, Jan. 17, 1716/7
Jonathan Phillip & Hephziba Parker, Feb. 27, 1716/7
Peter Oliver & Mary Maddock, of Cambridge, May 21, 1716
Richard Cudden of Cambridge & Elisabeth Johnson
of Woburn, Sept. 28, 1716
Ephraim Angier & Mrs. Elisabeth Goddard, Ap. 30, 1717
Joseph Cooledge & Elisabeth Bond, May 9, 1717
Benjamin Eddy & Elisabeth Phillip, Nov. 7, 1716
Obadiah Cooledge of Newton & Rachel Goddard, July 24, 1717
Sam'l Stone of Framingham & Hannah Seale of
Roxbury, May 21, 1716
Nathaniel Norcross & Jemima Abbut, Dec. 12, 1717
Ezekiel Richardson of Woburn & Lydia Ocking-
ham of Needham, Aug. 8, 1717
Ebenezer Hastings & Ruth Phillip, Aug. 12, 1717
Robert Goddard of Brookline & Mehetable Spring, Sept. 5, 1717
Richard Sautle & Abigail Whitney, Mch. 18, 1717
Allen Flegge & Abigail Fiske, Ap. 10, 1717
John Kembel & Mary Clerke, June 14, 1717
Joseph Stratten & Sarah Hagar, Aug. 19, 1717
Daniel Warren & Mehetabel Gearfield, Nov. 15, 1717
Israel Pierce & Sarah Holland, Jan. 16, 1717
William Cheever & Miriam Cleveland, June 21, 1717
Benjamin Child & Elisabeth Greenwood, both of
Newton, May 24, 1722
Jason Rice & Abigail Clark, both of Sudbury, May 31, 1722
Andrew Wilson of Cambridge & Sarah Sherman, June 7, 1722

Soloman Park & Lucy Laurence, both of Newton, June 21, 1722
Isaac Stone of Framingham & Elisabeth Brown of
    Sudbury,   July 24, 1722
Thomas Baker of Roxbury & Hannah Park of New-
    ton,   Aug. 2, 1722
James Whitney & Mary Flagg,   Nov. 8, 1722
Andrew White & Jane Dix,   Dec. 12, 1722
Daniel Dinney of Leicester & Mrs. Rebecca Jones
    of Worcester,   Feb. 14, 1722
John Whitney & Mary Hapgood, both of Sherburn, Ap. 10, 1688
James Smith & Prudence Harrison, both of Boston, Ap. 26, 1688
Thomas Woodward of Muddy River & Triphena
    Fairfield of Ipswich.   May 30, 1688
Thomas Knap & Mary Grout, both of Sudbury, Sept. 19, 1688
Richard Blosse & Anne Cutler of Cambridge, Sept. 26, 1688
Joseph Harrington & Joanna Mixer,   Nov. 7, 1688
Sam'l Newton & Rebeckah Newton, both of Marl-
    boro,   Sept. 8, 1688
Nathaniel Brigden & Elisabeth Waffe, both of
    Charlestown,   Dec. 13, 1688

WESTON

Jan. 1, 1712 West Precinct of Watertown established as Weston.

Joseph Adams of Cambridge & Rache—,   June 26, 1718
John Mirick & Abigail Harrington,   Sept. 18, 1718
James Beals & Hannah Coller of Natick,   Sept. 5, 1718
Benjam. Temple of Concord & Abigail Wait, Sept. 18, 1718
Joseph Merriam of Lexington & Mary Brewer, Oct. 9, 1718
John Brewer & Hannah Mirriam of Lexington, Oct. 9, 1718
Aaron Cutting & Mary Knapp,   March 20, 1718/19
Thomas Coller of Natick & Alice Alden of Need-
    ham,   April 9, 1719

WOBURN

Sept. 27, 1642 "Charlestowne village is called Wooborne."

James Parker & Elizabeth————,	March 23, 1643
William Simons & Judith Haward,	Jan. 18, 1643
Tho. Fuller & Elizabeth Tidd,	April 13, 1643
Nicho. Davis & Elizabeth Isaacke,	May 12, 1643
James Converse & An Long,	Aug. 24, 1643
Simon Thompson & Mary Converse,	Oct. 19, 1643
James Tompson & Mary Blodgit,	Dec. 15, 1643
Abraham Parker & Rose Whitlocke,	Sept. 18, 1644
John Wiman & Sarath Nutt,	Sept. 5, 1644
Francis Kendall & Mary Tidd,	Oct. 24, 1644
Francis Wiman & Judeth Peirce,	Oct. 30, ————
John Russell & Elizabeth Bakes,	March 13, 1645
Isacke Larned & Mary Sternes,	May 9, 1646
Henry Jefs & Ann Stowers,	July 13, 1647
Moses Cleiveland & Ann Winn,	July 26, 1648
Henry Jefs & Hama Birth,	March 21, 1649
George Polle & Elizabeth Win,	March 21, 1649
John Brookes & Eunice Mousall,	Sept. 1, 1649
Henry Baldwin & Phebe Richardsonne,	Sept. 1, 1649
—ward Winn & Sarah Beal,	June 10, 1649
Edw. Johnson & Kathrin Baker,	Nov. 10, 1649
Richard Post & Susan Sutton,	Dec. 27, 1649
William Pierce & Abigail Warren,	8-4-1690
Jonathan Wyman & Hannah Fowle,	July 31, 1690
John Holden & Sarah Pearse,	June 19, 1690
Timothy Carter & Anna Fisk,	May 3, 1680
James Wilson & Deborah Pierce,	Jan. 19, 1686/7
Abraham Cummins of Dunstable & Sarah Wright,	
	Feb. 28, 1686/7
Jacob Wyman & Elizabeth Richardson,	Nov. 23, 1687
Robert Fenton & Deborah Farrar,	Feb. 27, 1687/8

Joshua Kibby & Mary Comy,	May 24, 1688
Samuel Walker ? & Judith Haward of Concord,	June 1, 1688
Thomas Pierce & Mary Wyman,	Feb. 27, 1692/3
Benjamin Pierce & Hannah Bowers of Chelmsford,	April 3, 1693
Joseph Wright of Charlestowne & Elizabeth Bateman,	July 7, 1692
Henry Brooks & Mary Graves of Sudbury,	Dec. 9, 1692
William Brush & Elisabeth Gold, widow,	March 15, 1693
Josias Convers & Ester Champneys,	26-1-1651
Richard Gardiner & Anna Blanchard,	Aug. 18, 1651
George Read & Elizabeth Gennings,	Aug. 4, 1652
Theophilus Richardson & Mary Champney,	March 2, 1654
John Baker & Susan Martin,	March 28, 1654
Henry Tottingham & Allice Eager,	May 13, 1654
William Johnson & Hester Wiswall,	March 16, 1655
Michael Bacon & Mary Richardson,	Aug. 26, 1655
Willm. Lock & Mary Clarke,	Sept. 27, 1655
Jonathan Thompson & Susan Bloget,	Sept. 28, 1655
Samuel Bloget & Ruth Eggleden,	Oct. 13, 1655
Mathew Johnson & Hannah Palfrey,	Sept. 12, 1656
John Johnson & Bethia Read,	Feb. 28, 1657
Michael Knight & Mary Bullard,	Aug. 20, 1657
Isacke "Jack" Coale & Jane Britton,	1-2-1658
Jno. Richardson & Elizab. Bacon,	Oct. 22, 1658
George Brush & Elizab. Clarke,	————, 1659
Timothy Brooks & Mary Russells,	————, 1659
Michael Bacon, Jr. & Sarah Richardson,	March 22, 1660
John Berbine & Sarah Goold,	April 16, 1660
Samuel Convars & Judeth Carter,	June 8, 1660
Henry Sumers & Mable Read,	Nov. 21, 1660
John Russell, Jr. & Sarah Champneys,	Oct. 31, 1661
Joseph Wright & Elizabeth Hassull,	Nov. 1, 1661
John Craggin & Sarah Dawes,	Nov. 4, 1661
Henry Merrow & Jamis ? Willis,	Dec. 19, 1661
Edward Convars & Joanna Sprague,	Sept. 9, 1662
Samuel Walker, Jr. & Sarah Read,	Oct. 23, 1662
Mathew Johnson & Rebecca Wiswall,	Sept. 10, 1662
Richard Post & Mary Tiler,	Nov. 18, 1662

Jno. Smith & Abigail Carter,	March 7, 1674
Samuel Richardson & Hannah Kingsley,	July 30, 1674
Steeven Richardson & Abigail Wiman,	Nov. 2, 1674
Nathll. Davis & Mary Convars,	Jan. 31, 1675
Tho. Lepingwell & Sarah Knight,	March 11, 1676
Aaron Cleveland & Dorcas Wilson,	July 26, 1676
Moses Cleveland & Ruth Norton,	Aug. 4, 1676
Samuel Richison & Phebe Baldin,	Sept. 7, 1676
Matthew Smith & Mary Cutler,	April 20, 1684
Thomas Fuller & Sarah Wyman,	June 25, 1684
Edward Converse & Sarah Stone,	Sept. 5, 1684
Abraham Cosens & Mary Eames,	Sept. 19, 1684
Daniel Baldwin & Hannah Richardson,	Oct. 6, 1684
Samuel Chadwick & Mary Stocker,	Oct. 22, 1684
John Brooks & Mary Cranston,	Oct. 30, 1684
George Read & Abigail Peirce,	Nov. 18, 1684
Joshua Broadbent & Sarah Osburne,	Feb. 6, 1685
Peter Fowle of Charlestown & Sarah Winn,	Oct. 30, 1691
Josiah Converse & Ruth Marshall,	Aug. 8, 1685
Thomas Blogget & Rebekah Tedd,	Sept. 11, 1685
John Wyman & Hannah Farrer,	Oct. 14, 1685
James Simonds & Hannah Blogget,	Oct. 29, 1685
Seth Wyman & Esther Johnson,	Oct. 17, 1685
Samuel Snow & Sarah Parker of New Cambridge,	Aug. 9, 1686
Eliezer Bateman & Elizabeth Wright,	Nov. 2, 1686
Edward Johnson & Sarah Walker,	Jan. 12, 1686/7
Jacob Wyman & Elizabeth Richardson,	Nov. 23, 1687
Robert Fenton & Deborah Farrar,	Feb. 27, 1687/8
Nathanll. Cutler of Redding & Sarah Fatingham,	April 11, 1715
Abraham Chamberlin & Mary Shed, both of Bil- lerica,	July 23, 1718
Robert Fiske of Lexington & Mary Stimson of Red- ding,	May 26, 1718
John Center & Jane Foster, both of Chelmsford,	April 8, 1718
John Leatherby & Anna Holden, both of Charles- town,	April 17, 1718
John Merrow, Jr. & Rebeckah Davis, both of Red- ding,	Jan. 30, 1721/2

Phineas Parker & Elisabeth Bowers, Lancaster, June 14, 1722
John Lovejoy & Hannah Foster, both of Andover, June 25, 1722
Nathan Wyman & Huldah Simonds,   Jan. 29, 1722/3
Isaac Kent of Concord & Anna Barney of Billerica,
                                       Aug. 18, 1724
Adam Hart of Redding & Abigail Deal,   Sept. 29, 1725
John Swan of Cambridge & Elizebeth Cowdrey of
        Reading,   March 25, 1725
Isaac Baldwin & Mary Flegg,   March 24, 1725/6
Abraham Josling of Marlborough & Jemima Snow,
                                       May 9, 1728
Zurishaddai Peirce & Abigail Johnson,   July 24, 1728
James Richardson & Sarah Fowle,   Sept. 24, 1728
Saml. Cole of Framingham & Sarah Boutel of Read-
        ing,   Sept. 25, 1728
Isaac Richardson & Elizeboth Richardson,   July 2, 1728
Ebenezer Thompson & Hannah Converse,   Sept. 27, 1728
Edward Richardson & Jerusha Wyman,   Feb. 24, 1729/30
Joseph Wright & Rachael Brooks,   Nov. 19, 1729
William Hincher & Priscilla Reed,   March 8, 1739
Rev. Ebene. Wyman & Mary Wright,   May 22, 1739
James Baldwin & Ruth Richardson,   May 29, 1739
John Coolidge & Ann Russell,   May 29, 1739
Richard Snow & Abigail Coggin,   May 31, 1739
John Holt & Sarah Wright,   Nov. 26, 1739
David Alexander & Elisabeth Evans,   Jan. 10, 1739
Jonathan Bacon & Elisabeth Wyman,   Sept. 22, 1739
Samuel Nevers & Susannah Williams,   Aug. 2, 1739
Joseph Johnson & Sarah Tompson,   July 5, 1739
Samuel Dean & Martha Wyman,   Sept. 6, 1739
Thomas Underwood & Elisabeth Wyman,   Nov. 1, 1739
Joseph Walker & Elisabeth Wyman,   Dec. 4, 1739
Samuel Buckman of Maldon & Elisabeth Wyman,
                                       Sept. 19, 1738
Samuel Farley & Mary Adams, both of Reading, Feb. 22, 1738
Jonathan Smith of Kingston & Sarah Peirson of
        Wilmington,   April 12, 1739
Jonathan Williams of Stoneham & Martha Peirce, Feb. 26, 1739

Jonathan Reed & Kezia Converse, Feb. 26, 1739
Joseph Upham of Reading & Elisabeth Richardson,

Feb. 28, 1739
Joshua Wright & Abigail Richardson, March 6, 1739
Jacob Snow & Abigail Wyman, April 8, 1740
Amos Lampson of Concord & Esther Thompson, April 8, 1740
Edward Dean & Patience Wyman, May 1, 1740
Joseph Barret of Reading & Rebekah Peirce of Wil-
mington, Oct. 21, 1740
John Wrightson & Jane Lunagin of Reading, Nov. 25, 1740
Nathaniel Wyman & Elisabeth Evans, April 10, 1740
David Evans of Reading & Hannah Nevers, Aug. 5, 1740
David Richardson & Mary Ann Dupee, Sept. 1, 1740
Timothy Kendall & Esther Walker, Nov. 13, 1740
James Kendall of Lancaster & Lydia Richardson,

March 1, 1740
James Fowl & Susannah Wyman, Oct. 22, 1741
Zachariah Symmes & Judith Eams, Oct. 29, 1741
Samuel Hathorn & Grace Walker, Feb. 11, 1741
Isaac Gleason & Elisabeth Harrington, June 26, 1740
Joseph Whittmore & Mary Merron, Dec. 24, 1741
Abiel Richardson & Sarah Smith, Jan. 14, 1742
Benjamin Nutting & Ruth Wood, March 3, 1742
Jonathan Reed & Mary Wyman, Sept. 9, 1742
Obadiah Sanders & Mary Snow, Sept. 14, 1742
Increase Winn & Elisabeth Knight, Oct. 5, 1742
Joseph Peirce & Abigail Green, Nov. 10, 1742
Nehemiah Wyman & Elisabeth Winn, Dec. 7, 1742
Thomas Barney & Martha Bruce, Jan. 13, 1742
Jacob Winn & Sarah Buck, March 2, 1742
Ebenezer Fisk & Katherine Baker, March 16, 174—
Thomas Richardson & Sarah Brooks, Oct. 18, 1742
Joshua Simonds & Jerusha Waters Feb. 1, 1742
James Perry of Scituate & Anna Carter, Jan. 11, 1742
John Lane of Bedford & Martha Flagg, Oct. 28, 1747
Thomas Alexander & Phebe Parker of Reading, May 17, 1748
Reuben Barret & Sarah Fletcher, of Chelmsford, June 19, 1751
Jacob Gold & Elisabeth Holding, of Stoneham, Nov. 25, 1751

Samuel Johnson & Hannah Wyman,	Dec. 25, 1751
Joseph Peirce & Susannah Gleason,	Feb. 21, 1751
Benjamin Bigelow & Mary Wyman,	June 13, 1751
Thos. Locke & Rebekah Lawrence,	June 27, 1751
Thos. Ross, Jr. & Peggy Turner,	Dec. 11, 1751
Simeon Spaulding & Abigail Willson,	Nov. 13, 1751
Joseph Wyman, Jr. & Mary Johnson,	April 16, 1752
Solomon Wood & Martha Johnson,	Sept. 20, 1752
Aaron Mason & Abigail Reed,	Oct. 24, 1752
William Buck & Mary Wyman,	Jan. 11, 1753
Elkanah Welch & Mercy Skilton,	Jan. 18, 1753
Benja. Flagg & Hannah Thompson,	March 8, 1753
Thos. Smith & Sarah Raymond,	April 12, 1753
Joshua Kendall & Susannah Johnson,	May 2, 1753
Josiah Walker & Mary How,	May 3, 1753
Eliphas Reed & Sarah Newell,	May 24, 1753
Isaiah Fay & Abigail Symonds,	May 29, 1753
Phineas Bloget & Joanna Lock,	Oct. 10, 1753
Amos Wyman & Elizabeth Peirce,	Feb. 21, 1754
William Hopkins & Rebekah Reed,	March 23, 1754
Lott Brewster & Lucy Reed,	April 4, 1754
Joshua Danforth & Keziah Reed,	July 25, 1754
Jono. Fowle & Mehitabel Rossum,	Aug. 1, 1754
Josiah Brown & Desire Batchellor, both of Bedford,	Nov. 6, 1754
William Prentice of Sutton & Abigail Willson of Bedford,	Oct. 29, 1754
John Nutting & Hannah Reed, both of Bedford,	July 10, 1754
Samuel Preston & Hannah Frost, both of Wilmington,	May 27, 1754
Thomas Wright & Elizabeth Chandler,	March 2, 1756
Abraham Ozburn & Elizabeth ———,	March 6, 1756
Oliver Richardson & Eunice Peirce,	March 30, 1756
Ebenezer Bearman & Sarah Lilly,	May 28, 1756
James Carr of Boston & Lois Converse,	Oct. 4, 1756
John Giles of Medford & Lydia Atwood,	Nov. 25, 1756
James Snow & Persis Reed,	Dec. 28, 1756
Jesse Richardson & Jemima Brooks,	Dec. 29, 1756
Jabez Carter, Jr. & Lydia Dean,	Feb. 17, 1757

Nathl. Gowing of Sutton & Patience Richardson,

	March 17, 1757
Ephraim Flagg of Wilmington & Ruth Converse,	———, 1757
Samuel Belknap & Abigail Lewis,	Dec. 15, 1757
John Munroe & Anna Kendall,	Dec. 23, 1757
Josiah Converse & Hepzibah Brooks,	March 28, 1758
Nathl. Evans & Mary Tidd,	April 18, 1758
Barnabas Richardson & Rebekah Tidd,	June 14, 1758
Nathl. Cutter & Sarah Wyman,	Oct. 21, 1758
John Cutter, Jr. & Martha Richardson,	Nov. 28, 1758
Edward Wyer of Charlestown & Abigail Reed,	Nov. 30, 1758
Walter Russell of Charlestown & Mary Wyman,	Dec. 14, 1758
Joseph Bruce & Abigail Wyman,	Dec. 20, 1758
Reuben Richardson & Jerusha Kendall,	March 3, 1757
Phineas Richardson & Hannah Richardson,	Feb. 27, 1759
Isaac Belknap & Bridget Richardson,	Jan. —, 1759
Edward Johnson & Sarah Willson,	Feb. 19, 1755
John Fay & Susannah Peirce,	March 1, 1755
James Hunnewell & Esther Reed,	March 27, 1755
Jabez Damon & Lucy Wyman,	April 3, 1755
Noah Wyman & Ruth Thompson,	June 18, 1755
David Willson & Judith Johnson,	July 9, 1755
Jonathan Fisk & Abigail Lock,	Sept. 4, 1755
Ebenezer Farly & Hepzibah Wyman,	Oct. 16, 1755
Nathaniel Brooks, Jr. & Esther Wyman,	Jan. 16, 1756
Ebenezer Johnson, Jr. & Deborah Bowles,	April 30, 1756
Ebenezer Carter, Jr. & Esther Wood,	March 21, 1757
Joseph Kendall & Sarah Johnson,	Aug. 18, 1757
Seth Breuister & Hannah Carter,	Sept. 13, 1757
Azel Johnson & Rebekah Willson,	Oct. 13, 1757
John Wyman & Mary Johnson,	Nov. 17, 1757
Jonathan Lawrence & Elizabeth Johnson,	Dec. 13, 1757
Ezra Wyman & Eunice Perkins,	May 3, 1758
Nathaniel Dunklee & Ruth Johnson,	Nov. 23, 1758
Ebenezer Lock & Lucy Wood,	Feb. 22, 1759
Jonathan Harwood & Judith Reed,	May 2, 1759
Abraham Alexander & Jerusha Thompson,	July 4, 1759
Joseph Johnson & Hannah Snow,	July 26, 1759

Joshua Reed & Rachel Wyman,	Nov. 28, 1759
Reuben Willson & Sarah Mann,	Feb. 21, 1760
Joseph Johnson, Jr. & Mrs. Ruth Kendall,	
William Cutter & Mary Trask,	April 17, 1760
Ezekiel Reed & Mary Lock,	
John Trull & Esther Wyman,	July 3, 1760
Edward Winn & Joanna Carter,	July 5, 1759
Ezra Thompson of Dunstable & Mary Wyman,	July 31, 1759
Benjamin Richardson & Rebekah Wyman,	Aug. 16, 1759
Jonathan Wyman, Jr. & Abigail Wright,	Nov. 29, 1759
Abijah Thompson & Esther Snow,	Dec. 13, 1759
Silas Richardson & Mary Cochrane,	Dec. 20, 1759
John Fowle & Bridget Burbean,	Dec. 28, 1759
Bartholomew Richardson & Sarah Converse,	April 10, 1760
Joshua Wyman & Mary Fowle,	April 24, 1760
Jesse Wyman & Esther Burbeen	May 1, 1760
William Johnson, Jr. & Sarah Kendall,	July 9, 1760
Daniel Thompson & Phebe Snow,	Oct. 29, 1760
Andrew Evans, Jr. & Sarah Center,	—— 25, 1760
Josiah Johnson & Sarah Gardner of Charlestown,	Dec. 2, 1760
Samuel Converse & Mary Tyler,	Oct. 9, 1760
Ebenezer Frost, Jr. of Cambridge & Ruth Wright,	
	March 18, 1761
Jeduthan Richardson & Mary Wright,	March 24, 1761
Nathaniel Wyman of Lancaster & Submit Brown,	
	March 14, 1761
Titus Vespatian & Peggy Gregorie, (negroes),	——, 1761
Jacob Watson of Cambridge & Mehitabel Skinner,	June 4, 1761
William Patton & Rebecca Bowen, of Billerica,	June 16, 1761
John Wright & Phebe Tidd,	June 18, 1761
William Abbot, Jr. of Andover & Elizabeth Tay,	June 18, 1761
Abel Richardson & Mary Thompson,	Nov. 26, 1761
John Parker of Dracutt & Lydia Reed,	Dec. 31, 1761
Jonathan Brooks & Ruth Fox (?),	Feb. 18, 1762
Amos Richardson & Bethia Richardson,	April 15, 1762
Zadock Richardson of Reading & Sall Brooks,	April 27, 1762
John Wesson of Reading & Mary Atwood,	July 8, 1762
Joshua Tay & Susannah Richardson,	Dec. 3, 1762

James Bruce & Mary Russell,	Jan. 13, 1763
Bill Center & Hannah Evans,	March 22, 1763
Joseph Boutell of Wilmington & Hannah Eaton,	April 12, 1763
Josiah Brooks & Betty Flagg,	Aug. 11, 1763
Edward Richardson & Sarah Tidd,	Oct. 6, 1763
Zachariah Brooks & Hannah Wilde,	Oct. 13, 1763
Samuel Belknap & Abigail Flagg,	Oct. 20, 1763
Nathaniel Hutchenson of Charlestown & Rebecca Center,	Dec. 15, 1763
Lazarus Hubbard & Abigail Gillmore,	Feb. 23, 1764
Zebadiah Wyman & Elisabeth Brooks	Jan. 6, 1764
John Winship of Cambridge & Ruth Carter,	April 26, 1764
Samuel Willson of Newton & Martha Wyman,	Oct. 4, 1764
Shubael Johnson & Mary Cutler,	Dec. 9, 1760
Timothy Willson & Rebekah Wyman,	Dec. 11, 1760
Jacob Caldwell & Sarah Perry,	Feb. 24, 1761
David Tweed & Mary Ross,	Nov. 3, 1761
James Johnson & Judith Willson,	Dec. 3, 1761
Simon Blodget of Lexington & Susanna Skilton,	Dec. 24, 1761
William Barron of Wilmington & Olive Johnson,	March 18 1762
Benjamin Man & Martha Dean,	March 18, 1762
Nathan Simonds & Abigail Cutler,	April 22, 1762
Simon Eames & Sarah Willson,	Sept. 2, 1762
Reuben Kimble & Sarah Kendall,	Nov. 25, 1762
Silas Wyman & Susanna Wood,	Dec. 30, 1762
Stephen Twist & Sybill Wyman,	Jan. 11, 1763
Thomas Fox & Elisabeth Reed,	March 31, 1763
John Townshend of Wilmington and Mary Reed,	April 12, 1763
Nathan Simonds & Abigail Reed,	June 2, 1763
Nathaniel Haywood & Amy Richardson of Billerica,	July 12, 1764
Jesse (?) Wyman of Billerica & Abigail Johnson,	Sept. 18, 1764
David Johnson & Mary Richardson,	Jan. 10, 1765
William Fox & Abigail Wyman,	June 6, 1765
Jonathan Wright & Ruth Wyman,	June 6, 1765
Thomas Reed & Hannah Richardson,	Aug. 22, 1765
Abraham Belknap of Newbury & Molly Richardson,	Oct. 6, 1765

John Williams of New Marlborough & Sarah Tot-
    tingham,   Oct. 24, 1765
Benjamin Wyman, Jr. & Elisabeth Swain,   Jan. 23, 1765
Joel Fisk of Cambridge & Ruth Reed,   Sept. 4, 1766
Hezkiah Richardson of Townshend & Elisabeth
    How,   Sept. 4, 1766
Giles Johnson & Elisabeth Brooks,   Oct. 14, 1766
Nathan Peirson of Wilmington & Rebeka Tay, Oct. 24, 1766
James Fowle, 3rd. & Ruhamah ——,   Oct. 23, 1766
Silas Simonds & Mrs. (?) Dean,   Nov. 20, 1766
Michael Taylor of Stoneham & Mary Richardson,
                              Nov. 25, 1766
Hiram Thompson & Bridget Snow,   Oct. 3, 1767
Ebenezer Whitney & Anna ————,   June 3, 1767
Caleb Richardson of Stoneham & Sarah Richardson,
                             July 9, 1767
Caleb Parker of Reading & Kezia Reed,   ————, 1767
Zachariah Richardson & Elizabeth Brooks, Dec. 30, 1767
Jonathan Green, Jr. & Dorcas Hay, both of Stone-
    ham,   May 9, 1769
John White & Susanna Eaton of Reading, April 28, 1768
Benjamin Peirce of Bedford & Ruth Smith, May 24, 1768
James Wright & Ruth Tidd,   Oct. 6, 1768
Benjamin Comee of Malden & Hannah Richardson,
                              Oct. 17, 1768
Joseph Skinner & Sarah Brooks,   Nov. 1, 1768
Joseph Knight of Stoneham & Sarah Holdin, April 6, 1769
Joseph ——— & Mary Richardson,   April 20, 1769
Samuel Tay & Mary Johnson,   April 27, 1769
Doctr. John Flagg & Susanna Fowle,   June 21, 1769
Leonard Richardson & Ruth Wright,   June 22, 1769
Oliver Richardson & Betty Tidd,   June 22, 1769
Abraham Skinner & Susana Brooks,   July 6, 1769
Samuel Brooks & Martha Peirce,   Aug. 8, 1769
Jonathan Monro & Abigail Kendall,   Aug. 10, 1769
Reul Baldwin & Kezia Wyman,   Oct. 4, 1769
John Flagg & Hannah Tidd,   Nov. 6, 1769
Samuel Marble, Jr. of Sutton & Lucretia Richd., Nov. 16, 1769

Samuel Tidd & Lucy Gardner of Charlestown,   Dec. 28, 1769
David Fitch of Bedford & Mary Fowle,   April 3, 1770
Zebulon Richardson & Abigail Tidd,   April 11, 1770
Elisha Sawyer of Lancaster & Mary Belknap,   May 3, 1770
Ichabod Richardson & Sarah Wyman,   June 6, 1770
Jonathan Fowle, Jr. & Sarah Richardson,   June 7, 1770
Moses Tyler & Ann Munro,   June 28, 1770
Deacn. Samuel Eames & Joanna Fasset of Bedford,
  July 4, 1770
Stephen Richardson & Martha Wyman,   July 9, 1770
David Eames & Deborah Holt,   July 24, 1770
James Thompson, Jr. and Esther Reed,   Sept. 25, 1770
Aaron Tay & Phebe Locke,   Oct. 4, 1770
Edmund Richardson & Mary Lathe,   March 19, 1771
Nathaniel Evans of Reading & Mary Hayden, March 12, 1771
Daniel Green Brown of Stoneham & Reuben Smith,
  May 2, 1771
Samuel Simes & Susanna Richardson,   June 4, 1771
Francis Johnson, Jr. & Abigail Fowle,   June 27, 1771
Samuel Winn & Mehitable Bruce,   Dec. 12, 1771
Josiah Johnson, Esq. & Susanna Brooks,   Aug. 5, 1771
Jonas Brooks & Joanna Cummings,   Nov. 19, 1771
William Tay 3d. & Hannah Pollard of Billerica,   July 26, 1771
Nathaniel Watt & Patience Wright,   April 21, 1772
Ebenezer Wade & Elizabeth Lathe,   May 26, 1772
Joseph Trask & Hannah Simonds of Bedford,   June 10, 1772
Loami Baldwin & Hannah Fowle,   July 9, 1772
Jesse Wright & Lydia Parker,   Aug. 4, 1772
Benjamin Converse & Sarah Wright,   Aug. 6, 1772
William Fox & Mary Wright,   Sept. 24, 1772
Doctr, Samuel Blodgett & Jean Gillam,   Oct. 2, 1772
Josiah Brown of Stoneham & Judith Richardson, Oct. 8, 1772
Isaac Warren of Medford & Abigail Brooks,   Oct. 29, 1772
Jethro ——— & Hannah Richardson,   Nov. 19, 1772
Reuben Reed & Elisabeth Barron,   Feb. 2, 1773
Josiah Wright & Lydia Bucknam of Cambridge, Feb. 2, 1773
James Atwood & Phebe Richardson,   Feb. 10, 1773
Ashael Simonds & Mary Tidd,   March 19, 1773

Thomas Skilton, Jr., & Elisabeth Johnson,	May 10, 1768
Timothy Twist & Elisabeth Winn,	July 12, 1768
Nathaniel Cutler, Jr. & Betty Bennet,	Sept. 20, 1768
Henry Reed & Prudence Haywood,	Sept. 22, 1768
Edward Twist & Sarah Eames,	Oct. 4, 1768
Eliphas Wyman & Sarah Johnson,	Dec. 20, 1768
Jonathan Fox & Surviah Tidd,	April 18, 1769
William Young & Elisabeth Johnson,	June 8, 1769
John Caldwell & Sarah Trask,	Aug. 3, 1769
Matthew Skilton & Sarah Wyman,	Sept. 6, 1769
Amos Lock & Sarah Lock,	Oct. 19, 1769
Jesse Simonds & Elisabeth Simonds,	Nov. 16, 1769
Nathan Dix & Elisabeth Wyman,	Nov. 16, 1769
Thomas Phillips & Hannah Reed,	Dec. 8, 1769
Thomas Dean, Jr. & Isabel Johnson,	April 4, 1770
Daze Skilton & Ruth Hartwell,	June 19, 1770
Benjamin Burton & Susannah Richardson,	Aug. 23, 1770
Benjamin Tay & Sybill Marrion,	Sept. 17, 1770
Joseph Lakin & Jerusha Simonds,	Oct. 23, 1770
Samuel Johnson & Rebecca Coñella,	Nov. 8, 1770
John Bruce, Jr. & Sarah Johnson,	Nov. 29, 1770
Benjamin Gloyd & Patience Dean,	Dec. 27, 1770
Joseph Whittemore & Ruhamah Holden,	Sept. 10, 1771
Jonas Wyman & Elisabeth Gleason,	Dec. 19, 1771
Benjamin Gleason & Deborah Beard,	Feb. 4, 1772
Benjamin Nutting & Lucy Wyman,	June 30, 1772
Nathaniel Wyman & Catherine Tufts,	July 2, 1772
Amos Blodgett & Ruth Cutler,	Oct. 7, 1772
Jacob Winn & Molly Twist,	Oct. 27, 1772
Jonathan Jaquith & Lydia Johnson,	Jan. 14, 1773

✓ SPRINGFIELD

June 2, 1641. A letter from the General Court to Mr. Pinchen and others of "Agawam now Springfield."

The following early marriages of Connecticut people are found on the Springfield, Mass. city records.

Marriage intentions are indicated by an *.

William Bradley of New Haven & Alice Prichard Dec. 18, 1644
John Pynchon and Anne Willis at Hartford,   Aug. 30, 1645
Joseph Parsons & Mary Bliss at Hartford,   Sept. 26, 1646
John Lumbert & Johan Prichard at New Haven, July 1, 1647
William Grave of Standford & Widow Dibble,   Oct. 7, 1646
George Lancton of Wethersfield & Widow Haynes, April 29, 1648
Nathaniel Gun of Hartford & Sarah Day,   Oct. 17, 1658
John Barbar of Winsor & Bathsheba Coggin   Sept. 2, 1663
John Root of Farmington & Mary Ashley,   Oct. 18, 1664
Richard Lord of Hartford & Mary Smyth,   April 25, 1665
Eliakim Hitchcock of New Haven & Sarah Mirrick, Nov. 4, 1667
Benj. Waite & Martha Leonard at Hartford,   June 8, 1670
Obadiah Cooley & Rebecca Williams at Windsor, Nov. 9, 1670
Joseph Harman of Southfield (?) and Hannah Philly
        of Windsor,   Jan. 22, 1673
David Lumbard of Springfield & Margerett Philly
        of Windsor,   April 7, 1675
James Pease of Enfield & Hannah Harmon of Suffield,
                                                  Oct. 18, 1695
William Pritchard & Rebeca Tailor, both of Suffield,
                                                  Jan. 22, 1695/6
Zachariah Booth of Endfield & Mary Harmon,   May 28, 1696
John Beamont & Abigail Eggleston of Endfield,   Oct. 29, 1696
Robert Old of Suffield & Elizabeth Lamb, widow, Jan. 23, 1696/7
Sammuel Gillett of Suffield & Rebecca Bancroft, Jan. 22, 1701/2
Henry Chapin Junr. of Springfield & Mary Garnzy,
        late of Milford,   Feb. 19, 1701
Francis Griswold of Paquanuck Colony, Conn., &
        Abigail Colton,   Dec. 8, 1703

Solomon Fere of S. & Lydia Peck of New Haven,
                                    Feb. 7, 1704/5
Samuel Bliss 3rd of S. & Elishebah Brace of Hartford,
                                    Oct. 3, 1705
Nathaniel Baldwin of Milford, Conn. and Alice
    Beamon,   Nov. 22, 1705
Caleb Munson of Wallingford, Conn., and Elisabeth
    Harman,   Mch. 26, 1706
David Burt of S. & Martha Heal of Enfield,   June 27, 1706
Eliakim Cooley Junr. of S. & Griswold Beckwith
    of Lyne, Conn.,   *Sept. 14, 1706
Timothy Hale of Suffield & Hannah Barber,   Jan. 2, 1706/7
Benj. Dorchester of Springfield & Abigail Meriman,
    of Wallinsford, Conn.,   Nov. 19, 1706
Jerome Dorchester, Jr. of Springfield and Lydia
    Preston of Wallinsford,   Nov. 19, 1706
Nathan Wheeler of Strafford, Conn. and Mary
    Stebbins,   Dec. 17, 1706
John Hitchcock of Colchester, Conn. & Elisabeth
    Jones,   Feb. 13, 1706/7
William Hendrick of Wallinsford, Conn. & Abigail
    Sikes,   Jan. 7, 1707/8
John Hale of S. & Elisabeth Clarke of New Haven, Dec. ——, 1707
Ebenezer Bliss Senr. of S. & Mary Gaylord of
    Winzor, Conn.,   *Jan. 10, 1707
Jonathan Smith of Farmington, Conn. & Hannah Bor-
    durtha,   *May 6, 1708
William Spurham of S. & Mary Winchell of
    Suffield,   *Feb. 19, 1708/9
Ebenezer Dewey of Lebanon, Conn., & Elisabeth
    Wright,   Nov. 8, 1709
John Fere of S. & Elisabeth Hall of Wallinsford, *May 13, 1710
Samuel Miller of Springfield, widower, and Kath-
    arine Halliday, late of Suffield, widow,   June 20, 1710
Joseph Loomis of Windsor & Mary Cooly,   June 28, 1710
Jonathan Curtiss, late of Lebanon, & now of Spring-
    field & Sarah Loomis of Lebanon, Conn.,   *July 22, 1710
Samuel Wright of S. & Mary Case of Lebanon, *Sept. 22, 1710

John Burt, Jr. & Abigail Rix of Windsor, *Oct. 7, 1710
Japhet Chapin of S. & Dorithy Root of Enfield, May 31, 1711
Samuel Cooley of S. & Mary Clark of Windsor, Oct. 24, 1711
William Niccoles of S. & Sarah Rumerry of Enfield,
*Mch. 15, 1711/12
Ebenezer Thomas of Lebanon & Sarah Warriner,
*Oct. 21, 1712
Born Vonhorn & Sarah Smith of Suffield, *Jan. 9, 1712/13
John Worthinton & Mary Prat of Seabrook, *April 25, 1713
Thomas Maccraney & Elisabeth Granger of Suffield,
*Dec. 24, 1713
Thomas Haill of Enfield & Mary Miller, *March 27, 1714
John Barber of S. & Sarah Smith of Suffield, *Nov. 19, 1714
David Burt & Widow Joanna Allin of Suffield, *July 2, 1715
John Bush of Endfield & Hannah Fowler, *Aug. 6, 1715
Joshua? Loamess of Windsor & Deborah Cooley,
*Sept. 8, 1715
John Miller & Priscilla Hail of Endfield, *Nov. 26, 1715
Nathaniel Miller of S. & Rebecca Pritchard of Suf-
field, Nov. 10, 1716
Henry Wolcat of Windsor & Abigail Cooley, Nov. 17, 1716
Samuel Lamb of Springfield & Ann Rizby of Hart-
ford, Feb. 2, 1716/17
Ebenezer Lombard of Springfield & Rachel Loomis
of Windsor, *May 17, 1717
James Beckwith of Lyme & Rebecca Lamb, *July 4, 1717
Daniel Grant of Windsor & Sarah Burt, Nov. 20, 1717
Benj. Smith, Jun. of S. & Sarah Colton of Enfield,
*Nov. 2, 1717
John Mors of S. & Sarah Tudor of Windsor, *Nov. 9, 1717
Rev. Steven Williams of S. & Abigail Davenport-
of Stanford, *April 26, 1718
Hezekiah Porter of Hartford & Sarah Wright, *June 19, 1719
Benj. Smith of S. & Sarah Smith of Farmington,
*April 28, 1720
Jabez Loomis of Windsor & Mary Fere, Dec. 28, 1720
Obadiah Miller of S. & widow Dorathy Chapen
of Enfield, *Mch. 18, 1720-21

Thomas Tery of S. & widow Mary Meacham of
Enfield,   May 18, 1722
Peletiah Bliss, Jr. & Ann Stoughton of Windsor, May —, 1722
Isaac Colton of S. & Esther Marshfield of Hartford,
                                      *June 6, 1722
Edward Kibbe of Enfield & widow Rebecca Cooley, Oct. 4, 1722
Thomas Miller of S. & Sarah Meekins of Hartford,
                                      *Dec. 29, 1722
Thomas Lamb of S. & Sarah Beckwith of Lime, *Oct. 5, 1723
Hezekiah Parsons of Enfield & Rebeca Burt,   *Nov. 15, 1723
Joseph Parsons of S. & Hannah Penne of Windsor,
                                      *April 18, 1724
Benj. Smith of S. & Mary Buttolyth of Simes-
berry,   *Oct. 7, 1725
Timothy Phelps of Suffield & Abigail Mirick,   Jan. 18, 1726
Benj. Smith of S. & widow Hannah Phelpes of Wind-
sor,   *Jan. 24, 1726
Benj. Crofoot of S. & Abigail Spencer of Suffield,
                                      Sept. 14, 1726
Jonathan Warriner of S. & Marcy Burnham of
Hartford,   Oct. 26, 1726
David Smith of Suffield & Experience Chapin,   Dec. 14, 1726
Paul Tompkins of Springfield & Abigail Hais of
Simesbury,   *Nov. 12, 1726
Samuel Chandler of Enfield & Hepziba Colton,   Dec. 22, 1726
Samuel Taylor of S. & Joanna Smith of Suffield,
                                      *Nov. 26, 1726
Thomas Bliss of S. & Lois Cadwell of Hartford, April 21, 1727
Rev. Samuel Hopkins & Esther Edwards of Wind-
sor,   *May 13, 1727
Ezekiel Mighill of Killingley & Elisabeth Hitch-
cock,   *May 22, 1727
Ebenezer Thomas of Lebanon & Sarah Warriner,   Dec. 1, 1712
Henry Woolcut of Windsor & Abigail Cooley,   Dec. 27, 1716
Thomas Hale of Enfield & Mary Miller,   June 23, 1714
John Davis of Coventry & Hannah Root of West-
field,   Dec. 30, 1714
Josiah Farnam of Saybrook & Sarah Atcheson, May 10, 1725

Samuel Meacham & Sarah Pope, both of Enfield,   Nov. 7, 1726

David Chandler of Enfield & Sarah Keep,   Jan. 4, 1728

Azariah Allen of Enfield & Martha Burt,   *Nov. 30, 1727

Obadiah Miller of S. & Mary Purkins of Enfield,
                                      *Sept. 14, 1728

Jonathan Bird of Farmington & Huldah Lamb,
                                  *March 6, 1728/9

Samuel Crowfoot of Springfield & Johannah Scovil
  of Middletown,   *Sept. 11, 1729

John Peale of Enfield & Elizabeth Bliss (widow), Nov. 12, 1729

David Norton of Enfield & Mary Fowler,   *Oct. 23, 1730

Abel Leonard of S. & Esther Austin of Suffield,   Dec. 11, 1730

Isaac Griswold of Killingsworth & Jemima Keep, April 13, 1731

Hezekiah Porter of Windsor & Eunice Colton,   *May 6, 1731

  Banns forbidden,   May 11, 1731

John Frost of Springfield & Damarus Howard of
  Stafford,   May 24, 1731

Joseph Bewell of Killingsworth & Maud Anna Colton,
                                      April 10, 1733

John Jones of S. & Hannah Perkins of Enfield, *Nov. 2, 1732

Abraham Peale of Enfield & Abigail Warner,   August 28, 1733

James Rising of Suffield & Lydia Killum,   Feb. 20, 1733-4

Ebenezer Colton of S. & Deborah Chandler of-
  Enfield,   *July 16, 1733

Jonathan Purchase of Wallingford & Margaret
  Worthington,   *Dec. 1, 1733

David Rose of Durham & Elizabeth Fowler,   *Aug. 24, 1734

Luke Day of S. & Jerusha Skinner of Windsor,   *Nov. 9, 1734

Nicholas Holbrook of Lebanon & Mary Bliss,   Feb. 3, 1736

David Rockwell of Windsor & Margaret Vanhorne,
                                        Feb. 11, 1736

Christopher Fowler of S. and Experience Hollibert
  of Woodbury,   *April 10, 1736

Samuel Cutler of Killingsly & Huldah Lamb,   *May 20, 1736

Ephraim Pierson of Windsor & Abigail Dorchester, Nov. 1, 1736

John Pynchon of S. & widow Mary Levit of Suffield,   *March 19, 1737

Ebenezer Bliss of Lebanon & Rebecca Colton, May 7, 1737
Jonathan Allen of Suffield & Rebecca Cooper, Sept. 15, 1737
Jonathan Wright of Windsor & Abiah Keep, June 9, 1737
Silas Kent of Suffield & Jerusha Miller, March 15, 1738
Timothy Scott of Windsor & Thankful Dorchester,
*Dec. 9, 1738
William Hale of Enfield & widow Mary Barker, *Dec. 15, 1738
Joseph Pinney of Windsor & Sarah Bartlet, *Feb. 3, 1738/9
Aaron Hitchcock of S. & Experience Kent of Suf-
field, *Aug. 6, 1739
Thomas Perkins of Enfield & Eunice Bidwell, *Dec. 2, 1739
James Ferman of Enfield & Johanna Stebbins,
*Jan. 7, 1739/40
Caleb Ely of S. & Mary Edwards of Hartford, *May 2, 1740
James Wood of Enfield & widow Thankful Sikes,
*July 17, 1740
William Wright of Middletown & Lucy Richardson,
*Feb. 10, 1740-41
Ebenezer Redford of Killingsworth & Hannah Col-
ton, *Aug. 3, 1741
Noah Bissell of Windsor & Silence Burt, Oct. 28, 1741
Daniel Phelps of Uper-Houseatonick & Eunice
Parsons, *Apl. 10, 1742
John J. Shaim of Windsor & Ruth Ball, *June 19, 1742
Nathan Bliss of S. & Mary Cooley of Somers, *Oct. 30, 1742
Samuel Roberts of Canaan & Lydia Purchase, *Mar. 4, 1743
Jedediah Stow of Middletown & Elizabeth Day,
*April 19, 1743
Daniel Foot of Colchester & Margaret Parsons, *May 7, 1743
Samuel Pease of Enfield & Zerviah Chapin, *May 19, 1743
Caleb Johnson of Middletown & Anne Downing, *Aug. 12, 1743
Jonathan Chapin of S. & Mehitable Chandler of
Enfield, *Dec. 8, 1743
Luke Hitchcock 3rd of S. & Abigail Norton of Kens-
ington, *May 26, 1744
Ezekiel Loomis of Lebanon & Elizabeth Colton, March 1, 1742/3
Aaron Stebbins of S. & Mary Wood of Somers,
*June 21, 1744

Rev. Noah Mirick of S. & Abigail Brainerd of Had-
dam,   *Sept. 27, 1744
Daniel Birchard of Norwich & Elizabeth Cooley, Oct. 8, 1745
Benjamin Rising of Cornwall & Lydia Hooker, *Mch. 14, 1744
Jonathan Chapin of S. & Sarah Morse of Walling-
ford,   *June 10, 1745
Jacob Brooker of Killingsworth & Miriam Philips,
                                                   *Aug. 2, 1745
Simeon Phillips of S. & Hannah ——— of Suffield,
                                                   *Mch. 5, 1745
Elias Camp of Middletown & Ruth Taylor,   July 1, 1746
Isaac Kibbee Junr. of Enfield & Eunice Miller, Mch. 11, 1746
Wm. Clark of Colchester & Mary Parsons,   May 12, 1747
Samuel Trescott of Canaan & Hannah Purchase, July 23, 1747
Joseph Warriner of S. & Sarah Howard of Mans-
field,   *Nov. 28, 1747
Titus Sikes of Suffield & Rhoda Miller,   June 16, 1748
Henry Curtis of Coventry & Widow Elizabeth Ed-
wards,   Oct. 28, 1748
Thomas Colton of Springfield & Deborah Dickenson
of Saybrook,   *Sept. 15, 1748
Eleazer Chapin of S. & Elenor Smith of Suffield,
                                                   *Oct. 13, 1748
Joseph Chapin, Jr. of S. & Elizabeth Field of Som-
ers,   *Dec. 8, 1748
Peletiah Glover of S. & Widow Hannah Burt of
Hartford,   *March 31, 1749
Ruben Woolworth of Suffield & Abigail Winchel, Dec. 7, 1749
Joseph Sexton, Jr. of Somers & Rebeckah Chapin, Nov. 8, 1749
Ebenezer Burt of S. & Elizabeth Bond of Somers, *Oct. 4, 1749
George Wood, Jr. of Somers & Sarah Morgan,   Jan. 11, 1750
Josiah Chapin of S. & Martha Woolcott of Windsor,
                                                   *Oct. 21, 1749
Elijah Williams of Enfield & Mrs. Margaret Pynch-
on,   Jan. 1, 1749-50
Henry Bliss of S. & Rubie Brewster of Lebanon, *Dec. 22, 1749
Deacon John Pierce of New Castle & Hannah Burt,
                                                   *March 3, 1749

Benajah Stevenson of S. & Almy Long of Winsdor,
*April 20, 1750
Gideon Morgan of S. & Rachel Kibbee of Enfield,
*July 19, 1750
Samuel Stebbins, Jr. of S. & Sarah Jones of Som-
ers,   *Oct. 18, 1750
Phinehas Pelton of Middletown & Esther Seldon,
*Oct. 17, 1750
Gideon Jones of S. & Rebeckah Parsons of Enfield,
*Oct. 26, 1750
Nathan Phillips of S. and Esther Meacham of Suf-
field,   *Feb. 16, 1750
Henry Chandler of Enfield & Mercy Colton,   *April 2, 1751
Preserved Leonard of S. & Sarah Keep of Westford,
*April 19, 1751
Samuel Kent, Jr. of Suffield & Mrs. Thamar Barber,
*July 20, 1751
Benjamin Stebbins, Jr. of S. & Seabury Minor
of Lyme,   *Oct. 4, 1751
Simeon Hitchcock of S. & Rachel — of Chichester,
*Nov. 30, 1751
Hezekiah Cooley of S. & Charity Clark of Lebanon,
*Jan. 11, 1752
Moses Hale of S. & Mary Meacham of Enfield,   *Jan. 25, 1752
Ebenezer Bliss, 4th of S. & Mary Boothof Enfield,
*Feb. 12, 1752
William Hancock of S. & Hannah Long of Windsor,
*March 14, 1752
Josiah Farnum of S. & Rebeckah Gillet of Suffield,
*May 15, 1752
Joseph Hitchcock of S. & Sarah Morris of Somers,
*May 23, 1752
John Willard of Guilford & Mary Horton, 3rd,   *Aug. 1, 1752
Noah Bouker of Somers & Hepzibah Willard,   *Jan. 2, 1753
Abel Morley of S. & Mary Miller of Somers, *March 17, 1753
Luke Parsons of Somers & Sarah Chapin,   *April 3, 1753
George Hitchcock of S. & Hannah Johnson of Mid-
dletown,   *June 9, 1753

Stephen Cooley of S. & Mary Field of Enfield,
*Sept. 26, 1753
John Morgan, Jr. of S. & Dorothy Belding of Suf-
field, *Oct. 12, 1753
Ebenezer Selden of S. & Jerusha Pomroy of Suf-
field, *Oct. 24, 1753
John Frost of S. & Deborah Harris of Road-
town, *March 29, 1754
William Stebbins of S. & Mrs. Thankful Pond of
Branford, *March 29, 1754
Joseph Pomroy of Suffield & Dorcas Atchinson, Jr.,
*May 10, 1754
George Pynchon of S. & Mrs. Abigail Pease of En-
field, *July 6, 1754
Benoni Chapin of S. & Esther Lewis of Farming-
ton, *July 20, 1754
Stephen Warriner of S. & Hepzibah Chandler of
Enfield, *Oct. 5, 1754
Daniel Hancock of S. & Lucy Long of Windsor,
*Oct. 12, 1754
Abiel Abbot of Windsor & Mrs. Abigail Field, *Oct. 19, 1754
Israel Phelps of S. & Priscilla Jones of Somers,
*Nov. 22, 1754
Samuel Weld of S. & Abigail Rumral of Enfield,
*Feb. 22, 1755
Noah Webster of Lebanon & Margaret Chapin, *May 8, 1755
Hezekiah May of Weathersfield & Mary Lamb, *June 28, 1755
David Bissell of Windsor & Sarah Williston, *Sept. 26, 1755
Samuel Lamb, Jr. of S. & Hannah Dudley of Say-
brook, *Dec. 25, 1755
John Farnam of S. & Sarah Dunk of Saybrook,
*April 8, 1756
Rev. Josiah Whitney of Pomfret & Mrs. Lois Breck,
*July 20, 1756
Edmund Lewis of Stratford & Martha Leonard,
*Sept. 24, 1756
Daniel Kent of Suffield & Sarah Bedortha, *Sept. 29, 1756
James Nelson of Simsbury & Ruth Stevenson, *Oct. 13, 1756

Abiel Pease of Somers & Esther Cooley, *April 14, 1757
John Fox of Weathersfield & Mercy Day, *Sept. 24, 1757
Nathan Chapin of S. & Mary Smith of Hunts-
    town, *Nov. 16, 1757
Wm. Welch of Windsor & Thankful Wright, *Nov. 18, 1757
Simeon Granger of S. & Abigail Dudley of Say-
    brook, *Nov. 26, 1757
Samuel Wright of S. & Mary Adams of Suffield,
    *Feb. 3, 1758
Thomas King, Jr. of Suffield & Lucy Flower, *Feb. 3, 1758
Elihu Dwight of Somers & Eunice Horton, *March 24, 1758
Noah Ball of S. & Anna Granger of Suffield, *April 5, 1758
John Anderson of Windsor & Mary Cooley, *Nov. 28, 1758
Samuel Raynolds of Somers & Mrs. Martha Williams,
    *Dec. 15, 1758
Sampson Wood of S. & Thankful Field of Somers,
    *Jan. 5, 1759
Joseph Dorchester of S. & Ruth Dickinson of Som-
    ers, *Jan. 25, 1759
Elijah Leonard of S. & Anne Adams of Suffield,
    *Feb. 8, 1759
Asahel Kent of Suffield & Mary Barnard Brooks,
    *April 13, 1759
Samuel Meacham of S. & Deborah Bliss of Som-
    ers, *April 13, 1759
Roger Woolcott, Jr., of Windsor & Mrs. Eunice Ely,
    *May 3, 1759
Daniel Chandler, Jr. of Enfield & Esther Bliss, *June 10, 1759
Capt. Luke Bliss of S. & Mrs. Rebeckah Stough-
    ton of Windsor, Oct. 1, 1759
Charles Wright of Enfield & Dinah Terry, *Oct. 11, 1759
Jonah Gleason of Enfield & Sarah Hale, *Nov. 9, 1759
Luke Parsons, Jr. of Somers & Elizabeth Ely, *July 11, 1760
Ebenezer Taylor, Jr. of S. & Ruth Spencer of Somers,
    *Oct. 9, 1760
Aaron Parsons & Mary Fisk, both of Somers, June 14, 1746
Thomas McClintock of S. & Sarah King of Kings
    town, Oct. 29, 1747

BERKSHIRE COUNTY

Marriages found on the records of the Clerk of Courts at Pittsfield.

✓ ADAMS

Oct. 15, 1778. The plantation called East Hoosuck established as Adams.

Theophilus Luther & Rhobe Smith,	Jan. 7, 1787
Luke Brown & Mary Butler,	Feb. 22, 1787
Nathan Sherman & Rebeckah Williams, both of Bullocks,	Mch. 8, 1787
Geo. Richmond of Wallingford, Vt. & Rachel Haile,	Mch. 18, 1787
Reuben Sheldon & Jain Fenner,	Ap. 2, 1787
Moses Parsons & Cloe Bridges,	Ap. 5, 1787
Sam'l Catlin of Litchfield, Ct. & Esther White,	Ap. 8, 1787
Paul Griffiths & Margaret Burden,	Ap. 19, 1787
Justus Collings of Manchester, Vt. & Cynthia Baker,	Aug. 26, 1787
Wm. Williams, Jr. & Anna Rogers, both of Bullock, grant,	Nov. 22, 1787
Benj. Buffington & Huldah Curtis,	Dec. 2, 1787
David Yean? & Lydia Prescott,	Dec. 9, 1787
Josiah Alger, Jr. & Joanna Yean ?,	Dec. 27, 1787
Sam'l Power & Lydia Bennet,	Jan. 7, 1788
Caleb Vincen? of Little Hoosick, N. Y. & Nancy Samson,	Jan. 13, 1788
Moses Woolcot & Olive Russel of Lanesboro,	Oct. 27, 1787
Perygreene Buck & Abigail Brown,	Oct. 31, 1787
Abraham Balm & Mary Ash, of the Province Gore,	Nov. 1, 1787
Jenkes Seamons & Rebeckah Luther,	Jan. 27, 1788
Alexander Conke Maset & Olive Hinmon,	Feb. 21, 1788
David Brown & Mary Carpenter,	Mch. 9, 1788
Thos. Jenkes & Mary Herenden ?,	Mch. 9, 1788

Henry Olden of Shaftsbury & Lois Richardson,	Mch. 20, 1788
Rufus Werden & Tabitha Cook,	Mch. 16, 1788
John Russel & Barbara Harris,	Mch. 27, 1788
Gilbert Hathaway & Vashti Seymour, both of Bullocks Grant,	Ap. 6, 1794
Elisha Kingsley & Hannah Anthony,	June 24, 1792
Wm. Stead & Susanna Cole,	Aug. 16, 1792
Jeremiah Smith, Jr. & Rachel Hathaway,	Nov. 1, 1792
Isaac Jones & Hannah Henry of New Ashford,	Jan. 7, 1793
Thos. Bazil Wills of Varman Town & Elisa Tibbits of Windsor,	Feb. 7, 1793
Sam'l Bowen & Mercy Slocum ?,	Ap. 25, 1793
Joseph Goodenow of Pownal & Filey Fullar,	May 13, 1793
Benajah Alger & Mary Reynolds,	July 10, 1793
Laban Jencks & Prudence White of Cheshire,	Sept. 22, 1793
Chas. Briggs & Priscilla Aldridge,	Sept. 29, 1793
Jabez Safford of Windsor & Azubah Hickson of Cheshire,	Sept. 29, 1793
James Mason & Hopy Smith,	Oct. 20, 1793
Joshua Wells of Cheshire & Casandra Callam,	Dec. 15, 1793
Robt. Nesbit, Jr. & Rachel Reed,	Dec. 23, 1793
Jas. Fullar & Elisa. Alsworth,	Jan. 3, 1794
Ephraim Whipple & Sarah Mixture,	Jan. 26, 1794
John Brown of A. & Phebe Brayton of Cheshire,	Jan. 30, 1794
Jesse Scott of Cheshire & Susanah Chapin,	Feb. 7, 1794

CHESHIRE

Mar. 14, 1793. Parts of Adams, Lanesborough, Windsor, and the district of New Ashford established as Cheshire.

Caleb Fisk & Lydia Whitaker,	June 16, 1793
Isaac Hatheway of Adams & Hannah Fuller,	Aug. 20, 1793
Peckham Barber & Sarah Carpenter,	Dec. 12, 1793
Aberdeen Smith & Nancy Mixture,	Jan. 12, 1794
Joseph Tibbitts & Sarah Merril,	Mch. 2, 1794

Jas. Grinman of Stephentowne & Lois Mason,   Nov. 14, 1793
Solomon Powel of Lanesboro & Ruth Miller,   Dec. 5, 1793
Isaac Burdon of C. & Susanah Rice of New Ashford,   1794
Ziba Newland ? & Lucy Henry of New Ashford, Mch. 2, 1794
Welcom Eddy & Roby Bennet,   Nov. 1793
Gott. Writt & Betsy Lane,   Feb. 18, 1794
Ebenezer Sergeant of W. Springfield & Betsey Ad-
    ams,   May 4, 1794
Jona. Lincoln of Lanesboro & Amy Northrup,   Dec. 11, 1794
Pardon Arnold & Sally Carpenter,   May 4, 1794
Curtis King & Cynthia Hillard,   Jan. 8, 1795
Seth Sherman & Anna Wilber, both of Bullocks
    Grant,   Sept. 11, 1794
Jacob Kennedy & Urania (?) Miner,   Sept. 25, 1794
Benj. Cooper & Jerusha Bucklin, both of Adams, Nov. 13, 1794
John Russell & Cynthia Brown, both of Adams, Dec. 25, 1794
Abijah Willington & Sarah Matthewson,   Jan. 25, 1795
Howland Kimball & Hannah Brown,   Mch. 5, 1795
Asa Southwick & Elisabeth Sherman, both of Ad-
    ams,   Ap. 2, 1795
Waterman Manchester & Lydia Daily, both of Ad-
    ams,   June 11, 1794
Elisha Pettebone & Elisabeth Blakesley, both of
    Lanesboro,   July 11, 1794
Nathan Stoddard & Sibbill Cole,   Nov. 11, 1794
Smith Grosvenor & Betsy Burden,   Jan. 8, 1795
Wm. Hathaway of Bullocks Grant & Anna Barker,
                                             Feb. 8, 1795
David Willington & Phebe Tibbits,   Feb. 22, 1795
Selah Root & Eunice Russell,   Mch. 25, 1795

DALTON

Mar. 20, 1784.   The New Plantation of Ashuelet Equivalent established as Dalton.

Sam'l Brown of Chesterfield & Olive Brown,   Dec. 6, 1787
Jacob Chamberlain & Dolly Cleveland,   Nov. 30, 1788
Caleb Goff & Lydia Skinner,   Mch. 6, 1789
Thad. Hulbert, late of Pittsfield, now of Dalton, &
    Mahitabel Gallup,   Mch. 22, 1789
Jesse Saxton of Pittsfield & Anna Candell, alias Cong-
    don, late of Washington & Pittsfield,   Ap. 9, 1789
Mr. Nath'l Hill & Miss Mercy Goodrich,   June 27, 1790
Dr. John Wright & Sally Cady,   Aug. 22, 1790
Abner Mason of Lanesboro & Priscilla Gallup,   Oct. 3, 1790
Joel Bradley & Lucy Dewey, both of Lanesboro, Nov. 24, 1790
Jared Foot, Jr.? & Lucinda Jennings,   Nov. 25, 1790
Amos Spofford & Spedee? Lawrence,   Dec. 1, 1791
Azariah Haskin of Pittsfield & Patty Merriman, Feb. 19, 1792
Mr. Levi Day of Freehold, N. Y. & Albiah Chamber-
    lain,   Feb. 23, 1792
Sam'l Baldwin Jr. of Windsor & Lois Chamberlin, Feb. 23, 1792
Simeon Read of Windsor & Thankful Hovey,   Mch. 8, 1792
Solomon Bacon & Rebeckah Gallup,   Ap. 15, 1792
Sam'l Armstrong & Grace Brown,   Oct. 25, 1792
Dan. Chamberlain of D. & Rhoda Chamberlain of
    Pittsfield,   July 10, 1794
Reuben Bill & Rhoda Cheeseman ?   Sept. 2, 1794
Elijah Jones of Stephentown, N. Y. & Sybil Newell,
                                            Dec. 29, 1794
Aaron Cleveland & widow Lydia Wright,   Oct. 27, 1795

✓ EGREMONT

Feb. 13, 1760. Certain common lands lying West of Sheffield established as the district of Egremont.

Dr. Amasa Bucknum & Mrs. Anna Karner,	Ap. 12, 1793
Ebenezer Smith & Mrs. Cloe Kellogg,	Aug. 8, 1793
Aaron Gale & Mrs. Achsah Race or Raw?,	Oct. 13, 1793
Jacob Southwell & Mrs. Sylva Karner,	Oct. 14, 1793
Arba Doolittle & Mrs. Prudence Stephenson,	Ap. 27, 1794

✓ GREAT BARRINGTON

June 30, 1761. Part of Sheffield established as Great Barrington.

Isaac Van Dusen, 3rd & Christian Spoor,	Jan. 15, 1789
John Van Deusen, Jr. & Hannah Hawk,	Feb. 7, 1789
Andrew Burghart & Catharine Van Deusen,	Feb. 26, 1789
Dan'l Younglove & Peggy Bolton,	Aug. 24, 1788
Wm. Pixley, Jr. & Lydia Root,	Ap. 9, 1789
Silas Jones & Sarah Laird,	May 20, 1788?
Jacob Walker & Dinah Ogden,	Jan. 25, 1787
Andrew Loomis & Hannah Stewart,	Jan. 8, 1789

HANCOCK

July 2, 1776. The plantation called Jericho established as Hancock.

Griffin Reynolds, son of Jas. & Marthy Gardner, da. of
    Nath'l,   Sept. 22, 1793
Willard, son of Wm. Smith & Hannah & Amy, da.
    of Palmer Gardner,   Dec. 26, 1793

Isaac, son of Widow Hadsell? & Isabel, da. of Thos. Eldred,	Aug. 7, 1794
Josiah Perry & Rebecca Church,	Dec. 4, 1794
Ward King & Sarah Walker,	Feb. 26, 1795
Elisha Becket of Stephentown & Mary Walker,	Feb. 26, 1795
Stephen Potter of Cheshire & Esther Harwood of Windsor,	Oct. 27, 1794

LANESBOROUGH

June 21, 1765. The Plantation of New Framingham established as Lanesborough.

Francis Gitteau, Jr. & Hannah Wilson,	Aug. 20, 1789
Seeley Bennet & Amy R ———,	Sept. 17, 1789
Nathl. B. Torrey & Sally Hall,	Nov. 8, 1789
Augustus Tripp & Polly Walker,	Nov. 26, 1789
Philo Pittibone & Lucy Barton,	Dec. 31, 1789
Alexander Sloan & Sally Lyon,	Dec. 31, 1789
Alvin Wolcott & Lois Terrill,	Jan. 7, 1790
Wait Squier & Hannah Powel,	Jan. 18, 1790
Levi Warren & Abigail Hammond,	Feb. 18, 1790
Ezra Hoyt & Sarah Smith,	Feb. 27, 1790
Asahel Jarvis & Abigail Griswold,	Mch. 18, 1790
John Seymour & Mary Squier,	Mch. 25, 1790
Sam'l Penfield & Elizabeth Farnum?,	Ap. 7, 1790
Jas. Green & Hope Short,	Ap. 8, 1792
Lyman Warren & Mercy Whipple,	May 29, 1792
John Barker & Betsy Leland,	Oct. 17, 1792
John Mason & Phebe Starkweather,	Nov. 19, 1792
Isaac Williams & Sally Westcoat,	Dec. 22, 1792
Wm. Card & Elisa Brundage,	Jan. 13, 1793
Luther Hill & Mercy Clark,	Feb. 13, 1794
Reuben Hinman & Dasy Phittiplan?	Feb. 27, 1794
Sam'l Jencks & Lurana Blin ?,	Mch. 30, 1794
Ezra Barker & Sally B. Witt,	Mch. 17, 1793
Sam'l Ingalls & Anne Wheeler,	Nov. 30, 1793

LENOX

Feb. 26, 1767. Part of Richmont established as the district of Lenox.

Simeon Hayward of Lenox & Chloe Galpin of Stock-bridge,	Nov. 25, 1784
Ephraim Hollister of Lee & Laurana Canfield,	Dec. 15, 1785
Jacob Washburn & Phebe Northrup,	Ap. 13, 1786
Edward Perrin & Lydia Nash,	Oct. 29, 1786
Wm. Lovelon ? & Martha Stebbins,	Oct. 30, 1786
Stephen Leonard & Lois Willcox, both of Lee,	Jan. 10, 1788
John Briggs & Martha Gibbs,	Jan. 1, 1789
Wm. Hollister of Pittsfield & Ora Willard,	Oct. 28, 1790
Justus Baker & Ruth Porter,	Dec. 1, 1791

MOUNT WASHINGTON

June 21, 1779. The plantation called Tauconnuck Mountain established as Mount Washington.

Henry Ryan & Huldah Lord,	Nov. 30, 1794

PERU

July 4, 1771. The new plantation called Number Two established as Patridgefield.
June 19, 1806. The name of the town of Patridgefield changed to Peru.

Peter Stanton ? & Lucy Loomer,	Nov. 12, 1786
Jedediah Ross of Dalton & Phebe Hibbard,	Dec. 24, 1795

PITTSFIELD

April 21, 1761. The plantation called Pontoosuck established as Pittsfield.

Jas. Colt & Sally Root,	May 8, 1791
₵ Calvin Wood & Diantha Tuttle,	Oct. 23, 1791
Matthew Millard, Jr. & Sopha Smith,	Nov. , 1791
Adin Denning & Patty Phelps,	Nov. 29, 1791
Elisha Tracy & Jane Fisher,	Dec. 5, 1791
Elijah Bagg & Sally Churchill,	Dec. 22, 1791
Robt. Stanton & Anne Tracy,	Jan. 7, 1792
Rufus Johnson & Anne Merrill,	Feb. 7, 1792
James? Robbins & Hannah Fairfield,	Feb. 9, 1792
⌇ Joel Wood & Betsey Howard,	Feb. 9, 1792
Henry Collins & Lucy Noble,	
Martin Bagg & Alive Goodrich,	Mch. —, 1792

TYRINGHAM

Mar. 6, 1762. The new plantation called Number One established as Tyringham.

Manassa Fairbanks & Otave? Taylor,	———, 1793
Elijah Hall & Elizabeth Abbott,	——— 1793
⌐ Sam'l Barber, 3rd & Widow Eunice Bradly,	——— 1793
Thos. Canfield & Martha Underwood,	——— 1793
Sam'l Thompson, Jr. & Jemima Chapin,	——— 1793
Saml. Bunn & Isabel Brann,	——— 1793
Reuben Webb & Polly Perkins,	——— 1793
Geo. Brown & Jerusha Markham,	——— 1793
Loudowick Gardner & Christian Gearfield,	——— 1793
Sam'l Hulet & Susannah Wadsworth,	——— 1789
Thos. James & Prudence Heath,	——— 1789
Reuben Davis & Polly Abbott,	from Apr. 1790 to 1791

John Morcey ? & Jemime Hurd,	Ap. 1790-1791
Reuben Phillip & Zillah Kimball,	Ap. 1790-1791
Rev. Jonathan Judd & Wid. Ruth Bidwell,	Ap. 1790-1791
Lawrence Fosdick & Wealthy Warren,	Ap. 1790-1791
Timothy Alden & Lois Willcox,	Ap. 1790-1791
James Davidson & Hannah Baldwin,	Ap. 1790-1791
Jeremiah Leaming ? & Sarah Hawley,	Ap. 1790-1791
Rodman Clark & Huldah Leaming,	Ap. 1790-1791
Stephen Markham & Dolly Joslin,	Ap. 1790-1791
Briant Milliman & Susannah Rathbun,	from 1791 to 1792
Ebenezer Jackson & Hannah Brewer,	fr. 1791-1792
Barzillai Northrup & Margory Rockwood,	fr. 1791-1792
Joshua Stowers ? & Phebe Rockwood,	fr. 1791-1792
Reuben Marsh & Lydia Rathbun,	fr. 1791-1792
Roswell Stanton & Anna Abbott,	fr. 1791-1792
Benj. Howard & Betsey Howard,	fr. 1791-1792
Abraham Milliman & Elizabeth Park,	fr. 1791-1792
Joshua Hervey & Betsey Lewis,	fr. 1791-1792
Simeon Culver & Anna Green,	fr. 1791-1792
Jonathan Townsend & Louis Scripture,	fr. 1791-1792
Lemuel Tillotson & Temperance Hawley,	fr. 1791-1792
Wm. Jencks ? & Sally Cook,	fr. 1791-1792
Ede Mercy ? & Levine Culver,	from Ap. 1792 to 1793
John Curtis & Naomi Spring,	Ap. 1792-1793
Noah Allen, Jr. & Elizabeth Larned Partridge,	Ap. 1792-1793
Abraham Northrup & Widow Anna Culver,	Ap. 1792-1793
Silas Clark & Rebekah Chapman,	Ap. 1792-1793
Nathan Underwood & Dianthy Curtis,	Ap. 1792-1793
Noah Langdon, Jr. & Phebe Ward,	Ap. 1792-1793
Geo. Paterson & Sylvia Tillotson,	Ap. 1792-1793
Darius Powell & Electa Hall,	Ap. 1792-1793
Allen Taylor & Polly Myre,	Ap. 1792-1793
Joel David & Sally Johnson,	Ap. 1792-1793
Barnabas Hoos ? & Parmele Stone,	Ap. 1792-1793
Ezekiel Wadsworth & Zada Taylor,	Ap. 1792-1793
Jonathan Foot & Temperance Hawley,	Ap. 1792-1793
Dan'l Chapman, Jr. & Eunice Hall,	Ap. 1792-1793
Justus Markham & Submit House,	Ap. 1792-1793

Dan'l Hobbs, Jr. & Sally Leaming,   Ap. 1792-1793
Varnum Gardner & Mitchell Tuttle,   1794
Isaac Cowles & Polly Brookins,   1794
Ebenezer Hall & Elizabeth McGregory,   1794
Jonathan Tuttle & Anna Battle,   1794
Isaac Doud of New Haven, Ct. & Polly Johnson, June 4, 1795

WEST STOCKBRIDGE

Mar. 9, 1774, Part of Stockbridge established as the district of West Stockbridge.

Dan. Williams & Mary Park,
Obadiah French & Sarah Warner,
Jeremiah Minclair & Margaret Thomas,   1789
Theodore Devereux & Hannah Moffit,   May 27, 1790
Sam'l Dryer & Philene Robbins,   Nov. 8, 1790
Ezra Wilmarth & Polly Boughton,   Feb. 17, 1791
Joseph Jackson & Margaret French,   Mch. 7, 1793
Azor Boughton & Katharine Rees,   Feb. 7, 1793
Enoch Wilcox & Nancy Woodruff,   Mch. 7, 1793
John Rice ? & Mabel French,   Mch. 21, 1793
Eben. Havins ? & Zilpha Robinson,   Oct. 29, 1792
Nathl. Young & Polly Ashley,   ————, 1792
John Winter & Surviah Fullar,   1792
Matthew Calkins & Lois Smith,   1792
Jonathan Niles & Sybil Johnson,   1793
John Paterson & Sophia Briggs,   1793
John Jaquin & Lovina Stevens,   1794
Joseph Persons & Deborah Rowley,   1794
Nathl. Ford & Caroline Kees,   1794
John Ras ? & Martha Lard   1794

WILLIAMSTOWN

June 21, 1765. The plantation called West Hoosuck established as Williamstown.

Robt. Miller of Pawling Precinct & Sarah Sherman,

	May 27, 1789
Jas. Sherwood & Huldah Stratton,	Jan. 1, 1789
Gideon Seldon & Polly Cook,	July 28, 1789
Wm. Younger & Hannah Ladd,	Oct. 18, 1789
Salmon Gregory & Anner Clark,	Nov. 5, 1789
Reuben Read & Esther Horsford,	Dec. 31, 1789
Timothy Sabin & Abigail Hicock,	Jan. 7, 1790
John Wood & Mary Foster,	Jan. 14, 1790
Oliver Lampson & Hannah Foster,	Jan. 12, 1790
David Gilmore & Sarah Seelye or Seely,	Feb. 3, 1790
Sylvanus Eaton & Almira Sloan,	Feb. 28, 1790
Edmond Lamb & Rebeckah McMaster,	Mch. 2, 1790
Nathan Raymond & Elizabeth Jones,	Mch. 8, 1790

WINDSOR

July 4, 1771. The new plantation called Number Four established as Gageborough, Oct. 16, 1778. The name of the town of Gageborough changed to Windsor,

Ebenezer Still? & Susannah Preston,	Oct. 9, 1792
Dan'l Felshon? & Lydia Safford,	Nov.—, 1792
Jonathan Ball & Huldah Taft,	Nov.—, 1792
Oliver Harwood & Fear Ripley,	Jan.—, 1793
Nath'l Luther & Widow Lucy Hammon,	June 27, 1793
Asa Warner of Amherst & Molly Eddy,	Aug. 8, 1793
James Dodge & Cynthia Preston,	Nov. 6, 1793
Zebulon Packard & Abiatha Bannister,	Mch. 13, 1794
Ely? Fullar & Eunice Dunbar,	Mch. 13, 1794

Oliver Town & Sarah Dodge,   Ap. 1, 1794

Abiathar Chafey & Miriam Clark,   Jan. 16, 1797

Aaron Cleveland & widow Lydia Wright, both of
     Dalton,   Oct. 27, 1795

Wm. Cady of the Equivalent & Margaret Read,   Ap. 11, 1781

Geo. Wales & Mrs. Irena Pouree? both of Lanesboro,
                                    May 9, 1781

Chas. Thrasher & Susanna Higgins, both of New
     Ashford,   Sept. 20, 1781

Nehemiah Richardson & Deliverance Worden, both
     of Adams,   Nov. 25, 1781

Sam'l Baker & Huldah Green of Lanesboro,   Ap. 4, 1782

David Stafford of Adams & Sarah Baker of Lanes-
     boro,   Ap. 4, 1782

Sam'l Ingraham & Rosanna Staples of Adams,   Dec. 30, 1788

Dr. Phillips of Windsor & Lucy Ludden,   Feb. 16, 1786

Ichabod Shearlock & Anna Welsh, both of Lanes-
     boro,   Oct. 30, 1785

Theophilus Grovenor of Windsor & Bathsheba
     Thornton of Lanesboro,   Oct. 28, 1784

Ebenezer Smith & Ann Thornton of Lanesboro, Nov. 11, 1784

Benj. Stafford & Lydia Lockwood, both of Adams,
                                  Nov. 28, 1784

Lemuel Durfee of Cambridge & Prudence Hath-
     away of Adams,   Aug. 29, 1784

John Green of Lanesboro & Sarah Straight,   Oct. 9, 1782

Stephen Westcott of Lanesboro & Anstress Green, Oct. 17, 1782

Simon Brown ? & Elisabeth Topliff,   Oct. 17, 1782

Levi Cole & Anna Camp of Adams,   Dec. 23, 1782

Tho. Pearse & Molly Frey? both of Adams,   Feb. 6, 1783

Nathan Westcott & Ezibu? Greene?, both of Ad-
     ams,   Mch. 26, 1783

William ———? & Asenath Jencks? of Adams,   July 27, 1783

Jas. Wheeler & Molly Phillips,   Aug. 13, 1790

Asa Kent & Elisabeth Miller, both of Lanesboro, Mch. 21, 1790

Benj. Bliss & Amey Brown,   Ap. 22, 1790

John Banister & Serviah Davis,   Nov. 6, 1794

Nathan Andrews & Polly Banister,   Ap. 2, 1795

Simeon Miner? & Betsey Cole,   Ap. 5, 1795
Amos Bowen & Ruth Smith, Int.   Sept. 9, 1798
Timothy Smith & Elisabeth Miner, Int.,   Oct. 27, 1801
Ebenezer Blanchard of Windsor & Abigail Gillet of
    Savoy, Int.,   July 13, 1801
Willard Morse & Olive Convers, Int.,   Feb. 4, 1802
Jephthah Turner of Cummington & Mrs. Hannah
    Beals,   Nov. 19, 1802

PLYMOUTH COUNTY

Additions to Book II. The following marriages have been found in an unnumbered volume of the Court of General Sessions of the Peace, Plymouth County and are added here to complete that issue.

✓ MIDDLEBOROUGH

Joseph Haskell & Sarah Braley,	Mar. 27, 1729
Joseph Leonard & Hannah Pratt,	Apr. 9, 1729
Willm. Hack of Taunton & Mary Tinkham,	Aug. 21, 1729
Eleazer Pratt, Jr. & Hannah Short,	Sep. 10, 1729
Joshua Combs of Rochester & Elizabeth Pratt,	Sep. 10, 1729
Joshua Peirce of Pembroke & Hopestill Holloway,	Nov. 20, 1729
Nathan Holloway of Taunton & Elizabeth Makepeace,	
	Dec. 25, 1729
Seth Howland & Elizabeth Delano,	May 24, 1728
Ebenezer Redden & Joanna Vaughan,	Sep. 10, 1728
David Miller & Susannah Holmes,	Oct. 31, 1728
Ignatius Elmes and Sarah Bennett,	Dec. 4, 1728
Jonathan Snow of Bridgewater & Sarah Soul,	Dec. 18, 1828
Willm. Hooper of Bridgewater & Lois Thomas,	Jan. 1728
Thomas Wood & Hannah Alden,	Apr. ult. 1728
Coombs Barrows & Joanna Smith,	May 15, 1728
Robert Ransom & Sarah Chyles,	May 27, 1728
John Savery & Mary Thomas, da. of Jonathan Thomas, dec. ,	Jul. 17, 1728
John Eaton of Kingston & Elizabeth Fuller,	Jul. ult., 1728
Rev. John Wadsworth of Canterbury & Mrs. Abigail Sprout,	Dec. 11, 1728
Jonathan Fuller & Hannah Harlow,	Dec. 17, 1728
Cap. Ichabod Tupper & Hannah Tinkham,	Dec. 23, 1728
Dea. Thomas Pratt of Easton & Desire Bonney,	Mar. 5, 1729/30
Isaac Billington & Mary Donham,	Mar. 5, 1729/30
Robert Barrows & Fear Thomas,	Mar. 12, 1730
Peter Tinkham & Eunice Thomas,	Apr. 1, 1739

Benjamin Leonard & Elizabeth West,	Sep. 16, 1730
Elections Reynolds, Jr. & Charity Caswell,	Apr. 1, 1731
Francis Gayward of Rochester & Anna Morse,	July 10, 1730
Samuel Wood & Sarah Howland, widow,	Aug. 7, 1730
Josiah Hatch of Pembroke & Mercy Redding,	Nov. 12, 1730
Jacob Tomson & Elizabeth Holmes,	Jan. 7, 1730
John Wood & Hannah Chiles,	Feb. 18, 1730
Jacob Soul & Mary Thomas,	Mar. 31, 1731
Thomas Holmes & Mary Sprout,	Apr. 1, 1731
Francis Miller & Experience Sprout,	Nov. 22, 1731
Obadiah Sampson & Mary Soul,	Dec. 14, 1731
Elias Miller & Sarah Holmes,	Feb. 17, 1731
Thomas King & Mary Gaunt (?),	Apr. 12, 1732
Thomas Tomson & Martha Soul,	Apr. 25, 1732
John Miller, Jr. & Waitstill Clap,	Jun. 26, 1732
Isaac Bennett & Mary Drew,	Aug. 24, 1732
James Winslow of Plymouth & Susanna Conant,	Dec. 7, 1732
Jesse Griffeth & Elizabeth Bent,	Jan. 4, 1732
Samuel Eddy, Jr. & Lydia Alden,	Feb. 5, 1732
Ebenezer Reed of Abington & Hannah Tompson,	Feb. 21, 1732
Noah Thomas & Mary Alden,	Feb. 22, 1732
Stephen Donham & Lydia Taylor of Taunton,	May 10, 1733
Nathaniel Holloway & Mehitabel Bassit of Bridge-water,	Jun. 20, 1733
James Bumpas & Rachel Hanks,	Mar. 1732-3
Benjamin Wood & Presulla Rickard, both of Plimpton,	Apr., 1733
Francis Eaton & Lydia Fuller,	Jun. 12, 1733
Zacheriah Whitman of Bridgewater & Eleanor Bennet,	Nov. 1, 1723
Samuel Shaw of Plimpton & Desire Southworth,	Apr. 21, 1731
Benjamin Gurney & Sarah Morse,	Jun. 14, 1731
Elkanah Sherman of Dartmouth & Margaret Pitts,	Jan. 16, 1731
Combs Barrows & Mary Dwelly,	May 29, 1732
Samuel Thomas & Lydia Richmond,	Jun. 9, 1732
Nathaniel Richmond of Taunton & Alice Hacket,	Nov. 2, 1732
Thomas Ramsdale & Mary Peirce,	Nov. 2, 1732
Eleazer Lyon & Bethiah Allen,	Jun. 27, 1732

Jotham Caswell & Mary Renolds,   Jan. 11, 1732
Timothy Rogers & Damarus Macumber of Taun-
    ton,   Jan. 31, 1732

✓ PLYMOUTH

Rev. Robert Ward of Wenham & Margaret Rogers,
                                    Feb. 16, 1726-7
Barnabas Shurtleff of Plimpton & Jemina Adams,
                                    Mar. 16, 1726-7
Joseph Bartlett & Sarah Morton,   Apr. 4, 1727
Samuel Totman & Experience Rogers,   Apr. 17, 1727
Ebenezer Cobb, Jr. & Lydia Stephens,   Dec. 14, 1727
Benjamin Lothrop, Jr. of Barnstable & Experience
    Howland,   Dec. 22, 1727
Ebenzer Cobb & Mary Thomas of Middleborough,
                                    Feb. 8, 1727
Samuel Doty & Marcy Cobb,   Apr. 10, 1727
Joshua Finney & Hannah Curtis,   Sep. 28, 1727
Nehemiah Ripley & Sarah Atwood,   Jun. 6, 1728
Thomas Scarret & Alse Ward,   Aug. 6, 1728
Elkanah Delano & Mary Saunders,   Oct. 31, 1728
Ephriam Sampson of Duxborough & Ruth Sheperd,
                                    Nov. 14, 1728
Samuel Cole & Mercy Barnes,   Nov. 14, 1728
Timothy Burbank of Boston & Mary Kempton, Dec. 12, 1728
Jonathan Freeman of Plimpton & Sarah Ryder, Dec. 19, 1728
Thorton Gray & Katherine White,   Dec. 20, 1728
James Holmes & Content Silvester,   Jan. 30, 1728
Matthew Lemote & Mercy Billington,   Feb. 18, 1728
Edward Stevens & Marcy Silvester,   Apr. 3, 1729
Rodolphus Hatch of Province Town & Esther Holmes,
                                    Apr. 3, 1729
Thomas Doane of Chatham & Sarah Barnes,   May 20, 1729
Thomas Totman & Lucretia Ross,   May 30, 1729

Jack & Mariah, negroes of Mr. Jonathan Bryant, Jun. 30, 1729
Jacob Lewis & Bathsheba Mallis, Jul. 8, 1729
John Watson, Esq. & Mrs. Priscilla Thomas, Jul. 8, 1729
Jacob Taylor of Barnstable & Mary Atwood, Jul. 14, 1729
Seth Doggett & Elizabeth Delano, Sep. 9, 1729
Isaac King & Hannah Harlow, Oct. 28, 1729
John Cushing, Esq. of Scituate & Mary Cotton, Nov. 20, 1729
John Hambleton & Elizabeth Jones, Feb. 10, 1729
Thomas Ward & Joanna Donham, Mar. 4, 1729
Ephraim Churchill & Priscilla Manchester, Mar. 27, 1730
Thomas Weston & Prudence Conant, May 4, 1730
William Dyre of Boston & Hannah Phillips, May 18, 1730
Deac. John Atwood & Experience Pierce, Jun. 8, 1730
Nicholas Drew & Lydia Doggett, Aug. 10, 1730
Ebenexer Finney of Barnstable & Rebecca Barnes, Sep. 22, 1730
John Studley & Elizabeth Doten, Sep. 24, 1730
Jabez Holmes & Rebecca Harlow, Sep. 30, 1730

ROCHESTER

Nicholas Hicks & Hannah Coombs, Jun. 24, 1729
Stephen Ellis & Ruth Turner, Jun. 27, 1729
Seth Winslow & Abigail Whiteridge, Oct. 23, 1729
Jonathan Hunter & Hopestill Hamblin, Nov. 29, 1729
Archelaus Hammond & Elizabeth Weeks, Dec. 10, 1729
Nathaniel Parker & Sarah Parker of Dartmouth, Jan. 25, 1729
George Barlow & Ruth Barrow, Feb. 19, 1729
Seth Ellis & Mary Bumpas, Feb. 26, 1729
James Steward & Hannah Dexter, Apr. 16, 1730
Samuel Hammond & Deliverance Admister, Nov. 5, 1730
Benjamin Hammond & Priscilla Sprague, Nov. 12, 1730
Lowis Deneranville & Susanna Crapo, Dec. 8, 1730
Ebenezer Keen & Mercy Whiteridge, Dec. 31, 1730
Stephen Goodspeed & Bethiah Wooding, Mar. 1, 1730
Edward Doty & Mary Andrews, Nov. 17, 1726

Seth O'Riley of Yarmouth & Mehitabel Wing,	Nov. 23, 1726
John Grass & Penelope White,	Feb. 28, 1726
James Pratt & Frances Combs,	Apr. 15, 1727
Joseph Ashely & Mary Whetredge,	Jan. 1, 1728
James Foster & Lydia Winslow,	Jul. 10, 1729
Abiel Sprague & Elizabeth Ashely,	Jun. 18, 1730
Chillingsworth Foster of Harwich & Marcy Winslow,	Oct. 10, 1730
Benjamin Cole of Swansey & Elizabeth Nelson of Middleborough,	Nov. 19, 1730
James Whitcomb & Sarah Linkhorn,	May 31, 1731
John Ross & Sarah Clifton,	Jun. 22, 1731
Micah Sprague & Elizabeth Turner,	Aug. 22, 1731
Ebenezer Lothrop of Mansfield & Elizabeth Hammond,	Oct. 13, 1731
Hinkman Vaughan of Middleborough & Desire Hicks,	Oct. 21, 1731
Ithamas Comes & Hannah Andrews,	Nov. 3, 1731
Robert Whitcomb & Joanna Lawrence	
Samuel Dexter & Mary Clark,	May 18, 1732
Joseph Barlow & Abigail Wyatt,	Jul. 23, 1732
Barnabas Sears & Thankful Freeman,	Sept. 25, 1732
Benjamin Clap & Katherine Nye,	Oct. 6, 1732
Josiah Bump & Hannah Bump,	Dec. 21, 1732
Cornelius Connor & Hittee Haskell,	Jan. 5, 1732
Ebenezer Luce & Sarah Doty,	Oct. 18, 1733
David Nye & Elizabeth Briggs,	Oct. 25, 1733
Abraham Ashley & Elizabeth Rogers,	Nov. 22, 1733
Barzillai Randall & Jerusha Hammond,	Nov. 25, 1733
Thomas Whetredge & Hannah Haskell,	Nov. 25, 1733
Andrew Haskell & Jane Clark,	Nov. 25, 1733
Jonathan Spooner & Mary Crapo,	Dec. 31, 1733
Samuel White & Elizabeth Ashley,	Mar. 14, 1733
William Randall, Jr. & Rest Sumer,	May 28, 1732
Nathaniel Chabbuch, Jr. & Tabitha Besse of Agawam-Plymouth,	Sep. 18, 1732
Caleb Benson of Middleborough & Deborah Barrow of Plimpton,	Jan. 11, 1732

William Ashley & Elizabeth Ashley, Feb. 12, 1732
Samuel Edward & Rebecka Burge, Aug. 16, 1733
Ebenezer Luce & Sarah Doty, Oct. 18, 1733
Jedidiah Briggs & Jedidah Ellis, Oct. 19, 1733
David Nye & Elizabeth Briggs, Oct. 25, 1733
Abrah Ashley & Elizabeth Rogers, Nov. 22, 1733
Barzillai Randall & Jerushe Hammond, Nov. 25, 1733
Thomas Wetteridge & Hannah Haskell, Nov. 25, 1733
Andrew Haskell & Jane Clark, Nov. 25, 1733
Jonathan Spooner & Mary Crapoo, Dec. 31, 1733
Samuel White & Elizabeth Ashley, Mar. 14, 1733
James Lake of Dartmouth & Elizabeth Crapoo, Oct. 31, 1734
Samuel Bumpas & Abigail Bumpas, Oct. 13, 1737
Isaac Doty & Elizabeth Blackmer, Oct. 19, 1737
Samuel Robinson & Elizabeth Doty, Oct. 20, 1737
John Barrows & Joanna Dexter, Nov. 22, 1737
Ebenezer Briggs & Betta Gibbs, Feb. 16, 1737

√ HANOVER

David Bryant, Jr. of Scituate & Hannah Turner, Jan. 16, 1728
Richard Hill & Jemimah Ramsdil, Feb. 20, 1728
Benjamin Barstow & Sarah Bardin, May 15, 1729
Jonathan Potter & Margaret Frank, Jul. 7, 1729
Ezekiel Palmer & Martha Pratt, Oct. 9, 1729
Joseph Ramsdell & Mary Homer, Apr. 23, 1730
Clemond Bate & Agatha Merritt, Jun. 15, 1730
Matthew Stetson of H. & Hannah Lincoln of Scituate, Sep. 24, 1730
Melatiah Dillingham & Phebe Hatch, Feb. 18, 1730
John Low of Pembroke & Susanna Gilford, Apr. 22, 1731
Eliab Turner & Martha Barstow, May 12, 1731
Isaac Barden & Deborah Tobey, June 4, 1731
Richard Bowker & Sarah Palmer, Aug. 4, 1731

BRIDGEWATER

———— Field & Mary Haward,	Nov. 15, 1726
———— Whitman & Elizabeth Rickard,	Nov. 29, 1726
Solomon Snow & Bathsheba Mahurin,	Apr. 8, 1724
Joseph Byram & Martha Perkins,	May 13, 1724
Zacheus Packard & Mercy Allden,	Oct. 21, 1725
Hugh Mahurin & Mary Snell,	Dec. 17, 1725
Joseph Carver & Elizabeth Snow,	May 4, 1725
Stephen Leach & Sarah Hooper,	May 5, 1725
Samuel Phillips & Lydia Bassett,	Nov. 17, 1726
Joseph Drake & Alice Hayward,	Apr. 5, 1727
Elisha Dunbar & Mercy Hayward,	Apr. 6, 1727
Henry Kingham & Mary Allen,	Nov. 24, 1726
Recompense Cary & Sarah Brett, widow,	Jan. 17, 1726
Josiah Snell & Abigail Fobes,	Jan. 23, 1728
John Wormal & Mary Bryant,	Jun. 10, 1729
Samuel Packard & Susanna Kinsley,	Jul. 22, 1729
Benjamin Washburn & Martha Kingham,	Aug. 6, 1729
Joseph Perry & Mary Chandler,	Oct. 17, 1729
Nathl. Davenport & Lucy Wyeman,	Dec. 22, 1729
Ephraim Dunham & Elizabeth Bump,	Dec. 9, 1729
Christopher Askins & Susanna Robinson,	Oct. 15, 1729
John Whitman & Elizabeth Cary,	Nov. 10, 1729
Caleb Brand & Damaras James,	Nov. 13, 1729
Samuel Pratt & Bithia Byram,	Dec. 30, 1729
Benjamin Allen & Mehitabel Cary,	Jan. 7, 1729
Zachariah Whitmarsh & Hannah Washburn,	Jan. 28, 1729
William Davenport & Sarah Richards,	Apr. 16, 1730
Timothy Hayward & Mary Reed,	Nov. 12, 1730
Arthur Harris & Mehitabel Rickard,	Nov. 12, 1730
John Johnson & Peggy Holman,	Oct. 21, 1731
Jocob Allen & Abigail Kingman,	Jan. 1, 1730
Isaac Kingman & Jane Kingman,	Jan. 13, 1730
Joseph Davis & Ruth Bassett,	Mar. 23, 1730

Christopher Askins & Susanna Robinson,	Oct. 15, 1729
John Whitman & Elizabeth Cary,	Nov. 10, 1729
Caleb Brand & Damaris James,	Nov. 13, 1729
Samuel Pratt & Bethiah Byram,	Dec. 30, 1729
Benjamin Allen & Mehitabel Cary,	Jan. 7, 1729
Zachary Whitmarsh & Hannah Washburn,	Jan. 28, 1729
William Davenport & Sarah Richards,	Apr. 16, 1730
Shubal Waldow & Abigail Allen,	Oct. 14, 1730
David Snow & Joanna Hayward,	Mar. 11, 1730
Zachariah Snell & Abigail Hayward,	Mar. 11, 1730
Thomas Ames & Keziah Hayward,	Jun. 20, 1731
Samuel Soper & Esther Littlefield,	Jun. 23, 1731
Israel Alger & Rachel Wade,	Jun. 24, 1731
John Snow & Hannah Hayward,	Jul. 11, 1731
Wright Bartlett & Bethia Packard,	Jul. 29, 1731
David Kingman & Mercy Hayward,	Mar. 1, 1731
Jonathan Kingman & Mercy Keith,	Mar. 1, 1731
William Gillemer & Mary Willis,	Nov. 24, 1732
Jonathan Alden of Marshfield & Mehitabel Allen,	
	Nov. 25, 1731
Benjamin Mahurin & Lydia Pratt,	Dec. 23, 1731
Solomon Washburn & Martha Orcutt,	Jan. 13, 1731
Benjamin Johnson & Ruth Holman,	Feb. 8, 1731
Shepherd Fisk & Alice Alger,	Feb. 24, 1731
Joseph Cary & Anna Brett,	15th Jun., 1732
John Randall & Experience Willis,	May 17, 1732
William Brett & Bethiah Kingsly,	May 15, 1732
Benjamin Curtis & Experience Hayward,	May 25, 1732
Isaac Willis & Hannah Pratt,	Aug. 4, 1732
Ephraim Keith & Sarah Washburn,	Sep. 21, 1732
Joseph Gannett & Hannah Brett,	Oct. 21, 1732

DUXBOROUGH

David Seabury & Abigail Seabury,	Jan. 3, 1726
Abraham Pierce of Pembroke, Jr. & Abigail Peterson,	Sep. 25, 1729
Thomas Prince & Judea Fox,	Nov. 25, 1729
Joseph Trebble & Anna Jones, both of Plymouth,	Dec. 19, 1729
Amaziah Delano & Ruth Samson,	Jan. 8, 1729
Abner Weston & Sarah Standish,	Mar. 2, 1729
Ebenezer Sherman & Bathsheba Foord, both of Marshfield,	May 4, 1730
John Soul & Mabel Partridge,	Aug. 5, 1730
Ebenezer Bartlett & Jerusha Samson,	Oct. 8, 1730
Benjamin Simmons, Jr. & Fear Samson,	Oct. 26, 1731
Reuben Peterson & Rebekah Simmons,	Jul. 6, 1732
Ezra Arnold & Rebaca Sprague,	July 27, 1732
Isaac Simmons & Lydia Cushman,	Oct. 24, 1732

MARSHFIELD

Ebenezer Howland & Sarah Green,	Mar. 28, 1723
James Dexter of Rochester & Lois Sherman,	Mar. 29, 1723
Thomas Tracy & Susanna Waterman,	Jun. 3, 1723
Benjamin Kent & Persis Doggett,	Oct. 31, 1723
John Logan & Margaret Carr,	Jan. 7, 1723
Joshua Rose & Elizabeth Gibson,	Jan. 30, 1723
James Warren of Plymouth & Penelope Winslow,	Jan. 30, 1723
Samuel Sherman & Mary Williamson,	Feb. 17, 1723
Francis Crooker & Patience Childs,	Mar. 11, 1723
Benjamin Hanks & Mary White,	Apr. 23, 1724
Joshua Samson & Mary Oakman,	May 23, 1724

Thomas Stockbridge of Scituate & Hannah Rogers,

Jul. 8, 1724

John Thomas & Mary Ray, Oct. 8, 1724

Caleb Oldham of Scituate & Bethiah Stephens, Oct. 21, 1724

William Stephens & Patience Jones, Oct. 9, 1724

Thomas Phillips & Mary Sherman, Feb. 23, 1724

Anthony Eames & Anna Barker, Mar. 25, 1725

Ichabod Washburn of Plymouth & Bethiah Phillips,

Jun. 2, 1725

William Lucas & Sarah Thomas, Oct. 21, 1725

Israel Hatch of Scituate & Bethiah Thomas, Oct. 27, 1725

Nathaniel Keen of Pembroke & Thankful Winslow,

Oct. 27, 1725

Ebenezer Damon of Scituate & Abigail Thomas, Oct. 27, 1725

William Hambelton & Jane Hopkins, Oct. 7, 1725

Adam Hall & Sarah Sherman, Jan. 6, 1725

Silvanus Hall of Plymouth & Elizabeth Doggett, Jan. 13, 1725

John Winslow of Plymouth & Mary Little, Feb. 16, 1725

John Polan & Thankful Atkins, May 26, 1726

Josiah Phinney of Plymouth & Mercy Thomas, Sep. 14, 1726

Samuel Baker & Hannah Foord, Nov. 9, 1726

Seth Joyce & Rachel Sherman, Nov. 9, 1726

John Deyre & Mary Trouant, Apr. 5, 1727

Thomas Oldham of Scituate & Desire Wormall, May 8, 1727

Robert Waterman of Plimpton & Abigail Gingley, Jun. 8, 1727

Ebenezer Taylor & Sarah Carver, Jan. 11, 1727

Stephen Stoddard of Hingham & Rebecca King, Jan. 24, 1727

Isaac Phillips & Sarah White, Jan. 25, 1727

Ebenezer Jones & Jane King, Mar. 19, 1727

Bezaliel Palmer of Scituate & Anna Jones, Mar. 19, 1727

Isaac Taylor of Pemproke & Jerushe Tiden, May 28, 1728

Joshua Carver & Martha Foord, Jul. 4, 1728

Tobias Payne of Boston & Sarah Winslow, Oct. 14, 1728

William Foord & Hannah Barstow, Oct. 30, 1728

Snow Winslow & Deborah Bryant, Nov. 6, 1728

Samuel Kent & Desire Barker, Nov. 14, 1728

John Magoun of Scituate & Abigail Waterman, Nove. 28, 1728

Thomas Doggett & Joannah Fuller, Dec. 11, 1728

Joseph Hewitt & Sarah Dingley,	Dec. 19, 1728
Benjamin Phillips & Desire Sherman,	Jan. 18, 1728
Joshua Eames & Abigail Doggett,	Jan. 18, 1728
Samuel Foord & Sarah Rogers,	Jan. 16, 1728
Anthony Eames & Grace Oldham of Scituate,	Dec. 11, 1724

HAMPSHIRE COUNTY

√ BELCHERTOWN

June 30, 1761. The plantation called Cold Spring established as "Belcher's Town."

Silas Thayer & Rachel Hanks,	Mar. 21, 1786
Thomas Brown & Abigail Thayer,	Apr. 6, 1786
Humphrey Grise & Patty Grise,	June 14, 1786
Joel Rice & Sarah Barton,	Apr. 10, 1788
Mark Stacy & Julia Root,	July 3, 1788
Israel Russell, of Sunderland & Phoebe Smith,	Aug. 20, 1788
Daniel Barton & Lois White of Granby,	Aug. 21, 1788
Heman Kentfield & Sarah Knolton,	Nov. 27, 1788
Josiah Kentfield & Sally Burding,	Dec. 26, 1788
Daniel Hannum & Phoebe Bags,	Jan. 29, 1789
Jonathan Smith & Phoebe Squire,	Apr. 9, 1789
Artemas Green, & Esther Warner of Granby,	Nov. 20, 1788
Reuben Prentiss of Somers & Olive Green,	Apr. 23, 1789

√ BLANDFORD

April 10, 1741. Suffield Equivalent land, commonly called Glasgow, established as Blandford.

Amos Kingsley & Mary Wadsworth,	Feb. 3, 1758
James Richard & Abigail King,	Feb. 3, 1758

Alexander Clark of Colrain & Elisa Donaghy,	Apr. 11, 1754
John Beard & Agnes Brown,	June 27, 1754
David Boyse & Rachel Crooks,	Feb. 6, 1755
David Fleming of Palmer & Sarah Loughead,	May 22, 1755
Matthew Bircherd & Mary Messenger,	Aug. —, 1756
Samuel Loughead & Mary Caldwell,	Mar. 17, 1757
John Davis & Jane Brown,	Feb. 16, 1758
John Carnahen & Rebecca Gibbles,	July 28, 1757
Solomon Steward & Sarah McConoghey,	Apr. 13, 1758
John Dalrimple & Elisabeth Young,	June 22, 1758
David McConoughey, Jr. & Anna Carnahan,	Sep. 21, 1758
William Watson & Ruth Beard,	Nov. 23, 1758
Solomon Brown & Jean Anderson,	June 18, 1759
James Clark & Sarah Scoot,	June 26, 1759
William Carnahen & Mary Clark,	July 26, 1759
William Loghead & Isabel Black,	Aug. 23, 1759
Glory McMurrey & Susanna Tagart,	Oct. 6, 1759
John Scoot & Rachel Steward,	Oct. 25, 1759
James Fergeson & Hannah McConoughey,	Sep. 22, 1759
Israel Gibbs, Junr. & Agnes Clark,	Dec. 12, 1759
James Campbel & Jean Knox,	Jan. 10, 1760
John Gibbs & Rachel Boies,	Jan. 24, 1760
John Kenney of Glassenbury & Susanna Phillips,	Feb. 11, 1760
James Beard, Jr. & Martha More,	July 11, 1760
John White, M. D. & Sarah Carnahen,	Sep. 4, 1760

✓CHARLEMONT

June 21, 1765. The new plantation called Charlemont established as the town of Charlemont.

Elnathan Baker, & Thesime Butler, of Zoar,	Aug. 28, 1782
John Gould & Olive Thompson,	Oct. 10, 1782
Solomon Haywood & Polly Ward,	Mar. 27, 1783
Seth Temple & Martha Hunt,	May 24, 1783
Luke White & Eunice White,	Nov. 30, 1783

Joshua Warfield & Prudence Buck,	Mar. 25, 1784
Parla Hunt & Persis Gleason,	July 1, 1784
Jonas King & Abigail Leonard,	Jan. 30, 1783
Amos Avery & Azubah Hawks,	Jan. 30, 1783
Ichabod Hawks & Molly Avery,	May 28, 1783
Benjamin Comstock & Sarah Rice,	Mar. —, 1782
Silas Becket & Esther Fales,	Dec. 30, 1782
Zebulon Benton & Louise Avery,	July 3, 1783
Silas Holbrook & Tirzah Taylor,	Aug. 21, 1783
Amos Avery & Eunice Avery,	Sep. 25, 1783
Thomas Totman & Rachel Rice,	Oct. 2, 1783
Asa Nichols & Sylvia Brooks,	Nov. 13, 1783
Noah Reed & Abigail Rice,	————, 1784
Nathel Colman & Eleanor Comstock,	Nov. 24, 1784
William Taylor & Abigail Giles,	Dec. 30, 1784
James Tynny & Thankful Shippe,	Apr. 14, 1785
Lebbeus Rudd & Sarrah Fales,	Aug. 25, 1785
Israel Shippe & Rhoda Bass,	Oct. 6, 1785
Jona Hastings, Jun. & Anna Nash,	———— 16, 1785
Josiah Holly & Lucinda Taylor,	———— 18, 1785
Rufus Hawks & Rowena Nichols,	Jan. 31, 1786
Abisha Rogers & Sarah Hawks,	Feb. 2, 1786
Lemuel Crocker & Mary Pike,	Mar. 16, 1786
Daniel Harris & Mary Harris,	Apr. 5, 1785

DEERFIELD

Oct. 22, 1677. "Deerfield" is mentioned.

Jeremiah West & Patty Williams,	Feb. 27, 1787
James Upham & Elisabeth Barnard,	Apr. 1, 1787
Ebenezer Barnard & Abigail Catlin,	June 17, 1787
Jonathan Arms & Sarah Wells,	July 26, 1787
Elihu Smead & Mercy Bardwell,	Aug. 2, 1787
John Catlin & Huldah Bangs,	Nov. 11, 1787

Rufus Wells & Prudence Newton,	Dec. 21, 1787
Silvester Stebbins & Elisabeth Dwelly,	Feb. 7, 1788
Eli Abbot & Eunice Newton of Shelburne,	Feb. 28, 1788
Joseph Bradley & Lydia Sexton,	Jan. 5, 1789
Cotton Partridge & Sophia Arms,	May 4, 1788
Joshua Sweet & Polly Hawks,	July 6, 1788
Joel Wells & Abigail Hawks,	July 17, 1788
Daniel Chapin & Joanna Arms,	Jan. 1, 1789
Abiather Joy & Elisabeth Burt,	Jan. 4, 1789
Abijah Harding & Lydia Dickinson,	Jan. 8, 1789
John Newton & Abigail Parker,	Jan. 29, 1789

✓ GREENFIELD

June 9, 1753. Part of Deerfield established as the District of Greenfield.

Elijah Smith & Mary Stebbins,	Jan. 1, 1784
Joseph Stanhope & Bethia Smalley,	——— 13, ———
Adam Wellman & Mary Loveland,	——— 29, ———
Benja Kneeland Carrier & Jerusha Ballard,	Mar. 25, ———
George Loveland & Hannah Combs,	June 29, ———
Selah Hastings & Susanna Smith,	Oct. 27, ———
Abner Darling & Chloe Derby,	Apr. 3, 1785
Jonas Stanhope & Mary Allen,	——— 21, ———
John Sawteel & Anna Denio,	June 9, ———
George Darling & Jane Severance,	——— 27, ———
Jesse Johnson & Hannah Cohoon,	Nov. 16, ———
Eliezer Wells & Anna Wells,	——— 24, ———
Hull Nims & Hannah Newton,	Dec. 1, ———
Amos Cornwell & Abigail Severance,	——— 14, ———
Joel Allen & Abigail Smead,	——— 15, ———
Giles Webster & Huldah Thornton,	Feb. 22, 1786
Elihu Atherton & Hepzibah Leach,	Jan. 18, 1785
Frederick Loveland & Rhoda Combs,	May 6, ———
William Jonier & Judeth Heart,	June 24, ———

Joshua Combs, Jun. & Anna Loveland,	July 26,	——
Moses Bardwell & Sarah Ransom,	Sept. 11,	——
John Kemp & Hannah Wells,	March 29, 1786	
Reuben White & Rachel Herdin,	Apr. 20,	——
Moses Mawley & Joanna Whetten,	Mar. 30, 1786	
Solomon White & Lydia Amsden,	May 24,	——
Joseph Phelps & Martha Bascom,	July 5,	——
Elias Bardwell & Irena Allen,	Oct. 19,	——
Abner Arms & Mary Denio,	—— 26,	
Robert Cone & Sarah Cook,	Dec. 6,	——
John Mellis & Hannah Turner,	Feb. 1, 1787	
John French & Elisabeth Bascom,	—— 29,	
Ephraham Hastings & Widow Hitchcock,	Apr. 30,	——
Aaron Field Wells & Abigail Burnham,	May 10,	——
Oliver Atherton & Mary Bascom,	—— 15,	
John Crosset & Olive Carpenter,	July 11,	——

Jonathan Sheldon & Naoma Fox, both of Bernardston,

July 22, 1787

Wm. McHard & Temperance Whipell,	Aug. 24,	——
Nathan Jacobs & Sarah Clerk,	Sep. 13,	——
Edvardas Allen & Hannah Brown,	Oct. 23,	——

Elisha Worden of Halifax & Lucy Hale of Bernardston,

Oct. 23, 1787

Eber Hambleton & Katharine Sexton,	Nov. 8,	——
Elihu Knight & Mehitabel Welman,	—— 25,	
Oliver Cone & Esther Welman,	—— ——	
Wm. Smalley & Susanna Bascom,	—— 29,	
Salmon Howland & Wealthy Wise,	—— ——	
Reuben Ingram & Tabitha Arms,	Dec. 27,	——

Parley Streeter of Guilford & Elianor Brooks of Bernardston,

Feb. 21, 1788

Mulford Philips & Thankful Smalley,	Feb. 18, 1788

Nathan Nichols of Bernardston & Polly Newcomb,

Mch. 6, 1788

Amasa Skinner & Salome Burnell,	Mar. 13,	——
Quintus Allen & Dorothy Stebbins,	June 1,	——
Uriah Weeks & Susanna Woods,	—— 12,	——
Barre Wing & Leucy Clary,	Aug. 25,	——

Samuel Newton & Sybel Weld,	Oct. 1, ———
Stephen Taylor & Mindwell Taylor,	Nov. 13, ———
John Wells & Anne Arms,	Jan. 13, 1789
Charles Evans & Asenath Foot,	Feb. 2, ———
Benja Hastings, Jun. & Rachel Strickland,	Mar. 7, ———
Job Allen & Phoebe Picket,	——— 14, ———
Jonathan Allen & Cloe Bascom,	Apr. 9, ———
John Alvord & Abigail Smead,	Dec. 14, 1786
Mathew Severance & Mary Wells,	Nov. 25, ———
John Frazer & Dinnis Wells,	Jan. 22, 1787
Joseph Nutting & Hulday Converse,	——— 27, ———
Elijah Allen & Eunice Smead,	Nov. 29, ———
John Allen & Lucretia Risley,	Feb. 6, 1788
Jonathan Hall & Marcy French,	——— 19, ———
John Foster & Mindale Atherton,	Apr. 24, ———
George Dickinson & Anna Whiting,	June 26, ———
Selah Allen & Thankful Allen,	Nov. 25, ———

✓ # HATFIELD

May 31, 1670. Part of Hadley established as "Hattfield."

William Morton & Hannah Chambers,	Jan. 23, 1783
Nathan Bliss & Submit White Jun.,	Feb. 19, 1783
Ebenezer Dwight & Bethia Truesdale,	——— 27, do
Joel Day & Martha Murray,	Mar. 10, 1783
Benjamin Morton & Electa White,	June 26, 1783
Henry Wilkee & Anna Tucker,	July 24, 1783
Levi Smith & Ruth Morton,	Aug. 6, 1783
Abner Loomis & Zilpha Field,	——— 24, do
Benja Wait 3d & Zilpha Howard,	Oct. 16, do
Moses Hubbard & Martha Frary,	Dec. 11, do
John Rogers & Jerusha Alvord,	Feb. 17, 1784
Luke Packard & Rebecca Morton,	Sep. 23, do
Reuben Judd & Submit Graves,	Dec. 22, do

Joseph Church Jun & Lydia Wait,	——— 27, do
James Preston & Martha Meekins,	Feb. 3, 1785
Salmon Dickinson & Phoebe Baker,	Apr. 17, do
Israel Chapin, Jun. & Abigail Nash,	May 3, do
Rufus Smith & Levina Bangs,	——— 5, do
Benja Wells & Anna Chapin,	June 23, do
Perez Morton & Dorothy Morton,	Aug. 11, do
John Clary & Mary Frary,	Nov. 17, do
John C. Williams & Lucretia Williams,	Feb. 15, 1786
Elisha Sheldon & Elisabeth Wells,	May 25, do
Ebenr Morton & Hannah Ingraham,	June 22, do
Augustus Dickinson & Submit Dickinson,	Dec. 13, do
Oliver Hastings & Clarissa Allis,	May 10, 1787
Silas Porter & Mary Graves,	June 26, ———
Asa Ludden of Williamsburg & Sarah Morton,	Nov. 27, ———
Jonatha Bagley & Betsey McCollat,	Feb. 7, 1788
Elijah Smith of Whately & Miriam Morton,	Apr. 9, ———
Frederick Chapin & Lucretia Morton,	Sep. 11, ———
Joseph Smith 2d & Lois White,	Feb. 19, 1789
Amasa Wells & Eunice White,	Mar. 1, ———
Abijah Bliss & Orinda Herrick	Apr. 23, ———

√ MONSON

Apr. 28, 1760.   Part of Brimfield established as the District of Monson.

William Hudson & Tabitha Kibbee,	Sep. 17, 1782
Samuel Davis & Eunice Trask,	Feb. 20, 1783
Benja. Blodget & Molly Riddle,	Apr. 3, do
John Squire, Jr. & Susanna Riddle,	May 1, do
John Atcheson & Pheebe Kibbe,	Oct. 5, do
Stephen Bush & Zilpha Thresher,	Jan. 29, 1784
Aaron Bliss & Lucy Shaw,	Dec. 5, 1783
Abner Sabin & Joanna Colton,	Dec. 7, 1783
Joseph Smith & Sally Cooley,	Dec. 11, do

Joshua Blodgett & Increase Childs,	do ——— do
Stephen Wood & Cloe Newell,	do ——— do
Robert Barker & Mary Squire,	Jan. 5, 1784
Isaac Meacham & Dorcas Hail,	Dec. 30, do
Timo. Danielson & Elisabeth Sykes,	Feb. 17, 1785
Francis Sykes & Rose Bishop,	June 30, do
Noah Merick & Elisabeth Bishop,	do ——— do
Nye Peckham & Patience Anderson,	Sep. 28, 1783
John Streator & Elisabeth Kibbe,	Nov. 7, 1785

NORTHAMPTON

May 14, 1656. The towns of Springfield and North Hampton are mentioned.

Jehiel Alvord & Dorothy French,	June 11, 1778
Christopher Ely & Esther Hunt,	Oct. 12, ———
Christopher Kneep & Meribah Miller,	Nov. 17, ———
Justin Edwards & Elisabeth Clark,	Nov. 26, ———
Samuel Phelps & Phoebe Clark,	Dec. 17, ———
Frederick Bonestead & Thankful Cotes,	Jan. ———, 1779
Eliphaz Wright & Anne Moseley,	Mar. 22, ———
Joseph Warner & Jerusha Edwards,	Mar. 25, ———
Solo Williams & Mary Hooker,	Apr. 22, ———
Thomas Craige & Elisabeth Allen,	May 17, ———
Elijah Allen & Keziah Wright,	June 10, ———
Jonathan Bartlett & Dorcass Bartlett,	June 10, ———
Jedediah Clark of Sunderland & Lucy Parsons,	June 15, ———
Timothy Wright & Martha Wright,	June 16, ———
John Allin of West Springfield & Rachel Hendrick,	
	July 23, ———
Moses Bartlett & Hannah Wright,	Sep. 7, ———
Solo Pomeroy & Rachel Alvord,	Oct. 6, ———
Elisha Clap & Rachel Brown,	Nov. 24, ———
Rev. Noah Williston of Westhaven & Eunice Hall,	
	Nov. 25, ———

Lyman Clark & Susanna Wright,	Dec. 2,	——
Matthew Fenton & Levina Bigelow,	Dec. 7,	——
William Ingram, West Springfield & Eleanor Farnum,	Dec. 14,	——
Josiah Wait & Patty Strong,	Jan. 19,	1780
Seth Sheldon of Marlborough & Sarah Parsons,	Feb. 8,	——
Giles Lyman & Phoebe Lyman,	Feb. 24,	——
David Graves of Sunderld & Sarah Clap,	May 4,	——
Timothy Edwards & Thankful Strong,	May 31,	——
Seth Wright & Sarah Clark,	Sep. 13,	——
John Brown & Tabitha Porter,	Nov. 30,	——
Job Strong & Lydia Clap,	Dec. 14,	——
Luke Lyman & Susanna Hunt,	Jan. 21,	1781
Ephraim Wooster of Litchfield & Abigail Lyman,	Feb. 12,	——
Benja Mills of Chesterfield & Eunice Lyman,	Mar. 6,	——
Nathl. Phelps, Jun. & Lucy Strong,	July 5,	——
Oliver Clap & Patty Edwards,	July 25,	——
William Shearer of Greenwich & Eleanor Kentfield,	Oct. 2,	——
Nehemiah Cleaveland of Williamsburgh & Hannah Parsons,	Oct. 3,	——
Daniel Warner, Jun. & Phoebe Alvord,	Oct. 11,	——
Medad Strong & Eunice Parsons,	Oct. 18,	——
Daniel Strong & Tryphena Bush,	Nov. 5,	——
Eliphalet Phelps & Betsi Clap,	Nov. 6,	——
Amos Marsh & Jerusha Doolittle,	Nov. 12,	——
Elihu Wright & Mary Pomroy,	Dec. 13,	——
Henry Purkitt of Boston & Eunice Wright,	Jan. 1,	1782
Alvord Edwards & Eunice Root,	Jan. 16,	1782
Eleazer Alvord & Eunice Clark,	Feb. 21,	——
Daniel Bush & Penelope Cook,	Mar. 14,	——
Hezekiah Hutchins & Deborah Clap,	Apr. 18,	——
Thaddeus King & Naomi Warner,	June 19,	——
Benja Clark & Wid. Mary Hunt,	June 20,	——
Simeon Root & Betsi Clark,	June 27,	——
Phineas Alvord & Rachell Judd,	July 5,	——
Jona. Dwight & Meriam Wright,	Aug. 1,	——
Saml. Henshaw & Patty Hunt,	Aug. 8,	——
Levi Kellogg of Amherst & Cynthia Wright,	Aug. 30,	——

George Bryant of Chesterfield & Peggy Clap,	Oct. 24, ——
Noah Cook & Polina Baker,	Nov. 20, ——
Job Clark & Esther Burt,	Nov. 21, ——
Israel Barnard & Theodosia Lyman,	Nov. 21, ——
Oliver Edwards & Rachel Parsons,	Jan. 15, 1783
Fortune Prescott & Phoebe Bartlett,	Jan. 30
Daniel Crocker & Susanna Baker,	Feb. 6
Jared Hunt & Asenath Clark,	Mar. 6
Elijah Hubbard & Abigail Clap,	Mar. 13
Daniel Alvord & Susanna Judd,	Mar. 20
William Stone & Mehitabel Phelps,	June 18
Ebenr. Lane & Patty Phelps,	July 6
Gaius Pomroy & Betsey Clark,	Aug. 14
Elisha Baker & Ruth Fernum,	Sep. 25
Simeon Clap Junr. & Patty Root,	Oct. 9
Rev. Noah Atwater & Rachel Mather,	Oct. 16
Warham Parsons & Priscilla Parsons,	Dec. 25
Daniel Wright & Roxana Hunt,	Jan. 6, 1784
Paul Clark & Submit Phelps,	Jan. 15
Solo Clark & Sarah Turner,	Feb. 19
Simeon Day & Eleanor Hulbert,	Apr. 7
Shubael Wilder & Sarah Wright,	Apr. 19
Medad Strong & Wid. Rachel Clap,	June 2
Elam Clark & Dorcas Brown,	June 10
Simeon Darling of Mendon & Anna Phelps,	June 24
David Goodale & Mercy Clark,	July 14
George Langford & Nabby Elliot,	Oct. 25
Thomas Lyman & Dolly Clark,	Oct. 28
Simeon Edwards & Lydia Edwards,	Nov. 25
Joseph Cook & Esther Edwards,	Dec. 16
Caleb Tuttle & Molly Masters,	Dec. 23
Samuel Kellogg & Lucy Clap,	Dec. 30
Belah Strong, & Sally Parsons,	Dec. 30
Ariel Clark & Hannah Janes,	Dec. 30
Edward Williams & Rachel Barnard,	Jan. 2, 1785
Elisha Graves & Nabby Parsons,	Jan. 26, ——
Mathew Clark & Irena Strong,	Jan. 27, ——
Medad Parsons & Dorothy Clap,	Mar. 16, ——

Moses Grouch & Elenor Judd,	Apr. 12, ———
John Elliot & Rebecca Gardiner,	May 5, ———
Zenas Clark & Charlotte Lyman,	June 14, ———
Eli Edwards & Dorcas Wright,	Aug. 8, ———
Job White & Mindwell Clap,	Oct. 6, ———
Lewis Smith & Eunice Judd,	Nov. 3, ———
Oliver Clark & Damaris Strong,	Dec. 13, ———
Elijah Parker & Jerusha Brown,	Dec. 20, ———
Eliakim Clap & Pamelia Wright,	——— 20, ———
Joseph Parsons, Jr. & Dolly Clap,	Jan. 12, 1786
Silas Brown, Junr. & Jemima Clark,	Jan. 25, ———
Lynde Lord, Jr. & Polly Lyman,	Jan. 30, ———
Ebenezer Davis & Sarah Allen,	Mar. 8, ———
Thomas Cone & Mehitabel Lyman,	Mar. 13, ———
Moses Bartlett & Wid. Patience Frost,	Apr. 12, ———
Simeon Day & Phoebe Goff,	Apr. 13, ———
Amasa Parsons & Hannah Bartlett,	May 8, ———
George Hunt & Cynthia Day,	May 17, ———
Levi Gale & Hannah Dickinson, both of Hadley, May 21, 1786
Samuel Hinckley & Dolly Strong,	June 8, ———
Justin Lyman & Patty Clap,	June 19, ———
Eli Smith & Catharine Sheldon,	June 21, ———
Aaron Dickinson & Experience Cooley, both of Hadley,
	July 27, 1786
Eleazer Clark & Sally Clark,	Aug. 21, ———
Elihu Clap & Esther Cook,	Oct. 3 ———
Samuel Porter & Lucy Hubbard, both of Hadley, Oct. 25, 1786
Benajah Strong & Sarah Brown,	Oct. 31, ———
Medad King, Jr. & Susanna Warner,	Nov. 2, ———
Daniel Edwards & Dorcas Parsons,	Nov. 16, ———
Lewis R. Morris & Polly Dwight,	Dec. 2, ———
Matthew Murray & Hannah Elwell,	Jan. 18, 1787
Daniel Kingsley of Southampton & Polly Edwards,
	June 20, ———
William Clark, Junr. & Jerusha Wright,	July 19, ———
Patrick Welch & Acsha Wright,	Aug. 30, ———
Justin Clark & Temperance Pomroy,	Sep. 27, ———
Elijah Taylor & Rachel Hulbut,	Oct. 11, ———

Zachariah Field of Amherst & Philena Clark, Oct. 28, ———

Joseph Clark & Lydia Cook, Nov. 13, ———

Ezra Dewey & Martha Kent, Nov. 23, ———

Timothy Jewett & Elisabeth Phelps, Nov. 29, ———

Elijah Scott of Deerfield & Eunice Strong, Nov. 29, ———

Joshua Abel, Junr. of Goshen & Dolly Parsons, Dec. 12, ———

Abner Miller of West Springfield & Lois Edwards, Jan. 31, 1788

Timothy Pomroy of Southampton & Anna Burt, Apr. 8, ———

Moses Stebbins of Deerfield & Experience Clark, June 18, ———

Jeremiah Carrier of West Springfield & Sarah Ball,

July 31, ———

Aaron Wales of Westminster & Eunice Edwards, Oct. 5, ———

Elihu Bartlett of Westhampton & Rachel Edwards,

Nov. 27, ———

James Wales & Phoebe Burt, Dec. 4, ———

David Turner & Achsah Clark, ——— 10, ———

Samuel Parsons & Esther Pomroy, Jan. 7, 1789

Joseph Day of West Springfield & Lois Lyman, ——— 8, ———

Moses Wright & Eunice Parsons, Feb. 5, ———

David Strong & Esther Thayer, ——— 12, ———

Thaddeus Potter & Amy Kindall, Feb. 26, 1789

Caleb Smith of Athol & Abigail Baker, Mar. 3, ———

Oliver Parsons & Rhoda Parsons, ——— 10, ———

Levi Cleflin & Mercy Bridgman, Apr. 2, ———

√ ORANGE

Oct. 15, 1783. Parts of Athol, Royalston, Warwick, and certain common lands called Ervingshire established as the district of Orange.

Amos Woodward & Cata Goddard, Aug. 3, 1783

Humphrey Atherton Chapney & Sally Fisher, both

of Warwick, Aug. 19, 1783

William Crosby & Mary Higgins, May 30, 1784

Hezekiah Goddard & Anne Durham Oliver, of Athol,

Aug. 15, 1784

Asa Hemingway & Louise Knap of Winchester, Sep. 16, 1784

Jonathan Lampson of Randolph & Sally Morton, Sep. 19, 1784
Jacob French & Sally Duncan,   Feb. 14, 1785
Jacob Briggs Junr. & Lydia Bradish,   Oct. 18, 1784
Stephen King & Sarah Demon, both of New Salem,
      Nov. 18, 1784
John Love & Anner Burnet, both of Warwick,   Apr. 3, 1785
Abner Twichell of Athol & Hannah Brown of New
      Salem,   Apr. 14, 1785
Simon Chase & Sarah Town, both of New Salem, May 5, 1785
Benajah Aldrich & Huldah Metcalf,   Dec. 27, 1785
Elijah Ball & Prudence Rice,   May 10, 1786
Daniel Curtiss & Keziah Smith, both of New Salem,
      July 13, 1786
Noah Pheney & Elisabeth Pulsipher, both of New
      Salem,   Sep. 14, 1786
Benjamin Morton, Junr. of Guilford & Hannah
      Dexter,   Nov. 29, 1787
Samuel Knowles & Sally Woodward,   Nov. 29, 1787
David Harrington & Sarah Lord,   Oct. 14, 1787
Fra Babbit & Susanna Woodcock,   Nov. 4, 1787
Nathan Ellis & Hannah Lord,   Nov. 29, 1787
Ellis Whiting & Dorothy Woodward,   Dec. 31, 1787
Timothy Sow & Mary Kendall,   Jan. 10, 1788
Seth Thompson & Sarah Stow,   Jan. 10, 1788
Jephtha Johnson & Lydia Lusckcomb,   Feb. 14, 1788
David Cheney & Elisabeth Jones,   June 15, 1788
Barnabas Paine & Lois Woods,   Jan. 12, 1789
Aaron Chase & Priscilla Harrington,   Mar. 22, 1789
Hezekiah Cotter & Hannah Merick Briggs,   Mar. 10, 1789

SOUTHAMPTON

Jan. 5, 1753.   Part of Northampton established as the district of Southampton.

Frones Elliot & Lydia Kellogg,   June 8, ——
Eliakim Danks & Zebiah Dewey,   —— ——, ——

Timothy Clap & Salle Stone,   July 12, ———

Asahel Packard of S. & Martha French of Mont-
     gomery,   Aug. 12, ———

Stephen Maynard of Norwich & Elisabeth Wright,
     of Montgomery,   Oct. 17, ———

Stephen Allen & Silve Clap,   ——— 25, ———

Shem Trimmon & Mercy Lee,   Nov. 20, ———

SUNDERLAND

Nov. 12, 1718. "The Place" made a township and ordered that "the name of the township be henceforth called Sunderland."

Thomas Morton of Amherst & Sarah Barrett,	Apr. 29, 1762
Stephen Ashley & Elisabeth Billing,	Nov. 10, 1762
John Gould & Mary Barrett,	Dec. 14, 1762
Israel Chauncy & Elisabeth Petty,	Feb. 16, 1763
Caleb Smith & Katherine Harwood,	Feb. 17, 1763
Jonathan Field & Elisabeth Cooley,	Nov. 29, 1764
Benoni Farrand & Mary Campbell,	Dec. 5, 1764
Jonathan Ballard & Lucy Graves,	Oct. 5, 1765
Hekh Belding of Amherst & Martha Field,	Apr. 21, 1767
Giles Hubbard & Editha Field,	Apr. 23, 1767
Seth Field & Mary Hubbard,	May 26, 1767
John Gunn & Jerusha Oaks,	Oct. 1, 1767
Jona Russel & Anna Ashley,	Dec. 10, do
Eber Allis & Sarah Mann,	———, 1768
Moses Graves & Experience Oaks,	Jan. 12, do
Saml Clary & Mircah Barrit,	——— 19, do
Nathan Adams & Sybbil Ward,	Mar. 14, 1769
Moses Scott of Bennington & Mary Ballard,	Sep. 14, do
Abraham Sanderson & Lydia Smith,	Jan. ———, 1770
Josiah Cowls & Christian Graves,	June 7, do
Gideon Ashley & Mary Russell,	Nov. 1, do
Daniel Russel & Lucy Clark,	Feb. 6, 1771
Abner Cooley & Martha Russell,	June 18, 1771

Jonathan Graves, Junr. of S. & Jemima Scott of
   Whately,   Aug. 15, 1771
Miles Alexander & Wid. Mary Warner,   Nov. 21, do
Noah Graves & Ruth Wilde,   June 10, 1773
David Scott & Bethiah Esterbrooks,   June 30, 1773
Benjamin Dickinson & Sarah Ashley,   Oct. 21, 1773
Daniel Cooley & Mary Clary,   Nov. 14, do
Timothy Parsons of Northampton & Martha Hubbard,
                                    Dec. —, do
Ezekiel Woodbury of Barre & Anna Hubbard, Oct. 25, 1774
Ebenezer Barnard & Lydia Clark,   Mar. 12, 1775
Jonathan Hubbard & Hannah Barnard,   June —, do
Israel Russell & Eunice Montague,   July 16, do
Samuel Wright of Windsor & Eunice Ballard, Sep. 22, do
Oliver Williams & Zeruiah Ballard,   Nov. 19, do
Joseph Shattuck of Deerfield & Chloe Scott, Nov. 22, do
William Tryon & Susanna Spafford,   Feb. 9, 1777
John Montague & Abigail Hubbard,   Oct. 8, 1777
Martin Cooley & Irena Montague,   Oct. 9, do
Ebenezer Marsh, Junr. of Montague & Eunice
   Sprague,   Dec. 18, 1777
Avery Powers of Northampton & Lucy Ballard, Feb. 26, 1778
Samuel Smead of Montague & Wid. Hannah Scott,
                              Apr. 14, 1779
Stephen Gunn of Montague & Sarah Baker, Nov. 23, 1778
Lemuel Clark & Keziah Hubbard,   Oct. 14, 1779
Aaron Fisher of New Braintree & Elisabeth Ware, Feb. 24, 1780
Rinnah Cooley & Lucy Field,   Apr. 27, 1780
Caleb Hubbard & Tryphena Montague,   June 15, do
Joseph Barnard of S. & Wid. Sarah Cummings of
   Deerfield,   June 11, do
Gideon Cooley & Eunice Rowe,   July 6, do
Melzar Hunt & Mercy Cooley,   July 13, do
Jeremiah Graves & Lucinda Hubbard,   May 14, 1781
Isaac Sanderson & Submit Montague,   July 11, 1781
David Montague & Sarah Clark,   Sep. 23, do
Elijah Harmon & Rebecca Clark,   Nov. 28, 1782
Simeon Graves & Huldah Hubbard,   Feb. 2, 1783

Moses Frary of Ashfield & Wid. Hannah Graves, Feb. 12, do
Medad Clark of Northampton & Martha Warner, Mar. 20, do
Samuel Russel & Esther Harvey, May 19, do
Leml Graves & Deborah Battle, Sep. 12, 1783
Nathel Twing of Whately & Asenath Billings, Jan. 22, 1783
Ebenezer Stebbins of Deerfield & Rebecca Leonard,

May 19, 1785

Eliphalet Hale of Chesterfield, N. H., & Marcy Ballard,

July 28, do

John Russel & Miriam Graves, Sep. 22, 1785
Saml Hawks of S. & Mary Smead of Deerfield, Apr. 26, 1786
William Montague & Persis Russell, June 8, ———
Heman Farnum & Mary Field, Sep. 4, ———
Nath Smith 2d & Thankful Graves 2d., Nov. 15, ———
Spencer Russel & Ruth Cooley, Dec. 14, ———
Saml Belding, of Swansey, N. H. & Naomi Ballard,

Feb. 20, 1787

✓ WENDELL

May 8, 1781. Part of Shutesbury and part of the common lands called Ervingshire
established as Wendell.

Nathl. Wilder, Junr. & Anna Johnson, Jan. 29, 1784
Josiah Houghton & Elisabeth Weatherbee, Mar. 24, ———
Thomas Sawyer & Zebiah Hare, Sep. 6, ———
William Knight of New Salem & Rachel Stephens, Oct. 14, ———
Benja. Upton & Hannah Hixon, Mar. 24, 1785
Elihu Osgood & Mary Osgood, Nov. 9, ———
Ephraim Ross & Silence Osgood, ——— —— ——
Ephraim Howe & Esther Drury, Mar. 8, 1786
Samuel Osgood & Patty Dow, June 11, ———
Paul Sawyer & Sibbil Higgins, Sep. 11, ———
Richard Caswell & Rhoda Randboth, Dec. 17, ———
James Houghton & Lois Farr, May 26, 1787
Silas Wright & Sarah Caswell, Nov. 29, ———

Aaron Dresser of Montague & Abigail Munroe, ———— ——— ———
Ebenezer Burt of Deerfield & Wid. Barbara Paine,

Jan. 24, 1788

Moses Dresser of Montague & Lois Crosbie, Feb. 27, ———
Moses Lock & Hannah Lock, May 19, 1788
William Washburn of W. & Huldah Clark of New
Salem, Aug. 21, ———
Joel Crosbee & Phoebe Needham, Dec. 21, ———
Zedekiah Fisk & Lucy Sweetser, ——— 29, ———
Eli Rugg of New Salem & Abigail Higgins, Jan. 4, 1789
Josiah Ballard & Jane Zuil, ——— 20, ———
Timothy Blodgett, Junr. of Montague & Elizabeth Stiles,

Apr. 26, ———

Daniel Putnam & Polly Putnam, both of New Salem,

WESTFIELD

May, 9, 1669. Part of Springfield called Woronoake established as Westfield.

Eli Root & Mindwell Sackett, July 10, 1755
Reuben Noble & Ann Ferguson, July 17, 1755
Joseph Leonard & Mary Ashley, May 13, 1756
Nicholas Brown & Mary Root, June 14, 1756
Silas Noble & Bethiah Dewey, Nov. 25, 1756
Daniel Fowler & Eleanor Williams, Dec. 11, 1757
William Jones & Eleanor Noble, Sep. 22, 1757
Medad Dewey & Elisabeth Noble, Dec. 8, 1757
Dan Cadwell & Abigail Phelps, Dec. 29, 1757
Ichabod Lee & Martha Root, Dec. 29, 1757
Robert Smith of Palmer & Margaret Mawhorter,
of Greenwich, Dec. 13, 1759
Ebenezer Cooley of Petersham & Lydia Russell of
Greenwich, Jan. 9, 1760

WESTHAMPTON

Sept. 29, 1778.   Part of Northampton established as Westampton.

Ebenr. French, Junr. & Lucy Berwick,	Jan. 11, 1781
Gad Pomroy of Southampton & Lucy Herring,	Aug. 12, 1782
Cornelius Bartlett & Sarah Fisher,	June 19, 1783
John Potsinger & Rhoda French,	Oct. 23, do
Heman Pomroy & Rachel Howard,	Jan. 22, 1784
Andrew Malory & Abigail Smith,	Mar. 31, 1785
John Christian Baker of Northampton & Mary Howard,	Apr. 14, ——
Isaac Butard & Wid. Katharine Meriam,	Oct. 13, ——
Russell Clark & Phoebe Thayer,	Feb. 9, 1786
John Butard 2d. & Ruth Tyler,	Nov. 16, ——
Seth Parsons of Northampton & Rachel Wales,	Oct. 28, 1787
Zebulon Rust of Southampton & Aurela Norton,	Jan. 24, 1788
Timo. Warren of Hatfield & Sibel French,	May 29, 1788
Joseph Rhodes, Junr. of Chesterfield & Salome Rust,	Dec. 11, ——
Elisha Burt of Northampton & Chloe Wales,	—— 18, ——
Aaron Searl of Breadport & Mary Post,	Feb. 12, 1789
Reuben Wright & Dorcas Alvord,	Mar. 12, ——

BRISTOL COUNTY

✓ ATTLEBOROUGH

Oct. 19, 1694. Part of the land called the North Purchase established as Attleborough.

Benjamin Aengres (Heugres?) & Elizabeth Hill,	Nov. 9, 1758
Henry Alexander & Anna Hacker of Providence,	Nov. 4, 1779
Daniel Allen of Walpole & Patience Carpenter of Rehoboth,	Nov. 1, 1795
David Allen, Jr. of Ashford & Silva Briggs of Berkley,	April 1, 1779
Stephen Andrews, Jr. & Mary Bolckum,	Jan. 1, 1756
Jeremiah Armsbury & Hannah Clafflen,	Dec. 21, 1762
Consider Atherton & Sarah Carpenter,	Jan. 6, 1783
Daniel Atherton of New York & Phebe Bradford,	Aug. 27, 1795
Daniel Atherton of Walpole & Polly Bradford,	Jan. 13, 1791
Samuel Atherton & Sarah Robinson,	Dec. 1, 1757
Ebenezer Bacon & Caty Gay,	Nov. 13, 1795
William Balkcum, Jr. & Nancy Capron of Norton,	Dec. 6, 1791
Thomas Bardean of Middleboro & Susannah Riggs,	Feb. 11, 1763
Samuel Barden & Elizabeth Fuller,	Nov. 10, 1763
Elijah Barnes & Sarah Braman,	Mar. 25, 1762
Benaiah Barrows & Hopestil French,	Feb. 4, 1787
Ira Barrows of Richmond, N. H. & Abigail Guild,	Jan. 30, 1794
Joseph Barrows & Hannah Sweeting,	May 6, 1742
William Barrows & Patience Barrows,	July 19, 1795
Aaron Barrus (Barrows?) & Mary Read,	Dec. 29, 1768
Elijah Barrus (Barrows?) & Sarah Braman,	Mar. 25, 1762
Alvin Basset & Hannah Thayer, both of Norton,	May 17, 1792
Comfort Bates & Sarah Brown,	Nov. 27, 1780
Elijah Bates & Chloe Tyler,	Dec. 3, 1767
Michael Bates of Mendon & Chloe Atwell,	Feb. 21, 1793

Solomon Bates & Hannah Bolckum,   Sept. 4, 1755
Zimrhode Bicknell & Remember Ingraham,   Sept. 18, 1777
John Biggs & Sarah Woodward,   Nov. 29, 1769
Agabus Bishop of Fitzwilliam & Betty Sweetland, Feb. 22, 1790
Demos Bishop & Lydia Sweeting,   Jan. 30, 1783
Elkanah Bishop & Lydia Robinson,   Aug. 10, 1769
Samuel Bishop & Elizabeth Bishop,   June 2, 1731
Timothy Bishop & Hannah Lane of Norton,   Mar. 5, 1767
Otis Blackington & Ruth Richardson,   June 4, 1795
David Blackington & Lydia Chellay,   Dec. 25, 1794
Dorcas Blackington & Peter Hopkins,   Jan. 25, 1753
George Blackington & Mary Wolcot,   Mar. 1, 1770
Penticost Blackington & Margaret Robinson,   May 19, 1768
Peter Blackington & Margaret Everett,   April 24, 1755
Richard Blackington & Margaret Everit,   April 24, 1755
Ebenezer Blake of Wrentham & Petronella Peck, Dec. 11, 1729
Samuel Blake of Wrentham & Hannah Wilkerson,
    April 22, 1790
Daniel Blanding of Rehoboth & Sarah Lane,   Jan. 5, 1758
Joseph Blanding & Huldah Marting,   Sept. 30, 1790
Noah Blanding & Bridget French,   Nov. 23, 1758
Noah Blanding & Bethiah Thacher,   June 23, 1791
Newman Bliss of Rehoboth & Sally Starkey,   Jan. 6, 1792
Charles Bobbins of Providence & Nancy Ingraham,
    Oct. 19, 1794
David Bolckom & Fanna Phillips,   Apr. 10, 1781
Alexander Bolckum & Hannah Sheperdson,   Jan. 17, 1750
John Bolckum, Jr. & Bathsheba Daggit,   May 18, 1742
Enoch Bolkcolm & Sally Bishop,   Mar. 19, 1795
Alexander Bolkcom & Martha Okintun,   May 14, 1725
Benjamin Bolkcom & Martha Richardson,   May 16, 1793
Jno. Bolkom & Sarah Grover of Norton,   May 29, 1733
Joseph Bolkom & Mary Perminter,   Mar. 21, 1733-4
William Bolkom & Mary Tiler,   Oct. 3, 1717
Moses Bowen & Huldah Read of Rehoboth,   Sept. 6, 1781
Isaac Bowers (negro) & Betty Chace (mulatto), May 1, 1792
John Bradford & Phebe Stearns,   June 10, 1761
Joseph Bradford & Bethiah Morse,   Mar. 2, 1758

Henry Bragg & Sarah Luther,	Nov. 6, 1717
Josiah Brayman of Norton & Mary Jilson,	Oct. 2, 1729
Jesse Briggs of Norton & Mary Parmenter,	Aug. 21, 1766
Consider Brown & Peggy Robinson,	Oct. 24, 1776
John Brown & Bathsheba Barrows,	Aug. 13, 1741
John Brown & Priscilla Bishop of Cumberland,	Oct. 11, 1767
John Brown, Jr. & Nobby Wilson, both of Rehoboth,	
	Feb. 7, 1791
Lemuel Brown of Wentham & Sarah Draper,	April 11, 1775
Noah Brown & Judith Short,	Dec. 17, 1778
Noah Brown & Deborah Wilmarth,	April 9, 1752
Stephen Brown & Sarah Wilmarth,	Mar. 16, 1790
Baruck Bucklen of Rehoboth & Hannah Read,	Aug. 11, 1731
Nehemiah Bucklen & Beriah Read,	Dec. 10, 1730
Barak Bucklin of Rehoboth & Hannah Reed,	Aug. 11, 1731
Benjamin Bucklin & Rebeca Bowin,	Mar. 19, 1729-30
Solomon Buller & Patronella Blake,	Mar. 11, 1756
Richard Bullock & Polly Robinson,	July 6, 1794
Peter Burbee & Margaret Annis, ?	July 21, 1757
Peter Burbee & Margaret Curnio, ?	July 21, 1757
Andrew Burn & Sarah Cummins,	Apr. 13, 1769
Solomon Buttler ? & Patronella Blake,	Mar. 11, 1756
Elijah Capron & Abigail Stanley,	July 20, 1769
John Capron & Deborah Woodcock,	Sept. 26, 1723
Capt. Joseph Capron & Mary French,	Nov. 12, 1754
Otis Capron & Rachel Sweet,	Jan. 3, 1794
Seth Capron & Eunice Man,	Sept. 9, 1790
Caleb Carpenter of Rehoboth & Lucy Carpenter,	
	April 28, 1768
Caleb Carpenter of Rehoboth & Hannah French,	April 7, 1757
Charles Carpenter & Sarah Hutchins,	April 17, 1777
Cyrel Carpenter, Jr. & Mary Tyler,	April 15, 1790
Cyrial Carpenter & Lucy Lane of Norton,	Nov. 28, 1765
Daniel Carpenter, Jr. & Alice Richardson,	Mar. 6, 1794
Daniel Carpenter & Elizabeth Tyler,	Jan. 30, 1766
Ebenezer Carpenter & Mehitabel Bishop,	Oct. 31, 1717
Elihu Carpenter of Rehoboth & Martha Hutching,	
	June 14, 1783

Elisha Carpenter, Jr. & Anna Freeman,   Mar. 6, 1768
Elkanah Carpenter & Experience Sweet,   Jan. 9, 1794
John Carpenter, 2nd. & Molly Tyler,   Feb. 21, 1793
Joseph Carpenter & Mary Nason,   Dec. 25, 1754
Josiah Carpenter, Jr. & Chloe Carpenter of Reho-
    both,   June 27, 1793
Josiah Carpenter & Hepzebeth Wilmarth,   Sept. 21, 1769
Nathan Carpenter & Lucinda Ingraham,   Oct. 26, 1794
Nathan Carpenter & Patience Tower,   Dec. 26, 1723
Nehemiah Carpenter & Elizabeth Sweet,   Sept. 16, 1752
Noah Carpenter & Martha Follet,   June 24, 1756
Obadiah Carpenter & Amy Lee of Rehoboth,   Nov. 27, 1766
Obediah Carpenter, Jr. & Marcy Tyler,   Dec. 9, 1790
Oliver Carpenter, Jr. & Betty Draper,   April 2, 1792
Oliver Carpenter, Jr. of Rehoboth & Sarah French,
    Nov. 15, 1759
Peter Carpenter of Rehoboth & Amy French,   Dec. 6, 1759
Barnabas Cary of Providence & Mary Short,   April 5, 1759
Berry Chace, Jr. of Longmeadow & Mary Bowen, Nov. 7, 1793
John Chadwick & Elizabeth Wheting,   Feb. 15, 1732-3
Daniel Chaffee & Widdo. Ormsby,   Nov. 3, 1757
Noah Chaflin & Hannah French,   Jan. 10, 1733-4
Noah Chaflin, Jr. of Wrentham & Patty Willmarth,
    Dec. 12, 1793
Daniel Cheever & Joana Titus,   Mar. 28, 1793
John Chidell of Providence & Meribah Lealand, April 15, 1790
Daniel Chittenden & Rebecca Starkey,   Jan. 12, 1792
Calven Clafflen & Polly Welman,   Aug. 8, 1790
Eliphalet Clafflen & Amy Jilson,   Nov. 29, 1769
Nehemiah Clafflen & Mehitable Starkee,   Dec. 29, 1768
Noah Clafflen, Jr. & Keziah Carpenter of Rehoboth,
    Nov. —, 1756
Phineas Clafflenton ? & Marcy Fuller,   Dec. 15, 1761
Ebenezer Claflen & Bethiah Tiffany,   Nov. 16, 1749
Noah Claflen of Wrentham & Elizabeth Bullock of
    Rehoboth,   Sept. 24, 1789
Allorton Claflon & Sally Newell,   April 1, 1793
Jonathan Clark & Experience Weddge,   Oct. 29, 1724

Peter Clark of Cumberland & Zerviah Sweetland,
Dec. 27, 1759
Uriah Clark & Margaret Slack, Jan. 16, 1755
Eliphalet Clofflin & Anny Jilson, Nov. 29, 1769
Aaron Cole of Rehoboth & Susannah Smith, Oct. 26, 1791
Curtis Cole of Warren & Mary Briggs, Sept. 2, 1781
Noah Cole & Abilene Freeman, Mar. 7, 1794
Nathaniel Cooper, Jr. of Rehoboth & Hannah Bishop,
Apr. 3, 1777
Oliver Cotting & Keziah Clafflen of Wrentham, Nov. 29, 1787
Agreen Crabtree & Sarah Ingraham, July 20, 1758
Richard Crownenshield & Mary Lane, Nov. 12, 1761
James Crowningshield & Persis Carpenter, Dec. 1, 1757
Abraham Cummins, Jr. & Mary Bowen,? June 7, 1781
Peter Church, Col. of Bristol & Hannah Gay, Nov. 29, 1787
Joseph Cushman & Nancy Sheldon, Nov. 24, 1791
Nathaniel Daget & Lydia Tifany, April 30, 1724
Daniel Dagget & Margaret Woodcock, Apr. 14, 1763
James Dagget of Rehoboth & Rebeckah Stearns, Oct. 20, 1757
Jesse Dagget & Lois Robinson, Mar. 6, 1792
John Dagget, Jr. & Judith Capron, Dec. 13, 1781
Mayhew Dagget & Martha Newell, Nov. 20, 1766
Simeon Dagget & Anna Dean, June 8, 1779
Daniel Daggett, Jr. & Hannah Event, Nov. 20, 1794
Jacob Daggett of Rehoboth & Lydia Slack, June 2, 1791
Mayhew Daggett & Lucy Daggett, Mar. 5, 1789
Mayhew Daggett & Martha Newel, Nov. 20, 1766
Samuel Daggett & Lydia Stephens, Dec. 20, 1787
Daniel Day & Mary Fairbrother, Mar. 6, 1760
John Day & Hannah Robbins, Oct. 15, 1730
Joseph Day & Hannah Hoppin, Jan. 13, 1731-2
Ephraim Dean & Lydia Capron, June 1, 1790
Ebenezer Draper & Sally Capron, Sept. 26, 1793
Ellis Draper & Lydia Miller, April 20, 1789
Fisher Draper & Hannah Maxcy, Mar. 5, 1789
Isaac Draper & Chloe Tingley, Feb. 8, 1770
John Draper & Mary Reed, Oct. 5, 1749
Lewis Draper & Lucy Orne, Sept. 25, 1788

John Drown of Providence & Lucy Woodcock, April 18, 1775
John Dryer, Jr. of Rehoboth & Keziah ——, April 21, 1778
William Dryer, Jr. of Rehoboth & Ruth Hawes, Dec. 8, 1778
Abiel Dunham & Ruth Cobb, July 16, 1761
Solomon Dunham of Norton & Sarah Hill, Nov. 4, 1756
Benjamin Eastey & Elizabeth Reed, Jan. 11, 1787
Richard Everet & Drusilla Shurtlief, Aug. 27, 1761
Joshua Everett & Patience Stanley, June 24, 1756
Joshua Everett, Jr. & Molly Titus, June 22, 1764
Timothy Everett of Wrentham & Sarah Pitcher, Nov. 22, 1787
William Everett & Rebecka Allen, June 23, 1791
Peter Fales of Walpool & Avis Bicknell, Nov. 17, 1763
Thomas Fance & Rebecca Briggs, Oct. 23, 1766
Jonathan Felt & Love Well, Feb. 5, 1746-7
Ebenezer Field & Miriam Lane, Nov. 20, 1794
Alexander Fillebrown of Mansfield & Naomi Daggett,
June 16, 1789
David Fisher of Boylston & Sophia Thayer of Mans-
field, Dec. 9, 1790
Joel Fisher & Elizabeth Cummins, Sept. 21, 1768
John Fisher & Mary Bolckom, May 23, 1751
John Fisher of Norton & Mary Bolkom, Mar. 30, 1732
John Fisher & Betty Tiffany, Dec. 1, 1757
Samuel Fisher, Jr. of Wrentham & Olive Ellis, June 9, 1791
William Fisher & Abigail Grover, Oct. 3, 1754
Asa Fisk of Providence & Susannah Clark, Dec. 27, 1759
Abraham Follet & Susannah Cook, June 8, 1769
Abraham Follet & Dorcas Wise, May 12, 1726
Jonathan Follet & Mary Brown of Rehoboth, Sept. 23, 1763
William Follet & Rebecca Everet, Mar. 19, 1760
Alexander Foster, Jr. & Esther Pratt, Mar. 6, 1761
Ebenezer Foster & Desire Cushman, Sept. 17, 1730
Ebenezer Foster & Maria Orne, Dec. 13, 1792
Edward Foster, Jr. & Margaret Bridge, ? Jan. 12, 1763
John Foster & Abigail Richardson, July 21, 1763
Josiah Foster of Johnstone, R. I. & Elizabeth Rich-
ardson, May 2, 1791
Robert Frank & Catherine Fisher, Nov. 2, 1753

Solomon Franklin of Wrentham & Keziah Richardson,
Apr. 10, 1793
Ebenezer Freeman & Hannah Tyler, Feb. 23, 1750
Jeremiah Freeman, Jr. & Susannah Fairbrother, Nov. 15, 1764
Samuel Freeman & Anna Atwell, Jan. 10, 1760
Christopher French & Ame Carpenter, Oct. 11, 1753
Joseph French & Sibbil Carpenter, June 12, 1755
Nathaniel French & Bethiah French, Dec. 18, 1777
Aaron Fuller of Ashford & Hannah Pidge, Feb. 12, 1733-4
Abiel Fuller & Patience Read of Rehoboth, Apr. 16, 1778
Caleb Fuller of Winsor, Conn. & Hannah Weld, Oct. 28, 1762
Francis Fuller & Priscilla Day, Oct. 15, 1730
Jeduthun Fuller, Jr. & Achel Claflon, Jan. 29, 1793
John Fuller & Mary Martin, Nov. 12, 1755
Jonathan Fuller & Elizabeth Wise, Mar. 30, 1725
Nathan Fuller & Phebe Harris, Nov. 4, 1757
Noah Fuller, Jr. & Rebecca Sweet, Jan. 21, 1768
Stephen Fuller & Jemima White, Dec. 1, 1761
Zelotes Fuller & Esther Martin, Oct. 27, 1791
David Fulton & Ruth Foster, July 22, 1725
Samuel Gardner & Nabby Tabor, Nov. 4, 1790
Ephraim Gay, Jr. & Deleny Atwood, Aug. 27, 1788
Hannah Gay & Col. Peter Church of Bristol, Nov. 29, 1787
William Gay & Nabby Carpenter of Cumberland, Feb. 19, 1792
Preston George & Joanna Jackson, April 21, 1791
William George & Elizabeth French of Cumberland,
Oct. 16, 1760
William Gilmore of Franklin & Nancy Fales, Nov. 27, 1791
Tirall Gilmore of Franklin & Sally Fales, Jan. 27, 1790
Jonathan Green of Coventry & Lucretia Bans, ? Mar. 18, 1762
Benjamin Grover of Mansfield & Lucy Bolkcom, Feb. 13, 1777
Ebenezer Grover of Norton & Sarah Pratt, May 29, 1733
Jesse Grover & Phebe Braman both of Mansfield, Mar. 23, 1787
Benjamin Guild & Jemime Mors, Feb. 1, 1753
David Guild & Olive Day, Feb. 6, 1792
Ebenezer Guild, Jr. & Molley Lane, Dec. 13, 1782
John Guild & Margrett Dagget, May 1, 1788
Joseph Guild & Hannah White, Nov. 10, 1741

Napthali Guild & Elize. Howes of Wrentham,	Nov. 1, 1787
Napithali Guild & Joanna Richardson,	Dec. 9, 1742
Daniel Hall & Ruth Marshall,	Aug. 7, 1741
Edward Hall & Rebekah Robinson,	Oct. 13, 1723
Ephraim Hall & Hannah Fuller (widow),	Dec. 8, 1791
Ephraim Hall & Elizabeth Hutchins,	Mar. 8, 1753
William Hambleton & Mary Richardson,	Mar. 10, 1741/2
William Hancock of Wrentham & Sarah Tower,	July 19, 1733
Job Harding of Midway & Dorcas Reed,	April 25, 1787
Nathan Harvey & Martha Stephens,	April 30, 1741
Abner Haskel & Grace Day,	Jan. 15, 1746/7
Abner Haskel & Grace Peck, 2nd.,	Jan. 15, 1746/7
Peter Haskins of Taunton & Susannah Eddy,	Mar. 24, 1763
Elijah Hawes & Betsy Tingley,	Nov. 1, 1792
William Haws of Wrentham & Eunice Dagget,	Nov. 7, 1793
Ebenezer Healey & Hannah Fuller,	Nov. 11, 1730
Ezra Healy & Ruth Day,	Feb. 21, 1760
James Heddon of Rehoboth & Martha Fuller,	May 3, 1764
Benjamin Hughes & Elizabeth Hill,	Nov. 9, 1758
Benjamin Hill & Lois Carpenter, both of Cumberland,	Nov. 17, 1790?
Nathaniel Hills & Hannah ———,	June 11, 1753
Nathaniel Hills & Malatiah Woodcock,	Apr. 4, 1793
James Hodges of Norton & Abigail Daggett,	Nov. 30, 1749
Joseph Hodges & Miriam Bishop,	Nov. 30, 1749
James Holmes & Lydia Barrows,	June 18, 1741
Peter Hopkins & Dorcas Blackington,	Jan. 25, 1753
Benjamin Hoppen & Mary Day,	April 22, 1731
John Hoppen & Elizabeth Ide,	May 13, 1772
John Hoppin & Elizabeth Ide,	May 13, 1742
Peter Hoskins of Taunton & Susannah Eddy,	Mar. 24, 1763
Daniel Hunt of Norton & Sarah Jackson,	June 30, 1757
Amos Ide & Sally Carpenter,	Dec. 17, 1795
Amos Ide & Huldah Tyler,	Mar. 22, 1753
Benjamin Ide, Jr. & Abigail Sweet,	Sept. 16, 1752
Jacob Ide, Jr. & Sarah Ide,	Nov. 13, 1744
John Ide, Jr. & Lydia Lane,	Oct. 27, 1757
Josiah Ide of Rehoboth & Jemima Sweet,	Oct. 26, 1775

Nathan Ide & Martha Carpenter of Rehoboth,   Feb. 25, 1768
Nathaniel Ide & Hannah Daggett,   Apr. 13, 1792
Nicholas Ide & Rachel Day,   Oct. 13, 1743
Timothy Ide of Cumberland & Abigail Robins, Nov. 23, 1758
John Inde & Anna Short,   May 4, 1786
Comfort Ingraham & Molly Cheney,   July 3, 1765
Elijah Ingraham & Sarah Ide,   Dec. 3, 1730
Elijah Ingraham & Rebeckah Sweet,   Feb. 2, 1792
Nancy Ingraham & Charles Robbins of Providence,
                                             Oct. 19, 1794
Isaac Jackson & Ruth Tallman,   Sept. 15, 1755
Joseph Jackson & Zipporah Tower,   Jan. 28, 1730/31
Ephraim Johnson of Stratford, Conn. & Mary Dagget,
                                             May 19, 1776
Henry Joslin & Mary Whipple,   May 21, 1724
Thomas Keepers & Hannah Martin,   Nov. 16, 1749
John Kent & Rachel Carpenter,   Mar. 30, 1726
John King & Elizabeth Alexander,   June 16, 1768
Keziah Lane & Micah Packard of St. George,   Oct. 31, 1769
Robert Laurl (negro) & Jemime Sly (negro),   Jan. 25, 1793
Rev. Ebenezer Lazel & Chloe Richardson,   Jan. 15, 1793
Joseph B. Lealand & Nabby Healy,   May 26, 1790
Daniel Lothrop, 3rd. of Bridgewater & Sally Whiting,
                                             May 21, 1787
Samuel Luscombe & Deborah Read,   Sept. 5, 1776
Henry Lyon of Ashford & Anna Everet,   Feb. 18, 1767
Benjamin Macey & Esther Fuller,   Dec. 25, 1794
John Macomber of Rehoboth & Olive Shepherdson,
                                             Apr. 10, 1777
Lemuel Macomber of Rehoboth & Tabitha Capron,
                                             Apr. 24, 1777
Bazaliel Man & Polly Field,   Mar. 31, 1796
Dr. Bezeliel Man & Bebe Carpenter,   Feb. 15, 1753
Newton Mann & Abigail Maxcy,   May 10, 1792
Lieut. Josiah Maxcey & Mary Robinson,   June 14, 1759
Abel Martin & Huldah Fisher,   Mar. 19, 1776
Amos Martin & Esther Chaffe,   April 27, 1757
Dr. Calvin Martin of Rehoboth & Susanna May, June 13, 1793

Job Martin & Susannah Fisher, Dec. 9, 1779
John Martin & Margaret Richardson, Jan. 27, 1767
Robert Martin & Elizabeth Wellman, April 30, 1741
David Mathews & Eleoner Burn both of Norton, Oct. 11, 1781
Benjamin Maxcey & Sarah Fuller, Oct. 20, 1763
Levi Maxcey & Ruth Newel, April 23, 1766
Joseph Maxcy & Hannah Pidge, Mar. 11, 1788
Joseph Maxcy & Rebekah Stacey, Feb. 8, 1727/8
Josiah Maxcy & Chloe Daggett, July 5, 1789
Joseph Maxey & Mary Stanley, Nov. 3, 1752
Lieut. Josiah Maxcy & Mary Robinson, June 14, 1759
Levi Maxey & Ruth Newil, Apr. 23, 1766
Elisha May & Ruth Medcalf, Sept. 22, 1763
Ebenezer Medcalf & Elizabeth Stanley, Jan. 25, 1770
Joseph Millard & Mary Reed, Jan. 8, 1767
Josiah Miller, Jr. of Cumberland & Mary Bicknel, Apr. 14, 1794
Comfort Moore & Chloe Reed, July 20, 1769
Alexander More & Allin Chafey, July 23, 1741
Comfort More & Margaret Fuller, June 10, 1790
Elijah Morse of Mansfield & Ruth Fisher, July 11, 1793
Henry Morse & Esther Pidge, Mar. 20, 1755
Noah Morse & Betty Hill, Nov. 15, 1764
Wm. Morse, Jr. & Lucy Tingley, Apr. 2, 1795
Samuel Newell, Jr. & Philena Hissany, Apr. 4, 1793
Rev. Oliver Noble of Coventry & Lucy Weld, May 15, 1760
Jonathan Nutting of Wrentham & Deborah Whipple,
May 5, 1731
James Orn & Esther Everet, May 28, 1760
James Orne, Jr. & Chloe Hunt Brown, June 25, 1792
Dr. Cardee Parker of Coventry, Conn. & Mary Weld,
Apr. 15, 1762
Obadiah Parker & Rhoda Briggs, Dec. 2, 1741
Caleb Parmenter, Jr. & Elizabeth Round, May 18, 1780
Joshua Parmenter & Sarah Fuller, Nov. 3, 1742
Jeremiah Pearce & Patty Tingley, Sept. 29, 1791
Henry Peck & Anna Richardson, Jan. 18, 1781
Jeremiah Peck of Cumberland & Elizabeth Gains, Dec. 25, 1792
John Peck & Rebeca Richardson, May 26, 1724

Joseph Peck & Elizabeth Reed,	Feb. 6, 1766
Solomon Peck of Cumberland & Esther Wiswal,	Dec. 7, 1758
Ezra Perry of Rehoboth & Jemima Tittus,	Apr. 29, 1762
Joseph Perry & Chloe Towns,	Mar. 25, 1790
Timothy Perry of Rehoboth & Huldah Hill,	Nov. 29, 1769
Jno. Philamore, Jr. of Norwich & Leah Day,	Nov. 12, 1747
Jonathan Philbrook of Boston & Dorothy Weld,	Aug. 7, 1759
Samuel Philips & Rachel Kirkland,	April 15, 1725
John Phillimore, Jr. of Norwich & Leah Day,	Nov. 12, 1747
Samuel Phillips & Rachel Kirkland,	Apr. 15, 1725
Abijah Pitcher & Sarah Ellis,	Mar. 11, 1783
Keziah Pitcher & Azariah Tingley,	Jan. 16, 1766
Samuel Pitcher & Hannah Follet,	Apr. 30, 1752
Stephen Pullen & Mary Blackinton,	Jan. 12, 1769
James Pulling & Lydia Woodcock,	Mar. 1742/3
Ebenezer Read & Betty Stanley,	Feb. 11, 1790
Joel Read & Chloe Stanly,	Oct. 14, 1779
Nathan Read of Rehoboth & Sally Robinson,	Nov., 1795
Nathaniel Read & Huldah Carpenter,	Dec. 28, 1758
Noah Read & Dorcas Chaffe,	Dec. 10, 1761
Noah Read & Widdo. Hannah Richardson,	Jan. 17, 1760
Samuel Read, Jr. of Rehoboth & Dille Carpenter,	
	Aug. 10, 1762
Timothy Read & Priscilla Hatch of Walpole,	July 24, 1766
Timothy Read & Martha Pidge,	Apr. 7, 1760
William Read & Cylinda Tingley,	May 24, 1792
Samuel Redaway of Rehoboth & Abia Follet,	Feb. 21, 1760
Daniel Reed, Jr. & Bebe Peck,	Apr. 23, 1765
Daniel Reed & Mary White,	Apr. 2, 1741
Ichabod Reed & Elizabeth Robinson,	April 12, 1763
Nathaniel Reed & Huldah Carpenter,	Dec. 28, 1758
Noah Reed & Abigail Robins,	Mar. 11, 1741/2
Samuel Reed & Mary Maxcey,	Nov. 17, 1763
Thomas Reed & Rachel Titus of Rehoboth,	May 28, 1783
Timothy Reed & Priscilla Hatch of Walpole,	July 24, 1766
Timothy Reed & Elizabeth Tyler,	Jan. 31, 1765
Ezeblon ? Rhodes of Stoughtonham & Sarah Bishop of Cumberland,	
	Nov. 11, 1779

Avery Richards & Zelpha George,	May 19, 1790
Calvin Richards & Lydia Walcut,	Feb. 22, 1787
Edward Richards, Jr. & Ame Bucklin,	Jan. 7, 1790
Luther Richards & Lydia Wilmarth,	Nov. 13, 1787
Aaron Richardson & Ruth Tingley,	Jan. 17, 1765
Caleb Richardson, Jr. & Huldah Hatch,	June 21, 1787
Caleb Richardson & Esther Tiffany,	Nov. 19, 1761
Daniel Richardson, 2nd & Olive Franklin of Wren-	
them,	Apr. 10, 1793
Daniel Richardson & Sarah Read,	Oct. 12, 1762
Ebenezer Richardson & Esther Cheney of Norton,	
	Jan. 15, 1765
Ebenezer Richardson & Sarah Cummings,	Aug. 2, 1750
John Richardson, Jr. & Patty Everett,	Apr. 15, 1792
John Richardson & Elizabeth Wilmarth,	Apr. 21, 1742
John Richardson & Ruth Woodcock,	Nov. 17, 1768
Jno. Richardson & Elizabeth Wilmouth,	Apr. 21, 1742
Stephen Richardson & Hannah Fuller, 2d.,	April 30, 1761
Stephen Richardson & Mary Fuller,	May 16, 1765
Wm. Richardson & Mary Coy,	April 15, 1742
Nathaniel Richmond of Providence & Sally Mann,	
	May 22, 1783
John Riggs & Sarah Woodward,	Nov. 29, 1769
Ezekiel Robbins & Lydia Titus,	Jan. 7, 1755
Jack Robbins & Hannah Eason of Norton,	Dec. 13, 1787
Job Robbins & Cynthia Cushman,	April 2, 1767
John Robbins, Jr. & Martha White,	May 20, 1742
Jonathan Robbins & Jane Yeats,	Feb. 22, 1759
Jno. Robin, Jr. & Martha White,	May 20, 1742
Amos Robinson & Hepzebeth Wilmurth,	Mar. 30, 1758
Comfort Robinson & Widow Rachel Robinson,	Apr. 26, 1764
Elijah Robinson & Esther Fuller,	Dec. 19, 1793
Elijah Robinson & Sarah Smith,	Apr. 17, 1755
Enoch Robinson & Mindwell Shepard,	Dec. 17, 1761
Geo. Whitefield Robinson & Silena Richardson,	July 26, 1791
Geo. Robinson of Norton & Ruth Slack,	June 2, 1791
Jesse Robinson & Lavinia Gardner,	Oct. 24, 1793
Joel Robinson & Margaret Blackington,	Nov. 17, 1791

John Robinson & Thankfull Newel,	May 28, 1723
John Robinson & Mary Shurtliff,	Jan. 3, 1750
Nathan Robinson & Lois Briant,	Apr. 18, 1793
Nathaniel Robinson & Hannah Woodcock,	Mar. 30, 1775
Nathaniel Robinson & Hannah Woodcock,	Apr. 13, 1775
Noah Robinson & Patience Daggett,	Oct. 4, 1723
Samuel Robinson & Elizabeth Capron,	Sept. 14, 1752
Samuel Robinson & Joy Newell,	Jan. 31, 1764
Zephaniah Ross of Wrentham & Phebe Bolckum,	Oct. 31, 1765
Moses Rowley & Mehitable Weeks,	July 3, 1724
John Sabin, Jr. of Rehoboth & Zerviah Fuller,	Dec. 31, 1767
John Sadler & Hannah Morse, (More?)	May 15, 1783
James Sally & Nelly Little,	Oct. 19, 1779
Samuel Sanford & Eleona Pullin,	Dec. 24, 1795
Ichabod Sever of Midway & Rebecka Richardson,	
	Aug. 15, 1787
Ichabod Shaw, Jr. of Norton & Zilpah Bolckum,	Sept. 15, 1763
Rev. Oakes Shaw & Elizabeth Weld,	July 19, 1764
Ephraim Sheldon & Margaret Fenner,	April 15, 1725
Amose Shepardson & Margaret Pidge,	Mar. 30, 1732
Daniel Shepardson, Jr. & Mary Peck,	Nov. 12, 1753
Daniel Shepardson & Hannah Richardson,	Dec. 9, 1725
Jonathan Shepardson, Jr. & Miriam Follet	
Amos Shepardson & Margaret Pidge,	Mar. 30, 1732
Stephen Shepherdson & Lucy Fisher of Norton,	Mar. 15, 1759
Manassah Short of Rehoboth & Anna Peck,	July 27, 1780
Silvanus Shurtleff & Sarah Wood,	Jan. 31, 1760
Comfort Slack & Sarah Love,	Dec. 11, 1769
Joel Slack of Wrentham & Easter Richardson,	Mar. 22, 1792
John Slack, Jr. & Betsy Ide	
John Slack & Abigail Gould,	Aug. 18, 1768
Samuel Slack & Ruth Stearns,	Dec. 12, 1765
David Smith & Martha Dagget,	Jan. 3, 1782
Eleazer Sprague of No. Providence & Eunice Read,	Dec. 24, 1778
John Sprague & Mary Everett,	Sept. 30, 1756
Joseph Sprague of Smithfield & Phillis Jilson,	Dec. 29, 1768
Artemas Stanley & Betsy Daggett,	Nov. 24, 1795
Benjamin Stanley & Abigail Spear,	April 1, 1760

Benjamin Stanley & Anna Tiffany,   April 23, 1766
Jeremiah Stanley & Abigail Ward,   April 2, 1761
Penticost Stanley & Experience Fairbank,   Jan. 8, 1767
Solomon Stanley & Patience Perry,   June 11, 1767
Stephen Stanley & Martha Stanley,   Feb. 7, 1792
Timothy Stanley & Ruth Clarke,   June 24, 1767
Lieut. Timothy Stanley & Rebeckah Maxey,   May 13, 1761
Wm. Stanley & Zilpha Daggett,   Oct. 6, 1752
Thomas Starkee & Rebeckah Capron,   Sept. 18, 1755
Thomas Starkey, Jr. & Irena Pond of Wrentham, Oct. 25, 1787
William Starkey & Sarah Martin,   Nov. 29, 1764
John Stephens & Rachel Freeman,   Nov. 22, 1727
John Stephens & Sarah Titus,   Dec. 6, 1733
Lemuel Straton of Foxborough & Abigail Stearns, Dec. 4, 1787
John Streeter & Meriam Day,   Oct. 31, 1733
Joseph Streeter & Elizabeth Titus,   June 4, 1717
Amos Sweet & Hannah Richardson,   Nov. 18, 1762
Calvin Sweet & Nancy Tylor,   May 26, 1793
Ebenezer Sweet & Naomi Daggett,   June 5, 1764
Henry Sweet & Bathsheba Bolkcom,   Feb. 27, 1746/7
Henry Sweet, Jr. & Lucinda Tyler,   May 21, 1787
John Sweet & Sarah Maclaflen,   Nov. 11, 1730
Michael Sweet & Rachel Foster,   Feb. 9, 1762
Thomas Sweet, Jr. & Margaret Foster,   Oct. 31, 1766
Thomas Sweet, Jr. & Nancy Tyler,   Nov. 17, 1791
Henry Sweeting & Elizabeth Barrows,   Nov. 23, 1758
John Sweeting & Ruth Reed,   Dec. 17, 1767
George Sweetland & Nancy Walker, Jr. of Cumberland,
    Dec. 30, 1794
Samuel Sweetland of Rehoboth & Esther Robbins,
    Sept. 30, 1733
John Tallman & Anna Miller,   June 2, 1768
Peter Thacher, Jr. & Nanne Tyler,   Apr. 16, 1778
John Thatcher & Sarah Richardson,   Dec. 7, 1780
Moses Thatcher & Sarah Reed,   Apr. 1, 1793
Obadiah Thatcher & Elizabeth Richardson,   Jan. 6, 1783
Samuel Thatcher & Betsy Carpenter,   Feb. 4, 1793
John Thayer & Mary Spencer,   Jan. 10, 1770

Noah Tiffany & Hannah Carpenter of Cumberland,
Mar. 22, 1781
Daniel Tiffany & Mary Woodcock, May 25, 1762
Ebenezer Tiffany & Molley Carpenter, Feb. 9, 1758
James Tiffany & Elizebeth Allen, Nov. 11, 1725
Joseph Tiffany & Charlotte Capron, Nov. 25, 1790
Thomas Tiffany & Malatiah Tingley, June 10, 1779
William Tiffany & Betty Swain, April 12, 1787
Samuel Tiler & Mary Capron, Dec. 19, 1717
Josiah Tingley & Jemima Crabtree, Nov. 22, 1759
Thomas Tingley & Alathea Day, Nov. 28, 1754
Thomas Tingley & Martha Day, Nov. 28, 1754
Thomas Tingley, Jr. & Elizabeth Tylor, Oct. 15, 1792
Timothy Tingley & Nabe Capron, Aug. 12, 1790
John Titus, Jr. & Lydia Bates, Jan. 5, 1764
John Titus & Mary Daggett, Jan. 18, 1727/8
Robert Titus & Elizabeth Foster, May 1, 1755
Robert Titus & Esther Wilmarth, May 28, 1741
Samuel Titus of Rehoboth & Rachel Fisher, June 13, 1777
Samuel Titus & Chloe Tingley, June 25, 1789
Simeon Titus & Hannah Allen, Nov. 24, 1766
William Toleman & Chloe White of Mansfield, Nov. 20, 1777
John Tollman & Anna Miller, June 2, 1768
Abisha Town & Lucinda Wellman, April 18, 1793
Benjamin Tree & Hannah Streeter, Feb. 20, 1723/4
Thomas Turner & Betsy Horse, April 5, 1795
David Tyler & Hannah Read, Jan. 24, 1794
Ebenezer Tyler & Hannah Read, May 1, 1762
John Tyler & Mercy Thacher, June 30, 1768
Moses Tyler & Thankful Reed, Feb. 23, 1758
Nathan Tyler & Rebekah Eastee, Mar. 22, 1753
Samuel Tyler & Lucy Daggett, Feb. 25, 1783
Walter Tyler & Bathshaba Sweet, Oct. 28, 1790
Zelotes Tyler & Molly Robinson, Dec. 27, 1791
William Tyler & Eleonar White, Oct. 18, 1787
William Tyler & Submit Woodcock, Dec. 4, 1792
Ebenezer Walcott of Winthrop & Molly Titus, Mar. 20, 1788
Michael Walcut & Eunice Pitcher, May 10, 1787

Comfort Walker of Rehoboth & Mehitable Robinson,

Nov. 24, 1762

David Walker of No. Providence & Mary Sweetland,

Aug. 11, 1791

Timothy Walker & Elizabeth Carpenter, Dec. 10, 1741

Moses Ware of Norton & Elizabeth Lane, June 23, 1731

William Ware & Mary Maxey, May 4, 1726

Abisha Washburn & Mary Willmarth, Dec. 19, 1776

David Wedge & Joanna Headle, Dec. 16, 1723

Richard Weeks & Mary Leonard, Aug. 10, 1724

Rev. Ezra Weld & Anna Weld, Feb. 9, 1764

Elijah Wellman & Rhoda Sweet, June 28, 1759

Lot Wellman & Mercy Jencks, Sept. 13, 1795

Thomas Wellman of Lynn & Martha Follet, June 29, 1769

John Welman & Mary Attwell, May 24, 1753

Jerahmel B. Wheeler of Vermont & Sibbel French, Feb. 3, 1791

Simeon Wheeler of Rehoboth & Elizabeth Titus, Mar. 29, 1780

Preserved Whipple & Eliza Hewes, Mar. 19, 1795

Hezekiah White & Anne Skinner, both of Mansfield,

Sept. 6, 1793

Jonathan White, Jr. of Mansfield & Lucy Woodcock,

Apr. 6, 1775

William White & Susannah Robinson, Oct. 20, 1763

Zechariah White of Mansfield & Hephziba Woodcock,

May 14, 1778

David Whiting, Jr. & Patty Daggett, Oct. 9, 1792

David Whiting, & Hannah Walcot, Dec. 4, 1766

Otis Whiting, & Lowis Willman, Sept. 25, 1794

David Whitney & Hannah Walcot, Dec. 4, 1766

Rev. John Wilder & Easter Tyler of Preston, Sept. 2, 1790

John Wilkerson & Hannah Fisher, May 24, 1763

John Williams of Concord & Molly Everet, Sept. 26, 1769

Jonathan Williams of Dudley & Esther Wilmarth,

Oct. 31, 1768

Solomon Willis & Mary Chaffee, Oct. 26, 1780

Amos Wilmarth & Eunice Buttler, Apr. 18, 1777

Ebenezer Wilmarth & Molly Capron, Jan. 23, 1777

Ebenezer Wilmarth & Sarah Sweet, July 4, 1764

Eliphalet Wilmarth, Jr. & Bethiah Crane,		Mar. 12, 1778
John Wilmarth, Jr. & Bethana Bishop,		Apr. 5, 1787
John Wilmarth, & Phebe Briggs, of Rehoboth,		June 4, 1761
Stephen Willmarth & Lurana Willmarth,		Apr. 13, 1790
Elkanah Willmarth & Alice Briggs,		Oct. 7, 1755
John Willson of Newton & Mehitable Metcalf,		Apr. 30, 1761
Benjamin Wilmarth & Susanna Capron,		Jan. 11, 1787
Benoni Wilmarth & Lydia Crane,		Mar. 21, 1776
Elkanah Wilmarth & Sally Hall,		Aug. 9, 1791
Deacon Nathan Wilmarth & Rebeckah Brown of Rehoboth,		Aug. 19, 1756
Stephen Wilmarth & Hannah Reed,		Mar. 3, 1741/2
Eliphalet Wilmurth & Hannah Sweet,		Mar. 15, 1752
Abial Wood & Phebe Smith both of Taunton,		Sept. 30, 1795
David Woodcock & Abigail Holmes,		Sept. 17, 1765
Israel Woodcock & Jemima Whipple,		June 15, 1732
John Woodcock & Elizabeth Capron,		June 15, 1775
Jonathan Woodcock & Abigail Hills,		May 9, 1751
Joseph Woodcock, Jr. & Mercy Richardson,		July 29, 1776
Joseph Woodcock & Martha Tripp,		May 4, 1769
Nathaniel Woodcock, & Mary Brewster,		Aug. 18, 1731
Noadiah Woodruff & Esther Capron, both of W. Stockbridge,		Feb. 9, 1792
John Yarman & Mary Alexander,		Aug. 6, 1769
Elisha Brown & Anna Kennicut, both of Barrington, R. I.,		Mar. 26, 1778

ERRATA, Book I

P. 71.   Gershom **How** of Northboro and Levina Bartlett.

P 88.   Isaac **How** and Hannah Fay.

P. 89.   Eliab Wheelock and **Persis** Gaschet.

INDEX.

EARLY MASSACHUSETTS MARRIAGES.

PLYMOUTH COUNTY MARRIAGES

1692-1746

LITERALLY TRANSCRIBED FROM THE FIRST VOLUME OF THE
RECORDS OF THE INFERIOR COURT OF COMMON PLEAS,
AND FROM AN UNNUMBERED VOLUME AND VOLUME
ONE OF THE RECORDS OF THE COURT OF
GENERAL SESSIONS OF THE PEACE,
PLYMOUTH COUNTY,
MASSACHUSETTS

REPRINTED FROM VOLUMES ONE AND TWO OF "THE GENEALOGICAL ADVERTISER"

1898-1899

CAMBRIDGE, MASS.
LUCY HALL GREENLAW, PUBLISHER
1900

NOTE.

The publication of Plymouth County Marriages was begun in THE GENEALOGICAL ADVERTISER in March, 1898, and the sheets of this pamphlet were reprinted from that magazine from time to time as the several installments appeared. It was the intention of the publisher to issue an indexed volume of these marriages as soon as their publication in the magazine was completed. The fact that these records were being printed was generally known, and has been widely advertised during the past three years. Rev. Frederic W. Bailey, B. D., "Member New England *Genealogical* and *Biographical* Society," has recently forestalled the balance of this intended work by publishing abstracts of the larger part of the Plymouth County Marriages, as the second volume of his Early Massachusetts Marriages. One volume of the Court Records at Plymouth, however, seems to have escaped his notice. It is an unnumbered volume of the Records of the Court of General Sessions of the Peace, and contains records of marriages for the years 1723 to 1737, none of which are found in Mr. Bailey's volume.

The purpose of issuing this pamphlet now is to supply such of Mr. Bailey's subscribers, as do not have a set of THE GENEALOGICAL ADVERTISER, with that portion of the Plymouth County Marriages contained in the unnumbered volume but not printed in his book. These occupy pages three to nineteen of this pamphlet. As this is intended for a supplement to his work, it is not thought necessary to index it. Scanning the pages for the name wanted is only a step beyond scanning the pages of an index in which the arrangement of names seems to have been determined by chance, Trask being the first name found under its initial and Thurston the last.

CAMBRIDGE, October, 1900.

PLYMOUTH COUNTY MARRIAGES.

FROM THE FIRST VOLUME OF THE RECORDS OF THE

INFERIOR COURT OF COMMON PLEAS,

AT PLYMOUTH, MASS.

[1] 1693 Registry of marriages within yᵉ Town of Plimouth

John Dotey junʳ And mehetabel Nelson were married ffebruary yᵉ 2ᵈ : 1692-3

Joseph ffinney of plimouth marryed to mary Bryant of yᵉ same june 14ᵗʰ 1693 :

John Nelson of plimouth marryed to patience Morton of yᵉ same may 4ᵗʰ 1693 :

Joseph Bucland was married to Deborah Barrow, October 17ᵗʰ 1693.

Jodathon Robbins & Hannah Pratt were marryed yᵉ 11ᵗʰ day of January 1693-4

Samˡ Dunham senʳ & Sarah Watson Widdow was marryed yᵉ 15ᵗʰ day of January 1693-4

Hugh Cole senʳ & mary morton Widdow were marryed yᵉ 30ᵗʰ of January 1693-4

1694 John Dotey senʳ and Sarah Jones were married the 22ᵈ of Novembʳ 1694 :

George Barrow & patience Simmons were married the 14ᵗʰ of ffebruary 1694-5

Wᵐ Little & Hannah w [not finished, entry erased.]

[2 Blank.]

[3] 1693 Registry of marriages within yᵉ Town of Duxborough

James Thomas and mary Tilden were married January yᵉ 3ᵈ 1692-3

Richard Waste and Mary Samson were marryed Octobʳ 26ᵗʰ 1693

James Soul was marryed to Lidia Tomson Decembʳ 14ᵗʰ : 1693

1694 Samuel Hill married to phebe Leonard Novembr 6th 1694

Elisha Wadsworth married to Elizabeth Wisewall ye 9th day of December 1694 :

1695 Saml Samson and Assadiah Eedey were marryed ye 29th day of may 1695

James Bonney and Abigail Bishop were married the 14th day of June 1695

[4 Blank]

[5] 1693 Registry of marriages within ye Town of Scituate

John Dwelley and Rachell Buck were married January ye 4th : 1692-3

Robert Stetson (son of Joseph Stetson) and mary callomer were married ye 12th of January 1692-3

Samuel Stodder and Elizabeth   were married ye 1st of march 1692-3

John Buck of Scituate married to Sarah Dotey of plimouth Aprill 26th 1693

[6 & 7 Blank]

[8] 1693 Registry of marriages within ye Town of marshfield

Thomas Tilden junr married to Hannah mendall the 20th day of December 1692 :

[9] Registry of maryages within ye Township of Bridgwater 1694 :

James Harris and Elizabeth Bayley both of bridgwater marryed ffebry 14th 1692-3

Richard Holt & Lidia wormwood of Bridgwater marryed may ye 10th 1693

James Washbourn & mary Bowden of Bridgwater marryed December ye 20th 1693 :

John Whitemore and Ruth Bassett were married ye 22d of Decembr 1692

Benjamin Snow and Elizabeth Alden were marryed the 12th of December 1693

John Emerson and Elizabeth Leech were married ye 27th of December 1693 :

[10 Blank]

[11] Registry of marriages within the Township of Middleborough

1693 : James Wood Marryed to Experience ffuller Aprill
12th 1693

Jacob Tomson married to Abigaii Wadsworth Decembr 28th :
1693

1694 Samuel Eaton and Elizabeth ffuller were married
ye 24th of May 1694.

FROM THE UNNUMBERED* VOLUME OF THE COURT OF GENERAL
SESSIONS OF THE PEACE.

[124]　Marriages in the Town of Middleborough.

1729 March 27th Josiah Haskell and Sarah Brayley both
of the Town of Middleborough—

April the 9th Joseph Leonard and Hannah Pratt both of the
Town of Middleborough—

August 21st William Hack of Taunton and Mary Tinkham of
Middleborough—

September 10th Eleazer Pratt Junr and Hannah Short both of
Middleborough—

September 10th Joshua Combs of Rochester and Elizabeth Pratt
of Middleborough—

November 20th Joshua Peirce of Pembroke and Hopestill Holloway of Middleborough—

December 25th Nathan Holloway of Taunton and Elizabeth
makepeace of Middleborough—

　　By the Revd Benjamin Ruggles.

1728—May 24th Mr Seth Howland and Elizabeth Delano
both of Middleborough—

September 10th Ebenezer Redden and Joanna Vaughan both of
Middleborough—

October 31st David Miller and Susannah Holmes both of Middleborough—

December 4—— Ignatius Elmes and Sarah Bennett both of
Middleborough—

December 18 —— Jonathan Snow of Bridgwater and Sarah Soul
of Middleborough—

William Hooper of Bridgwater and Lois Thomas of Middleborough January 30th 1728

1729　April ultimo, Thomas Wood and Hannah Alden both
of Middleborough—

---

*See Report on Custody and Condition of the Public Records of [Massachusetts]
Parishes, Towns and Counties, page 354.

[125] May 15th Coombs Barrows and Joanna Smith both of Middleborough—

May 27— Robert Ransom and Sarah Chyles both of Middleborough—

July 17— John Savery Junr and Mary Thomas Daughter of Jonathan Thomas deceased both of the Town of Middleborough—

July ult : John Eaton of Kingston and Elizabeth Fuller of Middleborough—

December 11th The Rev.d Mr. John Wadsworth of Canterbury and Mrs. Abigail Sprout of Middleborough—

December 17— Jonathan Fuller and Hannah Harlow both of Middleborough—

December 23 — Captain Ichabod Tupper and Hananh Tinkham both of the Town of Middleborough—

1729-30 March 5th Deacon Thomas Pratt of Easton and Desire Bonney of Middleborough—

March 5th Isaac Billington and Mary Donham both of Middleborough—

1730 March 12th Robert Barrows and Fear Thomas both of Middleborough —

April 1st Peter Tinkham and Eunice Thomas both of Middleborough —

By the Revd. Peter Thatcher

A true Copy Transcribed from Middleborough Town Book Attest Jacob Tomson *Town Clerk.*

1730 — September 16. 1730 — Benjamin Leonard and Elizabeth West both of Middleborough—

1731—April 1st Electious Reynolds Junr and Charity Caswell both of the Town of Middleborough—

By Benja Ruggles

1730 July 10th Francis Gayward of Rochester and Anna Morse Junr of Middleborough—

August 7th Mr Samuel Wood and the Widow Sarah Howland both of Middleborough—

November 12th Josiah Hatch of Pembroke and Mercy Redding of Middleborough—

[126] January 7th Mr. Jacob Tomson and Mrs. Elizabeth Holmes both of Middleborough—

February 18th John Wood and Hannah Chiles both of Middleborough—

1731—March 31 — Mr Jacob Soul and Miss Mary Thomas both of Middleborough—

April 1—Thomas Holmes and Mary Sprout both of Middleborough—

November 22ᵈ Mʳ Francis Miller and miss Experience Sprout both of Middleborough—

Decʳ 14—Obadiah Sampson and Mary Soul both of Middleborough—

February 17ᵗʰ Elias Miller and Sarah Holmes both of Middleborough—

1732 April 12—Thomas King and Mary Gaunt[?] both of Middleborough—

April 25—Mʳ Thomas Tomson and miss Martha Soul both of Middleborough—

June 26—John Miller Junr—and Watistill Clap both of Middleborough—

August 24—Mʳ Isaac Bennett and miss Mary Drew both of Middleborough—

December 7ᵗʰ James Winslow a Seafaring Resident of Plymouth and Susanna Conant of Middleborough—

January 4—Jesse Griffeth and Elizabeth Bent both of Middleborough

February 5ᵗʰ Samuel Eddy Junʳ and Lydia Alden both of Middleborough—

February 21ˢᵗ Mʳ Ebenezer Reed of Abington and miss Hannah Tompson of Middleborô.

February 22—Noah Thomas and Mary Alden both of Middleborough

By the Revᵈ Peter Thatcher

1733 May 10ᵗʰ Stephen Donham of Middleborough and Lydia Taylor of Taunton—

[127] June 20—Nathaniel Holloway of the Town of Middleborough and Mehetabel Bassit of Bridgwater—

By Benjᵃ Ruggles

March 1732-3—James Bumpas and Rachel Haŋks both of the Town of Middleborough—

April 1733—Benjamin Wood and Presulla Rickard both of the Town of Plimpton

Francis Eaton and Lydia Fuller both of the Town of Middleborough June 12ᵗʰ 1733—

November 1ˢᵗ 1733 Zacheriah Whitman of Bridgwater and Eleanor Bennet of Middleborough

By Benjᵃ White Justice of Peace.

A true Copy Transcribed from Middleborough Town Book —Attest Jacob Tomson *Town Clerk*

1731 Samuel Shaw of Plimpton and Desire Southworth of Middleborough April 21st 1731—

June 14—Benjamin Gurney and Sarah Morse both of Middleborough—

January 16—Elkanah Sherman of Dartmouth and Margaret Pitts of Middleborough—

1732 May 29—Combs Barrows and Mary Dwelly both of Middleborough—

June 9th Samuel Thomas and Lydia Richmond both of Middleborough—

Novr 2d Nathaniel Richmond of Taunton and Alice Hacket of Middleborough—and also Thomas Ramsdale and Mary Peirce both of Middleborough—

By Benja Ruggles

1732 June 27—Eleazer Lyon and Bethiah Allen both of Middleborough By Benja White Just: of Peace

January 11th Jotham Caswell and Mary Renolds both of the Town of Middleborough—

January 31st Timothy Rogers of Middleborough and Damaras Macumber of Taunton

By the Revd Benja Ruggles—

A true Copy Transcribed from Middleborough Town Book Att. Jacob Tomson *Town Clerk*

[128] Marriages in the Town of Plymouth—

1726-7 February 16—The Reverend Mr Robert Ward of Wenham and miss Margaret Rogers of Plymouth—

March 16—Barnabas Shurtleff of Plimpton and Jemima Adams—

1727—April 4—Joseph Bartlett and Sarah Morton both of Plymouth—

April 17—Samuel Totman and Experience Rogers both of Plymouth—

December 14—Ebenezer Cobb Junr and Lydia Stephens both of Plymouth—

December 22—Benjamin Lothrop Junr of Barnstable and Experience Howland of Plymouth—

February 8th Ebenezer Cobb of Plymouth and Mary Thomas of Middleborough—

The above Marriages were solemnized by the Reverend Nathl Leonard—

1727 April 10—Samuel Doty and Marcy Cobb both of Plymouth—

September 28th Joshua Finney and Hannah Curtis both of Plymouth—

The above two Marriages were Solemnized by Isaac Lothrop Esqr—

1728 June 6—Nehemiah Ripley and Sarah Atwood both of Plymouth—

August 6th Thomas Scarret and Alse Ward both of Plymouth—

October 28th Jo a Negro Man belonging to Mr Nathaniel Thomas and Phebe a Negro Woman belonging to Mr Haviland Torrey—

October 31—Elkanah Delano and Mary Sanders both of Plymouth—

November 14—Ephraim Sampson of Duxborough and Ruth Shepherd of Plymouth—

November 14—Samuel Cole and Mercy Barnes both of Plymouth—

December 12th Timothy Burbank of Boston now residing in Plymouth and Mary Kempton of Plymouth—

[129] December 19—Jonathan Freeman of Plimpton and Sarah Rider of Plymouth—

December 20—Thorton Gray and Katherine White both of Plymouth—

January 30—James Holmes and Content Silvester both of Plymouth—

February 18—Matthew Lemote and Mercy Billington both of Plymouth—

By the Reverd Nathl Leonard—

A true Copy Transcribed from the Records of the Town of Plymouth—Attest John Dryer *Town Clerk*

1729 April 3d Edward Stevens and Marcy Silvester both of Plymouth—

April 3d Rodolphus Hatch of Province Town and Esther Holmes of Plymouth—

May 20—Thomas Doane of Chatham and Sarah Barnes of Plymouth—

May 30—Thomas Totman and Lucretia Ross both of Plymouth—

June 30th Jack and Mariah Negroes belonging to Mr Jonathan Bryant—

July 8—Jacob Lewis and Bathsheba Mallis both of Plymouth—

July 8th John Watson Esqr and Mrs Priscilla Thomas both of Plymouth—

July 14 — Jacob Taylor of Barnstable and Mary Atwood of Plymouth—

September 9th Seth Doggett and Elizabeth Delano both of Plymouth—

October 28 — Isaac King and Hannah Harlow both of Plymouth—

November 20 — John Cushing Esqr of Scituate and Miss Mary Cotton of Plymouth—

February 10 — John Hambleton and Elizabeth Jones both of Plymouth—

March 4 — Thomas Ward and Joanna Donham both of Plymouth

[130] 1730 March 27 — Ephraim Churchill and Priscilla Manchester both of Plymouth—

May 4 — Thomas Weston and Prudence Conant both of Plymouth

May 18 — Mr William Dyre of Boston and Miss Hannah Phillips of Plymouth—

June 8 — Deacon John Atwood and miss Experience Pierce both of Plymouth—

August 10th Nicholas Drew and Lydia Doggett both of Plymouth—

September 22 — Ebenezer Finney of Barnstable and Rebecca Barnes of Plymouth—

September 24 — John Studley and Elizabeth Doten both of Plymouth—

September 30 — Jabez Holmes and Rebecca Harlow both of Plymouth—

The Foregoing Marriages were Solemnized by the Revd Nathl Leonard—

A true Copy Transcribed from the Records of the Town of Plymouth—

Marriages in the Town of Rochester—

1729 June 24 — Nicholas Hicks and Hannah Coombs both of Rochester—

June 27 — Stephen Ellis and Ruth Turner both of Rochester—

October 23d Seth Winslow and Abigail Whiteridge both of Rochester—

November 29 — Jonathan Hunter and Hopestill Hamblin both of Rochester—

December 10 — Archelaus Hammond and Elizabeth Weeks both of Rochester—

January 25th Nathaniel Parker of Rochester and Sarah Parker of Dartmouth—

[131] February 19th George Barlow and Ruth Barrow both of Rochester were married—

February 26 — Seth Ellis and Mary Bumpas both of Rochester were married—

1730 April 16 — James Steward and Hannah Dexter both of Rochester were married—

November 5th Samuel Hammond and Deliverance Admister both of Rochester—

November 12th Benjamin Hammond And Priscilla Sprague both of Rochester—

December 8th Lowis Deneranville and Susanna Crapo both of Rochester—

December 31 — Ebenezer Keen and Mercy Whiteridge both of Rochester were married—

March 1st Stephen Goodspeed and Bethiah Wooding both of Rochester

The foregoing Marriages were Solemnized by the Reverend Timothy Ruggles—

1726 November 17th Edward Doty and Mary Andrews both of Rochester were married—

November 23 — Seth ORiley of Yarmouth and Mehitabel Wing of Rochester—

February 28th John Grass and Penelope White both of Rochester were married—

1727 April 15th James Pratt and Frances Combs both of Rochester were married—

1728 January 1st Joseph Ashely and Mary Whetredge both of Rochester were married—

1729 July 10th James Foster and Lydia Winslow both of Rochester—

1730 June 18 — Abiel Sprague and Elizabeth Ashely both of Rochester—

October 10th Chillingsworth Foster of Harwich and Marcy Winslow of Rochester—

November 19th Benjamin Cole of Swansey and Elizabeth Nelson of Middleborough—

The above Marriages were Solemnized by Edward Winslow Justice of the Peace—

A true Copy of all the Marriages that have been to me Returned S Wing T *Clerk*

[132] 1731 May 31st James Whitcomb and Sarah Linkhorn both of Rochester were married—

June 22 — John Ross and Sarah Clifton both of Rochester were married—

August 22 — Micah Sprague and Elizabeth Turner both of Rochester—

October 13 — Ebenezer Lothrop of Mansfield and Elizabeth Hammond of Rochester—

October 21 — Hinkman Vaughan of Middleborough and Desire Hicks of Rochester—

November 4 — Ithamas Comes and Hannah Andrews both of Rochester—

January 13 — Robert Whitcomb and Joanna Lawrance both of Rochester—

1732 May 18 — Samuel Dexter and Mary Clark both of Rochester

July 23 — Joseph Barlow and Abigail Wyatt both of Rochester—

September 25 — Barnabas Sears and Thankful Freeman both of Rochester—

October 6 — Benjamin Clap and Katherine Nye both of Rochester—

December 21st Josiah Bump and Hannah Bump both of Rochester—

January 5th Cornelius Connor and Hitte Haskell both of Rochester—

By the Revend Timothy Ruggles

1733 October 18 — Ebenezer Luce and Sarah Doty both of Rochester—

October 17 — Jedidiah Briggs and Jedida Ellis both of Rochester were married—

October 25 — David Nye and Elizabeth Briggs both of Rochester—

November 22 — Abraham Ashley and Elizabeth Rogers both of Rochester—

November 25 — Barzillai Randall and Jerusha Hammond both of Rochester—

November 25th Thomas Whetredge and Hannah Haskell both of Rochester—

November 25th Andrew Haskell and Jane Clark both of Rochester—

[133] December 31 — Jonathan Spooner and Mary Crapoo both of Rochester were married—

March 14 — Samuel White and Elizabeth Ashley both of Rochester—

1732 — May 28 — William Randall Junr and Rest Sumer both of Rochester—

September 18 — Nathaniel Chabbuch Junr and Tabitha Besse Agawam Plymouth—

January 11 — Caleb Benson of Middleborough and Deborah Barrow of Plympton—

February 12 — William Ashley and Elizabeth Ashley both of Rochester—

1733 August 16 — Samuel Edward and Rebeckah Burge both of Rochester—

October 18 — Ebenezer Luce and Sarah Doty both of Rochester—

October 19 — Jedidiah Briggs and Jedidah Ellis both of Rochester—

October 25 — David Nye and Elizabeth Briggs

November 22 — Abraham Ashley and Elizabeth Rogers both of Rochester

November 25 — Barzillai Randall and Jerusha Hammond both of Rochester—

November 25 — Thomas Wetteridge and Hannah Haskell both of Rochester—

Novr 25 — Andrew Haskell and Jane Clark both of Rochester—

December 31 — Jonathan Spooner and Mary Crapoo both of Rochester—

March 14 — Samuel White and Elizabeth Ashley both of Rochester—

1734 October 31 — James Lake of Dartmouth and Elizabeth Crapoo of Rochester—

1737 — October 13th Samuel Bumpas and Abigail Bumpas both of Rochester—

October 19 — Isaac Doty and Elizabeth Blackmer both of Rochester—

October 20 — Samuel Robinson and Elizabeth Doty both of Rochester—

November 22d John Barrows and Joanna Dexter both of Rochester—

February 16 — Ebenezer Briggs and Betta Gibbs both of Rochester—

By the Revd Timothy Ruggles—

Copy examined pr Noah Sprague T *Clerk*—

[134]   Hanover Marriages.

1728   January 16 — David Bryant Junr of Scituate and Hannah Turner of Hanover—

February 20 — Richard Hill and Jemimah Ramsdil both of Hanover—

1729   May 15 — Benjamin Barstow and Sarah Bardin both of Hanover—

July 7 — Jonathan Potter and Margaret Frank both of Hanover—

October 9th Ezekiel Palmer and Martha Pratt both of Hanover—

1730   April 23 — Joseph Ramsdell and Mary Homer both of Hanover—

June 15th Clemond Bate and Agatha Meritt both of Hanover—

Sept 24 — Matthew Stetson of Hanover and Hannah Lincoln of Scituate—

February 18 — Melatiah Dillingham and Phebe Hatch both of Hanover—

1731   April 22d John Low of Pembroke and Susanna Gilford of Hanover —

May 12 — Eliab Turner and Martha Barstow both of Hanover—

June 4th Isaac Barden and Deborah Tobey both of Hanover—

August 4th Richard Bowker and Sarah Palmer both of Hanover—

By the Revd Benjamin Bass—

A true Copy of the Records of Hanover Exam^d p^r William Withrell Town *Clerk*

[135]   Marriages Solemnized in the Town of Bridgwater—

1726   November 15th   Field and Mary Haward both of Bridgwater were married—

November 29 —   Whitman and Elizabeth Rickard both of Bridgwater were married—

By the Revd Daniel Perkins

1724 — April 8 — Solomon Snow and Bathsheba Mahurin both of Bridgwater —

May 13 — Joseph Byram and Martha Perkins both of Bridgwater—

1725 — October 21 — Zacheus Packard and Mercy Allden both of Bridgwater—

December 17 — Hugh Mahurin and Mary Snell both of Bridgwater—

May 4th Joseph Carver and Elizabeth Snow both of Bridgwater—

May the 5th Stephen Leach and Sarah Hooper both of Bridgwater—

1726 — November 17th Samuel Phillips and Lydia Bassett
both of Bridgwater—

1727—Joseph Drake and Alice Hayward both of Bridgwater
— April 5th

April 6 — Elisha Dunbar and Mercy Hayward both of Bridgwater—

By Josiah Edson Justice of Peace—

1726 Novr 24 — Henry Kingman and Mary Allen both of
Bridgwater —

January 17 — Recompense Cary and the Widow Sarah Brett—
By the Revd John Angier—

1728 January 23d Josiah Snell and Abigail Fobes both of
Bridgwater—

1729 — June the 10th John Wormal and Mary Bryant both
of Bridgewater—

July 22d Samuel Packard and Susanna Kinsley both of Bridgwater—

August 6 — Benjamin Washburn and Martha Kingman both of
Bridgwater—

October 17 — Joseph Perry and Mary Chandler both of Bridgwater—

December 22d Nathl Davenport and Lucy Wyeman both of
Bridgwater—

December 9th Ephraim Dunham and Elizabeth Bump both of
Bridgwater—

By the Revd Daniel Perkins

[136] October 15th Christopher Askins and Susanna Robinson both of Bridgwater—

November 10 th John Whitman and Elizabeth Cary both of
Bridgwater—

November 13 — Caleb Brand and Damaras James both of Bridgwater—

December 30 — Samuel Pratt and Bithia Byram both of Bridgwater—

January 7th — Benjamin Allen and Mehitebel Cary both of
Bridgwater—

January 28 — Zachariah Whitmarsh and Hannah Washburn
both of Bridgwater—

1730 — April 16th   Davenport and Sarah Richards both of Bridgwater—

November 12th Timothy Hayward and Mary Reed both of
Bridgwater—

November 12th Arthur Harris and Mehitabel Rickard both of
Bridgwater—

1731 October 21st John Johnson and Peggy Holman both
of Bridgwater—

By the Revd John Angier—

1730 — January 1st Jacob Allen and Abigail Kingman both
of Bridgwater—

January 13 — Isaac Kingman and Jane Kingman both of
Bridgewater—

March 23 — Joseph Davis and Ruth Bassett both of Bridgwater—

By the Revd Daniel *Perkins*

1729 — October 15th Christopher Askins and Susanna
Robinson were married — both of Bridgwater—

November 10 — John Whitman and Elizabeth Cary both of
Bridgwater—

November 13 — Caleb Brand and Damaris James both of Bridgwater—

December 30 — Samuel Pratt and Bethiah Byram both of
Bridgwater—

January 7th Benjamin Allen and Mehitabel Cary both of Bridgwater—

[137] January 28 — Zachary Whitmarsh and Hannah
Washburn both of Bridgwater were married—

1730 — April 16 — William Davenport and Sarah Richards
both of Bridgwater—

By the Revd John Angier—

1730 — November 12th Timothy Hayward and the Widow
Mary Reed both of Bridgwater—

November 12 — Arthur Harris and Mehetable Rickard both of
Bridgwater—

1731 — October 21st John Johnson and Pegge Holman both
of Bridgwater—

1730 — October 14 — Shubal Waldow and Abagail Allen
both of Bridgwater—

March 11 — David Snow and Joanna Hayward both of Bridgwater—

March 11 — Zachariah Snell and Abigail Hayward both of
Bridgwater—

1731 June 20th Thomas Ames and Keziah Hayward both of Bridgwater—

June 23 — Samuel Soper and Esther Littlefield both of Bridgwater—

June 24 — Israel Alger and Rachel Wade both of Bridgwater—

July 11th John Snow and Hannah Hayward both of Bridgwater—

July 29 — Wright Bartlett and Bethia Packard both of Bridgwater—

March 1st 1731 — David Kingman and Mercy Hayward both of Bridgwater—

March 1st Jonathan Kingman and Mercy Keith both of Bridgwater—

By the Revd Daniel *Perkins*—

1732 — November 24th William Gillemer and Mary Willis both of Bridgwater—

1731 — November 25 — Jonathan Alden of Marshfield and Mehetable Allen of Bridgwater—

December 23 Benjamin Mahurin and Lydia Pratt both of Bridgwater—

January 13 — Solomon Washburn and Martha Orcutt both of Bridgwater—

[138] February 8th Benjamin Johnson and Ruth Holman both of Bridgwater—

February 24 — Mr Shepherd Fisk and miss Alice Alger both of Bridgwater—

1732 — June 15th Joseph Cary and Anna Brett both of Bridgwater—

By the Revd John Shaw—

1732 — May 17 — John Randall and Experience Willis both of Bridgwater—

May 15th William Brett and Bethiah Kingsly both of Bridgwater—

May 25 — Benjamin Curtis and Experience Hayward both of Bridgwater—

August 14 — Isaac Willis and Hannah Pratt both of Bridgwater—

September 21 — Mr Ephraim Keith and Miss Sarah Washburn both of Bridgwater —

October 21th Joseph Gannett and Hannah Brett both of Bridgwater—

By the Revd Daniel *Perkins*—

Duxborough Marriages

1726 — January 3ᵈ David Seabury now resident in Duxborough and Abigail Seabury of Duxborough—

By the Revᵈ John Robinson—

1729 — September 25 — Abraham Pierce of Pembroke Junʳ and Abigail Peterson of Duxborough—

November 25 — Thomas Prince and Judea Fox both of Duxborough —

December 19 — Joseph Trebble and Anna Jones both of Plymouth—

January 8ᵗʰ Amaziah Delano and Ruth Samson both of Duxborough—

March 2ᵈ Abner Weston and Sarah Standish both of Duxborough—

1730 — May 4ᵗʰ Ebenezer Sherman and Bathsheba Foord both of Marshfield —

August 5 — John Soul and Mabel Partridge both of Duxborough—

By Edward Arnold Justice of *Peace*

[139] October 8ᵗʰ Ebenezer Bartlett and Jerusha Samson both of Duxborough—

1731 — October 26 — Benjamin Simmons Junʳ and Fear Samson both of Duxborough—

1732 — July 6 — Reuben Peterson and Rebakah Simmons both of Duxborough—

July 27 — Ezra Arnold and Rebaca Sprague both of Duxborough—

October 24 — Isaac Simmons and Lydia Cushman both of Duxborough—

By Edward Arnold Justice of *Peace*

Marriages in the Town of Marshfield—

1723 — March 28 — Ebenezer Howland and Sarah Green both of Marshfield were married—

May 29 — James Dexter of Rochester and Lois Sherman of Marshfield—

June 3ᵈ Thomas Tracy and Susanna Waterman both of Marshfield---

October 31 — Benjamin Kent and Persis Doggett both of Marshfield---

January 7 — John Logan and Margaret Carr both of Marshfield—

January 30 — Joshua Rose and Elizabeth Gibson both of Marshfield—

January 30 — James Warren of Plymouth and Penelope Winslow of Marshfield—

February 17 — Samuel Sherman and Mary Williamson both of Marshfield—

March 11 — Francis Crooker and Patience Childs both of Marshfield—

1724—April 23 — Benjamin Hanks and Mary White both of Marshfield—

May 23 — Joshua Samson and Mary Oakman both of Marshfield.

July 8th Thomas Stockbridge of Scituate and Hannah Rogers of Marshfield

[140] October 8 — Mr John Thomas and Miss Mary Ray both of Marshfield—

October 21 — Caleb Oldham of Scituate and Bethiah Stephens of Marshfield—

October 9th William Stephens and Patience Jones both of Marshfield—

February 23 — Thomas Phillips and Mary Sherman both of Marshfield—

1725 March 25 — Anthony Eames and Anna Barker both of Marshfield—

June the 2d Ichabod Washburn of Plymouth and Bethiah Phillips of Marshfield—

October 21st William Lucas and Sarah Thomas both of Marshfield—

October 27th Israel Hatch of Scituate and Bethiah Thomas of Marshfield—

October 27 — Nathaniel Keen of Pembroke and Thankful Winslow of Marshfield—

October 27 — Ebenezer Damon of Scituate and Abigail Thomas of Marshfield—

October 7th William Hambelton and Jane Hopkins both of Marshfield—

January 6th Adam Hall and Sarah Sherman both of Marshfield—

January 13 — Silvanus Hall of Plymouth and Elizabeth Doggett of Marshfield—

February 16 — John Winslow of Plymouth and Mary Little of Marshfield —

1726 — May 26 — John Polan and Thankful Atkins both of Marshfield—

September 14 — Josiah Phinney of Plymouth and Mercy Thomas of Marshfield—

Novembr 9th Samuel Baker and Hannah Foord both of Marshfield—

November 9th Seth Joyce and Rachel Sherman both of Marshfield—

1727 April 5th John Deyre and Mary Trouant both of Marshfield—

[141] May 8th Thomas Oldham of Scituate and Desire Wormall of Marshfield—

June 18 — Robert Waterman of Plimpton and Abigail Dingley of Marshfield—

January 11 —Ebenezer Taylor and Sarah Carver both of Marshfield—

January 24 — Stephen Stoddard of Hingham and Rebecca King of Marshfield

January 25 — Isaac Phillips and Sarah White both of Marshfield

March 19 — Ebenezer Jones and Jane King both of Marshfield—

March 19 — Bezaliel Palmer of Scituate and Anna Jones of Marshfield—

1728 — May 28 — Isaac Taylor of Pembroke and Jerusha Tilden of Marshfield—

July 4 — Joshua Carver and Martha Foord both of Marshfield—

October 14 — Tobias Payne of Boston and Sarah Winslow of Marshfield —

October 30 — William Foord and Hannah Barstow both of Marshfield —

November 6 — Snow Winslow and Deborah Bryant both of Marshfield —

November 14 — Samuel Kent and Desire Barker both of Marshfield—

November 28 — John Magoun of Scituate and Abigail Waterman of Marshfield —

December 11 — Thomas Doggett and Joannah Fuller both of Marshfield—

December 19 — Joseph Hewitt and Sarah Dingley both of Marshfield—

January 18 — Benjamin Phillips and Desire Sherman both of Marshfield—

January 18 — Joshua Eames and Abigail Doggett both of Marshfield—

January 16 — Samuel Foord and Sarah Rogers both of Marshfield—

1724 December 11th Anthony Eames and Grace Oldham
of Scituate—

The Forgoing Marriages were Solemnized by the Revd.
Mr Gardner—

FROM VOLUME ONE OF THE COURT OF GENERAL SESSIONS OF
THE PEACE.

[101] Duxborough Marriages from 1734 To 1737,

Robert Samson and Else Samson both of Duxborough were
Maried December the 19. 1734.

Hartale Jaffere & Betty Tom both of Plymouth were Maried
December 23. 1734.

John Wadsworth Junr. and Mary Allden both of Duxborough
were Maried December 31. 1734.
pr. Edward Arnold Just peace.

[102] Duxborough Mariages.

Nathaniel Phillips and Joanna White both of Marshfield were
Maried Jany 16. 1734.

James Arnold & Joannah Sprague both of Duxborough were
maried February 19. 1734.

Ichabod Brewster of Duxborough & Lidiah Barstow of Pembroke were Maried June 3. 1735.

Seth Bartlet & Charity Cullifer both of Duxborough were maried
the 27th of February A. D. 1735–6.
The aforesd persons were Maried pr. Edw Arnold Just
peace

Nathaniel Dunham of Plymouth & Anne Peterson of Duxborough
were Maried at Duxborough April 7. 1735 pr. John
Robinson.

Joseph Morgan of Preston in the Colony of Conneticut & Ruth
Brewster of Duxborough were maried at Duxborough May
8. 1735. pr John Robinson Clerk.

John Pryer & Mercy Dellano both of Duxborough were maried
in Duxborough Oct. 14. 1735. pr. me John Robinson.

Mr Joanathan Trumble of Lebanon in the Collony of Conneticut
& mrs Faith Robinson of Duxborough were maried at Duxboro. Decemr. 9. 1735 pr me Jno. Robinson

Ichabod Wadsworth Junr. & Anne Hunt both of Duxborough
were maied in Duxborough November 25. 1736. pr John
Robinson Clerk.

Asa Hunt and Sarah Partridge both of Duxborough were maried at Duxborough December 2ᵈ. 1736.
pr John Robinson Clerk.

Ichabod Wormwell and Lydia Dellano both of Duxboro were Maried at Duxborough December 13, 1736. pr John Robinson Clerk.

Samuel Drew Junr. of Kingston and Anne White of Duxborough were maried at Duxborough December 28. 1736 pr Jno. Robinson Clerk

Sylvanus Curtiss of Plymouth and Dorothy Dellano of Duxboro were Maried at Duxborough November 26, 1734 pr me John Robinson

John Hanks and Mary Delano both of Duxborough were Maried in Duxboro January 16. 1734-5 pr me Jno. Robinson

Allerton Cushman of Plymton & Allathea Sole of Duxborough were Maried in Duxborough January 30. 1734-5 pr me Jno. Robinson

Samuel Wormwel and Mary Forest 17 January 1736-7.

May 11. Isaac Simmons & Elizabeth Sams.

Seth Bartlet & Martha Bourn 23ᵈ. November.

Experience Holmes of Dartmouth & Hannah Samson of Rochester maried December 13. 1737.

Caleb Jenney of Dartmouth & Patience Standish of Duxborough maried April 6. 1738

[103] Rochester Mariages.

1. Samuel Ruggles & Allis Sherman were Maryed June 25. 1738.
2. Josiah Jenkins of Barnstable & Mary Ellis of Rochester Maryed July 6. 1738.
3. Joseph Edwards Junr. & Sarah Burge were Maried July 13. 1738.
4. David Bessey Junr. & Dinah Maxum were Maryed July 20. 1738.
5. Nathaniel Whitcomb & Phœbe Blackmer maried July 27. 1738.
6. Uriah Savory & Deborah Bumpass were maried September 3. 1738.
7. Nathan Bumpas & Lydia Bumpas were maried October 19. 1738.
8. Zaccheus Bumpas & Reliance Morey were maried October 19. 1738.
9. Samuel Hix of Dartmouth & Ruth Hoskens of Rochr. maried Janry. 9. 1738-9.

10. Samuel Doty & Zerviah Lovel were Maried Jany. 18. 1738-9.

 By me Timothy Ruggles.

 Recorded in R^r. Town Book p^r. Noah Sprague T. Cler

[112] Mariages in the Town of Pembrooke From 1724. To 1738.

Jacob Ellis of Herwich & Elizabeth Foster of Pembrooke were maried August 20. 1724.

Ichabod Bonney & Elis^a. Howland 29th. October 1724.

Samuel Parris and Ruth Bonney Janry 21. 1725.

Isaac Sole & Egatha Parry March 11. 1725.

Josiah Foster Junr. & Mary Bonney July 29. 1725.

Thomas Holloway and Rebecca Tubs Sep^{tr}. 14th. 1725.

John Mackfarland Junr. & Mary Foster March 28. 1726.

Benj^a. Hanks and Mary Ripley of Bridgwater March 23. 1727.

Nath^o. Pearce and Keturah Newland April 27. 1727.

M^r. Jacob Norton of Chilmark & M^{rs}. Hannah Barker June 8. 1727.

Andrew Miller and Jane Macklucas December 19. 1727.

Joseph Stetson jun^r. & Abigail Hatch December 26. 1727.

Ezekiel Turner of Scituate & Batheba Stockbridge December 27. 1727.

Joseph Parry & Rebecca Joslyn both of Hanover April 24. 1728.

Thomas Partin & Margrett Gorden May 30. 1728.

John Franckley of Rehoboth & Hannah Record October 16. 1728.

John Lambert Junr. & Sarah Staples both of Hanover Novr. 4. 1728.

Anthony Winslow of Marshfield and Deborah Barker June 7. 1729.

Eben^r. Bonney & Elis^a. Parriss Oct^o. 16 1729.

Joseph Chandler & Deborah Bonney Novr. 27. 1729.

Rouse Howland & Ann Bonney Novr. 27: 1729.

Elisha Bonney & Elis^a. Lincoln Decr. 10. 1729.

Joseph Tubs jun^r. & Eliz^a. Randall Decr. 11. 1729.

James Hayes & Abigail Knapp Feb^{yr}, 25. 1730.

Joshua Baker & Sarah Cushing Sep^{tr}. 3 1730.

Lott Thacher of Barnstable & Rebecca Keen Sep^{tr}. 29. 1730.

Benj^a. Thomas of Marsfield & Gennet Stetson Novr. 5. 1730.

Sol^o. Beals jun^r. & Ann Howland Novr. 10. 1730.

Isaac Wadsworth & Susanna Nichols Decr. 16. 1730.

Joshua Turner & Sarah Winslow of Scituate Janry. 28. 1731.

Abraham Howland junr. & Sarah Simmons of Plympton March 11, 1731.

Zechariah Simmons of Duxboro. & Deborah Bishop May 27. 1731.

Nicholas Webster & Content Bishop Septr. 7. 1731.

Nehl. Pearce and Eliza. Hanks Octo. 27. 1731.

Isaac Oldham junr. & Mary Stetson Novr. 11. 1731.

Isaac Mackfarland & Sarah Foster Decr. 8. 1731.

Isaac Foster & Francees Joslyn of Hanover Janry. 6. 1732.

Thomas Elmour of Hanover and Elisa. Russell Mar. 16. 1732.

Barnas. Perry & Alce Sole of Duxboro. Mar. 30. 1732.

[113] Isaac Little Esqr and Mrs. Abigail Thomas Novr. 29. 1732.

George Russel and Hannah Mackfarland Decr. 18. 1732.

Andrew Linsey & Jane Curbe April 5. 1723.

Job Bonney & Ruth Bisbe May 9. 1733.

Daniel Hayford & Deliverance Boles May 24. 1733.

Thomas Tracy & Lidia Barstow of Hanover May 28. 1733.

John Bisbe junr. & Abiah Bonney Septr. 6. 1733.

Jesse Foord & Mary Crooker Octo. 17. 1733.

Aaron Sole junr. & Lidia Peterson of Duxborough Decr. 26. 1733.

Thomas Hayford & Susanna Perry Septr. 23. 1734.

Samuel Parry & Unice Wethrel of Hanover Septr. 24. 1734.

Willlam Mackfarland & Sarah Peterson of Duxboro. Novr. 18. 1734.

John Stetson & Abigail Crooker Novr. 28. 1734.

Ezekiel Bonney and Hannah Bryant Decr. 26. 1734.

Joseph Foord Junr. and Hannah Nichols Mar. 6 1735.

Joseph Stetson & the Widdow Mary Parry Mar. 1 1736.

Job Randall and Mary Jennings Mar. 4. 1736.

Danll. Crooker & Mary Ramsdell April 28. 1736.

Elijah Cushing and Hannah Barker of Hanover May 3. 1736.

Jedediah Lincoln of Hingham and the Widdow Mary Barker June 10. 1736.

Daniel Lewis Junr. & Sarah Bisbe Junr. Septr. 30. 1736.

Austin Bearse of Halifax and Hannah Stetson Octo. 21. 1736.

Joseph Osyer and Mercy Thomas Decr. 8. 1736.

By Elisha Bisbe Esqr.

Josiah Bishop and Sarah Crooker Decr. 16. 1736.

Samuel Keen & Margaret Reddin of Scituate Janry. 4. 1737.

Benja. Jacob of Scituate and Mary Thomas May 12. 1737.

James Randall & Ruth Magoon June 15. 1737.

Elijah Bonney & Susanna Tubbs June 27. 1737.

Deacon Joseph Foord and the Widdo Sarah Dogget of Marshfield Septr. 7. 1737.

Jedediah Beals & Deborah Boles April 5. 1738.

> All but One Maried by the Reverd. Mr. Daniel Lewis the 19th. of December 1737 all but the last, and Recorded pr. Thomas Burton Town Clerk for Pembrooke.

> Received Sept. 6. 1738 pr. Edward Winslow Cler.

[153] A list of Middleboro. Mariages. from 1733. To 1740.———

May 10. 1733. Then Stephen Donham of Middleboro. & Lydia Taylor of Taunton was maried by me——— Benja. Ruggles———

June 20. 1733 Then Nathll. Holloway of the Town of Middleboro. & Mehitable Bassett of Bridgewater was Maried by me—— Benja. Ruggles———

James Bumpas & Rachell Hanks both of the Town of Middleboro. were maried March 14. 1732–3 By me, Benja. White Just peace.

Benja. Wood & Priscilla Rickard, both of the Town of Plymton were maried April 12. 1733. By me Benja. White Just Peace

Francis Eaton & Lydia Fuller both of the Town of Middleboro. were maried June the 12th 1733. by me
    Benja White Just of peace.

Middleboro. Novembr. 1st. 1733. Then was maried at Middleboro. aforesd. Zachry. Whitman of Bridgwater & Elinor Bennet of Middleboro.
        pr. me Benja. White Just of peace

March 20. 1733–4 Then Ebenr. Hayford of Middleboro. & Mary Brooman of Taunton were maryed by me.   Benja. Ruggles

May 3. 1734 then Caleb Cowing of Rochester & Anna Richmond of Middleboro. was maried by me———
        Benja. Ruggles———

[154] July 4th. 1734. Then William Smith & Elisabeth Renolds both of Middleboro. was maried by me—Benja Ruggles———

July 30. 1734 Then Ephraim Pratt of Seabrooke and Beulah Williamson of Middleboro. was maried by me—Benja. Ruggles.

Transcribed from Middleboro. Town Book by me. Jacob
Tomson   Town Clerk

Novr. 7. 1734. then Benja. Waldron of Dighton & Hannah
Hackett of Middleboro. was maried by me—— Benja. Ruggles.

Jany. 30. 1734–5 Then John Montgomery & Mary Strawbridge
both of the Town of Middleboro. was maried by me
————————————————————————Benja. Ruggles.

Middleboro. March 20. 1734–5 then was mared at Middleboro.
aforesd.——Edmond Weston & Eliza. Smith both of Middleboro.——
pr me Benja White Just Peace.

Middleboro. June 19. 1735 Then was maried at Middleboro.
aforesd. Thomas Tupper & Rebecca Bumpas both of Middleborough——
pr me Benja. White Just Peace

May 5th 1735. Then Isaac Peirce Junr. & Deliverance Holla-
way both Middleboro. was Maried by me — Benja Ruggles——

Transcribed From Middleboro. Town Book by me Jacob Tomson   T Cler.

February 7th. 1733–4 Willm. Redding & Bennett Eddy both of
Middleboro. after lawfull publication in presents of parents
were maryed.   Peter Thacher

April 2. 1734. Nathan Cobb of Plymo. & Joanna Bennet of
Middleboro. after lawfull publication & Consent of parents
were maryed. by Peter Thacher

June 13. 1734. Samll. Warren junr. & Rebecca Donham both of
Middleboro were maryed — by Peter Thacher

Augt. 6. 1734 Joseph Jennings & Hannah Thomas both of
Middleboro. were maryed————————— By Peter Thacher

Nov. 6. 1734. Ephraim Tompson of Hallifax & Joanna Thomas
of Middleboro. were maryed —— by Peter Thacher——

Novr. 7. 1734. John Cannady & Anna Hathaway both of Middleboro. were maryed —— by Peter Thacher

Febry. 6. 1734–5 Nathll. Foster of Plymo. & Mercy Thacher of
Middleboro. were maryed by their ffather ——
Peter Thacher

Mar 25. 1735 Moses Eddy & Jedediah Wood both of Middleboro, were maryed —— By Peter Thacher—— ——

Apr 23. 1735 Elnathan Wood & Patience Cushman both of
Middleboro. were maryed ——by Peter Thacher

May 1 : 1735 Nathan Thomas & Abigail Allden both of Middleboro. were maryed —— by Peter Thacher

July 13. 1735 Silvanus Brimhorn of Plymoth & Mary Bennet of Middleboro. were maryed——— Peter Thacher

Augt 12. 1735. Daniel Vaughn & Sarah Cushman both of Middleboro. were maryed——————by Peter Thacher

Augt. 19. 1735. John Jackson & Joanna Bate both of Middleboro. were maryed——————By Peter Thacher—

Septr. 11. 1735 Peter Bennet jun^r. & Sarah Stephens both of Middleboro. were maryed ——— By Peter Thacher——

Oct^o. 7. 1735. Hezekiah Purrington of Truro & Mercy Bate of Middleboro. were maryed by Peter Thacher———

[155] Oct^o. 30. 1735. John Miller & Priscilla Bennet both of Middleboro. were maryed by———Peter Thacher

Novr. 6. 1735. Simeon Leonard & Abigail Morss both of Middleboro. were maryed ——— by — Peter Thacher

Decr. 25. 1735. Willm. Cushman & Susanna Samson both of Middleboro were maryed——————— By Peter Thacher———

Decr. 25. 1735 W^m. Cushman & Susanna Samson both of Middleboro. — were maryed ———By Peter Thacher

Transcribed from Middleboro. Town book. by me Jacob Tomson Town Clerk

Middleboro. Novr. 13. 1735. Then Nath^{ll}. Macomber of Taunton & Priscilla Southworth of Middleboro. was maryed by me — Benj^a. Ruggles———

Mar. 10. 1737. Then Benj^a. Renolds & Sarah Smith both of Middleboro. were maryed by me. Benj^a Ruggles

May 12. 1737. Then Willm. Holloway of Middleboro. & Sarah Walker of Taunton were maryed by me ——— Benj^a Ruggles———————

Febr^y. 2. 1737-8 Then Robt. Sprout & Hannah Samson both of Middleboro. were maryed by me — Benj^a. Ruggles

May 1. 1738 Then Benj^a Samson jun^r. of Plymton & Mary Williamson of Middleboro. were maryed by me – Benj^a. Ruggles.

Septr. 20. 1738 Then Daniel Tayler jun^r. & Mary Russell both of Middleboro. were maryed — by me Benj^a. Ruggles ———

Novr. 2. 1738 Then George Williamson Junr. & Fear Eddy both of the Town of Middleboro. were maryed by me Benj^a. Ruggles

July 7th. 1737. Samuel Holloway & Rebecca Treuant both of Middleboro. was maried — by me Benj^a Ruggles —

Augt. 16. 1737. Shadrach Peirce of Middlebor⁰. & Abigail Hoskins of Taunton was maried—by me Benj^a. Ruggles——

Oct⁰. 25. 1737. James Keith of Bridgwater & Deborah Bennet of Middlebor⁰. were maried — by me Benj^a Ruggles.

Novr. 17. 1737. Charles West & Deborah Williamson both of Middlebor⁰. were maried — by me Benj^a Ruggles.

Janr^y. 6th. 1737-8 Phillip Leonard & Mary Richmond both of Middlebor⁰. were maried —— —— by me Benj^a. Ruggles

Novr. 23. 1738. Then John Hayford of Fretown & Thankfull Finney of Middlebor⁰. were maried by me — Benj^a Ruggles ——

Janr^y. 4 1738-9 Then Ephraim Keen of Fretown & Mercy Allen of Middlebor⁰. were maryed — by me Benj^a Ruggles

Mar 2 1738-9 Then John Hodson & Sarah Renals both of Middlebor⁰. were maryed by me—————— Benj^a Ruggles

Augt. 16. 1739 Then Ephraim Renolds & Alice Braley both of Middlebor⁰. were maryed — by me Benj^a Ruggles

Novr. 29. 1739 Then Josiah Holloway & Hannah Parris both of Middlebor⁰. were maried by me – Benj^a. Ruggles.

[156] June 18. 1740. Then M^r. Mark Haskell of Rochester & M^rs. Abiah Nelson of Middlebor⁰. were maryed by me. Benj^a Ruggles.

October 2. 1740 Then William Nelson & Eliz^a. Howland both of Middlebor⁰. were maryed by me —————— Benj^a. Ruggles.

Janr^y. 29th. 1735-6 Then was maried at Middlebor⁰. Josiah Woods & Mary Holmes both of s^d. Town
P^r. me Benj^a White Just peace

Febr^y. 20. 1735-6 Then was maried at Middlebor⁰. John Smith & Deborah Bardin both of s^d. Town —
p^r me Benj^a White Just peace

July 27. 1737. Then was maried at Middlebor⁰. John Warren & Ann Reed both of s^d. Town——p^rme Benj^a White Just peace

Septr. 6. 1737. Then was maried at Middlebor⁰. Jon^a. Smith Junr. & Experience Cushman both of s^d. Town. p^r me Benj^a White Just Peace

January the 25th. 1738-9 Then was maried at Middlebor⁰. Seth Howland & Lydia Cobb both of s^d. Town. p^r me Benj^a White Just peace.

May 4th. 1739. Then was maried at Middlebor⁰. Nathan Caswell & Hannah Shaw both of Middlebor⁰. p^r me Benj^a White Just peace

Febr^y. 28. 1739-40 then was maried at Middlebor⁰. Gersham Cobb Junr. & Meriam Thomas, jun both of s^d. Town
p^r. me Benj^a White Just peace

Febr͟y. the 28ᵗʰ 1739-40 then was maried at Middlebo͟r. Nathˡˡ. Washburne of Bridgwater & Mary Pratt of Middleboro. p͟r. me Benjᵃ White Just peace

Augᵗ. 11. 1740. Then was maried at Middleboro. Manaseh Donham of the Town of Plymouth & Sarah Hanks of Middleboro. p͟r. me Benjᵃ White Justice of peace

Augᵗ. the 26ᵗʰ. 1740. Then was maried at Middleboro. Willᵐ Lyon & Martha Knowlton both of Middleboro. p͟r. me
Benjᵃ White Just peace

Septʳ. 1. 1740. Then was maried at Middleboro. Benjᵃ Washburn the 3ᵈ. & Zerviah Packard both of Bridgwater
p͟r. me Benjᵃ White Just peace

Septʳ. 1. 1740. Then was maried at Middleboro. Willᵐ. Roach & Mary Kingman both of Bridgwater Pʳ me
Benjᵃ White Just Peace

The Before written is Transcribed from Middleboro. Town Book by me Jacoᵇ Tomson Town Cler

[167] A list of middleborough marriages From 1740. To 1743-4—

June 2 1740 William Reed and Sarah Warren Both of middleborough were married at middleborough in The County of Plymʰ. p͟r. Benjᵃ. White Justice of peace

March 18. 1740-1 Samˡˡ. Pratt 3ᵈ. & Wibray Bumpas Both of middleboro. Were married at middleboro. in The County of Plymʰ. — — —   pʳ Benjamin White Justice of peace

Novʳ. 5. 1741 Phineas Pratt and Sarah White Both of Middleborough Were married at middleborough in the County of Plymouth — — —   p͟r. Benjamin White Justice of peace

Novʳ. 30. 1741 Ephraim Donham and mercy Tinkham Both of middleboro. Were married At middleboro. in the County of Plymʰ — — — —   p͟r. Benjᵃ. White Justice of peace

Decʳ. 31. 1741 Benjᵃ Warren and Jedidah Tupper Both of middleboro. in the County of Plymʰ. — — pʳ. Benjᵃ. White Justice of peace

January 28. 1741 Joseph Bumpas and mehitable Tupper Both of middleboro. Were married at middleboro. in the County of Plymʰ — pʳ. Benjᵃ. White Justice of peace.

[168] Aprill 1. 1742. Joseph Alden of middleborough and Hannah Hall of Bridgwʳ. Were married at middleboro. in yᵉ. County of Plymʰ — — — pʳ. Benjᵃ. White Justᵗ. of peace

Aprill 1. 1742 Jacob Barden and Elinor Hackett Both of middleboro. Were married at middleboro. in the County of Plymʰ — — — Pʳ. Benjᵃ. White Just. of peace

may 24. 1742 Joshua Lazel and Elizabeth Ames Both of mid-

dlebor⁰. Were married at middlebor⁰. in yᵉ. County of
Plymʰ. — — pʳ. Benjᵃ. White Justice of peace

octoʳ. 14. 1742 Samuel Thurber of Swanzey & Egatha Bryant of
middlebor⁰ Were married at middlebor⁰. in the County of
Plymʰ – — — pʳ. Benjᵃ. White Justice of peace

octoʳ. 28. 1742 Israel Thomas and Phebe lyon Both of middleborough Were married at middlebor⁰. in yᵉ. County of
Plymʰ — — pʳ. Benjᵃ. White Justice of peace

Novembʳ. 11. 1742 Peter Walker of Taunton and Sarah Samson
of middlebor⁰. Were married at middlebor⁰. in yᵉ. County
of Plymʰ. — — pʳ. Benjᵃ. White Justice of peace.

Decembʳ. 20. 1742 Simon Lazel and Joanna Wood Both of
middlebor⁰. Were married at middlebor⁰. in yᵉ. County of
Plymʰ — pʳ. Benjᵃ. White Justice of peace

January 27. 1742-3 Jn⁰. Tinkham Junʳ. and Jerusha Vaughan
Both of middlebor⁰. Were married at middlebor⁰. in yᵉ.
County of plymʰ — — pʳ. Benjᵃ. White Justice of peac

February 9. 1742-3 Jn⁰. Harris and marcy Torrey Both of middlebor⁰. Were married at middlebor⁰. in yᵉ. County of
Plymʰ. — — pʳ. Benjᵃ. White Justice of peac

Novʳ. 24. 1743 Jedediah Lyon and mary Cushman Both of
middlebor⁰. Were married At middlebor⁰. in The County of
Plymʰ — — pʳ. Benjᵃ. White Justice of peac

Decembʳ. 19. 1743 Jn⁰. Thurber Junʳ. of Swanzey and Ann
Bryant of middlebor⁰. Were married at middleborough in
yᵉ. County of plymʰ — — pʳ. Benjᵃ. White Justice of peace

0 February 16. 1743-4 Ichabod Wood and Thankfull Cobb
Both of Middlebor⁰. Were married at middlebor⁰. — pʳ.
Benjᵃ. White Justice of peace

February 21. 1743 Barnabas Eaton and Elizabeth Clemons
Both of middlebor⁰. Were married at middlebor⁰. in yᵉ.
County of Plymʰ — — pʳ. Benjᵃ. White Justice of peace

Aprill. 10. 1744 Jesse Bryant and Susanna Winslow Both of
middlebor⁰. Were married at middlebor⁰. in yᵉ. County
of Plymʰ — — pʳ. Benjᵃ. White Justice of peace

August. 10. 1743 Then I married Isaac Reynolds Junʳ. and
mercy Niles Both of middlebor⁰. — — pʳ. Benjᵃ. Ruggles ——

June 9. 1743 Then I married Josiah Richmond of Taunton and
Elizabeth Smith of middlebor⁰. — — pʳ. Benjᵃ. Ruggles ——

octoʳ. 6 1743 Then I married Joseph Richmond Junʳ. of Taunton
and Elizabeth Hacket of middlebor⁰. — pʳ. Benjᵃ. Ruggles

Novʳ. yᵉ. 4. 1743 Then I married mallachy Howland and Hopestill Dwelley Both of middlebor⁰. — — — — pʳ. Benjᵃ. Ruggles

February y^e. 16. 1743-4 Then I married Nathaniel Sprout and Esther Thrasher Both of middleborough —— —— p^r. Benj^a. Ruggles —— ——

The above & written written is a True Copy From middleborough Town Book   Seth Tinkham Town Clerk——

[169] 1738 A list of Bridgwater marriages From 1738. To 1742 ——

July 13 David Whitman and Susanna Hayward ——

oto^r. 11 Josiah Hayward and Sarah more——

Novr. 22 Eleazer Washburn and Anna Alden
   Ephaim Cary and Susanna Alden
   Ebenezer Byram and Abigal Alden
   Benajah Smith of Easton & Mary Hill of Bridgw^r.

Decr. 21 Seth mitchell and Ann Latham ——
   26 James Radsford and margaret Bells —— ——

1739
march 27 Jonathan Allen of Braintry and y^e. widdow Alice Latham of Bridgwater

May 16 Samuel Harden and Elizabeth Wade

Novr. 20 Bridgwater and Cate Co^ll. Homans Negroes

Decr. 10 Charles Cushman and mary Harvey ——
   21 Benjamin Vickory and mary kingman —— were Joyned Together in wedlock p^r. The Rev^d. M^r. John Anger

1738
Jany. 4 John Pain and Hannah Pool ——
   24 Caleb orcutt and mehetable Harvey

1739
aprill 19 Solomon Leach of Bridgwater and Jerusha Bryant of Plymton
   26 Jeremiah Conant and mary Packard ——

may 10 John Freelove of Freetown and abigail Washburn Bridgwater
   23 Lieu^t. Daniel Hudson and The Widdow Abigail Fobes
   30 moses orcutt and mercy Allen ——

Aug^st. 16 Thomas Drew of Hallifax and abigail Harris of Bridgwater

Novr. 27 Ebenezer leach of Bridgwater and Lydia Tillson of Plymton
   Joseph Whesley and Jean Gillmore

Jany. 1 Seth Alden and mehetable Carver
   3 Israel Washburn and Leah Fobes
   10 Benjamin Leach and Hannah keith
   24 Josiah Leonard and Jemimah Washburn

Feby. 6 Joseph Bolton and Deliverance Washburn

march 5 Josiah Fobes and Freelove Edson ——

      6 Robert Washburn and Mary Fobes

     24 Nathaniel Bolton and The Widdow Deborah Ripley

1740

may 29 Joshua Fobes and Esther Porter

oct^r. 7 Elisha Hayward and Elizabeth Washburne

    22 Abraham Hardin of Bridgwater and Ruth Perry of Scituate

Novr. 7 Jonathan Benson and martha Snell were married p^r. The Rev^d. m^r. John Shaw

    11 Jonathan Pratt and Elizabeth French

Decr. 7 Henery Chamberlain and Susanna Hinds

Feby. 17 Israel keith and Betty Chandler

    19 Ephraim Holmes of Hallifax and margaret Washburn of Bridgwater

    24 Nehemiah Bryant of middleborough and Beth^h. Washburne of Bridgwater

[170] 1740

march 4 Robert keith and Tabitha Leach ——

    23 Jabez Cowing and Susanna Bolton were married By The Rev^d. m^r. John Shaw

1738

Septr. 26 Samuel Edson 3^d. and martha Perkins

Feby 27 Nathan Edson and mary Sprague -- married p^r. Benj^a White Justice of peace

1741

May 13 John Cary and mary Harden married p^r. Dan^ll. Johnson Justice of peace

1740

Septr. 16 Daniel Rickards and mary Packard and William Packard and Sarah Rickards

1741

Aprill 28 Josiah Allen and Sarah orcut

May 20 Arthur Harris and Bethiah Hayward

June 23 Seth Whitman and Ruth Reed

Novr. 11 Jonathan Bass and Susanna Byram

Decr. 3 Ichabod Cary and Hannah Gannett

Jany. 6 Benjamin Hayward and Sarah Cary

    28 Daniel Cary and martha Cary were married By The Rev^d. m^r. Jno. Angier

1740

July 9 Jonathan mahurin and Widdow mary Packard

August 15 Ebenezer Kingman and Content Turner

1741
Aprill 2 Abisha Willis and Zeruiah Willis
Novr. 11 Thomas Willis and Susanna Ames were married By
The Rev^d. m^r. Daniel Perkins

1741
Novr. 19 Benjamin Peterson of Easton and Hannah Perry of
Bridwater married p^r. Daniel Johnson Justice of The
peace————

1742
Novr. 19 Joseph Peterson of Duxborough and Lydia Howell of
Bridgwater married p^r. Dan^{el}. Johnson Justice of peace

June 4 Jessie Byram and abigail Thurston —
Augst 4 Hugh Orr and mary Bass
Novr. 9 Eleazer Whitman and Abigail Alden
10 James Allen and Ann Pryer
11 Zachariah Cary and Susanna Bass —

Decr. 13 Japhet Byram and Sarah Allen
16 Joseph Alden and Susanna Packard
John Whitman and Hannah Snow were married p^r. The
Rev^d m^r, John Angier
A True Copy attest Jonah Edson Junr Town Clerk————

[171] A List of Abington marriages From 1733. To 1742
Samuel Petingill and martha Jackson was married December y^e.
14. 1733
Jacob Reed and Hannah Noyes was married December The 21.
1733
Ebenezer Joslin and Easther Hersey was married June The 5.
1733
Samuel Pool and Rebekah Shaw was married November the 15.
1733
Jacob Ford and Sarah Pool was married November the 22. 1733
Hezekiah Ford and Deborah Beal was married November the
22. 1733
Eleazer Bate and Rachel Ager was married march 17. 1735
Nicholas Shaw and Ruth Beal was married February The 6.
1735
Peter Nash and mary Noyes was married November the 13. 1735
Jonathan Tory and Deborah Shaw was married December the
18. 1735
Joseph Pool and Ruth Ford was married November The 27.
1735
Benjamin Negro and Sarah Jonas was married march the 17.
1737

James Torey and Sarah Nash was married December The 25. 1735

John Reed and Abigail Niels was married December the 28. 1738

John Shaw and Lydia Shaw was married Aprill the 14. 1737

Samuel Reed and Elizabeth Hayward was married aprill the 28. 1737

James Richards and Hannah Shaw was married November. the 10. 1737

John Cobb and Ruth Chard was married February the 1. 1737

John Shaw and Silence Bate was married December The 14. 1738

Daniel Bate and Lydia Symmys December The 14. 1738

Peter Bate and Sarah Randall was married December the 14. 1738

William Tirrell and Hannah Whitmarsh was married January the 25. 1738-9

John Dyer and mary Reed was married aprill The 17. 1739

James Reed and Abigail Nash was married may The 10. 1739

Benjamin Edson and Anna Thayer was married october the 1. 1739

Samuel Noyse and Rebeckah Harden was married march the 3. 1736

Samuel Tirrell and Sarah Gurney was married November the 1. 1739

Barnabas Tomson and Hannah Porter was married march 13. 1740

James Rickards and Susana Pratt was married may the 15. 1740

Ephraim Spooner and Ruth Whitmarsh was married July The 24. 1740

James Reed and Ruth Pool was married august The 30. 1741

Alexander Nash and mary Tirrell was married october 22 1741

Isaac Tirrell and mary Whitmarsh was married october 22. 1741

Abraham Joslin and Rebeckah Tirrel married october 29. 1741

Jacob Reed and mary Ford was married November The 26. 1741

Edmond Jackson and Silence Allen was married February 24. 1741

Ezekiel Reed and Hannah Beal was married November 25. 1742

Andrew Ford and Sarah Shaw married November 25 1742

A True Copy of The Records of marriages in abington That Has Been Given in To me Ever Since I have Kept The Book of Records which Began in yᵉ. year 1733

Transcribed By me

Jacob Reed Town Clerk

[172] A list of marshfield marriages From 1739 To 1743

Elnathan Fish of Kingston and Lydia Adams married Decemb^r. 12. 1739.

Thomas Ford and Jane Thomas of This Town were married Janu^y. 2 1739-40.

Michael Harny and Gail Rogers of This Town married January 14. 1739-40

Michael Samson of Kingston and Deborah Gardner of marshfield married February 1739-40

Seth Ewell and Jane Eames of This Town married February 21. 1739-40

Job Winslow and Elizabeth macumber were married march 20. 1740

Samuel Silvester and Sarah mori were married may y^e. 8. 1740

Benjamin Hatch Junr. of Scituate and mercy Phillips of This Town married June 25. 1740

Robert Shareman and The widdow mary Eames were married Septr. y^e. 23. 1740

Mathew Simonton of Falmouth and marcy oakman of this Town were married march 12. 1741

Benjamin Hatch of Scituate and Jerusha Phillips of This Town married aprill 7. 1741

Thomas Silvester and Hannah Harris married aprill 16. 1741 —

Elisha Kent and Susannah Ford married Jun y^e. 11. 1741

Elisha Rogers and margaret mackfarland married December y^e. 2. 1741

John Tilden the 3^d. and Rachel Hall married march y^e. 4. 1741

Derby Fits Patrick and Joanna Rogers married may y^e. 1. 1742

James Sprague Junr. and Patience Ford and Jno. Baker and Ruth Barker were married February The 24. 1742-3 ———

Benjamin White and Hannah Decro married aprill y^e. 3^d. 1743

Joseph Stetson of Scituate and mary Eames of this town married Septr. y^e. 15. 1743

James Lewis and Lydia Rogers of This Town married December y^e. 1. 1743

Ignatious Vinall of Scituate and mary Tilden of this Town married Decr. 15. 1743

A True list of The marriages Consummated Before me Atherton Wales.

Joseph Bruster of Duxborough and Jedidah White of marshfield were married Novr. 26. 1740

Ezekiel Kent and Susanna Winslow Both of marshfield were married Decem^r. 22 1740

John Tilden and Lydia Holmes Both of marshfield were married February 12. 1740

Nehemiah Thomas and Bial Winslow Both of this town were married July 6. 1741

Joseph Soul Junr. of Duxborough and mary Fullerton of marshfield were married march 18. 1742

Thomas Eames and margaret Dugles Both of marshfield were married June 10. 1742

William Winslow of middlebor^o. & Hannah Loe of marshfield were married Novr. 11. 1742

Snow Winslow and Lydia Crooker Both of marshfield were married Novr. 24. 1742

Jno. Tilden of Hanover and Sybil Thomas of marshfield were married Decr. 2. 1742

Robert Boath of Norwich and Lydia Hewett of marshfield were married march 21. 1743

Benj^a. Phillips and Else Thomas Both of marshfield were married Novr. 15. 1743

Jedediah Bourn and Sarah Thomas Both of marshfield were married octo^r. 24. 1743

Thomas Ford of marshfield and Hannah Turner of Pembrook were married Septr. 8. 1743

Amoss Ford and Lillis Turner Both of marshfield were married January 3. 1743-4

Thomas Little and Abigail Howland Both of This Town were married march 9. 1742

Jabez Whittemore and Elizabeth Howland Both of marshfield were married Sept^t. 26. 1743
p^r. me Samuel Hill Clerk

[173]   A List of Kingston mariages from 1735. to 1734 viz.
1735
Octr. 2 — Joshua Sherman & Deborah Croade were maried

1736. Feby. 17.   Joshua Bradford & Hannah Bradford were maried

1737. Jany. 11 Jon^a. Tilson and martha Washburn were maryed.

1742. Feb^{ry}. 22 Cornelius White & Sarah Ford were maried.

april 26 Elisha Stetson jun^r. & Sarah Adams were maried.

1743. Sepr. 14 Thomas Phillips & Mary Mitchel were maried
By me Nic^o Sever Just peace

1737. Decr. 15 Timothy morton & Mary Wilson were maried.

1737. Feb. 23 Eben^r. Chandler & Anna his wife was maried.

1738. May 30. Charles Cooke & Hannah Faunce was maried.

1738 June 12. Andrew Samson & Sarah Phillips was maried
Before me Joshua Cushing Just peace

1736 Jan^ry. 6 Peter Tinkham and Mary his wife was maried
Before me Joshua Cushing J Peace

1736. June 26 James Claghorn & Elizabeth Ring was maried.

1736. Octr. 21. John Simmons & Hopestil Stutson was maried.
Octr. 21. Zachr^y. Chandler & Zerviah Holmes were maried

1736. Decr. 7. Nathan Wright & Hannah Cook was maried.

1736. Jany. 31 Edmund Hodges & mercy Cook were maried

1736 Augt. 18 John Wright & mercy Coomer was maried.
Before Joseph Stacy

1737. Augt. 30. Samuel Wade & Mary Curtiss was maried. ——
Before Jo^s. Cushing Jus^t. peace

1742. Decr. 30. Abner Hall of Kingston to Sarah Hatch of Pembrooke

1742. Jan^ry 27 Benj^a. Eaton to Mary Tilson both of Kingston.

1743 apr. 5. Jno. Finney of Kingston to Betty Lovel of Abbington

May. 5. Eben^r. Morton to Susanna Holmes both of Kingston.

Novr. 25 Ichabod Bradford to Mary Johnson both of Kingston.
David Eaton to Deborah Fuller both of Kingston

1744. June 27. Ignatius Cushing of Hallifax to Tabitha Fish of Kingston—— were maried p^r. Thaddeus Mackarty Minister

[191]—A List of Pembrooke mariages from 1738. To. 1742. viz.

1 James Johnson of Scotland in Great Britain & Bethia Barker jun^r. of pembrooke were maried July 31. 1738.

2 Jonah Bisbee & Ruth Briant both of Pembrooke were maried Augt. 24th. 1738.

3 Willm. Richards of Pembrooke & Hannah Simmons of Duxbor^o. were maried Sepr. 7. 1738

4 Richard Bordman of Duxbor^o. & Ester Samson of Pembrooke negroes were maried Octr. 12. 1738.

5. Samuel Howland & Sarah Joy both of Pembrooke were maried Octr. 13. 1738.

6 William Curtis & Martha Macfarld Junr. both of Pembrooke were maried Novr. 14. 1738.

7 Henry Munroe of Swanzey & Hannah Joslyn jun^r. of Pembrooke were maried Novr. 16 1738

8   Robert Stetson jun^r. of Scituate & Hannah Turner of Pembroke were maried Novr. 23. 1738.

9   Isaac Crooker & Desire Bates jun^r. both of Pemb : were maried Novr. 23. 1738.

10 Elisha Barker & Eliz^a. Bowen both of Pembrooke were maried Janr^y. 25 1738

11 Gideon Soule & Mercy Silvester both of Pembrooke were maried mar. 5th. 1738-9

12 Caleb Turner Junr. of Scituate & Ruth Briggs of Pembrooke maried May 1. 1739.

13 Francis Keen & Margret Hunt both of Pembrooke were maried Novr. 1. 1739

14. Richard Tillah a molatto & Peg a Negro Girl both Servants to M^r. Josiah Cushing of Pembrooke December 11th. 1739.

15. Solomon Russel & Dorothy Tubs were maried Decr. 27. 1739

16 Jno. Orcut of Bridgwater & Mary Webster of Pembrooke were maried mar. 31. 1740.

17 John Jordan of Scituate & Mercy Damon of Pemb. were mari^d. Decr. 23. 1740.

18. Nathaniel Baker & Susannah Lincoln jun^r both of Pemb. mar^d. Decr. 29 – 1740

19. Jno. Lincoln Junr. of Pemb. & Content Turner of Hanover maried Febr^y. 25. 1740.

20 Jno. Allen of Bridgw^r. & Bethia Crooker of Pemb. were maried Mar. 5. 1740

21 Hutson Bishop & Eliza Keen both of Pembrooke. maried Septr. 3. 1741

22 Nehemiah Cushing jun^r. & Sarah Humphreys both of Pemb. maried Novr. 18th. 1741.

23 Abr^a. Joslyn & Mary Soule both of Pemb. were maried Decr. 16. 1741.

24 Jno. Wallis of Pemb. & Eliz^a. Patteson of Hanover maried Decr. 29. 1741.

By the Rev^d. M^r. Daniel Lewis——

[192] 25 Joseph Ramsdell jun^r. of Pembrooke & mary Daws of Bridgwater were maried Decr. 30. 1741.—

26 Elisha Palmer of Hanover & Jerusha Stetson of Pembrooke were maried December 31. 1741.——

27 William Page & Agatha Stetson both of Pemb. were maried May 31. 1742

28 Joshua Brigs & Zervia Dellano both of Pemb : were maried June 3^d. 1742

29 Gideon Bisbee & Rebecca Turner both of Pemb. were maried Septr. 7. 1742.

30 Shubal Munroe & Mary Joslyn both of Pemb : were maried Nov[r]. 10. 1742

31 Benj[a]. Tailer of Hanover & Mery Russel of Pemb : were maried Dec[r]. 23. 1742.

The above mariages were Consumated p[r]. the Rev[d]. M[r]. Daniel Lewis————

32 Samuel Peirce & Rachel Cordwell both of Hanover were maried June 12. 1742.

33 Recompence Magoune & Ruth Crooker both of Pembrooke were maried July 20. 1742.

34 John Ransom of Kingston & Desire Bishop of Pembrooke were maried October 11th. 1742.

35 Job Simmons of Plimton & Abigail Parris of Pemb : were maried Oct[r]. 20. 1742

36 Job Crooker & Abigail Winslow both of Marshfield Dec[r]. 15. 1742

37 Nath[l] Croade & Eliz[a]. Carter both of Plymouth were maried Dec[r]. 29. 1742

By Joshua Cushing Justice of the peace A True Copy Transcribed from the Records of the Town of Pembrooke attest Daniel Lewis Jun[r]. Town Cler

The following is a list of the marriages Solemnized by the reverend m[r]. Jonathan Parker ——— viz.

1 Febr[y]. 23. 1741. Robert Avery to Anna Cushman.
2 24 Isaac Lobdel to Ruth Clarke
3 and Thomas Loring unto Sarah Lobdel
4 May 12. 1742 Plilemon Samson unto Rachel Standish
5 June 9. 1742. David Darling unto Ruth Faunce
6 Novemb[r]. 10. 1742. Asa Cook unto Susanna Bryant
7 11. 1742 Ichabod Churchel unto Rebecca Curtis
8 1. Benjamin Shaw unto Mary Attwood.
9 25. Ephraim Paddock unto Sarah Bradford
10 and Robert Cook unto Hannah Bisbe
11 april 7. 1743. Elkanah Cushman unto Hannah Standish
12 August 12. 1743. John Holmes unto Joanna Adams
13 October 6. 1743 Eleazer Richard unto Martha King.
14 Dec[r]. 1. 1743. Simeon Holmes unto Abiah Stertevant
15 January 19. 1743. James Whiten Jun[r]. unto Molly Lucas Plymton February 20. 1743.

A True Copy p[r] me Josiah Perkins Town Cler

A List of Mariages Solemnized by Edward Arnold Esq[r] Just peace viz.

1   July 20. 1738 Eliakim Willis of Dartmouth & Lydia Fish of
    Duxbor⁰.

2   December 12ᵗʰ 1738 Jethro Sprague & Patience Bartlett both
    of Duxbor⁰.

3   Decembᵣ. 17. 1738 Miles Standish junᵣ. of Duxbor⁰. & Me-
    hitable Robins of Plym⁰.

4   March 1. 1738-9 Hezekiah Herrington & Hannah Southworth
    both Marshfield

5   Nathaniel Simmons & Mercy Simmons both of Duxbor⁰ June
    12ᵗʰ. 1739

6   Isaac Tinkham of Plym⁰. & Keziah Wormall Duxbor⁰. July
    26. 1739

    [193] 7 William Wilson of Scituate & Hannah Bourne of
    Marshfield Novᵣ. 28. 1739

8   Decᵣ. 3. 1739. Hezekiah Ripley & Abigail Hunt both of
    Duxborough

9   1739-40 March Eleazer Harlow of Duxbor⁰. & Abigail
    Thomas of Marshfield

10 May 22 1740. Nathˡˡ. Blackmer of Dartm⁰. & Rebecca Samson
    of Duxbor⁰. Maried

11 June 23. 1740. William Tolman of Scituate & Abigail Wil-
    liamson of Marshfield

12 Novᵣ. 4. 1741. Jedediah Soule & Tabitha Bishop both of
    Duxbor⁰.

13 July 8. 1742. Samuel Sprague junᵣ. & Sarah Oldham both of
    Duxbor⁰.

14. Febrʸ. 10. 1742-3 Benjᵃ Howland of Pembrooke & Experi-
    ence Edgartown of Hallifax

15 Thomas Gullifer & Keturah Samson both of Duxbor⁰. Octᵣ.
    26. 1743.

16 Novᵣ. 4. 1743. John Chandler 3ᵈ. & Sarah Weston Both
    Duxbor⁰.

    The Following Mariages Solemnized by the Revᵈ. Mᵣ. Sam-
    uel Veazie viz.

1. May 28. 1740 David Delano & Abigail Chandler both of
    Duxbor⁰.

2   May 31. 1740. Micah Soule & Mercy Southworth both of
    Duxborough

3   Decᵣ. 31. 1740 Joseph Russel & Abigail Wadsworth both
    Duxbor⁰.

4   May 14. 1741 Abisha Sole & Abigail Delano both of Duxbor⁰.

5   July 9. 1741 Lemuel Delano & Lydia Bartlett both Duxbor⁰.

6   Octᵣ. 8. 1741 Charles Rider of Plym⁰. & Rebecca Bartlett of
    Duxborough

7 Novr. 19. 1741 Briggs Allden & Mercy Wadsworth both of Duxboro.

8 April 20. 1742 Simeon Curtis of Scituate & Asenath Sprague of Duxboro.

9 June 10. 1742 Nathaniel Bartlett & Zenobe Wadsworth both of Duxboro.

10 Janry. 14. 1742-3 Jona. Crooker junr. of Pembrooke & Bethia Lowden Duxboro.

11 March 17. 1743. Nero Negroman & Patience Indian Woman both Duxboro.

The following Mariages were Consummated at Plymouth By Samuel Bartlett Just of ye Peace ———— viz

1. Janry. 21 1735. James Wood & Deborah Fish both of Plymouth

2. June 13. 1738. Simeon Totman & Sarah Little John both of Plymo.

3. William Clarke & Experience Doty both of Plymouth

4. Augt. 3. Edward Doten & Phebe Phinney both of Plymouth

Septr. 5. William Harlow & Hannah Bartlett both of Plymouth

6 March 21. 1738-9 Joshua Swift of Sandwich & Jane Faunce of Plymouth

7 David Morton & Rebecca Finney both of Plymo. May 8th.

8 John Jones & Sarah Barnes both of Plymouth Augt. 18. 1740

9 April 16. 1741. Edward Sparrow & Jerusha Bradford both of Plymo.

10 June 30. Mr. Ezra Whitemarsh & Mrs. Dorothy Gardner both Plymo.

11 July 3. Jona. Sanders of Warham & Eliza. Tinkam of Plymo.

12 May 13. 1742. William Wood & Elizabeth Finney both of Plymo.

13 19. Ephraim Holmes & Sarah Finney both of Plymouth —

14 March 3. 1742-3 Peleg West & Lydia Keen both of Kingston

15 14.— Gideon Gifford of Rochester & Lois Jackson of Plymouth

16 July 7. Silvanus Bartlett & Martha Waite both of Plymo.

The above is a true Copy of Record from Plymo. Town book Attest Samll. Barlett Town Clerk

1743 June 7 Cornelius Holmes & Mary Doten both of Plymo. maried by Josiah Cotton Esqr Just peace

A true Copy of Record attest Samuel Bartlett Town Cler —

[194] Mariages Solemnized by the revrd. Mr. Nathll. Leonard of Plymo. Viz.

1 June 14. 1742. Benj^a. Barnes & Experience Rider both of Plymouth

2 M^r. Samuel Veazie of Duxbor^o. & M^{rs}. Deborah Samson of Kingston Augt. 6. 1742.

3. Septr. 6. 1742. Barzilla Stetson & Ruth Kempton both of Plymouth

4 Robert Shattuck & Ruhama Cooke both of Plym^o. Septr. 9th. 1742.

5 The^o. Cotten & Martha Sanders both of Plym^o. Octr. 29. 1742.—

6 Lemuel Bartlett & Mary Dotey both of Plym^o. Novr. 25. 1742.

7 Henry Saunders Junr. of Warham & Mary Hambleton of Plym^o. Decr. 13. 1742.

8 Joseph Shurtleff & Sarah Cob both of Plym^o. Decr. 9th. 1742

9 Jan^{ry}. y^e. 13. 1742-3 Joseph Ruggles of Hardwick & Hanah Cushman of Plym^o.

10 Jan^{ry}. 20. 1742-3 Thomas Faunce 4th. & Sarah Bartlett both of Plym^o.

11 Job Hammond Negro, & Hannah Quoy Indian Febr^y. 17. 1742-3

12 March 10. 1742-3 Noah Bradford & Hannah Clarke both of Plym^o.

13 March y^e. 17. 1742-3 William Keen & Ruth Sergeant both of Plym^o.

14 May 2. 1743. Doct^r. Lazarus Lebaron & m^{rs}. Lydia Cushman both of Plym^o.

15 May 26. 1743. Jonah Whetemore of Charlestown & Mary Hatch of Plym^o.

16 May y^e. 30. 1743. Francis Perriss & Mary Thomas Indians —

17 Septr. 22. 1743. David Curtice of Scituate & Hannah Ward of Plymouth

18 Novr. 10. 1743. John Bradford of Plymton & Eliz^a. Holmes of Plym^o.

19$^5_2$Decr. 8. 1743. Mr. Jno. Greenleaf of Boston & m^{rs}. Priscilla Brown of Plymouth

20 Peter Daniel & Sarah Waterman Indians Decr. 18. 1743. both of Plym^o.

21 Febr^y. 13. 1743-4 Amos Donham & Ann Mackleroy both of Plym^o.

22 Febr^y. 14. 1743-4 Ephraim Ward & Sarah Donham both of Plym^o.

23 Febr^y. 23. 1743-4 Gideon White of Marshfield & Joanna Howland Plym^o.

A True Copy of Record from Plym^o. Town book ——
Attest Saml. Bartlett Town Cler

A List of Marriages by Edward Winslow of Rochester Just of peace viz.

1 April 10. 1740. Elisha Tupper & Mary Hommond both of Rochester.

2 Novr. 26. 1740. Daniel Wing & Mary Cliften both of Rochester.

3 Augt. 6. 1741. Marke Haskell ye 3^d. & Elizabeth Witredge both of Plym^o.

4 Oct^o. 15. 1741. Jno. Penny of Harwick & Eliz^a. Dellano of Rochester.

5 Decr. 20. 1741. Simon Burge & Deborah Edwards both of Rochester

6 Samuel Rider Junr. & Mary Chapman both of Roch^r. April 13. 1742

7 Novr. 16. 1742. William Tereth & Dinah Dexter both of Rochester

8 March 15. 1742. Lemuel Claghorne & Deborah Wing both of Roch^r.

9 May 2. 1743. Elijah Caswell & Hannah Freman both of Rochester

10 July 12. 1743 Job King & Uniss Hammond both of Rochester

11 July 13. 1743 Joshua Lawrence & Jane Haskell both of Rochester

12 Octr. 20. 1743. Amos Mendal & Susanna Church both of Rochester.

13 January 4. 1743 Haneniah Gifford & Joanna Mendal both of Rochester

[195] 14 January 4th. 1743 John Mattkelf & Rebecca Crapoo both of Rochester

15 Received Febr^y. 14. 1743. & Entered in Town Book of Records of Rochester
p^r Sam^{ll}. Wing T. Cler.

Peleg Dexter & Catherine Cosby both of Rochester were maried p^r Ivory Hovey Past^r.

[196] 1 Thomas Weeks of Hardwick & Katharine Clarke of Rochester were maried the 3^d. of April 1743.

2 George King & Lydia Snow were maried Augt. 4. 1743.

3 James Francis & Hosea Nummuch Ind^{ns}. Septr. 28. 1743.

4   David Paker of Newporte & Dorothy Robinson maried Oct⁰. 27. 1743.

5   Joseph Tharp & Charity Andrews maried Janʳ. 1. 1743.

6   John Goodspeed & Mercy Hamond maried Febrʸ. 5. 1743.— by me Tim⁰. Ruggles.

Samuel Savory & Elizabeth Bumpas of Warham were maried December 25ᵗʰ, 1739. pʳ. me Timothy Ruggles.

A List of Marriages by mʳ. Rowland Thacher of Warham.

1   Septʳ. 6. 1741. Gersham Morss of Middlebor⁰. & Elizᵃ. Swift of Warham

2   Josiah Swift & Mary Besse both of Warham Novʳ. 19. 1741.

3   Decʳ. 9. 1741. Jonᵃ. Dillano of Rochʳ. & Rachel Bump of Warham

4   March 15. 1741-2 Josiah Man of Scituate & Mary Chubbuck of Warham

5   Daniel Raymond & Elizᵃ. Doty March 21. 1741.

6   Octʳ. 22. 1742. Hezekiah Bourne aged 65, & Mehitable Hinckley aged 25.——

7   Novʳ. 4. 1742. Joseph Landen Junʳ. & Sarah Lovell.

8   Novʳ. 3. 1743. Jonᵃ. Earle & Hannah Dotey.

9   Decʳ. 22. 1743. Joshua Besse & Lydia Sanders— were maryed pʳ. me Rowland Thacher

[199] Marshfield April 17. 1745. A List of Mariages Compleated before me Since December 15, 1743. viz.

1   Onesimus Macumber of this Town & Lucy Barker of Hingham were maried January 15. 1744.

2   Robert Cushman of Kingston and Prudence Sherman of this town were maried February 2ᵈ. 1744.

3   Elisha Sherman and Lydia Walker both of this town were maried Febrʸ. 5. 1744.

4   Jn⁰. Hamilton of Worster & Mercy Simenton of this town were Maried Febrʸ. 7. 1774 —— pʳ. Atherton Wales.——

[211] A List of Marshfield Mariages Solemnized by?

Thomas Phillips Junʳ, of Duxborough & Lydia Carver of this town were maried January 24. 1744-5.

Joseph Kent & Lydia Thomas were maried Febrʸ. 28ᵗʰ. 1743.

Jonathan King of Plimouth & Deborah Carver of this Town were maried Febrʸ. 21. 1744-5.

[212] A List of Mariages Solemnized by the Revᵈ. Mʳ. Samuel Veazie of Duxborough viz.——

1   John Sprague & yᵉ widdow Deborah Simmons Decʳ. 5. 1744.——

2 John Goold of Hull & Huldah Brewster of Duxbor⁰. June
  13. 1745.

3. Eleazer Harlow of Duxborough & Abigail Clarke of Plimouth
  were maried Sepʳ. 11. 1745.

4 Ichabod Simmons & Lydia Soule were maried Decʳ. 8ᵗʰ. 1743.

5 Thomas Prince of Kingston & Lydia Delano of Duxborough
  Decʳ. 8. 1743
    were maried p Samˡ Veazie

1 Jabez Cole & Grace Keen both of Duxbor⁰. were maried
  august 23ᵈ. 1744.

2 Amos Samson & Deborah Samson were maried Octʳ. 19.
  1744—

3. Ebenezer Delano & Lydia Wormall were maried May 16. 1745.
  Pʳ. Edward Arnold Just of peace

    [213] The following is a List of Mariages Consumated by
    Mʳ. Othniel Campbel

July 31. 1744. Ephraim Tilsen and Deborah Ransom both of
  Plimpton were maried —

September 25. 1744. Abraham Jackson of Plimouth & Bethiah
  Whitin of Plimpton were Joind together in Mariage——

January 4. 1744. Samuel Thomas of Middlebor⁰. & Mehitable
  Barows of Plimton were Joynd together in Mariage——

April 25. 1745 Mʳ. John Doten of Plimton & Hannah Sherman
  of Plimouth were Joynd together in mariage —

    Plimton Decʳ. 16. 1745. a true Copy pʳ. me Josiah Perkins
    Town Cler

    [226] A List of Mariages of the Town of Bridgwater—viz.
    1743

Novʳ. 30. Nathan Allen and Rebecca Reed.

Janrʸ. 18 Daniel Howell & Deliverance Latham

Febrʸ. 7 John Edson and Mary Gannet were Maried pʳ. the
  Revᵈ. Mʳ. John Angier

    1743

April 13. Isaac Lathroop and Patience Alger.

May 5 Thomas Wade & Elizᵃ. Hanmer

  26. David Johnson & Susannah Willis

    1744.

April 19 Daniel Lathroop and Rhoda Willis
  were Maried pʳ. Danˡ. Johnson Esqʳ

    1741.

April 21 Elijah Edson and Ann Packard.

May 4 James Clansey and Ruth Ballaney.

26 Eben^r. Leach of Bridgwater & Mary Wilbore of Raynham
— Benanuel Leach & Betty Perkins —
July 29. Ruben Hall & Ruth Gilbert
Augt. 11 Stoughton Willis and Hannah Harlow
Octr. 12 William Leach & Mary Cohoone
Decr. 3. M^r. Eliab Byram & M^rs. Phebe Leonard
22 Joseph Wilbore of Raynham & Susanna Harris of Bridgwater.
— Benj^a. Pratt & Lydia Harlow
Febr^y. 11 Josiah Hayward & Mary Perkins
Mar. 5. James Wickett & Betty Moses Indians
1742.
May 5. James Perkins & Bethiah Dunham
June 3 Jonathan Allen of Brantrey & Mary Latham Bridgwater
[227] July 20. Ezra Washburne and Susanna Leach —
Augt. 5. William Gilmore and Margarett Stewart
Octr. 25 Samuel Bolton Bridgwater and Rebecca Simmons Hallifax
1743.
April 5. Nathaniel Hayward Bridgwater & Eliz^a. Curtiss Hallifax
Sepr. 29 Jabez Carver & Sarah Perkins
— Abraham Perkins & Mary Carver
Octr. 17 Benjamin Price & Silence Hayward
Novr. 3 Benjamin Peirce of Scituate & Charity Hayward of Bridgwater
— 7 William Snow & Hannah Hill
Decr. 20 Isaac Pool & Sarah Leonard
Janr^y. 12 Arthur Bennet of Middlebor^o. & Keziah Keith of Bridgwater
— 24 Jonathan Allden & Experience Hayward
Febr^y. 17. Lot Conant of Bridgwater & Betty Homes of Middlebor^o. —
March. 8 Robert Hoar of Middlebor^o. & Sarah Willis of Bridgw^r.
1744
April 10. Joseph Hayward of Raynham & Mary Cahoone of Bridgwater
June 14 Daniel Keith & Elizabeth Conant
Sepr. 20. Joseph Bozworth of Hallifax & Sarah Cobb of Brigw^r.
Novr. 15 Abiezer Edson & Mary Packard.
— 24 Joseph Cowing of Scituate & Jean Keith of Bridgw^r.
Decr. 10. Nathan Kingsley of Easton & Betty Dunbar of Bridgw^r.
Mar. 4. Joab Willis and Martha Bolton

Were maried by the rev^d. m^r. John Shaw

1741.

Mar. 1 Joel Edy & Rachel Vosse

1742. Novr. 11 Jacob Hayward & Tabitha Hayward

1743.

April 21. James Stacey of Easton & Mehitable Willis of Brigw^r.

July 19 Thomas Willis of Taunton & Bethiah Hayward of Bridgw^r.

Augt. 26. William Hall & Ann Chasta

Octr. 13. Benoni Hayward & Hannah Page

1744

June 14 Seth Thayer & Hannah Pray.

Novr. 22. Oliver Cheney of Pomphret & Hannah Hayward of Bridgw^r.

Decr. 3. James Linsey & Hannah Turner
were maried by the Rev^d. M^r. Danl. Perkins.

1744

May 28. Robert Dawes & Lydia Harden

June 7. Joseph Gannet and Betty Latham

Sepr. 27. Naphtali Byram and Hannah Pratt
were maried by the Rev^d. M^r. John Angier
A True Copy from the Town Record Examined
p^r Josiah Edson jun^r. Town Cler

[228] The following Couples were Maried in Middleborough by me the Subscriber at the times perticulerly Mentioned (Viz)

Nathan Bennet and Jemima Samson both of Middlebor^o. Decr. 5.

1745.

Eben^r. Briggs of Taunton & Margerey Leonard of Middleb^o. February 6. 1745-6

Thomas Weld Minister of the Gospel in Middleborough

Decr. 13. 1745 Then John Hall & Lydia Hacket both of Middlebor^o. was maried

Jany. 2. Then m^r. Saml. Southworth & m^rs. Eliz^a. Caswell Junr. were maried

By me Benjamin Ruggles.

The above written is a True Copy Transcribed from Middlebor^o. Town Book ——— Attest Jacob Tomson Town Cler.

[230] Marshfield July 7th. 1746. A List of Persons maried by me Samuel Hill Clerk.———

Benjamin Barnes & Mary Gullifer were maried Sepr. 16. 1745.

M^r. Anthony Thomas of this Town & M^rs. Abigail Allden of Duxborough were maried Jan^ry. 23. 1745-6—

John Fullerton of this town & Rebecca Dellano of Duxbor⁰. were
    maried April 17ᵗʰ. 1746

Anthony Sherman & Silence Foord were maried April 17ᵗʰ. 1746.

[231] Marriage Consummated by the Revᵈ. Mʳ. Jonathan
Ellis —

1740.

Augᵗ. 24. Ebenezer Harlow & Meriah Morey both of Plimouth mar-
    ryed a Ditt⁰.

Novʳ. 13. Nathaniel Morton & Mary Elles both of Plimouth
    married at D⁰.

Febrʸ. 19 Jonᵃ. Tobey of Sandwich & Deborah Swift of Plim-
    outh marryed at Plim⁰.

1742. Mar. 18. Thomas Clarke & Ruth Morton both of Plim-
    outh marryed at D⁰.

April 22. Jonathan Harlow & Sarah Holmes both of Plim⁰.
    marryed at D⁰.

1743. Augᵗ. 11. Joseph Morton the third & Experience Morton
    both of Plim⁰. marryed.

Sepʳ. 29 Edward Tinkham of Kingston & Lydia Rider of Plim⁰.
    married at Plim⁰.

Decʳ. 14. Eleazer Holmes Junʳ. & Esther Ellis both of Plim⁰.
    married a D⁰.

1744. Mar. 11 Joseph Croswell of Groton & Jerusha Bartlett of
    Plim⁰. married at D⁰.

Novʳ. 29. Joslyn Sepit & Joanna Sepit Indians both of Plim⁰.
    married a D⁰.

1745. Apr. 11 Ebenʳ. Holmes the 3ᵈ. & Susanna Holmes both
    of Plim⁰. marryed at D⁰.

1744. Augᵗ. 5 William Fish & Mercy Morey both of Plim⁰.
    maryed a D⁰.

Mariage Solemnized by Samuel Bartlett Esqʳ Just Peace
for the County of Plimouth.

1744-5. Joseph Fulgham & Rebeccah Young both of Plym⁰.
    March 1

1745.

Sepʳ. 26. Jacob Decoster & Elizᵃ. Cole both of Plimouth mar-
    ryed at D⁰.

Mariages Consummated by the Revᵈ. Mʳ. Nathaniel Leonard.

1745.

April 11 Elkanah Shaw of Middlebor⁰. & Joannah King of
    Plim⁰. marryed.

—25 Eleazer Donham of Plimpton & Phebe Lucas of
    Plim⁰. married a D⁰.

July 28. Jire Fish of Sandwich & and Hannah Finney of Plim⁰. marryed

Augt. 15 Caleb Sherman & Rebecca Rider both of Plim⁰. marryed at D⁰.

Sepr. 10. Azariah Whiten of Plimton & Rebecca Holmes of Plimouth marryed a D⁰.

1745-6. 23. Joseph Churchel & Meriah Rider both of Plim⁰. maryed a D⁰.

Febr^y. 10. Stephen Doten & Hannah Bartlet both of Plim⁰. maried at D⁰.

Mar. 6. Benj^a. Delano of Duxbor⁰. & Lydia Jackson of Plim⁰. marryed a D⁰.

Mariages Solemnized By the Rev^d. M^r. Thomas Frink of Plim⁰.

1745.

Octr. 3. Daniel Robins & Sarah Sanders Indians of Plim⁰. marry'd at D⁰.

Octr. 4. Thomas Ling & Eliz^a. Mackfun both of Plim⁰. marryed a D⁰.

— 31 Amaziah Churchel & Eliz^a. Silvester both of Plim⁰. marryed a D⁰.

1745-6. Febr^y. 25. Thomas Burge & Patience Dotey both of Plim⁰. maried a D⁰.

1745-6 A True Copy of Record attest Samuel Bartlet Town Clerk

Peleg Sprague &   Chanler both of Duxborough were Joyned together in Marriage

Samuel Winsor & Rhoda Delano both of Duxborough were Joyned together in mariage

By me Edward Arnold Just Peace

[232] Mariages Consummated by Elijah Cushing Esqr one of the Justices of the Peace for the County of Plimouth viz.

1736.

Augt. 23. William Estes of Hanover & Eliz^a. Stetson of Scituate were maried

Sepr. 30 Andrew Linsey & Ruth Parrish both of Pembrooke were maried

1737. June 1. John Barker of Hanover & Grace Turner of Scituate were maried

1738 June 29. Ebenezer Rogers & Sarah Stetson both of Marshfield were maried

1739 July 4 Ebenezer Woodward & Hannah Stetson both of Hanover were maried

1740. July 8. Shedrak Keen & Eliz^a. Turner both of Hanover were maried

1741 July 2. Caleb Rogers of Scituate & and Mary Harlow of Hanover were maried

1742 June 30 James Hanks of Pembrooke & Abigail Phillips of Bridgw^r. were maried

Janr^y. 27. Theophilus Cushing & Hannah White both of Pembrooke were maried

1743. Janr^y. 11 Silas Stetson & Mary Brackit both of Scituate were maried

1744 Janr^y. 29. Joshua Staples of Hanover & Eliz^a. Conaway of Pembrooke were maried

March 7 Ebenezer Record & Joanna Bowls both of Pembrooke were maried

1746. Sepr. 19. Prince Palmer of Scituate & Ruth Bowker of Hanover were maried
      p^r. Elijah Cushing Just Peace

The following Mariages were Consumated by the Rev^d. mr. Benj^a. Bass of Hanover — viz.

1744
March 29. Joshua Ripley & Alice Stetson both of Hanover were maried

April 28 Eleazer Donham of Plimouth & Eliz^a. Conner of Hanover were maried.

Decr. 6. Jesse Torrey & Mary Buker both of Hanover were maried

1746. May 31 Daniel Cotherel of Bridgw^r. & Hannah Rose of Hanover were maried
      p^r. me Benj^a. Bass Past^r. of Hanover

[236] 1 Nathan Pratt & Sarah Harlow were maried Octr. 15. 1745——

2 Benj^a. Benson & Keziah Snell Octr. 30. 1745——

3 Thomas Thomson & Jane Washburne Octr. 31. 1745 —

4 Thomas Conant & Mary Wood Octr. 29. 1745.

5 Nathl. Pratt & Hannah Conant Novr. 5. 1745

6 Eleazer Cary & Betty Fobes Novr. 12. 1745.

7 Elijah Leach & Jemima Snow Decr. 4. 1745.——

8 James Dunbar & Hannah Benson Janr^y. 22. 1745 —

9 Josiah Washburne & Abigail Curtiss Janr^y. 29. 1745 —
      [237] 10 Eleazer Carver jun^r. & Hepsiba Perkins April 3. 1746—

11 John Sprague & Susanna Cob June 20 : 1746 —

12 Joseph Lathrop & Content Washburne Octr. 24. 1746
13 Jonathan Carver & Sarah Homes Octr. 13. 1746 ——
14 John Hooper & Sarah Carver Decr. 1. 1746.
15 Joseph Clap & Sarah Carver Decr. 23. 1746
16 Joseph Carver & Sarah Hartwell Decr. 25. 1746 ——
    were maried —— By the Rev^d Jno. Shaw.

1745. March 26 Charles Snell & Susanna Packard.
May 23. Jonathan Chandler and Abthia Wade ——
Augt. 29. George Haward & Abigail Copeland.
Febr^y. 11. Samuel Dunbar & Mary Haward
    were Maried by m^r. Daniel Perkins.

1745. May 27. Nathaniel White & Susanna Crosman ——
June 6. Benanuel Leach & Elizabeth Edson
Octr. 3. Thomas Lindsey & Eliz^a. Turner
Decr. 11. John Whitman & Margrett Willis
1745/6. Janr^y. 22. Edward Wentworth Stoughton & Sarah Winslow.
Febr^y. 4 Terah Whitman of Easton & Anna Willis ——
Mar. 3. Jno. Conant & Abigail Pratt ——
    Were maried p^r Daniel Johnson Esqr

1745
Feb^{ry}. 7. William Shurtleff & Sarah Kingman ―――
― 20 Isaac Allen & Joanna Packard
25. Joseph Pettingail & Mary Edson.
Mar. 15. Jno. Alden & Rebecca Nightingail
28. Peter Edson & Sarah Southworth
Isaac Packard & Abigail Porter
Apr. 18. Amos Cordner & Abigail Calley Molattoes
1746 Janr^y. 1. David Edson & Susanna Ganett.
Febr^y. 25. Ebenezer Packard Sarah Perkins.
were maried p^r m^r. Jno. Porter

1745
Octr. 17. Samuel Beals & Eliz^a. Blackmer.
24. Elisha Allen & Rebecca Pratt.
Decr. 17. Joseph Byram & Mary Bowditch
1746. June 30. Doct^r. Isaac Otiss & Mehitable Bass
Octr. 7. Joseph Keith Junr. & Ann Turner
were maried p^r. the rev^d. Jno. Angier

[238] Marriages Consumated By the Rev^d. M^r. Nathl. Leonard

1746.
April 28. Lemuel Holmes & Abigail Rider both of Plim^o. marryed at Plim^o.
June. 19 John Howard & Unice Curtis both of Plimouth marry^d. at Plim^o.
July 3. Jabez Mendall of Plim^t. & Mariah Churchell of Plimouth marryd at Plim^o.
― 29 James Watkins & Jerusha Rider both of Plim^o. marry'd at Plimouth
Aug^t: 28 William Jerman and Elenor Thomas both of Plimouth marry'd at Plim^o.
Octr. 28. Benj^a. Eaton of Kingston & Mary Tinkam of Plim^o. marry'd at Plim^o.
Novr. 6. Josiah Bradford & Hannah Rider both of Plim^o. marry'd at Plim^o.
24. Nathl Bradford & Sarah Spooner both of Plim^o. marryed at Plim^o.
Decr. 11 James Howard Junr. & Thankfull Branch both of Plim^o. marry'd at Plim^o.
15. Samuel Harlow & Mercy Bradford both of Plimouth marry'd at Plim^o.
25 Nathaniel Goodwin & Lydia Lebaron both of Plim^o. marry'd at Plim^o.

1746/7.

Janr^y. 1. Thomas Paterson & Susannah Beale both of Plim^o. marry'd at Plim^o.

. 22. Josiah Carver jun^r. & Jerusha Sparrow both of Plim^o. marry'd at Plim^o.

27 Edward Wright & Eliz^a Decoster both of Plim^o. marryd at Plim^o.

March 19. Isaac Morton & Meriah Lewen both of Plim^o. marryed at Plim^o.

[239] Marriages Consummated by the Rev^d. Mr Thomas Frink
1746.

Octr. 21. Thomas Swift Junr. & Rebecca Clarke both of Plim^o. marry'd at Plimouth

Novr. 3. Benj^a. Churchel & Ruth Dellano both of Plim^o. marry'd at Plimouth

20 Perez Tilson & Eliz^a. Doty both of Plimouth marry'd at Plim^o. ——

Janr^y. 8. Doughty Randall of Scituate & Eliz^a. Tillson of Plim^o. marry'd at Plim^o.

Febr^y. 5. Jacob Tinkam & Lydia Donham both of Plim^o. marry'd at Plim^o.

Marryages omitted Ent^d. p^r. m^r. Frink which ought first to have been Entred viz.

1746.

May 5. Nathaniel Hatch & Ruth Rider both of Plim^o. marry'd at Plimouth

30 Amaziah Harlow & Lois Doten both of Plimouth marry'd at Plimouth

July. 24. Ezekiel Morton & Abigail Morton both of Plim^o. marry'd at D^o.

Marriages Consummated By Samuel Bartlett Esqr Just Peace
1746

April 7. Joshua Benson & Sarah Shurtleff both of Middleborough marry'd at Middleborough ——
A true Copy of Record, From Plimouth Town Book. Attest Saml Bartlet T. Clerk.

[240] 1744

Septr. 27 M^r. James Read of Camebridge & M^rs. Hannah Stacey of Kingston was maried.

Octob^r. 4 M^r. Jacob Gould of Hull & M^rs. Deborah Samson of Kingston was maried.

Decr. 13. Dea John Washburne of Kingston & M^rs. Mehitable Wright of Plimton was maried.

Janr^y. 8. M^r. Amos Cortis of Scituate to M^rs. Mary Faunce of King-ston was maried.

1745.
Octr. 3. M^r. Isaaiah Thomas of Newporte & M^rs. Keziah Holmes of Kingston was maried —
The last five mariages was by the rev^d. m^r. Thadeus Macarty of Kingston

1746.
June 16 Isaac Holmes & Mary Atherton both of Kingston was maried —

July 14. Thomas Hall & Hannah Edgartown both of Kingston was maried

Augt. 14. Timothy Briggs of Taunton & Bersheba Mitchel of Kings-ston were maried —— These three last by the rev^d. m^r. Willm. Rand Minister in Kingston ——

A true Copy Comp^d. with the Record
    Attest Francis Adams Town Cler

[245] John Bump 3^d. & Alice English both of this Town may 20. 1744.

Adonijah Muxum of Sharon & Keziah Benson of this Town Octr. 31. 1744.

Nathan Leonard of Bridgw^r. & Thankfull Besse of this town Novr. 22. 1744

Jeremiah Bump ju^r. & Judith Randal both of this town Decr. 20. 1744/5

Peleg Landers & Eliz^a. Bishup both of this town Janr^y. 24. 1744/5 —

Nathan Briggs of Rochester & Sarah Perry of this town Febr^y. 28. 17445.

Nathl White of Rochester & Mary Raymont of this town May 20. 1745.

Rowland Swift & Mary Dexter both of this town Decr. 5th. 1745.——

John Gibbs & Sylvia Hunter both of this town Octr. 9. 1746

Saml Briggs ju^r. of Rochester & Eliz^a. Besse of this town Octr. 9. 1746.

Phillip Bump & Mary Burge both of this town Decr. 18. 1746 ——
    The above persons were all married p^r. me Rowland Hamond.

[246] February: 6. 1745/6 Then Josiah Richmond & Lydia Crocker both of the Town of Middleborough was maried was maried by me Ben Ruggle

1745/6
Febr^y. 19. Joseph Peirce of Middlebro, & Phebe Smith of Tounton were maried

April 17. Aaron Sekins & Hannah Westcoat were maried both of Middlebro.

1746.

May 8. 1746. Jacob Caswell of Middlebro, & Deliverance Caswell of Taunton were maried

May 29 Caleb Jenne of Dartmouth & Silence House of Middlebro, were maried.

June 20. Samuel Allen jun^r. & Betty Willis both of Middlebro, were maried.

Sepr. 18. Joseph Phinney of Middlebr°. & Phebe Cole of Berkley were mared

Sepr. 23. Then Ithamer Hoskins of Middlebro & Mercy Fry ju^r. of Taunton were maried

Janr^y. 27. 1746.7 John Macumber & Elizabeth Phinney both of Middlebr°. was maried

Febr^y. 12. Thomas Richmond of Middlebr°. & Mary Dodson of Fretown was maried

March 5. John Richmond ju^r. & Hannah Paddock both of Middlebr°. was maried
p^r Benj^a. Ruggles —

Novr. 4. 1746. Then Phillip Wapquish & Abiah Hosuit both of Middlebro. Indians were maried by me Ezra Clap Justice of peace over the Indians ———

The above written is a True Copy Transcribed from Middlebro. Town Book — Attest Jacob Tomson town Cler.

[249] The Record of Mariages Since 1742. ———

Samuel Nash & Abigail Hearsey were Maried Novr. 10. 1743.

Daniel Noyse and Hannah Thayer were maried Novr. 24. 1743

Isaac Hearsey & Mary Gurney were maried Janr^y. 5. 1743/4 ———

Samuel Green & Hannah Jackson were maried April 25. anno. 1745 ———

Jon^a. Shaw & Susanna Hearsey were maried Augt. 17. 1744 ———

Elexander Robinson & Abigail White were maried the 26th. 1744———

Thomas White & Rachel Lincoln were maried Octr. 3. 1745.

Willm. Hearsey & Lydia Gurney were maried Novr. 7th. A. D. 1745.

Ebenezer Bisbee & Bathsheba Whitmarsh, Joseph Terril & Rebecca Gurney were maried Janr^y. 9th. A. D. 1745./6 ———

Joseph Bate & Sarah Pettingale were maried Janr^y. 9. 1745/6 ———

Thomas Moore of Bridgw^r. & Mary Hamblin were maried Septr. 24. 1746.

Isaac Hamblin & Sarah Shaw were maried Janr^y. 23. A. D. 1746/7.

Transcribed from the Record of Abbington
By me Jacob Reed Town Cler

[253] Thomas Macomber & Mercy Tilden both of this Town May 9th. 1745

John Sherman & Mercy Lucas both of this Town Decr. 3. 1745.

Seth Vinal of Scituate & Hannah Tilden of this town Janr^y. 9. 1745/6

Willm. Clift Junr. of this town & Bethiah Hatch of Scituate Apr. 17th. 1746

John Hall ju^r. & Zilpha Crooker both of this town Sepr. 1. 1746.

Israel Smith of Scituate & Abigail Foord of this town Octr. 24. 1746

Joshua Brimhall of Hingham & Katharine Hall of this town July 30. 1747 —

 [254] Deacon Samuel Hatch of Scituate and the widdow Mercy Silvester of this town Octr. 27. 1747

Amos Steward and Hannah Moses both of this town Octr. 27th, 1747

 Mariages Consumated by the Rev^d. M^r. Nathl Leonard — viz

1747.

April 23. M^r. Joseph Lebaron & M^{rs}. Sarah Leonard both of Plimouth

May 14 M^r. Nathl Torrey & M^{rs}. Ann Leonard both of Plimouth

July 16. Edward Stephens ju^r. & Phebe Harlow both of Plimouth

Sepr. 24 Jonathan Samson & Sarah Drew both of Plimouth

Octr. 29 Eleazer Stephens & Sarah Silvester both of Plimouth

Novr. 5. M^r. Thos. Foster ju^r. & M^{rs}. Mercy Wethrel both of Plim^o.

 12 Job Morton & Mary Barnes both of Plimouth

 16 Samuel Morton & Ruth Rogers both of Plimouth

 16 Josiah Johnson & Patience Faunce both of Plimouth

 23 Eben^r. Churchell & Mercy Branch both of Plimouth

 Guiney & Hagar (Negroes) were maried at Plim^o. Decr. 10th. 1747

 Attest Saml Bartlett Town Cler

Mariages Consumated By the rev^d. m^r. Thos. Frink —

1747.

June 3. M^r. Willm. Greenleaf of Boston & M^{rs}. Mary Brown of Plimouth

Octr. 13. Lemuel Churchell & Lydia Silvester both of Plimouth

Novr. 26 Joseph Bramhall & Sarah Tilson both of Plimouth

1747.

Mar. 8. Elkanah Churchell ju^r. & Susanna Bartlett both of Plim^o.

 Attest Saml Bartlett Town Cler.

[286] Josep Bumper Ruth Reed both of Wareham Marryed October 20 — 1749 —

John Randall of Rochester Lois Bump of Wareham Mared March 11 — 1749 —

 Wareham May 11 — 1750

 pr Me Rowland Thacher

Wheeler, Anne Lanesborough
New Farmin pg 140

Wheeler, James, Windsor Shan pg 146

Wheeler, Abraham Worcester 7
" Mary " 8
" Ebenezer Mendow 15
" Adam & Marc Rutland 23
" Pensis Ashburnham 43
" Matilda Bolton 48
" Mary HARVARD 52
" Amos of Worcester Leicester 60
" Abel Spencer 65
" JR. Jonathan Holden 68
" Abigail " 69
" Moses " "
" Nathan " "
" Thomas " 72
" Lucy " "
" Persis Shrewsbury 79
" DINAH " 79
" Miriam " 80
" Lucy " 81
" Jonathan " "
" Ephraim " 82
" Solomon 83
" Lois " "
" Jacob " 84

too Mary

Lots of Wood upton 8.48
" " Middleborough 70

CPSIA information can be obtained at www.ICGtesting.com
Printed in the USA
BVOW03s1713230614

356883BV00019B/109/P

9 780806 300085